The Coast of British Columbia

1	2	3

1
2
3

1	2	3
4	5	6

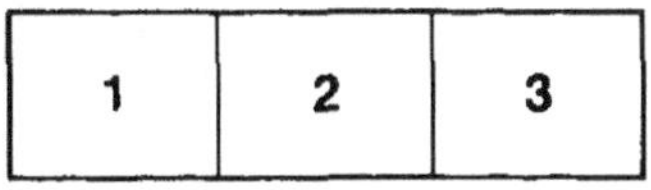

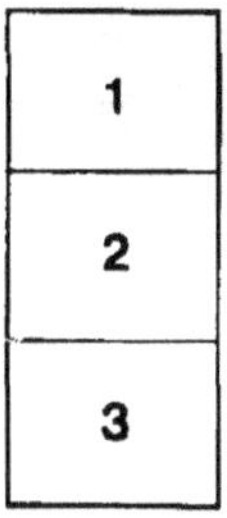

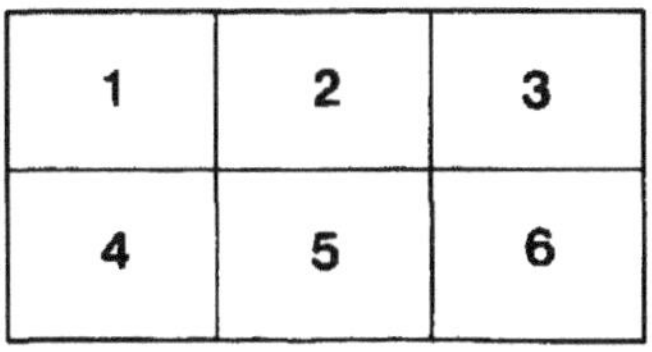

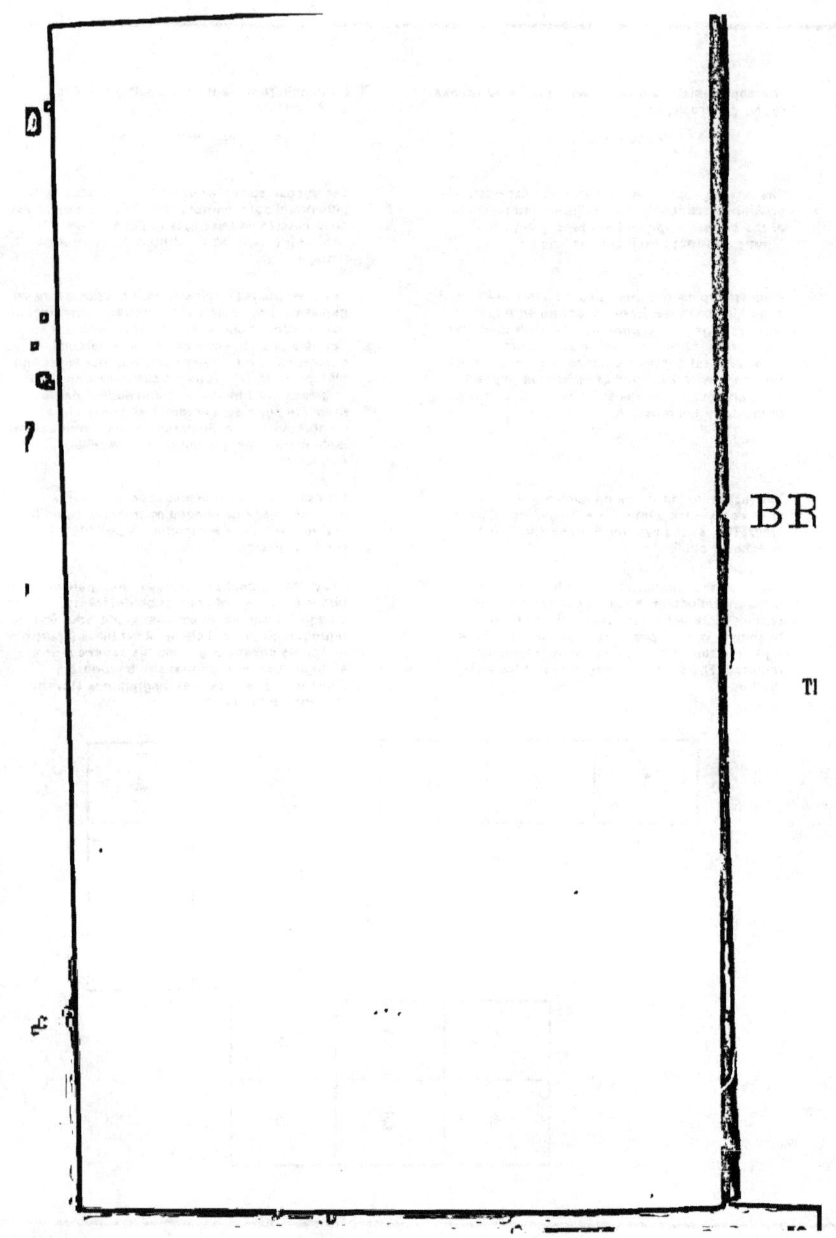

No. 96.

THE COAST

OF

BRITISH COLUMBIA

INCLUDING

THE JUAN DE FUCA STRAIT, PUGET SOUND, VANCOUVER
AND QUEEN CHARLOTTE ISLANDS.

COMPILED BY

R. C. RAY, U. S. NAVY,

Under the direction of

RICHARDSON CLOVER, HYDROGRAPHER.

Price $1.50

WASHINGTON:
GOVERNMENT PRINTING OFFICE.
1891.

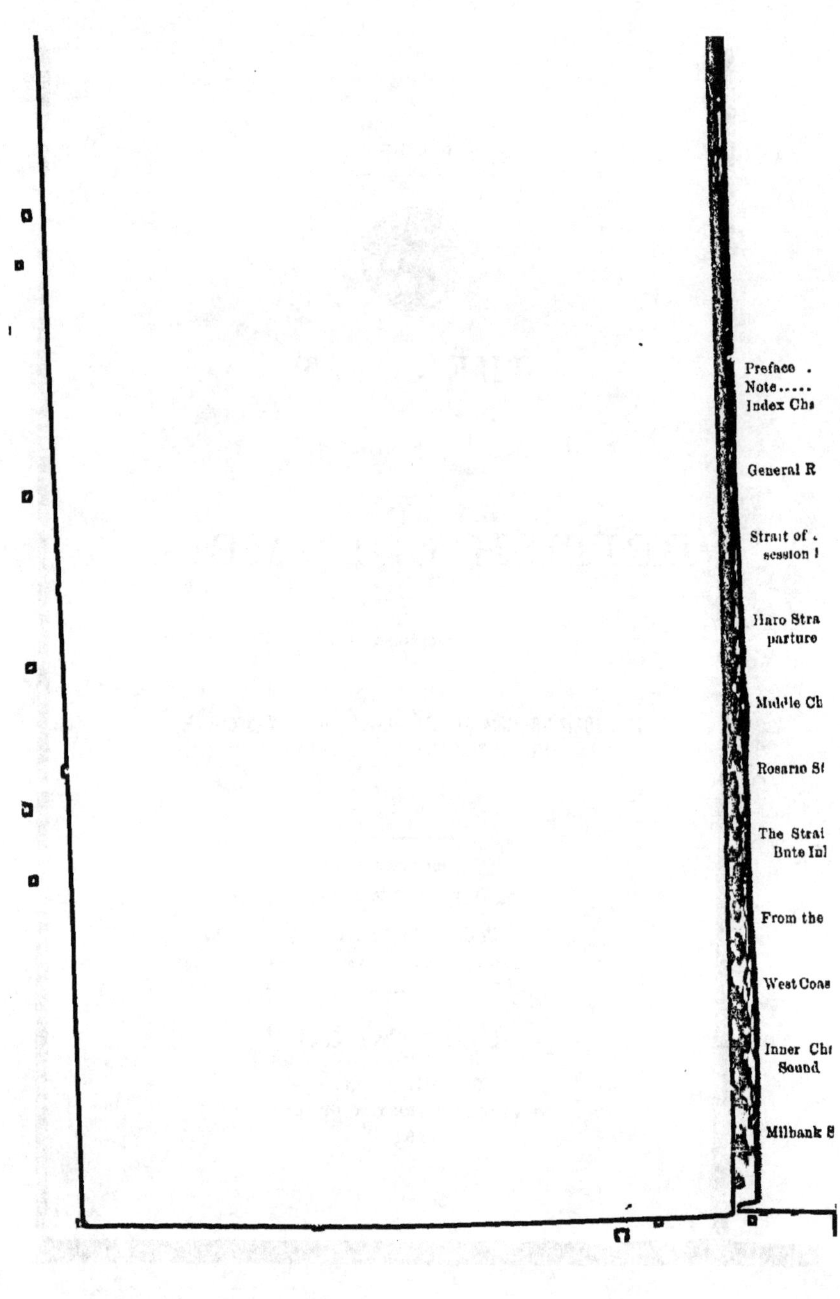
Preface .
Note.....
Index Cha
General R
Strait of
session
Haro Stra
parture
Middle Ch
Rosario St
The Strai
Bute Inl
From the
West Coas
Inner Ch
Sound
Milbank S

CONTENTS.

PREFACE.

This edition contains sailing directions for the Strait of Juan de Fuca, Admiralty Inlet, Puget Sound, and Hood's Canal; Haro and Rosario Straits and the Western Channels; Strait of Georgia and the inner waters of British Columbia; the coast of Vancouver and Queen Charlotte Island, together with Portland Inlet and Canal and Observatory Inlet.

In the compilation of this volume the following authorities have been consulted:

Pacific Coast Pilot of California, Oregon, and Washington, U. S. Coast and Geodetic Survey.
Pacific Coast Pilot, Alaska, Part I, U. S. Coast and Geodetic Survey.
British Columbia Pilot, British Admiralty.
Archives, U. S. Hydrographic Office.
Office of Naval Intelligence, Navy Department.
Consular Reports, State Department.
Dock Book, British Admiralty.
Port Charges of the World, Hunter.
Hydrographic Office Charts.
Coast and Geodetic Survey Charts.
British Admiralty Charts.

The information has been principally taken from the Pacific Coast Pilot of California, Oregon, and Washington, Coast Survey, and the British Columbia Pilot, Admiralty, together with such information as has been from time to time furnished by officers of United States vessels.

RICHARDSON CLOVER,
Hydrographer.

U. S. HYDROGRAPHIC OFFICE,
Washington, D. C., 1891.

NOTE.

The bearings, courses, and trend of the land are true. The direction of the winds, the point from which they blow; of currents, the point toward which they set. Distances are expressed in nautical miles; soundings, unless otherwise stated, are reduced to mean low water.

lirection
ıe point
l miles;
vater.

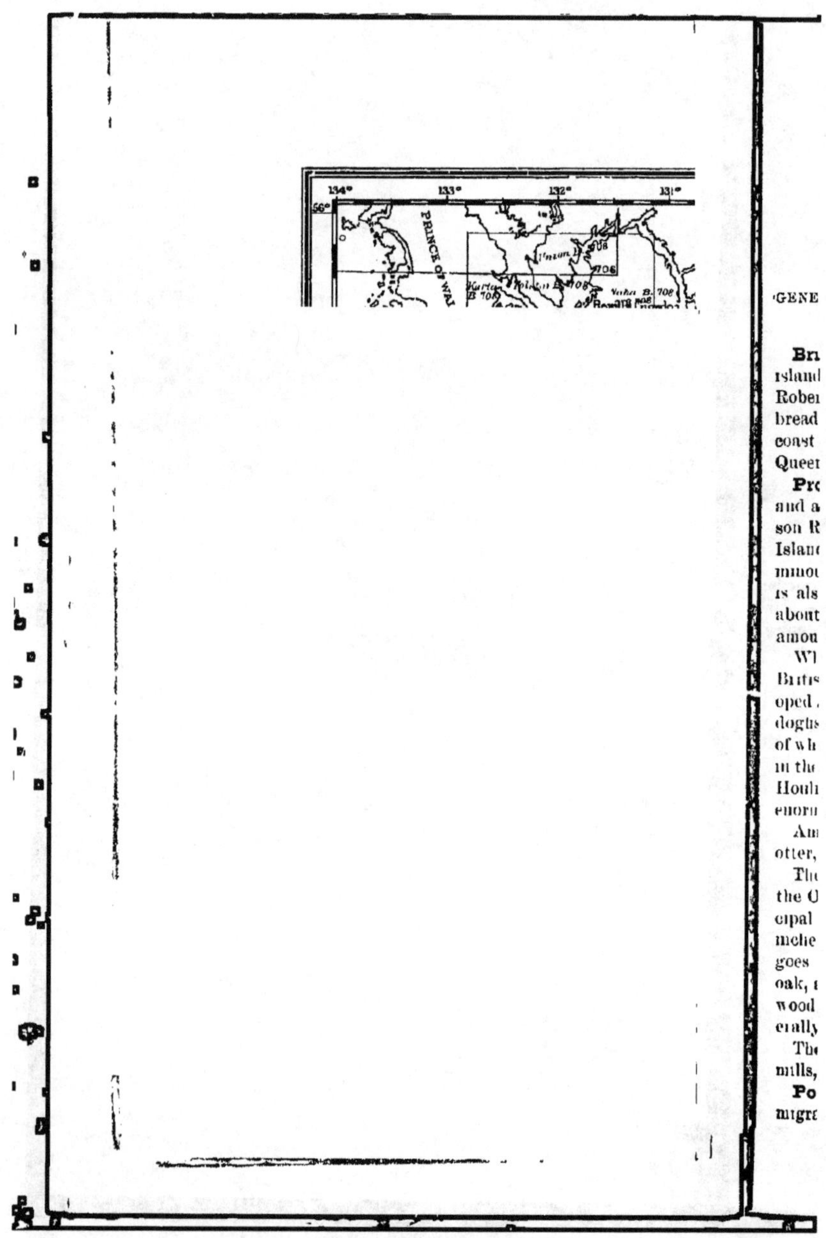
134°
133°
132°
131°
56°
PRINCE OF WAL

INTRODUCTORY CHAPTER.

GENERAL REMARKS.—CLIMATE, METEOROLOGY.—PRODUCTS.—PASSAGES.

British Columbia includes Vancouver Island, also the numerous islands and adjacent mainland of North America lying between Point Roberts, in the Strait of Georgia, and Portland Canal. The average breadth of British Columbia is about 250 miles, and the length of its coast line about 450 miles; the area, including Vancouver Island and Queen Charlotte Islands, is roughly estimated at 466,000 square miles.

Products.—British Columbia contains extensive tracts of arable land and a large auriferous district. Gold was first discovered on Thompson River in 1858. Coal is found on the mainland and on Vancouver Island; the mines at Nanaimo and Departure Bay, which yield bituminous coal, being the principal places on the island. Anthracite coal is also found, especially in Queen Charlotte Islands. During 1870 about 30,000 tons were exported; in 1884 the value of coal exported amounted to $2,000,000, and in 1886 to $973,000.

Wheat, barley, oats, potatoes, peas, vegetables, and fruits flourish in British Columbia. The fisheries are very rich, but are not yet developed; whaling is, however, being carried on to a small extent, and the dogfish catch is steadily progressing. Salmon is abundant, the export of which, chiefly in tins, constitutes one of the principal sources of wealth in the country; it is also an important part of the food of the Indians. Houlican, somewhat resembling the sardine, cod, herring, halibut (of enormous size), sardines, anchovy, haddock, and oysters are also found.

Among the numerous fur-bearing animals the principal are the sea otter, marten, silver fox, black fox, and red fox.

The forests are of great extent, producing valuable timber, of which the Oregon pine, white pine, maple, Scotch fir, and cedar are the principal; the former, yielding spars 100 to 150 feet in length, and from 20 inches to 2 feet in diameter, is that principally exported in large cargoes. Besides the above, the yellow cypress, poplar, arbor vitæ, yew, oak, arbutus, alder, dogwood, cherry, crab apple, willow, and cottonwood are found. Cattle, horses, sheep, and farm animals thrive generally in all parts.

The manufactures of British Columbia consist of sawmills and flour mills, breweries, and distilleries; they are rapidly increasing.

Population.—The population of British Columbia is to some extent migratory; in 1871 it amounted to 10,586, exclusive of Indians, and was classed as follows: 8,576 whites, 462 negroes, and 1,548 Chinese; but in 1885 the population of Victoria alone reached to nearly 12,000, and continues to increase with rapidity. The Indian population is estimated at about 30,000 or 40,000, 17,000 being on Vancouver Island, but they appear to be gradually diminishing in numbers, consequent on tribal wars, feuds, and the ravages of smallpox and measles, both of which diseases are deadly amongst the natives.

The Indians along the coast have great skill in the building and management of canoes; they are a polygamous race, and subsist chiefly by hunting and fishing; those of southern Columbia are dark, and wear their hair long, while those of the more northern districts are of a clearer tint. The coast Indians live in substantial one-story dwellings of ax-hewn timber, divided into several compartments, of which one is occupied by each family. In the interior the houses, or wigwams, are made of skins, old tent cloths, and mats; in severe weather they take shelter in underground houses (circular pits) from 20 to 40 feet in diameter and 8 or 10 feet deep, covered over with a substantial earthed roof, with a 3 foot circular aperture in the center, forming the only outlet for the inhabitants and smoke.

Railways.—The Canadian Pacific Railway is 3,054 statute miles in length between Quebec and Vancouver town, in Burrard Inlet, the western terminus. The railway is in course of construction from Vancouver town to English Bay, and a branch line has been made from Port Moody to New Westminster.

A railway has also been constructed on Vancouver Island, between Victoria, Esquimalt, and Nanaimo, and there is now daily communication between these places.

Telegraphs.—Esquimalt is in telegraphic communication with England through Canada, by way of Nanaimo and Burrard Inlet. Also through the United States, by way of Seattle.

Climate.—The climate of British Columbia varies considerably according to the locality; in the southern parts and on Vancouver Island it is temperate during summer, the thermometer seldom, if ever, rising on the hottest day above 80°, or falling below 20° in winter. In the central part of the province, however, the drought, heat, and cold are greater, the heat sometimes being very intense. It is, however, remarkably healthy both in summer and winter, there being no malaria or ague either during the hottest weather or in the dampest localities. Generally speaking, the summers are dry at Vancouver Island, but with occasional showers, the winters bring a good deal of rain, and snow falls more or less each year.

In the northern part of the province, along the coast, the atmosphere is excessively humid, and rains fall heavily.

The climate of the mainland coast opposite Vancouver Island differs somewhat from that of the SE. portion of the island. In summer the temperature averages slightly higher, and in winter somewhat lower, while the rainfall is greater immediately along the coast. The lower Fraser Valley (New Westminster district) does not receive in summer the cold breezes from the Olympian Mountains which blow across Victoria, nor does it receive in winter so much of the genial warmth of warm ocean air. As a general thing ice forms on the river for a short time, and snow begins to fall in January, and continues to do so intermittently until March, the ground not being continuously covered with it. Observations for seven consecutive years—1874 to 1880—at New Westminster give the highest maximum temperature, 92° in July, and the lowest 7° in January, the mean annual rainfall being 59·66 inches.

Taken as a whole, the climate, differing widely as it does in places, is salubrious and invigorating. No miasmatic infection from ague-breeding marshes taints the atmosphere, whatever locality may be selected for a residence, whether one of moist air and equable temperature along the coast, or the drier and more varying one of the interior; the climate will be found healthy, invigorating, and calculated to inspire activity, comparing more than favorably with the same latitude on the Atlantic slope.

Thermometer.—At Esquimalt the highest summer temperature averages 72° (in August), June, July and August being the warmest months of the year. The lowest temperature averages 23½°, the coldest months being December, January and February. The greatest daily range occurs in March and the smallest in October.

The temperature on Vancouver Island during summer is lower than on the mainland, owing to the prevailing SE winds blowing from the snow capped mountains on the American side and across the sound. The waters of the sound are peculiarly cold at this season

Barometer—The barometric variations are neither great nor frequent, the range for the year averaging about 1.5 inches.

Port Simpson.—The climate at Port Simpson is uncertain, no two seasons being precisely the same or appearing to follow any general law.

During one summer fine weather may be experienced for six weeks at a time, and on such occasions a serene atmosphere, with magnificent sunsets, will be experienced. The following summer may prove one of almost constant rain, with a succession of gales from the southeastward Along the shores of Chatham Sound the rainfall is not so great as within the inlets. The temperature during July and August, 1869, varied from 37° to 64°; during June, July and August, 1868, it varied from 48° to 73°. The mean temperature of the sea was 4° lower than the mean temperature of the atmosphere at Port Simpson during these periods, but at Metlah catlah and Nass Bays it was 8° lower than the atmosphere, probably due to the influence of the cold water from the rivers which flow into those bays

Birds—During the month of May humming birds in great numbers arrive, and remain until the end of August.

At the beginning of October, large flocks of wild geese and ducks are seen flying southward, and the winter season is then assumed to have commenced.

Temperature.—From observations taken in 1868, during the four months mentioned, the maximum and minimum registrations of temperature were as follows: June, 65°, 50°; July 71°, 48°; August, 70°, 54°; September, 64°, 41°.

Portland Canal.—The sun's rays in August, between 9 a. m. and 3 p. m., were very powerful, and, reflected from the snow, caused occasionally intense heat. When the sun was obscured by the mountains, the atmosphere at once conveyed a sensation of chilliness. During that month, just before sunrise, the thermometer registered 32°, water left in basins within the tent being frozen during the night. The vapor developed by the heat of the sun during the early portion of the day, becoming condensed on the mountainous shores of the inlet, usually fell as a drizzling rain from 3 p. m. to about midnight.

Temperature of the surface water, within 20 miles of the head of the canal, was 35°. At that distance from the mouth of the Bear River the water on the surface was fresh.

Queen Charlotte Islands.—The climate of Queen Charlotte Islands and the off lying islands of the coast of British Columbia is influenced by the warm body of water which washes their shores, and the winter is less severe and the climate is milder on the islands than within the inlets. The vapor arising from this body of warm water is condensed upon the high mountains which form the shores of the mainland, and falls in the drizzling rain so prevalent in these waters.

Ice.—The Frazer River is, as a rule, frozen over at New Westminster from January to early in March, during which time sleighs run to Langley. The lakes in the vicinity are frozen over, and ice forms at the head of the several inlets where the water is comparatively fresh, but on the coast it does not form sufficiently thick to impede navigation.

Within the inlets on the coast, north of Vancouver Island, ice is formed during the winter of from 8 to 12 inches in thickness, and occasionally extends as far as 25 miles from the heads of the inlets.

The Skeena and Nass Rivers are frozen over during the winter, the former as far as 6 miles below port Essington, and the latter, in severe weather, down to its mouth.

Rainfall.—The average rainfall appears to be about 55 inches; heavy rains generally occur in December and January.

The following table shows the principal meteorological features at Esquimalt, Vancouver Island, during the years 1870 and 1871.

Month	Barometer (mean height)	Thermometer		Temperature of sea	Prevailing wind.	Remarks.
		Maximum	Minimum			
January	30 021	51 5	23 5	43 4	North and northeasterly	
February	29 070	50 0	20 5	43	Easterly.	
March	20 021	59	34	45.4	Southeasterly and westerly	Rainy month
April .	30 037	61 5	43 5	48.2	Southeasterly and southwesterly	
May .	30 009	62 5	46 5	51 7	Southeasterly and southerly	
June	29 989	68	50 5	53 2	Southeasterly and southwesterly	
July	30 043	68 5	54 5	57 4	Southeasterly to westerly	
August	30 039	72	55	58 9	Southeasterly to westerly	
September	30 018	65	50	55.1	Southwesterly, variable	Fogs during latter part of month
October	30 037	60 5	45 5	49 1	Variable . . .	Fogs and frequent rains
November	30 059	61	40 5	46 7	Easterly, northeasterly to southeasterly	
December .	30 006	59	28 5	45.1	Easterly	

Fogs.—Juan de Fuca Strait.—Although fogs in this region are not of such frequent occurrence as on the neighboring coast of California (where they prevail almost uninterruptedly during summer and as late as the middle of October), yet from July to November they occur in Juan de Fuca Strait, and are sometimes very dense over the entrance for several days together. They are generally accompanied by calms or very light winds from NW., which renders them the more dangerous to sailing vessels closing the land.

Coast North of Vancouver Island.—Fogs are prevalent especially during the summer months. The NW. winds which prevail during that season condense the vapor which arises from the comparatively warm water surrounding Queen Charlotte Islands and the coast of Alaska. During the prevalence of NW winds this vapor is dispersed, but during calms or with light winds, and especially with southwesterly winds succeeding NW. winds, it approaches quickly from seaward in the form of dense fog or drizzling mist and rain.

At times fog will be found at the entrances to the sounds during the forenoon, dispersing near noon by the heat of the sun, the afternoons becoming clear and fine.

Smokes from forest fires cause much inconvenience during the dry season, and are a great impediment to navigation. In some seasons they have extended from the Gulf of Georgia to Portland Inlet

Vancouver Island to San Francisco (sailing).—Keep between 50 and 100 miles off shore to obtain the benefit of the current and to avoid the fogs. Take advantage of either tack upon which the most latitude can be made. In summer make the land to the northward of the port, in winter to the southward. Use every opportunity to observe for latitude and longitude, as fogs prevail near the land. Allow generally for a southerly set of ½ mile per hour until within 50 miles of the coast, after which it is not appreciable. With the above precaution vessels may shape a course for the south Farallon.

From November to April vessels are liable to have head winds from SW. as far south as the parallel of Cape Mendocino. These winds, however are variable, and blow frequently from the NW. To the southward of 40° N., the NW. winds will become more frequent.

From April to November, the good season, NW. winds prevail, and there is no difficulty in making the passage.

The wind often blows from SW. in the morning, and NW. in the afternoon.

San Francisco to Vancouver.—From November to April, the bad season, the passage should commence by putting well out to sea, the wind generally being from the NW. When far enough from the land to have nothing to fear from SW. or NW. squalls, make as much to the north as possible. North of the parallel of Cape Mendocino SW. winds prevail at this season, and enable vessels to finish the passage without difficulty.

From April to November the wind almost invariably blows from the northward, between NW. and NE., but generally from the NW. Both SE. and SW. winds have been met in this locality. After leaving San Francisco run about 100 or 150 miles to sea and then make to the northward, profiting by every shift in the wind, and always standing on the most favorable tack.

Uniform System of Buoyage.—Throughout the ports of British Columbia all buoys on the starboard side of the channel, entering from seaward, are painted *red*, and, if numbered, marked with *even numbers*, and must be left on the starboard hand when passing in.

All buoys on the port side, entering from seaward, are painted *black*, with *odd numbers*, if any, and must be left on the port hand when passing in.

Buoys painted with *red* and *black horizontal bands* will be found on obstructions or middle grounds, and may be left on either hand.

Buoys painted with *white* and *black vertical stripes* will be found in mid-channel, and must be passed close to, to avoid danger.

All other distinguishing marks to buoys are in addition to the foregoing, and indicate particular spots; a detailed description of which is given when the mark is first established.

Perches with balls, cages, etc, will, when placed on buoys, be at turning points, the color and number indicating on which side they are to be passed

Spar buoys will in some cases be surmounted by a ball, which will invariably be painted *red*, and will indicate that it is a starboard buoy, and must be left on the starboard or right hand when entering a channel or harbor.

The rule for coloring buoys is equally applicable to beacons, spindles, and other day marks, so far as it may be practicable to carry it out.

STRAI

Str
cithe h
which
bearin
the st
It gra
and S
miles ;
miles,
Rosari
the G
at the
and is
forms
Whidl
water
in its
is clos
miralt
Haro,
ing be
an ave
not le
Head
with a
may b
rock, w
Bay or
On t
places,
outwar
ern sid
Bay, V
harbor

CHAPTER I.

STRAIT OF JUAN DE FUCA, ADMIRALTY INLET, PUGET SOUND, HOOD'S CANAL, AND POSSESSION SOUND.

Strait of Juan de Fuca.—The entrance to this strait from the Pacific lies between Cape Flattery and Cape Bonilla, on Vancouver Island, which forms the northern shore. Its width is about 12 miles, and the bearing from Tatoosh Island to Cape Bonilla N. 5° E. From this line the strait runs ESE. for 40 miles, with a uniform width of 11 miles. It gradually contracts to 8 miles, between Beechey Head on the north and Striped Peak on the south; changes its direction to E. ½ S. for 15 miles; then expands to the northward, attaining a width of 18 to 20 miles, and divides into two ship channels, the Canal de Haro and Rosario Strait, leading through the Archipelago de Haro northward to the Gulf of Georgia It is terminated on the east by Whidbey Island; at the southeast it passes into Admiralty Inlet and Puget Sound, and is bounded on the south by the mainland of Washington, which forms the entire southern shore of the strait. From the ocean to Whidbey Island the mid channel distance is 83 miles The depth of water throughout the strait is remarkably great, no bottom being found in its deepest parts with 150 fathoms of line, and the 10 fathom line is close under the shores. It is the main artery for the waters of Admiralty Inlet, Puget Sound, Possession Sound, Hood's Canal, Canal de Haro, Rosarlo Strait, Bellingham Bay, and the Gulf of Georgia, extending between Vancouver Island and British Columbia for 120 miles, with an average width of 20 The currents run with an average velocity of not less than 3 miles per hour, and off the Race Island and Beechey Head over 6 miles an hour. Its shores are bold, abrupt, and covered with a heavy growth of varied timber and dense underbrush. They may be approached safely within ½ mile; there is only one breaking rock, which lies nearly that distance off the western point of Crescent Bay on the southern shore.

On both sides of the strait there are several anchorages or stopping places, which may be taken advantage of by vessels, either inward or outward bound, when meeting with adverse winds; those on the southern side are Neéah and Clallam Bays, Port Angeles, New Dungeness Bay, Washington Harbor, and Port Discovery, before reaching the harbors of Admiralty Inlet and Puget Sound; on the northern side are

Port San Juan, Sooke Inlet, and Becher Bay, before rounding the Race Islands, after which excellent anchorage may be always obtained with westerly winds.

On the northern or Vancouver Island shore of the strait the hills rise gradually and are densely wooded, but near the coast attain to no great elevation; on the southern side the almost perpetually snow clad mountains known as the Olympian range rise more abruptly and vary.

At the eastern limit of the strait the western face of Whidbey Island is very steep; it is about 250 feet high, and appears flat, as does the whole country eastward to the sharp cut outline of the Cascade range, stretching its serrated ridge northward, where the snow peak of Mount Baker is distinctly seen, and to the southward, where the higher peak of Mount Rainier attracts the eye.

During dry summers the forest fires envelop the country in a vast smoke that lasts for two or three months. At such times it is frequently impossible to make out the shore at ½ mile distance. The strong westerly winds coming up the strait disperse it for a while, but only to fan the fires, and give them renewed force and activity.

Tides.—It is high water, full and change, at Cape Flattery, at noon, the ebb stream commences to run strong at 2h. p. m. and continues for about 6 hours.

In the outer part of Juan de Fuca Strait there is no very great strength of tide; it varies from one to 4 knots near Cape Flattery, but when approaching the more contracted part in the neighborhood of the Race Islands, eddies, races, and irregularities occur.

The result of observations continued throughout an entire year at Esquimalt, and partially on other parts of the coast during three seasons, appears to warrant the following conclusions, viz:

The flood tide sets to the northward along the outer coast of the continent and Vancouver Island. It enters the Strait of Fuca at Cape Flattery, running with considerable velocity, sometimes 3 or 4 knots, over Duncan and Duntze Rocks; it then turns sharply into the strait, passing through the various channels of the Haro Archipelago into the Strait of Georgia, and within about from 5 to 20 miles of Cape Mudge, where it is met by a flood from the northward, which, sweeping the western coast of Vancouver Island, enters Goletas Channel and Queen Charlotte Sound at its northern extreme, in latitude 51°, thence southerly down the narrow waters of Johnstone Strait and Discovery Passage, meeting the tide which enters by Fuca Strait, and reaches about midway between the northern and southern extremes of Vancouver Island, or close to the spot where the broad expanse of the Strait of Georgia merges into the narrow channels adjoining it.

On the western side of the island the tides were found to be regular—flood and ebb of six hours' duration, the times of high water on the full and change at Nootka Sound, and at the entrance of Goletas Channel varying very little, and occurring near noon, the greatest range 13 feet; nor is any marked irregularity observable in Johnstone Strait, and Discovery Passage, except the not unusual circumstance that the ebb stream continues to run to the northward for two hours after it is low water by the shore, the water rising at the same time; the ebb stream being of seven hours' duration, the flood about five hours

The great and perplexing tidal irregularities may therefore be said to be embraced between the Strait of Fuca, near the Race Islands, and Cape Mudge, a distance of 150 miles; and a careful investigation of the observations made at Esquimalt, and among the islands of the Haro Archipelago, shows that during the summer months, May, June, and July, there occurs but one high and one low water during the twenty four hours, high water at the full and change of the moon happening about midnight, and varying but slightly from that hour during any day of the three months; the springs range from 8 to 10 feet, the neaps from 4 to 5 feet The tides are almost stationary for two hours on either side of high or low water, unless affected by strong winds out side.

During August, September, and October, there are two high and low waters in the twenty four hours; a superior and an inferior tide, the high water of the superior varying between 1h. and 3h. a. m., the range during these months from 3 to 5 feet, the night tide the highest.

During winter almost a reversal of these rules appears to take place; thus, in November, December, and January, the twelve hour tides again occur, but the time of high water is at or about noon instead of mid-night.

In February, March, and April, there are two tides, the superior high water occurring from 1h. to 3h. p. m. Thus it may be said that in summer months the tides are low during the day, the highest tides occurring in the night, and in winter the tides are low during the night, the highest tide occurring in the day.

The ebb stream has always been found to run southward through the Haro Archipelago, and out of Fuca Strait for two and one half hours after it is low water by the shore, the water rising during that time; the ebb is stronger than the flood, and generally two hours' longer duration.

The tides during those months when two high and two low waters occur in the twenty four hours, are far more irregular than when there is only one twelve hour tide, and another anomaly exists, viz., the greatest range not infrequently occurs at the first and last quarters, instead of at the full and change of the moon

Currents.—A southerly current has been found to prevail on the western coast of Vancouver Island more or less throughout the year, particularly from August to November This current joining the ebb tide out of Fuca Strait has been known to set vessels between 4 and 5 miles an hour to the southward, and during fogs there is great risk of being drifted on to Cape Flattery, or some of its off lying dangers;

extreme caution should therefore be observed in entering the strait at such times, especially near the full and change of the moon, when the tides are at their strongest. A northerly set has been experienced with winds from the southward and eastward.

Winds.—Within the strait of Juan de Fuca, in the winter season, the winds usually assume its direction either up or down. During summer, the prevailing winds from NW. or SW take a westerly direction within the strait; while the SE. gales of winter blow directly out and create a heavy cross sea off the entrance to the strait.

Although a westerly wind may be blowing within the strait, it frequently during the change of the seasons blows heavily outside at the same time from SSW., or sometimes suddenly changes to that direction, from a light easterly wind on opening the entrance, which makes that part of the coast of Vancouver Island between Port San Juan and Bonilla Point a dangerous lee shore to a ship without steam power.

The coast winds in summer prevail from SW and NW., the former during the early months, and the latter blow fresh and with great regularity during June, July, and August. In September and the early part of October the winds are very uncertain and there is generally a great deal of calm, gloomy weather.

The barometer usually stands above 30 inches during summer; should it fall to 29.90, a southeasterly wind with thick rainy weather may be expected, but of short duration, clearing up with a westerly wind as soon as the barometer rises.

The winter winds are SE. or SW., more frequently the former; they set in towards the end of October, and continue until the middle of April. SE. gales are generally preceded by a short interval of calm, cloudy weather, they spring up gradually from E. or ESE., veering to the southward, accompanied by rain and thick weather, the barometer falling rapidly, when the barometer becomes stationary the wind shifts suddenly to SW. and blows heavily with clear weather, but frequent squalls of rain; the barometer begins to rise immediately the wind veers to SW., from which quarter it generally blows from twelve to twenty hours.

The violence and duration of these SE. gales is always proportioned to the fall of the mercury; with the barometer at 29.50 a strong gale may be looked for from this quarter; it seldom falls below 29.20, when very bad weather is certain to follow.

A SE. gale sometimes springs up, though very seldom, with the barometer above 30 inches On such occasions the wind has always been preceded by calm, cloudy weather and rain, with a high but falling barometer; such gales are not violent and of short duration.

SE gales are always accompanied by thick dirty weather, and rain; they seldom continue from that quarter for more than twelve or eighteen hours, unless the barometer falls very low, and almost always shift to SW

When the SW. gale of winter is not preceded by the southeastern, the barometer seldom falls; it either remains stationary, when the gale may be expected to continue longer, or rises slowly, when it will gradually subside and fine weather follow. SW. gales are accompanied by heavy banks of clouds, and passing showers of rain, sometimes snow.

The barometer has been known to fall during winter as low as 29.45 and has been followed by no gale or bad weather, but on such occasions there has been a heavy fall of snow on the hills, and a sudden fall of 15 degrees in the temperature.

A fine northerly or NE. wind frequently occurs at intervals during the months of December, January, and February; it is always accompanied by a high barometer, above 30, and at such times a continuance for several days together of clear, cold, frosty weather may be looked for; the barometer on these occasions will sometimes rise as high as 30.70, and the fine weather will then probably last a fortnight or more.

Fogs.—Fogs occur occasionally in Juan de Fuca Strait, from July to November, and are sometimes very dense, over the entrance, for several days together. They are generally accompanied by calms or very light winds from NW., which renders them more dangerous to sailing vessels closing the land.

PILOT LAWS.

(Approved February 2, 1888; took effect April 1, 1888.)

SEC. 11. That every pilot on boarding a vessel shall, at the request of the master, exhibit his license, and on refusal to do so shall be liable to pay a penalty of fifty dollars.

SEC. 16. That it shall be the duty of every pilot in charge of a vessel arriving at any of the ports of Puget Sound or its branches to have the vessel safely moored or anchored in such a position as the master of the vessel may direct, when his responsibility shall cease.

SEC. 18. That no person except those licensed by the commissioners shall pilot vessels in and out of the bays or harbors of Puget Sound or Juan de Fuca Strait or to or from the Pacific Ocean through said strait for hire, under penalty of three hundred dollars fine for each and every offense. This penalty is not incurred where the master of a vessel acts as his own pilot; provided, that the master or owner of any vessel shall not be compelled to take a pilot under the provisions of this act.

SEC. 20. That pilots taken to sea against their wills, when a boat is in attendance ready to receive them, shall be entitled to receive five dollars per day while absent, which sum shall be paid by the master or owner of the vessel by which the pilot was taken away.

SEC. 21. That if any pilot offers himself to any vessel requiring his services as pilot, outside of a line drawn from the west end of Waaddah Island to Observatory Point on the east side of Port San Juan, British Columbia, if inward bound, he shall have the preference, if a pilot's services are required by the vessel where bound to sea, or a pilot from the same pilot-boat.

SEC. 23. That the hull and appurtenances of all vessels shall be held liable for pilot's dues.

SEC. 24. That the pilots shall at all times keep a boat, in good condition, cruising on the Strait of Fuca or at sea. The number of pilots to be on any one boat to be determined by the commissioners.

SEC 26 The board of pilot commissioners shall fix the rate of pilotage between the open sea and the ports on Puget Sound, but such rate shall not exceed eight dollars per foot draught to vessels who engage pilots outside of Waaddah Island to port of entry or other ports on Puget Sound, to vessels from British Columbia to port of entry or other ports on Puget Sound not to exceed six dollars per foot draught. To vessels from Port Townsend to any of the ports on Puget Sound not to exceed four dollars per foot draught *Provided*, That nothing in this act shall be construed as requiring half pilotage to be paid when services are not actually performed *And provided further*, That every pilot bringing a vessel from sea shall take her to her port of destination if required when that port is above the port of entry without additional charges But after twenty-four hours of delay at the port of entry the pilot shall be entitled to additional pay of five dollars per day for every day so delayed

EXTRACTS FROM THE BY LAWS OF THE PILOT COMMISSIONERS

SEC 12 Pilot boats, while cruising, must have a white signal lantern displayed in a conspicuous manner during the night, and the number of the boat displayed on the mainsail as a day signal

SEC 13 Neither pilots nor their boats shall be permitted to leave their peculiar service whether in port or at sea, unless to assist vessels in distress, more than thirty miles north or south of Tatoosh light without first obtaining permission of this board and any boat infringing this * * *

SEC 15 That rates of pilotage shall be as follows Inward bound, six dollars per foot draught from any point on a line drawn from Cape Beale, British Columbia, and Flattery Rocks, Washington; five dollars per foot draught from any point on a line drawn from Waaddah Island to the most westerly point of San Juan harbor, British Columbia, four dollars per foot draught from any point west of a line drawn from Port Angeles light, Washington, to Race Rocks, British Columbia, three dollars per foot draught from Port Townsend to any port on Puget Sound, and *vice versa*. Any fraction of a foot over six inches, a foot; under six inches, not counted Draught to be measured when vessel draws most Should vessel be detained in Port Townsend harbor more than twenty-four hours before proceeding to any other port on Puget Sound, the pilot to be paid five dollars per day for every day of detention above said twenty-four hours. Outward pilotage to be five dollars per foot draught from Port Townsend to the sea, and six dollars per foot draught from any port on Puget Sound to sea Outward-bound vessels allowed forty-eight hours' detention without charge for delay

It is reported (August 13, 1889) that these laws and regulations are a dead letter, because no persons have qualified under the law which does not allow half pilotage when vessels decline a pilot.

Cape Flattery is a remarkable point of land, distinctly seen at a distance of 35 miles, rising gradually from the sea to a thickly wooded mountain nearly 2,000 feet high, with an irregular shaped summit, and falling again at the distance of 3 or 4 miles to the eastward. When seen from the southward or southwest it has the appearance of an island, being separated by a stretch of lowland from hills of the same or greater elevation, which rise again immediately southward of it.

On a nearer view, the headland itself, with its wild off-lying rocks, over which the sea is almost constantly breaking, presents no inviting appearance; it is a rugged, sea worn cliff of no great elevation, and rising gradually to its more prominent feature, a densely wooded mountain. From the cape the coast trends eastward for 4 miles to Neéah

Bay. There is generally a heavy swell with irregular tides, and vessels should not approach it within a mile.

Tatoosh Island, lying ½ mile off Cape Flattery, is a steep, almost perpendicular, rocky islet, bare of trees, and 108 feet high, with some reefs extending a short distance off its western side. The lighthouse, known among seamen as Cape Flattery light, stands on the summit of the island, which, with its outlying reef is the most western portion of the United States. Sailing vessels should not approach the lighthouse inside of 2 miles.

Fuca Pillar, 140 feet high and 50 feet in diameter, lies $\frac{9}{10}$ mile S. 15° E. of the lighthouse on Tatoosh Island. It is a leaning, rocky column, and only 120 yards from the cliffs, which are 120 feet high. It shows well when a vessel is approaching Tatoosh Island from the northwestward, and is last seen from the strait when the face of the cape is just open by the eastern tangent of Tatoosh Island.

Duncan Rock lies N. 14° W. one mile from Tatoosh Island light; it is a few feet above water, but the sea always breaks over it. There is deep water between it and the island, but vessels should not use the passage unless compelled to do so.

Duntze Rock, with 3 fathoms water over it, lies about ¼ mile N. 19° W. of Duncan Rock, and the sea frequently breaks on it. The cross sea which is created in this neighborhood during bad weather strongly resembles heavy breakers, extending a considerable distance across the strait. In the immediate neighborhood of Cape Flattery, and among these rocks, the tides are strong and irregular.

Directions.—Vessels from the southward or westward, bound for Fuca Strait, should make Cape Flattery; there is no inducement to hug the coast, on which a long rolling swell frequently sets, and this swell, meeting the southeasterly gales of winter, causes a confused sea. The cape and its off lying rocks should not be approached within a distance of at least 3 miles, as the tide occasionally sets over Duncan and Duntze Rock with great velocity. It is necessary either in entering or leaving the strait to avoid the coast of Vancouver Island between Port San Juan and Bonilla Point when there is any appearance of bad weather.

It is recommended to pass at the distance of at least 10 miles from the coast, unless working to windward against a fine northerly wind, when it may be safely approached within 3 miles or less.

To vessels making the strait in bad weather it will be more desirable to run in and seek shelter than to remain outside. If the land has been made either to the southward of Cape Flattery or on the Vancouver Island shore within a moderate distance of the entrance, or if the latitude can be relied upon within 2 or 3 miles, it will be advisable to run for the strait. The powerful light of Cape Flattery will, unless in very thick weather or fog, be seen at the distance of 5 miles, and as soon as a vessel is actually within the strait she will have comparatively smooth water, with sufficient sea room, and may run boldly up the center for the

Race light, or by the assistance of that on Cape Flattery maintain her position in the strait if preferred. It is to be remarked that when Cape Flattery light is brought to bear to the northward of west it becomes shut in by the land about Neéah Bay, and that the Race Island light from a similar cause becomes obscured by Beechey Head when brought to bear to the southward of S. 83° E.; therefore, when either of these lights are obscured the distance from either coast will be accurately judged, and in the latter case a ship will be getting too close to the northern shore.

Coming from the westward with a heavy westerly or northwest gale, thick weather, and uncertain of the latitude, it would be prudent to lay by at not less than 30 miles from the entrance of the strait or on the edge of the bank of soundings. These gales seldom last more than twelve hours, and if they veer towards the SW. the weather will clear, and vessels may immediately bear up for the strait.

With a SE. gale it is recommended to close the land, smoother water will be obtained, and the bank of soundings off the Vancouver Island shore will give vessels pretty accurately their distance from the land. Gales from this quarter sometimes continue in the winter season thirty hours, and when a vessel strikes soundings on the edge of the bank in 90 fathoms and carries them in to 60 she may put her head to WSW. and have plenty of room for drift.

It is of great importance in making the strait during bad weather to strike the outer edge of the bank of soundings, as the ship's distance from the land will then be accurately known.

Should sailing vessels be overtaken by one of the dense fogs which sometimes hang over the entrance of the strait they should not close the land, but stand off sufficiently far to avoid being set by the southerly current too near Cape Flattery. If a steamer has made the land or light, and is certain of her position, she should get the Vancouver Island shore aboard, when, with the assistance of the chart and lead, she may feel her way in. When 8 or 10 miles eastward of Port San Juan there is anchoring ground in 12 fathoms a mile from the shore, and if the fog is very dense strangers should anchor; it must be remarked, however, that not unfrequently the weather is clear a few miles within the strait while the entrance is totally obscured.

Neéah Bay is between Koitlah Point and Waaddah Island; which is a narrow high ridge, covered with pine trees. Koitlah Point is 3.7 miles East of the lighthouse on Tatoosh Island. The bay offers a safe and convenient anchorage to vessels meeting SW. or SE. gales at the entrance of the strait, and is sheltered from W. and N. round by south to ENE. The western shore is steep and cliffy, a reef extends for more than 200 yards off Koitlah Point, and within the point a sand [illegible], which dries, extends off ¼ mile at low water from abreast the cliffs. The head of the bay is a low sandy beach, on which there is generally some surf rolling. On the eastern side of the bay, off the southwestern side of Waaddah Island, a rocky ledge and shoal water extends for 600 yards, and the holding ground is not so good on the island side.

A good berth will be found in Neéah bay, in 6 fathoms sandy bottom, with the outer point of Waaddah Island N. 56° E., and Koitlah Point N. 56° W.; a short distance within this position kelp grows in large patches all over the bay, and care is necessary in selecting a berth. Large sailing vessels may anchor in 7 or 8 fathoms a little outside the above bearings, in the center of the bay, with the outer point of the island N. 79° E.

Vessels should leave this bay on any indication of a northeast wind, and if too late and unable to weather Waaddah Island, they may run between it and the main; the passage is 400 yards in breadth, and the [illegible] 21 feet; they must be careful to avoid the ledge off the southwest end of Waaddah, and in hauling out should give the eastern side of the island a berth of at least $\frac{1}{4}$ mile. Vessels have ridden out northwest gales close to the southeast end of Waaddah in 6 fathoms, but it is more prudent to get out into the strait at the commencement of the gale. During strong westerly or southwesterly gales, or after they have been blowing outside, a considerable swell rolls into the bay, which renders it at such times a disagreeable though not unsafe anchorage; small vessels may go close in and get smooth water, even among the kelp which grows in 4 and 5 fathoms.

Clallam Bay.—From Neéah to Clallam Bay the coast is nearly straight, and the shore bold, the only remarkable feature being Klahosloh (Seal Rock), 150 feet high, which lies a short distance off the shore, 2 miles southeastward of Waaddah Island. If vessels reach as high as Clallam Bay and meet an easterly or southeasterly wind, they may obtain anchorage and shelter in the center of the bay, but this can only be considered as a stopping place; it is easily recognized by Slip Point, its eastern [illegible], which is the western termination of a bold coast ridge.

The Coast from Clallam Bay continues in the same direction to Pillar Point, which terminates in a bare, columnar-shaped rock. The coast on the eastern side of this point forms a small bight, in which there is a considerable stream, and then trends S. 79° E. with a gentle curve to Striped Peak; a small river, the Lyre, empties just eastward of Low Point, about 6 miles westward of the peak.

Striped Peak is rather remarkable from a landslip occurring down its face; this mark is being rapidly obliterated by the growth of vegetation.

Crescent Bay.—Tongue Point lies about one mile northwestward of Striped Peak, and forms the eastern side of a slight indentation of the shore line, extending a mile to the westward, where another low point extends out $\frac{1}{3}$ mile to form Crescent Bay. Tongue Point has several visible rocks extending $\frac{1}{4}$ mile to the westward. The western point has a sunken rock $\frac{1}{3}$ mile northward with 15 feet water over it and upon which the swell breaks at low water. There is a depth of 8 fathoms close outside, and 6 fathoms on the east and west. This is the only known hidden danger on the south side of the strait. There is no good anchorage, the bottom is not good, and the currents between the rock and the reef off Tongue Point are treacherous.

Fresh Water Bay.—About $1\frac{2}{3}$ miles east of Striped Peak is the moderately low wooded extremity of the land stretching from the peak and forming the western point of Fresh Water Bay. This is known as Observatory Point, a[illegible] has several visible and sunken rocks running nearly $\frac{1}{4}$ mile to the [illegible]d.

The eastern point of the [illegible] the low delta named Angeles Point, under the western side of which empties the Elwha River by several mouths.

Angeles Point bears N. 82° E., 3 miles from Observatory Point, and from the line joining these the southern shore recedes a little over a mile, with an irregular outline. On the line of the two points the depth of water is about 15 fathoms; inside of it the depth decreases to 6 fathoms at about $\frac{1}{2}$ mile from the shore, which is clean except toward the western part, where there is a narrow line of kelp for $1\frac{1}{4}$ miles to Observatory Point. Off the delta the depth increases from one fathom to 10 fathoms in a mile; and to the eastward of Angeles Point a great bank, having from 5 to 10 fathoms of water upon it, stretches northward a mile, and eastward towards Ediz Hook.

The spit off Point Angeles must be approached with great care in thick weather, because there are no trees on the extreme point, and therefore it cannot be seen; the lighthouse near its extremity serves to mark it.

Fresh Water Bay is an open roadstead, but anchorage may be had in moderate weather. It affords no shelter from the easterly swell except close under the lee of the rocks off Observatory Point, where a vessel may find comparatively smooth anchorage with good holding ground close up to the kelp. In the eastern part of the bay the bottom is smooth rock, on which the anchor will not hold. The Elwha River is reported to be one of the most convenient places for obtaining fresh water; it is a very rapid mountain stream and brings down a large amount of material in suspension.

Port Angeles.—At $6\frac{1}{2}$ miles S. 85° E. of Angeles Point is the lighthouse upon the eastern extremity of the Ediz Hook.

This hook is a long, low, very narrow sand spit stretching out from the clay bluff 3 miles N. 78° E. with a regular sweeping curve swelling a little to the northwest. The extremity lies $1\frac{1}{2}$ miles off the main shore, and thus an excellent and extensive harbor is formed, protected from the north round by the west and south, but open to the eastward, with deep water from 25 to 30 fathoms over a sandy bottom close under the inside of the sand spit almost to the head of the bay. Through the center of the bay is found a line of 15 fathoms over sticky bottom, and between that and the main shore it shoals very regularly, with the same kind of bottom. The 3-fathom line lies as much as ¼ mile from the south shore, and there is a broad low-water beach; but in places the clay bluff, which is about 75 feet high, comes almost directly to the high-water line, except in a few localities. The bluff and the flat country back of it are densely wooded.

Fresh water is found at several places on the southern shore, but the extensive flats render it difficult to obtain.

On the southern shore is the town of Port Angeles, stretching for 1½ miles east and west; abreast Taylor's or Norman's Creek a wharf extends 700 feet into the bay, with a T, 100 feet long. There is a depth of 16½ feet of water at the end of the wharf. On the outside of the spit very deep water is found close to it, and the hook may be rounded within 200 yards in 25 fathoms.

In foggy and smoky weather, with no wind and the currents unknown, a vessel on this side of the strait must be vigilant and keep the lead going.

Vessels coming up the strait and bound for Departure Bay may go into Port Angeles and telegraph to Port Townsend for a tug.

At the head of the bay and connected therewith by a small outlet there is a large salt-water lagoon, and the beach affords a capital place for heaving down.

The hook is covered with coarse grass, and in many places with drift-wood, showing that the sea sometimes washes over it. Although it lies well out of the line of vessels bound either in or out of the strait, it has been deemed necessary to mark it with a light-house. In thick, hazy weather it would be readily distinguished if clumps of trees were planted upon it. From the middle of the strait it can not be seen, and its position is ascertained by the light-house building or the peculiarities of the bluff beyond.

New Dungeness Bay.—The shore from the head of Port Angeles runs in a slightly curving line for 9 miles to the eastward, and at 7 miles from Ediz Hook it runs nearly straight for 6 miles to the new Dungeness light-house.

The slightly projecting point in the deepest part of this bight and 4⅓ miles from Ediz Hook light-house is Green Point. It has 5 fathoms of water at ¼ mile outside. To the east of it there is no kelp; to the westward for 4 miles there is a field of kelp reaching out to 7 fathoms of water.

Northeastward 4¼ miles from Green Point another long, low, narrow sand spit, covered with coarse grass and very similar to Ediz Hook, leaves the high clay bluff shore and stretches in a general northeast direction for 3⅞ miles. This spit forms the northwestern shore of the roadstead of New Dungeness.

The south shore is distant 2 miles from the light-house, and runs 6 miles southeastward to Washington Harbor. This leaves the bay broad open to the east.

The depth of water along the outside of the spit is very great, at ⅓ mile this depth is 10 fathoms over hard sand and gravel bottom, and it drops off very suddenly to 30 fathoms within ½ mile. Along the outer southern part of the spit toward the bluff the 10 fathom curve stretches out 1½ miles and the 20-fathom curve runs on nearly a straight line to within 2 miles of Ediz Hook

Off the northeastern extremity of the spit a long gravel reef extends over ¾ mile from the light to the northeast, dropping off suddenly from 5 and 10 fathoms to 30 fathoms of water with heavy rips at the change of tides and currents The extremity of this spit is marked by a buoy.

The depth of the bay to the westward is much inferior to that at Port Angeles, because on the inside of the main spit and at 1⅛ miles from the extremity a second spit makes out SSW. for 1¼ miles and reaches to within ¼ mile from the southern bluff This second spit divides the bay into the outer or eastern harbor proper and the inner shoal bay, which is 2¼ miles long northeast and southwest by ⅞ mile wide. It is occupied by marsh and extensive flats Through the narrow channel connecting the two the water passes as over a rapid at low tide.

Abreast of this point is a narrow passage, which is the opening of the Dungeness River, under a bluff 60 feet high, upon which is a large village of the Clallams An abundance of fresh water is to be had at this stream, but boats must obtain their supply at low tide and come out when the tide has risen sufficiently The eastern shore of the Dungeness river is low, swampy, and covered with trees and brush. It forms the main or southern shore of the roadstead, and off it lie the extensive mud flats, which are bare at low water for ⅝ mile to the northward and continue as far as Washington Harbor. The area of the outer harbor is restricted by the flats ¼ mile in width lying under the east side of the secondary spit, and by the extensive mud flats on the southern shore, where the 3-fathom line is ½ mile from the low shore.

Beyond these flats the depth of the water throughout the harbor ranges to 10 fathoms with soft, tenacious, muddy bottom The deepest water is under the extremity of the spit, where a depth of 20 fathoms is found ⅛ mile from the light house The best anchorage is close under the spit in 10 fathoms of water ⅛ mile from the beach to the northwest, with the light-house bearing N. 39° E. distant ½ mile A steamer may anchor closer in, to the northwest of this location

A southeast wind drawing out of the strait blows directly into this harbor, but the bottom will hold any vessel with good ground tackle. The only difficulty is to get the anchors out of the mud after riding out a gale for two or three days. In the position mentioned for anchorage, a vessel can readily get under way when the southeast wind comes up and clear the point and the danger off it.

Eastward of New Dungeness to the entrance of Admiralty Inlet, 14 miles, there is a deep recession of the general shore-line for 5 miles to the southeastward, with openings into Washington Harbor and Point Discovery.

Light.—The lighthouse is near the eastern end of the spit, is conical, and has a keeper's dwelling attached.

Washington Harbor.—From New Dungeness roadstead to the entrance of the harbor the immediate shore line is nearly straight for $5\frac{1}{2}$ miles, with a slightly projecting angle midway, called Kulo Kala Point. The shore is low and flat and bordered by an extensive mud flat, averaging nearly one mile wide. The harbor is of little importance, the entrance being nearly closed by a low sand spit, stretching across from the east almost to the western side, where there is a narrow channel, about 200 yards in width, with a depth of 2 fathoms. Inside the general depth is from 10 to 20 fathoms, over a muddy bottom, and 6 fathoms can be carried nearly to the head. The breadth of the harbor is a little over a mile and its depth $3\frac{1}{2}$ miles.

Protection Island.—This island is about $1\frac{5}{8}$ miles long and $\frac{3}{8}$ mile wide across the middle. Its general direction is ENE. and WSW., and it lies $1\frac{5}{8}$ miles squarely off the entrance to Port Discovery. There is a long, low point at each end of the island. That at the west is rocky and sandy; that at the east all sand. The highest part is near the western extremity and reaches an elevation of 215 feet but the fir trees which cover this end of the island make it look much higher. The sides are very steep, and rise from 90 to 130 feet. The seaward crest of the eastern part is covered with a narrow fringe of stunted pines. The eastern slope is steep and grassy, and that toward Port Discovery is undulating and covered with fern. The principal part of the eastern half of the island is cultivated.

Midway up the face of the cliff toward the northwest and near the angle of the northern shore there is a horizontal streak of gray glacial clay almost 3 feet broad, which is a local feature easily recognized.

On the inside of Protection Island there is a good broad passage round either end. In the eastern passage the width of the channel between the 5-fathom lines is $1\frac{1}{4}$ miles, with good water close under Cape George and very deep water off the point of Protection Island. There is a depth of 53 fathoms in this channel. The width of the western passage between the black buoy off the western point of Protection Island and the nearest bluff to the SW. is $1\frac{1}{4}$ miles. The greatest depth of this channel is 65 fathoms.

Vessels bound into Port Discovery from the strait with a southerly wind enter by the western passage, because the southerly wind draws out of Washington Sound and gives a fair working breeze to reach Point Clallam.

On the inside shore of the island there is moderately deep water close under the banks, and anchorage may be had in 10 fathoms about 300 yards off the shore. There is no kelp off this shore except in the middle of the summer, when there is a little near the buoy. North of the island an extensive shoal makes out to the northward known as the Dallas Bank. Directly off the shore the 3 fathom line extends fully ½ mile out, and the outer line of the kelp marks the 4-fathom line. The limit of the 10 fathom line of this bank is 2½ miles to the northward or ½ mile outside of the line between New Dungeness lighthouse and Point Wilson lighthouse; the breadth is about 1½ miles. This 10 fathom line runs sharply to the east point, but it swings ¾ mile off the west point and is beyond the black buoy. This bank affords anchorage when a vessel is baffled with light airs and strong adverse currents. The bottom is irregular, full of huge bowlders toward the island, and sand and gravel toward the strait. The bottom falls off suddenly on the east side of the bank to 30 and 40 fathoms, and on the west side to 20 and 30 fathoms.

The charts do not give a shoal spot of 3 and 4 fathoms, formerly reported, near the outer northern limit of the bank.

Port Discovery.—This landlocked bay lies in the eastern part of the bight between New Dungeness and Point Wilson. It is not readily made out by vessels in the strait because the entrance appears blocked by Protection Island. Clallam Point, the western point of the port, is low, but rises quickly to a moderate height and slopes to the southward. Cape George, the eastern point, is a steep cliff and rises directly from the water which is very deep under the south side; under the north side the 3 fathom curve is not over 200 yards from shore. The average width is nearly 1¾ miles until near its head, when it decreases rapidly to the Salmon River. It makes four turns from the entrance to the head, a distance of about 10 miles. The shores are abrupt and covered with wood and the projecting parts are all terminated by low points stretching out short distances with deep water off them. The great drawback to this port is the great depth of water, which, in mid channel, is not not less than 25 fathoms and in some places 40 fathoms.

Anchorage may be had in 20 fathoms, soft bottom, on the western shore 2 miles south of Clallam Point and abreast a low swampy beach. In the deepest part of the bight between Clallam Point and this anchorage, off the mouth of Eagle Creek, there is good anchorage in 10 fathoms about 400 yards offshore.

At the head of the bay it contracts in width, the water shoals, a large mud flat exists for the last mile and the shores become higher.

A large sawmill has been built on Point Discovery, the bay is here scant one mile wide with a depth of 22 fathoms in mid channel. There is good anchorage in the bay near the sawmill.

Middle or Rocky Point.—Midway between Cape George and Point Wilson is a sharp point projecting out nearly ¼ mile. The whole shore line lies at the base of high yellow clay cliffs, which reach 400 or 500 feet elevation.

Current.—The currents off the point are conflicting from its proximity to the entrance of Admiralty Inlet, the Dallas Bank, and the passage to Port Discovery.

Rock.—A buoy has been placed ⅛ mile northeast of the point, and marks a small sunken rock which is awash at the lowest tides. This buoy should not be approached within 100 yards.

Point Wilson.—This point lies at the entrance to Admiralty Inlet, of which it forms the western point. It is also the northwestern point of the entrance of Port Townsend.

The high yellow clay cliffs surmounted by heavy forest run from Port Discovery to Port Townsend, and reach a height of 400 or 500 feet near Rocky Point; they are very steep and break down suddenly under a hill 250 feet high ⅜ mile before reaching the extremity of Point Wilson. This point stretches out toward Admiralty Head and is formed of low sandy hillocks covered with coarse grass.

On the extremity of the point are the lighthouse buildings.

Between Rocky Point and Point Wilson the 5-fathom line is less than ¼ mile distant, except within ⅜ mile of Point Wilson, where it reaches out ½ mile over a very rough, rocky, and shingly bottom, with a field of kelp to mask it. The kelp field is well off the point on the north side of the bight just west of the low extremity. The 10-fathom line lies about ⅜ mile from the shore. Directly off the point towards Admiralty Harbor, a depth of 20 fathoms is found 100 yards from the beach, and the currents make by it with great velocity. During the ebb tides a very strong eddy current sets to the eastward along shore from Middle or Rocky Point, and even as far as Port Discovery. Vessels working out from Port Townsend, with the strong summer winds, hold well under the southeast shore of Point Wilson, carrying 3 fathoms within 250 yards of the beach southwest of the lighthouse, and round the point close aboard.

Quimper Peninsula.—Between Port Discovery and Port Townsend lies a peninsula averaging 3 miles in breadth and 10 miles long. It is reasonably undulating land and has many large farms.

Point Partridge.—This is the western point of Whidbey Island, the eastern boundary of the Strait of Juan de Fuca. It may be considered the northern part of the entrance to Admiralty Inlet and Puget Sound, although Admiralty Head and Point Wilson are, strictly considered, the two points of the entrance.

The seaward slope is very steep and shows large areas of sand and sandy soil. The coast line is level on the summit, which is covered with spruce, fir, and cedar. There are two noticeable cultivated farms on the shore about 3 miles to the northward of the point. The point is so rounding that it is not easily recognized on coming from the westward, but from the south and north it is well marked and prominent. Its face is composed of yellow sand, which, being blown up the hill by the strong west winds, has formed a very peculiar ridge on the outer face of the top. This is so narrow that it can hardly be traveled, and in many places it is 35 feet above the ground inside; yet being overgrown with bushes the ridge is now permanent.

The highest part of the point is about 260 feet above low water.

Although the water off this point is quite bold, yet the bottom drops off so suddenly that in foggy or smoky weather vessels running by the lead may be unexpectedly upon a bowlder reef which extends out ½ mile from the point and is marked by kelp very nearly to that depth. The line of the shore south of the point runs southeast and in line with the direction of Partridge Bank, so that the 10 fathom lines are hardly a mile apart, yet there is a depth of 30 fathoms in that width.

Off the end of the bowlder reef in 5 to 10 fathoms the currents are very strong and there is much boiling and overfall at the changes.

Buoy.—To mark the outer end of the bowlder reef which lies close under the shore of Point Partridge a buoy has been placed in 31 feet of water just outside the kelp and about ½ mile west of the extreme outer part of the point. Vessels passing northward under the western shore of Whidbey Island must leave it on the starboard hand. A vessel coming from Rosario Strait to Admiralty Inlet must have it on the port hand.

ADMIRALTY INLET, PUGET SOUND, AND HOOD'S CANAL.

General description.—Under special names the great body of water now known to the commercial world under the general designation of "Puget Sound" may be described as a series of vast interior canals giving unsurpassed facilities for navigation in the very heart of a prosperous section of the country.

"Puget Sound," in the broad acceptation of the term, lies between latitudes 47° 03′ and 48° 11′, and between longitudes 122° 10′ and 123° 10′.

Admiralty Inlet, Puget Sound and Hood's Canal, have an aggregate shore line of not less than 908 statute miles, and Possession Sound 200 miles, yet the number of dangers known to exist in them is remarkably few.

Admiralty Inlet, at the southeastern extremity of Juan de Fuca Strait, extends in a general southeasterly direction for about 60 miles, to the southern end of Vashon Island; it has for this distance an average width of 3½ miles, and numerous broad branches from it on both sides form other straits, channels, bays, and harbors. At 16 miles within the entrance Hood's Canal opens out to the westward, and 9 miles farther Possession Sound opens to the eastward and runs to the northwestward behind Whidbey Island and leads into the strait through Deception Pass.

At the south end of Vashon Island the Puget Sound of Vancouver commences; the channels are decreased in width to one or 2 miles, but they ramify by eight principal arms through an area of 22 miles square. The extreme northwestern arm, named Case's Inlet, reaches within 2 miles of the head of Hood's Canal, and between them lies comparatively low ground and a large lake.

The shores of these inlets are generally bluffs, ranging from 50 to 500 feet in height; their sides are kept bright from the wearing action of the water and their tops are covered with trees and thick undergrowth to the very edges. It is difficult to recognize the different points from the sameness in the appearance in the shores.

The depth of water is everywhere great and anchorages are difficult to obtain at any distance from the shore.

Directions (general).—From the entrance a S. 45° E. course for 6½ miles will take a vessel to abreast Marrowstone Point; here change course to S. 11° E., and when off Double Bluff a S. 51° E. course for 10 miles will reach the entrance to Possession Sound; thence the mid-channel course to Point Vashon is S. 6° W.

The channel on either side of Vashon Island may be used; to the eastward of the island the currents are moderately strong. The chances for anchoring few, and it is sometimes calm, while in Colvos Passage a fine breeze is blowing. When through the narrows and in Puget Sound, a mid-channel course is almost always free from danger. Off Steilacoom there is a 14-foot shoal, upon which the tide rip is very great and dangerous to small boats. The navigation of Puget Sound should not be attempted without a pilot unless well acquainted with the various channels.

Admiralty Head.—A vessel going into the sound from the Strait of Fuca, when off New Dungeness Lighthouse, sees ahead the high, bright cliffs between Port Discovery and Port Townsend, and the broad side of Whidbey Island beyond. There is little or no sign of passage in that direction, but when she is 8 or 10 miles eastward of New Dungeness the entrance to Admiralty Inlet opens; the high point to the northward, crested with trees, is Partridge Point, the low point with a cluster of white buildings to the south is Point Wilson; and directly ahead is a comparatively low, treeless headland standing out fairly well to the westward, with low land and water directly behind it, but the higher wooded lands beyond.

This headland is Admiralty Head; it lies 5½ miles southeast of Point Partridge and just inside the entrance to the inlet or sound of the eastern shore; and it is directly opposite the entrance to Port Townsend. It is a nearly vertical, rocky cliff, 80 feet high, standing well out at the extremity of the broad triangular point. The area of the summit is limited and marked by the cluster of white lighthouse buildings; it falls away to the north to low marshy ground and a large lagoon. Towards the northwest the shore, alternately cliffs and low, runs nearly straight for 5½ miles to Point Partridge. Inside of it the low pebbly beach at its base sweeps to the northeast for 2 miles, gradually curving eastward and finally southeast to form Admiralty Bay. Behind this beach for 2 miles from the head is a large lagoon more than ½ mile wide. Behind that the land rises and is wooded.

Admiralty Bay is formed by a great sweep of the shore line, forming a semicircle with a diameter of more than 3 miles. It is only used occasionally for anchorage just to the east of the light-house, where the bottom is hard and sandy in irregular ridges, and with depths of from 15 to 25 fathoms of water. It is an uncomfortable anchorage, for it is open to the full sweep of the southeasters, and at all times the current is running out. This current is so strong that even in the summer winds a vessel rides to it. With the wind from the southward a vessel would lie in the trough of the sea.

Sailing vessels should not approach this head or Admiralty Bay, because in calm weather they encounter the strong and irregular currents near it, or they may be embayed under the eastern shore.

Port Townsend is just within the entrance of Admiralty Inlet, now almost universally known as Puget Sound, and is a port of entry for the Puget Sound district. It is a safe harbor, but from its extent it is subject to a disagreeable sea in heavy winds, and with a strong southeaster landing is oftentimes impracticable and the sea dangerous for boats.

The entrance to the harbor itself lies between Point Wilson and Marrowstone Point, the latter distant 3⅝ miles from the former. Inside of the line between Point Wilson and Marrowstone Point the width of the port is contracted by Point Hudson, which lies S. 8° E. 1⅝ miles from Point Wilson. From the entrance line the mid-channel direction of the ports is nearly SW. for 3 miles, with an average width of 2 miles to abreast the most westerly indentation, and then S. by E. for 3½ miles, with an average width of 1¼ miles.

The shores of the port are moderately high bright cliffs, with some breakdowns. The summits are covered with forest trees, except near the town.

Point Hudson is a broad, low gravel spit, stretching out ¼ mile from the high cliffs of the town of Port Townsend. Part of the town is built on this low point, and the custom-house is but a short distance from the wharves. A large sawmill is on the extremity of the point; extensive wharves project from the front of the town into deep water, and landing is readily and safely made. A quarter of a mile off these wharves there is a deep channel carrying 10 to 16 fathoms of water, through which the currents run with considerable velocity. Off the north side of the point the 3-fathom line extends out over ½ mile for ¾ mile to the NNW.

Within recent years a shoal has made out 250 to 300 yards north of Point Hudson.

To mark the outer edge of this shoal a spar buoy has been placed in 21 feet of water. It is about 250 yards NE. of the high-water end of Point Hudson.

Between Point Wilson and Point Hudson there is a deep bight, the bluff shore receding ¼ mile westward, and carrying deep water for more than ¼ mile inside the line of the points, except near Point Hudson. The NW. head of Marrowstone Island, on the eastern side of the bay, is a high, bright clay cliff, terminating at the NE. in the low Marrowstone Point, and on the SW. in a low narrow sand spit one mile long, masking the entrance to Kilisut Inlet. This spit runs nearly SW.

Parallel with this part of the port, and under the SW. point, there is an opening and a channel through shoals into Kilisut or Long Harbor, on which lies the western shore of Marrowstone Island. At high water this harbor communicates by a crooked boat channel, 6 miles long, with Oak Cove, at the southward.

Kala Point, on the west side of the bay, and within 1¾ miles of the head, is a low point, projecting ¼ mile from the steep high hillside out into very deep water; it lies S. 11° W. 3⅔ miles from Point Hudson. Half a mile south of Kala Point a small stream, called the Chimikim Creek, opens between two high and steep cliffs; the shoal water lies ¼ mile ou[illegible]e this mouth.

W[illegible] Point is a very low and marshy projection on the eastern side [illegible]ay, and stretches ¼ mile out into very deep water. It lies south 2¾ miles from Point Hudson. Between it and Kala Point, on the western side, the bay is a mile wide, and the depth of water 14 and 15 fathoms, over soft sticky bottom.

The head of the bay is visible from Point Hudson over Walan Point, and is distant 5¼ miles in a straight line. It is ¾ mile between the high cliffs on the east and west, and deep water continues to the head. In the SW. angle there is a shoal pocket, formed by a low and very narrow spit ⅓ mile long, with a rocky islet at the entrance In the SE. angle there is a narrow channel opening into a large flat, mostly bare at low water, and bounded by a beach nearly 100 yards across and ½ mile long, which separates Port Townsend from Oak Cove. Across this creek there is a portage frequently used by the Indians.

Directions.—Vessels bound into Port Townsend from the Strait of Fuca must keep clear of the rocky shoal off the northern side of Point Wilson, but as soon as Point Hudson is opened by Point Wilson the latter may be passed within 120 yards with a depth of 20 fathoms, hard bottom; through this deep channel a strong current runs. When abreast of Point Wilson a steamer should steer S. 12° E. to clear the shoal ground to the NW. of Point Hudson; but a sailing vessel may keep a little inside this course until within ½ mile of Point Hudson, and then gradually keep away about ¼ mile from the shore in from 5 to 10 fathoms of water over hard bottom, and as the point opens run quite close, with the summer wind directly offshore, to save making a tack. There is a depth of 10 to 15 fathoms a little more than ⅓ mile offshore. Keep along about ½ mile to the SW., parallel with the city front, and anchor anywhere off the wharves in from 10 to 12 fathoms, and ¼ mile distant. In winter anchor farther out, to clear Point Hudson, in getting under way with a southeaster.

When sailing vessels are coming down the sound bound into this port with the ebb current, they should pass Marrowstone Point nearly ¾ mile before heading in for the town, and so avoid a very strong eddy which comes out of the bay along and under the high shore west of this point. If the wind be light and the ebb current strong, pass the point quite close to; run along the outside of the current rip, and try to get upon the mid-channel bank as soon as practicable, to avoid being set up the sound by the next flood.

In summer, sailing vessels not employing tugs will frequently drift about the entrance for days without a breath of wind and with very strong currents. In winter, the SE. storms blow with great violence in this high latitude, and a vessel must move to an anchorage under the cliffs of the old military post to get a comfortable berth, in 10 fathoms of water, soft bottom.

The mid-channel bank lies upon and even outside of the line joining Point Wilson and Marrowstone Point. Within the 10 fathom curve it stretches halfway from the base on Marrowstone Island towards Point Wilson, and the least water found upon it is 5¾ fathoms. The bottom is clear, hard sand.

Marrowstone Point is a low sandy point, extending out 300 yards from the bluff and forms an indentation on its southern face, where anchorage may be had in 12 fathoms, with a current or eddy invariably running ebb.

Craven Rock lies close to shore, about 1⅛ miles south of Marrowstone Point.

Bush Point lies on the eastern shore. It is low and projects ½ mile from the general direction of the shore, and has one or two clumps of trees and bushes, with low ground behind, and the ground rising therefrom and densely wooded. There is very deep water close to the point, and anchorage may be had on the north side in 15 fathoms, sandy bottom, but the currents are strong and irregular.

Nodule Point, abreast Bush Point, on the opposite shore, is a rounding bluff point, covered with trees, 1⅛ miles north of the southern end of the island which forms the NE. shore of Oak Bay. Directly off this point there is good anchorage in 12 to 15 fathoms of water.

Oak Bay opens to the northwestward and extends nearly to Port Townsend. It has bluff shores nearly all around, the SW. face being limestone. In beating out of the inlet with a favorable current do not work into the bay for the sake of a long tack.

Basalt Point, the south entrance point of Oak Bay, is a rounding jagged point, covered with trees to the shore line and rising to a moderate hillock covered with wood.

Klas Rock lies ¼ mile N. 30° E. of Basalt Point and the same distance offshore. It is a patch of rocks 175 yards in extent and marked with kelp. There is deep water all around this danger and 16 fathoms may be carried inside of it.

Mutiny Bay, on the eastern side of the inlet, in the deep indentation between Bush Point and Double Bluff, has a narrow bank of 11 fathoms in its northern part, which affords good fishing.

Double Bluff.—This is a mesa promontory one mile wide and $1\frac{1}{2}$ miles long, lying between Mutiny Bay on the west and Useless Bay on the east. The cliffs are 300 to 400 feet in height, and the greater part of the surface back from the face is covered with trees, but near the water it is destitute of trees, except one large clump which marks it conspicuously in going up the sound. The NW. point of this spur is the higher.

Useless Bay.—On the east side of the point of Double Bluff the shore runs to the northeastward for $2\frac{1}{4}$ miles, and then swings round in a long curve to the east and to the southeastward to Indian Point, one mile NW. of Scatchet Head. This forms a bay nearly 5 miles broad at the mouth and $2\frac{1}{2}$ miles deep to the northeastward. It lies broad open to the SSW., and looks directly upon Point No Point. The shores of this bay are in part bluff and in part low, with a fringe of marsh nearly around the whole bay. There is deep water in this bay, the 40-fathom curve reaching into it and the 20-fathom curve running nearly to the deepest part of the shore. The shoalest water is under the east shore, where the 10-fathom curve stretches out one mile, with a bottom of sand. At the head of the bay there are two long narrow sand spits, behind which lies Deer Lagoon, a large shallow sheet of water, full of marsh islets and having a shoal outlet between the sand spits. At the eastern part of this lagoon is the settlement of Useless.

Scatchet Head.—This is the southwestern point of the long and irregular Whidbey Island and is visible for 25 miles from the southward: it stretches as a promontory into a broad part of Admiralty Inlet; it is directly abreast of Point No Point. The southern entrance of Possession Sound is on its eastern side and Useless Bay on the western. It is a double-headed promontoy with a length of 6 miles and an extreme breadth of $2\frac{3}{4}$ miles between Useless Bay and Possession Sound.

The two heads have each a face of about $\frac{3}{4}$ mile in breadth exposed to the south; they are bold yellow clay cliffs; the eastern one rises about 300 feet above the water, and is covered with wood, and the western one rises 140 feet or more. The western head has become locally known as the False Scatchet. Off the base of the bright cliffs there are seen great erratic granite bowlders.

Possession Point.—The lower part is a nearly vertical white-clay cliff; the bank slopes at an angle of 45°, with a partially broken whitish front, until it reaches 140 feet elevation. There are a few scattered trees on the lower part of the slope, and the summit level is covered with them.

The shore under the eastern side of the head is bordered by a low narrow beach.

The eastern shore of the entrance to Possession Sound abreast this head rises from a low narrow beach with deciduous trees on the lower slope and Oregon pine on the summit. Yellow bluffs show in patches through the trees.

Between the two heads there is a shallow pocket running back 1½ miles, called Cultus Bay. It is in part overflowed at high tide, and then presents the appearance of a bay. An extensive sand bank and shoal makes out nearly 3 miles to the southward, with the breadth of the heads as a base. From the eastern head round the western, and a mile toward Useless Bay, the low-water line makes out ½ mile, the shore being bare, where older maps have deep water. For over a mile south of the western head a depth of 8 and 10 fathoms of water and smooth sandy bottom can be found; while the 20-fathom line runs out 3 miles directly for Apple Tree Cove, with a bottom of sand, gravel, and shells. Off the eastern head a strong undercurrent runs into Possession Sound, and an upward current setting to the westward at all tides.

Off the south side of Possession Point on the line of 3 fathoms, is a rock awash at the lowest tides. It is about 250 yards off the front of the cliffs.

Possession Sound.—(See page 56.)

Port Ludlow.—South of Basalt Point and 2 miles directly west of Foulweather Bluff is the broad opening to Port Ludlow on the west side of the entrance to Hood's Canal. This bay has a broad entrance open towards the NNE. The two points of the entrance are Basalt Point to the north and Tala Point to the south, the former lying 1⅞ miles exactly SSE. of the latter.

The general direction of the western shore of the bay from Basalt Point is south for 2⅜ miles to the sawmill.

It is in part low, broken bluff, with a gently rising country behind, covered with Oregon pine. The low-water beach is about 50 yards wide, and the 3-fathom line is from 100 to 200 yards from the shore, except near Snake Rock, which it nearly reaches. The general direction of the eastern side of the bay from Tala Point is SW. by S. for 1¼ miles; the shore is high under Tala Point and decreases to the southward in the bay. Abreast the Sawmill Point the width of the bay is ⅝ mile, but the channel is narrowed by a shoal from the southeastern shore, stretching fully ½ mile toward Sawmill Point. Inside the Sawmill Point the bay affords a good anchorage in 6 to 8 fathoms of water over soft mud for ½ mile to the southward and westward. This small basin is completely landlocked, and is protected from gales from every quarter by the high land and high trees about it.

Tala Point is a bright bluff head less than ¼ mile broad, covered on top with Oregon pine.

From Tala Point there is a bar of hard sand nearly ¾ mile wide within the 5-fathom line, stretching in an outward curve to Colvos Rocks, which lie one-third the distance from Basalt Point to Tala Point.

The 3-fathom curve stretches nearly ⅝ mile, with a width of ¼ mile, from Tala Point to the northward, reaching to the black buoy; the bottom is hard sand. The low-water line is 200 yards from the cape, and kelp lies for ¼ mile to the northward.

Abreast Tala Point the width of the bay is ¾ mile, with good water and good holding ground.

The approaches to this harbor are marked by Klas Rock and Colvos Rocks.

Colvos Rocks are a cluster of three rocks; the nearest one to the shore lies nearly ½ mile S. 26° E. of Basalt Point. It is 25 feet high and of small extent; the largest rock is ⅛ mile farther on in the same course. The third one is 200 yards northwards of the outer one. There is deep water around the northwest rock, but a long shoal stretches to the southeast from the largest. The bottom around these rocks is rocky and hard sand. From these rocks there is a bar nearly ⅓ mile wide, of less than 5 fathoms, reaching in an outward curve toward Tala Point.

There is deep water on the north, west, and east sides of the northeastern rock of the Colvos group.

There is very shoal ground for 250 yards SSW. from the southeast Colvos Rock, and from this there is a long tail of hard sandy bottom stretching over ¾ of a mile nearly SE. towards the red buoy.

Abreast the Colvos Rocks, and nearly ¼ mile from the shore, there is a large rock. This is the Snake Rock 150 yards in extent and just awash at high tide. There is a narrow line of 3 fathoms of water just inside of it.

Directions.—The deepest channel into this bay lies outside the Klas Rock, and between the inner Colvos Rock and Snake Rock, where the channel is 600 yards wide between the 5-fathom lines, and carries 16 fathoms of water over sticky bottom. Thence everything is clear to the head of the bay, gradually reducing the depth to 8 and 7 fathoms inside the Saw Mill Spit, and having good water under each shore, but the better water is under the western shore. There is a broad foreshore, or low water beach, under the eastern shore.

The usual channel is between the Colvos Rocks and Tala Point, crossing the bar in 4½ fathoms of water, over hard sandy bottom, between the red and black buoys.

This passage is ⅜ mile wide, and the buoys lie N. 13° E. and S. 13° W. of each other.

If the wind and currents do not suit for entering by this buoyed channel, a vessel must run inside of the Colvos Rocks, carrying good water over a soft muddy bottom. The approaches to both channels are good.

Hood's Canal.—(See page 51).

Foulweather Bluff.—This is one of the most noticeable of the many cliffs in Puget Sound. It is the northern extremity of a 7-mile peninsula which separates Admiralty Inlet from the entrance to Hood's Canal. It is the landmark for making Port Ludlow at the entrance to that canal, and Port Gamble, 5 miles inside. The northern face is about a mile broad, with nearly vertical sandy clay cliffs about 225 feet high, and covered on the summit with heavy firs and a very dense undergrowth. It slopes toward the east to a bluff 40 feet high, but on the side next to Hood's Canal the cliff is steep Hood's Canal is here almost 1¾ miles wide, and the inlet across to Double Bluff is barely 3 miles across.

On the southwestern side of the bluff two small points make out, with a little recession between them. The northern one is low

Rock.—A rock awash at the lowest tides lies off the face of the bluff, a little to the east of the middle of the face, and 3 fathoms water is found outside this danger It is intended to place a buoy outside of the rock in 5 fathoms of water

Point No Point.—This is one of the turning points in the broad waters of the sound The point itself is low and just above high water, with a gully and small stream open just at the western part. To the westward the broken cliffs run in a concave curving line to Foulweather Bluff. To the southward the shore is nearly straight for 10 miles, with increasing height to the cliffs, and a low narrow marshy line under them to Pilot Point, 2½ miles distant The land behind it is 200 or 300 feet high and moderately wooded Deep water runs close to the point, and one third of the way across the channel abreast it there is a depth of 114 fathoms Under the south side of the point there is good anchorage in 10 fathoms

Apple Tree Cove lies 6¼ miles S 18° E. of Point No Point, and is a low point rising behind to higher ground, which is wooded From this point there is a soft muddy flat extending several hundred yards up the sound, with good water over it. From 5 to 12 fathoms of water and sticky mud bottom are found fully ½ mile from the shore, and a depth of 6 fathoms is carried well into the cove, which is formed by a broad receding of the shore for nearly one mile to the westward The head of the cove is 1½ miles from the point, and vessels may avoid adverse currents by anchoring on the muddy bank The head of the bay is marshy, no fresh water is obtainable here. The south shore of the cove runs almost southeast for a mile and then trends more to the southward for President Point. There is very deep water close under the southern shore of this cove

Edmund Point.—Directly abreast of Apple Tree Cove, on the east side of the inlet or sound, is Edmund Point It is a low, rounding point with a lagoon inside its shores and it makes out from the low narrow valley behind it. There is a bluff to the southward Thence to Elliot Point, on the east side of the entrance of Possession Sound, the direction is almost NNE. for 9¼ miles The shore north of it is low and the water deep; off the point itself the water is very deep. The inlet is here 3¾ miles wide.

Point Wells, south of Edmund Point, is low and makes out from the high bluff behind it. There is a slight recession of the shore between the points, and the 10-fathom line is outside of the line joining them, but there is anchorage in the bight, although contracted. The 30-fathom line is close under the point.

President Point and Point Jefferson.—On the west side of the sound and on the north side of the entrance to Port Madison, there is a line of moderately high, straight bluff shore, with the land rising behind it and covered with trees; it commences at President Point and continues one mile south to Point Jefferson, when the shore makes a sharp turn and runs to the west for more than 3 miles. This southern face of Point Jefferson is a low, bright cliff in places. When abreast Point Jefferson it shows broken white cliffs decreasing to the northward and to the southwestward, and then from the latter rising again. Stretching broad off the shore between President Point and Point Jefferson for more than ½ mile there is a 9-fathom bank which affords excellent anchorage for vessels when drifting with light airs and adverse currents. Close under the south side and extending out to 4½ and 5 fathoms of water, there is a compact mass of kelp ¼ mile long parallel with the shore southwest and northeast.

Port Madison.—This is a broad and deep recession of the western shore of the inlet. Under the north shore it stretches in 3 miles west, and the entrance toward the inlet is 2 miles wide. There is deep water throughout this large bay, ranging from 80 fathoms at the SE. part to 20 fathoms at the NW. part, but there is a narrow bank stretching one mile south of Point Jefferson with 15 fathoms of water, sandy bottom.

The northern shores of the bay are broken white cliffs and intervening low beaches. The western face is moderately low bright cliffs, with the white buildings of the Indian reservation in the SW. angle at the entrance to Agate Passage. The south shores are broken cliffs, except at the entrance to the Port Madison docks. The mills are ¾ mile inside the NE. point of the entrance, with very ample wharf facilities and mooring dolphins for vessels to haul out to. The channel is narrow and carries 13 feet of water. Outside the entrance to this inner port the water deepens to 15 fathoms in less than ½ mile, except to the west, where there is a long spit with only 15 to 18 feet of water upon it for ⅜ mile from the shore.

Point Monroe.—The SE. point is a low, narrow sand spit, curving inward from the outer shore to the westward and merely outlying the cliffs ⅓ mile.

Buoy.—A buoy is placed just outside the 3-fathom bank, which makes out northward ⅛ of a mile from the low sandy hook of Point Monroe. Very shoal water is carried out very nearly to the 3-fathom line, and then the depth increases to 10 fathoms in 50 yards and to 20 fathoms in 200 yards.

Bainbridge Island.—This island lies in a deep bight of the Great Peninsula, and its eastern shore forms the western side of the inlet or sound directly abreast West Point and Duwamish Bay. The north shore forms the south side of Port Madison. It is a little over 9 miles long N by W. and 3½ miles wide. It is moderately high, has some high bluffs along the eastern shore, but this is broken by several indentations, forming anchorages and harbors. To the westward of the island is a long sound, which, with its arms, is nearly 30 miles long and one mile wide, with a good depth of water close to the shores.

Port Orchard has its entrance in the southwestern part of Port Madison. This entrance is very narrow and somewhat crooked, but has from 3 to 4 fathoms of water in it. Vessels must enter under easy sail and keep the lead going on each side to find the deepest water. When through, give Point Bolin a berth of nearly ½ mile, to avoid the shoal making out eastward from it. Around Point Bolin, Dogfish Bay opens to the NW., and near the head of the port, Dye's Inlet opens to the northward and westward.

Rich's Passage, the southern entrance to Port Orchard, is obstructed by rocks and is difficult of navigation. The winds are light and variable, and at its narrowest part, where it makes a sharp turn, the current is swift.

Skiff Point.—This is the first point, 3¼ miles south of Point Monroe, on the west side of the sound. It is directly abreast of West Point light house, where the channel is 2¼ miles wide. The point is moderately broad and rounding, and projects fully ½ mile into the channel. It is low at the water line, and rises regularly to a ridge to the westward; the bluff to the northward is moderately high. The water off the point is quite bold.

Murden's Cove.—This is a wide recession of the western shore of the sound, just under Skiff Point, the shore sweeping to the westward for nearly a mile and then southeastward for 1½ miles to Yemoalt Point. The northwestern shore is low, the southern shore has steep clay cliffs. The inner part of the cove has shoal water, but inside of the line of the two points there is anchorage in 10 to 15 fathoms.

Yemoalt Point is the southern point of Murden's Cove. It is a low point, with gently rising land behind it. The cliffs to the northward and southward are moderately high and broken. There is deep water off the point.

Eagle Harbor.—This is a narrow, deep indentation in the eastern shore of Bainbridge Island. At the mouth the entrance is barely ½ mile wide, and the 3 fathom curve extends nearly a mile into the harbor. A depth of 8 fathoms is ⅜ mile inside from the north point. The north side of the entrance is Wing Point, it overlaps the south side ¼ mile, and is a very narrow, low point. It is nearly in the line of the latter point, Yemoalt Point, and Skiff Point.

A long, pebbly beach makes out 300 or 400 yards SE. from Wing Point, and late surveys have developed a direct connection from this ledge to the Blakely Rock, running parallel with the shore. For ¾ mile from the point on a line to Blakely Rock there is found as little as 2½ fathoms of water. Outside of this ledge the bottom drops very suddenly to 50 fathoms. Vessels bound into Port Blakely must not haul too close to the shore until they are within ⅛ mile of [illegible] es- sels are bound [illegible] he [illegible] ep [illegible] of [illegible] al [illegible] le [illegible] h [illegible] s [illegible] s [illegible] inside the north [illegible] nearer the southern shore than the northern, in 9½ fathoms of water, over hard bottom. Here the width, under the northern and southern shores, is only 300 yards, and that width decreases farther in.

Blakely Rock.—In the outer road there is a ledge of rock nearly ¼ mile in extent, and a large part of it is above water. The middle and highest part is 15 feet above water. There is shoal water and foul ground for 260 yards to the northward of the rock, with a bank of kelp extending out to 7 fathoms of water all around it. On the south side there is deep water close under it, with a passage between it and the northern shore of Restoration Point, ⅜ mile wide; this passage has 25 fathoms of water with sticky bottom. The passage between the north point and Blakely Rock is ½ mile wide between the 10-fathom curves and has 26 fathoms of water over sticky bottom, so that vessels from the north always pass between the rock and the north point. The approach from the north is over the long ledge which runs from Wing Point to Blakely Rock. A little less than ½ mile north of Blakely Rock this ledge can be crossed in 9 fathoms water, sandy bottom; but thence to Wing Point the depth of water on the ledge decreases, and as little as 2½ fathoms is fo[illegible], with deep water inside. Outside of the ledge the depth increases rapidly to 50 fathoms.

Restoration Point is in some respects very peculiar; no other point in these waters, except Battery Point, presents the same formation. For 300 yards it is flat, about 10 feet above high water, and has a foot depth of soil covered with grass, over a limestone rock upheaved nearly on edge, the direction of the strata pointing toward Battery Point, or a little southwestward of it. Inshore the land rises sharply about 100 feet, its sides covered with grass and its summit with fir trees. Around the whole southeastern face of the point these peculiarities exist. On the upper levels of the high land adjacent are small lakes of water.

Decatur Reef.—From the extremity of the point, a ledge, bare at low

sound directly abreast West Point and Duwamish Bay. The north shore forms the south side of Port Madison It is a little over 9 miles long N by W and 3½ miles wide It is moderately high, has some high bluffs along the eastern shore, but this is broken by several indentations, forming anchorages and harbors. To the westward of the island is a long

(1728) **WASHINGTON—Puget sound—Port Orchard—Bremerton naval station — Hydrographic information.** — Commander V. L Cottman, U. S. Navy, Puget Sound naval station, reports under date of October 18, 1905, that the piers at the naval station are numbered as follows:

The first pier eastward of the coaling wharf is pier No 1 The pier where the receiving ship lies is No 2 The pier forming the western side of the entrance to the dry dock is No 5. The eastern side of the entrance to the dry dock is pier No 6 About 50 yards eastward of No 6 is pier No 7

The mooring buoy on the eastern side of the dock entrance is No. 1; on the western side is No. 2. The stern buoy, 350 yards to the southward, is No. 3. (N. M. 43, 1905.)

by rocks and is difficult of navigation The winds are light and variable, and at its narrowest part, where it makes a sharp turn, the current is swift.

Skiff Point —This is the first point, 3¼ miles south of Point Monroe, on the west side of the sound It is directly abreast of West Point light house, where the channel is 2¾ miles wide The point is moderately broad and rounding, and projects fully ¼ mile into the channel It is low at the water line, and rises regularly to a ridge to the westward; the bluff to the northward is moderately high. The water off the point is quite bold.

Murden's Cove —This is a wide recession of the western shore of the sound, just under Skiff Point, the shore sweeping to the westward for nearly a mile and then southeastward for 1½ mues to Yemoalt Point The northwestern shore is low, the southern shore has steep clay cliffs The inner part of the cove has shoal water, but inside of the line of the two points there is anchorage in 10 to 15 fathoms.

Yemoalt Point is the southern point of Murden's Cove It is a low point, with gently rising land behind it. The cliffs to the northward and southward are moderately high and broken. There is deep water off the point

Eagle Harbor —This is a narrow, deep indentation in the eastern shore of Bainbridge Island At the mouth the entrance is barely ½ mile wide, and the 3 fathom curve extends nearly a mile into the harbor A depth of 8 fathoms is ¾ mile inside from the north point. The north side of the entrance is Wing Point, it overlaps the south side ¼ mile, and is a very narrow, low point. It is nearly in the line of the latter point, Yemoalt Point, and Skiff Point

A long, pebbly beach makes out 300 or 400 yards SE. from Wing Point, and late surveys have developed a direct connection from this ledge to the Blakely Rock, running parallel with the shore For ¾ mile from the point on a line to Blakely Rock there is found as little as 2½ fathoms of water. Outside of this ledge the bottom drops very suddenly to 50 fathoms. Vessels bound into Port Blakely must not haul too close to the shore until they are within ½ mile of Blakely Rock. If large vessels are bound into Eagle Harbor, they would have to enter from the southward, close under shore, and pass through the narrow but deep channel between the ledge and the shore.

Port Blakely is a moderately deep indentation on the north side of Restoration Point, which is the mark for the entrance. The actual length of the port is ⅞ mile, and it carries 3 fathoms fully ⅝ mile inside the opening, which is ⅜ mile wide.

The usual outer anchorage of Port Blakely is S. 11° E. of the north point of the entrance, a little nearer the southern shore, in 13 fathoms of water, over sticky bottom. The deepest water in the entrance is 18 fathoms. The inner anchorage is from ¼ to ½ mile inside the north point and rather nearer the southern shore than the northern, in 9½ fathoms of water, over hard bottom. Here the width, under the northern and southern shores, is only 300 yards, and that width decreases farther in.

Blakely Rock.—In the outer road there is a ledge of rock nearly ¼ mile in extent, and a large part of it is above water. The middle and highest part is 15 feet above water. There is shoal water and foul ground for 260 yards to the northward of the rock, with a bank of kelp extending out to 7 fathoms of water all around it. On the south side there is deep water close under it, with a passage between it and the northern shore of Restoration Point, ⅜ mile wide; this passage has 25 fathoms of water with sticky bottom. The passage between the north point and Blakely Rock is ½ mile wide between the 10-fathom curves and has 26 fathoms of water over sticky bottom, so that vessels from the north always pass between the rock and the north point. The approach from the north is over the long ledge which runs from Wing Point to Blakely Rock. A little less than ½ mile north of Blakely Rock this ledge can be crossed in 9 fathoms water, sandy bottom; but thence to Wing Point the depth of water on the ledge decreases, and as little as 2½ fathoms is found, with deep water inside. Outside of the ledge the depth increases rapidly to 50 fathoms.

Restoration Point is in some respects very peculiar; no other point in these waters, except Battery Point, presents the same formation. For 300 yards it is flat, about 10 feet above high water, and has a foot depth of soil covered with grass, over a limestone rock upheaved nearly on edge, the direction of the strata pointing toward Battery Point, or a little southwestward of it. Inshore the land rises sharply about 100 feet, its sides covered with grass and its summit with fir trees. Around the whole southeastern face of the point these peculiarities exist. On the upper levels of the high land adjacent are small lakes of water.

Decatur Reef.—From the extremity of the point, a ledge, bare at low tides, makes out broad into the sound for 300 yards, the depth of the water is 6 fathoms 100 yards off its extremity, and 16 fathoms at ¼ mile. South of the point, anchorage may be had in 15 fathoms of water over sticky bottom, ¼ mile from shore, or, as a rule for finding anchorage, bring the Blakely Rock north of the point to range just over and inside of it. Kelp exists along the southern face.

Point Orchard.—This is the low rocky point at the south side of the entrance to Rich's Passage into Port Orchard. Behind it the land rises into a moderate hillock with a low neck to the southward, and a cove inside the passage to the WNW. Off this point the water is deep.

Meadow Point, nearly opposite Point Monroe on the western shore of the sound, is a small low grassy point, with a marshy lagoon inside and higher ground rising behind.

West Point is a sharp low grassy point projecting nearly a mile into the channel. It has a light-house on its extremity.

Shilshole Bay and **Creek**.—Between the two latter points is Shilshole Bay, and at the bottom of the bay Shilshole Creek empties, draining Union Lake 3 miles to the eastward.

Under the broken cliffs between the Shilshole Creek and West Point the low water beach is shingle, but outside of the 3 fathoms the bottom is sticky. On the line between the two points the depth midway is 25 fathoms directly abreast the opening of the creek. One third of a mile inside this line is the 3 fathom curve. The shoal water makes out farthest at the mouth of the creek. Two feet can be carried into the mouth of this small stream at low water.

Anchorage may be had in Shilshole Bay in 15 fathoms of water over sandy bottom, with the light house bearing S 22° W distant ¾ of a mile.

There is a good anchorage in 7 to 10 fathoms about 250 yards from the shore between West Point and Shilshole Creek, and good protection from southeasters.

It has been proposed to excavate a channel from the sound to Union Lake and thus have a safe port in fresh water. Locally, this bay is known as Salmon Bay.

Duwamish Bay.—On the eastern side of the sound and on the south side of West Point, Duwamish Bay opens with a width of 5¼ miles, contracts rapidly to 2⅜ miles both from the northern and southern shores, and then continues with that width for 2 miles to the edge of the extensive flats at the mouth of the Duwamish River.

On the south side of the high wooded bluff commencing just east of West Point there is a long bright horizontal cut, which is halfway between the water and the top; it is a good landmark. This bluff is named Magnolia Bluff and it makes a long rounding sweep for 1¼ miles to the southeastward from the light house. It reaches nearly 400 feet elevation and continues with decreasing height for 1⅜ miles nearly ESE to a sharp recession of the shore which makes in to the northward for ¼ mile. This recession forms a moderately wide cove, bare at low water, called Smith's Cove. Under the foot of Magnolia Bluff and nearly ¾ mile SSE. of its highest break, there is a large granite erratic bowlder inside the low-water line, and locally known as Four Mile Rock. The broken bluff abreast this rock is 220 feet high and the land behind it rises to nearly 400 feet. From the eastern side of Smith's Cove the shore for 3 miles to Seattle, is nearly straight and runs southeast. It is comparatively low but the land behind rises rapidly to the top of the ridge between this bay and Union Lake, the extreme height being 410 feet. After rounding West Point a vessel keeps about ½ mile off the northern shore, and the general course to Seattle is S. 57° E., and the distance is 5¼ miles from the light on West Point.

Duwamish River.—This is a moderately large stream in the Cascade range of mountains, and running a general course to the northwest to Duwamish Bay. A tributary from the north drains the extensive lakes, Washington and Sammamish; and in its valleys and at the lakes there have been developed extensive deposits of coal and iron. The whole country is well wooded. The great mud flats at the head of Duwamish Bay are formed from the sediments brought down by this river.

Seattle.—In the northeastern part of the bay is an extensive town. Vessels can obtain all kinds of supplies. It is the shipping port for the coal mines in the vicinity and large quantities are exported. Vessels are rapidly coaled at the wharves by chutes, price $6.50 per ton. Wheat is largely exported and the lumber business extensive.

There is an extensive system of wharves in the extended frontage of Seattle, and steamboats and vessels go directly there to discharge and load. These wharves reach out to 3 and 4 fathoms of water. Vessels anchoring off the town find the best ground near the southern part of the town, where a depth of 15 to 20 fathoms over muddy bottom is found, 400 yards outside the wharves. It drops off suddenly from 15 fathoms.

Directions.—When a sailing vessel is getting under way from her anchorage off Seattle, the usual summer winds compel the first tack to be to the southward towards the edge of the great mud flat. If it be high water this flat can not be distinguished, and the lead must be kept going. When a depth of 15 fathoms is struck a vessel must go about, for the water shoals to 3-fathoms very suddenly, and keeping on would soon bring her up on the flat. If the current be ebb, vessels bound out of the sound should stand well into the inlet; and if bound up the sound should work close under and around Duwamish Head to Battery Point. If the current be flood, vessels bound out of the inlet should work under the north shore and close to West Point; if bound up the sound, they should work under the north shore about 3½ miles to Magnolia Point, or to the Four Mile Rock, or until they can fetch well clear of Battery Point. If calms prevail, the tug is employed to tow vessels in or out. The tug service throughout the sound is good.

Duwamish Head is steep, about 320 feet high, and the summit is sparsely covered with the Oregon pine. The western side of the head is broken to the height of 260 feet at the highest point and 200 feet at the extreme point. On the inside it is very steep but not broken for ¼ mile. The beach at low water stretches out ½ mile to the northward, when the shoal water is continued to the 3 fathom line, which is 600 yards from the bluff, the drop to 20 fathoms is within 250 yards. Along the east face of the bluff the water is very deep close inshore. Uner the eastern side of the head is the town of West Seattle, with an extensive sawmill and wharfage facilities. Seven-eighths of a mile inside the head is a small settlement called O'Connor, within the outer edge of the great flats.

Battery Point.—The south point of the entrance to Duwamish Bay is Battery Point, which is 5¼ miles nearly south of West Point light-house. From the northwestward just before reaching West Point, Battery Point is seen as a moderately low, bare, nearly flat-topped mound, with a steep cliff nearly 60 feet high towards the water, and a short, low point outside of it, which is the real point. Inside of the curiously shaped mound there is a low neck with large straggling pine trees, and behind this the land again rises. From the southeastward beyond Brace Point, the same characteristics are seen with one lone pine trunk standing in the middle of the gently sloping surface of the mound. This tree shows now only the bare trunk; formerly it was a good mark. On the north side of Battery Point a vessel anchoring in 20 fathoms of water over sandy bottom can not have a greater scope of chain than 35 fathoms, without being too close to the shore. The beach is smooth and very regular, being composed of sand and gravel.

Point Williams.—This point, on the east side of the sound, is the first small low sandy and gravel point, 2¾ miles from Battery Point. The land rises rapidly behind it and it is pine covered. Between it and Battery Point the shore retreats ¼ mile to the eastward and is nearly straight. It is not a notable point to vessels going up or down the sound because it retreats inside the line of Brace Point. It is the north point of Fauntleroy Cove.

Brace Point forms the south side of Fauntleroy Cove. It is a small low sandy gravelly point, backed by rapidly rising ground, covered with Oregon pine. In running north, before a vessel reaches Point Pully, Brace Point is seen as a moderately high wooded point just to the eastward of Battery Point; the land behind the first rise falling a little and then rising to the eastward.

Fauntleroy Cove.—This slight indentation is between Point Williams and Brace point; the distance apart of these points is a little over ¾ mile, and the shore recedes ¼ mile to the eastward. The immediate shore is low except under Point Williams, where the bluff reaches the water. Good anchorage may be had here in 10 and 12 fathoms of water; but when on a range of the two points the depth increases and the bottom drops away very suddenly outside. Fresh water is easily obtained in the vicinity.

Point Pully lies 4¼ miles from Brace Point. Between Brace Point and Point Pully the shore retreats more than a mile to the eastward, with low shores bordering the higher pine-covered land. Two or three small streams enter this bight, and the depth of the water is very great. Point Pully projects more than ⅓ mile into the sound; it is sharp and narrow.

It is a low point with a flat rounding hillock behind it, and upon which stands one large high tree in the middle and two or three smaller ones straggling on each side. The extremity of the point is sand and gravel and it pitches sharply off into very deep water, the 50-fathom curve lying but a short distance outside with 120 fathoms in mid-channel. There is deep water on the north and south sides; strong currents sweep by it. Under Point Pully to the eastward the bluff breaks down to brown slopes without trees, and at one mile from the point a stream comes in from a moderately broad valley. Off this valley a flat makes out some distance, with deep water at its edge.

Blake Island.—This island is at the northern entrance to Colvos Passage. It is about one mile in extent, not high, but covered with wood, except at the eastern point, which is low and pebbly. The eastern side of the island is low, with straggling trees, and the land rises to near the western side. There is deep water generally around the island, the 20-fathom curve being close under the south and west sides and off the east point. Off the north side the 10-fathom curve makes out ⅓ mile towards the broad shore of Restoration Point, and there is anchorage in 17 to 18 fathoms close under the east point, with bottom of soft mud.

Allen Bank.—Stretching from the SE. face of Blake Island there is a bank with less than 20 fathoms of water reaching all the way across to Point Vashon at the NE. part of the entrance to Colvos Passage. The bottom is variable: in some places mud and in others hard sand. The depth is greater near the island and decreases to as little as 8½ fathoms one mile N. 17° E. of Point Vashon. This bank has proven of great service to vessels losing the wind and having adverse currents: the more especially when the Colvos Passage was the channel used by all vessels.

Vashon Island.—This is the largest island in the waters of Admiralty Inlet and Puget Sound. It is high, with steep shores, covered with wood and undergrowth. Its surface is marshy, in many parts quite elevated. It is 11 miles in length, north and south, and ranges from one to 6¾ miles in breadth. It may be considered as lying in a great expansion of the sound 12 or 14 miles long and 10 miles wide. Between the east and SE. sides of the island and the mainland is the 2-mile-wide channel of the main inlet, reaching as far as Commencement Bay. The shore line of the island is 47 miles, and around the shores of the island there is a belt of kelp in the latter part of the summer and autumn, but it is torn away by the storms of the winter and spring.

The easternmost projection of the shore of Vashon Island is a curiously shaped peninsula, called Maury Island, 4½ miles long and 1½ miles wide, lying underneath the SE part of Vashon Island This peninsula is high, wooded, and has compact, bold shores.

The NW part is connected with Vashon Island by a low sandy neck of land only 100 yards wide The bight at the north side of this neck is Tramp Harbor, broad open to the NW The deep bay on the south side of the neck and between Vashon Island and Maury Island is 3½ miles long and over ½ mile wide, with 5 to 10 fathoms of water over gray sand and mud at the north extremity This bay is an excellent shelter at 2 miles inside the entrance with good water and good holding ground. It is named Quartermaster's Harbor

In the earlier years of the navigation of these waters by large sailing vessels, the Colvos Passage was universally used, but in recent years the development of Tacoma and the use of tugs have changed the whole traffic to the main channel between Vashon Island and the main shore to the eastward In this channel the currents are not strong, the chances for anchoring are few, and it is sometimes calm while there is a fine breeze blowing through Colvos Passage

The main channel on the east side of this island is the best to work in with a head wind.

Point Vashon—The northern point of Vashon Island is named Point Vashon, it is a high rounding bluff, covered with Oregon pine, forming the NE point of the entrance to Colvos passage

Anchorage—Broad off the north face of Vashon Island there is good anchorage from ¼ to ½ mile offshore, with protection from southeasters

Dolphin Point is the eastern point of the north end of Vashon Island It is a high, sharply rising bluff, covered with Oregon pine to the base, where there is a clump of trees to the water's edge, forming a little projection. Under Dolphin Point the shore line runs a mile to the SSW, and then 2 miles to the SE. by S to Point Beals, the depth of water is very great, and in the bight to the southward the depth is still greater The 20 fathom curve is close to the point, and the mid channel depth is 108 fathoms.

Good anchorage is reported, however, in from 7 to 14 fathoms

In the bight between this point and Point Beals there are three rocks above water close under the shore The southernmost is on the NW side of Point Beals, and is 14 feet above the water, the other two in the bight are 7 and 6 feet high

Point Beals is 2¾ miles from Dolphin Point It is a wooded point, rising gradually to several hundred feet, but it does not project far into the channel There is deep water close off it and deep water under the slightly receding shore to the north and to the south

Point Robinson is the prominent and noticeable point forming the easternmost projection of Maury Island. It stretches well over toward the eastern shore of the channel, which it reduces in width to 2 miles. The extremity of the spit is a low point 150 yards outside the trees, with intervening marshy ground, and then a bluff, which is about 30 feet high, and bright on the south side, but covered on the top with trees. The bluff rises to about 70 feet behind.

Upon the point are three inconspicuous houses, being part of the fog-signal buildings. To the northwest of the point the shore runs nearly west for 3 miles, then with a sweeping curve to the north for one mile to Point Heyer, thence N. by W. for nearly 3 miles to Point Beals. On the south of the point the bluff shore runs 4½ miles southwesterly, in a receding curve to Point Piner.

Under the south side of Point Heyer is a broad open bight called Tramp Harbor, with a very low shore on the southern part and nearly connected with the head of Quartermaster's Harbor. In this bight there is anchorage in 15 to 18 fathoms of water over fine gray sand, with deep water of more than 60 fathoms on the line between Point Heyer and Point Robinson. This is a good anchorage and there is fresh water.

Off Robinson Point the water is very deep; and between this and Point Brown it is said that, when the weather is calm, there is always a lot of old seaweed and stuff afloat, as if there was very little current movement.

Point Brown.—This forms the north point of the entrance to Commencement Bay. On the outermost point to the north it is low and gravelly with gently rising wooded ground behind a marshy spot inside the low point. On the south face of the point the shore rises gradually and irregularly in exposed white clay cliffs from 25 to 200 feet high within ⅜ mile from the point. There is very deep water 100 yards off the point.

Dash Point.—The low point 1⅛ miles N. 30° E. of Point Brown is Dash Point, slightly breaking the general line of the shore to the northeastward. There is a slight bight with deep water between them.

Commencement Bay.—South of Point Robinson the width of the inlet or sound expands to 3½ miles, with high bluff wooded shores on both sides; on the northwestern shore the bluffs are unbroken; on the southeast they are broken by small streams entering the sound. In this expansion of the sound the water is deep to either shore, and in the center it is about 100 fathoms. At the southern part of this basin Commencement Bay opens from the southeast with an entrance of 2⅛ miles between Point Brown on the north side and the main shore east of Point Defiance to the southward. The head of the bay is 3 miles inside of Point Brown and somewhat increases its width, but at its head there is a broad and extensive mud flat and low marsh land formed by the deposits brought down by the Puyallup River. This is a large stream coming in from the flanks of the Cascade range and nearly parallel with the Duwamish or White River.

Throughout the bay the depth of the water is very great, ranging from 88 fathoms in the middle of the entrance to 30 fathoms close under either shore, and carrying 20 fathoms close up to the edge of the mud flats, which are bare at low water. No special directions are needed to enter or leave this bay. The anchorage off Tacoma is not good, because the depth of water is too great and increases very rapidly offshore. There is good anchorage under the north shore in the slight recession beginning ¾ of a mile eastward of Point Brown. Half a mile offshore and ½ mile ESE. of the highest bright bluff of Point Brown there is a depth of 20 fathoms over brown mud, and the 3 fathom line is 100 yards offshore. This anchorage is well sheltered from all but the southeasters of winter.

The eddy currents are so very irregular in Commencement Bay that courses to steer by in thick weather are almost useless. There is a peculiar film of whitish water on the surface of the bay during the ebb tides and first quarter of the flood tides; this rarely leaves the bay and is said to come from the glacial waters brought down by the Puyallup River. When in or off the entrance to this bay the snow-covered summit of the massive Mount Rainier shows wonderfully distinct over the low middle ground at the head of the bay.

Tacoma, on the southwestern side of the bay, is the terminus of the Northern Pacific Railroad. Its principal trade is in wheat, coal, and lumber. Supplies of all kinds may be obtained. Vessels coal from alongside of wharves.

Colvos Passage.—Before the general use of steam tugs on these waters and before the development of Tacoma as the terminus of a transcontinental railroad, this passage was the almost invariably used ship channel for vessels to and from Puget Sound. It is formed by the western shore of Vashon Island and the eastern shore of the Great Peninsula. It is 11½ miles long and nearly straight on a course S. by W., and has a very regular width of one mile, with high bluff shores, varied by numerous small low sand points making out a short distance from the face of the bluff and all having very deep water off them. The mid-channel depths are from 30 to 60 fathoms over fine gray sand and gravel. A vessel may anchor anywhere under either shore if she has room to swing. The best anchorage is under the eastern shore, near the north entrance, about 1½ miles inside of Point Vashon. There is here a slight receding and breaking down of the bluff and a vessel will find excellent anchorage in 5 to 10 fathoms of water. This anchorage is known as Fern Cove, and the low point forming the southern shore is Point Peter.

There is usually more wind in this passage than in the broad passage to the eastward of Vashon Island, and much stronger currents, while at the north entrance, between Point Vashon and Blake Island, is the anchoring ground of Allen Bank, already described. There are no known dangers in this passage.

Point Southworth.—The northwest entrance of the Colvos Passage is one mile wide between Point Vashon and Point Southworth, the latter bearing nearly west from the former. It is low near the water but rises to a high wooded bluff. It has deep water close under its southeast side, but anchorage may be had off the north face with strong currents.

Dalco Point.—This is the southwestern point of Vashon Island, where the Colvos Passage opens to the southward. The southernmost point of the island is Neill Point, which is nearly a mile to the eastward of Dalco Point. The former point is a moderately high wooded bluff with no definite point, being a rounding shore.

Neill Point, as seen when off Point Defiance, is a high sloping bluff covered with trees to the beach without any bright exposed part. There is a very narrow beach at high water.

Dalco Passage.—The passage between Neill Point and Point Defiance is known as Dalco Passage. The currents in it are very variable.

The Narrows.—There is a relatively narrow passage leading from the more expansive channels of the Admiralty Inlet proper to the narrower but greatly ramified inlets of Puget Sound. Through it pass all the waters of Puget Sound. This passage is called The Narrows, at the entrance it is one mile wide; for 2 miles the course is S. 27° E., curving gradually with a slightly decreased width to S. 28° W. for 3 miles, when the waters of the sound open to the southward and westward. The average width of The Narrows is about ¾ mile; the shores are high, bold, and in some places rocky. The summit of the cliffs is wooded. The depth of water through the mid-channel ranges from 30 to 40 fathoms, with deep water close under the shores. The eastern shore is the bolder, having 20 fathoms of water within 200 yards of the cliffs; the 3-fathom line is close under the shore. Midway through The Narrows the high long rounding point on the west side is Point Evans, and close under it is a sunken rock with kelp around it and in other patches along the shore. This danger is called Evans Rock, and lies about 130 yards off the shore, and is just a little NNE. of Point Evans. It has about 4½ feet of water upon it at extreme low tides, and the pilots of the steamboats have special marks and ranges for its location when passing close to it. It is locally known as the "Bowlder." At the extreme low tides of the year, about June, this rock shows just above the water for a few minutes at the stand.

The Currents in The Narrows.—In mid-channel the regular flood and ebb currents are always found to run from ½ to one hour after the rise or fall of the tide. There are generally considerable current rips, especially at the spring tides, with strong swirls, which make the water very rough and dangerous for small boats, more particularly when the winds are contrary to the currents.

On the east side of The Narrows and south of Point Defiance a strong eddy current is found on the flood tide from about abreast of Point Evans to Point Defiance. This eddy is much used by small steamers, but great care must be exercised when close to Point Defiance, if bound through the Dalco Passage to Tacoma, to haul out gradually to meet the strong flood at the point either bow on or quartering on the starboard bow, instead of running into it almost at right angles. The line between the flood and the eddy is well marked by the rip, and as both currents are strong care is demanded.

On the west side of The Narrows, between Point Evans and Gig Harbor, there is a strong eddy current on the ebb tide. This eddy is always taken advantage of by steamboats and small craft, but the pilots of boats using this eddy must be careful to keep clear of the "Bowlder," or Evans Rock. On the west side of The Narrows, between Point Evans and Point Fosdick, there is slackwater very close under the shore during the flood, but only the smallest craft can take advantage of it. In densely smoky weather the steamboats use the echo of the steam whistle to learn their distance from shore and when they make Point Defiance.

Point Defiance.—This head is the NE. point of the northern entrance to The Narrows. It rises by several steps. Between high and low watermark there is a narrow ledge or shelf of rock bare at low water. The face of this rock is almost perpendicular, with 5 fathoms of water alongside, and at 70 yards off 10 fathoms over rocky bottom. Above this rocky ledge there is a rise of 40 feet, a slope reaching 50 feet higher, and a third rise of 100 feet, above which the head is densely wooded, and the ground rises gradually inland. The face of the cliff is too steep for trees, and is a bright yellow color. The north face of the point looks directly into Colvos Passage. On the east side of the point the trees come down to the beach, which is very narrow and covered at high water. There is very bold water close under the point, and the currents and strong eddies exist around the point on the flood.

Gig Harbor.—On the western side of The Narrows, at the north entrance, and directly opposite Point Defiance, there is a small boat harbor, with a depth of 10 feet of water in the entrance and 5 fathoms inside. The entrance is very narrow.

Day Island Anchorage.—At the south entrance to The Narrows, on the eastern side, there is a small narrow projecting point from the eastern shore, which forms a little cove or indentation on the north side. The main shore itself is low and recedes slightly, thus adding to the size of this little cove. Anchorage is had in 15 fathoms of water, but there are strong swirling currents which make it an uncomfortable berth. On the south side of this little peninsula and outside the kelp, anchorage may also be had but the currents are strong. There is a small patch of kelp, with bowlders, close off Day Island.

Puget Sound.—This name is applied in its original meaning for the sake of subdividing these waters. Up to the Narrows the channel had been broad, open, and nearly straight; south of the Narrows the shore line of the sound and of the islands in it amounts to 280 miles, with deep water along almost every mile. The main body of the inlet lies to the southward and westward. The general width of the main channels is one mile, and the depth of the water is sufficient for the largest vessels throughout, and reaches 100 fathoms. The dangers in all these channels are few, and only two are in the main channels and require marking.

The navigation is very simple in good weather, but in thick and foggy weather it requires a full local knowledge of the currents and the peculiarities of the echoes from all points passed by the steamboats. With a knowledge of the tides and currents the captains and pilots run in foggy or thick smoky weather by courses and time-distances, and when approaching any point they ascertain its distance and bearing by the echo of their steam whistle signal from the shores. No minute sailing directions could be drawn up to take the place of the local knowledge and experience of the pilots, and general directions are only suggestive in good weather, for the chart is the best guide.

Fox Island is 4⅓ miles long NW. by N. and SE. by S., with an average width of one mile. The passage between it and the mainland to the north is over a mile wide at the eastern entrance, abreast of Day Island, and ½ mile wide at the western entrance, where it is known as Hale's Passage. There is deep water and no known dangers through the whole of this passage. The northeasternmost part of the island is a bright yellow cliff, estimated to be 70 feet high, and covered with Oregon pine to the edge.

Whollochet Bay.—This is a moderately wide bay, opening into the north side of Hale's Passage, opposite the middle of the north shore of Fox Island, and one mile west of Point Fosdick, at the south entrance of the Narrows. The immediate shores of this bay are low, rising to wooded high land. It carries deep water for 1⅓ miles, when 8 fathoms is found. The 3 fathom curve is never more than 200 yards from the shores. For ¾ mile the bay runs to the northward, and then curves gradually to the NW., and affords a good and sheltered anchorage.

Toliva Shoal.—This danger lies directly in line of the southern entrance to the Narrows. It is one mile from Gibson Point at the southeast part of Fox Island, one mile from the eastern main shore, and 1½ miles from Steilacoom.

Vessels bound up the sound to Steilacoom or direct to or from Olympia by Balch's Passage must beware of this shoal. The extent within the 3 fathom curve is about 150 yards, and there are two spots on it 60 yards apart in line with the point of Fox Island, which have 14 feet of water upon them. One of these shoal patches is 60 yards in extent to the 3-fathom limit. The bottom of the shoal and around it is foul and marked by a patch of kelp. Outside of it the water is very deep, the 20-fathom curve coming close up to and around it. From the west side of the shoal this 20-fathom curve reaches nearly to Point Gibson, on Fox Island. The current rip upon the shoal is very great, and with a little wind it raises a confused short swell sufficient to swamp a small boat.

This danger is now marked by a buoy; it is placed in 27 feet of water at the center of the shoal and may be passed on either hand by giving it a good berth

Steilacoom.—On the eastern shore of Puget Sound, 9 miles south from Point Defiance, is the town of Steilacoom, situated upon a rising bluff The ground rises to 150 feet and is patched with trees; behind the crest, on the level land, is the Oregon pine There is a wharf for the steamboat landing, and in approaching in thick weather the echo of the vessel's steam whistle is very good

Vessels approaching this from the northward keep along under the eastern shore, when abreast the south entrance to the Narrows a broad passage opens to the west, with the southeastern end of Fox Island forming the western shore of the main channel into the sound This main channel is here about ⅞ mile wide The shores of the mainland and of the island are bold, high, and of nearly uniform elevation, and covered with trees. A vessel keeps the eastern shore close aboard to avoid Tolmia Shoal, and if bound for Steilacoom, anchors off the town in 15 fathoms of water over hard bottom about 400 yards off the shore The current up in the channel abreast of the town is frequently sufficient, with a little wind, to swamp a small boat

Steilacoom River is a small stream emptying into the sound one mile north of the town, but is now locally known as Chambers Creek.

Ketron Island.—This is a narrow island 1¼ miles long, lying parallel with the main shore, a mile south of Steilacoom, with ½ mile wide passage on the east side called the Cormorant Pass, carrying 25 fathoms of water over muddy bottom, and the sound on the west side, 1½ miles wide towards Anderson Island This main passage has 75 fathoms of water over fine gray sand and mud The island is from 60 to 100 feet high, with steep sides, and is covered with tall Oregon pine.

Off the south end of the island the 3 fathom curve reaches out 150 yards; off the north end of the island there is kelp for ¼ mile, but the 3 fathom curve is only 200 yards from the point. There is a narrow beach around the island at low water

McNeil Island.—The island is about 3 miles in its longer diameter east and west and 2¼ miles north and south Between its north side and the south side of Fox Island there is a channel 1½ miles wide running for some miles into Carr Inlet Between the south side of the island and the north side of Anderson Island there is a comparatively narrow channel, known as Balch's Passage. McNeil Island is high and wooded, with high bluff shores broken at the east end

Anderson Island is moderately high and wooded, with deep water around the shores and no known dangers It is a little over 3 miles from Steilacoom and is 4 miles long, north and south, and about 2½ miles broad The southern end reaches well down into the southern part of the sound opposite the mouth of the Nisqually River, only ⅘ mile from the Nisqually Flats. There are good passages all around the island, with the broadest towards Nisqually, forming the Nisqually Reach and the narrowest towards McNeil Island, this latter forming Balch's Passage

In the southeast side of Anderson Island there is a deep indentation of ¾ mile, and nearly one mile wide between the points of entrance The line of soundings across the entrance is 25 fathoms, with good water close to either point, but deeper under the south point The 5 fathom line reaches nearly ½ mile into the bay, with muddy bottom

Caution—In rounding the south point of Anderson Island, give it a good berth, as foul bottom exists there

Nisqually Reach—Between the south end of Anderson Island and Nisqually Flats the passage is known as the Nisqually Reach It is one mile wide, with a depth of 42 fathoms ¾ mile off the edge of the bank where 10 fathoms is found The south end of Anderson Island opposite the bank is called Tutku Point, or Lyle Point; a long, rounding, moderately low point, with trees coming down to the high water mark There is a depth of 10 fathoms of water for 250 yards to the SSE. of the point, and under the west side there is a slight indentation called Thompson Cove, with anchorage in 5 and 6 fathoms of water Off Tutku Point there are strong current rips on the flood.

Nisqually Flats.—These extensive flats lie in the broad southern bend of the sound south of Anderson Island They are 3½ miles in extent WSW and ENE, and about ¾ mile wide They lie off the broad low, marshy valley through which the Nisqually River and its ramifications reach the sound There is very deep water along the northern edge of the flats, but especially towards the eastern limit

Nisqually.—This place is 5 miles south of Steilacoom, on the same side of the sound. It is at the mouth of a small stream and at the eastern edge of the extensive Inskip Bank or Nisqually Flats.

Nisqually Landing—It is one mile north of the Nisqually River, where the Signahlchew Creek empties There is one sawmill on the creek This creek is the natural outlet of the chain of lakes on the prairies; one of these lakes, American Lake, is several miles long.

Devil's Head—This is a bluff about 80 feet above the water and covered with trees that reach a height of 100 feet. There are trees under the bluff down to the very narrow sand beach It is the southern point of the unnamed peninsula between Carr's Inlet, on the east, and Case's Inlet on the west Abreast of it the channel is 1¼ miles wide with bold water under either shore, and reaching 50 fathoms close under the head The 3 fathom curve is within 200 yards of the shore, except at a small point about one mile NE. from the head, where the 3 fathom curve is ¼ mile out and at the edge of the low-water line. This part of the sound is the entrance to Case's Inlet and stretches NNW. 7 miles from Devil's Head and then nearly north for 8 miles farther, with an average width of 1¼ miles, and depths ranging from 35 fathoms to 5 at the head. To the SE. of the Devil's Head this broad arm reaches to the Nisqually Narrows

As the Devil's Head is approached from the west Mount Rainier is opened just clear of it, showing three nearly equally high summits.

Moody Point.—This is the extremity of the promontory between the broad waters towards Drayton Passage and Nisqually Reach, and the narrow arm of the sound on the west called Henderson's Inlet. It points directly towards the middle of Case's Inlet. It is a low, sandy point of almost 100 or 200 yards extent, with some unpainted shanties under the trees and bluff, which are inside and behind the low shore. There is good water off the point, the 20-fathom curve being less than ¼ mile out Across Case's Inlet to the NE the breadth of the channel is 1½ miles wide. Across Dana's Passage to the west the width is the same, with the Itsami Shoal in the middle. Moody's Point is locally known as Johnson's Point.

Itsami Shoal.—This danger lies one mile from the northern most extremity of Moody or Johnson's Point and ½ mile from the nearest shore of Hartstene Island to the west. Between it and Hartstene Island the main channel runs with 22 fathoms of water and good water close under the western shore. It is a rocky patch having as little as 9 feet of water on it with kelp spreading out to 3½ fathoms of water. There is 10 fathoms of water between the shoal and the west shore of Moody Point and 6¼ fathoms between it and Dickerson's double point, ½ mile to the south. This danger is marked by a buoy It is placed in 24 feet of water over rocky bottom on the north side of the kelp patch Vessels bound to Olympia should leave it on the port hand.

Dana Passage—From the Itsami Shoal the passage is contracted to about ½ mile wide with mid channel depths of 20 to 15 fathoms of water over coarse gray sand, shells, and gravel, and good water close to the shores. Its general direction is SW. by W and NE by E for 2 miles The eastern shore is indented and moderately low, but covered with Oregon fir; the western shore is formed by the south side of Hartstene island and is higher than the eastern shore. There are very strong currents during spring tides in this passage There is foul bottom close to Brisco Point and the edge of the channel is steep to.

Brisco Point is a sharp narrow point 60 feet high on the westward side of Dana's Passage, and nearly 2 miles WSW. of Itsami Shoal. It is wooded and has good water close to it on the east side, but the 3-fathom line extends 300 yards south from the point, with a fringe of kelp in 4 fathoms of water and with a narrow, low neck on the north. The channel immediately on the west side of the point is Peale's Passage, ½ mile wide, and with 12 to 13 fathoms in it; it leads to the NW completely around Hartstene Island.

Dofflemyer Point is low and cleared on the north with cliffs 80 feet high to the southward The 3 fathom curve is close to it, but lies 300 yards outside of Jeal's Point, ⅓ mile to the NE

Point Cooper, at the western side of the entrance to Budd's Inlet, projects to the northward: it is low and sharp and rises to 80 feet in ½ mile towards the south. It divides Budd's Inlet from Eld Inlet and the 3 fathom curve spreads out 300 yards from the point and narrows the entrance to Eld Inlet

Budd's Inlet.—This long arm at the head of the sound is ¼ mile wide at the entrance, one mile wide inside, and then gradually narrows to ¾ mile at the head. It is 6 miles long, and its general direction is south. For 1½ miles before reaching Olympia the bay or inlet is occupied by an enormous mud flat, of which one fourth is bare at low water, and this shoal within the 3 fathom line extends from the head of the bay for 1½ miles to the northward, and then continues under the east shore for 2 miles towards Wepusec Inlet The bluffs on the west shore average about 60 feet high, are steep, and generally covered with Oregon pine. The bluffs on the east shore are higher for the first mile, and then decrease towards the head.

The average depth of the water is 6 fathoms, and is quite uniform over a bottom of mud. There is only one danger inside the inlet, and that is 3¼ miles south of Cooper Point, under the western shore. It is a stony patch, in part bare at low water, and surrounded by hard bottom in one to 3 fathoms of water. The total area of this shoal spot is 100 yards north and south and 300 east and west, and it lies a little over ¼ mile from the western shore, abreast the 60-foot bluff ¾ mile north of Butler's Cove. There is a good channel carrying 8 and 9 fathoms on the west side of it, and a broader channel on the east carrying 8 to 4 fathoms of water. This shoal is marked by a buoy. There is good water on either side of the buoy, but less than halfway from it, towards the eastern shore, the 3 fathom line is reached. A depth of 3 fathoms can be carried one mile farther up the inlet than the buoy by keeping close under the western shore. Large vessels pass this shoal and anchor nearly a mile S. by E. of it in 3½ fathoms of water. Many vessels go to the wharf at Olympia at high water and lie there in the soft mud at low water. Steamboats run up to the wharves at high water, but if intending to move during the time of low water they must lie nearly a mile to the NNW., under the west shore, where there is a wharf, and whence there is a good road along the shore to Olympia.

Olympia is the county seat and also the capital of Washington. The United States land offices and the office of the United States collector of internal revenue are located here. It has large private educational institutions, manufacturing establishments, sawmills, etc The lumber output of the country is large. Extensive deposits of coal have been discovered and located.

Olympia Wharf.—A new wharf has been projected northward from the town of Olympia, through the middle of the great flats, ⅝ mile beyond the old wharf. It reaches 3 or 4 feet of water at the lowest tides.

Tumwater is a village about one mile south of Olympia, on the Des Chutes River, where the water-power of the falls is utilized by mills for various products of manufacture

Olympia—Directions.—It would be almost useless to attempt to describe the route between Olympia and Steilacoom, because a pilot or a chart is absolutely necessary to make the passage. The mid-channel course from wharf to wharf is 21 miles in length, and the width of the passage from ½ to 1½ miles. In fine clear weather a stranger would see nothing but land close around him, as if he were in an irregularly shaped lake with arms leading in every direction In foggy weather, or in the dense smoky weather of a dry summer, it is impossible to see a ship's length ahead, with irregular currents to add to the difficulty The chart is then almost useless, and a thorough local knowledge of every mark on the beaches and of the peculiarities of the echo of the steam whistle from every cliff and point are necessary to enable the pilot to make his trips. Steamboats and tows do not take the broader channel from Steilacoom between Ketron and Anderson Islands through the Nisqually Reach, but the first course is through Balch's Passage The entrance to this passage is nearly 3 miles from Steilacoom, and the passage itself 2 miles long and ½ mile wide for the middle part of the pass There is plenty of water in this passage and the shores are steep too Midway in the pass is a small rocky islet known as Eagle Island; it is nearer the south shore, but there is good water on either side of it

The island is only 280 yards long north and south and 100 yards wide It is about 10 feet above high water and covered with Oregon pine 70 feet high. The 3 fathom curve is 100 yards off the eastern side, where kelp is found out to 4 and 5 fathoms. The Eagle Island shoal, within the 3 fathom line, extends ¼ mile to the NW. parallel to the shore of the passage. It is marked by plenty of kelp. A depth of 5 to 6 fathoms can be carried through the southern channel between Eagle Island and Anderson Island, keeping rather closer to the latter, and this channel is preferred by the large steamboats, because at night and in thick weather they can much better keep the courses and distances which they run in clear weather. Ten fathoms can be carried through the northern and wider channel between Eagle Island and McNeil Island by keeping rather close to the shore under the latter.

After passing through Balch's Passage there is a narrow channel called Pitt Passage, ⅓ mile wide, on the west side of McNeil island, to the northward; a bay named Titusi Bay, one mile deep, with an entrance nearly ½ mile wide with good water, directly ahead, and to the south opens the broad Drayton Passage, 1½ miles wide, decreasing to one mile in width in 1½ miles, and then opening into the broader waters of the sound. This passage is 3 miles long, and at the southern entrance there is Point Treble on the east on Anderson Island, and Park Point or the Devil's Head on the west There is a depth of 18 to 30 fathoms in it, with good water up to either shore The direction of the channel is north and south.

Remarks.—It would require an immense amount of detail to describe the intricacy of all the inlets, passages, and islets throughout Puget Sound south of the Narrows The principal navigation is from Olympia by the route just described to Steilacoom, and thence to Tacoma and

Seattle. There are now small towns and settlements growing upon the shores of these inlets, also small sawmills. There is good water through the narrower inlets, which have bold shores and pine-covered country. Case's Inlet and Carro Inlet are the two principal arms, each being about 12 miles long and from one to 2 miles wide, with 30 to 50 fathoms in them and no dangers; the peninsula between these has no lakes through it. The chart gives all that is at present needed for the navigation of these waters.

Hood's Canal.—This great arm of Admiralty Inlet commences 14¼ miles inside the entrance to the inlet on Point Wilson; opening on the west side of the great channel, between the Foulweather Bluff on the east of the entrance and Basalt Point on the west. At 3¾ miles from the entrance there is passed on the starboard hand a high round wooded peninsula ¾ mile long north and south, and ½ mile wide east and west. It is connected with the mainland by a narrow neck of low sand beach. This peninsula is frequently mistaken for an island, and is named Hood's Head. Between this head and Port Gamble the canal changes its course and runs in nearly a straight line SW. by S. for 40 miles, with an average width of 1½ miles. In latitude 47° 21′ N. the canal makes an abrupt turn and runs 12 miles nearly NE., where it heads within 2 miles of the head of Case's Inlet, in Puget Sound.

At 15 miles from Port Gamble there is a slight crook in the line of the canal, and at 17 miles another broad arm stretches to the N. by W. for 10 miles, with a peninsula 1½ miles in width between it and the canal. This is the Toandos Peninsula. The shore line of the canal amounts to 192 miles.

The shores of the canal are bold, high, and wooded, rising to much greater heights than anywhere else on the inlet or sound. This is particularly so on the western shore, where the west shore of the Dabop Bay attains an elevation of 2,600 feet in less than 2 miles from the water. These high flanking mountains of the Olympus Range are called Jupiter Hills.

Southward from Point Misery, at Seabeck Harbor, the canal runs in nearly a straight line S. 31° W. for 21 miles, with a nearly uniform and average width of 1¼ miles. It has bold, rocky shores on either side, the eastern land of the Great Peninsula being of moderate height; the western land rising boldly and rapidly to 7,000 feet at the eastern peaks of the Olympus Range. "The Brothers" and Mount Ellinor, with elevations over 6,000 feet, lying only 7 or 8 miles to the westward, and Mount Constance 10½ miles, but reaching 7,777 feet elevation. The water is very deep close under the shores, except where streams make out, and through mid-channel the depths range from more than 90 to 50 fathoms. The bottom is mud throughout.

Hood's Head.—This is the islandlike mass on the western side of Hood's Canal, 3 miles inside of Foulweather Bluff. It is about ⅞ of a mile long N. by E. and S. by W., and ⅜ of a mile wide. It is joined to the western main shore by a low narrow strip of sandy beach ½ a mile long, which has moderately deep water on the north side and a contracted shallow cove on the south. A vessel may anchor to the northwestward of the head in 15 fathoms of water over muddy bottom at ⅓ of a mile from the shore.

The north face of the head is a very steep bare cliff, nearly ⅜ mile frontage east and west, and the south face is a rounding, high, bare cliff. All behind the cliffs is covered with pine. At the NE. point of the head, a low sandy point makes out 300 yards and terminates in a very sharp point; towards the higher point the ground is marshy. This is Point Hannon, and off it deep water is found with strong swirling currents

Port Gamble is a land locked bay 2¼ miles long north and south, with a nearly uniform width of ⅜ mile. It narrows at the entrance between two low grassy sand spits only 300 yards apart, and with a channel way of 120 yards width between the 3 fathom lines. The deepest water in the bay is 9 fathoms, and it may be said to have a nearly uniform depth of 5 fathoms. On the western point of the entrance is a sawmill, and the buildings reach to the rise of the bluff to the westward. The wharves on the western point are built out so that vessels have deep water between them and East Point.

Outside of the entrance to the bay there is a hard sand flat on either side; that from the east shore reaches westward 300 yards, that on the west stretches out to the N. by W. from the mill parallel with the east shore Between these two flats is the channel way, 90 yards wide between the 3 fathom curves. Westward of the entrance for 1¼ miles there is a remarkably straight shore line, partly cliff and partly low ground, towards the west, where Salsbury Point marks the turn of the shore line to the southward

Directions—Vessels from the northward after leaving Marrowstone Point pass Nodule Point, 6 miles from Foulweather Bluff, on a S. 59° W. course, steering for Hood's Head if it is recognized This course passes more than a mile to the westward of Foulweather Bluff and nearly halfway between Foulweather Bluff buoy and Colvos Rock buoy. After passing Foulweather Bluff keep closer to the eastern shore than the western to avoid the strong and irregular current passing around the low point which makes out 275 yards eastward from Hood's Head. Then run for the sawmill plainly in sight on the west side of the entrance, and when within a mile of it, approach the eastern shore within ⅛ mile. When it is foggy or smoky steamboats get their distance fron the shore by the echo of their whistles. Outside of this entrance the bottom is sticky out to 15 fathoms; beyond that it falls off rapidly A vessel may anchor in 8 fathoms with the mill bearing south, distant ¾ mile and the eastern shore distant ⅝ mile. When a vessel is going in she must have either good local knowledge of the channel and natural ranges, or must keep the lead going smartly. In summer the wind generally blows into the harbor lightly; in the winter [illegible] SE. gales prevail and draw directly out. When entering under sail the vessel must drop in with the early flood. Loaded vessels are towed in and out by the tug; when without the tug they must warp out in summer with the last of the ebb or trust to a light southerly air in the morning, with an ebb current. None but small, smartly working vessels can beat out, and very few of them have done so within channel limits. When a small vessel is beating out she should go out on the ebb.

Inside the sawmill and Indian Village points there is good water in mid-channel for anchorage. On the western side there was formerly a crib in 3½ fathoms of water, around which a shoal has formed with only 10 to 15 feet; between this crib and the lumber wharf there is from 17 to 22 feet of water; if a vessel has to anchor, she can do so just beyond this crib in 5 fathoms over soft muddy bottom. On the east side of the steamboat wharf there is a depth of 5 to 22 feet, the shoaler water being at the northern end. On the south side of the wharf, where the lumber vessels lie to receive their cargoes, there is a depth of from 21 to 24 feet at 20 feet from the wharf. Inside of the steamboat wharf, with an opening to the northward, there is a "gridiron," upon which small vessels are taken out at high water for repair or examination. It has 12 feet of water on it at high tide. The shores of the bay are steep but not high and are bordered by a pebbly beach, offering capital chances for heaving down a vessel.

Squamish Harbor.—The point on the western shore, nearly one mile SSW. of Hood's Head, is Termination Point, with high wooded land behind it and a low narrow beach in front. At Termination Point the shore continues WSW. for nearly one mile and then sweeps west for 2 miles to the head of Squamish Bay. From this head of the bay the west shore runs SSE. for 2 miles, thus forming a large triangular open bay with moderately low shores, a low valley and stream at the head, and marshy land under the shore, with a broad low-water beach. A large sand bank parallel with the west side one mile long and nearly ½ mile wide lies within ⅓ mile of the west shore. There is a 6-fathom channel inside of this shoal and around the north end. On the east side of this shoal, and under the north shore and across the mouth of the bay there is good water. In thick weather the approaches to the shoal, which is in part bare, are detected by the lead; the soundings decrease with fair regularity; from 20 fathoms the bottom is muddy.

The Sisters.—From Termination Point the 10-fathom curve runs nearly SSW. for ¾ mile to the rocks called The Sisters, which lie north and south of each other. These rocks are 120 yards broad off the south face of Termination Point, and are, therefore, nearly one-quarter the width of the channel from the western shore. Each is about 150 yards in extent, and they are covered at half tide; the tide ranges from 10 to 12 feet. They lie NE. and SW. from each other, and are 80 yards apart. There is a depth of 7 fathoms between them, and good water all around. The walls are bold, and they are marked by a patch of kelp around them. The southern rock lies 1¼ miles from Salsbury Point and ⅓ mile from Termination Point. These rocks are also known as the Squamish Rocks. The north shore of the harbor is called Yulkat Bluff. The shoal in the west part of the harbor is known as Case's Bank.

Seabeck Bay.—Southward from Termination and Salsbury Points the canal runs for 12 miles in a SW. by S. direction, with a general width of 1½ miles, gradually decreasing to the point of the Toandos Peninsula on the west side of the canal. The shores are bold, and there is good water close under them and no known danger. The bottom ranges from 30 fathoms in depth, to 72 at the narrowest point; the currents are strong.

The eastern point of the Toandos Peninsula is Hazel Point, and here the canal takes a direction nearly W. by S. for 5 miles. Under the eastern shore of this reach and directly abreast Oak Head lies the Harbor of Seabeck. This bay is an indentation of one mile in a southerly direction and is therefore open to the N. by E. At its narrow head there is the mouth of a small stream. On the east side of the bay the shore is moderately low; on the west there is a long point which forms the protection to the bay. On the old charts this projection was called Seabeck Point; on the recent ones it is named Point Misery. At the entrance the harbor is more than ¾ mile wide with 15 fathoms over sandy bottom in the middle; near the head it is contracted, but a depth of 5 fathoms of water is carried well up to the mill which is on the eastern side.

Oak Head is the southernmost projection of Toandos Peninsula. It is high and abrupt with deep water close under the shore. It is almost 2 miles north from Point Misery, with 60 fathoms of water in mid-channel.

Fisherman's Bay.—Just on the east side of Oak Head there is a long narrow cove making in to the NW. by W. for ¾ mile. There is a little spit at the west side of the entrance and the water is not deep.

Dabop Bay.—From Oak Head the shore runs NW. for a mile, and then nearly N. by E. for 9 miles, with a broad arm of Hood's Canal extending that far in and ending in two smaller arms. This bay has very bold shores, deep water, and very high hills on the west side. The western arm at the north is named Quilcene Bay and is shallow and marshy at the head, where there is a small settlement called Quilcene on the left bank of Big River. The large mountain stream entering Quilcene Bay has its rise in the northeast flank of Mount Constance by two tributaries, and a third tributary comes from a large lake midway to Port Discovery and nearly reaches Crocker Lake, which empties into Port Discovery.

Dusewallips River.—Abreast of Oak Head, on the west side of Dabop Bay, the river empties and has formed a flat delta and a broad shoal in front. This shoal is 2 miles long and ½ mile wide with deep water close up to it. Between this shoal and Tskuls'

Point, the nearest part of the Toandos Peninsula, the width of the bay is 1¾ miles and the depth of the water is 80 fathoms over muddy bottom. On either side of this river the mountains rise to 510 feet and to 2,300 feet within 1½ miles.

Quatsap Point.—Four miles WSW. of Oak Head and on the west side of the canal is a moderately low head, under the south side of which is a broad open bay one mile wide with an extensive flat extending out of the line of the northeast and southwest points. This bay receives the Duckabus River, which brings down much detritus.

Hamahama River.—This stream empties on the west side of the canal 12 miles S. 48° W. of Oak Head. It is marked by a broad flat one mile long and ½ mile wide in front of it with 15 fathoms of water close outside; but the 20-fathom curve reaches out to mid-channel to the southeastward. This river drains a large lake 4 or 5 miles behind the high mountains over the shore and into this lake a large stream comes from the Olympus range.

The Great Bend of Hood's Canal is 22½ miles by the mid-channel course from Point Misery. Here the breadth of the canal expands to 2 miles for the same distance and thence runs nearly 15 miles to the head in a general northeast direction, decreasing in width to ½ mile at Sister's Point on the north side. The shores are bolder on the port hand going up; the depth of water continues large to within 2½ miles of the head where there is a depth of 3 fathoms only. The head has mud flats and the width decreases to ⅓ mile.

Annas Bay.—This is the southernmost part of Hood's Canal at the Great Bend and it receives the water of the Skokomish River, which has brought down so much sediment that a square mile of the bay is a great sand and mud flat with deep water around the outer edge to the west and north. There is deep water between the western edge of this bank and the western main shore one mile distant. On the point at the south side of the shore of the inlet and forming the east side of Annas Bay is the village of Union City, which has a road through to Oakland on Hammersly's Inlet. The Skokomish is a large mountain stream coming around the southeast flank of the Olympus Mountains. It drains a large lake named Cushman, high up the flanks of Mount Ellinor.

Ayers' Point is the head which forms the farthest projection of the Great Peninsula from the northward into the canal at Annas Bay. It is a high rounding point and has deep water close under it.

Sister's Point is a high rounding bluff on the north shore of the canal 4 miles east of Ayers' Point at the Great Bend. It projects from the northward and nearly shuts the canal, leaving a channel only ⅛ mile wide with deep water over gravelly bottom.

Clifton—This village is at the extreme head of Hood's canal, with a long sand and mud flat for 2½ miles down the canal. There is a road thence to Oakland, another to Lightville, at the head of Case's Inlet, and a third to Seabeck Harbor.

Possession Sound.—The southern entrance to this now important and extensive series of broad deep channels lie between Possession Point, the southernmost point of Whidbey Island, and the main shore opposite, unmarked by any special projection or object. Scatchet Head and Possession Point have already been described. The northern entrance to this sound is the intricate, narrow, and deep Deception Pass. The sound is formed by the irregularly shaped Whidbey Island on the west and the main shore on the east, with Gedney and Camano Islands between them. The sound receives several important water courses, the Snohomish River in the southeast, the Stillaguamish River about the middle, with the Skagit River in the northeast. It also connects at the north by the Swinomish Slough with Padilla Bay, and thence with Guemes Channel and Bellingham Bay. The depth of water throughout the sound is great, except at the deltas of the rivers, which bring down an immense amount of alluvial material which forms mud flats. That from the Snohomish River has nearly filled in across the sound and reduced the channel to ¼ mile wide with only 1 to 6 fathoms of water. There are numerous villages and towns on the rivers and shores and sound, and beside the traffic in sailing vessels, regular communication is kept up by steamer from Seattle with all the towns and settlements. The shores present the general features of Puget Sound, but the channels are narrower, averaging about 2 miles in width, and the depth of water inside the southern entrance reaches 65 fathoms. There are no known dangers in the channels. The shores of the deltas of the rivers are low and muddy, and behind them there is a dense forest and undergrowth.

Port Gardner.—The southern part of the sound runs almost north from Possession Point for 3½ miles to abreast Point Elliot on the east, when it widens out into a nearly circular basin 5½ miles in diameter, with Gedney Island in the middle; this basin is locally known as Port Gardner, although the chart restricts that name to the southeast part. The shores are high and bold and wooded on the summit of the flat mesa-like lands. There is deep water and no dangers close under either shore. This port receives the Snohomish River in the northeast part. The river in its lower course comes through a marshy valley 2 miles wide. Behind Point Elliot is the town of Mukilteo; and 4 miles farther along the shore to the northeast is the town of Port Gardner.

In the NW. part of the port the high SE. point of Camano Island, called Point Allen, divides Port Gardner into two channels, leading to the NW.; the one to the east, 2 miles wide, leads to Port Susan and Stillaguamish River; the one to the west is the Saratoga Passage, and leads [illegible] one deep broad channel 15 or 16 miles long, between the west side of Camano Island and the east side of Whidbey Island, to the north end of the former. Point Allen, at the south end of Camano Island, and Sandy Point on Whidbey Island, 1¾ miles south of the former, are the entrance points to Saratoga Passage.

Gedney Island, lying in the middle of Port Gardner, is 1½ miles long SE. by E. and NW. by W. When seen from the NW., coming out of Saratoga Passage, it shows a moderately steep bluff to the west and a low slowly rising bluff to the east, both covered with Oregon pine. There is one prominent tree on this east point where a low sand spit shows out about 50 yards as it is approached. As seen from the northward, broadside on, the ridge line of Gedney Island looks moderately level, about 80 feet high, and covered with Oregon pine. The trees are the higher on the NW. end.

Off the SE. end of the island there is a great erratic bowlder visible at low water. There is moderately deep water around the island. A bank with 15 fathoms is reported by the steamboat captains to lie more than ¼ mile off the NW. point of the island towards Allen Point or Camano Head. Around the south shore there is a depth of 10 fathoms nearly ½ mile off; and on the prolongation of the axis to the SE. of the SE. point there is a shoal, which extends out a little more than ½ mile, with a depth of only 3½ fathoms at the end. Outside of these the depths increase to as much as 65 fathoms.

Tulalip lies on the main shore nearly abreast of Allen Point, at the entrance to Port Susan. The west point of the entrance has a bright patch of bluff with pines upon it; the bluff is about 40 feet high and 60 yards long. The SE. point has a bluff with trees, and a low neck of land towards the buildings of the Sisters of Charity. The bay is protected by two points, and somewhat restricted by a shoal making out from the NW. point to the middle of the opening. The entrance is open to the SW., and the two points are about ¼ mile apart.

Tulalip Bay Buoys.—Two buoys have been placed to mark the entrance to this anchorage. The one is a black spar buoy and the other is a red spar buoy.

Stillaguamish Slough Buoy.—Two spar buoys have been placed off the NE. shore of Camano Island to mark the channel into Stillaguamish Slough, at the north end of Port Susan.

Davis Slough Buoys.—Six spar buoys have been placed to mark the channel leading into Davis Slough, one of the mouths of the Snohomish River.

Saratoga Passage.—This is the fine, broad, deep strait, leading from Port Gardner to the northwestward between Camano Island on the east and Whidbey Island on the west. This strait, from Camano Head to the Mills of Utsalady is 18 miles long. The eastern shore is continuous, whereas into the western shore penetrate Holmes Harbor, Penn's Cove, Oak Harbor, and Duncan's Bay. The strait averages 2 miles in width: the shores are bluffs covered with Oregon pine, but not so densely as before the sawmills depleted the forests. There are prairie openings on either side. The channel is from 25 to 50 fathoms deep, with good water close under the shores. No steamboat navigation could be better in good weather. In smoky and in foggy weather the steamboats run by courses and time, according to the currents, and use the echo of the steam-whistle to determine their proximity to the land.

Allen Point.—This is the south end of Camano Island, and forms the north point of the entrance to Saratoga Passage. It rises inland to the tops of the trees, which are estimated at 160 feet above the water. A great landslide has taken place here, and 3 or 4 acres of the point have slid away, leaving a low outer white cliff with a few trees upon it; then the surface falls back to the base of the second or inner white-clay cliff, which rises to about 100 feet above the water, and is covered on the summit with high pine trees. There is deep water off Point Allen. This point is known to steamboat captains as Camano Head.

Sandy Point, on Whidbey Island, abreast of Allen Point, and forming the south part of the entrance to Saratoga Passage, is moderately long, low, and has no bushes. The bluff behind it rises by three steps, with straggling trees. There is a house at the inner or western end of the low beach of the point, with a cleared space on the sloping, rising ground, and a white house in the upper part of the clearing. There is bold water close under this point. It is locally known as Joe Brown's Point.

East Point is on the west side of Saratoga Passage, 6 miles from Sandy Point. The point on the opposite side of the channel, distant 1½ miles, is Point Lowell, on Camano Island. East Point is a short, low, grassy spit, backed by a high bluff well wooded. The tops of the trees are estimated to be 150 feet above the water. There is very deep water off the point. Point Lowell has very deep water off it. One and one-third miles west of East Point is Rocky Point, the turning point into Holmes Harbor, which runs south for 4½ miles; it is 1¼ miles wide, and has 20 fathoms of water to the head, which is only one mile from Mutiny Bay.

Rocky Point is low at the water's edge and rises gradually to 80 feet. The trees have been cut away and scrub now covers it. About 100 yards off the point is a rocky islet covered with scrub. It is about 50 yards in extent at low water, and is then connected with the point.

Watsak Point lies on the west side of the Saratoga Passage, and 9½ miles N. 35° W. of East Point, where the passage widens to 4 or 5 miles. Towards the west, around point Watsak, is the beautiful harbor of Penn's Cove, 3½ miles long and one mile wide, with 15 to 7 fathoms of water, and heading within 1½ miles of Point Partridge; towards the north are the broad bays of Oak Harbor and Duncan's Bay; to the northwestward, just beyond point Demock, is Utsalady. There is deep water along all these shores except off Point Watsak, where a narrow shoal runs to the northward for fully ½ mile, with fully 21 fathoms of water on the east side and 16 fathoms on the west side.

Watsak Point Buoy.—At the extremity of Point Watsak there is a buoy placed in 4 fathoms of water about 50 yards off the end of the spit, which has only one fathom upon it at low water. This point is locally known as Snakeland Point.

Point Polnell is on Whidbey Island, and forms the eastern boundary of Duncan's Bay; it lies 4 miles N. 39° E. of Watsak Point. Between it and Utsalady the broad Saratoga Passage may be said to end at the turn around point Demock, the NW. point of Camano Island. Point Polnell is a long narrow point jutting out to the southward from the rounding shore behind it. When seen from the southward it looks like a bluff-faced islet. Locally this point is known as Miller Point.

Utsalady.—This is the most important place on Possession Sound. It lies on the north side of Camano Island, 27 miles by mid-channel course from the southern entrance of Possession Sound. The channel to it through Saratoga Passage averages nearly 2 miles wide; the water is deep, the shores are bold, and there are no known dangers. The chart is a good guide for a vessel, but vessels are usually towed either way.

Oak Harbor and Duncan Bay are two bays on Whidbey Island, in the NW. part of Saratoga Passage. There is the town of Oak Harbor at the head of the former. Forbes Point is a broad peninsula 1½ miles long, lying between the two bays. Around this broad point is shoal water, and buoys have been placed to enable the steamboats to avoid it in foggy and smoky weather.

Skagit Bay.—The entrance to Skagit River is marked by buoys as is also La Conner, at the south entrance of Swinomish Slough.

VANCOUVER ISLAND.

North Shore of Juan de Fuca Strait.—From Point Bonilla to Owen Point the shore runs 10 miles S. 72° E. It is nearly straight, rocky, and bluff, with high mountains rising immediately behind it, all heavily wooded.

(1190) **BRITISH COLUMBIA—Vancouver island—Juan de Fuca strait—Port San Juan—Whistling buoy established.**—The Canadian Government has given notice that an automatic whistling buoy, on the Courtenay principle, has been established at the entrance to port San Juan, Vancouver island.

The buoy is painted red and is moored in 14 fathoms of water.

Approx. position: Lat. 48° 31′ 46″ N., Long. 124° 29′ 45″ W.

(N. M. 31, 1906.)

than 200 yards from it a low flat rock, named Owen ... high water.

Observatory Rocks, off the eastern entrance point, are high pinnacles, with two or three trees growing on them and some smaller rocks off, the outermost of which lies 300 yards from the shore. At 800 yards within these rocks and 200 yards from the shore is another reef, partly out of water, named Hammond Rocks.

The port runs nearly straight for 3½ miles, and carries its breadth almost to its head, which terminates in a round beach, composed of muddy sand. Gordon River enters the port through the north end of this beach, and Cooper Inlet penetrates its southern; very small coasters may enter them towards high water, and find depth and shelter within.

run by courses and time, according to the currents, and use the echo of the steam-whistle to determine their proximity to the land.

Allen Point.—This is the south end of Camano Island, and forms the north point of the entrance to Saratoga Passage. It rises inland to the tops of the trees, which are estimated at 160 feet above the water. A great landslide has taken place here, and 3 or 4 acres of the point have slid away, leaving a low outer white cliff with a few trees upon it; then the surface falls back to the base of the second or inner white-clay cliff, which rises to about 100 feet above the water, and is covered on the summit with high pine trees. There is deep water off Point Allen. This point is known to steamboat captains as Camano Head.

Sandy Point, on Whidbey Island, abreast of Allen Point, and forming the south part of the entrance to Saratoga Passage, is moderately long, low, and has no bushes. The bluff behind it rises by three steps, with straggling trees. There is a house at the inner or western end of the low beach of the point, with a cleared space on the sloping, rising ground, and a white house in the upper part of the clearing. There is bold water close under this point. It is locally known as Joe Brown's Point.

East Point is on the west side of Saratoga Passage, 6 miles from Sandy Point. The point on the opposite side of the channel, distant $1\frac{1}{3}$ miles, is Point Lowell, on Camano Island. East Point is a short, low, grassy spit, backed by a high bluff well wooded. The tops of the trees are estimated to be 150 feet above the water. There is very deep water off the point. Point Lowell has very deep water off it. One and one-third miles west of East Point is Rocky Point, the turning point into Holmes Harbor, which runs south for $4\frac{1}{2}$ miles; it is $1\frac{1}{4}$ miles wide, and [illegible] to the head, which is only one mile from Muti[illegible]

R[illegible] feet. [illegible] 100 [illegible] 50 y[illegible]

W[illegible] $9\frac{1}{2}$ miles N. [illegible] W. of East Point, where the passage widens to 4 or 5 miles. Towards the west, around point Watsak, is the beautiful harbor of Penn's Cove, $3\frac{1}{2}$ miles long and one mile wide, with 15 to 7 fathoms of water, and heading within $1\frac{1}{2}$ miles of Point Partridge; towards the north are the broad bays of Oak Harbor and Duncan's Bay; to the northwestward, just beyond point Demock, is Utsaludy. There is deep water along all these shores except off Point Watsak, where a narrow shoal runs to the northward for fully $\frac{1}{4}$ mile, with fully 21 fathoms of water on the east side and 16 fathoms on the west side.

Watsak Point Buoy.—At the extremity of Point Watsak there is a buoy placed in 4 fathoms of water about 50 yards off the end of the spit, which has only one fathom upon it at low water. This point is locally known as Snakeland Point.

Point Polnell is on Whidbey Island, and forms the eastern boundary of Duncan's Bay; it lies 4 miles N. 39° E. of Watsak Point. Between it and Utsalady the broad Saratoga Passage may be said to end at the turn around point Demock, the NW. point of Camano Island. Point Polnell is a long narrow point jutting out to the southward from the rounding shore behind it. When seen from the southward it looks like a bluff-faced islet. Locally this point is known as Miller Point.

Utsalady.—This is the most important place on Possession Sound. It lies on the north side of Camano Island, 27 miles by mid-channel course from the southern entrance of Possession Sound. The channel to it through Saratoga Passage averages nearly 2 miles wide; the water is deep, the shores are bold, and there are no known dangers. The chart is a good guide for a vessel, but vessels are usually towed either way.

Oak Harbor and Duncan Bay are two bays on Whidbey Island, in the NW. part of Saratoga Passage. There is the town of Oak Harbor at the head of the former. Forbes Point is a broad peninsula 1½ miles long, lying between the two bays. Around this broad point is shoal water, and buoys have been placed to enable the steamboats to avoid it in foggy and smoky weather.

Skagit Bay.—The entrance to Skagit River is marked by buoys as is also La Conner, at the south entrance of Swinomish Slough.

VANCOUVER ISLAND.

North Shore of Juan de Fuca Strait.—From Point Bonilla to Owen Point the shore runs 10 miles S. 72° E. It is nearly straight, rocky, and bluff, with high mountains rising immediately behind it, all heavily wooded.

Vessels are apt to lose much of their wind close to the shore.

Port San Juan is the first anchorage on the northern shore within the entrance of Fuca Strait. The opening, which is remarkable from seaward, is seen for a considerable distance, and makes as a deep gap between two mountain ranges.

Owen Point, at the western entrance to the port, has at a little more than 200 yards from it a low flat rock, named Owen Island, awash at high water.

Observatory Rocks, off the eastern entrance point, are high pinnacles, with two or three trees growing on them and some smaller rocks off, the outermost of which lies 200 yards from the shore. At 800 yards within these rocks and 300 yards from the shore is another reef, partly out of water, named Hammond Rocks.

The port runs nearly straight for 3½ miles, and carries its breadth almost to its head, which terminates in a round beach, composed of muddy sand. Gordon River enters the port through the north end of this beach, and Cooper Inlet penetrates its southern; very small coasters may enter them towards high water, and find depth and shelter within.

On the north side of the port some rocks and broken ground extend for one mile within Owen Point and nearly 400 yards from the shore; one rock, awash, lies 800 yards N. 70° E. of Owen Island, and is distant 550 yards from the shore.

Anchorage.—The port is entirely open to SW. winds, and a heavy sea rolls in when a moderate gale is blowing from that direction; and though it is possible that a vessel with good ground tackle would ride out a gale if anchored in the most sheltered part, it is by no means recommended to remain with any indication of such weather, but to weigh immediately, and if outward bound seek shelter in Neáah bay. There is a convenient depth of water all over Port San Juan, from 6 to 9 fathoms, the bottom fine muddy sand; when within ¾ mile of the head it shoals to 4 fathoms, and here in heavy gales the sea breaks; a flat runs off 600 yards from the head. In the outer part of the port there is generally a swell. Good anchorage will be found about 1¼ miles from the head, with Owen Island bearing S. 67° W., and Adze Head S. 45° E., in 7 fathoms.

The hill named Pandora Peak does not show as a peak within the port.

The Coast.—From Port San Juan the shore is thickly wooded, and the land rises to a considerable elevation. Providence Cove, fit for boats, lies 3 miles eastward of San Juan; at the distance of about 4 miles farther east, in a small bight, is a stream named Sombrio River. The River Jordan, a considerable stream, is 5½ miles westward of Sherringham Point.

Eastward of Sherringham Point the shore makes a bight, and at the distance of 4½ miles is Otter Point. The points on this side the strait are not remarkable nor easily distinguished unless close in shore. Vessels running or working up the strait at night should be careful not to get so near the northern shore as to shut in Race Island light by Beechey Head. From Otter Point to the entrance to Sooke Inlet, the intervening coast forms rather a deep indentation, named Sooke Bay, in which vessels may anchor in fine weather a little more than ½ mile from the shore in 8 fathoms.

Sooke Inlet is little over ½ mile in breadth, and the bar has only a depth of 14 feet on it at low water. Within the bar, the entrance proper, between Whiffin Spit and Entry Ledge, has 7 fathoms water, but is only 70 yards across, with a sharp turn and strong tide. Thence a narrow and tortuous channel 2½ miles in length, with a general north direction, leads to a beautiful land-locked basin, nearly 2 miles in extent east and west and one mile north and south, with a depth of from 8 to 16 fathoms all over it. Independently, however, of strong tides and several sharp turns, which vessels would have to make in entering, the breadth of the deep channel seldom exceeds 100 yards, and is consequently only adapted for coasting vessels or small steamers.

Anchorage.—Vessels may anchor outside in 10 fathoms ½ mile off the entrance; or, if necessary, run inside Whiffin Spit, where there is sufficient space to anchor; care must, however, be taken as to the depths on the bar, and to the state of the tide in the entrance proper, where the ebb at springs runs about 3 or 4 knots.

Whiffin Spit is low, gravelly, and connected with the western entrance; it must be rounded close, as a reef (Entry Ledge) lies only 100 yards eastward from it. On rounding the point drop the anchor at 200 yards within, in 8 fathoms water; here there is a space of deep water 400 yards in extent.

Secretary Island, small and wooded, lies 350 yards off Possession Point, a mile to the southward of Sooke Inlet. There is a depth of 16 fathoms between it and the main shore, and from it Beechy Head bears S. 62° E., 2½ miles, with a bold steep shore between and deep water close-to.

Becher Bay.—Beechey Head is a bold wooded cliff, forming the western entrance point of Becher Bay, cape Church being the eastern one. Off the eastern side are several small wooded islands, named Bedford. At ⅝ mile within in a northerly direction are Wolf and Frazer islands, with some small islets off them. Between these two islands, Frazer being on the eastern side, is the channel, 800 yards wide, to the anchorage; anchor with the center of Frazer Island bearing S. 46° W., distant ¼ mile.

Becher Bay can not be recommended as a good anchorage, as it affords no great shelter with southerly or westerly winds. Vessels outward bound had better wait a fair wind in Parry Bay, to the northward of Race Islands.

Vessels bound up the strait should pass the land about Beechey Head at the distance of 2 miles, if intending to go outside the Race Islands.

Race Islands are a cluster of low bare rocks, the outermost of which lies a mile S. 23° E. of Bentinck Island, at the SE. point of Vancouver Island; but SE. for ½ mile from this rock the bottom is very irregular, with two points of sunken rocks. They occupy more than ½ mile in extent north and south, and the same east and west. The outermost and largest, or Great Race, is 300 yards in extent and 25 feet high; the others are smaller, a few feet above high water or awash. The tides among them run from 3 to 6 knots, and during bad weather heavy and dangerous races occur. The outer rock should be given a berth of a mile.

The farthest offlying danger is the Rosedale Rock, with 5 feet on it, lying S. 34° E. of the Great Race, distant 800 yards. In light winds sailing vessels should give these islands a good berth, especially when eastward of them, as the ebb sets strongly towards them.

Race Passage is a clear channel between the Race Rocks and Bentinck Island. This passage may be taken by steamers; but it is not recommended for sailing vessels on account of the strength of the tides, and races caused by the irregular rocky nature of the bottom. A case may arise, however, when vessels overtaken by a strong SE. wind would do better to run through than risk weathering the Great Race, by less than a mile; if so the Bentinck Island shore should be kept aboard at a distance of 400 yards, or just outside the kelp; for the northernmost rock, which forms the southern side of the passage, is covered at high water, and the strongest tides and eddies are found in its neighborhood.

The passage inside Bentinck Island is choked with rocks and should never be taken.

Bentinck Island, lying close off the southeastern point of Vancouver Island, is irregularly shaped, being almost divided in the center by a narrow neck. It is about 100 feet high, and, like the adjacent land, covered with pine trees; its southern and eastern sides are fringed with kelp, outside which there are no dangers beyond those described in the Race Channel. Between it and the mainland is a boat channel, and coasters acquainted with the locality find shelter at its eastern entrance; there are some settlers' houses in the neighborhood.

Between Bentinck Island and Esquimalt Harbor the coast is indented by several bays, and anchorage may be obtained in 8 to 10 fathoms anywhere within a mile of the shore, except immediately off William and Albert Heads; the only dangers are a reef lying about 200 yards off Albert Head, and Coghlan Rock in Royal Bay, lying 700 yards north of the same head.

Pedder Bay, the first of these indentations, has its entrance immediately northward of Bentinck Island, between Cape Calver and William Head, where its breadth is ⅔ mile. The bay, ½ mile within, is only fit for small craft, which may find good shelter at its head. Vessels of any size may anchor in the entrance, but though the holding ground is good, it is open to all winds from NE. round east to south, and with a SE. gale would neither be a desirable nor safe anchorage. The tides are irregular.

Parry Bay, immediately northward of William Head, affords good anchorage with all westerly winds. Vessels bound to sea and meeting with a strong wind from this quarter are recommended to return here. With a southeast wind there is ample room to weigh, which vessels should immediately do, and if not able to round the Race Islands and proceed to sea, run for Esquimalt Harbor.

Albert Head, the northern point of the bay, is moderately high, sloping to the sea, bare of trees at its extreme, but wooded immediately behind; a reef lies 200 yards off it. William Head somewhat resembles it, but is lower. The water is too deep for anchorage immediately off these heads.

Royal Bay or Roads, of which Albert Head is the southern point, and the entrance of Esquimalt Harbor the northern limit, is a fine sheet of water, 3 miles in extent and affords good anchorage with all winds

(1191) **BRITISH COLUMBIA—Vancouver Island—Albert head—Telegraph cable—Caution.**—Mr. R. T. Reid, superintendent of the Western Union Telegraph Company, furnishes the following information, which is published for the guidance of mariners:

The Western Union telegraph cable connecting Albert head, Victoria island, with the United States proceeds from the southern shore of Albert head, in approximately 123° 29′ 48″ west longitude. It crosses the meridian 123° 30′ W. in latitude 48° 21′ 42″ N., recrosses the same meridian to the eastward in approximately latitude 48° 20′ N., reaches its most easterly point, longitude 123° 27′ 45″ W., in latitude 48° 17′ 54″ N., then trends in a south-southwestward direction, crossing the meridian 123° 30′ W. in latitude 48° 15′ N.

The superintendent states that several vessels have fouled this cable and broken it, thereby causing annoying interruption to business and costly repairs.

Vessels are cautioned against anchoring in the vicinity of this cable.

(N. M. 31, 1905.)

ing vessels unless with a commanding wind should ... of more than a mile. The flood sets to the NE., and with light winds vessels are liable to be carried to the eastward, up Haro Channel, where the water is generally too deep for anchorage; therefore, with the flood, the coast of Parry Bay should be kept aboard, if possible, where good anchorage may be had in moderate weather and with all westerly winds, less than a mile from the shore in 10 fathoms.

By night, when Fisgard light bears N. 12° E., a vessel may steer for it. Remember to keep the *white* light in full view; should it become dim or shaded the shore is being too closely approached, and the vessel should immediately haul out to the eastward until it is again distinctly seen.

Entering Esquimalt Harbor the Fisgard light should be left about 300 or 400 yards to port. When it bears N. 37° W. the light changes from *white* to *red*, and shows red within the harbor. Anchor when the light bears S. 34° W., at a convenient distance, or stand into Constance Cove. The Scrogg Rocks on the eastern side of the entrance must be avoided. Royal Bay has good anchorage in 9 fathoms at ½ a mile from the light, bearing N. 12° E.

The entrance to Victoria Harbor is 2 miles eastward of Esquimalt Harbor, and the same precautions are necessary in running for it. The course from one mile off the Race Islands is N. 31° 30′ E. At night or in bad weather Victoria Harbor should not be attempted. It can only be entered at certain stages of the tide, and the anchorage outside is exposed and unsafe in dirty weather; but if it is decided to run for the harbor, remember that when Fisgard light changes from *white* to *red* a vessel is very near the shore.

Fisgard Light.—The white light is intended to guide a vessel in from seaward, and while visible clears the western coast between Race Islands and Esquimalt and Scrogg Rocks off the southern shore.

The red light will be found useful in coming from the eastward, if bound to Victoria or Esquimalt. After rounding Trial Island it will indicate a vessel's distance from the shore. If bound to Esquimalt, a

IMAGE EVALUATION
TEST TARGET (MT-3)

6"

Photographic Sciences Corporation

23 WEST MAIN STREET
WEBSTER, N.Y. 14580
(716) 872-4503

and 1
may
woul
by le
aboa
nortl
cove
its n
Th
neve
Be
ver l
a nar
cove ... southern and eastern sides are fringed with kelp, outside which there are no dangers beyond those described in the Race Channel. Between it and the mainland is a boat channel, and coasters acquainted with the locality find shelter at its eastern entrance; there are some settlers' houses in the neighborhood.

Between Bentinck Island and Esquimalt Harbor the coast is indented by several bays, and anchorage may be obtained in 8 to 10 fathoms anywhere within a mile of the shore, except immediately off William and Albert Heads; the only dangers are a reef lying about 200 yards off Albert Head, and Coghlan Rock in Royal Bay, lying 700 yards north of the same head.

Pedder Bay, the first of these indentations, has its entrance immediately northward of Bentinck Island, between Cape Calver and William Head, where its breadth is ⅝ mile. The bay, ½ mile within, is only fit for small craft, which may find good shelter at its head. Vessels of any size may anchor in the entrance, but though the holding ground is good, it is open to all winds from NE. round east to south, and with a SE. gale would neither be a desirable nor safe anchorage. The tides are irregular.

Parry Bay, immediately northward of William Head, affords good anchorage with all westerly winds. Vessels bound to sea and meeting with a strong wind from this quarter are recommended to return here. With a southeast wind there is ample room to weigh, which vessels should immediately do, and if not able to round the Race Islands and proceed to sea, run for Esquimalt Harbor.

Albert Head, the northern point of the bay, is moderately high, sloping to the sea, bare of trees at its extreme, but wooded immediately behind; a reef lies 200 yards off it. William Head somewhat resembles it, but is lower. The water is too deep for anchorage immediately off these heads.

Royal Bay or Roads, of which Albert Head is the southern point, and the entrance of Esquimalt Harbor the northern limit, is a fine sheet of water, 3 miles in extent and affords good anchorage with all winds which would prevent vessels from entering that harbor; they may anchor anywhere within ¾ mile from the western shore. A good berth is a mile S. 22° W. of Duntze Head with the entrance open, or the beacon on Dyke Point just open of Inskip Rock; the latter is also a leading mark for clearing Scrogg Rocks.

Caution.—Heavy tide races occur along the north shore of the strait from Esquimalt to Beechey Head.

Race Islands to Esquimalt Harbor.—The light-house on Fisgard Island, at the western entrance point of Esquimalt Harbor, is very conspicuous, and will be seen immediately on rounding the Race Islands; a course direct for it will clear all dangers, but attention must be paid to the set of the tides. The ebb runs almost directly from the Haro and neighboring straits towards the Race Islands, and sailing vessels unless with a commanding wind should give them a berth of more than a mile. The flood sets to the NE., and with light winds vessels are liable to be carried to the eastward, up Haro Channel, where the water is generally too deep for anchorage; therefore, with the flood, the coast of Parry Bay should be kept aboard, if possible, where good anchorage may be had in moderate weather and with all westerly winds, less than a mile from the shore in 10 fathoms.

By night, when Fisgard light bears N. 12° E., a vessel may steer for it. Remember to keep the *white* light in full view; should it become dim or shaded the shore is being too closely approached, and the vessel should immediately haul out to the eastward until it is again distinctly seen.

Entering Esquimalt Harbor the Fisgard light should be left about 300 or 400 yards to port. When it bears N. 37° W. the light changes from *white* to *red*, and shows red within the harbor. Anchor when the light bears S. 34° W., at a convenient distance, or stand into Constance Cove. The Scrogg Rocks on the eastern side of the entrance must be avoided. Royal Bay has good anchorage in 9 fathoms at ½ a mile from the light, bearing N. 12° E.

The entrance to Victoria Harbor is 2 miles eastward of Esquimalt Harbor, and the same precautions are necessary in running for it. The course from one mile off the Race Islands is N. 31° 30′ E. At night or in bad weather Victoria Harbor should not be attempted. It can only be entered at certain stages of the tide, and the anchorage outside is exposed and unsafe in dirty weather; but if it is decided to run for the harbor, remember that when Fisgard light changes from *white* to *red* a vessel is very near the shore.

Fisgard Light.—The white light is intended to guide a vessel in from seaward, and while visible clears the western coast between Race Islands and Esquimalt and Scrogg Rocks off the southern shore.

The red light will be found useful in coming from the eastward, if bound to Victoria or Esquimalt. After rounding Trial Island it will indicate a vessel's distance from the shore. If bound to Esquimalt, a west course will lead a safe distance outside Brotchy Ledge, until the light changes from red to white, when the light may be steered for, and *not* before.

Esquimalt Harbor is a safe and excellent anchorage for ships of any size, and with the aid of the light on Fisgard Island may be entered at all times with great facility. The entrance is 600 yards in breadth, opening out immediately within to an extensive harbor having a general depth of 6 fathoms over it, and extending $1\frac{1}{4}$ miles to the northwest. On the eastern side are Constance Cove and Plumper Bay, in the former of which, built on Duntze Head, are the Government naval establishments.

There is daily communication with Nanaimo by rail. The railway terminus is situated in Thetis Cove, from which there is an extension to Victoria; and a short branch runs down to a pier, which has been built out from the south point of Thetis Cove, into a depth of 15 feet at low water.

Above Dyke Point, 200 yards, the water shoals to 3 fathoms, and from thence to the head of the harbor is a flat with only a few feet on it at low water.

Dock.—A dock 450 feet long, and 65 feet wide at the entrance, with a depth of $26\frac{1}{2}$ feet over the sill at high water ordinary spring tides, has been constructed west of Thetis Island. This dock is closed by a caisson, which, if necessary, can be placed on the outer side of the outer invert, giving an additional length to the dock of 30 feet.

Winds.—The strongest and most frequent gales blow from SW. and SE., which are leading winds in, but rarely from NW. The SW. is a summer wind, generally fresh, and brings fine weather, unless it blows a gale. SE. winds may be looked for during the winter months, or between November and March, and generally a strong gale once a month with rain and thick weather. The NE. wind rarely blows with much strength, and always brings fine, clear weather, a direct south wind, to which some parts of the harbor are open, seldom blows, and there is never sufficient swell to render the anchorage inconvenient.

Supplies, with the exception of fresh beef and bread, must be obtained from Victoria.

Coal.—Independent of the supply kept at the naval establishment on Thetis Island a stock of 5,000 tons of coal is maintained at Esquimalt. Vessels of about 15 feet draft can coal alongside Thetis Island wharf; regard should, however, be paid to the 15 foot shoal, which lies 60 yards from the high-water mark of the island, in the direction of the pier. Vessels can also coal alongside a wharf; on the east side of which there is a depth of 25 feet at low water. Or coal can be taken on board at all times from colliers or boats alongside.

Water may be obtained during the winter months without difficulty from the many streams that flow into the different bays; but in summer, watering is a tedious process, and boats must be sent either to

Rowe stream, at the head of the harbor, or to the salt lagoon just outside the entrance. Both offer difficulties, unless at or near high water.

Pilotage and Dues.—Sailing vessels $3 per foot. Vessels in tow $2. Steamers $1.50. Half these rates when the services of a pilot are offered but not accepted.

Harbor dues on vessels under 500 tons, $4; over 500 tons, $5.

Population.—The population of Esquimalt in 1881 was 614

Beacon.—A white pyramidal wooden beacon 23 feet above high water. is erected on Dyke Point (at the head of the harbor).

Scrogg Rocks.—The only dangers lie on the eastern side of the entrance 600 yards south Duntze Head, and cover at three quarters flood. Inskip Islands kept well open of the head leads clear to the westward of them; but the best mark for entering with a leading wind is the beacon on Dyke Point, just open of the rocks off the western end of Inskip Islands, bearing N 8° E., which leads in mid channel

Fisgard Island should not be passed within less than 200 yards keeping just outside the kelp, which extends about 100 yards eastward from it, as a rock with only 7 feet water over it lies 150 yards N 68° E. of the light house.

Buoy.—The shoal with only 4 feet on it at low water, lying south of Village Rocks, is marked by a red nun buoy.

Whale Rock, with only 7 feet on it at low water, lies 400 yards N. 62° W. of the outer Inskip Island, or nearly midway between it and the western shore of the harbor. This rock is of small extent, and not marked by kelp; it has a clear passage on either side, that to the eastward being the wider Yew and Rodd Points just touching, point to the rock; Yew Point just touching the light-house on Fisgard Island, leads nearly 200 yards westward; and when Ashe Head is well shut in by Inskip Islands, a vessel will be clear to the northward. The rock is marked by a buoy colored red and black in vertical stripes, moored off its south side.

Anchorage.—The most convenient anchorage is in Constance Cove, on the eastern side of the harbor, immediately round Duntze Head, the general depth being 6 fathoms, and the holding ground good; vessels of war anchoring between Dockyard Jetty and Foster's Pier, or Village Rocks. There is, however, safe anchorage in any part of the harbor, in not less than 4½ fathoms, as far northward as Dyke Point.

Thetis Cove, in Plumper Bay, on the eastern side of the harbor immediately north of Constance Cove, is a snug anchorage in 4½ fathoms, with the harbor entrance just shut in by Inskip Rocks, but vessels proceeding above these rocks must take care to avoid the Whale Rock.

Directions.—Vessels entering the harbor at night with a strong wind after them, should take care to shorten sail in time, as the space for rounding to is somewhat limited; and it is desirable to moor if any stay is intended, as the winds are changeable.

The best time for sailing vessels to leave the harbor is early in the morning, when either a calm or light land wind may be expected; there is little strength of tide in the harbor, or for some distance outside, and it sets fairly in and out.

Victoria Harbor has its entrance between Ogden and McLaughlin Points. Macaulay Point, a remarkable projection nearly midway between the two harbors, is a bare flat point about 30 feet high, showing as a yellow clay cliff, worn by the action of the sea and weather into a rounded knob at the extreme. The coast for one mile on either side of this point is fringed with sunken rocks, and is dangerous for boats in bad weather, many fatal accidents having occurred.

The entrance to the harbor is shoal, narrow, and intricate, and with SW. or SE. gales a heavy rolling swell sets on the coast, which renders the anchorage outside unsafe, while vessels of draft can not run in for shelter unless at or near high water. Vessels drawing 14 or 15 feet water may, under ordinary circumstances, enter at such times of tide; and ships drawing 17 feet have entered, though only at the top of spring tides.

Victoria, the seat of the government, is the largest and most important town in British Columbia, and has a considerable foreign and coasting trade, which is annually increasing. The resident population according to the census taken in 1881 was 6,687, exclusive of Indians, but is now said to be nearly 12,000. Victoria has excellent educational institutions, hospitals, and library, and the streets are lighted by the electric light.

Harbor and pilot dues are charged; and there are sick mariners' dues of 2 cents a ton register three times a year on vessels of 100 tons and upwards, and once a year on vessels under 100 tons. There is a quarantine station for persons affected with infectious diseases; and a hospital for seamen who are recommended for admission by masters of vessels that have paid sick mariners' dues.

At the entrance of the harbor, on the south side of Shoal Point, there is a wharf which is used by the San Francisco steamers. The pier is 600 feet in length and has a depth of 24 at low water. Along the eastern side of the harbor in front of the town there are about 400 yards of fair wharfage, with a depth of from 10 to 16 feet at low-water spring tides. Between Songhies and Limit Points, on the opposite side of the harbor, is a small slip capable of receiving vessels of about 200 tons burden; larger vessels, however, may heave down alongside the wharves.

A submarine telegraph cable crosses the Strait of Georgia at Nanaimo and connects the city with the mainland of British Columbia, and another crosses Juan de Fuca Strait to Washington.

There is direct mail communication with San Francisco every week, a triweekly service to the east coast of Vancouver Island, and a daily service to Port Moody, except on Mondays; and steamers run daily, except on Sundays, to the ports in Puget Sound. There is daily communication with Nanaimo by rail.

Buoys.—The channel is marked by black buoys with odd numbers on the northern side, and red buoys with even numbers on the southern side.

The buoys marking the northern edge of the shoal extending from Shoal Point, as also Channel Rock (lying 100 yards southwest of Pelly Island), are of pyramidal shape, surmounted by a ball

Supplies.—Provisions of all kinds, and of an excellent quality, may be procured, and water is to be had from a floating tank capable of going outside the harbor Supplies for refitting and repairing vessels, except timber, are scarce and expensive, but of fair quality. Ordinary repairs to machinery of steamers can be effected.

Coal can be obtained at the price of $6 per ton but a large quantity is

(1754) **BRITISH COLUMBIA—Vancouver island—Victoria harbor—Laurel point—Light established.**—The Canadian Government has given notice that on October 16, 1905, a *fixed red* electric light, consisting of two 16 candlepower incandescent electric lamps suspended in a *red* globe, will be exhibited at a height of 25 feet above high water from a pole standing on the bare rock at high watermark, on the extremity of Laurel point, southern side of Victoria harbor, Vancouver island The light should be visible 1 mile from all points of approach by water

Approx. position. Lat. 48° 25′ 22″ N.. Long. 123° 23′ 02″ W.

(N. M. 44, 1905.)

when bad weather may be looked for with more warn

Pilots.—There are pilots attached to the port, who keep a good lookout for vessels off the entrance. Pilotage is compulsory to all merchant vessels, except coasters. The rates same as at Esquimalt. Pilots are seldom met with below the Race Rocks; but between January and July, in moderate weather, vessels approaching the Strait of Juan de Fuca and requiring a pilot, may obtain a man competent to take them to Royal Roads or Port Townsend from the schooners engaged in the seal fishery off the coast, between Cape Beale and Clayoquot Sound, at a distance of from 5 to 20 miles from the land Sometimes in Neéah Bay a pilot may be had if a gun is fired twice in quick succession. Guns are used by the sealing schooners in foggy weather, but only once in 10 or 15 minutes, so that a gun fired twice in quick succession would not be mistaken.

Harbor dues on vessels under 500 tons, $4, over 500 tons, $5. Tug-

Discharging cargo or ballast 50

(1346) **BRITISH COLUMBIA — Vancouver island — Victoria — Brotchy Ledge beacon—Fog bell established—Fog horn discontinued.**—The Canadian Government gives notice that a fog bell, operated by electricity, has been established on Brotchy Ledge beacon. The bell will give, during thick or foggy weather, *one stroke every ten seconds.*

The electric fog horn heretofore used has been discontinued, but is left in place so that in the event of any accident happening to the bell its operation can be temporarily resumed.

Whenever the electricity is shut off for any cause it will be impossible to operate either alarm.

(N. M 34, 1905)

morning, when either a calm or light land wind may be expected; there is little strength of tide in the harbor, or for some distance outside, and it sets fairly in and out.

Victoria Harbor has its entrance between Ogden and McLaughlin Points. Macaulay Point, a remarkable projection nearly midway between the two harbors, is a bare flat point about 30 feet high, showing as a yellow clay cliff, worn by the action of the sea and weather into a rounded knob at the extreme. The coast for one mile on either side of this point is fringed with sunken rocks, and is dangerous for boats in bad weather, many fatal accidents having occurred.

The entrance to the harbor is shoal, narrow, and intricate, and with SW. or SE. gales a heavy rolling swell sets on the coast, which renders the anchorage outside unsafe ...
shelter
may, u...
ships d...
tides.

Victo...
portant
coasting
accordin...
but is n... 12,000 Victoria has excellent educational institutions, hospitals, and library, and the streets are lighted by the electric light.

Harbor and pilot dues are charged; and there are sick mariners' dues of 2 cents a ton register three times a year on vessels of 100 tons and upwards, and once a year on vessels under 100 tons There is a quarantine station for persons affected with infectious diseases; and a hospital for seamen who are recommended for admission by masters of vessels that have paid sick mariners' dues

At the entrance of the harbor, on the south side of Shoal Point, there is a wharf which is used by the San Francisco steamers The pier is 600 feet in length and has a depth of 23 at low water. Along the eastern side of the harbor in front of the town there are about 400 yards of fair ... from 10 to 16 feet at low-water spring tides.
Bet...
is a
larg...

A...
and
othe...

Th...
a tri...
serv...
exce...
munication with Nanaimo by rail.

Buoys.—The channel is marked by black buoys with odd numbers on the northern side, and red buoys with even numbers on the southern side.

The buoys marking the northern edge of the shoal extending from Shoal Point, as also Channel Rock (lying 100 yards southwest of Pelly Island), are of pyramidal shape, surmounted by a ball.

Supplies.—Provisions of all kinds, and of an excellent quality, may be procured, and water is to be had from a floating tank capable of going outside the harbor. Supplies for refitting and repairing vessels, except timber, are scarce and expensive, but of fair quality. Ordinary repairs to machinery of steamers can be effected.

Coal can be obtained at the price of $6 per ton, but a large quantity is not kept in store. Vessels can coal alongside the wharves in the harbor, and also from the wharf on the south side of Shoal Point.

Anchorage.—Vessels anchoring outside the harbor to wait for the tide, or from other causes, should not come within a line between Ogden and MacLaughlin Points, the former bearing S. 62° E., the latter N. 62° W., midway between, or ¼ mile from either; this is a good stopping place with offshore winds or fine weather, but is by no means recommended as a safe anchorage for sailing vessels during the winter months, when bad weather may be looked for with little warning.

Pilots.—There are pilots attached to the port, who keep a good look out for vessels off the entrance. Pilotage is compulsory to all merchant vessels, except coasters. The rates same as at Esquimalt. Pilots are seldom met with below the Race Rocks; but between January and July, in moderate weather, vessels approaching the Strait of Juan de Fuca and requiring a pilot, may obtain a man competent to take them to Royal Roads or Port Townsend from the schooners engaged in the seal fishery off the coast, between Cape Beale and Clayoquot Sound, at a distance of from 5 to 20 miles from the land. Sometimes in Neéah Bay a pilot may be had if a gun is fired twice in quick succession. Guns are used by the sealing schooners in foggy weather, but only once in 10 or 15 minutes, so that a gun fired twice in quick succession would not be mistaken.

Harbor dues on vessels under 500 tons, $4; over 500 tons, $5. Tug-boat charges from Royal Roads, $50. Discharging cargo or ballast, 50 cents per ton. Labor per day, $2.50. The average price of stores is, for fresh beef 7 cents per pound; salted in barrels of 200 pounds, $10 per barrel. Pork, $18 to $24 per barrel. Ship bread, 5 cents per pound. Vegetables are always obtainable at from one to 2 cents per pound.

The UNITED STATES is represented by consul and vice-consul.

Brotchy Ledge is in the fair way of vessels entering Victoria Harbor from the eastward; it has only 5 feet water on its shoalest part, is covered with kelp, and about 200 yards in extent within the 5-fathom line. There are 9 fathoms water between the ledge and the shore.

Buoy.—This shoal is marked by a pyramidal buoy, colored red and black in horizontal stripes and surmounted by a cage, moored 300 yards S. 67° W. of the shoal of 5 feet. The buoy is occasionally washed away during the heavy winter gales

Fisgard Island light-house, north part of Brothers Island, and Macaulay Point in line bearing N. 59°, W., leads 200 yards northward of the ledge in 9 fathoms, between it and the shore; and Fisgard Island light-house, just open southward of Brothers Island bearing N. 53° W., leads 400 yards southward of the ledge in 21 fathoms water.

Directions.—The channel is buoyed, but it is necessary for a stranger to take a pilot, and the space is so confined and tortuous that a long ship has considerable difficulty in making the necessary turn; a large percentage of vessels entering the port, small as well as large, constantly run aground from these causes, or from trying to enter at an improper time of tide, or neglecting to take a pilot. Such accidents, however, are seldom attended with more than delay and inconvenience, as the shoalest and most intricate part of the passage is sheltered; when within, the port is perfectly landlocked, and vessels may lie in from 14 to 18 feet at low water, but the harbor accommodation is limited.

Victoria to Vancouver.—With flood tide and clear weather the following route is recommended, the distance being shortest, water smoothest, and tide of the most assistance:

Enterprise, Mayor, and Baynes Channels, Sydney Channel (passing to westward of Moresby Island and the islands to the southward of it); thence through Swanson Channel and Active Pass, and across to Burrard Inlet.

With the *ebb* tide the usual route is outside of Trial Island to the main channel of Haro Strait, following the latter to the Gulf of Georgia. This route is recommended in thick weather, and also, at all times, to navigators not familiar with the tides and dangers of the narrower channels

Some of the fastest steamers, after passing outside Trial Island and part way through Haro Strait, tide ebb, stand up Swanson Channel and through Active Pass

Victoria to Nanaimo and Departure Bay.—With *flood* tide and clear weather pass through Enterprise, Mayor, Baynes, Swanson, and Trincomalie Channels, and Dodd Narrows. By this route the smooth water and strong tide will be of great assistance. On the southward trip this route should also be followed when the tide is *ebb*.

With adverse tides the usual route is through the main channel of Haro Strait and the Gulf of Georgia.

The Coast from Victoria Harbor trends in a southeasterly direction to Clover Point, and is for the most part faced by white sandy cliffs, varying in height from 10 to 80 feet; a sandy beach extends along the whole way, and at 200 yards' distance off in many places are rocks and foul ground. Four hundred yards east of Holland Point, and 200 yards off shore, are the Glimpse reefs, which cover at three-quarters flood.

Beacon Hill, a gentle rise of the land, 400 yards from the water's edge, and a mile east of the harbor, is grassy and bare of trees; its height is 140 feet, and there is a staff or beacon on the summit.

Clover Point, 2 miles eastward of the entrance to Victoria Harbor, is low, bare of trees, and projecting; it is steep-to, and off it are some strong tide rips, dangerous to boats in heavy weather. Ross Bay to the eastward of it is open, but sometimes used by small craft if waiting for the tide.

Foul Bay, nearly one mile to the eastward of Clover Point, is of small extent and filled with rocks. Off its entrance are the Templar Rocks, about 4 feet under water, and marked by kelp.

Foul Point, on the eastern side of the bay, is rocky, but has not less than 4 fathoms at 200 yards distance; the land at the back of the point rises to a height of 230 feet, forming a rocky ridge or summit, known as Gonzales Hill.

Trial Islands, nearly 1¼ miles eastward of Clover Point, on the southern side of Enterprise Channel, are two in number, bare and rocky, but generally appear as one. The southern or largest island is 80 feet high, and steep to at its outer end; the northern one is low, and from it foul ground extends some distance. Strong tide rips prevail off the southern island, especially during the flood, which runs nearly 6 knots at springs just outside it.

Inner Channels.—The inner channels leading from Juan de Fuca Strait into the Haro Strait are the Enterprise, Mouatt, Mayor, and Baynes Channels, and Hecate and Plumper Passages.

Enterprise Channel, between Trial Islands and the Vancouver shore, is a narrow, tortuous, but deep channel, much used by steamers and coasters trading to Victoria Harbor, as a slight saving of distance is effected, and less tide experienced than by going south of the Trial Islands. Its length is about a mile, its width in the narrowest place 100 yards, and there are not less than 24 feet in the shoalest part.

McNeil Bay, on the northern side of the channel to the eastward of Foul Point, is 600 yards in extent, with from 2 to 6 fathoms water; it is open to the southward, and foul ground exists in its eastern part, but the bay is much used by small vessels waiting for the tide.

Mouatt Reef, in the eastern part of the channel, 600 yards from North Trial island and nearly 400 yards off shore, is about 200 yards in extent, and covers at one-quarter flood; this reef is dangerous for vessels using the Enterprise Channel, as it lies just north of the fairway.

Directions.—Bound through the Enterprise Channel to the eastward, when past Foul Bay, give Foul Point a berth of from 400 to 600 yards, and steer for the west side of McNeil Bay on a northerly course; approach it close to, after which steer direct for Kitty Islet, and when within 100 yards of the latter, haul quickly to the eastward, keeping McNeil farm just open west of Kitty Islet, bearing N. 64° W.;

this will lead safely through the narrowest part of the channel and south of Mouatt Reef. When Channel Point and the west side of Great Chain Islet come in line bearing N. 37° E. the vessel will be well east of the reef, and should alter course to the northward to avoid the Brodie Rock, proceeding up through any of the inner channels.

Brodie Rock, a patch of 3 fathoms least water, marked by kelp, lies nearly one mile N. 65° E. of the summit of the south Trial Island.

The north point of small Trial Island in line with Foul Point bearing west, leads north of Brodie Rock.

Foul Point seen between the Trial Islands bearing N. 76° W. leads south of the rock.

Cadboro Point in line with the east extreme of Great Chain Island bearing N. 12° E. leads eastward of the rock.

Gonzales Point forms the southeastern extremity of Vancouver Island. It is a low salient point, rocky, bare of trees, and steep to on the east side.

Oak Bay.—From Gonzales Point, the Vancouver shore trends to the northward, and at one mile from the point forms a sandy bay which is somewhat less than one mile in extent, and affords fair anchorage near its north part in from 3 to 4 fathoms.

The best anchorage is to the northward of Mary Todd Islet in the south part of the bay. This islet is bare, and about 30 feet high; east of it, is Emily Islet, 4 feet above high water, and south of Emily Islet lies the Robson Reef, which uncovers at low water.

Cadboro Bay, to the northward of Oak Bay, is about ½ mile in extent, and open to the southeast; no sea rises within it, and there is good anchorage in from 3 to 4 fathoms near the entrance.

The Vancouver shore from Gonzales Point to this bay is low and lightly timbered with dwarf oak and pine trees; to the northward of Oak Bay it is clear of danger at 200 yards distance.

Mayor Channel is to the eastward of Gonzales Point, and west of Chain Islets. The channel is bounded on the western side by Thames Shoal, Harris Island, and Fiddle Reef, and abreast the latter on its opposite side lies the Lewis Reef. The tide seldom runs more than 3 knots through this channel, and it is the one generally used.

Thames Shoal has 2 fathoms water over it, is of small extent, and marked by kelp, it lies nearly ½ mile N. 43° E. of Gonzales Point, at the southwestern part of the Mayor Channel. Channel Point in line with west side of Great Chain Islet bearing N. 36° E. leads east of the shoal and the highest part of Trial Island in line with Gonzales Point bearing S. 31° W. leads west of it.

Mouatt Channel—Lee Rock, which only uncovers at low water springs, lies 300 yards northwestward of Thames Shoal; it is marked by kelp and steep to on the eastern side. Between this rock and Thames Shoal is Mouatt Channel, 200 yards wide.

The highest part of Trial Island in line with Gonzales Point, S. 31°

W., leads midway between Thames Shoal and Lee Rock; also through the fairway of the northern part of Mayor Channel, between Fiddle and Lewis Reefs.

Fiddle Reef, at the northern extreme of Mayor Channel, and upwards of a mile from Gonzales Point, is of small extent, and awash at high water spring tides; it may be approached close to on the eastern side.

Beacon.—A beacon, consisting of a white conical structure 41 feet high, surmounted by a black pole and cage 10 feet high, has been erected on Fiddle Reef.

Todd Rock, at 300 yards NW. of Fiddle Reef, in the entrance to Oak Bay, covers at two thirds flood, and is marked by kelp.

Lewis Reef, at the northeastern part of Mayor Channel, lies 500 yards S. 34° E. of Fiddle Reef, covers at high water, and may be approached close to on the western side.

The passage between it and Chain Islets is filled with kelp, but has not less than 2 fathoms water.

Beacon, consisting of a round stone tower, colored black, 10 feet in height, surmounted by a cross 16 feet above high water, is situated on Lewis Reef.

Chain Islets, midway between Discovery Island and the Vancouver shore, are a bare rocky group. The largest, called Great Chain Islet, is about 200 yards in extent and 30 feet above high water; it is the southwestern one of the group.

Spencer Ledge, off their eastern side at a distance of 300 yards from the easternmost high-water rock, is marked by kelp, and has 9 feet water on its shoalest part; if going through Hecate Passage it requires to be guarded against. Cadboro Point, open west of Channel Point bearing N. 7° W., leads east of this ledge through Hecate Passage.

Caroline Reef, at the northern part of the group, and connected to it by a rocky ledge, is of small extent, and covers at one quarter flood, but is well out of the track of vessels using any of the channels. Foul ground with depths of from 3 to 4 fathoms, marked by kelp, extends upwards of 200 yards westward from it.

Discovery Island is at the junction of the Haro and Fuca Straits. It is wooded, about ⅞ mile in extent, and its shores on all sides are bordered by rocks, extending in some places more than 400 yards. Rudlin Bay, on its southeastern side, is filled with rocks, and should not be used by any vessel.

The Chatham Islands, to the northwest of Discovery Island, and separated from it by a narrow boat pass, are of small extent, forming an irregular group, low, wooded, and almost connected with each other at low water. Their western side is steep-to, and the tide rushes with great strength through the passages between them.

Leading Point, at the southwestern extreme, is a bare rocky islet at high water. To the eastward of it is a small boat cove. Channel Point, their western extreme, is also bare and steep to. The tide runs strongly past it.

Strong Tide Islet, the northwestern of these islands, is rocky, about 50 feet high, and wooded. Its northwestern side is steep to. The ebb tide runs very strongly past it, nearly 6 knots at springs.

Refuge Cove, on the northeastern side of the Chatham Islands, is small, and has 1½ fathoms in the center, coasters or small craft entangled among these islets may find shelter in it. Alpha Islet, the easternmost of the group, is bare, 10 feet above high water, and steep-to on the eastern side. Boats only ought to go westward, or inside it.

Fulford Reef, 600 yards northward of the Chatham Islands, is about 200 yards in extent, and covers at three quarters flood Vessels using the Baynes Channel should keep well to the westward to avoid this reef, as the tide sets irregularly in its vicinity.

Hecate and Plumper Passages—Discovery Island is separated from the Chain Islets by a passage ½ mile wide in the narrowest part, forming an apparently clear and wide channel. Near the middle of the southern part lies Center Rock, which has only 3 feet over it, and though marked by kelp, this from the strength of the tides is often run under and seldom seen There is deep passage on either side of this danger, the one to the westward being called Hecate, and the eastern one Plumper Passage. The latter is wider and better adapted for large steamers, but the tide sets very strongly through both of them.

Cadboro Point, open west of Channel Point N. 7° W., leads through Hecate Passage in mid channel, west of Center Rock.

Cadboro Point, well shut in, north of Leading Point, N. 15° W., leads through Plumper Passage in mid channel, east of Center Rock.

Baynes Channel, between Cadboro Point and the Chatham Islands, connecting these inner channels with Haro Strait, is upwards of one mile long and ½ mile wide; the depths in it are irregular, varying from 2¾ to 30 fathoms, and the tide at spring sets through it with a velocity of 4 to 6 knots, strongest along the eastern side.

Five Fathom Shoal, which lies in the center of the channel, is not marked by kelp Nearly 200 yards N 23° W of it is another shoal with only 16½ feet water on it, and extending about 83 yards north and south and 50 yards east and west. To avoid it a vessel should keep a little over on either side of mid channel.

Cadboro Point, on the Vancouver shore, at the termination of the inner channels, is nearly 3 miles NNE. of Gonzales Point, and ¾ mile N. 23° W., of the Chatham Islands It is about 50 feet high, rocky and bare of trees A small islet lies just off it, also a reef which covers; when passing do not approach the islet within 400 yards.

The coast west from Cadboro Point to Cadboro Bay is low, very much broken, and there are some off lying rocks.

Jemmy Jones Islet, which is bare and 15 feet above high water, lies … W. of Cadboro Point; foul …

Tides.—The high water … much influenced by prevailing winds; the greatest rise and fall of tide at Discovery Island is 12 feet. During summer months in these channels the flood stream commences at 11 15 a. m., running with great strength till nearly 3 p. m., after which but little tide is felt till 4 a. m. on the following day, when the ebb commences and runs strong till nearly 11 a. m., the time of low water by the shore.

Constance Bank, lying in the Fuca Strait, nearly 6 miles S. 34° E. of Fisgard Lighthouse, is upwards of one mile in extent with depths of from 9 to 14 fathoms, but a vessel should not anchor on it, as the bottom is rocky.

(253) **BRITISH COLUMBIA-WASHINGTON — Submarine telephone cable laid between Vancouver island and the mainland.**— Through the courtesy of Mr. William P. Anderson, Chief Engineer, Department of Marine and Fisheries, Ottawa, Canada, the following advance proof of Canadian Notice to Mariners No 7 of 1905 is published for the benefit of mariners:

A submarine telephone cable has recently been laid across the several channels between Vancouver island, British Columbia, and the mainland in Washington, United States of America. The parts cross the channels follows:

From a point in Telegraph cove near the southeast extreme of Vancouver island, in latitude 48° 27′ 55″ N, longitude 123° 17′ 11″ W., across Haro strait on a course N. 45° E. true (NNE mag), 8.45 miles, to a point in Andrews bay, in latitude 48° 32′ 30″ N, longitude 123° 10′ 00″ W., on the west shore of San Juan island.

From a point on the east shore of San Juan island, north of Friday harbor, in latitude 48° 33′ 03″ N., longitude 123° 01′ 00″ W., across San Juan channel on a course N. 77° E. true (NE. ¾ E. E′ly mag), 1.21 miles, to a point on the southwest shore of Shaw island, in latitude 48° 33′ 15″ N, longitude 122° 59′ 28″ W

From a point on the northeast shore of Shaw island, in latitude 48° 35′ 03″ N., longitude 122° 55′ 23″ W., across Harney channel on a course N. 1° W. true (NNW. ⅛ W mag.), 0 542 mile, to a point on the south shore of Orcas island, in latitude 48° 35′ 31″ N., longitude 122° 55′ 23″ W.

From Lawrence point the easternmost point of Orcas island, in latitude 48° 39′ 40″ N, longitude 122° 45′ 00″ W, across Rosario strait on a course N 48° E. true (NNE. ¼ E mag), 3 62 miles, to a point on the west shore of Lummi island, in latitude 48° 41′ 43″ N, longitude 122° 41′ 28″ W

From a point on the east shore of Lummi island, in latitude 48° 42′ 17″ N., longitude 122° 40′ 30″ W. across Hale passage on a course N. 57° E. true (NE. by N mag), 0.915 mile, to a point on the mainland, in latitude 48° 42′ 47″ N, longitude 122° 39′ 28″ W., in Lummi Indian Reservation, Washington, and 7 miles from Whatcom.

The geographical positions and bearings given are approximate.

Each landing is designated by a white monument sign 12 inches wide by 66 inches long, with the word "Cable" in black painted thereon. Mariners are instructed not to anchor in the vicinity of these cables. (N M 7, 1905)

marked by kelp. Nearly 200 yards N. 23° W. of it is another shoal with only 10½ feet water on it, and extending about 83 yards north and south and 50 yards east and west To avoid it a vessel should keep a little over on either side of mid channel.

Cadboro Point, on the Vancouver shore, at the termination of the inner channels, is nearly 3 miles NNE. of Gonzales Point, and ¾ mile N. 23° W., of the Chatham Islands. It is about 50 feet high, rocky and bare of trees A small islet lies just off it, also a reef which covers, when passing do not approach the islet within 400 yards

The coast west from Cadboro Point to Cadboro Bay is low, very much broken, and there are some off lying rocks.

Jemmy Jones Islet, which is bare and 15 feet above high water, lies 600 yards off shore, and 900 yards S. 33° W. of Cadboro Point; foul ground extends around it for upwards of 200 yards in some parts, and though there is deep water between it and the shore, none except small craft should go through that passage

Directions.—Though these inner channels are deep, they should not be used except by steamers of moderate size or by small craft, unless in cases of necessity, and a knowledge of the tide is indispensable. Coasters and small steamers, when taking advantage of them, generally proceed through the Mayor Channel. If using this channel, after passing Gonzales Point keep the west side of Great Chain Islet in line with Channel Point bearing N. 37° E till within 400 yards of the islet, when the north end of Mary Todd Island will be in line with the north point of Harris Island and the vessel will be clear of the Thames Shoal, after which steer to the northwest, bringing the highest part of Trial Island in line with Gonzales Point bearing S. 31° W., and with that mark on astern, steer N 31° E, which will lead between the Fiddle and Lewis Reefs, and on through Baynes Channel, to Haro Strait, taking care, however, to avoid the patch of 16½ feet lying close to the Five fathom Shoal, as this mark leads only 100 yards westward of the patch. When past Lewis and Fiddle Reefs, a vessel may steer N. 45° E. and pass out of Baynes Channel between Five-fathom Shoal and Strong Tide Islet, but the tides are much stronger this side of the channel.

Going through Monatt Channel, which is very narrow and seldom used, after rounding Gonzales Point at 200 yards distance, bring the highest part of Trial Island in line with the point bearing S 31° W., and keeping this mark on astern, and steering N. 31° E., will lead through clear of danger.

The Hecate and Plumper Passages are nearly straight, and better adapted for large steamers than those west of the Chain Islets. If using either of them, after passing either through Enterprise Channel, or southward of Trial Islands, bring the leading marks on, and keep them so till northward of the Center Rock, when steer up in mid-channel between Chain Islets and Chatham Islands, N. 34° W, towards Cadboro Bay, and through Baynes Channel into Haro Strait.

Tides.—The high water at full and change is irregular and much influenced by prevailing winds; the greatest rise and fall of tide at Discovery Island is 12 feet. During summer months in these channels the flood stream commences at 11.15 a m., running with great strength till nearly 3 p. m, after which but little tide is felt till 1 a. m. on the following day, when the ebb commences and runs strong till nearly 11 a. m., the time of low water by the shore.

ConstanceBank, lying in the Fuca Strait, nearly 6 miles S. 34° E. of Fisgard Lighthouse, is upwards of one mile in extent with depths of from 9 to 14 fathoms, but a vessel should not anchor on it, as the bottom is rocky.

Middle Bank, lying in the southern entrance of Haro Strait, 4 miles S. 79° E. of Discovery Island, and almost in mid channel, is a rocky patch about 2 miles in extent each way, and the least water found on it is 10 fathoms. In bad weather there are heavy tide rips on and in the vicinity of this bank, which are dangerous to boats or small craft

Hein (Fonte) Bank, within the depths of 10 fathoms, is about 1½ miles in extent; it has depths of from 3½ to 5 fathoms on it and is marked by kelp It lies nearly in the middle of Fuca Strait, 6¼ miles S. 27° W. of Cattle Point (San Juan Island), and 8 miles S. 57° E. of Discovery Island. This bank should be avoided, as there may be less water on it than shown on the chart.

Smith Island lies almost in the center of the eastern end of Fuca Strait. It is about ½ mile in length, cliffy at its western end and 50 feet high. A large kelp patch extends for nearly 1½ miles from the western extreme, and should be avoided. From the eastern end a sand spit extends for ¾ mile and is partially covered at high water. On the north side of the spit anchorage may be had in 5 fathoms, about ½ mile from shore, but no vessel should lie here with any appearance of bad weather.

Beacon.—A beacon has been erected on Minor Island at the extremity of the spit extending from the eastern end of Smith or Blunt island.

Partridge Bank, 3 miles S 31° W of the light-house on Smith's Island is the northwestern point of this bank within 10 fathoms of water. Inside this depth the bank is 3 miles long and 1½ in width. The bottom is generally sand, gravel, and bowlders, except near the shoalest spot, where it is rocky and thickly covered with kelp This dangerous rock is covered by 14 feet water at lowest tides, and lies on the northern side of the bank, 3¼ miles from the nearest shore of Whidbey Island. A considerable part of the bank is covered with kelp, which is much underrun by strong currents. The currents over the bank are irregular, except under the eastern extremity, when they set strongly from the north and NW. at flood and ebb tides. There are current rips on all the banks in the straits, which split the moving volumes of water, and these rips are heavier in westerly winds.

Hassler Bank lies N. 38° W. of New Dungeness light-house, on a line nearly midway to Victoria This is a 20 fathom bank, 2 miles long and ½ mile wide, with as little as 15 fathoms of water over it.

ꟼO

om

Fuca strait into the strait of Georgia, [illegible] for 18 miles; it then turns sharply to the ENE. round Turn Point of Stuart Island, for a farther distance of 12 miles, leaving Saturna Island to the westward, and Waldron and Patos Islands to the eastward, when it enters the Strait of Georgia between Saturna and Patos Islands.

It is for the most part a broad, and for its whole extent a deep navigable ship channel; but on account of the reefs which exist in certain parts, the general absence of steady winds, the scarcity of anchorages, and [illegible]ove all, the strength and varying direction of the tides, much care [illegible]d vigilance is necessary in its navigation, and it is far more adapted to steam than to sailing vessels.

Besides the main channel of the Haro Strait thus described, there are several smaller channels and passages branching from it by which vessels may enter the Strait of Georgia; thus the Swanson Channel leads into the strait by Active Pass, and the Trincomalie and Stuart Channels by the Portier Pass, or the Dodd Narrows.

These channels may be again entered by smaller ones; thus Sidney and Cordov[illegible] Channels, on the western side of Haro Strait, lead by Moresby, Colbourne, and Shute Passages into the Swanson, Satellite, and Stuart Channels, and finally into the Strait of Georgia. These channels are essentially adapted to steam navigation, or to coasting vessels; they afford smooth water, and many of them anchorages.

Zero Rock, one of the principal dangers in the southern part of Haro Strait, lies on the western side of the strait, is about 100 yards in extent, covers at three quarters flood, and its vicinity is marked by kelp; it lies 6½ miles N. 22° W. of the east point of D[illegible]scovery Island.

Beacon.—A whitewashed beacon, pyramidal in shape, 30 feet high, surmounted by a pole and frame, resembling an obelisk, 20 feet high, also colored white, has been erected on Zero Rock.

A Rocky Patch, part of which nearly uncovers at low water springs, lies 700 yards N. 5° W. of Zero Rock.

Discovery Island Light is obscured in the direction of Zero Rock, and westward of it.

Middle Bank, lying in the southern entrance of Haro Strait, 4 miles S. 79° E of Discovery Island, and almost in mid channel, is a rocky

(1063) **WASHINGTON—Juan de Fuca strait—Hein bank—Buoy changed in position.**—Referring to Notice to Mariners No 25 (923) of 1904, further notice is given by the lighthouse inspector that Hein Bank buoy, a red and black horizontally striped nun, was moved on June 10, 1904, about 1,300 feet to the southward in 35 feet of water, and is now (approximately) 50 feet N 16° E true (N ¼ W. mag.) from a pinnacle rock or bowlder having but 14½ feet over it at mean low water, on the following bearings

Smith Island lighthouse, S. 75° E. true (E. ¾ N. N'ly mag).
New Dungeness lighthouse, S. 14° W. true (S ⅞ E. mag.).
Discovery Island lighthouse (Canadian), N. 60° W. true (W ½ N. mag).

(N M 29, 1904.)

[illegible] It is about ½ mile in length, [illegible] high. A large kelp patch extends for nearly 1½ miles from the western extreme, and should be avoided From the eastern end a sand spit extends for ¾ mile and is partially covered at high water. On the north side of the spit anchorage may be had in 5 fathoms, about ½ mile from shore, but no vessel should lie here with any appearance of bad weather.

Beacon—A beacon has been erected on Minor Island at the extremity of the spit extending from the eastern end of Smith or Blunt island.

Partridge Bank, 3 miles S 31° W. of the light house on Smith's Island is the northwestern point of this bank within 10 fathoms of water. Inside this depth the bank is 3 miles long and 1½ in width The bottom is generally sand, gravel, and bowlders, except near the shoalest spot, where it is rocky and thickly covered with kelp. This dangerous rock is covered by 14 feet water at lowest tides, and lies on the northern side of the bank, 3¼ miles from the nearest shore of Whidbey Island. A considerable part of the bank is covered with kelp, which is much underrun by strong currents. The currents over the bank are irregular, except under the eastern extremity, when they set strongly from the north and NW. at flood and ebb tides. There are current rips on all the banks in the straits, which split the moving volumes of water, and these rips are heavier in westerly winds.

Hassler Bank lies N 38° W. of New Dungeness light-house, on a line nearly midway to Victoria. This is a 20 fathom bank, 2 miles long and ½ mile wide, with as little as 15 fathoms of water over it.

HARO STRAIT, THE WESTERN CHANNELS AND ISLANDS TO NANAIMO HARBOR AND DEPARTURE BAY.

Haro Strait, the westernmost of the three channels leading from Fuca strait into the strait of Georgia, trends in a N. by W. direction for 18 miles; it then turns sharply to the ENE. round Turn Point of Stuart Island, for a farther distance of 12 miles, leaving Saturna Island to the westward, and Waldron and Patos Islands to the eastward, when it enters the Strait of Georgia between Saturna and Patos Islands.

It is for the most part a broad, and for its whole extent a deep navigable ship channel, but on account of the reefs which exist in certain parts, the general absence of steady winds, the scarcity of anchorages, and above all, the strength and varying direction of the tides, much care and vigilance is necessary in its navigation, and it is far more adapted to steam than to sailing vessels.

Besides the main channel of the Haro Strait thus described, there are several smaller channels and passages branching from it by which vessels may enter the Strait of Georgia; thus the Swanson Channel leads into the strait by Active Pass, and the Trincomalie and Stuart Channels by the Portier Pass, or the Dodd Narrows.

These channels may be again entered by smaller ones; thus Sidney and Cordova Channels, on the western side of Haro Strait, lead by Moresby, Colbourne, and Shute Passages into the Swanson, Satellite, and Stuart Channels, and finally into the Strait of Georgia. These channels are essentially adapted to steam navigation, or to coasting vessels; they afford smooth water, and many of them anchorages.

Zero Rock, one of the principal dangers in the southern part of Haro Strait, lies on the western side of the strait, is about 100 yards in extent, covers at three quarters flood, and its vicinity is marked by kelp; it lies 6½ miles N. 22° W. of the east point of Discovery Island.

Beacon.—A whitewashed beacon, pyramidal in shape, 30 feet high, surmounted by a pole and frame, resembling an obelisk, 20 feet high, also colored white, has been erected on Zero Rock.

A Rocky Patch, part of which nearly uncovers at low water springs, lies 700 yards N. 5° W. of Zero Rock.

Discovery Island Light is obscured in the direction of Zero Rock, and westward of it.

Middle Bank, lying in the southern entrance of Haro Strait, 4 miles S. 79° E. of Discovery Island, and almost in mid channel, is a rocky

(1063) **WASHINGTON—Juan de Fuca strait—Hein bank—Buoy changed in position.**—Referring to Notice to Mariners No 25 (923) of 1904, further notice is given by the lighthouse inspector that Hein Bank buoy, a red and black horizontally striped nun, was moved on [illegible]

(799) **WASHINGTON—Juan de Fuca strait—Hein bank—Buoy established.**—May 10, 1904, a first class nun buoy, painted black and red in horizontal stripes, was established on Hein bank, Juan de Fuca strait, to mark the bank (N M 21, 1904)

Smith Island lighthouse, S 75° E true (E ¾ N. N'ly mag.).
New Dungeness lighthouse, S 14° W. true (S. ⅞ E. mag).
Discovery Island lighthouse (Canadian), N. 60° W. true (W. ½ N. mag.). [illegible] (N. M. 29, 1904)

[illegible] high. A large kelp patch extends for nearly 1½ miles from the western extreme, and should be avoided. From the eastern end a sand spit extends for ¼ mile and is partially covered at high water. On the north side of the spit anchorage may be had in 5 fathoms, about ½ mile from shore, but no vessel should lie here with any appearance of bad weather.

Beacon.—A beacon has been erected on Minor Island at the extremity of the spit extending from the eastern end of Smith or Blunt island.

Partridge Bank, 3 miles S. 31° W. of the light-house on Smith's Island is the northwestern point of this bank within 10 fathoms of water. Inside this depth the bank is 3 miles long and 1½ in width. The bottom is generally sand, gravel, and bowlders, except near the shoalest spot, where it is rocky and thickly covered with kelp. This dangerous rock is covered by 14 feet water at lowest tides, and lies on the northern side of the bank, 3¼ miles from the nearest shore of Whidbey Island. A considerable part of the bank is covered with kelp, which is much underrun by strong currents. The currents over the bank are irregular, except under the eastern extremity, when they set strongly from the north and NW. at flood and ebb tides. There are current rips on all the banks in the straits, which split the moving volumes of water, and these rips are heavier in westerly winds.

Hassler Bank lies N. 38° W. of New Dungeness light house, on a line nearly midway to Victoria. This is a 20 fathom bank, 2 miles long and ½ mile wide, with as little as 15 fathoms of water over it.

CHAPTER II.

HARO STRAIT, THE WESTERN CHANNELS AND ISLANDS TO NANAIMO HARBOR AND DEPARTURE BAY.

Haro Strait, the westernmost of the three channels leading from Fuca strait into the strait of Georgia, trends in a N by W. direction for 18 miles; it then turns sharply to the ENE. round Turn Point of Stuart Island, for a farther distance of 12 miles, leaving Saturna Island to the westward, and Waldron and Patos Islands to the eastward, when it enters the Strait of Georgia between Saturna and Patos Islands

It is for the most part a broad, and for its whole extent a deep navigable ship channel; but on account of the reefs which exist in certain parts, the general absence of steady winds, the scarcity of anchorages, and above all, the strength and varying direction of the tides, much care and vigilance is necessary in its navigation, and it is far more adapted to steam than to sailing vessels.

Besides the main channel of the Haro Strait thus described, there are several smaller channels and passages branching from it by which vessels may enter the Strait of Georgia; thus the Swanson Channel leads into the strait by Active Pass, and the Trincomalie and Stuart Channels by the Portier Pass, or the Dodd Narrows.

These channels may be again entered by smaller ones, thus Sidney and Cordova Channels, on the western side of Haro Strait, lead by Moresby, Colbourne, and Shute Passages into the Swanson, Satellite, and Stuart Channels, and finally into the Strait of Georgia. These channels are essentially adapted to steam navigation, or to coasting vessels; they afford smooth water, and many of them anchorages.

Zero Rock, one of the principal dangers in the southern part of Haro Strait, lies on the western side of the strait, is about 100 yards in extent, covers at three quarters flood, and its vicinity is marked by kelp, it lies $6\frac{1}{2}$ miles N 22° W. of the east point of Discovery Island.

Beacon.—A whitewashed beacon, pyramidal in shape, 30 feet high, surmounted by a pole and frame, resembling an obelisk, 20 feet high, also colored white, has been erected on Zero Rock.

A Rocky Patch, part of which nearly uncovers at low water springs, lies 700 yards N. 5° W. of Zero Rock.

Discovery Island Light is obscured in the direction of Zero Rock, and westward of it.

The Kelp Reefs, ¾ mile in extent, lie almost in the center of Haro Strait, 7 miles north from the east point of Discovery Island. They uncover at low springs, and are well marked by kelp, which extends in detached patches to Darcy Island.

A black spar buoy is moored in 6 fathoms water off the easternmost patch of the Kelp Reefs. The buoy is liable to drift.

The Unit Rock lies ¾ mile eastward of the south point of Darcy Island, and uncovers 2 feet at low tides.

Bare Island well open north of Sidney Island, bearing N. 25° W., leads east of Kelp Reefs and Unit Rocks.

Directions.—Vessels passing up Haro Strait to avoid the above dangers, after rounding Discovery Island at the distance of one mile, should steer north, or for Kellett Bluff of Henry Island, a remarkable steep rocky headland. This course will lead clear to the eastward of Kelp Reefs. In working up, when standing westward, a vessel should tack when the NW. extreme of Low Island comes in line with the SE. point of Sidney Island, which will give the Zero Rock a good berth; but when approaching the Kelp Reefs, Bare Island must be kept well open to the eastward of the same point to avoid them. The eastern or San Juan shore is steep close to.

When abreast Kellett Bluff, at from ½ to one mile distant, a N. 11° W. course will pass the same distance from Turn Point of Stuart Island There are no dangers off this point; but whirling eddies and tide rips, caused by the meetings of the streams from so many channels, are generally met with, particularly on the ebb. A vessel may reach this point with a fresh southerly wind, but will almost invariably lose it here, until having opened out the middle channel eastward of San Juan.

After rounding Turn Point, a N. 62° E. course for 10 miles will lead to the northern entrance of Haro Strait, between the east point of Saturna and Patos Islands. This passage is 2½ miles in breadth, but is subject to heavy tide rips and eddies, vessels when possible should pass through the center of it, steering for the white cliffs of Point Roberts (Orcas Nob, Orcas Island, well open east of Waldron Island bearing S 3° E. leads through in mid-channel), and should not bear away to the westward until the south end of Sucia is shut in with south end of Patos Island. At night, after passing between Saturna and Patos Islands, they should maintain a northerly course for about 2 or 3 miles, and then if the light on Georgina Point, at the entrance to Active Pass, is not visible, steer N. 45° W. until it is sighted; remembering that this light becomes obscured when it bears to the westward of N. 72° W., and as whilst it is in view all dangers on the southern shores of the strait will be avoided, they should be careful to keep it in sight and by no means stand to the southward of the above line of bearing.

The flood from the Rosario Strait, which is met with as soon as the passage between Orcas and Sucia Island is open, is apt to set a vessel towards the east point of Saturna, off which and Tumbo Island there is much uneven and broken ground, with heavy tide races. This point should be given a berth of 1½ miles; taking care to avoid a dangerous rock lying ¼ mile N. 45° E. of Race Point.

The ebb sets to the eastward even before the Strait of Georgia is well open, and a vessel finding herself not likely to weather Patos should pass between it and Sucia, where there is a good clear passage of above one mile in breadth; if this passage is taken, the Patos Island shore should be kept rather aboard. Beware of the Plumper and Clements Reefs; the former lies 1¼ miles S. 56° W. of the northwest bluff of Sucia Island, and has 10 feet water on it; the latter the same distance N. 62° E. of the same bluff, and has 9 feet water over it.

Entering the strait and having passed to the northward of Patos Island, if the ebb is running a vessel is extremely liable, unless with a commanding breeze, to be set to the eastward and down the Rosario Channel.

The northern shore of Sucia Island should by all means be avoided. If Alden Bank can be fetched it offers a good anchorage while waiting for a tide. Alden Point, the western point of Patos Island, in one with Monarch head, a bold cliffy bluff bearing S. 74° W., leads over the northern edge of this bank in from 6 to 9 fathoms. When Mount Constitution is in line with the center of Matia Island, bearing S. 3° E., 9 fathoms may be expected, and vessels should not anchor in much less than this depth, as in the shoaler parts rocky ground is found. The least water on the bank is 2¼ fathoms.

With a foul wind and ebb tide vessels should always work up on the eastern shore; there are no dangers, little tide when eastward of a line between Roberts Point and Alden Bank, and anchorage may always be had within a mile of the shore if necessary. Birch and Semiahmoo Bays offer good anchorage, and are easy of access. In working up the Strait of Georgia the western shore should never be approached within a mile, for the tides sweep strongly along this shore, and there are several outlying reefs between East Point and Active Pass.

As soon as the strait is entered from the southward, Roberts Point will show its eastern part as a bold white faced cliff, its western as a low shingle point. Its summit is covered with trees, and it would at first sight be taken for an island in consequence of the land on its northern side falling rapidly in elevation. After passing northward of this point, its low water extreme, or the trees just within it, must not be brought to bear southward of S. 62° E to avoid Roberts Bank, which extends 5 miles off the Fraser River entrance, is steep to, and shoals suddenly from 25 to 2 fathoms.

Tides.—The stream of tide runs fairly through the main channel of Haro Strait, outside the Kelp Reefs, from 3 to 6 knots, and inside them through the Cordova and Sidney Channels. Passing outside the Kelp Reefs, and eastward of Sidney Island a part of the flood stream will be found to branch off to the eastward, between San Juan and Stuart Islands, and there, meeting the flood from the Middle Channel, cause heavy races and eddies, so that although there are deep water channels between these islands, they are not recommended for sailing vessels. In like manner the flood runs to the NW. between the group of islands, northward of Sidney Island, and through Shute and Moresby Passages, though the main stream will be found to run fairly between Stuart and Moresby Islands.

Johnstone Reef midway between Cadboro Point and Gordon Head, is marked by kelp, and is of small extent.

Three Shoal Patches, with from 6 to 12 feet on them, lie one to 1½ miles distant from Zero Rock.

There is but little stream of tide in Cormorant Bay when within the Zero Rock, and the holding ground is good.

Cormorant Bay, between Gordon and Cowitchin Heads, on the western side of Haro Strait, is a good stopping place, easy of access under most circumstances.

Mount Douglas, a remarkable hill 696 feet high, with its summit bare of trees, rises immediately over the coast at the head of the bay.

Directions—To enter Cormorant Bay southward of Zero Rock, coming from the northward, bring Mount Douglas to bear S. 62° W. and steer for it, when the western points of Discovery and Chatham Islands are well shut in by Cadboro Point, a vessel will be westward of Zero Rock and can take up a berth in 9 or 10 fathoms water, at one mile off shore, with Mount Douglas bearing S 31° W.

To enter this bay northward of Zero Rock, the Kelp Reefs must be avoided. The positions of both rock and reefs will generally be easily distinguished from a vessel's deck one mile off. By steering for Cowitchin Head (a very remarkable high white cliff at the northern end of Cormorant Bay), on a N. 73° W. bearing, will lead in mid-channel, and a good anchorage will be found in 8 to 10 fathoms water, at from one to 2 miles off shore with the head on that bearing.

This anchorage is more exposed to SE. winds than the one last mentioned, but a vessel with good ground tackle will always be perfectly safe.

Anchorages—Although there are many harbors among the archipelago which form the Haro Strait and its tributary channels, yet the number eligible for sailing vessels overtaken by darkness or an adverse tide is comparatively small.

Between Cormorant Bay and the northern entrance of Haro Strait, Plumper Sound and Cowlitz Bay are the only eligible stopping places for a sailing vessel seeking shelter.

Stuart Island has two fair harbors, and Roche Harbor at the north west end of San Juan Island is a suitable anchorage for steamers or small coasters, but no sailing vessel of moderate tonnage could enter either under ordinary circumstances without great loss of time, as well as risk.

San Juan Island, the western coast of which forms for some distance the eastern boundary of Haro Strait, is of considerable size. Its western shores are steep and rocky, and afford no anchorage; depths of from 100 to 150 fathoms being found within ½ mile of the coast. Mount Dallas rises abruptly to a height of 1,086 feet. The eastern side of the island falls in a more gentle slope. Towards the southern end, and visible from seaward, are some white buildings, the farming establishment of the Hudson Bay Company; the southeastern extreme, which forms one of the entrance points of the middle channel, terminates in a white clay cliff, over which rises Mount Finlayson to a height of 550 feet, remarkable as being entirely clear of trees on its southern side, while it is thickly wooded on the northern. There is a clean gravel beach under Mount Finlayson where boats can generally land.

Henry Island lies off the NW. end of San Juan, being only separated from it by a narrow channel called Mosquito Passage The island would be taken as a part of San Juan, the passage appearing merely as an indentation in the latter. Kellett bluff, the southwestern point of Henry Island, makes as the most prominent headland on the eastern side of Haro Strait, when seen from the southward. Immediately eastward of it is Open Bay, which has more the appearance of a channel than the true one, Mosquito Passage There is no shelter either in the bay, or anchorage in the passage, for anything beyond coasters.

Mosquito Passage is studded with numerous reefs, which are marked by kelp. When a mile within the passage, Westcott Creek, an indentation in San Juan branches off to the ENE., and affords a haven for coasters. There is a 2-fathom channel through the passage and into this creek The only directions necessary are to avoid the kelp patches. The tide runs strongly through it.

Roche Harbor.—At the northern entrance of Mosquito Passage, the space between San Juan and Henry Islands opens out considerably, and the depth of water increases. This space forms Roche Harbor, which must be entered from the northward by vessels of burden Its entrance is somewhat confined but not difficult of access, and it affords good shelter when within.

Roche Harbor to Port Townsend.—With strong *flood* tide the following route is recommended:

Spieden Channel, President Channel, leave Barnes Island to the eastward, Rosario Straits. With *ebb* tide and clear weather use Spieden and San Juan Channels.

Morse Island, a small, flat, cliffy island, about 30 feet high, lies ¼ mile westward of the north point of Henry Island; and the entrance of Roche Harbor is ½ mile eastward of the former.

Directions.—To enter, pass as near as convenient northward of Morse Island, as there are no dangers outside it. The entrance will then open out between Henry Island and the western point of Pearl Island, which is wooded and lies in the center of the passage. Off the northern side of Pearl is a small island connected with it at low water. The breadth of the entrance is 400 yards, but the navigable channel is contracted to little over 100 yards by shoal water, which extends off both shores.

Scout Patch, a dangerous spit projecting from the western shore just south of Inman Point, has only a depth of 17 feet on it at low water; and although there is a depth of 5 fathoms in mid channel, great care must be exercised to avoid this patch by vessels drawing over 14 feet. Vessels of less draft may approach the shores on either side to within 150 yards, immediately within Pearl Island the harbor opens out to a considerable breadth.

Anchorage.—A good anchorage is in 6 fathoms, with the west end of Pearl Island bearing N. 22° W., distant about ¼ mile, and the north part of Henry Island just open of it. If working in, remember that a shoal of 15 feet lies 300 yards northward of Bare Islet, and that fair anchorage may be had in 9 fathoms off the entrance, but a vessel should get in far enough to be out of the tides of Spieden Channel. Small vessels leaving Roche Harbor, and bound southward, may take the Mosquito Passage.

Stuart Island, lying 3 miles northwestward of the northern part of the island of San Juan, is of an irregular shape and 642 feet high, the summits of the hills partially bare of trees, Turn Point, its northwestern extreme, a bold cliffy bluff, forms the salient angle of the Haro Strait, where it changes its direction suddenly from N. 12° W. to N. 68° E. before entering the Strait of Georgia. There are two anchorages in Stuart Island, Reid Harbor on its southern side and Prevost Harbor on its northern, but both are small and intricate for sailing vessels above the size of coasters.

Reid Harbor.—To enter Reid Harbor from the southward, beware of being drawn by the flood into the channel between San Juan and Stuart Islands, where there are several dangers, and the tides most irregular in their direction. The southwestern side of Stuart Island should therefore be first closed; it is bold and free from danger.

The harbor bears N. 22° W. one mile from Spieden Bluff, a remarkable bare grassy point, generally of a yellow color, the western extreme of the island of the same name. Gossip Island, from which a shoal extends 300 yards N. 56° W., lies in the entrance, leave it on the right hand in entering. The breadth of the channel is 300 yards, the depth from 4 to 5 fathoms, and no dangers but what are visible. The best anchorage is ½ mile within the entrance.

Prevost Harbor, on the northern side of Stuart Island, 1½ miles eastward from Turn Point has James Island lying in the center of it. The entrance is to the westward of this island, between it and Charles Point, and is about 400 yards in breadth, the harbor extending south for a short distance, and then taking an easterly direction. Anchor in 6 fathoms as soon as the eastern arm opens out, or if desired run up the arm into 4½ fathoms, here it is narrow, but perfectly sheltered. The passage to the eastward of James Island is a blind one, but a vessel may anchor, if necessary, at its entrance in 10 or 12 fathoms water.

Johns Island, with its numerous off lying reefs, lies to the southeastward of Stuart Island, and is separated from it by a navigable channel of 10 fathoms, but it is narrow and not recommended except for coasters acquainted with the locality.

Several islets and rocks, all above water, extend ¾ mile southward and eastward of the southeastern end of Johns Island; the most southern of these are called Cactus Islands, between which and Spieden Island is the east entrance to New Channel.

Gull Reef, 2 feet above high water, lies ½ mile N. 59° W. of Cactus Islands, rocks extend from it in a southeasterly direction for more than 200 yards.

Spieden Island, lying between San Juan and Stuart Islands, is 2¼ miles long and very narrow; its southern side grassy and bare of trees, its summit and northern side thickly wooded; Green Point, its eastern extreme, is a sloping grassy point.

There is a channel on both sides of Spieden Island; New Channel to the northward, and Spieden Channel to the southward. It may sometimes be convenient to take either of these channels when passing from the Middle Channel to Haro Strait, or *vice versa*, as the distance round Stuart Island will be saved. But from the strength and irregularity of the tides, and the number of hidden dangers which exist in certain parts of them, they can not be recommended for sailing vessels, nor indeed to any vessel without a pilot.

New Channel, to the northward of Spieden Island, though narrower than Spieden, is deep, more free from danger, and the navigation of it more simple. The northern shore of Spieden Island is bold and steep, and should be kept aboard, the narrowest part of the channel is ¼ mile wide between Spieden and Cactus Islands, and care should be taken not to get entangled among the reefs to the northward of the latter. The flood tide sets to the northeastward among them, but it also sets fairly through New Channel, and by keeping the Spieden Island shore aboard there will be no danger of being set to the northward; the ebb tide runs to the southwestward between Johns and Spieden Islands.

Spieden Channel, between the island of that name and San Juan, has a general east and west direction. Its eastern entrance, between Green Point and the northeastern point of San Juan, is ¼ mile wide, and for 2 miles the water is deep and clear of dangers. The meeting of the flood tide, however, from Haro Strait, with that from the Middle Channel, causes heavy rips and irregular eddies. These, together with the general absence of steady winds, render the navigation always tedious and dangerous for sailing vessels. Its western entrance is encumbered with numerous reefs and shoals with irregular soundings.

Sentinel Island stands in the western entrance of this channel. It is small, bare on its southern side, and about 150 feet high. The passage between it and Spieden Island is more than 200 yards wide. Vessels using the Spieden Channel are recommended to keep the Spieden Island shore aboard, and to pass between it and Sentinel Island. There is much less tide here than in the center of the channel or on the San Juan shore. Sentinel Rock lies 400 yards west of the island, the passage between being foul

Center Reef is a dangerous patch, awash at low water, and almost in the center of the channel. It bears from Sentinel Island S. 62° W nearly ½ mile. Kelp will generally be seen around the reef, but it is sometimes run under. Both the flood from Haro Strait and the ebb through Spieden Channel set on to the reef. When nearing it the San Juan shore should be kept aboard, avoiding the shoal 300 yards north of Bare Islet

Danger Shoal is also at the western entrance. It is marked by kelp, though not always to be distinguished. It lies about a mile from Morse Island, N 12° E

Bare Islet is a rock about 15 feet high, lying in the southern part of the channel S. 85° E one mile from Morse Island There is a shoal patch of 15 feet nearly 300 yards north of it. This patch is always covered with kelp, and is the last danger known in the channel.

Directions.—Vessels bound from Haro Strait to the eastward through the Spieden Channel should pass about ¼ mile to the northward of Morse Island and then steer N. 85° E for Green Point until Sentinel Island bears north; the dangers in the western entrance will then be passed and a straight course may be steered through, bearing in mind that less tide will be found near Spieden Island shore.

Bound westward through this channel, if the passage between Spieden and Sentinel Islands is not taken, the shore of Spieden Island should be kept aboard to avoid the tide races If Center Reef is awash, or the kelp on it is seen, pass ¼ mile south of it and steer to pass the same distance northward of Morse Island If Center Reef is not seen, take care not to bring Morse Island to bear to the southward of S 68° W. until Bare Islet bears S. 22° E.

Waldron Island lies in the northern entrance of the Middle Channel, and its anchorages are frequently available for vessels passing to or from Haro Strait

The island is thickly wooded, moderately high, and cliffy on its southern and eastern sides, but falling to the northward, where it terminates in low sandy points. Disney Point, its southern extreme, is a remarkably high stratified bluff.

Cowlitz Bay on the western side of Waldron, between Disney and Sandy Points, affords good anchorage with all winds, the depth of water from 5 to 8 fathoms, and the holding ground stiff mud; it may be sometimes more desirable for sailing vessels to anchor here than to work up into Plumper Sound, particularly for those coming up Middle Channel. If entering from the northward or westward, Sandy Point may be passed at a distance of $\frac{1}{8}$ of a mile, and standing into the bay anchor on the line between it and Disney Point in 5 or 6 fathoms. If a southeaster is blowing, a vessel may stand far enough in to get smooth water under shelter of Disney Point; no sea, however, to affect a vessel's safety gets up in this bay with any wind The only danger in the bay is Mouatt Reef with a depth of only 3 feet on it; it lies $\frac{1}{2}$ mile N. 17° W. of Disney Point with deep water between it and the shore.

If entering from the southward, Disney Point should be kept within less than $\frac{1}{2}$ mile, particularly with the ebb, for as soon as Douglas Channel is opened out, which is the continuation of Middle Channel and through which the tide runs sometimes 5 knots, vessels are apt to be set down on Danger Rock.

North Bay, on the northwestern side of the island, affords anchorage about $\frac{1}{4}$ mile offshore, but it is not by any means such a desirable place as Cowlitz Bay, the bank being rather steep and the tide felt more strongly

White Rock is 35 feet above high water and lies S. 66° W., $1\frac{1}{4}$ miles from Disney Point. There is a reef extending 300 yards N. 39° W. from it.

Danger Rock, a dangerous reef with only 5 feet on it, and on which kelp is rarely seen, lies S 40° E., $\frac{1}{4}$ mile from White Rock.

Caution.—It is particularly recommended to give these rocks a wide berth, as with strong tides the water is too deep for anchorage in case of getting entangled amongst them in light winds.

Plumper Sound.—If from any cause it should be found necessary to anchor in that bend of the Haro Strait between Stuart Island and the east point of Saturna Island, this sound is recommended as a safe and convenient harbor, easy of access with the wind from any quarter. It is formed between Pender and Saturna Islands Blunden Island, about 400 yards in length, and close to the shore, forms the western entrance point, and Monarch Head, a high, bold, rocky headland, the eastern. There is anchorage in a moderate depth of water in most parts of it, as well as several bays or harbors if preferred.

There are no dangers at the entrance, and but little tide is felt. A rocky patch lies about N. 56° W., distant 550 yards from Croker Point, in a spot where the charts indicate 13 fathoms. It is of small extent and steep-to, except on its northern edge, where it shoals gradually from 8 fathoms. Between this patch and Saturna Island the soundings are irregular, varying from 8 to 20 fathoms.

In coming from the southward, the western extremity of Fane Island in line with the northeastern extreme of Pender Island clears this patch, and Lizard Islet open of Elliott Bluff clears its western edge

The most convenient anchorage is off the entrance of Port Browning, on the western side of the sound, in 8 fathoms, $\frac{1}{2}$ mile from the shore. Above Port Browning the only danger is Perry Rock, with 6 feet on it, marked by kelp. It is 400 yards from the shore and N. 11° W., $\frac{3}{4}$ mile from Razor Point, the northern point of the port.

Port Browning is on the western side of Plumper Sound. The best anchorage is in the center, just above Shark Cove, which is a convenient creek with 4 fathoms in it, on the southern side of the harbor, ¾ mile within the entrance; here a ship might beach and repair on a sandy spit. The cove is separated by a narrow neck of land 150 yards wide from Bedwell Harbor, on the south coast of Pender Island.

Lyall Harbor lies on the eastern side of Plumper Sound, and is an indentation in the northwestern end of Saturna Island. The King Islets, two low, rugged islets, with a reef extending nearly 200 yards off their western end, form the northern entrance. The harbor terminates in a sandy beach, with a good stream of fresh water at its head. Crispin Rock, with 6 feet on it at low water, decreases its value as a harbor for sailing vessels. This rock is a mere pinnacle, nearly ½ mile within the entrance; there is no kelp to give warning of its position, and it lies exactly in the middle of the harbor. There is a clear passage on either side of it 300 yards wide, and vessels anchoring within it should drop their anchor in 5 fathoms, ½ mile from the beach at the head of the harbor. Boot Cove, on the southern side of the harbor, ⅓ mile within the southern point, has 3 fathoms water, and is a convenient spot for repairing a vessel. A small islet lies off its western entrance point.

Samuel Island, between Saturna and Mayne Islands, is almost connected with both, but leaving two passages by which boats or even small coasters may pass into the Strait of Georgia at proper times of tide. This island is indented on its southern side by several bays.

Winter Cove is formed between the southern side of Samuel Island and the northwestern point of Saturna, and is only ½ mile northward of Lyall Harbor. The depth of water in the cove being only from 2 to 3 fathoms, is only fit for small vessels The outlet to the Strait of Georgia is not over 90 feet in breadth and the tides rush through with great rapidity.

Water is easily obtainable, during the winter or rainy months, from streams in almost any part of Plumper Sound. At the head of Lyall Harbor or Port Browning, constantly in the former, a certain quantity may be procured during the driest months of summer, from June to August.

Navy Channel is a continuation of the western part of Plumper Sound, and leads, between Pender and Mayne Islands, into the Trincomalie Channel.

Independently therefore of its value as an anchorage, Plumper Sound becomes a high road for vessels bound into the Strait of Georgia or Frazer River, by the Active Pass, or to Nanaimo, or any of the northwestern ports of Vancouver Island

Concom and Enterprise Reefs—Concom Reef lies about midway through Navy Channel, 1¼ miles from Fane Island, and nearly 400 yards off the northern shore, and narrows the strait at that part to ⅓ mile.

It is a ledge of rocks extending in the direction of the channel for more than 200 yards, and covering at half tide; its vicinity is marked by kelp, and a patch of 2 fathoms extends nearly 400 yards westward from it.

The Enterprise Reefs are two rocky patches, the westernmost of which is covered at one quarter flood, and both are marked by kelp. The outermost of these reefs lies ⅝ of a mile S. 11° W. of Helen Point, the south point of Active Pass. A patch of 2 fathoms lies 400 yards S. 45° E. of the westernmost rocky patch.

Beacons.—A beacon 22 feet above high water has been erected on Enterprise Reef, near its western extremity; to the pyramidal framework of the beacon are fixed two disks at right angles to each other, having the appearance at a distance of upper and lower balls. The whole is colored white.

On Helen Point (nailed on a dead fir tree) is a diagonal white board, with a corresponding one on the opposite bight. These marks when in line, bearing N. 14° E., lead over northwestern extreme of Enterprise Reef; and when they come well open a vessel can steer for Active Pass.

Directions.—Vessels using Navy Channel should keep rather southward of mid channel. The shores of Pender Island are bold. When passing out of the western entrance, if bound through Trincomalie Channel or Active Pass, steer over towards Prevost Island until Pelorus Point (the east point of Moresby Island) is open of Mouatt Point (the west point of Pender Island) bearing S. 19° E.; then haul up N. 19° W., keeping the marks just open, which will lead over ⅛ mile to the westward of Enterprise Reefs.

When Helen Point, which is a low bare yellow point, bears N. 34° E., or the northern beacon comes well open west of the southern one, a vessel may steer for the entrance of Active Pass, or shape her course up the Trincomalie Channel.

Tides.—The flood tide from the Swanson Channel runs through Navy Channel to the eastward and meets the flood in Plumper Sound, causing a slight ripple at the east entrance, its strength is upwards of 3 knots.

Bedwell Harbor, the entrance to which bears N. 23° E. 3 miles from Turn Point of Stuart Island, is, on account of its narrower entrance, not so eligible a stopping place for vessels waiting the tide, but for steamers it is a good harbor. The only danger which does not show is the Drew Rock, with 10 feet on it, in the center of the harbor ¼ mile from its head; there is, however, no necessity for vessels to go as high as this, the most convenient anchorage being in a bay on the eastern shore ⅝ mile within the entrance, in 8 fathoms, midway between Hay Point and the Skull Reef, which always shows some feet above high water.

Camp Bay, between Bedwell Harbor and Plumper Sound, offers shelter as a stopping place to small craft, when not convenient to work into either of these ports.

The Western Channels of Haro Strait may be used with advantage by steamers or coasters bound from the southern ports of Vancouver Island to the Strait of Georgia, or to the districts of Saanich, Cowitchin, Nanaimo, and the numerous intermediate harbors. Their advantage over the Haro Strait consists in the strength of tide being less, besides sheltered anchorage being obtainable in almost all parts, while in the latter strait the depth of water is so great that it is impossible to anchor, and sailing vessels may frequently be set back into Fuca Strait, thus entailing great delay as well as risk. On the other hand the western channels are not free from danger; yet, with the assistance of the chart, and a good lookout from aloft for kelp, a precaution which should never be neglected, they may be navigated during daylight with ease and safety.

To vessels passing from the southward, and intending to take the western channels, the dangers to be avoided after passing Discovery and Chatham Islands are: Johnstone Reef, lying nearly one mile from the shore, midway between Cadboro Point and Gordon Head, Zero Rock, which lies in the fairway, and the shoals which extend off Darcy, Sidney, and James Islands.

Sidney Channel, between James and Sidney Islands, is the best; it is nearly one mile wide, and deep until near its northern end, where shoal patches with only 6 to 9 feet water on them, marked by kelp, lie from 600 to 1,000 yards off the western point of Sidney Island. Whale Islet, a small rock only 6 feet above high water, lies at the southern entrance to Sidney Channel, and is joined to Sidney Island by a sand spit. Sidney Spit, the northwestern extreme, is a low sandy tongue with a few trees on its extreme. A beacon 40 feet high, surmounted by a pole and cage, has been erected on the spit. There is good anchorage off the spit in 8 fathoms.

Cordova Channel, between James Island and the main island of Vancouver, is a fair passage with little tide; it is not, however, to be preferred to Sidney Channel, neither is any saving in distance gained by taking it, and it can not be recommended for vessels drawing over 14 feet. It has a sand bank over 200 yards in extent with 15 feet water on it lying in the center of the passage. A little northward of Cowitchin Head a low flat of swampy land extends for 2 miles in a northerly direction, and from ¼ to ½ mile off the high land; shoal water extends from 200 to 400 yards outside; this flat forms the western side of the southern entrance of the channel.

The southern face of James Island is a moderately high and steep white clay cliff, its summit covered with trees, towards the eastern part of this cliff are two remarkable notches on its summit. A bank, having from one to 3 fathoms water on it, extends one mile to the eastward, and nearly ½ mile to the southward, and westward from the SW. bluff of James Island. A shoal ¾ mile in extent, having depths of from 1½ to 3 fathoms on it, lies southeastward of the island; the center of it bears S. 39° E., distant 1¼ miles from the southwestern bluff of James Island.

Directions.—If the passage inside Discovery and Chatham Islands has been taken, and intending to take the Sidney Channel, when abreast Cadboro Point, steer north, keeping the passage between that point and Chatham Islands open astern until Mount Tuam (on the southern point of Admiral Island) is in line over the center between the two remarkable notches on James Island bearing N. 34° W.; this mark will lead nearly one mile eastward of Zero Rock, 600 yards westward of the 3-fathom patches off Darcy Island, and between them and the shoal of 9 feet extending southeastward from James Island.

When Morse Island is in line with the southeastern point of Sidney Island, bearing N. 60° E., alter course to north to avoid the shoal which extends one mile S. 84° E. from SW. bluff of James Island; pass about 600 yards westward of Whale Islet, and then steer up mid channel, and avoid the shoal patches off the northwestern end of Sidney Island, by not shutting Whale Islet in with Darcy Island, until the end of Sidney Spit bears N. 23° E.

If passing outside the Discovery and Chatham Islands, at about one mile off, steer N. 16° W. until the leading marks (Mount Tuam, in line between the two remarkable notches on James Islands), bearing N. 34° W., are on, when proceed as before directed.

Miners Channel.—Low and Bare Islands are two small islands lying off the eastern side of Sidney Island, and between them and the latter there is a good passage. The eastern side of Sidney Island is bold, and affords good anchorage in 8 fathoms, out of the tide, in a bay S. 45° W. of the north end of Bare Island. A 3 fathom shoal lies 500 yards off the eastern point of Sidney Island, and a similar shoal lies about the same distance S. 55° E. of Low Island.

Midway between Low and Bare Islands, and on the line between their northwestern points, is a reef which uncovers, and about ¼ mile to the eastward of this reef is a rock marked by kelp. There is a rock 3 feet above high water N. 50° W., distant ⅛ mile from the northwestern end of Bare Island. After passing this island a course should be steered between Sidney Spit and Jones Island.

Having passed to the northward of Sidney Island, either by Cordova, Sidney, or Miners Channels, the Shute or Moresby Passages may be taken as convenient; if bound for Saanich, Cowitchin, or through Stuart Channel, the former is preferable, while the latter offers a more direct course through the Swanson or Trincomalie Channels, or to Fraser River by Active Pass.

Shute Passage.—To enter this passage, after leaving Sidney Spit pass between Jones Island and the Little Group, then eastward of Coal and Pym Islands, and between Piers and Portland Islands, when the Satellite Channel will be entered, which leads directly to Saanich, Cowitchin, and the western ports of Vancouver Island. This is a good clear channel, and with the assistance of the chart may be used with much facility.

Jones Island lies N 22° E of Sidney Spit, $\frac{3}{4}$ mile, with a clear passage between, shoal rocky ground extends 200 yards westward of the northwestern point of Jones Island, and the tides set with considerable strength, from 2 to 5 knots round this point; detached rocks extend 400 yards off the southeastern end of the island and off the northeastern side

Tree, Hill, Domville, Comet, and Gooch Islands, which lie in the fairway between Sidney and Moresby Islands, are moderately low and wooded The passages between them are not recommended.

Reefs—North Cod Reef covers at one quarter flood, and lies 800 yards S 17° W. of the western end of Gooch Island

South Cod Reef has only 6 feet on it at low water; it lies 1,400 yards S. 17° W. of the western end of Gooch Island. Both reefs are marked by kelp.

A patch of 2 fathoms, marked by kelp, lies nearly midway between the southern end of Jones and Domville Islands, the passage between Gooch and Comet Islands is filled with kelp.

The Little Group lie $\frac{2}{3}$ mile N. 56° W. of Jones Island They consist of four rocky islets, $\frac{1}{3}$ mile in extent east and west, bare of trees, and connected by reefs; there is a good passage between them and Jones Island, and their eastern side may be passed at 200 yards.

Bird Islet, lying on the eastern side of Shute Passage, and $\frac{3}{4}$ mile north of the north point of Jones Island, is about 6 feet above high water, and has a cluster of reefs around it almost 200 yards in extent, marked by kelp; between it and Coal Island there is a clear passage one mile wide.

Coal Island, which helps to form the western side of Shute Passage, lies immediately at the entrance of Shoal Harbor; it is one mile in extent and thickly wooded, and its eastern and northern shores are free from danger.

When working up the passage between Bird Islet and Coal Island, a vessel should not stand to the westward of a line joining the east end of Little Group to the east point of Coal Island, as a rock which covers at one quarter flood lies nearly $\frac{3}{8}$ mile south of the east point of the island.

Reefs.—A small patch with 4 fathoms water over it, and probably less, and marked by kelp, lies one mile N. 70° E. of the east point of Coal Island When abreast the east point of Coal Island, and distant $\frac{1}{3}$ mile, a N. 45° W. course will lead through Shute Passage in mid channel, passing eastward of Pym Island, off the eastern side of which a reef, which uncovers, extends a little more than 200 yards length. Patches of kelp have been seen extending some distance off the south end of Pym Island.

Celia Reef has 8 feet of water on it. It is marked by kelp and lies N. 22° E, $\frac{2}{3}$ mile from the northern point of Pym Island.

Knapp and Pym Islands are small and wooded, lying between Piers and Coal Islands. The passage between Piers and Portland Islands is above a mile in breadth, with no dangers which are not visible; off the eastern side of the former, about 200 yards, is a rock always uncovered. Having passed westward between these islands a vessel is fairly in Satellite Channel.

Moresby Passage.—After leaving the northern end of Sidney Island, the directions for Moresby Passage are the same as those already given for Shute Passage, until abreast the eastern point of Coal Island. From about ¼ mile off this point, the direct course through the passage is N. 17° E. for 2½ miles, or until near its northern entrance, which lies between Portland and Moresby Islands. Turnbull Reef and Canoe Rocks, which extend off both these islands, narrow the channel at its northern entrance to little over ¼ mile.

The Sisters.—Off the eastern point of Portland Island are three rocky islets, the Sisters, which extend to a distance of nearly 400 yards. They are about 25 feet high, have a few stunted cedar trees on their summits, are joined by reefs, and will be immediately recognized either from the northward or southward.

Turnbull Reef.—Eastward from the Sisters, at a distance of more than ¼ mile, extends the Turnbull Reef in a semicircular direction towards the NW. point of Portland Island, and almost joining it; 2 fathoms is the least water found on its outer edge, and it is marked by a heavy bank of kelp, which, however, is not always visible until close to it, on account of the tide.

Canoe Rocks form a dangerous ledge, extending N. 65° W. nearly ½ mile from Reef Point, the northwestern point of Moresby Island. The outer rock of this ledge covers a little after half flood, and is not marked by kelp, though kelp grows between the point and the rock.

Beacon.—A stone beacon 25 feet high, surmounted by a cross, is erected on Canoe Rocks. A buoy has been bolted to the rock at the western extremity of the reef off Reef Point. Between the buoy and the point there is a rock with only 1½ feet over it. The channel between this rock and the point is 75 feet wide. Vessels using this channel should keep close alongside the point.

Directions.—When the beacon is visible, the passage is very easy, as the dangers may be passed as close as convenient, but when not seen, it is desirable in coming from the southward to borrow on the Moresby Island shore, passing Seymour Point, the western cliffy point of the island, at the distance of 400 yards.

From this point the Canoe Rocks bear N. 22° W., nearly a mile, and from a berth 400 yards off it, a N. 17° W. course direct for Beaver Point, the sloping bare southeastern point of Admiral Island, will lead almost in mid-channel. When Chads Island, just off the northwestern point of Portland Island, comes open of that point, then vessels will be well to the northward of both rock and reef.

If coming from the northward, and intending to take Moresby Passage, by keeping Beaver Point astern with the easternmost Channel Island in Ganges Harbor touching it, or just shut in by it, the Canoe Rocks will be cleared. The western Channel Island just touching Beaver point leads on to the rock

Prevost Passage lies between Moresby Island and the group of smaller islands to the southward of it, and leads by the Shute or Moresby Passages into Satellite Channel.

To vessels passing up the main stream of Haro Strait and bound for the Swanson Channel, the easiest and most direct route is between Stuart and Moresby Islands; but circumstances of wind or tide may render it convenient to take the Prevost Passage; for instance, with light winds they may be set into the passage by the flood, or, if near to Moresby Island, by the ebb tide from the upper part of Haro Strait, which runs here, as it does in all other parts of the channel, from two and one half to three hours after low water by the shore, and sets to the westward among the small islands, and down the Miners and Sidney Channels.

Arachne Reef.—The dangers to be avoided in Prevost Passage are Arachne and Cooper Reefs. Arachne Reef lies nearly in the center of the passage, in a direct line between Fairfax Point and the east point of Gooch Island This reef covers at one quarter flood, and has a good deal of kelp on its northwestern edge, which, however, is frequently run under by the tide.

Cooper Reef, lying ½ mile N. 13° W. of Tom Point, is marked by kelp, and uncovers at half ebb; there is a passage one mile wide between it and Arachne Reef, the channel being about the same width between the latter and Moresby Island, with deep water. There are no dangers off the southern or western sides of Moresby Island.

Tom Point, in line with the southeast point of Sidney Island, bearing S. 3° E., leads only just clear to the eastward of Cooper Reef.

North part of Portland Island, in line with south side of Moresby Island, bearing N. 47° W., leads to the northward of Cooper and Arachne Reefs.

Yellow Islet, a small bare islet 8 feet high, lies 1¼ miles S 79° W. of Fairfax Point, and should be passed on the north side to clear the shoal of 3 fathoms which extends nearly 400 yards westward from the islet, and to avoid the small patch of 4 fathoms (probably shoaler) marked with kelp lying ¼ mile S. 68° W. of it; having passed westward of this island either the Shute or Moresby Passage may be taken as convenient.

Satellite Channel is formed by Admiral Island on the north, and Moresby, Portland, and Piers Islands, and the northern shore of Saanich Peninsula on the south It leads to Saanich Inlet, Cowitchin Harbor, and by the Sansum Narrows to Stuart Channel. It is a good, deep passage with but few dangers, which are not always visible; among these are Shute Reef and Patey Rock. The general breadth of the channel is one mile, with depths of from 30 to 40 fathoms, and the strength of tide from one to 2 knots, and sometimes 3 knots.

Shute Reef is a ledge less than 100 yards in extent, with two rocks, one of which is covered at 8 feet flood, its vicinity being marked by kelp. It lies $\frac{3}{8}$ mile west of Harry Point, and nearly 600 yards N. 37° E. of Arbutus, a small islet with two or three of the red-stemmed arbutus growing on it, and lying $\frac{1}{2}$ mile westward of Piers Island.

Patey Rock, at the western end of Satellite Channel, is a single rock, covered at 6 feet rise with kelp around it, and is in the way of vessels working into Saanich Inlet or Cowitchin Harbor. It lies nearly 2 miles N. 39° W. of Coal Point, a remarkable nob point, the southern extreme of Deep Cove.

Clearing marks.—Harry Point, open northward of Arbutus Islet, bearing N. 79° E., leads 600 yards southward of Patey Rock; and the high round summit of Moresby Island, well open northward of Arbutus Islet, bearing east leads 700 yards to the northward of it.

Boatswain Bank, on the western side of the channel, affords good anchorage in from 4 to 9 fathoms, sandy bottom. It extends $\frac{3}{4}$ mile from the Vancouver shore, between Cherry and Hatch Points. The edge of the bank is steep.

Saanich Inlet is a deep indentation running in a nearly south direction for 14 miles, carrying deep water to its head, which terminates in a narrow creek within 4 miles of Esquimalt Harbor. The inlet forms a peninsula of the southeastern portion of Vancouver Island. The coast line is fringed with pine forests, but in the center it is clear prairie or oak land, and much of it under cultivation; seams of coal have also been found.

Off the eastern or peninsula side of the inlet there are some good anchorages, the center being for the most part deep. Immediately southward of James Point, the northwestern point of the peninsula, is Deep Cove, but no convenient anchorage.

Norris Rock, awash at half tide, lies S. 57° W. 400 yards from James Point, with 12 fathoms between it and the point. Vessels rounding this point should give it a berth of $\frac{1}{4}$ mile.

Union Bay, 2 miles southward of James Point, affords good anchorage in 8 or 9 fathoms $\frac{1}{4}$ mile from the beach. There is a stream of fresh water in the southeastern corner of the bay.

Cole Bay, immediately under Mount Newton, is small, but capable of affording shelter to a few vessels of moderate size; off its northern point are two small bare islets, the White Rocks.

These bays are somewhat open to SW. winds, but a gale rarely blows from this quarter, nor, from the proximity of the opposite shore, distant scarcely 3 miles, could much sea get up.

Tod Creek is 2 miles southward of Cole Bay. Senanus Island, a small wooded islet, 150 feet high, lies off its entrance; foul ground extends nearly 200 yards off the northwestern side of the island; on the other sides the water is deep. A small islet, and a rock lying 200 yards north of it, lies in the entrance to the southeastern part of the creek. A short distance inside it narrows rapidly and winds to the southward and southeastward for ¾ mile, with a breadth of less than 200 yards, carrying 6 fathoms nearly to its head.

There is anchorage in the outer part of the creek in 15 fathoms.

Squally Reach.—From Willis Point, the western point of Tod Creek, the inlet known as Squally Reach trends to the SW. for 2½ miles, the breadth of the arm here being ¾ mile, with no bottom at 100 fathoms. Finlayson Arm, its continuation, terminates Saanich Inlet. Beacon Rock, which covers at three quarters flood, lies 200 yards S 62° W of Elbow Point, Finlayson Arm. A small islet named Dinner, with deep water on either side, lies near the head of this arm. At 600 yards south of the islet the arm terminates in a flat, which dries at low water.

Mill Creek Bay is a fair anchorage and the only one on the western side of Saanich Inlet; a bank of sand and rock, which has only from one to 3 fathoms water on it, extends from the western shore across the bay; a large stream flows into the NW. corner of the bay. A rock with only 6 to 9 feet lies almost in the center of the bay.

Cowitchin Harbor is westward of Cape Keppel, the southern extreme of Admiral Island. Separation Point, its northern entrance point, is somewhat remarkable, being the termination of a high, stony ridge, dropping suddenly, and running off as a low, sharp point to the southward. The harbor extends to the westward from this point for 2 miles, and the general depth of water in it is 30 fathoms, which shoals suddenly as the flat is approached; this dries off for more than ½ mile from the head of the harbor.

In its NW. end is a considerable river, the Quamitchan, which flows through the fertile valley and is navigable for small boats or canoes for several miles. There is a settlement here, off which is a long pier (on the south side of the harbor). Coming from the southeastward the entrance is easily distinguished by the pier and lumber yard, just inside the point on the west side. Mail steamers call here twice a week.

Anchorage.—Snug Creek.—The only convenient anchorage to be obtained is in Snug Creek, on the northern side of Cowitchin Harbor, or off the outer village on the south side, 1¾ miles within the entrance; in the latter case a vessel must approach the shore within little more than 200 yards, and anchor cautiously, when 12 fathoms are obtained.

Snug Creek is a convenient anchorage for small craft or coasters, and one or two vessels of moderate size might obtain anchorage and shelter in it, it extends in a northerly direction for nearly one mile, and is ¼ mile in breadth. Nearly in the middle of the entrance is a rock which uncovers at low water in the center of the kelp; it is about 20 feet in extent, and has 1½ fathoms water around it. The western point of entrance can be passed close as it is bold, and has 10 fathoms water within 100 yards of it; when ¼ mile, or less, inside the point, anchor in the center of the creek in 6 fathoms.

Sansum Narrows take a general northerly direction between Vancouver and Admiral Islands for a distance of 6 miles, when they lead into Stuart Channel; the average breadth of the narrows is about ½ mile, but at their narrowest part, abreast Bold Bluff, they are contracted to ¼ mile. The high land on both sides renders the wind generally very unsteady; from this cause as well as from the somewhat confined nature of the channel, and the depth of water which prevents anchoring, the narrows can not be recommended except for steamers or coasting vessels. There are but few dangers to be avoided, and the strength of the tides has seldom been found to exceed 3 knots, generally much less.

Entering Sansum Narrows from the southward a kelp patch, with 9 feet on it, lies on the Admiral Island shore, 400 yards S. 45° W. of a small islet close to the coast, nearly a mile S. 79° E. of Separation Point; there are 20 fathoms between it and the small islet.

Another rocky patch extends nearly 200 yards off shore from the eastern side of the Narrows, ¼ mile northwestward of Entrance Point.

Burial Islet lies on the eastern side of the narrows, 1½ miles above Separation Point; pass outside of it as close as convenient to the kelp.

Bold Bluff, a smooth headland of bare rock, is steep-to. Rocky ground marked by kelp extends 200 yards off Kelp Point on the west

(1691) **BRITISH COLUMBIA—Vancouver Island—Southeast coast—Stuart channel—Oyster harbor—Dangers.**—During the resurvey of Oyster harbor by H. B. M. S. *Egeria*, Commander J. F. Parry, R. N., the following dangers were found:

A rock, with 6 feet over it at low water ordinary springs, was found to the eastward of Coffin island. From this rock Coffin Island lighthouse bears S. 85° W. true (SW. by W. ⅜ W. W'ly mag.), distant 260 yards.

Another head with 12 feet over it was also found 120 yards to the eastward of the above position. From this danger Coffin Island lighthouse bears S. 88° W. true (SW. by W. ⅝ W. W'ly mag.), distant 380 yards.

The "3¼ fathoms" referred to in Notice to Mariners No. 22 (1101) of 1903, was found on examination to be the outer extreme of a narrow ridge extending from the reef off the point in Evening cove lying 600 yards northwestward of Sharp point. This ridge has depths of from 2 to 3 fathoms over it and from its extreme point Coffin Island lighthouse bears N. 50° E. true (NNE. ¼ E. E'ly mag.), distant 520 yards.

Off the west end of the western Twin island the 3-fathom line was found to extend into the anchorage 260 yards to the southwestward in the direction of the head of the coaling wharf on the opposite shore, the 5-fathom line extending 120 yards farther in a similar direction. This extension is in the nature of a spit running off the above point. Vessels are cautioned against anchoring in this vicinity.

(N. M. 48, 1904.)

of Thetis Island.

Osborn Bay, the southernmost anchorage on the western side may be known by the Shoal Islands, a low wooded group, connected at low

tends nearly 200 yards off the northwestern side of the island; on the other sides the water is deep. A small islet, and a rock lying 200 yards north of it, lies in the entrance to the southeastern part of the creek. A short distance inside it narrows rapidly and winds to the southward and southeastward for ¾ mile, with a breadth of less than 200 yards, carrying 6 fathoms nearly to its head.

There is anchorage in the outer part of the creek in 15 fathoms.

Squally Reach.—From Willis Point, the western point of Tod Creek, the inlet known as Squally Reach trends to the SW. for 2½ miles, the breadth of the arm here being ¾ mile, with no bottom at 100 fathoms. Finlayson Arm, its continuation, terminates Saanich Inlet. Beacon Rock, which covers at three quarters flood, lies 200 yards S. 62° W. of Elbow Point, Finlayson Arm. A small islet named Dinner, with deep water on either side, lies near the head of this arm. At 600 yards south of the islet the arm terminates in a flat, which dries at low water.

Mill Creek Bay is a fair anchorage and the only one on the western side of Saanich Inlet; a bank of sand and rock, which has only from one to 3 fathoms water on it, extends from the western shore across the bay, a large stream flows into the NW. corner of the bay. A rock with only 6 to 9 feet lies almost in the center of the bay.

Cowitchin Harbor is westward of Cape Keppel, the southern extreme of Admiral Island. Separation Point, its northern entrance point, is
ridge, dr
southwai
miles, an
suddenly
from the

In its
flows thi
canoes fc
pier (on
the ertra
inside th

Anch
obtained
or off the
in the la
than 20(

Snug
one or t
in it; its
in bread ... middle of the entrance is a rock ... covers at low water in the center of the kelp: it is about 20 feet in extent, and has 1½ fathoms water around it. The western point of entrance can be passed close as it is bold, and has 10 fathoms water within 100

yards of it; when ¼ mile, or less, inside the point, anchor in the center of the creek in 6 fathoms.

Sansum Narrows take a general northerly direction between Vancouver and Admiral Islands for a distance of 6 miles, when they lead into Stuart Channel; the average breadth of the narrows is about ½ mile, but at their narrowest part, abreast Bold Bluff, they are contracted to ¼ mile. The high land on both sides renders the wind generally very unsteady; from this cause as well as from the somewhat confined nature of the channel, and the depth of water which prevents anchoring, the narrows can not be recommended except for steamers or coasting vessels. There are but few dangers to be avoided, and the strength of the tides has seldom been found to exceed 3 knots, generally much less.

Entering Sansum Narrows from the southward a kelp patch, with 9 feet on it, lies on the Admiral Island shore, 400 yards S. 45° W. of a small islet close to the coast, nearly a mile S. 79° E. of Separation Point; there are 20 fathoms between it and the small islet.

Another rocky patch extends nearly 200 yards off shore from the eastern side of the Narrows, ½ mile northwestward of Entrance Point.

Burial Islet lies on the eastern side of the narrows, 1½ miles above Separation Point; pass outside of it as close as convenient to the kelp.

Bold Bluff, a smooth headland of bare rock, is steep to. Rocky ground marked by kelp extends 200 yards off Kelp Point on the western side almost opposite to Bold Bluff.

Burgoyne Bay, the entrance to which is ½ mile eastward of Bold Bluff, is a narrow and rather deep indentation, terminating in a sandy head. Anchorage may be had if necessary.

Maple Bay.—From Grave Point the narrows take a northwesterly direction, and on the Vancouver Island shore is Maple Bay. Bowlder, the southern entrance point, is remarkable from a large bowlder stone standing at its low-water extreme. Although an inviting looking bay, the water is too deep for comfortable anchorage.

Bird's-eye Cove, which runs in a southerly direction for nearly a mile from Bowlder Point, affords fair anchorage, with the bowlder bearing N. 62° E., the cove at this point is not above ¼ mile across.

Stuart Channel.—Sansum Narrows extend 1½ miles northward of Maple Bay, when they lead into Stuart Channel, the westernmost of the ship passages which wash the eastern side of Vancouver Island. The principal dangers are the North and Escape Reefs, White Rock, and Danger Reef.

On the western or Vancouver Island shore there are some good harbors, viz, Osborn Bay, Horse-shoe Bay, Oyster Harbor, and Chemainos Bay; on the eastern side there are also some anchorages; Telegraph and Preedy Harbors on the western, and Clam Bay on the eastern side of Thetis Island.

Osborn Bay, the southernmost anchorage on the western side may be known by the Shoal Islands, a low wooded group, connected at low water by reefs and mud banks, and which form the northern side of the bay, the southeasternmost of these islands lies N. 33° W., a little over 2 miles from the northwestern entrance point of Sansum Narrows. The bay affords good anchorage, sheltered from the prevailing winds from the westward and southeast. The best anchorage is with the southeasternmost Shoal Island, in one with Southey Point, and the southern trend of the coast S. 50° E.

The coast northwestward of Osborn Bay, between it and Horse-shoe Bay, is shoal for some distance off, deepening suddenly when ½ mile from the shore, and vessels should not approach it within that distance. The northern point of the North Shoal Island has a remarkable flat sandy spit, on which is built an Indian village; there are no passages between the small islands northward of this, and the bank dries 400 yards at low water. A rock awash at high water lies nearly ½ mile north of the southeasternmost Shoal Island.

Horse-shoe Bay will be known by a rather remarkable sharp point (Bare Point) bare at its extreme, which forms its eastern entrance. There is convenient anchorage for small vessels off the sawmill on the west side of the bay or within ¼ mile of its head in 8 fathoms, and within this distance it shoals suddenly from 5 to 2 fathoms.

Bird Reef, a rocky ledge uncovering at half tide, extends 200 yards from the shore, northwestward of the western point of entrance, and bears from Bare Point N. 79° W., ½ mile.

Oyster Harbor is 4 miles from Horse shoe Bay, the intervening coast being free from danger; the harbor is nearly one mile wide at the entrance, narrowing gradually within. Entering from the northward, Coffin Islet should be given a berth of 400 yards; there are no other dangers which are not visible; at low water the oyster beds dry for 400 yards off the western shore.

A Reef which covers at half flood extends 200 yards southward from the Twin Islands; ½ mile above this the harbor narrows to ¼ mile in width; the deepest water, from 5 to 3 fathoms, will be found at 200 yards off the western side of Long Island on the northern shore; on the western side are the oyster beds; small vessels may go as far up as the NW. end of Long Island, where 3 fathoms will be found at low water.

Anchorage.—A good anchorage for a large vessel is one mile inside the entrance in 9 fathoms, mud bottom, with the SE. end of Long Island bearing N. 37° W., and eastern extreme of Twin Islands bearing N. 22° E.; good anchorage may also be had in 6 fathoms, mud bottom, nearly ⅜ mile farther up the harbor, with the SE. end of Long Island bearing N. 28° W., and west end of Twin Islands bearing N. 6[illegible]° E.

Chemainos Bay is 2½ miles northward of the entrance of Oyster Harbor, and about the same distance westward of Reef Point, the NW. point of Thetis Island.

Anchorage may be had in 8 fathoms at ½ mile from its head, on a bank which projects from the southern shore, with Deer Point at the northern entrance of the bay bearing N. 68° E., and the southern trend of the coast bearing S. 33° E. It is open and can not be recommended, unless in fine weather, or with offshore winds. There are no dangers in working into it.

Yellow Point, bare and grassy at its extreme, is the northern point of Chemainos Bay; thence to Round Island, at the southern entrance of Dodd Narrows, the coast is moderately bold and free from danger. At 1½ miles southward of Round Island is a boat harbor, at the entrance of which a vessel may drop an anchor in 8 to 10 fathoms if waiting for the tide, though there is equally good anchorage nearer to the narrows

North Reef.—From the northern entrance of Sansum Narrows, on the eastern side, to North Reef, there are no dangers, and both shores may be approached boldly in working up, except, as before observed, the coast of Vancouver Island from the Shoal Islands to Bare Point of Horseshoe Bay, which should be given a berth of ½ mile.

North Reef is a sandstone ledge running in a northwesterly and southeasterly direction, as all the reefs in this channel do. It bears from the SE. point of Tent Island S. 60° W., ½ mile. It is just awash at high water, and therefore easily avoided; its shoal part extends in a NW., direction for ⅓ mile, steep on its northern and southern sides.

Tent Island lies off the southern extreme of Kuper Island; 200 yards off its southeastern end are two remarkable worn sandstone rocks 8 or 10 feet above water; the breadth of the passage between them and North Reef is ⅓ mile. Eastward nearly 100 yards from the southeast- [illegible] of Tent, is a rock which uncovers 2 feet. In passing eastward

> ([illegible]558) **BRITISH COLUMBIA—Vancouver island—East coast—Stuart channel—Escape reef—Beacon established.**—A pyramidal [illegible] beacon, 12 feet square at the base, surmounted by a staff carrying a latticework drum 8 feet high and 8 feet in diameter, the whole painted white, and showing 20 feet above high watermark, has been erected by the Government of Canada on Escape reef, Stuart channel
>
> Approx. position. Lat. 48° 56′ 46″ N., Long. 123° 39′ 40″ W.
>
> The reef covers 4 feet at high water. The beacon stands on a bed of concrete 2 feet deep (N. M. 44, 1904.)

Leading mark.—Yellow Point, just open westward of Scott Island, off Preedy Harbor, bearing N. 25° W., leads 600 yards westward of the [illegible].

Alarm Rock is scarcely in the track of vessels working up Stuart Channel. It lies 200 yards S. 34° W of the SE. point of Hudson Island, the southeasternmost of the group of islands, which lie off the western sides of Kuper and Thetis Islands, facing Preedy and Telegraph Harbors. It just covers at high water, and is connected by a ledge with Hudson Island.

water by reefs and mud banks, and which form the northern side of the bay; the southeasternmost of these islands lies N. 33° W., a little over 2 miles from the northwestern entrance point of Sansum Narrows. The bay affords good anchorage, sheltered from the prevailing winds from the westward and southeast The best anchorage is with the southeasternmost Shoal Island, in one with Southey Point, and the southern trend of the coast S 50° E.

The coast no thwestward of Osborn Bay, between it and Horse-shoe Bay, is shoal for so ance off, deepening suddenly when ½ mile from the shore, and vess hould not approach it within that distance. The northern point of the North Shoal Island has a remarkable flat sandy spit, on which is built an Indian village; there are no passages between the small islands northward of this, and the bank dries 400 yards at low water. A rock awash at high water lies nearly ½ mile north of the southeasternmost Shoal Island.

Horse-shoe Bay will be known by a rather remarkable sharp point (Bare Point) bare at its extreme, which forms its eastern entrance. There is convenient anchorage for small vessels off the sawmill on the west side of the bay or within ¼ mile of its head in 8 fathoms, and within this distance it shoals suddenly from 5 to 2 fathoms.

Bird Reef, a rocky ledge uncovering at half tide, extends 200 yards from the shore, northwestward of the western point of entrance, and bears from Bare Point N. 79° W., ½ mile

Oyster Harbor is 4 miles from Horse shoe Bay, the intervening coast being free from danger; the harbor is nearly one mile wide at the entrance, narrowing gradually within. Entering from the northward, Coffin Islet should be given a berth of 400 yards; there are no other danger

400 yar

A Re

the Twi

width;

yards o

the wes

the NV

water.

Anchorage.—A good anchorage for a large vessel is one mile inside the entrance in 9 fathoms, mud bottom, with the SE. end of Long Island bearing N. 37° W., and eastern extreme of Twin Islands bearing N 22° E.; good anchorage may also be had in 6 fathoms, mud bottom, nearly ¾ mile farther up the harbor, with the SE end of Long Island bearing N. 28° W., and west end of Twin Islands bearing N. 62° E.

Chemainos Bay is 2½ miles northward of the entrance of Oyster Harbor, and about the same distance westward of Reef Point, the NW. point of Thetis Island.

Anchorage may be had in 8 fathoms at ½ mile from its head, on a bank which projects from the southern shore, with Deer Point at the northern entrance of the bay bearing N. 68° E., and the southern trend of the coast bearing S. 33° E. It is open and can not be recommended, unless in fine weather, or with offshore winds There are no dangers in working into it.

Yellow Point, bare and grassy at its extreme, is the northern point of Chemainus Bay; thence to Round Island, at the southern entrance of Dodd Narrows, the coast is moderately bold and free from danger. At 1½ miles southward of Round Island is a boat harbor, at the entrance of which a vessel may drop an anchor in 8 to 10 fathoms if waiting for the tide, though there is equally good anchorage nearer to the narrows.

North Reef—From the northern entrance of Sansum Narrows, on the eastern side, to North Reef, there are no dangers, and both shores may be approached boldly in working up, except, as before observed, the coast of Vancouver Island from the Shoal Islands to Bare Point of Horseshoe Bay, which should be given a berth of ½ mile.

North Reef is a sandstone ledge running in a northwesterly and southeasterly direction, as all the reefs in this channel do. It bears from the SE. point of Tent Island S. 60° W., ½ mile. It is just awash at high water, and therefore easily avoided; its shoal part extends in a NW., direction for ⅓ mile, steep on its northern and southern sides.

Tent Island lies off the southern extreme of Kuper Island; 200 yards off its southeastern end are two remarkable worn sandstone rocks 8 or 10 feet above water; the breadth of the passage between them and North Reef is ¼ mile. Eastward nearly 400 yards from the southeastern end of Tent, is a rock which uncovers 2 feet. In passing eastward of Tent, its eastern shore should be given a berth of ½ mile, as some rocky ledges extend off it. There is no ship passage between Tent and Kuper Islands, being only one fathom deep at low water.

Escape Reef at 2 miles N. 36° W. of North Reef, is a dangerous patch, which covers at quarter flood, and has no kelp to mark its position. It lies nearly ½ mile from the western shore of Kuper Island, with Josling Point, its southern point, bearing S. 70° E., 1¼ miles. There is a deep channel ⅛ mile wide between it and Kuper Island. The two entrance points of Sansum Narrows, just touching lead on to the reef.

Leading mark.—Yellow Point, just open westward of Scott Island, off Preedy Harbor, bearing N. 25° W., leads 600 yards westward of the reef.

Alarm Rock is scarcely in the track of vessels working up Stuart Channel. It lies 200 yards S. 34° W. of the SE. point of Hudson Island, the southeasternmost of the group of islands, which lie off the western sides of Kuper and Thetis Islands, facing Preedy and Telegraph Harbors. It just covers at high water, and is connected by a ledge with Hudson Island.

False Reef lies 700 yards N. 50° W. of Scott Island, the northwestward of the group just mentioned, and a long ½ mile S 62° W. of Crescent Point, the NE. point of Preedy Harbor; it covers at half flood

White Rock, about 30 yards long, and 15 feet above high water, lies one mile north of Reef Point, the northwestern extreme of Thetis Island; a bank having from 2 to 5 fathoms water on it extends 400 yards northwestward from the rock. This rock has a whitish appearance, and is readily distinguished from a vessel's deck at a distance of 2 or 3 miles. It should not be passed within 400 yards, and there is a good passage between it and Thetis Island, giving Reef Point a berth of ½ mile to avoid a rocky ledge extending nearly that distance northwestward from it

Ragged Island, a low rocky islet, with a few trees on it, lies ¼ mile N. 45° W. of Pilkey Point, the north end of Thetis Island, with a passage of 12 fathoms water between them. There are no dangers 200 yards from the islet.

Danger Reef, lying one mile N. 17° W. of White Rock, and 1½ miles N. 56° E. of Yellow Point, covers a space of ½ mile almost in the center of the channel. A small portion of it is generally awash at high water, at which time it is difficult to make out until within a short distance of it.

Directions.—When passing through Stuart Channel there is a clear passage one mile in breadth between Danger Reef and the Vancouver Island shore, and going either up or down the channel, White Rock kept in line with the NE. extreme of Thetis Island, bearing S. 45° E., leads to the westward of the reef. Bound southward through Stuart Channel from Dodd Narrows, pass at from 200 to 400 yards eastward of Round Island, and steer for the westernmost ragged tree summit of Thetis Island, S 30° E; this course leads in mid channel and over ½ mile westward of Danger Reef and White Rock; when the latter bears S 67° E., alter course to south for Stuart Channel, avoiding shoal water north of Reef Point.

Vesuvius Bay, on the western side of Admiral Island, immediately opposite Osborn Bay, has deep water, but shoals suddenly at its head.

There is anchorage inside Idol Islet, in Houston Passage. This islet is S. 80° E about one mile from the southern end of Tent Island, and is 600 yards from Admiral Island; with the islet bearing N. 56° W. midway between it and the shore, there is anchorage in 6 fathoms.

Grappler Reef, on the eastern side of Houston Passage, is 200 yards in extent and uncovers at very low water. It lies ¼ mile off the northwestern end of Admiral Island Passing through Houston Passage, the eastern point of Sansum Narrows kept well open of the points of Admiral Island to the northward of it, leads westward of the reef, and when the southern point of Secretary Island is open of Southey Point, it is cleared to the northward.

Telegraph Harbor, on the west side of Kuper Island, is a snug anchorage, and its entrance is between Hudson Island and Active Point, which are ½ mile apart. Entering from the southward, if passing inside Escape

Reef, the shore of the island should be kept aboard within ¼ mile, if outside or westward, keep Yellow Point just open westward of Scott Island until Upright Cliff of Kuper Island bears N. 68° E., when a vessel will be well to the northward of it, and may steer for the entrance of the harbor, which is free from danger, with the exception of Alarm Rock, extending from the southeastern point of Hudson Island.

There is good anchorage in 8 fathoms with the NW. end of Hudson Island bearing west and distant about ½ mile.

Preedy Harbor is separated from the one just described by a group of small islands and reefs; its entrance is to the northward of them between Scott Island and Crescent Point of Thetis Island, and is ¼ mile in breadth. When entering, the Thetis Island shore should be kept aboard to avoid False Reef

tt and

earing
Island

tward
east.
tween
orgia.

anson
h and
thern.
anges
harbor on its eastern side.

Over Burgoyne Bay, on the western side, Mount Baynes rises to an elevation of 1,953 feet, and is very remarkable, its southern face being a perpendicular precipice, visible a long distance from the southward or eastward. The Otter range, of somewhat less elevation, rises northward of Mount Baynes, from whence the island slopes away in a wedge-shape, its northern termination, Southey Point, being a sharp extreme. The island is for the most part thickly wooded, but there is a considerable extent of partially clear land both in the valley at the head of Fulford Harbor and at the northern end.

Fulford Harbor penetrates the southeastern side of Admiral Island in a northwesterly direction for 2½ miles. At its entrance is Russell Island, between which and Isabella Point, the western point of the harbor, is the best passage in.

Cecil Rock, with one fathom on it, lies S. 42° E., ⅛ mile from the southern point of Russell Island. The breadth of the southern entrance is ⅜ mile, with a depth of 20 fathoms until abreast North Rock; here the harbor narrows, and carries a general breadth almost to its head of something less than ½ mile.

False Reef lies 700 yards N. 50° W. of Scott Island, the northwestward of the group just mentioned, and a long ½ mile S. 62° W. of Crescent Point, the NE. point of Preedy Harbor; it covers at half flood.

White Rock, about 30 yards long, and 15 feet above high water, lies one mile north of Reef Point, the northwestern extreme of Thetis Island; a bank having from 2 to 5 fathoms water on it extends 400 yards northwestward from the rock. This rock has a whitish appearance, and is readily distinguished from a vessel's deck at a distance of 2 or 3 miles. It should not be passed within 400 yards, and there is a good passage between it and Thetis Island, giving Reef Point a berth of ½ mile to avoid a rocky ledge extending nearly that distance northwestward from it.

Ragged Island, a low rocky islet, with a few trees on it, lies ¼ mile N. 47° W. of Pilkey Point, the north end of Thetis Island, with a passage of

(1559) **BRITISH COLUMBIA—Vancouver Island—East coast—Stuart channel—Danger reef—Light on beacon.**—Referring to Notice to Mariners No 22 (1100) of 1903, the Canadian Government has given further notice that in consequence of the threatened collapse of the wreck of the steamer *Miami*, the light shown therefrom was, on October 1, 1904, discontinued, and has been replaced by a similar light shown from the summit of a small wooden tower, painted white, standing on a wooden framework foundation, painted black.

The light is shown from a 31-day Wigham lamp fixed inside the framework of the wooden beacon

Approx. position. Lat. 49° 03′ 42″ N., Long. 123° 42′ 43″ W

The light is a *fixed white* light, elevated about 24 feet above high watermark and should be visible 9 miles from all points of approach by water.

The illuminating apparatus consists of a pressed glass lens

The light is unwatched. When passing to southward, it should be given a berth of at least 600 yards (N. M. 44, 1904.)

[illegible] White Rock, when the latter bears S. [illegible] E., alter course to south for Stuart Channel, avoiding shoal water north of Reef Point.

Vesuvius Bay, on the western side of Admiral Island, immediately opposite Osborn Bay, has deep water, but shoals suddenly at its head.

There is anchorage inside Idol Islet, in Houston Passage. This islet is S. 80° E about one mile from the southern end of Tent Island, and is 600 yards from Admiral Island; with the islet bearing N. 56° W. midway between it and the shore, there is anchorage in 6 fathoms.

Grappler Reef, on the eastern side of Houston Passage, is 200 yards in extent and uncovers at very low water. It lies ¼ mile off the northwestern end of Admiral Island. Passing through Houston Passage, the eastern point of Sansum Narrows kept well open of the points of Admiral Island to the northward of it, leads westward of the reef, and when the southern point of Secretary Island is open of Southey Point, it is cleared to the northward.

Telegraph Harbor, on the west side of Kuper Island, is a snug anchorage, and its entrance is between Hudson Island and Active Point, which are ½ mile apart. Entering from the southward, if passing inside Escape

Reef, the shore of the island should be kept aboard within ¼ mile; if outside or westward, keep Yellow Point just open westward of Scott Island until Upright Cliff of Kuper Island bears N. 68° E., when a vessel will be well to the northward of it, and may steer for the entrance of the harbor, which is free from danger, with the exception of Alarm Rock, extending from the southeastern point of Hudson Island.

There is good anchorage in 8 fathoms with the NW. end of Hudson Island bearing west and distant about ½ mile.

Preedy Harbor is separated from the one just described by a group of small islands and reefs; its entrance is to the northward of them between Scott Island and Crescent Point of Thetis Island, and is ¼ mile in breadth. When entering, the Thetis Island shore should be kept aboard to avoid False Reef, a patch which covers at half tide.

Shoal water extends for 300 yards off the northern sides of Scott and Dayman Islands.

Anchorage will be found in 7 fathoms, with Crescent Point bearing N. 45° W., distant nearly ½ mile, and east point of Dayman Island bearing S. 34° W.

Swanson Channel leads from the Haro Strait to the northwestward between Admiral Island on the west and Pender Island on the east. Passing eastward of Prevost Island it enters the Active Pass between Galiano and Mayne Islands and thence into the Strait of Georgia. Northward of Active Pass it connects with Trincomalie Channel.

Admiral Island, separating Stuart from Trincomalie and Swanson Channels, is of considerable extent, being nearly 15 miles in length and varying in breadth from 2 miles at its northern end to 6 at its southern. It has two good ports—Fulford Harbor on its southeastern and Ganges Harbor on its eastern side.

Over Burgoyne Bay, on the western side, Mount Baynes rises to an elevation of 1,953 feet, and is very remarkable, its southern face being a perpendicular precipice, visible a long distance from the southward or eastward. The Otter range, of somewhat less elevation, rises northward of Mount Baynes, from whence the island slopes away in a wedge shape, its northern termination, Southey Point, being a sharp extreme. The island is for the most part thickly wooded, but there is a considerable extent of partially clear land both in the valley at the head of Fulford Harbor and at the northern end.

Fulford Harbor penetrates the southeastern side of Admiral Island in a northwesterly direction for 2½ miles. At its entrance is Russell Island, between which and Isabella Point, the western point of the harbor, is the best passage in.

Cecil Rock, with one fathom on it, lies S. 42° E., ⅛ mile from the southern point of Russell Island. The breadth of the southern entrance is ⅜ mile, with a depth of 20 fathoms until abreast North Rock; here the harbor narrows, and carries a general breadth almost to its head of something less than ½ mile.

North Rock is a small rocky islet lying close off the northern side of the harbor, a rock which covers at quarter flood lies westward of it, and more than 300 yards offshore, so that strangers entering should keep rather to the westward of mid channel until past it. Mount Baynes appears very remarkable from the harbor, rising immediately over its head almost as a perpendicular cliff. Immediately over the northern side of the harbor is Reginald hill, a stony elevation between 700 and 800 feet high; with this hill bearing east there is good anchorage in 10 fathoms in the center of the harbor; at the head of the harbor is a considerable fresh-water stream, from which shoal water extends for 600 yards.

The northern passage into the harbor between Russell Island and Eleanor Point, though in places not more than ¼ mile in breadth, is a safe channel.

Louisa Rock, with only one fathom on it, is the only danger; it lies 400 yards from the northern or Admiral Island shore, with the western end of Russell Island bearing S 17° E., 800 yards, and North Rock west the same distance; with a leading wind the Russell Island shore should be kept rather aboard.

Ganges Harbor is a safe and commodious port for vessels of any description or size. Its southern entrance in the Swanson Channel lies between Admiral and Prevost Islands, and has no dangers which are not visible. The Channel Islets may be passed on either side, but to the northward is by far the widest passage, they are two small wooded islands, 1½ miles within Beaver Point

Liddell Point, the southeastern extreme of Prevost Island, and the northern entrance point of the harbor, has a reef which is covered at half flood extending 400 yards southeastward from it.

The Acland Islands, two in number, lie to the northwestward of Liddell Point along the shore of Prevost Island, between which and them there is no ship channel.

Directions—The fair channel into the harbor, between the Channel and Acland Islands, is nearly ½ mile wide, having passed these islands, the harbor is nearly 1½ miles wide, and the general depth for 2 miles is from 20 to 13 fathoms.

There are but few dangers in working into the harbor, and they are easily avoided. A rocky patch with one fathom water on it lies 550 yards N. 65° W. of the west point of the westernmost Acland Island, and the same distance off shore. There is another one fathom patch which is more in the track of vessels. it lies nearly 2 miles N. 50° W. of the southernmost Channel Islet, and is ½ mile from the Admiral Island side of the harbor; there is a clear passage 600 yards wide, the depth being 14 fathoms, southward of the patch; to the northward of it the passage is ¼ mile wide, with depths of from 13 to 21 fathoms.

The Chain Islands are a group of 6 or 7 low narrow islets connected by reefs, extending from the head of the harbor in a SE. direction for

$1\frac{1}{2}$ miles. To the southward of these islands the ground is clear but to the northward of them are scattered reefs, and vessels are not recommended to anchor on that side above the outermost island

Anchorage.—A vessel may anchor as soon as a depth of 10 or 12 fathoms is found; a good berth is in 11 fathoms water with Peile Point, and the two entrance points of Long Harbor nearly in line bearing N. 56° E., and the easternmost Chain Island N. 45° W. If desirable, anchorage may be had in 6 fathoms, mud, midway between the Chain Islands and the south shore, the easternmost island bearing east, or in a still snugger berth one mile above, off the sandy spit on Admiral Island, in 4 or 5 fathoms. This latter berth is recommended for vessels of moderate size intending to make any stay

Captain Passage also leads into Ganges Harbor, to the northward of Prevost Island. It is a clear deep passage, $\frac{1}{4}$ mile wide; vessels from the northward intending to enter the harbor should always use it. There is only one danger, which is well inside Ganges Harbor, and which is almost equally in the track of vessels working up by the southern passage; it is a small patch of 2 fathoms lying 700 yards S. 79° W of the western entrance point of Long Harbor. Entering by Captain Passage, Peile Point should not be shut in by the entrance points of Long Harbor until the opening between Prevost and Acland Islands is shut in, when this reef will be well cleared. When working up by the southern channel, a vessel should not stand so far to the eastward, when in the neighborhood of this patch, as to open out the passage between Acland and Prevost Islands.

Long Harbor may be almost considered as part of Ganges Harbor. Its entrance is between two sloping, rocky points, similar to each other, on the northern side of Captain Passage. At $\frac{1}{4}$ mile within the entrance is a high, bare islet, which must be passed on its southern side; one mile within is another island, somewhat similar, which may be passed on either side At the head is a snug place for a ship to repair, etc, but as a harbor, it is only adapted to steamers or coasters.

Prevost Island, lying in the center of Swanson Channel, is moderately high, thickly wooded, and of an irregular shape. On its southern and western sides it is indented by several bays and creeks; its northern side is almost a straight cliffy shore.

Ellen Bay, on the southeastern side of Prevost, between Liddell and Red Island Points, affords fair anchorage with all but southeasterly winds in 10 fathoms, mud. The head of this bay is a grassy, swampy flat, the distance between which and the creeks on the western shore is only 200 yards.

There are two bays northward of Ellen Bay, but too small to afford any shelter.

Annette and Glenthorne Creeks, on the western or Ganges harbor side, are curious, narrow indentations running into the island for a mile in a S. 56° E. direction, and only separated from each other by a narrow, stony ridge. In the western one, Glenthorne, there are 3 fathoms, the other has 1½ fathoms; they are snug places for small craft or for a vessel to repair.

James Bay, in the northwestern side of the island, and on the southern side of Captain Passage, offers fair but confined anchorage in 10 fathoms for a vessel of moderate size sheltered from southerly winds. There are 18 to 20 fathoms in the outer part of the bay.

Hawkins Island is a small rocky islet with a few bushes on it lying close off a remarkable white shell-beach, on the northeastern side of Prevost Island. From 100 to 700 yards N. 62° W. of its northwestern point are the Charles Rocks, three smooth topped rocks, not marked by kelp, and uncovering towards low water

Active Pass.—From Discovery Island, in the southern entrance of Haro Channel, to the sand heads of Fraser River, by the Active Pass, is just 40 miles, and the line is almost a straight one. By adopting this route, not only the most dangerous and inconvenient part of the Haro Strait is avoided, viz., its northern entrance abreast the east point of Saturna Island and Patos Island, where the tides are strong and apt to set vessels down Rosario Strait or over on the eastern shore, but a distance of nearly 10 miles is saved.

The southern point of entrance to Active Pass, Helen Point, is low, bare, and of a yellowish color; over its northern side rise the high, stony hills on the southern side of Galiano Island; the entrance itself does not become very apparent until it is approached within a mile.

Active Pass takes an easterly direction for 1½ miles, and then turns north for the same distance, fairly into the Strait of Georgia. The average breadth of the channel is about ⅓ mile, and its general depth about 20 fathoms; there are no hidden dangers with the exception of a small rock off Laura Point, on which there is said to be a depth of only a few feet, and which should therefore not be closely approached; and at ¼ mile within the western entrance, and very close off the northern shore, a rock which uncovers at half tide. The great strength of the tides, together with the absence of steady winds, renders the pass unfit for sailing vessels, unless small coasters. It is an excellent channel for steamers, but it is advisable for large ships and those deeply laden to pass through at or near slack water.

Otter Bay, on the western side of Pender Island, would serve as a good stopping place if overtaken by night or waiting for the tide. A fair anchorage in 8 fathoms may be had in the center of the bay. Ellen Bay might also be used for this purpose.

Miners Bay, on the southern side of Active Pass, affords anchorage if necessary, but vessels must go close in to get 12 fathoms, and then are barely out of the whirl of the tide.

Directions.—After entering Swanson Channel, between Admiral and Pender Islands, steer to pass to the eastward of Prevost Island, and keep Pelorus Point (eastern extreme of Moresby Island) open of Monatt

Point (the western extreme of Pender Island) bearing S. 19° E., which will lead westward of Enterprise Reef, and when Helen Point bears N. 31° E., or the northern beacon comes well open west of the southern one, the reef will be cleared, and the entrance of the pass may be steered for. There is a passage inside Enterprise Reef which may be taken when both kelp patches can be seen. If coming out of Navy Channel, between Pender and Mayne Islands, a vessel should keep over for Prevost Island until Pelorus Point is open of Moncatt Point; these two points in line, or just touching, lead very close on Enterprise Reef. On the western side of Swanson Channel, the reef which lies 400 yards ... Red and Bright

berth

flood,
is the
sh un-

Pass,
int on
ctions
hence
The

dened
t time
essels

should
ide of

from
in the

tides,
y tide
ie tide
r less
kelp

Trincomalie Channel commences at Active Pass, from the southern entrance of which its general direction is NW for 24 miles, when it enters the Dodd Narrows.

This channel must be classed as a channel for steamers or coasters; it can only be used with advantage by vessels bound to the eastern ports of Vancouver Island below Nanaimo, or by such as choose to enter Nanaimo itself by the Dodd Narrows

row, stony ridge. In the western one, Glenthorne, there are 3 fathoms, the other has 1½ fathoms; they are snug places for small craft or for a vessel to repair.

James Bay, in the northwestern side of the island, and on the southern side of Captain Passage, offers fair but confined anchorage in 10 fathoms for a vessel of moderate size sheltered from southerly winds. There are 13 to 20 fathoms in the outer part of the bay.

Hawkins Island is a small rocky islet with a few bushes on it lying close off a remarkable white shell-beach, on the northeastern side of Prevost Island. From 400 to 700 yards N. 62° W. of its northwestern point [illegible] Rocks, three smooth-topped rocks, not marked by kelp.

(1761) **BRITISH COLUMBIA—Strait of Georgia—Active pass—Hydrographic notes.**—Commander J F Parry, R N., H B. M. surveying ship *Egeria*, reports the following notes consequent upon the resurvey lately by him of Active pass.

A rocky patch having several heads with 5 feet over them at low water was found 260 yards offshore in the bay on the Galiano Island side of the southern entrance to the pass, from which pass Helen point bears S 9° W true (S by E ⅛ E mag), 900 yards This shoal lies (approximately) in the position of the 17 fathoms shown in the center of the bay on H. O. chart No. 1769.

This danger is well marked by kelp in summer and autumn

A rocky head having a depth of 18 feet over it at low water was found lying 140 yards from the shore to the north of Helen point From this head Helen point bears S 44° W. true (S. by W. ¾ W. mag.), 260 yards. There is deep water close to on the outer side of this danger. This is not marked by kelp.

An examination of the shoals lying to the northward of Georgina point, a rocky head with 5 feet over it at low water, was found in the position of the 1½ fathoms shown on H O chart No 1769

The 7-fathom shoal shown in the center of the northern entrance to the pass was found to lie about 200 yards farther to the westward, and has a least depth of 30 feet over it at low water.

From this 30-foot head Active Pass lighthouse bears S 64° E true (E. ⅛ S. S'ly mag), 1,040 yards. This shoal is usually plainly marked by heavy tide rips.

Mary Anne point, the eastern extreme of Galiano island and opposite Miners bay, bearing S. 33° W. true (S. ¼ W. W'ly mag.), is a good line for entering or leaving the northern end of the pass

The rock immediately to the northward of and close under Helen point, shown on H O charts Nos. 1769 and 1815 as drying 2 feet, dries 6 feet at low water, and the rock on the opposite shore at Galiano island, shown as bearing N 12° W true (NW. ¾ N N'ly mag), 700 yards from Helen point, dries 8 feet at low water (N M 50, 1904)

might also be used for this purpose.

Miners Bay, on the southern side of Active Pass, affords anchorage if necessary, but vessels must go close in to get 12 fathoms, and then are barely out of the whirl of the tide.

Directions.—After entering Swanson Channel, between Admiral and Pender Islands, steer to pass to the eastward of Prevost Island, and keep Pelorus Point (eastern extreme of Moresby Island) open of Mouatt

Point (the western extreme of Pender Island) bearing S. 19° E., which will lead westward of Enterprise Reef, and when Helen Point bears N. 34° E., or the northern beacon comes well open west of the southern one, the reef will be cleared, and the entrance of the pass may be steered for. There is a passage inside Enterprise Reef which may be taken when both kelp patches can be seen. If coming out of Navy Channel, between Pender and Mayne Islands, a vessel should keep over for Prevost Island until Pelorus Point is open of Moatt Point; these two points in line, or just touching, lead very close on Enterprise Reef. On the western side of Swanson Channel, the reef which lies 400 yards eastward from Liddell Point must be avoided, and Red and Bright Islands, off the points to the northward of it, should be given a berth of 200 yards.

When passing through Active Pass to the westward against the flood, a vessel should keep rather on the southern shore of the pass, as the tide sets over towards the rock near the western entrance, which uncovers at half tide.

When entering or passing out of the eastern entrance of Active Pass, the point of Gossip Island on the west, and also Georgina Point on the east, should be given a good berth; indeed, the best directions which can be given are to pass through in mid-channel. From thence the sand heads of Fraser River bear N. 3° E., distant 11 miles. The sand-head buoys are visible from a distance of 2 or 3 miles.

Caution.—It is dangerous for vessels of heavy draft or deeply laden to attempt the passage at the full strength of the tide, as at that time an undercurrent has, in several instances, been felt and caused vessels to run ashore from refusing to answer their helms.

The Gossip Island buoys at the northern entrance of the pass should not be approached within 600 yards, as there is foul ground outside of them.

Tides.—The flood tide in Active Pass sets from west to east, or from the Swanson Channel into the Strait of Georgia; and the ebb in the contrary direction.

The velocity during springs is sometimes 7 knots; at ordinary tides, from 3 to 5. In the northern entrance there is sometimes a heavy tide rip, caused by a patch of 7 and 9 fathoms, and by the meeting of the tide through the pass with that in the strait; no favorable eddy, or less strength of tide, will be found on either side, unless within the kelp which lines the shores.

Trincomalie Channel commences at Active Pass, from the southern entrance of which its general direction is NW. for 24 miles, when it enters the Dodd Narrows.

This channel must be classed as a channel for steamers or coasters; it can only be used with advantage by vessels bound to the eastern ports of Vancouver Island below Nanaimo, or by such as choose to enter Nanaimo itself by the Dodd Narrows.

The eastern side of the channel is formed by the long narrow islands of Galiano and Valdes, and the western by Admiral, Kuper, and Thetis Islands; some smaller islands are scattered over it, and there are also several rocks which require to be known. Montague Harbor, on the western side of Galiano Island, is a good stopping place, also Clam Bay on the eastern side of Thetis Island.

Trincomalie Channel contracts in breadth when abreast Narrow Island, but the shores are bold on either side. On the shore of Galiano Island, N. 68° E., one mile from the southeastern point of Narrow Island, is Retreat Cove, offering shelter for boats or anchorage for coasters; an island lies in the center of it.

Portier and Gabriola Passes lead into the Strait of Georgia; both are intricate and dangerous, and the tides are so strong, and varying in their set, that vessels would not be justified in using the passes unless in cases of emergency.

Montague Harbor is formed between the southwestern side of Galiano Island and Parker Island, and its entrance, between Phillimore Point and the small island of Julia, is 1¾ miles N. 45° W. from the western entrance of Active Pass. The entrance is but little over 200 yards in breadth, but has deep water, and is free from danger; immediately within the points it widens out to ¼ mile, and anchorage may be obtained in the arm which leads to the harbor, which though small is a snug and secure anchorage, with good holding ground. There is a narrow passage to the northwestward from this harbor into the Trincomalie channel.

Several smaller islands extend NW. of Parker Island, viz, Sphinx, Charles, Wise, and Twin Islands, the latter two rather remarkable rocky islets about 30 feet high. A rock which uncovers at low water springs is said to be 400 yards N. 51° W. of the Twin Islands.

Atkins Reef lies on the western side of Trincomalie Channel, ⅓ mile from the shore of Admiral Island, and in the track of vessels working up or down. It is 200 yards in extent, and covers at 4 feet flood, its neighborhood being marked by kelp, which is rarely seen when there is any ripple on the water. The reef bears from Peile Point N. 50° W., 3⅓ miles; from the Twin Islands S. 17° W., 1⅛ miles. The SW. abrupt tangent of Galiano Island in one with Mount Parke, a remarkable bare-topped conical hill on the southern side of Active Pass, bearing S. 64° E., leads well outside Atkins Reef.

Walker Hook is formed by a peninsula or tongue of land projecting from Admiral Island, 4 miles northwestward of the Captain Passage. On its SE. side is fair anchorage for small vessels in 6 fathoms, but a shoal patch marked by kelp, ⅛ mile in extent, lies 400 yards eastward of the southeastern point of the peninsula; small vessels may pass between the shoal and the point in 5 fathoms, or between it and Atkins Reef, which is better, and anchor in 6 fathoms, 400 yards southward of the neck of the peninsula. There is also anchorage in 10 fathoms northward of the peninsula, but vessels must not go within the northern point of the tongue of land forming the hook, as it dries a long way out.

Governor Rock, a dangerous rocky patch lying almost in the center of Trincomalie Channel, has 4 feet on it at low water, is about 100 yards in extent, and though kelp grows on it, yet it is very difficult to make out until quite close to. It lies 1⅝ miles N. 76° W. of Twin Islands and 1¼ miles N. 11° W. of the SE. point of Walker Hook. Quadra Hill rises from the center of Galiano Island to the height of 750 feet, and a remarkable white basaltic cliff will be seen on the coast immediately

(1193) **BRITISH COLUMBIA — Trincomali channel — Walker rock — Change in color of beacon.**—The Canadian Government has given notice that the concrete lower portion of Walker Rock beacon, Trincomali channel, will be changed in color from black to *white*, without further notice, so that in future both the beacon and the tower surmounting it will be white.

Approx. position: Lat. 48° 55′ 28″ N., Long. 123° 29′ 40″ W.

and white on north and south, is erected on the Walke. (N. M. 31, 1905.)

These two rocks are the principal dangers to be avoided in the southern part of Trincomalie Channel; they are both steep-to, and may be passed if necessary at 100 yards.

Directions.—In passing up or down Trincomalie Channel, vessels may either take the passage westward of Governor Rock or that between it and Walker Rock, or eastward of the latter. In taking the western passage, after having cleared Atkins Reef and the shoal off Walker Hook, the shore of Admiral Island, which is bold, should be kept aboard within ½ mile, until Quadra Hill bears N. 68° E., when they will be to westward of both rocks, and may steer north over towards Galiano Island, giving the southeastern end of Narrow Island a berth of at least ½ mile, as a reef extends off it.

If passing between the two rocks, the marks for a mid-channel course ... point of Thetis Island kept well open of the east- ... with these ... not to open ... sland as to ... it on to the ... uld be kept just halfway between the eastern side of Narrow and ... stern side of Hall Islands; these marks are very clear and well defined, and are generally seen from a long distance. In passing to the southward, when the SE. point of Walker Hook bears S. 23° W. vessels will be well southward of the rocks.

If passing eastward of Walker Rock, when bound up the channel, keep Parker and Wise Islands aboard within ½ mile; there are no dangers off them. When abreast Twin Island, which may be passed within 600 yards, haul in to the northward until Mount Sutil on the southern end of Galiano Island is in line with Charles Island bearing S. 53° E.;

The eastern side of the channel is formed by the long narrow islands of Galiano and Valdes, and the western by Admiral, Kuper, and Thetis Islands, some smaller islands are scattered over it, and there are also several rocks which require to be known. Montague Harbor, on the western side of Galiano Island, is a good stopping place, also Clam Bay on the eastern side of Thetis Island

Trincomalie Channel contracts in breadth when abreast Narrow Island, but the shores are bold on either side. On the shore of Galiano Island, N 68° E, one mile from the southeastern point of Narrow Island, is Retreat Cove, offering shelter for boats or anchorage for coasters; an island lies in the center of it.

Portier and Gabriola Passes lead into the Strait of Georgia; both are intricate and dangerous, and the tides are so strong, and varying in their set, that vessels would not be justified in using the passes unless in cases of emergency.

Montague Harbor is formed between the southwestern side of Galiano Island and Parker Island, and its entrance, between Phillimore Point and the small island of Julia, is 1¼ miles N. 45° W. from the western entrance of Active Pass The entrance is but little over 200 yards in breadth, but has deep water, and is free from danger, immediately within the points it widens out to ½ mile, and anchorage may be obtained in the arm which leads to the harbor, which though small is a snug and secure anchorage, with good holding ground There is a narrow passage to the northwestward from this harbor into the Trincomalie channel.

Several smaller islands extend NW. of Parker Island, viz, Sphinx, Charles, Wise, and Twin Islands, the latter two rather remarkable rocky islets about 30 feet high. A rock which uncovers at low water springs is said to be 400 yards N. 51° W. of the Twin Islands

Atkins Reef lies on the western side of Trincomalie Channel ¼ mile

(1194) **BRITISH COLUMBIA — Trincomali channel — Atkins reef—Change in color of beacon.**—Referring to Notice to Mariners No. 34 (817) of 1899, the Canadian Government has given further notice that Atkins Reef beacon, including the staff and ball, will be changed in color from black to *white* without further notice.

Approx. position Lat 48° 53′ N., Long 123° 28′ W.

(N. M 81, 1905.)

[illegible] bare-topped conical hill on the southern side of Active Pass, bearing S. 64° E., leads well outside Atkins Reef.

Walker Hook is formed by a peninsula or tongue of land projecting from Admiral Island, 4 miles northwestward of the Captain Passage. On its SE. side is fair anchorage for small vessels in 6 fathoms, but a shoal patch marked by kelp, ⅛ mile in extent, lies 400 yards eastward of the southeastern point of the peninsula; small vessels may pass between the shoal and the point in 5 fathoms, or between it and Atkins Reef, which is better, and anchor in 6 fathoms, 100 yards southward of the neck of the peninsula. There is also anchorage in 10 fath-ons northward of the peninsula, but vessels must not go within the northern point of the tongue of land forming the hook, as it dries a long way out.

Governor Rock, a dangerous rocky patch lying almost in the center of Trincomalie Channel, has 4 feet on it at low water, is about 100 yards in extent, and though kelp grows on it, yet it is very difficult to make out until quite close to. It lies 1⅜ miles N. 76° W. of Twin Islands and 1¼ miles N. 11° W. of the SE. point of Walker Hook. Quadra Hill rises from the center of Galiano Island to the height of 750 feet, and a remarkable white basaltic cliff will be seen on the coast immediately

(1193) **BRITISH COLUMBIA — Trincomali channel — Walker rock — Change in color of beacon.**—The Canadian Government has given notice that the concrete lower portion of Walker Rock beacon, Trincomali channel, will be changed in color from black to *white*, without further notice, so that in future both the beacon and the tower surmounting it will be white.

Approx. position. Lat. 48° 55′ 28″ N., Long. 123° 29′ 40″ W.

and white on north and south, is erected on the Walke. (N. M. 31, 1905.)

These two rocks are the principal dangers to be avoided in the southern part of Trincomalie Channel; they are both steep to, and may be passed if necessary at 100 yards.

Directions.—In passing up or down Trincomalie Channel, vessels may either take the passage westward of Governor Rock or that between it and Walker Rock, or eastward of the latter. If taking the western passage, after having cleared Atkins Reef and the shoal off Walker Hook, the shore of Admiral Island, which is bold, should be kept aboard within ½ mile, until Quadra Hill bears N. 68° E., when they will be to westward of both rocks, and may steer north over towards Galiano Island, giving the southeastern end of Narrow Island a berth of at least ½ mile, as a reef extends off it.

If passing between the two rocks, the marks for a mid channel course are, the northeastern point of Thetis Island kept well open of the eastern side of Narrow Island, the latter bearing N. 50° W., steer with these marks on until Quadra Hill bears N. 68° E., taking care not to open the northeastern point of Thetis Island so much of Narrow Island as to bring the former on with Hall Island, as this would lead right on to the Walker Rock. The northeastern point of Thetis Island should be kept just halfway between the eastern side of Narrow and the western side of Hall Islands; these marks are very clear and well defined, and are generally seen from a long distance. In passing to the southward, when the SE. point of Walker Hook bears S. 23° W. vessels will be well southward of the rocks.

If passing eastward of Walker Rock, when bound up the channel, keep Parker and Wise Islands aboard within ½ mile; there are no dangers off them. When abreast Twin Island, which may be passed within 600 yards, haul in to the northward until Mount Sutil on the southern end of Galiano Island is in line with Charles Island bearing S. 53° E.;

The eastern side of the channel is formed by the long narrow islands of Galiano and Valdes, and the western by Admiral, Kuper, and Thetis Islands; some smaller islands are scattered over it, and there are also several rocks which require to be known. Montague Harbor, on the western side of Galiano Island, is a good stopping place, also Clam Bay on the eastern side of Thetis Island.

Trincomalie Channel contracts in breadth when abreast Narrow Island, but the shores are bold on either side. On the shore of Galiano Island, N 68° E, one mile from the southeastern point of Narrow Island, is Retreat Cove, offering shelter for boats or anchorage for coasters, an island lies in the center of it.

Po [illegible]
both [illegible]
ing n [illegible]
unless [illegible]

Mo [illegible]
liano I [illegible] ..., between Phillimore
Point [illegible] ...t of Julia, is 1¼ miles N 45° W. from the western entrance of Active Pass. The entrance is but little over 200 yards in breadth, but has deep water, and is free from danger; immediately within the points it widens out to ¼ mile, and anchorage may be obtained in the arm which leads to the harbor, which though small is a snug and secure anchorage, with good holding ground. There is a narrow passage to the northwestward from this harbor into the Trincomalie channel.

Several smaller islands extend NW. of Parker Island, viz, Sphinx, Charles, Wise, and Twin Islands, the latter two rather remarkable rocky islets about 30 feet high. A rock which uncovers at low water springs is said to be 400 yards N 51° W of the Twin Islands.

Atkins Reef lies on the western side of Trincomalie Channel, ¼ mile

(1194) **BRITISH COLUMBIA — Trincomali channel — Atkins reef—Change in color of beacon.**—Referring to Notice to Mariners No. 34 (817) of 1899, the Canadian Government has given further notice that Atkins Reef beacon, including the staff and ball, will be changed in color from black to *white* without further notice.

Approx. position. Lat. 48° 53′ N., Long. 123° 28′ W.

...gent of Galiano Island in one with Mount ... (N. M. 31, 1905.)

bare topped conical hill on the southern side of Active Pass, bearing S 64° E, leads well outside Atkins Reef.

Walker Hook is formed by a peninsula or tongue of land projecting from Admiral Island, 4 miles northwestward of the Captain Passage. On its SE. side is fair anchorage for small vessels in 6 fathoms, but a shoal patch marked by kelp, ¼ mile in extent, lies 400 yards eastward of the southeastern point of the peninsula; small vessels may pass between the shoal and the point in 5 fathoms, or between it and Atkins Reef, which is better, and anchor in 6 fathoms, 400 yards southward of the neck of the peninsula. There is also anchorage in 10 fathoms northward of the peninsula, but vessels must not go within the northern point of the tongue of land forming the hook, as it dries a long way out

Governor Rock, a dangerous rocky patch lying almost in the center of Trincomalie Channel, has 4 feet on it at low water, is about 100 yards in extent, and though kelp grows on it, yet it is very difficult to make out until quite close to. It lies 1$\frac{2}{3}$ miles N. 76° W. of Twin Islands and 1$\frac{1}{4}$ miles N. 11° W. of the SE. point of Walker Hook. Quadra Hill rises from the center of Galiano Island to the height of 750 feet, and a remarkable white basaltic cliff will be seen on the coast immediately southward of it. Governor Rock lies 1$\frac{1}{4}$ miles S. 45° W. of it.

Walker Rock lies $\frac{2}{3}$ mile N. 23° E. of Governor Rock, and covers at 4 feet rise. It lies 1$\frac{1}{3}$ miles S. 56° W. of Quadra Hill, and $\frac{3}{8}$ mile from the shore of Galiano Island.

A Beacon of stone, 8 feet high, surmounted by a staff 18 feet high, with cross pieces at right angles, painted black on east and west sides and white on north and south, is erected on the Walker Rock.

These two rocks are the principal dangers to be avoided in the southern part of Trincomalie Channel; they are both steep to, and may be passed if necessary at 100 yards.

Directions.—In passing up or down Trincomalie Channel, vessels may either take the passage westward of Governor Rock or that between it and Walker Rock, or eastward of the latter. If taking the western passage, after having cleared Atkins Reef and the shoal off Walker Hook, the shore of Admiral Island, which is bold, should be kept aboard within $\frac{1}{2}$ mile, until Quadra Hill bears N. 68° E., when they will be to westward of both rocks, and may steer north over towards Galiano Island, giving the southeastern end of Narrow Island a berth of at least $\frac{1}{2}$ mile, as a reef extends off it.

If passing between the two rocks, the marks for a mid channel course are, the northeastern point of Thetis Island kept well open of the eastern side of Narrow Island, the latter bearing N. 30° W.; steer with these marks on until Quadra Hill bears N. 68° E., taking care not to open the northeastern point of Thetis Island so much of Narrow Island as to bring the former on with Hall Island, as this would lead right on to the Walker Rock. The northeastern point of Thetis Island should be kept just halfway between the eastern side of Narrow and the western side of Hall Islands, these marks are very clear and well defined, and are generally seen from a long distance. In passing to the southward, when the SE. point of Walker Hook bears S. 23° W. vessels will be well southward of the rocks.

If passing eastward of Walker Rock, when bound up the channel, keep Parker and Wise Islands aboard within $\frac{1}{2}$ mile; there are no dangers off them. When abreast Twin Island, which may be passed within 600 yards, haul in to the northward until Mount Sutil on the southern end of Galiano Island is in line with Charles Island bearing S. 53° E.;

run up with these marks on astern (which will lead well inside Walker Rock) until Quadra Hill bears N 68° E, when a mid channel course may be steered between Galiano Island and the islands forming the western side of the channel.

Coming down Trincomalie Channel, and desiring to pass eastward of Walker Rock, keep over on the Galiano Island shore until the northeastern point of Thetis Island is well shut in by the south point of Hall Island; as long as these points are not opened vessels will be eastward of the rock, and when Quadra Hill bears N. 22° E. they will be well eastward of both it and the Governor Rock

Houston Passage.—Vessels intending to take it had better pass up westward or inside the Governor Rock The entrance is between the northern point of Admiral Island and Narrow and Secretary Islands; the western side of Narrow Island is foul, several small islets and rocks extend from 200 to 600 yards off it, at 1¾ miles S. 56° E. of Southey Point, a bank having from 2 to 3 fathoms water on it extends ⅓ mile off the shore of Admiral Island, narrowing the navigable channel between that island and Narrow Island to ¼ mile; the general depth of water in mid-channel is 20 fathoms, and anchorage within a moderate distance of the shore of Admiral Island may be obtained in 10 or 12 fathoms water, off Saltspring Settlement, at 2½ miles S 56° E of Southey Point.

Southey Point, the sharp northern extreme of Admiral Island, may be approached to within 200 yards At ½ mile S 45° W. of it, is the Grappler Reef; round it Houston Passage turns abruptly to the southward, and Stuart Channel may be entered either by the main passage between North Reef and Admiral Island, or if necessary, between North Reef and Tent Island. Give North Reef a moderate berth, as a shoal ridge of rocks extends ⅛ mile off its NW. and SW. ends.

Portier Pass, between Galiano and Valdes Islands, is the first outlet into the Strait of Georgia northward of Active Pass; the pass, though short (not exceeding one mile from its southern entrance until fairly in the strait) is narrow, and is rendered still more so by sunken rocks on its western side; the tides are very strong, running from 4 to 7 knots, and overfalls and whirling eddies are always to be met in the northern entrance. No vessel but a steamer commanding a speed of 8 knots should take it.

Black Rock, the first danger in the southern entrance, is just awash at high water; it is on the western side of the pass, 260 yards S. 45° E. of Native Point, the northwestern entrance point, and is easily avoided.

Virago Rock, the principal danger, is almost in the center of the channel, but rather on the western side; it only uncovers at low tides, and lies 400 yards S 84° E. of Native Point, and a little over 400 yards N. 84° W. of Race Point, the center projecting point on the east side of the pass; here is the narrowest part of the passage

Two-fathom Patch.—The third danger is a 2 fathom rocky patch, extending from one of the outer east points of the pass; it lies ¼ mile N. 48° E. of Race Point, and 600 yards N. 48° W. of Tongue Point, the outer east point; this patch is covered with kelp, which is generally visible.

Directions.—At any stage of the flood stream, steam vessels acquainted with the channel might pass out into the Strait of Georgia with facility, the eastern shore should be always kept aboard within 200 yards until beyond Race Point, which should be passed close, after which vessels with the flood stream should make for Canoe Islet, a bare yellow rock north ¾ mile distant. in order to clear the 2 fathom patch; Canoe Islet on its eastern side should not be approached within 600 yards.

In passing out of the channel with the ebb tide, the great danger to be avoided is the violence of the stream setting against and round Race Point, which, if vessels have not sufficient power to stem, will either take them on the port bow and set them on the point, or, which is still more probable, on the starboard, and set them on Virago Rock

Entering Trincomalie Channel from the Strait of Georgia by this pass, vessels should keep ¼ mile eastward of Canoe Islet, and then steer for Race Point, due allowance being made with the flood for the 2 fathom patch; if with the ebb, Race Point should be kept close aboard to avoid being set on Virago Rock, and having passed the point, hug the Galiano Island shore, which is clear of danger; the rule on all occasions should be to avoid the Valdes Island shore, the great strength of the tide ceases immediately on clearing the entrance points either way. From the Strait of Georgia the pass is always easily recognized at the distance of several miles, by the gap formed by its sloping wooded entrance points terminating in two low extremes, from most points of view overlapping each other

Tides.—The flood tide runs from Trincomalie Channel to the northward into the Strait of Georgia, and the ebb in the contrary direction. The ebb stream commences from one hour to one and one-half hours before it is high water by the shore, and runs for one hour after low water, or from seven to eight hours, the high water at the full and change of the moon occurs about 4 p. m., but is not very regular. At springs the tides run with a velocity of 4 to 7 knots with dangerous whirls and eddies.

Clam Bay is on the eastern sides of Thetis and Kuper Islands, opposite Reid Island The continuation of the bay separates these two islands at high water, when there is a boat channel into Telegraph Harbor on their western side.

White Spit, a remarkable point of broken clam shells which can be seen from a long distance, forms the southern entrance point of the bay; immediately southward of it is a considerable native lodge; a reef, having less than one fathom water on it in some places, extends over

600 yards in a S. 45° E. direction from White Spit Point; Leech Island off the northern point of the bay is a small wooded islet.

Center Reef, with 6 feet water on it, and marked by kelp, should not be approached nearer than 250 yards; it lies almost in the center of the entrance, nearly 600 yards N. 28° W. of White Spit.

Rocket Shoal, on which there is only a depth of 6 feet at low water spring tides, lies nearly in the center of the bay, with White Spit extreme in line with the highest part of Indian Island, bearing S. 65° E.; it is 100 yards in extent, with depths of from 2 to 4 fathoms around it.

Directions.—The best passage into Clam Bay from the eastward is eastward of Narrow, Secretary, and Indian Islands, between them and Hall Island; after passing Indian Island, steer in for White Spit on a S. 68° W. bearing, giving it a berth of 200 yards.

If desired, vessels may enter westward of Narrow and Secretary Islands, between them and Kuper Island, and there is fair anchorage in a moderate depth of water in this passage; there are, however, several dangers in this channel, previously described, also two rocks marked by kelp with less than one fathom water on them off the southwestern side of Indian Island; the southern lies 800 yards S. 73° W., of the south end of Indian Island, and the northern 300 yards S. 67° W., of the north end of the same island; therefore the west side of Indian Island should be kept aboard, and a vessel should not bear up round White Spit until its extreme bears S. 67° W., as rocks extend off more than 600 yards S. 45° E. of it. This channel is not recommended.

Entering from the northward there is a clear, deep passage of ¼ mile in breadth between Thetis and Reid Islands.

Anchorage may be had in Clam bay in 6 fathoms water, between Rocket Shoal and the shore.

Rose Islets, five small rocky islets, the northernmost about 20 feet high with a few bushes on it, lie ½ mile northwestward of the north end of Reid Island but with no ship passage between. Vessels bound to Clam Bay from the northward should pass westward of these islets.

Yellow Cliff Anchorage.—There is fair anchorage on the western side of Valdes Island, 2 miles above Porter Pass, immediately off a yellow cliff, 8 fathoms, sandy bottom, will be found with the cliff bearing N. 10° W. distant ½ mile.

It will also be known by Shingle Point, a low projection with a native village on its extreme.

Pylades Channel.—The De Courcy Islands are a group extending 4½ miles in a southeasterly direction from Mudge Island, and on their eastern side, between them and Valdes Island, is Pylades Channel, which leads by the Gabriola Pass into the Strait of Georgia, as well as to the entrance of the False Narrows.

False Narrows are full of kelp, and shoal at low water, affording only a boat passage into Northumberland Channel. The passages between the De Courcy Islands are deep and navigable; Ruxton Passage between the northern and middle island, is ½ mile wide and free from danger: the narrow pass between the middle and southern island is scarcely

(1126) **BRITISH COLUMBIA — Strait of Georgia — Gabriola pass—Uncharted rocks.**—The Canadian Government has given notice that Commander J. F. Parry, R. N., reports the existence of the following rocks in the approach to Gabriola pass:

On close examination of Gabriola reef, the southernmost danger was found to be a depth of 18 feet at low water, with Gabriola beacon bearing N. 25° E. true (North mag.), distant 1.3 miles.

A rock, with 4 feet over it at low water, was found off the eastern entrance to Gabriola pass, lying 440 yards S. 43° E. true (ESE. E'ly mag.) from the southeast extreme of the long island abreast of the pass. This places the danger about midway between the extreme of the island and the 3⅜ fathoms shown on the chart. (N. M. 30, 1905.)

shoal water extends ¼ mile S. 40° E. from the southeastern end of the island; the channel from the pass into the Strait of Georgia is between the southwestern side of this island, and a narrow ridge of low wooded islands on the west side, off which a chain of covering rocks marked by kelp extends nearly 400 yards to the eastward.

Directions.—Proceeding through the pass into the Strait of Georgia, when nearly ¼ mile east of the narrows, steer S. 30° E. for ⅜ mile, when alter course to the eastward.

There is also a passage in a northerly direction, from the pass into the strait, between the east extreme of Gabriola and the islands off it, but it is not recommended.

Telegraph.—Overhead telegraph wires are stretched across Gabriola Pass; vessels having masts over 30 feet high should not attempt to pass under the wires.

The shore end of the telegraph cable laid from Point Grey (connecting Vancouver Island with the mainland) is landed at Valdes Island, 2½ miles SE. of Gabriola Pass. Wires are thence carried to Nanaimo and Victoria.

Tides.—The tides in Gabriola Pass run from 5 to 6 knots.

Gabriola Reefs, a dangerous cluster of rocks, covering a space of 1½ miles, some of which cover at half flood, and others having only a few feet water over them, lie 2 miles off the eastern point of Gabriola Island. There is a passage inside the reefs, but it is not recommended. When the north extreme of the northernmost Flattop Island bears S. 80° W., a vessel will be one mile to the northward of the reefs. Nanoose

of Gab-

ward of

ameter

... **Rock.**—At nearly 1,200 yards N. 38° E. of the above beacon, and about 400 yards seaward of the end of the Gabriola Reefs, is a detached rock which dries 1½ feet at low-water spring tides, in the kelp which marks the neighborhood. There is 11 fathoms within 200

600 yards in a S. 45° E. direction from White Spit Point, Leech Island off the northern point of the bay is a small wooded islet.

Center Reef, with 6 feet water on it, and marked by kelp, should not be approached nearer than 250 yards; it lies almost in the center of the entrance, nearly 600 yards N. 28° W. of White Spit.

Rocket Shoal, on which there is only a depth of 6 feet at low water spring tides, lies nearly in the center of the bay, with White Spit extreme in line with the highest part of Indian Island, bearing S. 63° E.; it is 100 yards in extent, with depths of from 2 to 4 fathoms around it.

Directions.—The best passage into Clam Bay from the eastward is eastward of Narrow, Secretary, and Indian Islands, between them and Hall Island; after passing Indian Island, steer in for White Spit on a S. 68° W. bearing, giving it a berth of 200 yards.

If desired, vessels may enter westward of Narrow and Secretary Islands, between them and Kuper Island, and there is fair anchorage in a moderate depth of water in this passage; there are, however, several dangers in this channel, previously described, also two rocks marked by kelp with less than one fathom water on them off the southwestern side of Indian Island, the southern lies 800 yards S. 73°W., of the south end of Indian Island, and the northern 300 yards S. 67° W., of the north end of the same island; therefore the west side of Indian Island should be kept aboard, and a vessel should not bear up round White Spit until its extreme bears S. 67° W., as rocks extend off more than 600 yards S. 45° E. of it. This channel is not recommended.

Entering from the northward there is a clear, deep passage of $\frac{3}{8}$ mile in breadth between Thetis and Reid Islands.

Anchorage may be had in Clam bay in 6 fathoms water, between Rocket Shoal and the shore.

Rose Islets, five small rocky islets, the northermost about 20 feet high with a few bushes on it, lie $\frac{1}{2}$ mile northwestward of the north end of Reid Island, but with no ship passage between. Vessels bound to Clam Bay from the northward should pass westward of these islets.

Yellow Cliff Anchorage.—There is fair anchorage on the western side of Valdes Island, 2 miles above Portier Pass, immediately off a yellow cliff; 8 fathoms, sandy bottom, will be found with the cliff bearing N. 10° W. distant $\frac{1}{2}$ mile.

It will also be known by Shingle Point, a low projection with a native village on it[illegible]

(1125) **BRITISH COLUMBIA—Vancouver island—Pylades channel—Uncharted rock.**—The Canadian Government has given notice that Commander J. F. Parry, R. N., reports the existence of a rock, awash at low water, lying at a distance of 220 yards off the eastern extreme of the easternmost island of the De Courcey group, approximately just outside of the 2 fathoms shown on the chart.

(N. M. 30, 1905.)

False Narrows are full of kelp, and shoal at low water, affording only a boat passage into Northumberland Channel. The passages between the De Courcey Islands are deep and navigable, Ruxton Passage between the northern and middle island, is ½ mile wide and free from danger: the narrow pass between the middle and southern island is scarcely

(1126) **BRITISH COLUMBIA — Strait of Georgia — Gabriola pass—Uncharted rocks.**—The Canadian Government has given notice that Commander J. F. Parry, R. N., reports the existence of the following rocks in the approach to Gabriola pass:

On close examination of Gabriola reef, the southernmost danger was found to be a depth of 18 feet at low water, with Gabriola beacon bearing N. 25° E. true (North mag.), distant 1.3 miles.

A rock, with 4 feet over it at low water, was found off the eastern entrance to Gabriola pass, lying 440 yards S. 43° E. true (ESE. E'ly mag.) from the southeast extreme of the long island abreast of the pass. This places the danger about midway between the extreme of the island and the 3¾ fathoms shown on the chart. (N. M. 30, 1905.)

shoal water extends ⅛ mile S. 45° E. from the southeastern end of the island; the channel from the pass into the Strait of Georgia is between the southwestern side of this island, and a narrow ridge of low wooded islands on the west side, off which a chain of covering rocks marked by kelp extends nearly 400 yards to the eastward.

Directions.—Proceeding through the pass into the Strait of Georgia, when nearly ¼ mile east of the narrows, steer S. 39° E. for ¾ mile, when alter course to the eastward.

There is also a passage in a northerly direction, from the pass into the strait, between the east extreme of Gabriola and the islands off it, but it is not recommended.

Telegraph.—Overhead telegraph wires are stretched across Gabriola Pass; vessels having masts over 30 feet high should not attempt to pass under the wires.

The shore end of the telegraph cable laid from Point Grey (connecting Vancouver Island with the mainland) is landed at Valdes Island, 2½ miles SE. of Gabriola Pass. Wires are thence carried to Nanaimo and Victoria.

Tides.—The tides in Gabriola Pass run from 5 to 6 knots.

Gabriola Reefs, a dangerous cluster of rocks, covering a space of 1½ miles, some of which cover at half flood, and others having only a few feet water over them, lie 2 miles off the eastern point of Gabriola Island. There is a passage inside the reefs, but it is not recommended. When the north extreme of the northernmost Flattop Island bears S. 80° W., a vessel will be one mile to the northward of the reefs. Nanoose or Notch Hill just open of Berry Point (the northeastern point of Gabriola Island), bearing N. 72° W., also leads one mile to the northward of them.

A Beacon, 26 feet high, surmounted by a cage 8 feet in diameter stands on the largest ledge, which covers at 6 feet rise of tide.

Thrasher Rock.—At nearly 1,200 yards N. 38° E. of the above beacon, and about 400 yards seaward of the end of the Gabriola Reefs, is a detached rock which dries 1½ feet at low-water spring tides, in the kelp which marks the neighborhood. There is 11 fathoms within 200

600 yards in a S. 45° E direction from White Spit Point; Leech Island off th

Cer

not be

the e

Ro

spring

treme

it is 1

Di

eastw

Hall Island; after passing Indian Island, steer … S 68° W. bearing, giving it a berth of 200 yards.

If desired, vessels may enter westward of Narrow and Secretary Islands, between them and Kuper Island, and there is fair anchorage in a moderate depth of water in this passage, there are, however, several dangers in this channel, previously described, also two rocks marked by kelp with less than one fathom water on them off the southwestern side of Indian Island, the southern lies 800 yards S 73° W., of the south end of Indian Island, and the northern 300 yards S. 67° W., of the north end of the same island; therefore the west side of Indian Island should be kept aboard, and a vessel should not bear up round White Spit until its extreme bears S. 67° W., as rocks extend off more than 600 yards S. 45° E. of it. This channel is not recommended.

Entering from the northward there is a clear, deep passage of ⅜ mile in breadth between Thetis and Reid Islands.

Anchorage may be had in Clam bay in 6 fathoms water, between Rocket Shoal and the shore.

Rose Islets, five small rocky islets, the northermost about 20 feet high with a few bushes on it, lie ½ mile northwestward of the north end of Reid Island, but with no ship passage between. Vessels bound to Clam Bay from the northward should pass westward of these islets.

Yellow Cliff Anchorage.—There is fair anchorage on the western side of Valdes Island, 2 miles above Portier Pass, immediately off a yellow cliff, 8 fathoms, sandy bottom, will be found with the cliff bearing N 10° W distant ½ mile

It will also be known by Shingle Point, a low projection with a native village on its extreme.

(1125) **BRITISH COLUMBIA—Vancouver Island—Pylades channel—Uncharted rock.**—The Canadian Government has given notice that Commander J. F. Parry, R. N., reports the existence of a rock, awash at low water, lying at a distance of 220 yards off the eastern extreme of the easternmost island of the De Courcey group, approximately just outside of the 2 fathoms shown on the chart.

(N. M. 30, 1905.)

False Narrows are full of kelp, and shoal at low water, affording only a boat passage into Northumberland Channel. The passages between the De Courcy Islands are deep and navigable; Ruxton Passage between the northern and middle island, is ½ mile wide and free from danger; the narrow pass between the middle and southern island is scarcely 200 yards wide, but has a depth of 5 fathoms.

Gabriola Pass, between the south end of Gabriola Island and the north end of Valdes Island, is not recommended, unless for coasting vessels knowing the locality, or steamers, if necessary, for it is a narrow and intricate channel, something of the same character as Dodd Narrows, except that it is a much longer reach. Its direction is east for little over one mile, its narrowest part is not over 250 yards in breadth, and the shoalest water is 6 fathoms.

An island nearly one mile long in a northern and southern direction, lies over ½ mile eastward of the narrow eastern entrance of the pass; shoal water extends ¼ mile S. 45° E. from the southeastern end of the island; the channel from the pass into the Strait of Georgia is between the southwestern side of this island, and a narrow ridge of low wooded islands on the west side, off which a chain of covering rocks marked by kelp extends nearly 400 yards to the eastward.

Directions.—Proceeding through the pass into the Strait of Georgia, when nearly ¼ mile east of the narrows, steer S. 39° E. for ¾ mile, when alter course to the eastward.

There is also a passage in a northerly direction, from the pass into the strait, between the east extreme of Gabriola and the islands off it, but it is not recommended.

Telegraph.—Overhead telegraph wires are stretched across Gabriola Pass; vessels having masts over 30 feet high should not attempt to pass under the wires.

The shore end of the telegraph cable laid from Point Grey (connecting Vancouver Island with the mainland) is landed at Valdes Island, 2½ miles SE. of Gabriola Pass. Wires are thence carried to Nanaimo and Victoria.

Tides.—The tides in Gabriola Pass run from 5 to 6 knots.

Gabriola Reefs, a dangerous cluster of rocks, covering a space of 1¼ miles, some of which cover at half flood, and others having only a few feet water over them, lie 2 miles off the eastern point of Gabriola Island. There is a passage inside the reefs, but it is not recommended. When the north extreme of the northernmost Flattop Island bears S. 80° W., a vessel will be one mile to the northward of the reefs. Nanoose or Notch Hill just open of Berry Point (the northeastern point of Gabriola Island), bearing N. 72° W., also leads one mile to the northward of them.

A Beacon, 26 feet high, surmounted by a cage 8 feet in diameter stands on the largest ledge, which covers at 6 feet rise of tide.

Thrasher Rock.—At nearly 1,200 yards N. 38° E. of the above beacon, and about 400 yards seaward of the end of the Gabriola Reefs, is a detached rock which dries 1½ feet at low-water spring tides, in the kelp which marks the neighborhood. There is 11 fathoms within 200

yards of the rock on its seaward side, and between it and the Gabriola Reefs there appeared to be a depth of about 5 fathoms over a rocky bottom.

Berry Point, bearing N. 72° W. (well open of Flattop Point), leads about one mile northward of Gabriola Reefs and Thrasher Rock. The entrance points of Portier Pass, just touching on a S. 2° E. bearing, leads more than 1½ miles eastward of the reefs.

Buoy.—A black conical iron buoy, marked with the letters G Rfs. in white, is moored in 11½ fathoms, 200 yards N. 68° E. of Thrasher Rock.

Caution.—Westward of Flattop Island the shore of Gabriola is bold until near Berry Point and Entrance Island, when it should not be approached within a long ½ mile; foul ground extends for some distance eastward from the point of the island.

Dodd Narrows may be said to commence above Round Island, although the narrowest part is a mile distant from it. To small vessels or steamers of sufficient power that obey their helm quickly, this narrow pass offers no dangers. The strength of the tide at its greatest rush is above 8 knots, the least depth of water 7 fathoms, and the narrowest part of the channel is 80 yards wide; but this is for a short distance, and the pass being nearly straight, a vessel is carried through in a few moments. Vessels should, however, only pass through at or near the time of slack water. The ebb stream sets across the northern entrance of the narrows.

Anchorage.—If bound through Dodd Narrows, and having to wait for tide, there is fair anchorage with but little tide westward of Round Island in 6 fathoms, midway between it and the shore.

Percy Anchorage is a convenient stopping place to wait for the tide. It is immediately on the north side of the narrows between Gabriola and Mudge Islands.

Mudge Island separates Dodd Narrows from the False Narrows.

Directions.—When proceeding for Dodd Narrows from abreast Portier Pass, the mid-channel course is N. 45° W. for about 3 miles, or until Ragged Island and Reef Point of Thetis Island are in line bearing S. 56° W.

The most direct course is northward of Danger Reef, between it and Tree Island; the latter is a small round wooded islet lying off the south end of De Courcy Islands; this passage is ⅜ mile wide, with depths of from 25 to 30 fathoms.

Danger Reef consists of two rocky patches 200 yards apart, the eastern of which is generally awash, and it should not be approached within ⅛ mile; if the reef should not be seen it is recommended to pass ¼ mile to the southward of Tree Island.

The passage between White Rock and Danger Reef is likewise a very good one; it is ¼ mile wide, with depths of from 20 to 30 fathoms. White Rock is 15 feet high, and may be passed if necessary on either side at the distance of 500 yards. When the passage between Tree

Island and the south point of De Courcy Island is open, the former bearing east vessels will be northward of Danger Reef, when a mid-channel course for Dodd Narrows and Round Island, at the entrance, should be seen ahead.

When passing up, keep on the eastern side of Round Island at a convenient distance; the only directions necessary after this are to keep in mid-channel, and to attend the steerage quickly and carefully. When ... the strength of the tide ceases, and a vessel will ... only

... mis- ... they ... The ... from ... nade ... tides ... rait of ... Shoals ... R. N., ... British ... survey

... heads, ... weastle ... t on it,

... t 1,100

... 1 mile

...), dis-

Two shoals, ... yards apart, with least water of ... feet over them, surrounded by deep water, were found off Hammond bay. From the more westerly of these—

Five Finger Island summit bears S. 76° E. true (E. by N. mag.), distant 1 mile 900 yards.

Southern West rock, S. 49° E. true (ESE. ½ E. E'ly mag.), distant 1 mile 440 yards.

Lagoon head, S. 13° E. true (SE. ⅝ S. mag.), distant 1,040 yards.

From the more southerly—

Five Finger Island summit bears S. 81° E. true (ENE. ½ E. mag.), distant 1 mile 500 yards.

Southern West rock, S. 49° E. true (SSE. ¾ E. E'ly mag.), distant 1,940 yards.

Lagoon head, S. 12° 30′ W. true (S. by E. ⅛ E. mag.), distant 700 yards.

Hammond bay is not recommended as an anchorage, owing to the swell usually prevailing there at all seasons.

Ships should not pass between Five Finger island and the West rocks, several 18-foot patches having been found in this locality.

Ships with masts over 100 feet in height are warned of the existence of a telepone wire stretching across the Newcastle Island passage near "Stone quarry" marked on the chart. (N. M. 44, 1904.)

yards of the rock on its seaward side, and between it and the Gabriola Reefs there appeared to be a depth of about 5 fathoms over a rocky bottom.

Berry Point, bearing N. 72° W. (well open of Flattop Point), leads about one mile northward of Gabriola Reefs and Thrasher Rock. The entrance points of Portier Pass, just touching on a S. 2° E. bearing, leads more than 1½ miles eastward of the reefs.

Buoy.—A black conical ...

(93) **BRITISH COLUMBIA — Vancouver island — East coast — Stuart channel — Approach to Dodds narrows — Shoals located.**— Commander J. F. Parry, R. N., H. B. M. S. *Egeria*, reports the existence of the following shoals in the approach to Dodds narrows from Stuart channel:

A rock with 6 feet over it was found 180 yards from the northern point of Round island. This rock lies in the position of 4½ fathoms as shown on H. O. chart No. 1915. There is deep water close round this shoal except between it and Round island, where the ground is foul. This shoal is usually marked by kelp.

An isolated rock with 12 feet over it lies 140 yards off the south shore of Mudge island, at the southern entrance to Dodds narrows.

From this rock the north tangent of Round island bears S. 31° E. true (SE. by E. mag.), distant 1,740 yards, and the detached islet off the south side of Mudge island bears S. 76° E. true (E. by N. mag.), distant 800 yards. This rock is surrounded by deep water and is not marked by kelp.

A shoal, with least water of 24 feet, was found 500 yards to the southeastward of Round island.

From the shoalest head the small islet just south of Round island bears N. 76° W. true (W. by S. mag.), distant 540 yards, and the islet off the south side of Mudge island bears N. 18° W. true (NW. ¼ N. N'ly mag.), distant 1,800 yards. This shoal is of small extent, is surrounded by depths of from 7 to 12 fathoms and is not marked by kelp.

(N. M. 3, 1905.)

... Mudge Island separates Dodd Narrows from the False Narrows.

Directions.—When proceeding for Dodd Narrows from abreast Portier Pass, the mid-channel course is N. 45° W. for about 3 miles, or until Ragged Island and Reef Point of Thetis Island are in line bearing S. 56° W.

The most direct course is northward of Danger Reef, between it and Tree Island; the latter is a small round wooded islet lying off the south end of De Courcy Islands; this passage is ⅜ mile wide, with depths of from 25 to 30 fathoms.

Danger Reef consists of two rocky patches 200 yards apart, the eastern of which is generally awash, and it should not be approached within ¼ mile; if the reef should not be seen it is recommended to pass ¼ mile to the southward of Tree Island.

The passage between White Rock and Danger Reef is likewise a very good one; it is ½ mile wide, with depths of from 20 to 30 fathoms. White Rock is 15 feet high, and may be passed if necessary on either side at the distance of 500 yards. When the passage between Tree

Island and the south point of De Courcy Island is open, the former bearing east vessels will be northward of Danger Reef, when a mid-channel course for Dodd Narrows and Round Island, at the entrance, should be seen ahead.

When passing up, keep on the eastern side of Round Island at a convenient distance; the only directions necessary after this are to keep in mid channel, and to attend the steerage quickly and carefully. When through the narrows the strength of the tide ceases, and a vessel will be in Northumberland Channel, a fine wide passage leading to, and only 5 miles from, the anchorage at Nanaimo.

When taking the narrows from the northward, be careful not to mistake the False Narrows, on the northern side of Mudge Island; they are much wider than the real pass, but nearly dry at low water. The Dodd Narrows are not so easy to pass through from the north as from the south, as in the former case the slight bend that has to be made ... narrow part. The tides

(1557) **BRITISH COLUMBIA—Vancouver Island—Strait of Georgia—Nanaimo harbor and Departure bay approaches—Shoals located—Hydrographic information.**—Captain J F Parry, R N., H B M surveying ship *Egeria*, engaged in a resurvey of British Columbian waters, reports the following information from the resurvey of the approaches to Nanaimo harbor and Departure bay

A shoal of about 200 yards in extent and having several heads, was found outside the 10-fathom line off Angle point, Newcastle island. The outermost and shoalest of these heads has 18 feet on it, on the following bearings:

McKay point, N. 78° W. true (WSW. ⅝ W. mag.), distant 1,100 yards

Snake Island summit, N 35° E true (N ⅞ E mag), distant 1 mile 840 yards

Southern West rock, N. 22° W true (NW ⅛ W W'ly mag), distant 1 mile 1,460 yards.

Two shoals, 500 yards apart, with least water of 30 feet over them, surrounded by deep water, were found off Hammond bay. From the more westerly of these—

Five Finger Island summit bears S. 76° E true (E by N mag), distant 1 mile 900 yards.

Southern West rock, S. 49° E. true (ESE ½ E. E'ly mag), distant 1 mile 440 yards

Lagoon head, S 13° E true (SE ⅝ S. mag.), distant 1,040 yards

From the more southerly—

Five Finger Island summit bears S. 81° E true (ENE ½ E. mag.), distant 1 mile 500 yards.

Southern West rock, S. 49° E. true (SSE. ½ E. E'ly mag.), distant 1,940 yards.

Lagoon head, S 12° 30' W. true (S. by E. ⅛ E. mag.), distant 700 yards

Hammond bay is not recommended as an anchorage, owing to the swell usually prevailing there at all seasons

Ships should not pass between Five Finger island and the West rocks, several 18-foot patches having been found in this locality

Ships with masts over 100 feet in height are warned of the existence of a telepone wire stretching across the Newcastle Island passage near "Stone quarry" marked on the chart. (N M 44, 1904)

yards of the rock on its seaward side, and between it and the Gabriola Reefs there appeared to be a depth of about 5 fathoms over a rocky bottom.

Berry Point, bearing N. 72° W. (well open of Flattop Point), leads about one mile northward of Gabriola Reefs and Thrasher Rock. The entrance points of Portier Pass, just touching on a S. 2° E. bearing, leads more than $1\frac{1}{4}$ miles eastward of the reefs.

(93) BRITISH COLUMBIA — Vancouver island — East coast — Stuart channel — Approach to Dodds narrows — Shoals located.— Commander J F Parry, R N, H. B M. S. *Egeria*, reports the existence of the following shoals in the approach to Dodds narrows from Stuart channel

A rock with 6 feet over it was found 180 yards from the northern point of Round island This rock lies in the position of $4\frac{1}{2}$ fathoms as shown on H O chart No. 1915 There is deep water close round this shoal except between it and Round island, where the ground is foul. Thi

An isol
shore of M

From th
true (SE. b
the south s
distant 800
marked by

A shoal,
southeastw

From th
bears N 7
islet off th
$\frac{1}{8}$ N N'ly
is surroun
by kelp.

Directi
tier Pass,
until Rag
S. 56° W

The mos
Tree Islan
end of De
from 25 to

Danger
ern of whi
$\frac{1}{4}$ mile, if
mile to the

The pass
good one;
White Roc
side at the

Island and the south point of De Courcy Island is open, the former bearing east vessels will be northward of Danger Reef, when a mid-channel course for Dodd Narrows and Round Island, at the entrance, should be seen ahead.

When passing up, keep on the eastern side of Round Island at a convenient distance; the only directions necessary after this are to keep in mid channel, and to attend the steerage quickly and carefully. When through the narrows the strength of the tide ceases, and a vessel will be in Northumberland Channel, a fine wide passage leading to, and only 5 miles from, the anchorage at Nanaimo.

When taking the narrows from the northward, be careful not to mistake the False Narrows, on the northern side of Mudge Island; they are much wider than the real pass, but nearly dry at low water. The Dodd Narrows are not so easy to pass through from the north as from the south, as in the former case the slight bend that has to be made must be made immediately on entering the narrow part. The tides should be studied in passing either way. Vessels should not attempt it with the full rush of the stream; an hour before or after low water there is no difficulty to a steam vessel.

Tides.—It is high water in the narrows at full and change at 3h. 30m. p. m., and low water at 9h. 30m. a. m., and at that period the flood stream commences at low water and runs about 7 hours The first of the flood is the best time to pass the narrows. Vessels leaving Nanaimo and intending to pass down, should be at the narrows an hour before high or low water, as the tides are nearly an hour earlier at the narrows.

Northumberland Channel runs from Dodd Narrows in a northwesterly direction for over 3 miles The water is everywhere deep A rock which uncovers lies100 yards off the extreme of Sharp Point

A submarine cable crosses the channel ¾ mile westward of the narrows.

Nanaimo Harbor is formed by Protection Island to the eastward and Newcastle Island to the northward, this latter island approaching the shore of Vancouver to within a distance of 300 yards, and forming a narrow strait affording communication with Departure Bay to the northward.

The channels leading into Nanaimo Harbor from the eastward are marked by red buoys on their northern sides, and black buoys on their southern sides. These buoys are numbered.

The entrance to the harbor lies between Gallows Point on the north side and a bank of mud on the south side. A rocky ledge extends for 300 yards on all sides of the point, and in summer is marked by kelp, a large bowlder stands on the ledge off the point, distant 150 yards, and covers before high water. The south side of the channel is the northern edge of the great shallow bay to the southward, which, although it does not quite dry in this part, has only 2 to 3 feet on it at low water, and is steep to. The entrance is here marked by a red conical buoy off Gallows Point and a black buoy on the south side, a little over 200 yards apart. The harbor thence opens out, and when the banks are covered gives the idea of being a large sheet of water, but the deep part is limited.

The town of Nanaimo, which is rapidly increasing in importance, contains about 4,000 inhabitants, but it is being continually added to by immigration Extensive colliery works are in full operation, and the country around possesses exceptional natural facilities. Steamers call here from San Francisco, Portland, and Alaska, as well as from Victoria and coast ports, and there is communication with Victoria by rail.

Between San Francisco and Nanaimo two steamships make two trips a month each. Nanaimo is connected with Victoria and New Westminster by telegraph The wharf accommodation is excellent. Two or more steamers can be coaled at the same time, the depth alongside the wharf at low water being 28 feet.

Ships are often placed on the beach at the high rise of the tide, affording an opportunity for effecting any repairs to the hull.

Provision is made for sick seamen, who are either admitted to the Nanaimo hospital or transferred to the marine hospital at Victoria.

A steam ferry runs between Nanaimo and Departure Bay.

Middle Bank lies in the center of the harbor, and has a depth of only 3 feet on it in places; it is marked by a *black* conical buoy on its north end, and a *red* conical buoy with globe on its south end.

Beacon Rock lies nearly 200 yards offshore abreast the northern pier; a beacon, consisting of an iron staff surmounted by a ball, has been erected on this rock.

Nicol Rock, lies 300 yards S.45° E. of Beacon Rock, and is marked. by a buoy, colored *red* and *black* in *horizontal* stripes.

Directions—Two narrow winding channels, the North and South, lead into the usual anchorage, which is close off the town, and westward of the Middle Bank, both are buoyed in the vicinity of the latter, but strangers should not enter either channel without a pilot

The North Channel lies between the Middle Bank and the south edge of the Satellite Reef, which is marked by a *red* buoy with staff and ball; steer about WNW.' to pass between the latter and the black buoy off the north edge of the Middle Bank, then haul close round the southern buoy to avoid the 3 fathom patch, and steer for the mine chimney. The South Channel, though of sufficient depth for large vessels, has a somewhat sharp turn at its western end, but is very convenient for sailing vessels leaving with a northerly wind, when they would be obliged to warp out of the North Channel.

A *black* conical buoy is moored at the edge of the bank, which extends more than 400 yards from the shore at the entrance to Mill Stream, to the northward of the town.

Anchorage.—Anchor close off the town in 5 fathoms, midway between the black buoy on north edge of Middle Bank and Beacon Rock. Vessels can go alongside the wharves.

Supplies.—Beef and mutton may be procured, and the country around abounds in wild fowl and deer

Ship stores can be obtained; but material necessary for refitting a vessel must be procured from Victoria The facilities for repairing a ship's hull and machinery are limited, but small work connected with the latter might be executed at the machine shops belonging to the Vancouver Coal Company and R. Dunsmuir & Sons

Trade.—The chief exports consist of coal, and the imports of general merchandise

Coal—The mines of Nanaimo produce a fair bituminous coal, which answers well for steaming purposes. It is lighter by about 10 per cent. than Welsh coal, and its consumption proportionately rapid. The mines are now in full working.

The quantity of coal usually maintained on hand is 5,000 tons, and the price is about $3.50 per ton. Vessels can coal from lighters alongside at all times.

Newcastle Island also produces large quantities, and the mines there are being rather extensively worked.

A small creek on the north side of Douglas coal wharf affords excellent facilities for beaching a vessel, and is frequently resorted to for that purpose.

Pilots are necessary and pilotage compulsory.

Rates—(1) For vessels entering or clearing from Nanaimo (including Departure Bay) $3 per foot under 10 feet draft, $4 per foot over 10 feet draft. Vessels under steam or in tow of a steamer one-fourth less. (2) For sailing vessels from Royal Roads to Nanaimo or from Nanaimo $3 per foot, for steamers or sailing vessels in tow of a steamer the pilots shall receive $10 per day.

There are no legal rates for tugboats, the charge varies from $100 to $500 to Race Rock in Fuca Strait for vessels of from 1,000 to 2,000 tons This charge includes the service of the tug both ways.

Harbor dues, 2 cents per registered ton, payable three times a year, wharf dues 50 cents per ton on cargo landed or taken on board. No charge at coal company's wharves

Departure Bay—From Nanaimo the long narrow channel or arm between Newcastle Island and the main leads in a northwesterly direction to Departure Bay. It is 200 yards in breadth, with 12 feet at low water, except on a rock which has only 2 feet water on it lying in mid channel, and is marked by a black buoy Vessels of 15 or 16 feet draft may enter Departure Bay by this channel.

The northern entrance to Departure Bay is between Bowlder Point, the steep cliffy north point of Newcastle Island and Jesse Island. Very little less than 20 fathoms will be found in any part of the bay, and it is not nearly so sheltered as Nanaimo Harbor. When coming from the northward, care must be taken to avoid the reef which extends more than 300 yards from Horswell Bluff, the north entrance point of the bay. A *black* can buoy is moored off Horswell Bluff in 3½ fathoms water, at the eastern extremity of the reef.

There are coaling piers in the northwestern part of the bay, and two additional coaling wharves have been built in the southwestern corner. There is a depth of 5 to 6 fathoms at low water alongside all the wharves. Three warping buoys have been placed for the convenience of vessels about to coal. Fresh water can be obtained from Messrs. Dunsmuir's wharf.

Coal.—The coal is about the same weight as the Welsh; price $5 per ton.

The mining village of Wellington has a population of about 1,000, and when required 1,500 tons of coal can be put out in a day.

Buoy.—A red beacon buoy marks the reef in southeastern corner of Departure Bay.

Reef.—A reef extends from the east end of Jesse Island; it is marked by a *black* can buoy, moored in 7½ fathoms. A *red* can buoy is also moored in 3½ fathoms westward of Black Island, northern side of Departure Bay. These buoys are intended to mark the channel inside Jesse Island to the North Wellington coal wharves, which is frequently used by vessels proceeding to load.

Directions.—Vessels intending to load with coal should bring the steep NW point of Newcastle Island to bear N. 34° E., and anchor in not less than 18 fathoms off the coal mine, 400 yards from the shore (or make fast to the mooring buoy until ready to haul alongside the wharf); the bank runs up steep within the above depth, and shoals from 12 to 2 fathoms. Unless anchored well out, a vessel is liable, with NW. winds, to tail on the bank; and ships are not recommended to lie here after they have got their cargo in. Strangers should take a pilot for the coaling station in Departure Bay, either from outside or in Nanaimo Harbor.

West Rocks lie northeastward of Horswell Bluff. These islets and rocks occupy a space of ½ mile in a NW. and SE. direction; there is a passage 600 yards wide between them and Five Finger Island with irregular rocky bottom, the depths varying from 9 to 35 fathoms, the passage is not recommended, but, if used, Five Finger Island should be kept aboard.

Inner Channel lies between the above islets and the shore of the main, and being more direct, is convenient for steamers or small craft bound to or from the northward. Almost in the center of this channel are the Clarke Rocks, which dry 4 feet at low water. A *black* can buoy is moored on these rocks.

Tides.—It is high water, full, and change, at Nanaimo Harbor about 5 p. m., and the range of tide is sometimes 14 feet, which is as much as is met with anywhere on the coast, rendering this a most eligible spot for the construction of docks, for which it offers peculiar facilities. This great range of tide only occurs at midnight during winter, and in the daytime in summer. The superior and inferior tides exist here as they do at Esquimalt and among the Haro Archipelago.

Five Finger Island is a bare rugged islet 48 feet high, of about the same dimensions as Light-house Island; the five hummocks on it resemble knuckles more than fingers.

Middle Channel, over one mile wide, lies between Five Finger and [illegible] free from danger, and has a depth

(375) **BRITISH COLUMBIA—Strait of Georgia—Entrance Island—Tempor[illegible]y light.**—The lighting apparatus at Entrance Island lighthouse having been damaged by fire, until repairs are completed a 7th order lens will be used temporarily and the light shown will be a *fixed white* light. Further notice will be given when the apparatus is repaired and the former characteristic of the light resumed.

Approx. position: Lat. 49° 12′ 30″ N., Long. 123° 48′ 45″ W.

(N. M. 11, 1905.)

[illegible] point; the least depth [illegible] 21 feet on the southern. The ledge is generally covered w[illegible] kelp and has a channel of 7 fathoms of water between it and the isla[illegible].

The southern extreme of this ledge is marked by a *black* can buoy moored in 3½ fathoms. This buoy is intentionally colored black to show better; regarded as a danger buoy merely.

A *black* buoy is moored 250 yards S. 56° W. of the south point of the island.

Fairway Channel, between the shore of Gabriola and Light-house Island, is the most direct for vessels entering from the southward or eastward. A bell buoy has been placed in the channel with the southern end of Light-house Island bearing N. 39° W., distant ⅞ mile.

The channel, between this ledge and Rocky point of Gabriola Island, is fully ¾ mile wide; for a distance of 400 yards off the latter point are depths of from 4 to 7 fathoms, rocky bottom, where kelp occasionally grows; this ledge of uneven rocky ground should be avoided. A mid channel course is recommended, which from a position ½ mile off Entrance Island is S. 73° W. for 3 miles; the water is deep, and the bottom irregular, varying from 15 to 40 fathoms; if to the southward of mid-channel it will shoal to 15 fathoms and shortly to 8 fathoms off Rocky Point.

Entrance Island, off Berry Point, is rocky, 30 feet high, formed of sandstone, bare of trees, but has some vegetation on it. Vessels passing up the strait bound for Nanaimo should round this island; there is a deep passage between it and Berry Point, named Forwood Channel, a little more than 400 yards in breadth, which steamers or small craft may use; but the southern and western sides of Entrance Island must be avoided, as reefs and broken ground extend 400 yards off them.

Having rounded Entrance Island at the distance of ¼ mile or more, the entrance of Nanaimo Harbor will be distant 5 miles. Fairway Channel is the most convenient for vessels bound to Nanaimo from the

is not nearly so sheltered as Nanaimo Harbor. When coming from the northward, care must be taken to avoid the reef which extends more than 300 yards from Horswell Bluff, the north entrance point of the bay. A *black* can buoy is moored off Horswell Bluff in 3½ fathoms water, at the eastern extremity of the reef.

There are coaling piers in the northwestern part of the bay, and two additional coaling wharves have been built in the southwestern corner. There is a depth of 5 to 6 fathoms at low water alongside all the wharves. Three warping buoys have been placed for the conven[illegible] about to coal [illegible]

wharf [illegible]

Coa[illegible]

ton.

The [illegible]

when [illegible]

Buo[illegible] [illegible]eastern corner of

Depart[illegible]

Reef.—A reef extends from the east end of Jesse Island; it is marked by a *black* can buoy, moored in 7½ fathoms. A *red* can buoy is also moored in 3½ fathoms westward of Black Island, northern side of Departure Bay. These buoys are intended to mark the channel inside Jesse Island to the North Wellington coal wharves, which is frequently used by vessels proceeding to load.

Directions.—Vessels intending to load with coal should bring the steep NW. point of Newcastle Island to bear N. 34° E., and anchor in not less than 18 fathoms off the coal mine, 400 yards from the shore (or make fast to the mooring buoy until ready to haul alongside the wharf); the bank runs up steep within the above depth, and shoals from 12 to 2 fathoms. Unless anchored well out, a vessel is liable, with NW. winds, to tail on the bank; and ships are not recommended to lie here after they have got their cargo in. Strangers should take a pilot for the coaling station in Departure Bay, either from outside or in Nanaimo Harbor.

West Rocks lie northeastward of Horswell Bluff. These islets and rocks occupy a space of ½ mile in a NW. and SE. direction; there is a passage 600 yards wide between them and Five Finger Island with irregular rocky bottom, the depths varying from 9 to 35 fathoms; the passage is not recommended, but, if used, Five Finger Island should be kept aboard.

Inner Channel lies between the above islets and the shore of the main, and being more direct, is convenient for steamers or small craft bound to or from the northward. Almost in the center of this channel are the Clarke Rocks, which dry 4 feet at low water. A *black* can buoy is moored on these rocks.

Tides.—It is high water, full, and change, at Nanaimo Harbor about 5 p. m., and the range of tide is sometimes 14 feet, which is as much as is met with anywhere on the coast, rendering this a most eligible spot for the construction of docks, for which it offers peculiar facilities. This great range of tide only occurs at midnight during winter, and in the daytime in summer. The superior and inferior tides exist here as they do at Esquimalt and among the Haro Archipelago.

Five Finger Island is a bare rugged islet 48 feet high, of about the same dimensions as Light-house Island; the five hummocks on it resemble knuckles more than fingers.

Middle Channel, over one mile wide, lies between Five Finger and Light-house Islands; it is perfectly free from danger, and has a depth of 80 fathoms.

Light-house Island is a smooth-topped grassy sandstone island, 600 yards in extent north and south, and about 39 feet high. A ledge of rocks, 800 yards long in a north and south direction, lies to the southeastward of Light-house Island, with the north end 450 yards east of the south point and the south end 900 yards S. 33° E. of the same point; the least depth on this ledge is 7 feet on the northern edge and 21 feet on the southern. The ledge is generally covered with streaming kelp and has a channel of 7 fathoms of water between it and the island.

The southern extreme of this ledge is marked by a *black* can buoy moored in 3½ fathoms. This buoy is intentionally colored black to show better; regarded as a danger buoy merely.

A *black* buoy is moored 250 yards S. 56° W. of the south point of the island.

Fairway Channel, between the shore of Gabriola and Light-house Island, is the most direct for vessels entering from the southward or eastward. A bell buoy has been placed in the channel with the southern end of Light-house Island bearing N. 39° W., distant ¾ mile.

The channel, between this ledge and Rocky point of Gabriola Island, is fully ¾ mile wide; for a distance of 400 yards off the latter point are depths of from 4 to 7 fathoms, rocky bottom, where kelp occasionally grows; this ledge of uneven rocky ground should be avoided. A mid-channel course is recommended, which from a position ½ mile off Entrance Island is S. 73° W. for 3 miles; the water is deep, and the bottom irregular, varying from 15 to 40 fathoms; if to the southward of mid-channel it will shoal to 15 fathoms and shortly to 8 fathoms off Rocky Point.

Entrance Island, off Berry Point, is rocky, 30 feet high, formed of sandstone, bare of trees, but has some vegetation on it. Vessels passing up the strait bound for Nanaimo should round this island; there is a deep passage between it and Berry Point, named Forwood Channel, a little more than 400 yards in breadth, which steamers or small craft may use; but the southern and western sides of Entrance Island must be avoided, as reefs and broken ground extend 400 yards off them.

Having rounded Entrance Island at the distance of ½ mile or more, the entrance of Nanaimo Harbor will be distant 5 miles. Fairway Channel is the most convenient for vessels bound to Nanaimo from the southward or eastward, but Middle Channel is certainly the safest and most desirable for vessels from the northward.

Directions.—Having entered the Strait of Georgia, between east point of Saturna and Patos Island, a N. 45° W. course for 38 miles will lead nearly 3 miles outside Gabriola Reefs, and abreast Entrance Island, the latter bearing S. 68° W. distant 5 miles. A vessel proceeding through Fairway Channel, if northward of mid-channel, must keep a lookout for the kelp on Light-house Island Ledge; when Light-house Island bears N. 22° W., steer S. 25° W., which leads for the entrance of Nanaimo Harbor. Strangers should be careful not to mistake Northumberland Channel for it. Off Sharp Point, a remarkable narrow projection on the main, at the distance of 100 yards, is a rock which uncovers.

Having passed between Light-house and Gabriola Islands, there is a good working space of $1\frac{1}{2}$ miles in breadth, between Gabriola on the east, and Newcastle and Protection Islands on the west, but the water is too deep for anchorage. The shores of the latter islands should not be approached within $\frac{1}{4}$ mile, as shoal rocky ledges extend off them. Having brought Gallows Point (the southern extreme of Protection Island) to bear S. 73° W., the town will come in view.

A vessel may anchor if necessary with the high-water mark of Gallows Point bearing N. 45° W., distant $\frac{1}{4}$ mile, which will be in the fairway of the entrance, but it is difficult for a sailing vessel to pick up a berth here with a strong breeze, as the space for anchorage is confined.

CHAPTER III.

SAN JUAN (MIDDLE) CHANNEL.—LOPEZ SOUND.—ORCAS, WEST AND EAST CHANNELS.

San Juan (Middle) Channel is the center of the three passages lead-

(1064) **WASHINGTON—San Juan channel Salmon Bank buoy No. 1 changed in position.**—On June 10 the first-class spar buoy No. 1, marking Salmon bank, south entrance to San Juan channel, was moved 1,500 feet to the southward of its former position and moored in 41 feet of water on the following bearings:

Cattle Point post light, N. 24° E. true (North mag.).

Smith Island lighthouse, S. 42° E. true (SE. by E. $\frac{7}{8}$ E. mag.).

Discovery Island lighthouse (Canadian), West true (SW. by W. $\frac{7}{8}$ W. mag.). (N. M. 29, 1904.)

trends to the NW. for 7 miles to its junction with President (Douglas) Channel. The southern entrance lies between the southeastern point of San Juan and the southwestern point of Lopez Island; for $1\frac{1}{2}$ miles its direction is north, and the breadth of the passage for this distance varies from $\frac{3}{4}$ mile to 500 yards; abreast Goose Island, on the western side, it does not exceed the latter breadth. When entering, the danger to be avoided on the western side is the Salmon Bank, extending southerly from San Juan, and on the eastern the Whale Rocks, always out of water. The tides in this entrance set from 3 to 6 knots an hour, with eddies and confused rips; when within the entrance there is far less tide, and Griffin Bay, offering good anchorage, is easily reached.

Salmon Bank extends $1\frac{1}{2}$ miles south from Cattle Point, the southeastern extreme of San Juan Island; a bare point about 50 feet high, the sloping termination of Mount Finlayson, and the least depth of water found on it is 10 feet, with rocky patches, marked in summer by kelp; depths varying from 4 to 9 fathoms extend for a farther distance of $\frac{3}{4}$ mile in the same direction.

Whale Rocks, on the eastern side of the entrance, are two black rocks, 200 yards apart, and 3 or 4 feet above high water; a patch, on which kelp grows, with one fathom on it, extends 400 yards to the southward of them, otherwise they are steep-to, but it is not recommended to pass them nearer than $\frac{1}{4}$ mile, as the tides set strongly over them.

Directions.—Entering San Juan Channel from the westward or southward, Cattle Point should be given a berth of at least $1\frac{1}{2}$ miles. Mount Erie, a remarkable summit on Fidalgo Island 1,250 feet high, in line with

southward or eastward, but Middle Channel is certainly the safest and most desirable for vessels from the northward.

Directions.—Having entered the Strait of Georgia, between east point of Saturna and Patos Island, a N. 45° W. course for 38 miles will lead nearly 3 miles outside Gabriola Reefs, and abreast Entrance Island, the latter bearing S. 68° W. distant 5 miles. A vessel proceeding through Fairway Channel, if northward of mid-channel, must keep a lookout for the kelp on Light-house Island Ledge; when Light-house Island bears N. 22° W., steer S. 25° W., which leads for the entrance of Nanaimo Harbor. Strangers should be careful not to mistake Northumberland Channel for it. Off Sharp Point, a remarkable narrow projection on the main, at the distance of 100 yards, is a rock which uncovers.

Having passed between Light-house and Gabriola Islands, there is a good working space of 1½ miles [illegible] east, and [illegible] is too deep [illegible] be approac[illegible] Having bro[illegible] Island) to b[illegible]

A vessel [illegible] lows Point [illegible] way of the [illegible], but it is difficult for a sailing vessel to pick up a berth here with a strong breeze, as the space for anchorage is confined.

CHAPTER III.

SAN JUAN (MIDDLE) CHANNEL.—LOPEZ SOUND.—ORCAS, WEST AND EAST CHANNELS.

San Juan (Middle) Channel is the center of the three passages leading from the Strait of Fuca into that of Georgia, and is bounded by San Juan Island on the west, and the islands of Lopez, Shaw, and Orcas on the east. Although a deep navigable ship channel, and eligible for steamers of the largest size, the southern entrance is somewhat confined, and subject to strong tides, with a general absence of steady winds; the wide straits of Rosario and Haro, on either side of it, are therefore far to be preferred for sailing vessels above the size of coasters.

The general direction of the channel is north for 5 miles, when it trends to the NW. for 7 miles to its junction with President (Douglas) Channel. The southern entrance lies between the southeastern point of San Juan and the southwestern point of Lopez Island; for 1½ miles its direction is north, and the breadth of the passage for this distance varies from ¼ mile to 800 yards; abreast Goose Island, on the western side, it does not exceed the latter breadth. When entering, the danger to be avoided on the western side is the Salmon Bank, extending southerly from San Juan, and on the eastern the Whale Rocks, always out of water. The tides in this entrance set from 3 to 6 knots an hour, with eddies and confused rips; when within the entrance there is far less tide, and Griffin Bay, offering good anchorage, is easily reached.

Salmon Bank extends 1¾ miles south from Cattle Point, the southeastern extreme of San Juan Island; a bare point about 50 feet high, the sloping termination of Mount Finlayson, and the least depth of water found on it is 10 feet, with rocky patches, marked in summer by kelp; depths varying from 4 to 9 fathoms extend for a farther distance of ¾ mile in the same direction.

Whale Rocks, on the eastern side of the entrance, are two black rocks, 200 yards apart, and 3 or 4 feet above high water; a patch, on which kelp grows, with one fathom on it, extends 400 yards to the southward of them, otherwise they are steep-to, but it is not recommended to pass them nearer than ¼ mile, as the tides set strongly over them.

Directions.—Entering San Juan Channel from the westward or southward, Cattle Point should be given a berth of at least 1½ miles. Mount Erie, a remarkable summit on Fidalgo Island 1,250 feet high, in line with

Jennis Point bearing N. 82° E., leads 1¼ miles south of Salmon Bank in 13 fathoms; when the entrance to the channel is open, bearing north, or when Goose Island, a small islet on the western side of the entrance, is in line with Orcas nob, bearing N. 5° W., a vessel will be well to the eastward of the bank, and may steer in for the passage.

The bottom in the channel is rocky and irregular, causing overfalls and eddies which are apt to turn a ship off her course; but there are no positive dangers after passing the Salmon Bank; between this bank and Cattle Point there is a passage carrying 3½ fathoms, ¼ mile in breadth; 5 fathoms will be found within 200 yards of the point. The westernmost Whale Rock, seen in the center of the channel between Charles Island and the north side of Mackaye Harbor, leads through the middle of this narrow channel, which, however, is not recommended.

Griffin Bay is an extensive indentation on the eastern side of San Juan. There is but a limited portion of the bay available for anchorage, and this is in the southern angle, immediately off the remarkable prairie land between two forests of pine trees.

With winds from north or NE. the bay is considerably exposed, and landing is difficult in consequence of the long flat which extends off the beach. These winds, however, are not of frequent occurrence.

Half-tide Rock, just awash at high water, lies 1¼ miles N. 64° W. of Harbor Rock. There is another rock which covers at one-quarter flood, lying 900 yards S. 17° E. of Half-tide Rock.

Directions.—Entering by the southern passage, Harbor Rock on the western side, nearly one mile within Goose Island, may be passed at 200 yards, keeping outside the kelp, which extends some distance off it.

Anchorage.—The best anchorage is in 9 fathoms, mud bottom, with the southernmost of the white cliffs on Lopez Island kept well open of Harbor Rock, bearing S. 84° E., and the black, rocky extreme of Low Point just open northward of Half-tide Rock, bearing N. 45° W. From this position the water shoals rapidly towards the shore, and strangers should drop an anchor directly 12 fathoms is obtained.

North Bay, immediately under Park Hill, affords good anchorage in from 4 to 10 fathoms, mud bottom, with all winds but those from SE. The bottom here is more regular than in Griffin Bay, and it is a snugger anchorage, though less convenient, being 3 miles from the settlement.

Anchorage.—Anchor in from 6 to 9 fathoms, mud bottom, with the east point of Dinner Island bearing S. 5° E., distant 800 yards.

Tides.—The greatest rise and fall at the southern entrance of San Juan Channel at full and change is 12 feet; but little stream is felt at the anchorages. With the flood an eddy, of about one knot an hour, sets to the southward in Griffin Bay, and with the ebb in the opposite direction.

Turn Island.—Its eastern point, a cliffy bluff, makes as the extreme of the peninsula which forms the north side of Griffin Bay. The island should be passed at a distance of over ½ mile, particularly going northward with the flood; there is a channel for boats or small craft between it and the peninsula.

Turn Rock lies nearly ¼ mile N. 68° E. of the island, and covers at high water. The tide sets with great strength over this rock, and vessels passing up or down the channel should give it a good berth.

Friday Harbor is on the north side of the peninsula, immediately opposite to North Bay; it is rather confined, but offers good anchorage, and is easily accessible to steamers or small vessels. Brown Island lies in the entrance, and there is a passage on either side of it; that to the eastward is narrow, less than 200 yards in width, but with a depth of 14 fathoms. Vessels entering by this passage may find anchorage in the bight immediately south of it, and distant from the island ⅓ mile. There is a clear channel through, inside the island, of more than 200 yards in width, and a depth of 6 or 7 fathoms.

The passage in, westward of Brown island, is the widest, being 600 yards across. In the center of the entrance there is a rocky patch, with a depth of 3½ fathoms at low water. To avoid it keep 200 yards off the San Juan Island shore.

Anchorage.—Anchor in 9 fathoms, mud bottom, with the passage between the island and main open.

Reid Rock.—After rounding Turn Island, San Juan Channel trends to the northwestward, and Reid Rock, the least water on which is 12 fete, lies right in the fairway; it is surrounded by thick kelp, which, however, is sometimes run under by the tide. The rock lies 1$\frac{3}{10}$ miles N. 45° W. of the north point of Turn Island. The passage on the north side of the rock is recommended for vessels bound up or down San Juan Channel, as, having to give the Turn Rock a good berth, it is the more direct one.

After passing Reid Rock there are no dangers which are not visible. From Caution Point, one mile above the rock, on the western side, the channel gradually increases in breadth, and varies but little from a NW. direction, the depth of water increasing to 60 and 70 fathoms.

Wasp Islands are on the eastern side of the channel. Between and among them are several passages leading between Shaw and Orcas Islands, and communicating with the magnificent harbors and sounds which deeply indent the southern coasts of Orcas.

Rocky Bay, on the western side of San Juan Channel, 4 miles from Caution Point, does not afford much shelter, and vessels are not recommended to use it unless in case of necessity. The small island, O'Neal, lies in the center of it. There is a depth of 14 fathoms between the island and San Juan, but the bottom is rocky. A reef of rocks, on which the sea generally breaks, extends 300 yards off the San Juan shore, bearing S. 59° W. of O'Neal Island.

Jones Island lies in the northern entrance of the San Juan Channel, nearly ½ mile from Orcas Island, being separated from the latter by Spring Passage. The island is less than one mile in extent, mostly wooded, but its western points are bare and grassy.

Spring Passage is a safe deep-water channel, and saves some distance to a steamer passing up or down San Juan Channel, by the President Channel.

Some rocky patches extend 200 yards off the eastern side of Jones Island, and a rock which covers at 2 feet flood lies the same distance north of a small cove on the northeastern side of the island; a rocky patch, with 5 fathoms water on it, lies 400 yards off the west side of Orcas Island; therefore it is desirable to pass through in mid-channel.

Caution.—Passing up or down San Juan Channel, the NE. end of San Juan should be avoided, as the tides are strong, and a sailing vessel is apt to be drawn into the strong tide-rips and overfalls in the eastern entrance of Spieden Channel.

Flattop Island, in the northern entrance of San Juan Channel, is ¼ mile in length, wooded, and about 100 feet high. At 400 yards off its western side is a rock 25 feet above high water. Between it and the island is a deep passage.

President (Dougles) Channel may be said to be the continuation of San Juan Channel, and leads into Haro Strait, between Orcas and Waldron Islands. There are other passages leading into the Haro Strait, viz, westward of Flattop Island, between it and Spieden and Stuart Islands; and eastward of Flattop, between it and Waldron Island. In the former, the confused tides and eddies are liable to entangle sailing vessels among Spieden and the neighboring groups of small islands and rocks; in the latter, the White Rock with its off-lying dangers offers serious impediments to the safe navigation of the same class of vessels.

The narrowest part of the channel is 1¼ miles between Waldron and Orcas Islands; the depth varies from 90 to 168 fathoms, and both shores are free from danger. If necessary, vessels will find a temporary anchorage in 12 fathoms water, in the bay, about 800 yards southward of the Doughty Point (Bill of Orcas).

Directions.—The channel westward of Flattop Island is less than one mile in breadth at its narrowest part. Green Point of Spieden Island is steep-to; a tide-rip is generally met with off it. After passing Flattop Island the channel course is N. 11° W. until Skipjack Island opens of Sandy Point (Waldron Island), bearing N. 37° E., when a course may be shaped either up or down Haro Strait; with the ebb, be careful not to get set into the channel between Spieden and Stuart Islands.

The channel eastward of Flattop Island, between it and White Rock, is about the same breadth as the one just described, but Danger Rock, with 5 feet water on it, which lies ¼ mile S. 33° E., of the center of White Rock, must be carefully avoided.

After passing Flattop Island, keep its eastern side just touching the western point of Jones Island, bearing S. 24° E., and it will lead nearly ¼ mile westward of Danger Rock; when Skipjack Island opens out northward of Sandy Point, bearing N. 37° E., all the dangers are cleared.

If passing between White Rock and Disney Point, the latter should be kept well aboard if the ebb is running, or a vessel is liable to be set on the rock. The west bluff of Sucia should by no means be shut in by the southern part of Waldron Island until Monarch Head is well shut in with Sandy Point, the latter bearing N. 17° W.; steer through with these marks on, and when White Rock is in line with the west side of Flattop Island, bearing S. 29° W., a vessel will be clear of all dangers, and may steer either up or down Haro Strait, giving Sandy Point a berth of ½ mile.

Tides.—Sailing vessels working through President Channel should beware of getting too close over on the Waldron Island shore, near Disney Point, as with calm or light winds they would run the risk of being set by the ebb onto Danger Rock, on which the kelp is seldom seen. Both flood and ebb set fairly through San Juan and President Channels, at the rate of 2 to 5 knots.

The ebb tide, coming down between East Point and Patos Island, strikes the north point of Waldron Island, and one part of it, together with the stream between Patos and Sucia Islands, passes down President and San Juan Channels. The other part sets between the Skipjack and Waldron Islands; thence southerly through the groups in the neighborhood of Stuart Island into Haro Strait, as well as down San Juan Channel. The ebb stream continues to run down through the whole of the passages in the archipelago, for 2½ hours after it is low water by the shore, and the water has begun to rise.

Skipjack and Penguin Islands are small islands lying close off the north side of Waldron Island; the former is considerably the larger, and is wooded; the latter is small, grassy, and bare of trees. A reef which covers, and is marked by kelp, lies between the two, but between this reef and Skipjack Island there is a narrow passage of 8 fathoms. The tides, however, set strongly between the islands, and the passage is not recommended; neither, for the same reason, is the passage between them and Waldron Island.

Patos Island lies east of Saturna Island, the passage between them being the widest, and at present most frequented, though it is not always the best channel from Haro or San Juan Channels into the Strait of Georgia. Patos is 1¼ miles long in an east and west direction, narrow, wedge-shaped, sloping towards its western end, and covered with trees. Active Cove at its western end is formed by a small islet connected at low water, and affords anchorage for one or two small vessels in 2 fathoms, but a strong tide-rip at the point renders it difficult for a sailing vessel to enter.

The passage into the Strait of Georgia between Patos and Sucia

Islands, although narrower than the one just mentioned, is to be preferred, especially for vessels passing through San Juan Channel, or for sailing vessels with a NW. wind The tides are not so strong, more regular, and set more fairly through; the passage is almost free from tide rips.

Directions—If intending to take the passage between Patos and Sucia Islands, either up or down, an excellent mark for clearing the Plumper and Clements Reefs (dangerous patches lying southward and northward from Sucia) is to keep the remarkable round summit of Stuart Island just open westward of Skipjack Island, bearing S. 62° W.; this leads well clear of both the reefs, and the same marks would lead across Alden Bank in 5 fathoms water.

If taking the passage from the San Juan or President Channels, keep the white-faced cliffs of Roberts Point well open westward of Patos Island, the cliffs bearing N 59° W , until the marks before described are on, when steer through the passage If the ebb stream is running, it is better to keep the Patos Island shore aboard; 16 fathoms water will be found on the Sucia shore, but it is not recommended to anchor unless positively necessary

Standing to the northeastward, when the northern end of Clark Island is open of the east end of Matia, the former bearing S 45° E, a vessel will be eastward of Clements Reef.

Sucia Island is of a horseshoe shape, remarkably indented on its eastern side by bays and inlets, the largest of these, Sucia Harbor, affords fair anchorage. The island is from 200 to 300 feet high, thickly covered with pines, and its western side a series of steep wooded bluffs

Plumper Reef, with 10 feet water on it, lies 2½ miles north of the Doughty Point, and nearly 2 miles S 12° W of the east point of Patos Island There is a deep passage between Plumper Reef and Sucia Island, but it is not recommended.

Clements Reef, on which there is a depth of 9 feet, lies 1½ miles N. 65° E. of Lawson Bluff, and 2 miles S. 78° E of the east end of Patos. Some rocky patches covering at high water, and marked by kelp, lie between Clements Reef and Ewing Island, and it is not safe to pass between them. There is a deep channel of more than one mile in breadth between Sucia and Matia.

Directions—Entering Sucia Harbor from the northward, steer for it with the NW. point of Clark Island in line with Puffin Islet, about S. 40° E., which leads between Alden Bank and Clements Reef; when the SE. end of Ewing Island bears S 57° W., alter course to about S. 23° W. Give the point of the island a berth of at least 600 yards to avoid some rocky patches which extend 400 yards southeastward of it. When the harbor is well open steer up the center N. 73° W., it is better to keep the southern or Wall Island shore rather aboard, as it is quite steep, and there are some reefs extending 200 yards off the north shore. When the west point of Ewing is just shut in by the east point of Sucia bearing N. 57° E., anchor in the center in 7 or 8 fathoms, mud bottom. If intending to make any stay it is desirable to moor, as the harbor is small for a large vessel; it affords good shelter from westerly winds; with those from SE. some swell sets in but never sufficient to render the anchorage unsafe.

If entering from President Channel, keep Doughty Point just touching the south bluff of Waldron Island, bearing S. 60° W.; this leads well southward of Parker Reef. The SE. points of Sucia may be passed at 200 yards; they are a series of narrow islands the sides of which are as steep as a wall, with narrow deep passages between them; steer in, keeping the northernmost of these islands aboard, to avoid the reefs on the north side of the harbor. For a steamer it is recommended to pass in between the north and middle Wall Islands, as it gives more room to pick up a berth; this passage, though less than 200 yards wide, has 12 and 15 fathoms water in it, and the wall-like sides of the islands are steep-to.

If bound to Sucia Harbor from Rosario Strait, pass on either side of Barnes, Clark, and Matia Islands as convenient; if northward of the latter, as soon as the harbor is open steer for it, keeping the southern side aboard as before directed, or passing between north and middle Wall Islands; if southward of Matia Island, then do not stand so far to the westward as to shut in the north part of Sinclair Island with Lawrence Point, in order to avoid Parker Reef.

Parker Reef is of considerable extent, lying in the passage between Sucia and Orcas Islands; at low water it uncovers ¼ mile of rock and sand, but its eastern end always shows its rocky summit, which is just awash at high water. It lies 2½ miles N. 77° E. of Doughty Point (Orcas Bill), and 1½ miles S. 17° W. of the east point of Sucia. There is a passage on both sides of the reef; the one to the southward is ½ mile wide, with a depth of from 6 to 8 fathoms, but it is not recommended as the points of Orcas Island at this part run off shoal. If the northern passage is used, the north part of Skipjack Island kept in line with the south extreme of Pender Island bearing west, leads well clear of Parker Reef. A part of the ebb stream setting down between Sucia and Matia Islands runs to the westward strongly over Parker Reef, and through the channels on both sides of it; the flood sets in the contrary direction.

A patch of 3 fathoms lies at the distance of ¼ mile west of Parker Reef, with depths of from 4 to 5 fathoms extending for ⅛ mile from its western side.

Matia Island, a little more than one mile eastward of Sucia, is about one mile in extent, east and west, and has no dangers off it; on its southern side are several boat coves. Close off its eastern extreme is Puffin Islet, off which a flat rock extends for 300 yards.

Lopez Island, on the eastern side of San Juan Channel, is thickly wooded, but differs from all the other islands of the archipelago in being much lower and almost flat, except at its northern and southern extremes, where elevations occur of a few hundred feet. Its southern side is much indented by bays and creeks which can not be reckoned as anchorages; on its western side, in San Juan Channel, is a creek terminating in an extensive lagoon, the former offering great facilities for beaching and repairing ships. On the northern shore is Shoal Bay, affording anchorage; and on the east is the spacious and excellent Sound of Lopez.

Mackaye Harbor, on the south coast of Lopez Island, is entered between Iceberg (Jennis) Point on the south and Long and Charles Islands on the north; from the latter it takes an easterly direction for one mile, and then trends to the southward for a short distance, terminating in a low, sandy beach. In the entrance there are depths of from 8 to 12 fathoms, muddy bottom, but with the prevailing southwesterly winds the anchorage is a good deal exposed. Iceberg Point should be passed at about 600 yards; the anchorage is about 1½ miles from it.

Directions.—With southwesterly winds the coast and islands on the eastern side of the San Juan Channel entrance, between Whale Rocks and Iceberg Point, should be avoided, as then a considerable sea sets in; and when passing the coast between Iceberg Point and Watmough Head (Cape Colville), it is desirable to keep one mile offshore, as some straggling rocks exist, which will be treated of under the head of Rosario Strait.

Shark Reef, immediately within San Juan Channel, and ½ mile northward of White Cliff, consists of two rocks awash at low water, extending a little over 200 yards offshore. There are no dangers on the coast of the island for 2 miles north of this reef, but large vessels working up should not approach nearer than ¼ mile.

Careen Creek is on the west side of Lopez Island. The western entrance point is a low sandy spit, close around which there are 3 fathoms water, and on it a vessel might, in perfect shelter, be beached and repaired with much facility; the creek terminates in a large salt lagoon.

Upright Channel is a deep, steep passage, leading from San Juan Channel to the Sounds of Orcas and Lopez, and by several passages into Rosario Strait. The narrowest part of the entrance is between Flat Point and Canoe Island, and here for a short distance it is scarcely 400 yards in breadth.

Flat Point is a low shingle or sandy point, with grass and small bushes on it; it is steep-to, and may be passed at less than 200 yards.

Canoe Island.—The shore of Canoe Island is fringed by kelp, close outside of which a vessel may pass; a rock marked by kelp lies 200 yards S. 23° W. of its south point. The tides in Upright Channel are seldom over 3 knots, and the channel in all respects is safe.

Anchorage may be had in 6 or 7 fathoms in Indian Cove, northwestward of Canoe Island, with Flat Point in line with the south point of Canoe Island; the only precaution necessary is to avoid the kelp off the south point of the island.

Shoal Bay extends in a southerly direction for one mile to its head, which is separated from False Bay, in Lopez Sound, by a low neck of land. Although apparently a considerable sheet of water, the anchorage for large vessels is much limited by a shoal which extends more than half way across from just within Upright Point to the head of the bay, leaving the greater half on the western side, with no more than from 2 to 3 fathoms at low water.

Anchorage.—The best anchorage for large vessels is in 8 fathoms, with Upright Point in line with the east point of Shaw Island bearing N. 59° W. and the east point of Shoal Bay S. 33° E.; 200 yards inside this position there are 4 fathoms; the holding ground is good. Vessels desiring to proceed up the bay after rounding Upright Point, which may be passed close to, must steer for the east point of the bay, until within 200 yards of it, and then keep along the eastern cliffy shore at the same distance, when not less than 5 fathoms will be found until within ¼ mile from the head, where there is anchorage in 4 fathoms; the space between the eastern side of the shoal and the eastern shore of the bay is nearly 400 yards.

Lopez Sound extends in a southerly direction nearly the whole length of the Island, its head reaching within ½ mile of the waters of Fuca Strait. The average breadth of the sound is nearly 1½ miles, and there is a convenient depth of water for anchorage in almost every part of it.

Middle Bank, on which there are not less than 3 fathoms at low water, is the only impediment between Frost and Houston Islands. It is ½ mile in extent north and south, 400 yards east and west, and lies almost in the center of the sound, its north end being ¼ mile south of the south end of Frost Island. Between Frost Island and the bank there are from 9 to 14 fathoms, and between the south end of the bank and the west shore of Decatur Island there is a channel ½ mile wide, with a depth of from 6 to 20 fathoms; close off this part of Decatur Island is a ledge of rocks always awash at high water. Between Middle Bank and Houston Island there is anchorage in any part of the sound in from 5 to 7 fathoms, mud bottom.

Abreast Lopez (Maury) Pass the water deepens to 13 and 15 fathoms, and this depth is carried for 1½ miles, or as far as Crown Islet, a small steep rocky islet on the eastern side, within one mile of the head of the sound.

Tides.—There is but little stream of tide felt in Lopez Sound, unless in the immediate neighborhood of the narrow passages from Rosario Strait.

Entrance Shoal, with 2 fathoms water on it, and marked by kelp, lies 1½ miles eastward of Upright Point, and ½ mile from the shore of Blakely Island; there is deep water on either side of it.

False Bay, on the western side of the sound, is separated from Shoal Bay by a low narrow neck, the cliffy extreme of the peninsula being

IMAGE EVALUATION
TEST TARGET (MT-3)

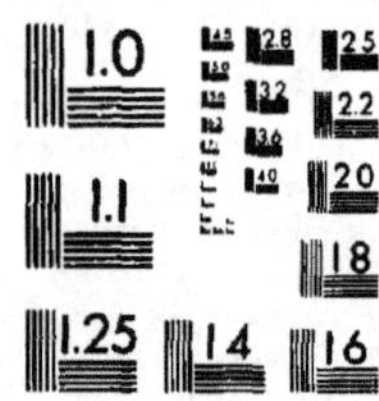

6"

Separation Point. A shoal, on which there is a depth of 2 fathoms, extends from the center of False Bay and connects with the small island of Arbutus, lying in its entrance, and it renders the bay unfit for anchorage, except for small vessels. Vessels may anchor in 8 fathoms southward of Arbutus, between it and Frost Island.

Half-Tide Rock, covering at half flood, and not marked by kelp, is in the track of vessels entering. It lies 800 yards northward of Arbutus Island. It is better to pass eastward of it; when it is not visible the point of Upright Hill kept just open of Separation Point, bearing N. 53° W. until the clay cliff of Gravel Spit is in line with the east point of Arbutus Island, bearing S. 12° W., will lead clear of it.

Frost Island, ½ mile long north and south, lies close off Gravel Spit on the western side of the sound; it is wooded, and its western side a steep cliff, between which and the spit end there is a narrow channel with a depth of 5 fathoms.

Black and Crown Islets.—The Black Islets are a ridge of steep, rocky islets, lying within and across the entrance of Lopez (Maury) Pass; at 400 yards S. 31° W. of the southernmost of these islets is a rock which covers at quarter flood There is a passage of 8 and 9 fathoms on either side of Crown Islet, and anchorage above it in 5 or 6 fathoms, but vessels should not proceed far above, as at a distance of ¼ mile it shoals to one and 2 fathoms, and dries for a considerable distance from the head of the sound, there is also good anchorage in 5 fathoms in the bight westward of Crown Islet.

Passing up the sound between Crown Islet and the western shore a rocky patch of 2 fathoms must be avoided; it lies ¼ mile N. 53° W. of Crown Islet, and 800 yards from the western shore of the sound; there are 12 fathoms close to it, and deep water in the passage on either side of it.

Lopez (Maury) Pass is the southernmost entrance to the sound from Rosario Strait. It is scarcely 400 yards wide at the entrance, with a depth of 12 fathoms; the Black Islets lie across the western entrance, and it is necessary to keep to the southward, between them and Lopez.

Thatcher Pass, between Blakely and Decatur Islands, is the widest and most convenient passage into Lopez Sound from Rosario Strait; it is 1½ miles in length, and its narrowest part 800 yards wide, with a general depth of from 20 to 25 fathoms.

The tides in Thatcher Pass run from 2 to 4 knots.

Lawson Rock, lying almost in the center of the eastern entrance, is the only danger, and covers at 2 feet flood. It lies 800 yards N. 11° W. of Fauntleroy Point, the southeastern entrance point. There is a good passage on either side of the rock, but that to the southward is the best.

Directions.—Entering Thatcher pass from the southward, if the flood is running, the south shore should be kept pretty close aboard, as until well within the passage it sets up towards Lawson Rock.

When the passage between Decatur and James Islands is shut in by Fauntleroy Point, a vessel will be shut westward or inside the rock

Vessels entering by Thatcher Pass, and drawing over 18 feet, to avoid the Middle Bank, keep the southern shore aboard within 400 yards. White Rock in line with the south point of Blakely Island leads over the tail of the shoal in 20 feet

The flood tide sets from Rosario Strait through Thatcher Pass both up and down the sound, a slight stream of flood also enters the sound from the northward.

Obstruction Passes.—Obstruction Island lies in the center of the channel, between Blakely and Orcas Islands and the passes on either side of it are safe. These passes are more adapted to steam than sailing vessels, although there would be no difficulty with a leading wind and fair tides. Small vessels would find no difficulty if the tides were properly taken advantage of

North Obstruction Pass is about 1¼ miles long, and its average breadth 400 yards; there are no dangers which are not visible In consequence of the bend in this channel it has more the appearance of a deep bay when seen from either entrance The eastern end of Obstruction Island should not be approached nearer than 200 yards, as shelving rocks extend a short distance off it, the best course for a steamer is to keep in mid channel The eastern entrance bears west from Cypress Cone, a remarkable bare peak on the north end of Cypress Island.

South Obstruction Pass, though narrower than the North, is perhaps the better channel of the two, as it is not more than ⅔ mile in length, and is perfectly straight in a ENE. and WSW. direction. Its narrowest part is not much more than 200 yards wide; the depth of water much the same as in the northern pass. On the south side of the eastern entrance two rocks extend off Blakely Island, the inner being always above high water; the outer, a long black rock, is nearly ¼ mile offshore, and is just awash at high water.

Entering from Rosario Strait the pass should be brought well open, bearing S. 68° W. before approaching it nearer than ½ mile; in like manner when passing into Rosario Strait, if the Black Rock is not seen, a N. 68° E. course should be maintained until at that distance from the eastern entrance. When the west point of Burrows Island opens out eastward of the east point of Blakely Island, bearing S. 22° E., a vessel will be ½ mile eastward of any dangers. The southern side of the pass appears like a round wooded island, in consequence of the land falling abruptly behind it, where there are two lagoons.

Tides—The flood tide in both passes sets to the westward from Rosario Strait, and the ebb to the eastward; the latter runs for nearly two hours after it is low water by the shore; the strength varies from 2 to 5 knots.

Shaw Island is much of the same character as Lopez, though considerably smaller It is the continuation of the eastern side of the San Juan Channel, and between it and Orcas Island lie the Wasp group.

Wasp Islands and Passages.—The Wasp Islands are five in number, besides some smaller islets and rocks.

Yellow Island, the westernmost of the group, is rather remarkable from its color, grassy and nearly bare of trees, the remainder of the group being wooded; from its west end a sandy spit extends 200 yards, having at its extreme a rock which dries at low water, and around which kelp grows

Brown and Reef Islands lie northward of Yellow Island; off the west side of the latter a reef extends for more than 200 yards, and several rocks, surrounded by kelp, extend over 200 yards off the west side of Brown Island Wasp Passage leads through this group to Orcas Sound and Rosario Strait With the assistance of the chart steamers will find but little difficulty in passing through it, though the passage by Upright Channel is to be preferred.

Crane Island, on the northern side of Wasp Passage, is wooded and much larger than either of the Wasp group A rocky reef extends for ¼ mile from the NE. point of the island in a northwesterly direction.

Knob Islet is a remarkable round islet 50 feet high, with two or three bushes on its summit, it lies just westward of Cliff Island.

Directions.—Passing between Brown and Reef Islands, where the channel is nearly ¼ mile wide, with a depth of 9 fathoms (a depth of 4 fathoms surrounded by kelp, lying between Reef and Brown Islands, has been reported), Bird Rock (awash at high water) may be passed on either side, the widest passage is to the eastward of it, between it and Crane Island, where the channel is ¼ mile across, and has a depth of 15 fathoms. The passage northward of Crane Island is so narrow that it appears joined to Orcas. After passing Bird Rock steer to the southward of Crane Island, between it and Cliff Island, and thence between Crane Island and the north end of Shaw Island.

For ¾ mile the channel is of a good breadth, with no dangers until approaching the east end of Crane Island, when it narrows to little more than 200 yards. The steep cliffy shore of Shaw Island must now be kept aboard to avoid the Passage Rock, which lies 300 yards eastward of Passage Island. Knob Islet, just touching the north end of Cliff Island, and just open southward of the south side of Crane Island, leads 200 yards south of Passage Rock, which is covered at 2 feet rise.

When Orcas Knob is just over the narrow passage between Double Islands and the west shore of West Sound, bearing N. 8° W., vessels are eastward of Passage Rock, and may steer up West Sound or eastward for East Sound or Rosario Strait. Passing out of West Sound the same marks are equally good; steer down just westward of Broken Point (a remarkable cliffy peninsula on the north side of Shaw Island) until the islands above mentioned touch, when steer for them, giving the south side of Crane Island a moderate berth, and passing out of Wasp Channel as before directed for entering it.

If desired, a vessel may pass into Wasp Channel to the southward of

Yellow Island, between it and Low Island (a small islet), thence northward of Knob Island, as before directed, between Crane and Cliff Islands

There is another passage into Wasp Channel southward of Cliff Island, between it and Neck Point, the remarkable western extreme of Shaw Island. The breadth between them is a little over 200 yards, but there is a patch of 4 fathoms, with kelp on it, in the center of the passage. If taking this channel there is a reef lying S 62° W., and extending more than ¼ mile from the SW. end of Cliff Island; this reef is sometimes covered, and is the only danger known that is not visible.

These two latter passages are the shortest into the Wasp Channel for vessels from the southward. The eye will be found the best guide, a good lookout is necessary and to steamers there are no difficulties. To the northward of Crane Island, between it and Orcas, there is a narrow channel, but though deep it is only fit for boats.

Tides.—The flood tide sets to the west in the eastern entrance of Wasp Channel, but in the western entrance the flood from San Juan Channel partially sets to the eastward and causes some rips among the islands, which may be mistaken for shoal water.

North Passage.—This clear deep channel leading to Deer Harbor, the westernmost port in Orcas Island, lies between Steep Point and Reef Island. It is nearly ¼ mile wide and 20 fathoms deep, and the only danger to avoid is the reef off the western side of Reef Island. To enter Deer Harbor After passing Jones Island keep Steep Point and the shore of Orcas aboard within 300 yards, until past Reef Island, when haul up to the northward and anchor as convenient.

Orcas Island is the most extensive of the group known as the Haro Archipelago, and contains the finest harbors. It is mountainous and in most parts thickly wooded. Its southern side is singularly indented by deep sounds, which in some places almost divide the island On the eastern side of the island Mount Constitution arises to an elevation of 2,420 feet, wooded to its summit; on the west side is the Turtle Back, a long wooded range 1,000 feet high, and west of it, rising immediately over the sea, is the singular bare top cone known as Orcas Knob.

On the western and northern sides there is no convenient anchorage. A vessel might drop an anchor, if necessary, southward of Doughty Point, where 12 fathoms water will be found within 200 yards of the shore; a small vessel might also anchor in 4½ fathoms, just inside a small islet in the bay ⅜ mile southward of Doughty Point

The northern coast is steep and precipitous, except between Doughty Point and Thompson Point, a distance of 2½ miles; here occurs the low land at the head of East Sound, and the points are shelving, with large bowlder stones extending some distance off.

Thompson Point is bare and cliffy; from it the coast forms a slight curve southeasterly to Lawrence Point, distant 6 miles.

Lawrence Point, the sloping termination of the high range of Mount Constitution, is the eastern extreme of Orcas Island; on its northern side it is a steep and almost perpendicular cliff, and from it the coast turns abruptly to the southward, forming the western side of Rosario Strait; 4 miles southward from the point is the entrance to North Obstruction Pass.

Deer Harbor, the westernmost of the three ports of Orcas, may be conveniently entered from the San Juan Channel by North Passage, and Brown Islands. The harbor is one mile long in a north and south direction, and about the same breadth at its southern end; it narrows rapidly, and terminates in a shoal creek and fresh-water streams fed from a lake

Fawn Islet lies off the steep cliffy shore of the west side of the harbor; below it the depth varies from 10 to 15 fathoms, abreast and above it from 5 to 8 fathoms, mud bottom.

Anchorage.—A convenient berth is in 7 fathoms, halfway between Fawn Islet and the eastern shore, or a snug anchorage in 5 fathoms will be found ¼ mile above the islet Between Fawn Islet and the western shore is a passage 200 yards wide with 9 fathoms. There are no dangers in this harbor except a reef of rocks extending from the north side of Crane Island. The west end of this island, in line with the west end of Cliff Island, bearing S. 39° W., leads on to the western edge of this reef, on which there is only one fathom water. If working up the harbor a vessel should not stand so far to the eastward as to shut in the east end of Cliff Island behind the west end of Crane Island; this will lead more than 200 yards clear of the reef.

West Sound may be entered from San Juan Channel, either by the Wasp or Upright Passages already described, or from Rosario Strait by either of the Obstruction Passes Having entered by the Wasp Passage, cleared the Passage Rock, and being off Broken Point, West Sound will be open, with Orcas Knob immediately over the head of it. The sound is about ¾ mile broad with depths of from 10 to 16 fathoms, and no hidden dangers.

Anchorage may be had in any part above Double Islands, which lie close off its western shore, but the snuggest anchorage, and the best for vessels intending to make any stay, is either in White Beach Bay, on the eastern shore, or in Massacre Bay, at the northwestern head of the sound.

White Beach Bay, so named from the quantities of white clam shells lying on its shores, and giving them the appearance of white sandy beaches, is on the eastern side of the sound, 2 miles above Broken Point. A small islet, Sheep Islet, lies in the middle of the bay, nearly connected with the shore at low water.

Anchorage.—There is good anchorage in 9 fathoms water, with Sheep Islet bearing N. 62° E. and Haida Point, the northern point of the bay, N. 34° W., distant ¼ mile.

Massacre Bay is between Haida and Indian Points. Harbor Rock, covering at one third flood, is almost in the center of the bay, between the two entrance points and nearly 600 yards east of Indian Point; it may be passed on either side in a depth of 9 fathoms. If to the eastward, Hada Point should be kept within 300 yards; if to the westward, the eastern cliffy part of Broken Point and the eastern side of Double Islands kept in line astern, bearing S. 17° E., leads westward of the rock When Indian Point bears S. 23° W good anchorage will be found in the center of the bay in 8 fathoms, mud bottom.

Harney Channel connects the West and East Sounds of Orcas. It commences at Broken Point, and takes an easterly direction for 3 miles, when it enters Upright Channel between Foster and Hankin Points; the former is a low sloping green point, the southern termination of the peninsula which separates the two sounds, the latter is the eastern bluff wooded point of Shaw Island

The north side of Harney Channel is a series of small bays with shingle beaches, and there is a deep cove ⅝ mile west of Foster Point, just westward of this cove is a rocky patch which lies more than 200 yards offshore, and covers at half flood.

Camp Cove is immediately northward of Foster Point, it is a convenient cove for boats, or a small vessel might anchor there in 6 fathoms; there is a good stream of fresh water running into it.

High Water Rock lies more than 200 yards from the shore, ½ mile northeastward of Foster Point; it is awash at high water, and there is a depth of 8 fathoms between it and the shore.

Blind Bay is on the southern shore, midway between Broken and Hankin Points. A small round islet partially wooded lies in the center of the entrance, and a reef of rocks covering at high water extends from its western point, almost choking the entrance on that side, but leaving a narrow passage close to the islet, a rock covering at one-quarter flood also lies off the eastern side of the islet, leaving a channel of 3 fathoms almost equally narrow on that side, so that the bay is only eligible for coasters, which should keep the island close aboard when entering; the eastern side is the best.

Anchorage in 4 or 5 fathoms may be had with the islet bearing north, distant 400 yards.

East Sound.—Entering this sound, remarkable conical hills over 1,000 feet high rise on both sides of the entrance, which is between Diamond and Stockade Points. From between these points the sound takes a northwesterly direction; it contracts at Cascade Bay to ½ mile, and opens out again above to more than one mile wide, the head of the sound terminates in two bays, separated by a jutting cliffy point. The depth of water in the sound is 15 fathoms.

Stockade Bay, on the eastern side of the entrance to the sound, nearly one mile north of Stockade Point affords anchorage in 8 fathoms, at about 600 yards from the shore, there is a good stream of fresh water running into the bay; with a strong SW. wind some swell sets into this anchorage

Green Bank, on the western side, immediately opposite Stockade Bay, is a bank of sand extending halfway across the sound; on it there are depths of from 5 to 9 fathoms, with one patch of 4 fathoms, and a vessel might anchor on it if necessary, as being more convenient than the deep water immediately off it. The best anchorage is in 6 fathoms at ½ mile north of Diamond Point, with a small green islet, which lies just off a white shell beach, bearing N. 67° W., distant about 800 yards.

Cascade Bay, on the eastern side of the sound, is formed by a small hook of land. Anchorage may be had 300 yards from the beach in 10 fathoms; but it would not be a desirable place to lay with a southeasterly wind.

Water.—A large stream falls by a cascade into the above bay, and it would be a convenient place at which to water a ship.

Fishing and Ship Bays.—Fishing Bay, the westernmost of the two bays at the head of the sound, has good anchorage in 10 fathoms, with Arbutus Point, the cliffy extreme of the jutting peninsula before mentioned, bearing N. 68° E., midway between it and the west side of the sound.

Ship Bay, eastward of Arbutus Point, runs off shoal for 400 yards or nearly to the extreme of the point; but it affords good shelter, perhaps better than Fishing Bay. There is good anchorage in 9 fathoms, mud bottom, with Arbutus Point bearing N. 55° W., distant 600 yards.

CHAPTER IV.

ROSARIO STRAIT AND SHORES OF GEORGIA STRAIT.

Rosario Strait is the easternmost and one of the principal channels leading from Juan de Fuca Strait into that of Georgia. Its southern entrance is between Lopez and Fidalgo Islands, and from thence its general direction is north and northwesterly for 25 miles, where it enters Georgia Strait.

Like Haro Strait, the Rosario has several smaller channels which branch off to the eastward, and lead between islands to the settlements in Bellingham Bay, or by a more circuitous route into the Strait of Georgia itself; among the principal of these channels are Guemes, Bellingham, and Lummi.

The principal dangers are the Bird and Belle Rocks, which lie almost in the center of the strait, 4 miles within the southern entrance. There are several anchorages available for vessels delayed by the tides or other causes. Shoal Bight (Davis Bay) on the eastern side of Lopez Island, 3 miles within the southern entrance; Burrows Bay, immediately opposite it, under Mount Erie, on the west side of Fidalgo Island; Ship Bay in Guemes Channel; and Strawberry Bay, on the western side of Cypress Island, are the principal. Vessels entering Fuca Strait, and bound to any of the ports of Puget Sound, or up Rosario Strait, either by day or night, should make New Dungeness light, and then Smith or Blunt Island.

Tides.—The tides in Rosario Strait are strong, from 3 to 7 knots in the narrower parts.

Directions.—Having made Smith Island, which vessels bound from sea up Rosario Channel should do on about a N. 73° E. bearing, it may be passed on either side, but to the northward appears most convenient. When Dungeness Light house bears S. 34° W. keep it on that bearing, astern, steering N. 34° E., which leads midway between Smith Island and the Hein (Fonte) Bank. (By day this bank will be always seen in time to avoid it.)

When the light-house on Smith Island bears S. 55° E. a vessel will be to the eastward of the bank, and a course may be steered for the entrance of the strait, which, however, should not be entered at night until there is a light on Bird or Belle Rocks, unless by those perfectly acquainted with the navigation and the state of the tide. If passing to the southward of Smith Island, remember to avoid Partridge Bank. The northwestern edge of the bank is marked by a buoy.

Vessels from the southern parts of Vancouver Island, bound up Rosario Strait, should of course pass northward of Smith Island. The only dangers to be avoided are the Salmon Bank, with 10 feet of water over it, off the south end of San Juan, and the Davidson Rock off Southwest Island. Mount Erie (on Fidalgo Island) in line with Iceberg Point, bearing N. 82° E., leads 1¼ miles south of the former, and it is not recommended to pass the southern side of Lopez Island at less than one mile, which will insure clearing the latter, moreover, the coast is rocky and the flood tide sets on to it.

Watmough Head (Cape Colville), the southeastern extreme of Lopez Island, is the western entrance point of Rosario Strait; Watmough Hill, flat-topped, and about 450 feet high, rises immediately over it

Southwest Island (Colville Island), small, and bare of trees about 40 feet high, lies one mile S. 45° W. of the cape; close to the cape and appearing from most points of view a part of it, is Castle Island, a high, precipitous rock. Entering the strait, Southwest Island should be given a berth of one mile.

Davidson Rock, on which is only a depth of 4 feet at low water, and occasionally uncovering at low springs, lies a little more than 600 yards S 67° E. of the east end of Southwest Island, and nearly one mile S 23° W. of Watmough Head; kelp grows about the rock, but the patch is so small that it is difficult to make out Kellett Island, or Cape St. Mary, kept open of the extreme of Watmough Head, bearing north, leads ½ mile to the eastward of the rock, and Eagle Point (San Juan) kept open of the south end of Lopez Island, bearing N. 64° W., leads one mile southward of it.

Kellett Island is a small flat-topped islet covered with grass, lying immediately northward, and close off the low extreme of Watmough Head.

Cape St. Mary, the next point northward of Watmough Head, and a little more than one mile from it, forms the southern point of Davis Bay.

Kellett or Hulah Ledge, with one fathom water on it, and marked by kelp, lies 600 yards N. 58° E. of Cape St. Mary; there is a deep passage between it and the cape. Vessels passing outside it should give the cape a berth of over ½ mile.

Shoal Bight (Davis Bay) Anchorage.—Shoal Bight affords good and convenient anchorage in a moderate depth of water. After rounding Hulah Ledge, a vessel may stand to the westward into the bay and anchor in 6 fathoms, mud bottom, at little more than ½ mile from the shore, with Cape St. Mary bearing S. 11° E., inside this the water shoals rather suddenly to 2½ and 3 fathoms. A kelp patch, on which there is shoal water, lies one mile N. 11° E. of the cape. There is anchorage in from 4 to 8 fathoms anywhere within one mile of the east shore of Lopez and Decatur Islands, from a little northward of Cape St. Mary, as far north as the white cliff of Decatur Island, avoiding the kelp patches just mentioned, or while the Bird Rock bears anything to the northward of S. 67° E., but little tide will be felt. With the Lopez (Maury) Pass open, bearing N. 67° W., there is good anchorage at from ½ mile to one mile from th shore, in from 6 to 8 fathoms.

Deception Pass is a narrow channel separating Fidalgo from Whidbey Island, and communicating with the waters of Puget Sound and Admiralty Inlet, but it is only eligible for such small vessels or steamers as are well acquainted with the locality. The tides set through it with great velocity.

Lawson Reef, on which there is only a depth of 3 fathoms at low water, is a ledge of small extent lying $1\frac{9}{10}$ miles S. 81° W. of the West point of Deception Island at the entrance to Deception Pass

Allan Island is ¾ mile in extent and 230 feet high. Its southern face is bare.

Burrows Island, separated from Allan Island by a channel ¼ mile wide, is 610 feet high, has a notably flat top, is wooded, and may be seen from the Strait of Fuca.

Burrows Bay, on the eastern side of the entrance to Rosario Strait, is well marked by Mount Erie, a remarkable conical hill, rising 1,250 feet immediately over it, at one mile from the coast. The bay is sheltered from westerly and southwesterly winds by Burrows and Allan Islands, and affords good anchorage.

Williamson's Rocks, a cluster of rocky islets, lie in the southern entrance of the bay, ½ mile south of Allan Island, with deep water close around them.

Directions—The best entrance, which is one mile in breadth, is to the southward of Williamson's Rocks, between them and Fidalgo Island. On the eastern side of Allan Island the water is deep for ⅛ mile off shore, having depths of from 18 to 25 fathoms. The eastern shore of the bay is shoal for 600 yards off the beach, and in one spot a bowlder, awash at low water, lies nearly 800 yards off.

Vessels from the northward may enter Burrows Bay by the passage northward of Burrows Island, or between the latter and Allan Island; they are about an equal breadth, a little over 400 yards at their narrowest part, free from danger, and lie nearly east and west.

Anchorage may be had in 6 fathoms, with the passage between Burrows and Allan Islands open bearing west, ½ mile from Young Island; but the most sheltered anchorage is in 12 fathoms at the north head of the bay, ½ mile from the eastern shore of Burrows Island, with the passage shut in, and Young Island bearing S. 40° W.

Tides.—The ebb tide sets to the eastward into both passages, at the rate of 3 to 4 knots during springs.

Denis Rock.—There is a deep channel ½ mile in breadth, between Williamson's Rocks and Allan Island, but vessels taking it, or working up westward of the latter island, must avoid Denis Rock, which has 2 feet on it at low water and rarely uncovers. It lies nearly 1,200 yards N 31° W. of Williamson's Rocks, and the same distance west of the south end of Allan Island.

Bird Rocks, lying almost in the center of Rosario Strait, nearly 4 miles N. 26° E. of Watmough Head, are composed of three detached rocks close together, the southernmost being the largest. There is deep water close to it, but on account of the strong tides, sailing vessels working up or down, particularly during light winds, should give it a berth of ½ mile. There is an equally good passage on either side of the rock; that to the eastward is the wider (2 miles across); to the westward it is one mile wide, with somewhat less tide. By taking the latter channel with a leading wind, strangers will more easily avoid the Belle Rock; passing Bird Rock at a convenient distance, steer just outside, or to the eastward of James Island, until the passage between Guemes and Fidalgo Islands is open.

Belle Rock, the most serious danger in the Rosario Strait, only uncovers near low water, and the tides set over it from 2 to 5 knots. It lies 1,200 yards N. 13° E. of Bird Rock, and in the passage between them are depths of 8 to 20 fathoms. Vessels should not pass between them except in cases of necessity The Belle Rock is easily avoided by day; if passing to the eastward of it, keep Lawrence Point (the eastern point of Orcas Island) just shut in by Tide Point (the western extreme of Cypress Island), bearing north, until the passage between Guemes and Fidalgo Islands is just open.

If taking the channel westward of Bird Rock, keep that rock well eastward of Watmough Head until Guemes Channel is open. The great danger of the Belle Rock to a sailing vessel is being left with a light wind in the center of the strait, as the water is too deep to allow of an anchor holding in so strong a tideway.

Buoy.—A bell-buoy, painted black, is moored in 9 fathoms, with Bird Rock S 45° W and Belle Rock N. 58° W

James Island, almost divided in the center, is a remarkable saddle island with two summits, 250 feet high, lying close off the east side of Decatur Island. There are no dangers on its off or eastern side.

White and Black Rocks are ¾ mile apart, and lie off the southeastern shore of Blakely Island. White Rock, the southernmost, is 16 feet above high water, and a little more than ¼ mile from the shore at the eastern entrance of Thatcher Pass. Black Rock, 10 feet high, lies ⅜ mile N. 57° E. of White Rock, and ½ mile from Blakely Island There is a deep channel between these rocks, as also between them and Blakely Island.

Bellingham Channel, between Guemes and Cypress Islands, is about 3½ miles long and ¾ mile wide in its narrowest part, between

East Point and Guemes Island. Abreast the northern end of Guemes Island, which is a steep bluff called **Clark's Point** and on the western side of the channel, are several small, high, wooded islets, called the Cone Islets. No dangers will be met with in navigating this channel. Pass north of Vendovi and south of Eliza Islands, and Bellingham Bay opens. Should the wind be light and the tide flood, pass close to Clark's Point to avoid being set past Sinclair Island.

Guemes Channel, south of Guemes Island, leads into Padilla Bay and eastward of the island to Bellingham Bay. At the western entrance, on the southern shore, is Ship Harbor.

Port Townsend to Bellingham Bay.—With strong *flood* tide and clear weather vessels pass through Guemes Channel instead of through Bellingham Channel. The usual route is through Bellingham Channel

(1065) **WASHINGTON — Bellingham bay—Bellingham — Information.**—Commander V. L. Cottman, U. S. Navy, commanding the U. S. S. *Wyoming*, reports under date of June 26, 1904, that the towns of Whatcom and Fairhaven have been united under the name of Bellingham. He also states that no coal can be obtained here as stated in the Sailing Directions. (N. M. 20, 1904.)

Bellingham Bay.—The general direction of this bay is north and south; it is 4 miles in width and 14 miles long, including the broad flats at either end. In the northeastern corner of the bay are the villages of Bellingham, Sehone, and Whatcom. There are coal mines near these villages, but the amount of coal is not great and the quality is poor. Half a mile from the shore there is good anchorage in 4 fathoms, soft sticky bottom. Underlying this soft bottom there is a stratum of sandstone, which prevents the anchor from holding, and vessels drag with southeasters, which blow strong up the bay and raise a rough sea.

Rocks and Shoals.—A single bowlder, with 8 feet of water over it, lies about midway between Point Frances and Eliza Island. This rock bears N. 8° 12′ W. from the north end of Eliza Island and S. 36° 48′ W. from Chuckanut Rock.

Starr Rock, a small ledge about 37 yards in length, in a N. 45° E. and S. 45° W. direction, with a least depth of 6 feet on it, is about 384 yards offshore, with from 5 to 6 fathoms inshore of it, and lies with the west end of warehouse on Whatcom Wharf bearing N. 24° 08′ E. and the south smokestack of Bellingham sawmill S. 8° 12′ E.

A small shoal spot, about 328 yards off Eliza Island, with a least depth of 5 feet, is 40 to 50 feet in length, and there is 15 fathoms outside and from 7 to 9 fathoms inside of it; it lies with the dead tree on extreme west point of Eliza Island bearing S. 8° 12′ E. and south point of Lummi Island S. 53° 59′ W.

A shoal spot on the east side of Lummi Island, about 1¾ miles from the south end, is about 110 yards offshore, and has a least depth of 8 feet on it, with from 4 to 6 fathoms inshore of it; it lies with the north end of Eliza Island S. 67° 16′ E.; tangent to east side of Point Frances N. 14° 18′ E.

Denis Rock.—There is a deep channel $\frac{1}{2}$ mile in breadth, between Williamson's Rocks and Allan Island, but vessels taking it, or working up westward of the latter island, must avoid Denis Rock, which has 2 feet on it at low water and rarely uncovers. It lies nearly 1,200 yards N 31° W. of Williamson's Rocks, and the same distance west of the south end of Allan Island

Bird Rocks, lying almost in the center of Rosario Strait, nearly 4 miles N. 26° E. of Watmough Head, are composed of three detached rocks close together, the southernmost being the largest. There is deep water close to it, but on account of the strong tides, sailing vessels working up or down, particularly during light winds, should give it a berth of $\frac{1}{2}$ [illegible] There is an equally good passage on either side of the rock; that [illegible]
ward it is [illegible]
channel w[illegible]
Rock; pas[illegible]
or to the e[illegible]
and Fidalgo Islands is open.

Belle Rock, the most serious danger in the Rosario Strait, only uncovers near low water, and the tides set over it from 2 to 5 knots It lies 1,200 yards N 43° E of Bird Rock, and in the passage between them are depths of 8 to 20 fathoms Vessels should not pass between them except in cases of necessity The Belle Rock is easily avoided by day; if passing to the eastward of it, keep Lawrence Point (the eastern point of Orcas Island) just shut in by Tide Point (the western extreme of Cypress Island), bearing north, until the passage between Guemes and Fidalgo Islands is just open.

If taking the channel westward of Bird Rock, keep that rock well eastward of Watmough Head until Guemes Channel is open. The great danger of the Belle Rock to a sailing vessel is being left with a light wind in the center of the strait, as the water is too deep to allow of an anchor holding in so strong a tideway.

Buoy—A bell buoy, painted black, is moored in 9 fathoms, with Bird Rock S. 45° W. and Belle Rock N. 58° W

James Island, almost divided in the center, is a remarkable saddle island with two summits, 250 feet high, lying close off the east side of Decatur Island. There are no dangers on its off or eastern side.

White and Black Rocks are $\frac{3}{4}$ mile apart, and lie off the south eastern shore of Blakely Island. White Rock, the southernmost, is 10 feet above high water, and a little more than $\frac{1}{4}$ mile from the shore at the eastern entrance of Thatcher Pass Black Rock, 10 feet high, lies $\frac{3}{4}$ mile N 57° E. of White Rock, and $\frac{1}{2}$ mile from Blakely Island. There is a deep channel between these rocks, as also between them and Blakely Island.

Bellingham Channel, between Guemes and Cypress Islands, is about $3\frac{1}{2}$ miles long and $\frac{3}{4}$ mile wide in its narrowest part, between

East Point and Guemes Island. Abreast the northern end of Guemes Island, which is a steep bluff called Clark's Point and on the western side of the channel, are several small, high, wooded islets, called the Cone Islets. No dangers will be met with in navigating this channel. Pass north of Vendovi and south of Eliza Islands, and Bellingham Bay opens. Should the wind be light and the tide flood, pass close to Clark's Point to avoid being set past Sinclair Island.

Guemes Channel, south of Guemes Island, leads into Padilla Bay and eastward of the island to Bellingham Bay. At the western entrance, on the southern shore, is Ship Harbor.

Port Townsend to Bellingham Bay.—With strong *flood* tide and clear weather vessels pass through Guemes Channel instead of through Bellingham Channel. The usual route is through Bellingham Channel and to the northward of Vendovi Island.

Bellingham Bay to Roche Harbor.—With *ebb* tide small vessels use Hale's Passage. With *flood* tide pass between Viti Rocks and Carter Point, then across to the northward of Orcas Island, passing between the island and Parker Reef.

Bellingham Bay.—The general direction of this bay is north and south; it is 4 miles in width and 14 miles long, including the broad flats at either end. In the northeastern corner of the bay are the villages of Bellingham, Sehome, and Whatcom. There are coal mines near these villages, but the amount of coal is not great and the quality is poor. Half a mile from the shore there is good anchorage in 4 fathoms, soft sticky bottom. Underlying this soft bottom there is a stratum of sandstone, which prevents the anchor from holding, and vessels drag with southeasters, which blow strong up the bay and raise a rough sea.

Rocks and Shoals.—A single bowlder, with 8 feet of water over it, lies about midway between Point Frances and Eliza Island. This rock bears N. 8° 12′ W. from the north end of Eliza Island and S. 36° 48′ W. from Chuckanut Rock.

Starr Rock, a small ledge about 37 yards in length, in a N. 45° E. and S. 45° W. direction, with a least depth of 6 feet on it, is about 384 yards offshore, with from 5 to 6 fathoms inshore of it, and lies with the west end of warehouse on Whatcom Wharf bearing N. 24° 08′ E. and the south smokestack of Bellingham sawmill S. 8° 12′ E.

A small shoal spot, about 328 yards off Eliza Island, with a least depth of 5 feet, is 40 to 50 feet in length, and there is 15 fathoms outside and from 7 to 9 fathoms inside of it; it lies with the dead tree on extreme west point of Eliza Island bearing S. 8° 12′ E. and south point of Lummi Island S. 53° 59′ W.

A shoal spot on the east side of Lummi Island, about 1¾ miles from the south end, is about 110 yards offshore, and has a least depth of 8 feet on it, with from 4 to 6 fathoms inshore of it; it lies with the north end of Eliza Island S. 67° 16′ E.; tangent to east side of Point Frances N. 14° 18′ E.

A shoal spot off the entrance to Inati Bay is about 110 yards long in a NNE. and SSW. direction. Its shoalest part is just bare at low water and lies with the north end of Eliza Island S. 57° 25′ E.; tangent to Point Frances N. 21° 20′ E.

Cypress Island forms a portion of the eastern side of Rosario Strait. It is thickly wooded with pine and white cedar trees; on its northern extreme a remarkable bare, rocky cone rises immediately over the sea to 720 feet. A reef of bowlder stones, some of which uncover, with kelp growing about them, extends ¼ mile off the SW point of the island; the outer bowlder covers at half flood. Between Cypress and Blakely Islands is the narrowest part of Rosario Strait, and here the tides during springs occasionally run between 6 and 7 knots.

Strawberry Bay, on the western side of Cypress Island, will be known by the small island of the same name, which lies immediately off it, 1¼ miles N. 22° W. of Reef Point, the southwestern extreme, and protects the bay from the westward; it is rather a confined anchorage, and at certain times of tide would be difficult of entrance for sailing vessels.

The bay is exposed to southerly winds, which, however, do not frequently blow; from SE it is sheltered, and there is no reason to doubt but that with good ground tackle a vessel would ride out any gale. There is a passage of 10 fathoms water to the northward between Strawberry and Cypress Islands; and in the event of parting or slipping, a vessel should run through this passage, and take shelter in Birch or Semiahmoo Bays, in the mainland.

Directions.—A sailing vessel should not attempt to enter the bay during the strength of the tide, unless with a commanding breeze, and should remember that the tides set with great strength against the points of Strawberry Island; it was remarked that, while the ebb was running strongly in Rosario Strait, which it continues to do for two and one half hours after low water, a stream of flood set to the northward through Strawberry Bay, as soon as it was low water by the shore.

Anchorage.—About 600 yards from the sandy bight of the bay, with the north bluff of Strawberry Island bearing N. 45° W and the south point of this island S. 56° W, is the best berth, in 7 fathoms, good holding ground, and nearly out of the tide, which sets with considerable strength inside Strawberry Island.

Water.—There is a belt of flat marsh-land in Strawberry Bay, through which several streams of good water run from the mountains.

Rock Islet, a small round islet covered with trees, lying nearly 400 yards northward of the north end of Cypress Island, has its shores strewn with large bowlder stones. There is a passage of 9 fathoms water between it and Cypress Island; but the ebb tide sets with great strength to the southward, and close round the western points of the latter island.

Cypress Reef, lying ¼ mile westward of Rock Islet, is a dangerous rocky patch with kelp growing about it, covering at half flood. James Island kept open of Tide Point, the west point of Cypress Island bearing S. 14° W., leads to the westward of the reef; and Rock Islet bearing S. 45° E., or either of the Cone Islands open of it, leads to the northward.

Sinclair Island, thickly wooded and comparatively low, lies to the northeastward of Cypress Island, with a deep passage of nearly one mile in breadth between them, leading to Bellingham Channel. Shelving rocks project a short distance off its western shores.

Bowlder Reef (Panama Reef), an extensive and dangerous shoal, extends nearly ½ mile in a northwestern direction off the NW. extreme of Sinclair Island, some parts of it uncovering at half tide; a large bowlder stands on the inner part of the reef. Great quantities of kelp grow in the neighborhood, but it is sometimes run under by the tide or concealed by the rips; there are 6 fathoms of water close to the edge of the kelp. By keeping Cypress Cone open to the westward of Rock Islet, or the strait between Cypress and Blakely Islands well open, vessels will clear it in passing up and down, and the centers of Vendovi and Barnes Islands in line leads clear to the northward and eastward of it.

The Peapods are two small rocky islets, bare of trees, lying ½ mile from the western shore of Rosario Strait, and from 1¼ to nearly 2 miles southward from Lawrence Point. They are ¾ miles apart in a NE. and SW. direction, the northernmost being the larger and higher. A little to the westward of a line drawn between them is a third rock which just covers at high water. There are no dangers about them which are not visible, and there is a passage 20 fathoms deep between them and Orcas Island.

The Eastern Side of Orcas Island between the Peapod Islets and Obstruction Pass, falls back in a bight, where there is considerably less tide than in the main stream of the strait, and if necessary vessels may anchor within ½ mile of the shore in about 16 fathoms water.

Lawrence Point, the eastern extreme of Orcas, is a long sloping point; immediately on its north side it rises abruptly in almost perpendicular cliffs, and trends to the westward, falling back for 3 miles in a somewhat deep bight, which is rocky, has deep water, and is unsheltered.

To the northward, Rosario Strait lies between Orcas and Lummi Islands, the direct channel being along the western shore of the latter. Anchorage may be had, if necessary, on the eastern side of the strait, within one mile of the shore, in 15 fathoms, between Sandy and Whitehorn Points, northward of Lummi Island.

Tides.—After passing northward of Lawrence Point, the ebb tide sets to the eastward between Orcas and the small islands to the northward of it, as well as to the SE. through the northern entrance of the strait; when in the vicinity of Alden Bank, or about 8 miles above

Lawrence Point, the strength of the tide sensibly decreases, and while vessels are eastward of a line between this bank and Roberts Point they will be entirely out of the strong tides of the archipelago and the Strait of Georgia. It is recommended with the ebb tide to work up on this shore.

Lummi Island is 8 miles long and very narrow On its southwestern side it is high and precipitous, a remarkable double mountain rising about 1,500 feet abruptly from the sea, there are no dangers off its western side; a small, high, double rocky islet, Lummi Rock, lies close off the shore, 3 miles from its southern point; foul ground extends from its northwestern point in a NW direction for more than ½ mile, and at about 1,600 yards SW. of Carter Point lies Viti Rock. A reef extends 600 yards from this rock in a southeasterly direction.

Rock.—A rock lies about ½ mile N. 39° W of Point Migley, and is marked by a buoy placed 50 feet SE. of it.

Hale's Passage, east of Lummi Island, connects with Bellingham Bay. A ledge extends across this passage from about the position of the stake light to the mainland. It has a least depth of from 12 to 15 feet.

Lummi Bay opens northeastward of Lummi Island, and is a shore bay backed by marshy ground. Into it by several mouths the Lummi River empties The main entrance of the river in the nort[illegible] part of the bay can only be reached by boats at high tide. Sandy P[illegible] the north entrance point of the bay, is low and grassy with a few bu[illegible]es upon it

Clark and Barnes Islands are two small wooded islands 2 miles NW. of Lawrence Point; two smaller islets, the Sisters, bare of trees, and a high rock lie immediately southward of Clark Island. There is a passage 1½ miles in breadth between these islands and Orcas with a depth of 45 fathoms; there is also a narrow channel with a depth of 20 fathoms between Clark and Barnes Islands, which a vessel may take if necessary.

The tides set strong about the Sisters, and the best and most [illegible]t channel is between Clark and Lummi Islands. When taking this channel the north point of Lummi Island should not be approached within one mile, as shoal and broken ground extends for some distance off it; Sinclair Island kept just open westward of the NW. point of Lummi leads to the westward of this foul ground in 15 fathoms water

Matia Island, 3 miles NW. of Clark Island, and one mile eastward of Sucia Island, is moderately high and wooded, and has some coves on its southern side, affording shelter for boats; close off its east point is Puffin Islet, and extending a short distance eastward of the islet is a flat rock which covers. Vessels bound through Rosario Strait are recommended to pass eastward of Matia.

Alden Bank, 3 miles in extent north and south and one mile east and west, lies in the center of the northern entrance of Rosario Strait; its southern limit is 2 miles north of Matia Island, and there is a channel 3 miles in breadth between it and the eastern shore.

The depth of water on this bank varies from 2¾ to 7 fathoms; the bottom is in some parts rocky, with patches of kelp growing on it; in other parts it is sandy, and offers a convenient anchorage for vessels becalmed or waiting for tide. It frequently happens that a vessel having passed to the northward between East Point and Patos Island, meets the ebb tide and is carried to the eastward; in such a case it would be desirable to anchor in 7 or 8 fathoms on Alden Bank, and thus prevent being set down Rosario Strait.

Vessels passing up or down are recommended to pass on the eastern side of the bank, Mount Constitution on Orcas Island kept just open eastward of Puffin Island, bearing S. 9° W., leads over the eastern edge of the bank in 13 fathoms; and the low west point of Patos Island in line with Monarch Head (Saturna Island), bearing S. 73° W., leads over the northern edge in 7 fathoms.

Whitehorn Point is a remarkable bold bluff about 150 feet high, its face showing as a steep white clay cliff. It is the southern point of Birch Bay, and is 9 miles NNW. of the north point of Lummi Island.

Birch Bay is between Whitehorn Point and Birch Point (South Bluff); the latter, which is a moderately high rounding point, forms the north entrance point of the bay; some large bowlder stones stand a short distance off it, and should not be rounded at a less distance than ½ mile. The bay is nearly 2 miles in breadth at a distance of one mile inside the entrance points; the head of the bay dries off a considerable distance at low water, and the 3 fathom line extends 1½ miles offshore in the center of the bay. The holding ground is good, and with southeast gales it affords excellent shelter. A good berth is in 4 fathoms, with Whitehorn Point bearing S. 23° W., distant one mile; the water shoals gradually from 14 fathoms at one mile off to 6 fathoms between the entrance points; inside this line, 4 fathoms only will be found for a farther distance of one mile towards the head of the bay. Both entrance points are buoyed.

Semiahmoo Bay, between Birch Point (South Bluff) and Kwomais Point (North Bluff), affords good anchorage in from 6 to 8 fathoms water, at about 1½ to 2 miles distance outside Drayton Harbor entrance; a good berth is in 6 fathoms, mud bottom, with Birch Point bearing S. 12° W. and Tongue Point bearing S. 78° E. This is always good anchorage, unless with a heavy Southwest gale, when vessels might take shelter in Drayton Harbor.

Supplies.—Wild fowl frequent this anchorage in considerable numbers during the winter months.

Drayton Harbor is formed by a remarkable low narrow spit over one mile long. The spit is covered with grass and drift timber, and a few pine trees grow on it; several wooden buildings were erected on it in 1858, and received the name of Semiahmoo town.

Directions.—Off the outside of Tongue Spit a bank extends for a considerable distance, and vessels should not approach the spit within

¾ mile until its extreme point bears S. 70° E., when it may be steered for and passed close to. There is only a depth of 4 fathoms at low water in the fair way, at from ¼ to ¾ mile outside the entrance; the channel is narrow, and vessels unacquainted with the locality should not enter before placing boats or poles on the edges of the shoals; when within, it opens out into a considerable sheet of water, but it is for the most part shoal, drying off from the main shore from ½ to one mile.

Anchorage.—The anchorage is in from 7 to 10 fathoms; it is perfectly sheltered, and affords room for 3 or 4 large vessels, as well as several small ones, and on the inside of the spit a vessel might be beached for repairs. The only landing at low water is at the spit end, which is steep-to.

Boundary Bay is an extensive sheet of water between the promontory of Roberts Point on the west and Kwomais Point (North Bluff) on the east. The bay extends in a northerly direction for nearly 7 miles, and is only separated from the south bank of Fraser River by a low delta 3 miles across, intersected by streams and swamps; it is very shallow and dries off for a distance of 3 miles at low water, the edge of the bank in 3 fathoms water extends 1½ miles off the whole of the north shore of the bay

Vessels should never stand so far to the northward as to bring the white bluff of Roberts Point to bear to the southward of S. 79° W., which line of bearing leads more than ½ mile outside the shoal edge of the bank; the general depth of water outside this line is from 7 to 15 fathoms, good holding ground, but this anchorage is exposed to all southerly winds, which send in a considerable sea

Roberts Point is the termination of a remarkable promontory, which stretches southerly from the delta of the Fraser River The eastern point of the promontory is a remarkable white faced cliff 200 feet high, its summit crowned with trees; from it the land gradually falls to the westward and terminates in Roberts Spit, a low shingle point, within which is a small space of level, clear land, where a few wooden buildings were erected on the first discovery of gold in the Fraser River and named Roberts Town; for a few months it served as a depot for the miners, but it has been long deserted.

From most points of view, and particularly from the southward, Roberts Point presents the appearance of an island; shoal water and rocky irregular bottom, on which kelp grows in summer, extends for more than one mile SW. from the white face of the point, and vessels should give it a good berth.

Boundary Mark.—There is a granite monument 25 feet high erected on the summit of the boundary bluff, which is only just visible from the anchorage on account of the trees; it marks the boundary between the United States and British possessions.

Anchorage will be found on either side of the promontory; to the eastward in 9 fathoms, sandy bottom, with the extreme of the white cliff bearing west, distant 1½ miles, and Roberts Spit, the western termination of the promontory, just shut in by the white cliff To the westward of the spit there is fair anchorage in 8 fathoms, good holding ground, with the spit extreme distant one mile, bearing S 30° E., and the bare bluff of the 49° parallel, or the monument on its summit N. 23° E., here the edge of the bank is distant ½ mile, and vessels should not anchor any farther to the northward, as the Roberts Bank trends rapidly to the westward.

Directions—Vessels should feel their way by the lead cautiously into this anchorage; the bank is very steep outside, and shoals suddenly within; a signal staff at present stands on the end of the spit.

Ships should not lie at this anchorage with strong southerly or westerly winds, but should shift round to the eastern one, or to Semiahmoo Bay, and give the southern face of Roberts Point a berth of 2 miles in rounding; neither of the anchorages at Roberts Point can be considered as more than stopping places, and during winter vessels should be prepared to weigh at short warning

Roberts Bank, formed by the alluvial deposits of the stream of the Fraser River, extends from the spit of Roberts Point in a N. 56° W. direction for 9½ miles, to the Sand Heads or river entrance, and at this point is 5 miles from the shore; it then takes a northerly direction for a farther distance of 12 miles, joining Point Grey on the north, as it does Roberts Point on the south. The portion of the bank northward of the Fraser is named the Sturgeon Bank; it is steep-to, there being depths of from 70 to 60 fathoms at one mile from its edge, shoaling suddenly to 20 and 2 fathoms.

Strait of Georgia.—Having passed out of Fuca Strait by either of the channels now described, when to the northwestward of a line drawn between east point of Saturna Island and Whitehorn Point (mainland) a vessel may be considered well in the Strait of Georgia.

General Remarks.—Of the channels leading into Georgia Strait, Haro Strait is the more tortuous, the water is so deep that it would be impossible for a vessel to anchor in the main stream, and for its whole length the tides, though not stronger, are more varying in their direction.

Rosario Strait leads by a very gentle curve almost a straight course into Georgia Strait, the depth of water, although considerable, is such that if necessary a vessel might anchor in it; in one part it is somewhat narrower than the narrowest parts of Haro Strait, and the tides run with equal strength, it has its sunken rocks and dangers in an equal degree with the Haro, and perhaps the anchorages in point of numbers and facilities for reaching them are equal in both; extreme care and vigilance are called for in navigating either with a sailing vessel; to one with steam power neither offer any difficulties.

To a vessel bound from sea, or from any of the southern ports of Vancouver Island to the Strait of Georgia, the Haro Channel is pref erable, while to reach the same destination from Admiralty Inlet or Puget Sound, Rosario Strait is the most direct and desirable. Having entered, however, by either channel, the promontory of Roberts Point will be immediately seen with its conspicuous white-faced cliff, appearing as an island

Dangers.—The dangers to be avoided in working through the Strait of Georgia are, on the northern shore, Roberts and Sturgeon Banks; and on the southern, the neighborhood of East Point and Tumbo Island, and the coast of Saturna and Mayne Islands, until beyond the entrance of Active Pass A chain of reefs and rocky islets lie parallel with this shore, in places extending nearly one mile off; and the bottom is rocky and irregular, with strong tides.

Extending one mile east from the east end of Tumbo Island is a ledge of foul, rocky ground, over which there are very heavy tide rips and dangerous overfalls. At ¼ mile N. 62° E. of Race Point is a rocky patch of 5 fathoms, about 400 yards in extent; and at about 200 yards to the northwestward of this patch there is a rock with only 14 feet water on it, possibly a shoal head of the 5 fathom patch. This rock lies ¾ mile N. 43° E. of Race Point. Orcas Knob kept well open to the eastward of the east point of Waldron Island, bearing S 3° E., leads in the fairway between Saturna and Patos Islands, 1¼ miles eastward of the rock; and Toe Point (Patos Island), in line with the north extreme of Sucia Island, bearing S. 64° E., leads nearly ¾ mile to the northward of it.

A rock lies 300 yards S. 56° E. of Edith Point, Mayne Island. The least depth on it is 2 feet, with irregular soundings around.

Caution.—As before observed vessels should when possible pass midway between Saturna and Patos Islands; they should on no account give the east point of Tumbo Island a berth of less than 1½ miles, and are recommended not to approach the northern shores of the islands lying between Haro Strait and Active Pass, within a distance of 2 miles; and they are strongly urged to adhere strictly to this advice.

The light on Georgina Point, at the entrance to Active Pass, becomes obscured when bearing to the southward of N. 73° W.; and it should be borne in mind that during the night while this light is in sight all the dangers off the northern shores of the above islands will be avoided.

It should also be remembered that the ebb sets to the SW., through Active Pass, and that tide races occur in its northern entrance. Roberts Bank is easily avoided. The extreme of Roberts Spit, or the tangent of the high trees immediately within it, should not be brought to bear to the southward of S. 67° E. If the weather is thick, when 50 fathoms is struck, vessels will be getting very near the edge.

The Tides, although not nearly so strong as among the Haro Archipelago, yet run with considerable strength (3 knots), particularly during the freshets of summer, when the Fraser River discharges an immense volume of fresh water, which takes a southerly direction over the banks almost straight for the entrance to Active Pass. This peculiar milky colored water is frequently carried quite across the strait, and is sometimes seen in the inner channels along the shores of Vancouver Island; at other times it reaches the center of the channel only, forming a remarkable and most striking contrast with the deep blue waters of the Strait of Georgia.

Below the mouth of the Fraser the tide is rather the stronger on the southern shore. On the northern side, within the line between Roberts and Sandy Points, scarcely any tide is felt; and vessels will gain by working up on that shore with the ebb, where good anchorage can also be found, if necessary.

Allowance must be made for the tide; this is not difficult when after having once entered the Strait of Georgia by daylight, and noted which tide was running. In the center of the strait above Saturna and Patos Islands, the strength of the tide varies from one to 3 knots, seldom more, unless close to the island shores, which are swept by the rapid currents out of Gabriola, Portier, and Active Passes. Above the mouth of the Fraser there is still less stream and plenty of sea room, the breadth of the strait being nearly 15 miles.

Fraser River possesses advantages over any other river on the coast; a sheltered strait, scarcely 15 miles across, receives its waters, and Vancouver Island serves as a natural breakwater, preventing the possibility of any sea arising which would prove dangerous to vessels even of the smallest class, unless they ground

The river is navigable to Hope, 80 miles from the entrance [illegible] steamers of light draft reach the [illegible] es above [illegible] nly and [illegible] l stream [illegible] it, and [illegible] rom the [illegible] gation. [illegible] mouth, [illegible] considerable strength of current, from 4 to 7 knots, at [illegible] ore; but at Langley the river becomes a broad, deep, and placid stream, and except during the three summer months the influence of the flood stream is generally felt, and vessels of any draft may conveniently anchor. The depth is 10 fathoms, the current not above 3 knots.

Midway between Langley and Hope the Harrison River flows into the Fraser, and by it and a long chain of lakes extending in a general north westerly direction a comparatively easy route has been established, by which the Upper Fraser may be reached at a point just below the Bridge River.

Vessels of 14 feet draft may enter the Fraser near high water, and proceed as high as Langley with ease, provided they have or are assisted by steam power, and are acquainted with the existing deep water chan-

erable, while to reach the same destination from Admiralty Inlet or Puget Sound, Rosario Strait is the most direct and desirable. Having entered, however, by either channel, the promontory of Roberts Point will be immediately seen with its conspicuous white-faced cliff, appearing as an island.

Dangers.—The dangers to be avoided in working through the Strait of Georgia are, on the northern shore, Roberts and Sturgeon Banks; and on the southern, the neighborhood of East Point and Tumbo Island, and the coast of Saturna and Mayne Islands, until beyond the entrance of Active Pass. A chain of reefs and rocky islets lie parallel with this shore, in places extending nearly one mile off; and the bottom is rocky and irregular, with strong tides.

Extending one mile east from the east end of Tumbo Island is a ledge of foul, rocky ground, over which there are very heavy tide rips and dangerous overfalls. At ¾ mile N. 62° E. of Race Point is a rocky patch of 5 fathoms, about 400 yards in extent; and at about 200 yards to the northwestward of this patch there is a rock with only 14 feet water on it, possibly a shoal head of the 5 fathom patch. This rock lies ⅝ mile N. 43° E. of Race Point. Orcas Knob kept well open to the eastward of the east point of Waldron Island, bearing S. 3° E., leads in the fairway between Saturna and Patos Islands, 1¼ miles eastward of the rock, and Toe Point (Patos Island), in line with the north extreme of Sucia Island, bearing S. 64° E., leads nearly ¼ mile to the northward of it.

A rock lies 300 yards S 56° E. of Edith Point, Mayne Island. The least depth on it is 2 feet, with irregular soundings around.

Caution.—As before observed vessels should when possible pass

(1127) **BRITISH COLUMBIA Strait of Georgia—Tumbo island—Rosenfelt (Tumbo) reef - Change in character of buoy.**—The Canadian Government has given notice that the black conical buoy marking Rosenfelt reef, off the eastern end of Tumbo island, moored in 12 fathoms of water 1¼ miles N. 27° E. true (N. ⅜ E mag.) from the lighthouse on the east point of Saturna island, has been replaced by an iron can buoy surmounted by a cage, the whole painted black.

Approx. position: Lat. 48° 48′ N., Long. 123° 02′ W.

(N. M. 30, 1905.)

... in mind that during the night while this light ... the dangers off the northern shores of the above islands will be avoided.

It should also be remembered that the ebb sets to the SW., through Active Pass, and that tide races occur in its northern entrance. Roberts Bank is easily avoided. The extreme of Roberts Spit, or the tangent of the high trees immediately within it, should not be brought to bear to the southward of S 67° E If the weather is thick, when 50 fathoms is struck, vessels will be getting very near the edge.

The Tides, although not nearly so strong as among the Haro Archipelago, yet run with considerable strength (3 knots), particularly during the freshets of summer, when the Fraser River discharges an immense volume of fresh water, which takes a southerly direction over the banks almost straight for the entrance to Active Pass. This peculiar milky colored water is frequently carried quite across the strait, and is sometimes seen in the inner channels along the shores of Vancouver Island; at other times it reaches the center of the channel only, forming a remarkable and most striking contrast with the deep blue waters of the Strait of Georgia.

Below the mouth of the Fraser the tide is rather the stronger on the southern shore. On the northern side, within the line between Roberts and Sandy Points, scarcely any tide is felt, and vessels will gain by working up on that shore with the ebb, where good anchorage can also be found, if necessary.

Allowance must be made for the tide, this is not difficult when after having once entered the Strait of Georgia by daylight, and noted which tide was running. In the center of the strait above Saturna and Patos Islands, the strength of the tide varies from one to 3 knots, seldom more, unless close to the island shores, which are swept by the rapid currents out of Gabriola, Portier, and Active Passes. Above the mouth of the Fraser there is still less stream and plenty of sea room, the breadth of the strait being nearly 15 miles.

Fraser River possesses advantages over any other river on the coast; a sheltered strait, scarcely 15 miles across, receives its waters; and Vancouver Island serves as a natural breakwater, preventing the possibility of any sea arising which would prove dangerous to vessels even of the smallest class, unless they ground.

The river is navigable to Hope, 80 miles from the entrance; steamers of light draft reach this point and even the town of Yale, 15 miles above it, during from six to nine months of the year. In June, July and August, the melting of the snow causes so rapid a downward stream that vessels even of high steam power are rarely able to stem it, and during these months numbers of large trees are brought down from the flooded banks, which offer another serious obstruction to navigation. Between Hope and Langley, the latter 30 miles from the river's mouth, there is always a considerable strength of current, from 4 to 7 knots, at times more; but at Langley the river becomes a broad, deep, and placid stream, and except during the three summer months the influence of the flood stream is generally felt, and vessels of any draft may conveniently anchor. The depth is 10 fathoms; the current not above 3 knots.

Midway between Langley and Hope the Harrison River flows into the Fraser, and by it and a long chain of lakes extending in a general northwesterly direction a comparatively easy route has been established, by which the Upper Fraser may be reached at a point just below the Bridge River.

Vessels of 14 feet draft may enter the Fraser near high water, and proceed as high as Langley with ease, provided they have or are assisted by steam power, and are acquainted with the existing deep water channel, which, it should be remembered, is subject to change. It must be remembered, however, that the tides of the Strait of Georgia sweep across the channel of the entrance, and large ships are recommended to enter or leave with the last quarter of the flood

The great quantity of deposit brought down by the freshets of summer has created an extensive series of banks, which extend 5 miles outside the entrance proper of the river. The main stream has forced a somewhat narrow channel, in which there is a sharp bend, through these banks, and at its junction with the current of the Strait of Georgia, which runs at right angles to it, has caused the wall edged bank before alluded to, extending to Roberts Point on the south and Grey Point on the north.

The river is at its lowest stage during the months of January, February and March. In April it commences to rise from the melting of the snows, and is perhaps 2 feet above its lowest level, the flood stream is strong enough to swing a ship at New Westminster up to the end of this month. In May the water rises rapidly the river is at its highest about the end of June, and remains up with trifling fluctuations until the end of July or middle of August. During these six weeks the banks are overflowed and extensive plains above Langley covered for a space of several miles; the strength of the stream between Langley and Hope being from 4 to 7 knots, and in the narrow parts even more. The usual rise of the river at Langley due to these floods is about 14 feet, but it has been known to reach 25 feet.

From the middle to the end of August the waters begin to subside, and in September the stream is not inconveniently strong. September, October and November are favorable months for the river navigation, as the water is then sufficiently high to reach Hope, and the strength of the current considerably abated The shallow stern-wheel steamers have got to Hope as late as December; between this month and April, owing to the shoalness of the water and the great quantity of ice formed, navigation, even by these vessels only drawing 18 inches, is attended with great difficulty, and rarely practicable at all. The snags or drift trees which become imbedded in the river also form a serious obstacle to navigation at this season.

In April the steamers commence again to run; in June, July and August the rapidity of the current is the great obstacle, but these high pressure vessels, commanding a speed of 11 and 12 knots, frequently accomplish the voyage, though at much risk The Harrison River route obviates some but not all of these difficulties.

Tides.—At New Westminster the freshets raise the level of the river about 6 feet, but the banks being high no inconvenience is felt, and the strength of the stream is rarely 5 knots, during the winter from 2 to 3; for some miles within the entrance the low banks are partially flooded for a month or six weeks The rise and fall due to tidal causes is from 8 to 10 feet at springs, between the Sand Heads and the entrance of

(1192) **BRITISH COLUMBIA—Strait of Georgia—Fraser river entrance—Light vessel to be established.**—A lightship will shortly be established by the Government of Canada off the Sandheads, to mark the entrance to Fraser river.

The light will be a *fixed white* light, visible all round the horizon. The fog signal will be a bell.

Due notice of the establishment of the lightship will be given
(N. M. 8, 1905.)

(2007) **BRITISH COLUMBIA—Strait of Georgia—Fraser river—Roberts bank—Bell buoy established.**—A bell buoy has been established by the Government of Canada on the extreme western shoulder of Roberts bank, 1 mile S. 1° 30′ W. true (SSE. mag.) from Fraser River lightship.

The buoy is moored in 15 fathoms; it is painted red and is surmounted by a bell rung automatically by the motion of the buoy.

Approx. position Lat. 49° 05′ 33″ N., Long. 123° 18′ 32″ W.
(N. M. 49, 1905.)

Anvil island within the sound, bearing N. 3° E., leads also clear of the edge of the Sturgeon Bank and about the same distance westward of the light house.

The South Sand Head dries at low water, and has frequently a ripple on it when covered; it is marked by a *red* buoy. The least depth in the old (south) channel is 5 feet at low water; as, however, the channel shifts from time to time, the *services* of a local pilot are *absolutely necessary*. Approaching the entrance, the buoy moored off the North Sand Head should be brought to bear N. 45° E., and then steer to leave it about 200 or 300 yards on the port side, which will lead in, nearly in mid channel.

New Channel—In 1884 a new channel through the sands at the mouth of the river had formed with a depth of 8 feet at low water, summer spring tides. This channel (to the northward of the old one) is marked with black spar buoys numbered consecutively from 1 to 9.

Directions.—Vessels making for the new channel should, to clear the Sand Heads, keep on the leading marks of Howe Sound until Garry Bush (Leading Tree)* bears N. 79° E., when it should be steered for; leave the black buoys 50 yards on the port hand, and after passing No. 9 buoy, steer for No. 15 (fairway buoy), which may be passed on either hand, and thence to Garry Point. The Sand Heads Light house bears S. 16° E. of No. 1 buoy, distant $1\frac{2}{10}$ miles.

New Westminster stands on the north or right bank of the Fraser River, just above the junction of the North Fork, and 15 miles in a general northeasterly direction from the entrance proper. It occupies a commanding position, is within an easy distance of the entrance, and has great facilities for wharfage along its water frontage, a good depth of water, and excellent anchorage.

The river bank is somewhat precipitous in places, and the country at the back is, like all the lower parts of the Fraser, densely wooded; a considerable clearing, however, of the timber has taken place in the vicinity of the town, which now assumes a prominent and thriving aspect. It has several public buildings of note, including a very good

* A remarkable isolated tree situated 430 yards N. 12° W. of Garry Point, but it is reported as having been cut down.

nel, which, it
remembered,
across the ch
enter or leav
The gr
mer has
side the
somewha
banks, an
which in
alluded to
the north

The river is at its lowest stage during the months of January, February and March. In April it commences to rise from the melting of the snows, and is perhaps 2 feet above its lowest level, the flood stream is strong enough to swing a ship at New Westminster up to the end of this month. In May the water rises rapidly, the river is at its highest about the end of June, and remains up with trifling fluctuations until the end of July or middle of August. During these six weeks the banks are overflowed and extensive plains above Langley covered for a space of several miles, the strength of the stream between Langley and Hope being from 4 to 7 knots, and in the narrow parts even more. The usual rise of the river at Langley due to these floods is about 14 feet, but it has been known to reach 25 feet.

From the middle to the end of August the waters begin to subside, and in September the stream is not inconveniently strong. September, October and November are favorable months for the river navigation, as the water is then sufficiently high to reach Hope, and the strength of the current considerably abated. The shallow stern wheel steamers have got to Hope as late as December; between this month and April, owing to the shoalness of the water and the great quantity of ice formed, navigation, even by these vessels only drawing 18 inches, is attended with great difficulty, and rarely practicable at all The snags or drift trees which become imbedded in the river also form a serious obstacle to navigation at this season

In April the steamers commence again to run; in June, July and August the rapidity of the current is the great obstacle, but these high-pressure vessels, commanding a speed of 11 and 12 knots, frequently accomplish the voyage, though at much risk. The Harrison River route obviates some but not all of these difficulties.

Tides.—At New Westminster the freshets raise the level of the river about 6 feet, but the banks being high no inconvenience is felt, and the strength of the stream is rarely 5 knots, during the winter from 2 to 3, for some miles within the entrance the low banks are partially flooded for a month or six weeks. The rise and fall due to tidal causes is from 8 to 10 feet at springs, between the Sand Heads and the entrance of the river proper at Garry Point; at New Westminster it is 6 feet, and at Langley scarcely perceptible.

Directions.—The light house on the North Sand Head enables a vessel to pick up the narrow entrance between the Sand Heads with accuracy. A large black buoy is placed off the the outer edge of the North Sand Head, and the edge of the channel inside is marked by buoys, colored red on the starboard hand (south bank), and black on the port hand (north bank), they are also numbered consecutively, the Sand Head buoy can be seen well from a distance of 2 miles.

Coming from the northward, Passage Island, at the entrance of Howe Sound, kept in line or just open eastward of a remarkable peak on Anvil Island within the sound, bearing N. 3° E., leads about one mile clear of the edge of the Sturgeon Bank, and about the same distance westward of the light house.

The South Sand Head dries at low water, and has frequently a ripple on it when covered; it is marked by a *red* buoy. The least depth in the old (south) channel is 5 feet at low water; as, however, the channel shifts from time to time, the *services* of a local pilot are *absolutely necessary*. Approaching the entrance, the buoy moored off the North Sand Head should be brought to bear N. 45° E., and then steer to leave it about 200 or 300 yards on the port side, which will lead in, nearly in mid channel.

New Channel.—In 1884 a new channel through the sands at the mouth of the river had formed with a depth of 8 feet at low water, summer spring tides. This channel (to the northward of the old one) is marked with black spar buoys numbered consecutively from 1 to 9.

Directions.—Vessels making for the new channel should, to clear the Sand Heads, keep on the leading marks of Howe Sound until Garry Bush (Leading Tree)* bears N. 79° E., when it should be steered for; leave the black buoys 50 yards on the port hand, and after passing No. 9 buoy, steer for No. 15 (fairway buoy), which may be passed on either hand, and thence to Garry Point. The Sand Heads Light-house bears S. 16° E of No 1 buoy, distant $1\frac{2}{10}$ miles.

New Westminster stands on the north or right bank of the Fraser River, just above the junction of the North Fork, and 15 miles in a general northeasterly direction from the entrance proper. It occupies a commanding position, is within an easy distance of the entrance, and has great facilities for wharfage along its water frontage, a good depth of water, and excellent anchorage.

The river bank is somewhat precipitous in places, and the country at the back is, like all the lower parts of the Fraser, densely wooded; a considerable clearing, however, of the timber has taken place in the vicinity of the town, which now assumes a prominent and thriving aspect. It has several public buildings of note, including a very good

* A remarkable isolated tree situated 430 yards N. 12° W of Garry Point, but it is reported as having been cut down

hospital, and large canneries which put up some 70,000 cases of salmon each season.

The population of New Westminster in 1881 was about 3,000.

Pilots.—Pilotage is compulsory; the rates subject to agreement, but not to exceed \$6 per foot. Vessels under steam or in tow of a steamer, one-fourth less. Tug-boat charges from Royal Roads, Vancouver Island, and return, for a vessel of 700 tons, about \$300. Harbor dues on vessels over 500 tons, \$5; under 500 tons, \$4.

Supplies of all descriptions are readily obtained, and salmon in abundance in the season. There are not many facilities for repairs to shipping and machinery.

Coal can be obtained at a price of \$6 per ton. About 500 tons are usually kept in stock, but any quantity can be procured at a short notice. Vessels can coal from barges, or they can go alongside a wharf which extends into a depth of 20 feet at low water.

Pitt River.—At 5 miles eastward of New Westminster is the entrance to the Pitt River, which trends in a general northeasterly direction for 28 miles, terminating in two remarkable lakes inclosed between almost perpendicular mountains, and navigable to the head for vessels of 14 feet draft, the depth in places being far too great for anchorage.

Derby or New Langley.—The landing place at Fort Langley is 12 miles above New Westminster in an easterly direction, on the south or opposite side of the river; the channel between is deep and there are no impediments to navigation. The depth of water here is 10 fathoms. Large vessels may proceed with ease 7 miles beyond Langley; the navigation then becomes somewhat intricate, and the current too rapid for any vessels but steamers of light draft and great power.

The North Fork is another entrance to the Fraser, navigable for vessels drawing 6 or 8 feet water, and is generally used by the natives proceeding to or from Burrard Inlet. A large, low, partially wooded island lies in its entrance and splits the channel into two arms.

In many parts of the North Fork the water is deep, in holes, and the bottom irregular; it can only be considered a boat channel.

Burrard Inlet has its entrance between Grey Point on the south and Atkinson Point on the north. Howe Sound immediately adjoins it on the north, Atkinson Point, the northern entrance point of the inlet, being the eastern limit of the sound.

The entrance to the inlet is well marked; Grey Point, a long, wooded promontory terminating in a rounded bluff, is very conspicuous from the southward, while Bowen Island, which lies at the entrance of Howe Sound, and may also be said to form the northern boundary of the inlet, is very remarkable; its high, round, and almost bare summit, Mount Gardner, reaching an elevation of 2,479 feet, is easily recognized from any point of view. Passage Island, small but prominent, lies in the eastern passage of Howe Sound, midway between Bowen Island and Atkinson Point, and is an excellent mark from the southward. As before observed, Anvil Peak, in line with or just open westward of this island, bearing N. 3° E., leads 1½ miles clear of the edge of the Sturgeon Bank, and at night the light on Atkinson Point should not be brought to bear westward of N. 23° E.

Burrard Inlet differs from most of the great sounds of this coast in being comparatively easy of access to steam vessels of any size or class, and in the convenient depth of water for anchorage which may be found in almost every part of it; its close proximity to Fraser River, with the great facilities for constructing roads between the two places, and its having become the terminus of the Pacific and Canadian Railway, likewise add considerably to its importance. It is divided into three distinct harbors, viz, English bay or the outer anchorage; Vancouver (formerly called Coal Harbor), above the First Narrows; and Port Moody, at the head of the eastern arm of the inlet.

There is communication by steamer daily and bi-weekly with provincial ports; weekly with San Francisco, and bi-weekly with ports in Puget Sound; and by railway to all parts of Eastern Canada and throughout the United States. There is also telegraphic communication with main points throughout the province, with the United States, and with Europe.

A submarine cable extends from Point Grey across the Strait of Georgia to Valdes Island.

English Bay is more than 3 miles in breadth at the entrance, and carries the same breadth for nearly its entire length, or almost 4 miles.

Spanish Bank, which extends in a northerly direction from Grey Point for ¾ mile, and then curves easterly, joining the south shore of the inlet at the distance of 2 miles within the point, contracts the entrance in some measure, however. This bank is composed of hard sand, and is dry at low water; its edge is steep-to, having off it from 20 to 7 fathoms and then on shore; when covered its existence would not be suspected; there is no ripple on it unless with strong westerly winds, and then only near low water. A red can buoy is moored off its north edge in 7 fathoms. A red can buoy, surmounted by a staff and cage, is moored in 10 fathoms westward of the bank.

The head of English Bay on the southern shore terminates in a shoal arm, named False Creek; on the northern shore it leads by the First

... in 6 fathoms, ... the bay (off ... 40° E., and ... anchorage is ... nd is also out ... nd farther to ... stands close ... s just shut in ... the point, bearing N. 6° E., a vess... ... h in.

hospital, and large canneries which put up some 70,000 cases of salmon each season.

The population of New Westminster in 1881 was about 3,000

Pilots.—Pilotage is compulsory, the rates subject to agreement, but not to exceed $6 per foot. Vessels under steam or in tow of a steamer, one-fourth less. Tug boat charges from Royal Roads, Vancouver Island, and return, for a vessel of 700 tons, about $300. Harbor dues on vessels over 500 tons, $5, under 500 tons, $4.

Supplies of all descriptions are readily obtained, and salmon in abundance in the season There are not many facilities for repairs to shipping and machinery.

Coal can be obtained at a price of $6 per ton. About 500 tons are usually kept in stock, but any quantity can be procured at a short notice. Vessels can coal from barges, or they can go alongside a wharf which extends into a depth of 20 feet at low water

Pitt River—At 5 miles eastward of New Westminster is the entrance to the Pitt River, which trends in a general northeasterly direction for 28 miles, terminating in two remarkable lakes inclosed between almost perpendicular mountains, and navigable to the head for vessels of 14 feet draft, the depth in places being far too great for anchorage.

Derby or New Langley—The landing place at Fort Langley is 12 miles above New Westminster in an easterly direction, on the south or opposite side of the river; the channel between is deep and there are no impediments to navigation The depth of water here is 10 fathoms. Large vessels may proceed with ease 7 miles beyond Langley; the navigation then becomes somewhat intricate, and the current too rapid for any vessels but steamers of light draft and great power.

The North Fork is another entrance to the Fraser, navigable for vessels drawing 6 or 8 feet water, and is generally used by the natives proceeding to or from Burrard Inlet. A large, low, partially wooded island lies in its entrance and splits the channel into two arms.

In many parts of the North Fork the water is deep, in holes, and the bottom irregular; it can only be considered a boat channel

Burrard Inlet has its entrance between Grey Point on the south and Atkinson Point on the north Howe Sound immediately adjoins it on the north. Atkinson Point, the northern entrance point of the ...

(1128) **BRITISH COLUMBIA—Strait of Georgia—Burrard inlet—Grey point—Change in character of buoy.**—The Canadian Government has given notice that the red can buoy surmounted by a cage, moored off Grey point, Burrard inlet, and known as Grey Point fairway buoy, has been replaced by a bell buoy of United States Government pattern

The buoy is of steel, painted red, and is surmounted by a bell rung by the motion of the buoy on the waves. It is moored about 1¼ miles N. 3° W true (NNW. ⅜ W. mag.) from Grey point

Approx position: Lat 49° 17′ 00″ N, Long. 123° 15′ 50″ W.

(N M 30, 1905.)

the eastern passage of Howe Sound, midway bet... and Atkinson Point, and is an excellent mark from the southward. As before observed, Anvil Peak, in line with or just open westward of this island, bearing N. 3° E., leads 1½ miles clear of the edge of the Sturgeon Bank, and at night the light on Atkinson Point should not be brought to bear westward of N. 23° E.

Burrard Inlet differs from most of the great sounds of this coast in being comparatively easy of access to steam vessels of any size or class, and in the convenient depth of water for anchorage which may be found in almost every part of it; its close proximity to Fraser River, with the great facilities for constructing roads between the two places, and its having become the terminus of the Pacific and Canadian Railway, likewise add considerably to its importance. It is divided into three distinct harbors, viz, English bay or the outer anchorage; Vancouver (formerly called Coal Harbor), above the First Narrows; and Port Moody, at the head of the eastern arm of the inlet.

There is communication by steamer daily and bi-weekly with provincial ports; weekly with San Francisco, and bi-weekly with ports in Paget Sound; and by railway to all parts of Eastern Canada and throughout the United States. There is also telegraphic communication with main points throughout the province, with the United States, and with Europe.

A submarine cable extends from Point Grey across the Strait of Georgia to Valdes Island.

English Bay is more than 3 miles in breadth at the entrance, and carries the same breadth for nearly its entire length, or almost 4 miles.

Spanish Bank, which extends in a northerly direction from Grey Point for ¾ mile, and then curves easterly, joining the south shore of the inlet at the distance of 2 miles within the point, contracts the entrance in some measure, however. This bank is composed of hard sand, and is dry at low water; its edge is steep-to, having off it from 20 to 7 fathoms and then on shore; when covered its existence would not be suspected; there is no ripple on it unless with strong westerly winds, and then only near low water. A red can buoy is moored off its north edge in 7 fathoms. A red can buoy, surmounted by a staff and cage, is moored in 10 fathoms westward of the bank.

The head of English Bay on the southern shore terminates in a shoal arm, named False Creek; on the northern shore it leads by the First Narrows to Burrard Inlet.

Anchorage.—There is good anchorage in English Bay in 6 fathoms, stiff mud bottom, at about ½ mile from the south shore of the bay (off Indian huts), with the extreme of Coal Peninsula bearing N. 40° E., and light-house on Point Atkinson bearing N. 47° W.; this anchorage is well protected from westerly winds by the Spanish Bank, and is also out of the influence of the current. Anchorage may also be had farther to the eastward if desired; a remarkable high Nine-pin Rock stands close off the west end of Coal Peninsula, and when this rock is just shut in by the point, bearing N. 6° E., a vessel will be far enough in.

Tides.—In English Bay during the winter months from September to March there is what is locally called a "short run out" during the day, and a "long run out" at night. The tide is consequently high during the day and low at night. The duration of the short run out is from 3 to 4 hours, that of the long 7 to 9 hours. This is entirely reversed during the summer months, when it is high water during the night, and low water during the day. The tides are very complicated, and can not be depended on, except at full and change of the moon.

Directions.—Entering Burrard Inlet from the southward, Grey Point should not be approached within one mile, when the extreme of the bluff bears S. 16° E. and the north end of Coal Peninsula is N. 79° E., steer in east, which will lead ½ mile clear of the Spanish Bank; a good lookout being kept for the buoy.

Vessels intending to pass above the narrows must attend to the tides, and strangers will do well to anchor in English Bay before proceeding farther up.

The First Narrows lie between the bluff of Coal Peninsula and the north side of the inlet, where the breadth of the channel is not more than 300 yards with a depth of from 10 to 12 fathoms; to strangers the entrance is not easily made out until close in. A flat composed of shingle and bowlder stones, covering with the early flood, extends from 200 to 600 yards off the north shore, so that the peninsula bluff must be kept pretty close aboard, rather less than 200 yards. From the entrance of the narrows, when abreast Peninsula Bluff, steer for Brockton Point for about a mile, then gradually alter course to pass Brockton Point at the distance of about 300 yards, when a S. 78° E. course will lead to the Second Narrows. To sailing ships a knowledge of the locality is necessary, as well as a commanding breeze, and the narrows should never be attempted with the full strength of the stream; and vessels must be quick and careful with the helm. Even for steamers, the strength of the current in the First Narrows necessitates unusual care.

The narrow part of the channel is ¼ mile in length, when it gradually opens out from 400 yards to ½ mile, which is the breadth abreast of Brockton Point, 1¼ miles within the Peninsula Bluff on the southern shore. When past the narrowest part, the southern shore should be kept aboard within 400 yards until abreast Brockton Point.

Shoal.—A shoal spot 240 yards in diameter, depth of 4 fathoms, has been found almost in mid channel off Brockton Point. The center of the shoal lies about 700 yards N. 25° W. of the eastern extreme of the point. Less water than charted is found north of the shoal, but south of it the depth is unaltered.

Beacons.—Three beacons have been erected on the northern side of the First Narrows.

Each beacon consists of a cluster of five piles, 8 feet in height above high water, painted black and surmounted by a triangle 10 feet high, placed base upwards and painted white.

The outer beacon stands in 6 feet at low-water spring tides, with Nine-pin Rock open of the bluff, bearing S. 41° 27′ W., and Hastings sawmill open of Brockton Point, bearing S. 47° 09′ E.

The middle beacon is situated 1,000 yards S. 55° 35′ E. of the outer beacon The inner (easternmost) beacon stands in 10 feet of water at low-water spring tides, 1,000 yards S. 64° E of the middle beacon.

Tides—The strength of the tide in the narrowest part of the First Narrows is from 4 to 8 knots. It is high water, full and change, at 6 p. m.; and the rise is 13 feet. The ebb stream commences directly it is high water by the shore, and runs out for two hours after it is low; there is consequently only 4 hours' flood stream.

Burnaby Shoal, about 400 yards in extent, marked by kelp, with 9 feet water on it, lies 650 yards S 70° E. of Brockton Point, the kelp, however, is frequently not seen until close upon it. The houses northward of Brockton Point open north of that point, lead north of Burnaby Shoal, and the pier at Vancouver, bearing S 6° W, clears it to the eastward. A red buoy is moored on this shoal, leave to the west in passing.

Vancouver Harbor, the first anchorage inside the First Narrows, is a bight formed by the land falling back from Brockton Point. At the northern side of the harbor is the Burnaby Shoal, and midway between Vancouver town and Hastings mill the Whiting Bank extends 350 yards from the shore, with 2¼ fathoms on its outer edge.

Vancouver, a rapidly increasing town which had in 1887 about 3,500 inhabitants, is on the east side of Vancouver Harbor, it is the terminus of the Canadian Pacific Railway, and trains leave daily for Montreal. It is in telegraphic communication with Vancouver Island and Montreal. There are excellent facilities for beaching vessels. A small steam vessel plies between this town and Moodyville sawmills on the northern side of Burrard Inlet. There is an establishment for herring curing here.

A pier has been constructed eastward of Buckland Point, with a depth alongside it at low water of 24 feet.

Vancouver is the center of the great lumber district which produces the supply for Hastings mill

At Hastings sawmill, on the east entrance point of Vancouver Harbor, several piers have been constructed for the convenience of vessels loading lumber, there is a depth of 25 feet alongside the largest of these piers.

Large quantities of timber are exported to Sandwich Islands, Australia, China, and San Francisco; vessels of 1,500 tons go alongside the piers to load. The steamers from China coal at Vancouver from a hulk.

Anchorage—The best anchorage in Vancouver Harbor is in the southeastern corner in from 10 to 12 fathoms, mud, with the north extreme of the piers at Hastings mill bearing S. 78° E., and the landing stage at Vancouver Town (a long floating stage) bearing S 23° W. This position is out of the influence of the strong tidal streams.

Supplies.—Wood for steaming purposes can be abundantly procured, and also ordinary supplies. Water is of bad quality.

Coal is obtained from Nanaimo, from which port it can be shipped at the rate of $1 per ton. A small quantity can be procured from the retail dealers; price, $8 per ton.

A powerful steam tug is available for towing vessels between Juan de Fuca Strait and Burrard Inlet.

Directions.—From about 300 yards off Brockton Point steer S 73° E., keeping the houses NW. of Brockton Point open north of that point until the pier at Vancouver Town bears S. 6° W., when Burnaby Shoal will be passed and the anchorage may be steered for

Hastings, a small village situated on the south side of the inlet, is 3 miles from Vancouver, and is connected with New Westminster by a stage road 9 miles long. It is much frequented during the summer months.

Moodyville.—At Moodyville, on the north shore, there is a steam sawmill, also a gridiron 180 feet long and 40 feet wide, capable at spring tides of taking a vessel drawing 12 feet; alongside it is a small wharf. Moodyville contained in 1884 about 250 inhabitants, principally employes of the sawmills. Two steam ferryboats ply between this place and the several other settlements in Burrard Inlet.

Second Narrows.—The Second Narrows are similar to the First, a bank of the same description, but more extensive, is caused by the deposit brought down from the high mountains by the numerous streams which flow into the inlet on the north side. This bank is dry at low water, and the breadth of the deep channel, at the narrowest part and for ½ mile on either side of it, varies from 300 to 400 yards, with a depth of from 10 to 20 fathoms The channel, however, is straight, and the tides, which run from 3 to 7 knots, set fairly through it. The only directions necessary are to keep the southern shore close aboard, and steer from point to point without going far into the bights which indent the coast on either side of the narrowest part The great strength of the tide ceases when ½ mile from the narrowest part of the narrows

Telegraph.—A submarine telegraph cable crosses the Second Narrows in the narrowest part, marked by three wooden painted posts placed on the mud flat; and the outer of these being on the southern edge of the flat is a good guide for the deep water channel.

Port Moody.—The entrance to this snug harbor is 4 miles eastward from the Second Narrows, at the head of the eastern arm of the inlet. At its entrance it is 400 yards across; there are no dangers, and there is a uniform depth of water, with good holding ground. It terminates in a muddy flat at its head, which reaches within 3 miles of the banks of Pitt River Wharfage accommodation for vessels of large tonnage is provided, the depth alongside of which is 30 feet at low water. A considerable settlement is being formed on the south shore at the head of the bay, which in 1884 contained about 250 inhabitants.

The sea worm is very destructive in the port.

Anchorage.—The best anchorage, in from 5 to 6 fathoms, is in the widest part of the harbor, just before reaching the arm which turns to the southward and eastward at about ½ mile from the road which leads to New Westminster. Abreast the turning point, and on the north shore, a bank dries off for nearly 400 yards at low water, on which good oysters are found.

North Arm, just before reaching Port Moody, branches off from the main inlet, and takes a general northerly direction. It is entirely different in its character from other portions of the inlet. The water is deep, and it is inclosed on both sides by rugged mountains rising from 2,000 to 5,000 feet almost perpendicularly, and down the steep sides of which the melting snow in summer forces its way in foaming cascades, rendering the surface water in the inlet below nearly fresh.

There is scarcely sufficient level land in this arm to pitch a tent, nor is there any anchorage except in Bedwell Bay, a narrow creek 2 miles within the entrance, on the eastern shore, where 7 to 9 fathoms are found near its head. North Arm is nearly one mile wide at the entrance, but one mile within it is contracted to a little over 400 yards, when it shortly opens out again, and maintains an average breadth of ¼ mile as far as Croker Island. There is a settlement on North Arm named Richmond with a population of about 250, and there are two salmon canneries there.

Croker Island is one mile from the head of the arm, and on both sides of it there are deep but narrow channels; that to the eastward is the wider. The head terminates in a delta of swampy rushes, through which some rapid streams find their way into the inlet from a deep and narrow gorge in a northerly direction.

Water.—During the winter months fresh water is to be obtained in all parts of Burrard Inlet, and probably the whole year round there would be no scarcity; in June there is abundance at the creek in English Bay, off which is the anchorage.

In Port Moody there is a fine stream close to the oyster bank.

CHAPTER V.

THE STRAIT OF GEORGIA, FROM NANAIMO HARBOR AND BURRARD INLET TO CAPE MUDGE AND BUTE INLET.

The Strait of Georgia, as already observed, commences at the northern end of the Haro Archipelago, and extends in a general northwesterly direction for 110 miles. There are many harbors, both on the Vancouver and continental shores; and several islands, some of considerable size, form other channels, all of which are navigable.

The tides are not strong, and between Nanaimo and Cape Mudge there are few dangers in the way of ships navigating the strait.

The smaller channels on the continental shore are Malaspina Strait and Sabine Channel.

On the Vancouver shore is Ballinac Channel, lying westward of the islands of the same name; also Lambert Channel and Baynes Sound.

Tides—The meeting of the tides takes place between Cape Mudge and Cape Lazo; that is to say, the flood entering by Fuca Strait meets that entering by the north end of Vancouver Island within 20 miles of the former cape, generally much nearer, but varying according to the phases of the moon and the state of the winds, and at the point of meeting a considerable race occurs, which would be dangerous to boats; there is generally such a race at the entrance of Discovery Passage It is high water, full and change, at Cape Mudge and Cape Lazo at about 5h. 30m., and the range during ordinary springs is from 12 to 14 feet. At the entrance of the passage during springs the tidal streams attain a velocity of 4 to 6 knots an hour, the flood, or easterly stream, being the strongest.

Winds—The prevailing summer wind is from NW, or the same as on the outside coast, and between May and September it blows strong and steady, commencing about 9 a. m and dying away towards sunset. These winds do not generally extend much below Point Roberts, among the Haro Archipelago they become variable and baffling, while in the main channels of Rosario and Haro, the westerly wind entering the Strait of Fuca is deflected to SW., and vessels running up these channels with a fair wind will almost always find it ahead on entering the Strait of Georgia. During winter there is a good deal of moderate calm, and gloomy weather, but gales from SE., and SW., are frequent.

Nanoose Harbor, 8 miles westward of Nanaimo, is easily recognized by Nanoose or Notch Hill, a remarkable hill immediately over its northern side, showing as a double or notch peak from the southward; the harbor or inlet indents the coast for over 3 miles, and is remarkably

(1316) **BRITISH COLUMBIA—Strait of Georgia—Nanoose harbor—Shoal at entrance.**—Commander J. F. Parry, H. B. M. S. *Egeria*, reports that on close examination of the 2¼ fathoms lying off Entrance rock in the narrowest part of the entrance to Nanoose bay, east coast of Vancouver island, this shoal was found to extend 100 yards to the westward, having a least depth of 6 feet on it at low water.

The kelp on this is only visible at and about low water.

A good mark for entering Nanoose bay, leading clear of the above shoal and North rock, is the southern extreme of Notch Hill peninsula in line with the foot of the slope from the northern shoulder of Mount Arrowsmith, bearing N. 86° W. true (WSW ⅛ W. mag.)

The back mark of this leading line is the southern part of the lowest dip in the farthest range of mountains in this vicinity.

Mount Arrowsmith is the highest mountain with several snow-capped summits, lying well back over the head of the bay.

(N. M. 36, 1904.)

he off the north point of Nanoose Harbor.

Maude Island, small, wooded, and about 100 feet high, is the southernmost of the group. Vessels working in may stand pretty close to it and to Blunden Point, but when inside the latter, a sand bank dries for a considerable distance off at low water, and the southern shore should not be approached within ¼ mile.

Entrance Rock, 2 feet above high water, lies 1½ miles west of Blunden Point, off a low maple flat on the southern side, almost into the middle of the harbor, and contracting the width of the passage to 600 yards; within this the harbor opens out to nearly one mile in width, terminating at a distance of 1⅜ miles in a shoal mud flat, which dries at low water more than ½ mile, and where quantities of oysters are found.

North Rock, the only danger on the northern shore when entering, lies nearly 400 yards from the shore, and has a depth of 5 feet on the outer part.

Directions.—When midway between Maude Island and Blunden Point, the fair course in is west. When the east point of Southey Island is shut in by the north entrance point, North Rock will be passed, and the northern shore should be kept rather aboard. Entrance rock should in no case be passed nearer than 200 yards, and it working in, beware of the North Rock, and the sand-bank already mentioned as extending off the southern shore, and which stretches also for ¼ mile westward from Entrance Rock: when that distance westward of the rock both shores of the harbor are clear of danger.

Anchorage.—No convenient anchorage in less than 18 fathoms will be found, until well up towards the head. When Nanoose Hill bears N. 23° E., anchor in 12 fathoms in the center of the harbor, or as near to either shore as desired. It is a spacious anchorage and well sheltered from all winds.

There is a convenient nook with a steep shingle beach, where a vessel might be laid for repairs if necessary, on the north side one mile from the head.

THE STR

The St
ern end o
erly direc
couver an
able size,

The tide ... Cape Mudge there are few da... of ships navigating the strait

The smaller channels on the continental shore are Malaspina Strait and Sabine Channel.

On the Vancouver shore is Ballinac Channel, lying westward of the islands of the same name; also Lambert Channel and Baynes Sound.

Tides—The meeting of the tides takes place between Cape Mudge and Cape Lazo; that is to say, the flood entering by Fuca Strait meets that entering by the north end of Vancouver Island within 20 miles of the former cape, generally much nearer, but varying according to the phases of the moon and the state of the winds, and at the point of meeting a considerable race occurs, which would be dangerous to boats, there is generally such a race at the entrance of Discovery Passage It is high water, full and change, at Cape Mudge and Cape Lazo at about 5h 30m, and the range during ordinary springs is from 12 to 14 feet. At the entrance of the passage during springs the tidal streams attain a velocity of 4 to 6 knots an hour, the flood, or easterly stream, being the strongest.

Winds.—The prevailing summer wind is from NW, or the same as on the outside coast, and between May and September it blows strong and steady, commencing about 9 a. m and dying away towards sunset. These winds do not generally extend much below Point Roberts; among the Haro Archipelago they become variable and baffling, while in the main channels of Rosario and Haro, the westerly wind entering the Strait of Fuca is deflected to SW, and vessels running up these channels with a fair wind will almost always find it ahead on entering the Strait of Georgia. During winter there is a good deal of moderate calm, and gloomy weather, but gales from SE., and SW., are frequent.

Nanoose Harbor, 8 miles westward of Nanaimo, is easily recognized by Nanoose or Notch Hill, a remarkable hill immediately over its northern side, showing as a double or notch peak from the southward; the harbor or inlet indents the coast for over 3 miles, and is remarkably clear of danger. The entrance is ⅓ mile wide, and the width of the harbor varies between 600 yards and over one mile There are depths of from 30 to 35 fathoms at the entrance, and deep water is carried up to within ½ mile of the head, when it shoals more rapidly.

The Coast for 6 miles westward of Nanoose is fringed with numerous small islands and reefs, the latter generally marked by kelp. The outermost of them, Winchelsea and Yeo Islands, extend between one and 2 miles from the land, and beyond these there are no hidden dangers.

Small vessels may find good shelter in Schooner Cove at 1½ miles NW. of the north point of Nanoose Harbor. There is a rock awash nearly in the center of the entrance, but nearer to the north point

Winchelsea and Ada Islands, a group of small wooded islands, lie off the north point of Nanoose Harbor.

Maude Island, small, wooded, and about 100 feet high, is the southernmost of the group. Vessels working in may stand pretty close to it and to Blunden Point, but when inside the latter, a sand-bank dries for a considerable distance off at low water, and the southern shore should not be approached within ¼ mile.

Entrance Rock, 2 feet above high water, lies 1¼ miles west of Blunden Point, off a low maple flat on the southern side, almost into the middle of the harbor, and contracting the width of the passage to 600 yards, within this the harbor opens out to nearly one mile in width, terminating at a distance of 1¾ miles in a shoal mud flat, which dries at low water more than ½ mile, and where quantities of oysters are found.

North Rock, the only danger on the northern shore when entering, lies nearly 400 yards from the shore, and has a depth of 5 feet on the outer part.

Directions.—When midway between Maude Island and Blunden Point, the fair course in is west. When the east point of Southey Island is shut in by the north entrance point, North Rock will be passed, and the northern shore should be kept rather aboard Entrance rock should in no case be passed nearer than 200 yards, and if working in, beware of the North Rock, and the sand bank already mentioned as extending off the southern shore, and which stretches also for ¼ mile westward from Entrance Rock; when that distance westward of the rock both shores of the harbor are clear of danger.

Anchorage.—No convenient anchorage in less than 18 fathoms will be found, until well up towards the head. When Nanoose Hill bears N. 23° E., anchor in 12 fathoms in the center of the harbor, or as near to either shore as desired. It is a spacious anchorage and well sheltered from all winds.

There is a convenient nook with a steep shingle beach, where a vessel might be laid for repairs if necessary, on the north side one mile from the head.

Supplies—Grouse are to be got here, and fresh water may be obtained from a cove at the head on the north side.

The Grey Rock, bare, 12 feet above high water, and rather remarkable, lies 400 yards east of the eastern end of the Winchelsea group.

Rudder Reef, with a depth of one fathom on it, lies ¼ mile S. 27° E. of Grey Rock, and has very little kelp on it. The southeastern end of the Winchelsea Islands should be given a berth of at least ½ mile.

Yeo and Gerald Islands lie northwestward of the Winchelsea Group, and are smaller. They may be safely passed to the northward, at the distance of ½ mile

Ballinac Islands, two in number, are larger than the groups just described, and lie 2¼ miles offshore. The northernmost has only two or three trees on it, and its summit terminates in a sharp, bare nipple; the southernmost is wooded. They have the appearance of being one island seen from all points, being only separated by a narrow passage, which at the eastern entrance is less than 200 yards wide, but opens out within, and forms a sheltered cove with anchorage for small vessels in 8 fathoms, close to its southern sandy beach; on the west side this channel is almost closed, and there is no passage into it. The islands are steep and bold on all sides, and are conspicuous after passing westward of Nanaimo, vessels bound through the Strait of Georgia would do well to steer for them.

Having passed Entrance Island, or gained an offing of one mile from Light-house or Five Finger Islands, a direct course for Ballinac Islands leads well outside all the small islands and reefs lying off the coast westward of Nanoose.

Ballinac Channel is a safe, clear passage, 1¼ miles in width at its narrowest part (abreast Gerald Island); the shores of the islands on both sides may be approached within 200 yards, if necessary.

To steamers, coasters, or vessels with a fair wind, Ballinac Channel is recommended. Large sailing vessels with a foul wind would find it an advantage to make long boards, and pass to the northward of the islands through the main strait.

Cottam Reef, the only danger in the channel, has 2½ fathoms water on it, and is generally marked by kelp; it lies on the southwestern side of the channel.

The northernmost of the Winchelsea Islands kept open of Yeo Islands, bearing S 61° E., leads well north of the reef.

Northwest Bay indents the coast for 2 miles in a southeasterly direction, making a peninsula of the land which separates it from Nanoose Harbor. It is much exposed to NW. winds and the water in it is very deep; a considerable stream flows into the bay at its western entrance.

Mistaken Island, low, wooded and ½ mile long, lies close off the entrance to Northwest Bay.

The Coast.—From Northwest Bay the land trends, with a slight indentation, westward to Denman and Hornby Islands, and to the southern entrances of Baynes Sound and Lambert Channel. This stretch of coast presents no remarkable feature; wooded bluffs, of moderate height, terminating in sandy or shingle points, off which for a very short distance the water is shoal.

Qualicum River is a small stream, only noticeable as affording shelter to canoes or boats within its entrance.

The entrance of Qualicum River has nothing to mark its position until within one mile of it, when the bowlder stones which fringe the ... somewhat farther off shore

rnby Island

of one mile.

e northward

diately west

r 10 fathoms

at ¾ mile from the shore, with the east point of Hornby Island bearing N. 18° E.; the holding ground is good, and northerly ...nds, which would make it a lee shore, seldom blow with any strength. From NW. winds it is in a great measure sheltered by the islands, but with those from SE. a considerable sea will get up, though there would be plenty of room and no danger of drifting with good ground tackle.

Denman and Horn... the coast; the

oast, and has an

n; on its west-

rkable flat-top

east side and

side is Tribune

e is a consider-

... the latter, also fresh water.

... is separated from the mainland by a good passage ...lled Baynes Sound, and Hornby Island from Denman by Lambert Channel. There is more tide felt in the channel than in the sound; in the former its rate is sometimes 2 knots, the flood coming from the southeastward. The prevailing winds are northwesterly; therefore, for sailing vessels from the southward, the main strait east of Hornby Island is to be preferred.

Baynes Sound has an average navigable width of over ½ mile. There are two very fair anchorages, Fanny Bay on the south or main side, and Henry Bay on the north or island side.

The exit into the Strait of Georgia by the northwestern entrance of the sound, between the north end of Denman Island and Cape Lazo, is nearly 2 miles in width, but a remarkable bridge or bar of sand, strewed with large stones, extends the whole way across, and at low water there is as little as 8 feet on it; during summer it is thickly covered with kelp,

Supplies.—Grouse are to be got here, and fresh water may be obtained from a cove at the head on the north side.

The Grey Rock, bare, 12 feet above high water, and rather remarkable, lies 400 yards east of the eastern end of the Winchelsea group.

Rudder Reef, with a depth of one fathom on it, lies ¼ mile S. 27° E. of Grey Rock, and has very little kelp on it. The southeastern end of the Winchelsea Islands should be given a berth of at least ½ mile.

Yeo and Gerald Islands lie northwestward of the Winchelsea Group, and are smaller. They may be safely passed to the northward,

(1318) **BRITISH COLUMBIA—Strait of Georgia—[illegible] South Ballinac island—Uncharted shoal.**—Commander [illegible] H. B. M. S. *Egeria*, reports the existence of a rocky shoal [illegible] feet over it at low water 500 yards off the southeast extreme of the South Ballinac island, with the lighthouse bearing N. 61° W. true (W. ⅝ N. mag.).

Depths of 10 fathoms were found between the shoal and the South Ballinac island, and 20 to 40 fathoms close-to on its other sides.

No kelp was visible on this rock. (N. M. 36, 1904.)

out within, and forms a sheltered cove with anchorage for small vessels in 8 fathoms, close to its southern sandy beach; on the west side this channel is almost closed, and there is no passage into it. The islands are steep and bold on all sides, and are conspicuous after passing westward of Nanaimo; vessels bound through the Strait of Georgia would do well to steer for them.

Having passed Entrance Island, or gained an offing of one mile from Light-house or Five Finger Islands, a direct course for Ballinac Islands

(1317) **BRITISH COLUMBIA—Strait of Georgia—Ballinac channel—Uncharted rock.**—Commander J. F. Parry, H. B. M. S. *Egeria*, reports the existence of an uncharted rock in Ballinac chan[illegible] line between the eastern extreme of the South Ballinac [illegible] Douglas island, being distant from the latter 800 yards.

The rock has 15 feet of water over it at low water with [illegible] of 20 to 40 fathoms close-to all round. No kelp was seen on the rock.

From the rock Ballinac lighthouse bears N. 1° W. true (NNW. ¾ W. W'ly mag.), $1\frac{1}{10}$ miles, and the north extreme of Mistaken island N. 78° W. true (WSW. ⅞ W. mag.), $2\frac{8}{10}$ miles. (N. M. 36, 1904.)

Cottam Reef, the only danger in the channel, has 2½ fathoms [illegible] on it, and is generally marked by kelp; it lies on the southwestern side of the channel.

The northernmost of the Winchelsea Islands kept open of Yeo Islands, bearing S. 61° E., leads well north of the reef.

Northwest Bay indents the coast for 2 miles in a [illegible]sterly direction, making a peninsula of the land which separates it [illegible] Nanoose Harbor. It is much exposed to NW. winds and the water in it is very deep; a considerable stream flows into the bay at its western entrance.

Mistaken Island, low, wooded, and [illegible] mile long, lies close off the entrance to Northwest Bay.

The Coast.—From Northwest Bay the land trends, with a slight indentation, westward to Denman and Hornby Islands, and to the southern entrances of Baynes Sound and Lambert Channel. This stretch of coast presents no remarkable feature, wooded bluffs, of moderate height, terminating in sandy or shingle points, off which for a very short distance the water is shoal.

Qualicum River is a small stream, only noticeable as affording shelter to canoes or boats within its entrance.

The entrance of Qualicum River has nothing to mark its position until within one mile of it, when the bowlder stones which fringe the whole of this coast will be seen to extend somewhat farther off shore than at other points. When the sharp east point of Hornby Island bears N. 12° E., it will be easily made out at the distance of one mile. A *black* can buoy is moored in 3 fathoms water, about ¼ mile northward of the river entrance.

Qualicum Bay is a slight indentation of the coast, immediately west of the river, where very fair anchorage will be found in 8 or 10 fathoms at ¾ mile from the shore, with the east point of Hornby Island bearing N. 18° E., the holding ground is good, and northerly winds, which would make it a lee shore, seldom blow with any strength. From NW winds it is in a great measure sheltered by the islands, but with those from SE. a considerable sea will get up, though there would be plenty of room and no danger of drifting with good ground tackle.

Denman and Hornby Islands lie immediately off the coast, the former is 9 miles long, in a direction parallel with the coast, and has an average width of 2 miles.

Hornby Island is about 4 miles across in every direction, on its western side rises rather abruptly Mount Geoffrey, a remarkable flat-top hill, 1,076 feet high, sloping gradually down on the east side and terminating in a low, bare, grassy point, on the eastern side is Tribune Bay, affording good anchorage. On both these islands there is a considerable quantity of good land particularly on the latter, also fresh water.

Denman Island is separated from the mainland by a good passage called Baynes Sound, and Hornby Island from Denman by Lambert Channel. There is more tide felt in the channel than in the sound; in the former its rate is sometimes 2 knots, the flood coming from the southeastward. The prevailing winds are northwesterly, therefore, for sailing vessels from the southward, the main strait east of Hornby Island is to be preferred.

Baynes Sound has an average navigable width of over ½ mile. There are two very fair anchorages, Fanny Bay on the south or main side, and Henry Bay on the north or island side.

The exit into the Strait of Georgia by the northwestern entrance of the sound, between the north end of Denman Island and Cape Lazo, is nearly 2 miles in width, but a remarkable bridge or bar of sand, strewed with large stones, extends the whole way across, and at low water there is as little as 8 feet on it; during summer it is thickly covered with kelp, which never altogether disappears. The bar is very narrow, and is always smooth; towards high water, vessels of 19 feet draught, by carefully paying attention to the leading marks and buoys, may safely pass either into or out of the strait by this channel

Buoys and Beacons—The northern and southern entrances to Baynes Sound are marked by buoys. A *black* can buoy is moored in 4 fathoms on the NE. side of Kelp Bar, and a similar buoy is moored in 3½ fathoms on the SW. side of the bar; these buoys bear, approximately, from each other N. 40° E. and S. 40° W. A course from one to the other leads over the bar in 2 fathoms water.

Maple Point beacon: A beacon consisting of three piles driven in a cluster, surmounted by two circular disks 7 feet in diameter, the one showing black from seaward, the other white when abreast of the beacon. The beacon stands in 18 feet on the extreme end of Maple Point bank, and its summit rises 16 feet above high-water mark.

Reef Bluff spar buoy: A red spar-buoy in 20 feet, on the western extremity of Reef Bluff Reef.

Base Flat beacon: Exactly similar in form and color to the Maple Point beacon This beacon stands in 12 feet on the outer extremity of the flat.

Village Point spar buoy A red spar buoy in 21 feet on the end of the reef.

Union Spit beacon A single pile, surmounted by a circular disk 7 feet in diameter, painted black. The pile is driven in 18 feet on the extremity of the spit, and the beacon stands 10 feet above high-water mark

Grassy Point beacon Similar to the last described. This beacon stands in 18 feet on the NE extremity of the flat extending out from Grassy Point, and rises 14 feet above high water.

Leading marks—On White Beach, leading marks consisting of white washed planks attached to trees have been erected.

These marks when in line, bearing S 40° W. present the appearance of an upper and lower cross, and may be seen from a distance of 4 miles; they lead across the bar at the western entrance, in not less than 12 feet at low water.

Yellow Island is small and bare, and generally of a yellow color. It lies close off the SE. point of Denman Island, is conspicuous, may be seen for several miles, and is a good object to steer for coming from the eastward, as it forms the eastern entrance point of the sound. A light has been put in operation on Yellow Island. The light, besides indicating the entrance to Baynes Sound, is useful for the general navigation of the Strait of Georgia.

Maple Point, which forms the western entrance point, is also very conspicuous; it is low and covered with maples, which in form and foliage bear a remarkable contrast to the pine, particularly in autumn and winter, when the leaf assumes a bright yellow or orange color.

A sand-spit, which dries at low water and is rather steep to, extends ⅓ mile north from Maple Point, and the 3 fathom line is the same distance from the shore as far eastward as Qualicum Bay; therefore, neither the coast nor the point should be approached within that distance.

Anchorage.—If desired there is good anchorage outside, in 6 fathoms, with Yellow Island in line with Norris Reef bearing N. 63° E., and Maple Point west.

Directions.—Entering Baynes Sound by the southeastern channel, some care is necessary to avoid the shoal sand spit extending off Maple Point, as well as some rocky patches and foul ground lying off the Denman Island shore, nearly 2 miles northwestward of Yellow Island.

Immediately opposite on Denman Island, northwest of Maple Point, is ... high clay cliff, with a bare grassy slope; off this cliff, for ... patches (Kelp Reef), marked by a *red* spar ... between them and Maple ... s recom ... e of Reef ... earing N. 61° W., until Maple ... eton is in line with or just shut in by Boyle Point, ... teer west, keeping these marks on astern, which will lead midway between Maple Point spit and the patches off the northern shore.

In coming down the Sound the light on Yellow Island must not be brought to bear to the eastward of S. 84° E. to clear Maple Bank.

Mount Tremeton, the summit of Lasqueti Island, is a very remarkable, bare, castellated knob, 1,056 feet high. When Maple Point bears S. 55° E. the first reach of the sound will be well open, and Base Flat, a low grassy point on the west side of Fanny Bay, will be seen open of Ship Point, then steer up mid-channel. Ship point, with the land one mile SE. of it, shows as two bold wooded bluffs, which should not be approached within 400 yards.

The western side of the sound between Maple Point and Fanny Bay for about 4 miles is low, and shoal water extends for a considerable distance off it; it is recommended not to stand so far over on this side as altogether to shut in Base Flat by the bluffs of Ship Point just mentioned.

Deep Bay.—Maple Point from the extremity of the trees turns sharp off at a right angle to the west for ½ mile and forms a low sandy spit, in shape resembling the long beak of a bird; westward of this is Deep Bay, in which the depth varies from 15 to 20 fathoms, irregular bottom, but sandy. It is a small, and not very desirable anchorage, and as the shoal extends off the back of the spit for its whole length to the distance of ⅓ mile; the extreme of it, which is steep to, can not be steered for until it bears S. 22° E.; if intending to anchor, the best berth is in 14 to 16 fathoms, near the center of the bay.

which never altogether disappears. The bar is very narrow, and is always smooth; towards high water, vessels of 19 feet draught, by carefully paying attention to the leading marks and buoys, may safely pass either into or out of the strait by this channel.

Buoys and Beacons.—The northern and southern entrances to Baynes Sound are marked by buoys. A *black* can buoy is moored in 4 fathoms on the NE. side of Kelp Bar, and a similar buoy is moored in $3\frac{1}{2}$ fathoms on the SW. side of the bar; these buoys bear, approximately, from each other N. 40° E. and S. 40° W. A course from one to the other leads over the bar in 2 fathoms water.

Maple Point beacon: A beacon consisting of three piles driven in a cluster surmounted by two circular disks 7 feet in diameter, the one

(324) **BRITISH COLUMBIA—Vancouver island—East coast—Baynes sound—Reef point—Distinguishing mark on buoy.**—A wooden triangle painted red has been placed on the top of the steel conical buoy moored off Reef point, Baynes sound, to serve as a distinguishing mark in foggy weather.

Approx. position: Lat. 49° 28′ 40″ N., Long 124° 43′ 24″ W.

Base Flat beacon: Exactly similar in form as (N. M. 10, 1904.)

Point beacon This beacon stands in 12 feet on the outer extremity of the flat.

Village Point spar-buoy A red spar-buoy in 21 feet on the end of the reef.

Union Spit beacon. A single pile, surmounted by a circular disk 7 feet in diameter, painted black. The pile is driven in 18 feet on the extremity of the spit, and the beacon stands 10 feet above high-water mark

Grassy Point beacon. Similar to the last described This beacon stands in 18 feet on the NE. extremity of the flat extending out from Grassy Point, and rises 14 feet above high water.

Leading marks—On White Beach, leading marks consisting of white washed planks attached to trees have been erected.

These marks when in line, bearing S. 40° W. present the appearance of an upper and lower cross, and may be seen from a distance of 4 miles, they lead across the bar at the western entrance, in not less than 12 feet at low water.

Yellow Island is small and bare, and generally of a yellow color. It lies close off the SE. point of Denman Island, is conspicuous, may be seen for several miles, and is a good object to steer for coming from the eastward, as it forms the eastern entrance point of the sound. A light has been put in operation on Yellow Island. The light, besides indicating the entrance to Baynes Sound, is useful for the general navigation of the Strait of Georgia.

Maple Point, which forms the western entrance point, is also very conspicuous; it is low and covered with maples, which in form and foliage bear a remarkable contrast to the pine, particularly in autumn and winter, when the leaf assumes a bright yellow or orange color.

A sand-spit, which dries at low water and is rather steep to, extends ½ mile north from Maple Point, and the 3-fathom line is the same distance from the shore as far eastward as Qualicum Bay; therefore, neither the coast nor the point should be approached within that distance.

Anchorage.—If desired there is good anchorage outside, in 6 fathoms, with Yellow Island in line with Norris Reef bearing N. 63° E., and Maple Point west.

Directions.—Entering Baynes Sound by the southeastern channel, some care is necessary to avoid the shoal sand spit extending off Maple Point, as well as some rocky patches and foul ground lying off the Denman Island shore, nearly 2 miles northwestward of Yellow Island.

Immediately opposite on Denman Island, northwest of Maple Point, is Reef Bluff, a high clay cliff, with a bare grassy slope; off this cliff, for 400 yards, extend some rocky patches (Kelp Reef), marked by a *red* spar buoy, which narrow the width of the entrance between them and Maple Point spit to something over 600 yards. When entering, it is recommended to steer in nearly mid-channel, or with the low extreme of Reef Bluff in line with the low part of Ship Point of Fanny Bay bearing N. 61° W., until Maple Point bears S. 23° W., or Mount Tremeton is in line with or just shut in by Boyle Point, bearing east; then steer west, keeping these marks on astern, which will lead midway between Maple Point spit and the patches off the northern shore.

In coming down the Sound the light on Yellow Island must not be brought to bear to the eastward of S. 84° E. to clear Maple Bank.

Mount Tremeton, the summit of Lasqueti Island, is a very remarkable, bare, castellated knob, 1,056 feet high. When Maple Point bears S. 53° E. the first reach of the sound will be well open, and Base Flat, a low grassy point on the west side of Fanny Bay, will be seen open of Ship Point; then steer up mid channel. Ship point, with the land one mile SE. of it, shows as two bold wooded bluffs, which should not be approached within 400 yards.

The western side of the sound between Maple Point and Fanny Bay for about 4 miles is low, and shoal water extends for a considerable distance off it; it is recommended not to stand so far over on this side as altogether to shut in Base Flat by the bluffs of Ship Point just mentioned.

Deep Bay.—Maple Point from the extremity of the trees turns sharp off at a right angle to the west for ½ mile and forms a low sandy spit, in shape resembling the long beak of a bird; westward of this is Deep Bay, in which the depth varies from 15 to 20 fathoms, irregular bottom, but sandy. It is a small, and not very desirable anchorage, and as the shoal extends off the back of the spit for its whole length to the distance of ⅛ mile; the extreme of it, which is steep-to, can not be steered for until it bears S. 22° E.; if intending to anchor, the best berth is in 14 to 16 fathoms, near the center of the bay.

Fanny Bay affords a good though somewhat limited anchorage. Base Flat, the delta of a considerable stream, having its rise in the Beaufort range of mountains, forms its western point; and Ship Point, a bold wooded bluff, its eastern. Entering from the eastward, give Ship Point, and the coast of the peninsula immediately south of it, a berth of ¼ mile.

Anchorage.—Anchor in 12 or 13 fathoms in the middle of the bay, with Ship Point distant a short ½ mile and in line with the Reef Bluff, bearing S. 61° E.; the latter will appear as the SE. extreme of Denman Island.

The southern part of the bay dries entirely at low water, and a sandy flat extends a considerable distance off all around the shores. Small vessels may stand in to 8 fathoms, from which depth it shoals very suddenly off Base Flat; a sand-bank dries for more than 600 yards at low water.

Village Point.—From Fanny Bay the trend of the sound alters slightly to the northward, and increases gradually in width from one mile to 2 miles, which latter it attains at the north end of Denman Island. Both shores are free from danger, with the exception of some rocky or bowlder ledges which extend from 200 to 400 yards off the points. Village point has on it a large native settlement, and a sand-spit extends a short distance off it.

Henry Bay.—Denman Island, towards its NW. end, falls away into a remarkable wedge shape, terminating in a singular sharp beak shaped extreme called Beak Point; the hollow of this beak, on the northwestern side of the island, forms Henry Bay, and is a safe and convenient anchorage, though it is somewhat limited in size. The shores are moderately high and wooded; its western extreme is a low but steep shingle spit, with one or two trees on it, and a clear beach of the same character extends all around the bay.

Anchorage.—The holding ground is very good, and the anchorage in 9 or 10 fathoms in the center of the bay, with Beak Point bearing N. 22° W., when a remarkable clump of trees on Sandy Island will be just open westward of it, here a vessel will be ¼ mile from the beach, where a considerable native village is built. The Indians resort to this bay in large numbers during summer to fish.

Sandy Island.—From Beak Point a series of sand banks, some of them above water, others covered, extend in a northwesterly direction for a little more than 2 miles. Sandy Island, the largest of them, is ⅜ mile from the point, and 6 feet above high water, with large bowlder stones dispersed over it; there is a good boat passage through at half tide.

White Spit.—Two thirds of a mile NW. of Sandy Island is White Spit, which almost covers, and is very remarkable from the number of clam shells collected on it, giving it an appearance of a white sandy beach; it is connected with Sandy Island at very low tides.

Kelp Bar.—The end of the shoal, which occasionally dries in patches, extends ¾ of a mile NW. from White Spit, and from it commences a remarkable kelp bar, which connects Denman Island with the land about Cape Lazo, distant nearly 2 miles. The bar is composed of sand, interspersed with large bowlders, which can be seen at low water; great quantities of kelp grow on it during summer, and it is rarely entirely without it. In shape it resemble an hour glass, very narrow in the center, not above 600 yards wide, and with a depth of 12 feet at low water. The western edge of this bar is steep, shoaling suddenly, and vessels working to the northwestward through Baynes Sound should not stand so far to eastward as to shut in a remarkable single tree on the shingle spit of Beak Point behind the clump of trees on Sandy Island, or avoid bringing White Bluff (which is 2½ miles southward from Cape Lazo and very conspicuous) to the westward of N. 22° W., and when within one mile of it, to the westward of north.

To cross the Kelp Bar over its narrowest part and in the deepest water, a vessel should stand 2½ miles through the sound, northwestward from Henry Bay, until the leading marks on the western shore are in line bearing S. 40° W., then steer out boldly N. 40° E., or on a direct course from one buoy to the other; two or three casts of 12 feet will be struck, at low water, but it will immediately deepen to 3, 4, and shortly 15 fathoms. the same directions will hold good for entering. The white beach may be distinctly seen at 3 or 4 miles distance, but when entering, until it is clearly made out and the buoys on the bar are visible, Cape Lazo should not be brought to the eastward of north, nor the clump of trees on Sandy Island to the eastward of south.

Port Augusta, in the northwestern corner of Baynes Sound, although appearing to be a large sheet of water, at high water, has its upper part entirely filled up by a mud flat, which almost dries at low tides, and is formed by the Courtenay River, which flows into it.

The small settlement of Comox, containing about 350 inhabitants, contains all necessary conveniences for settlers. There is a long wooden pier on the north shore with a depth of 14 feet alongside, and at about one mile off is a Hudson's Bay store and Indian village. Some number of English and Scotch farmers are settled in the neighborhood.

Oil wells have recently been discovered in the vicinity of Port Augusta.

Goose Spit, a remarkable elbow shaped tongue of land, projects to the southward and westward from White Bluff; it is grassy, with one or two hillocks, and bare, with the exception of two solitary small clumps of trees.

Grassy Point, the southern entrance point, is very low and swampy. the delta of a considerable stream; off it, at low water, sand and bowlders dry for 400 yards, and the water shoals suddenly from 10 to one fathom at the distance of 800 yards, leaving a width of less than one mile between the entrance points.

Directions.—Goose Spit is steep to at its western end, but shoal water extends 600 yards off its southern face; and if working in, the low western extreme must not be brought to the southward of N. 67° W. Steer in N. 67° W., passing ¼ mile from the spit, and anchoring in 13 or 14 fathoms, mud bottom. A little more than ½ mile westward from the spit the water shoals suddenly from 7 fathoms to a few feet.

Rounding the spit end, which may be done very close, a deep cove extends one mile to the eastward, or close up to White Bluff; its upper half dries at low water, but there is snug anchorage in its outer part, in 14 fathoms, with the spit end bearing S. 11° E. distant 400 yards. This is an excellent place during a SE. gale, though no sea to speak of could get up in any part of Port Augusta

Tides.—It is high water, full and change, in Port Augusta, at 5h. 0m.; springs rise 12 feet

Supplies—Fish and wild duck are plentiful

Courtenay River is a deep and rapid mountain stream, but, on account of falls and other obstructions, is only navigable for a few miles for boats and canoes, it has its rise in Mount Washington, from whence it flows in a southeasterly direction. Salmon and trout, at the proper season are found in large quantities.

Mount Washington is remarkable, and rises to 5,415 feet, it is the westernmost of a range 10 miles in length, terminating in Mount Beecher to the east.

Lambert Channel, a safe passage, is one mile wide at its southern entrance, gradually increasing to the NW. as it opens into the Strait of Georgia, the water is deep but shoals to 16 fathoms on either side within 400 yards of the shore. Coming from the southward, Yellow Island marks the western entrance point, while Mount Geoffrey rises over the eastern side of the channel; either of these may be steered for until approaching the entrance, when NW. is a mid channel course through. Yellow Island and the western shore are free from danger

Norris Rock, on the eastern side, is of considerable extent at low tide, but at high a mere patch 6 feet above water. From Norman Point, some reefs and foul ground extend nearly 800 yards towards Norris Rock, leaving a narrow passage of 8 fathoms water pretty close to the latter, but it is not recommended.

The eastern side of Lambert Channel, between Norman Point and Shingle Spit, a distance of 2 miles, has two groups of rocks which cover at high water, extending nearly 400 yards off, and the shore should not be approached within ¼ mile; on these rocks the sea generally breaks when there is any wind, and they are marked by kelp in summer.

Shingle Spit is a remarkable low point on the eastern side of the channel; shoal water extends off its extreme, which should be given a berth of 200 yards; temporary anchorage will be found on either side of it, according to the wind; to the northward, in 13 fathoms, at less than 400 yards from the shore; to the southward, in 9 or 10 fathoms.

One patch of the rocks which cover, before mentioned, lies 800 yards S. 45° E of the spit end.

After passing Shingle Spit the width of the channel increases, and there are no dangers which are not visible. On the western side there is anchorage in 12 fathoms off a low maple flat, a little over 2 miles NW. of Shingle Spit, with the high bowlder of Hornby Island bearing N. 68° E., with NW. winds it would be exposed.

Two miles northwestward of this flat is Komas Bluff, a bold wooded headland, from whence the coast trends away to the northwestward and terminates in Beak Point. This stretch of land is shelving, with kelp patches and shallow water extending some distance off, and vessels should give it a berth of ½ mile, after passing Komas Bluff, a good limit in standing to the westward is Shingle Spit of Hornby Island in line with the SE point of Denman Island bearing S 25° E; it is better not to stand so far to the westward as to open out the channel between these two points, in order to avoid the shoal ground in the neighborhood of Sandy Island and the eastern side of Kelp Bar; these marks are very prominent, and answer equally for vessels bound through Lambert Channel from the northward

Off the north end of Hornby Island is a remarkable bowlder rock, 7 or 8 feet high, with smaller ones near it, and vessels should not approach the shore in this neighborhood within a long ½ mile

Tribune Bay, on the southeastern side of Hornby Island, affords good anchorage with all but easterly or southeasterly winds, to which it is exposed It is easy to enter or to leave, and conveniently situated as a stopping place for vessels bound either way, being 35 miles west of Nanaimo, and 40 eastward of Cape Mudge and the entrance of Discovery Passage At its head are two bays, separated by a jutting point; the northern has a clean, white, sandy beach

The eastern end of Hornby Island terminates in a rather remarkable point (St John), grassy and bare of trees. Off it are two or three small low islets Some reefs on which the sea generally breaks extend nearly ½ mile outside the islets, and vessels should not pass nearer than ½ mile to the northeastern coast of Hornby Island. The entrance of Tribune Bay is one mile west of St John Point; its eastern shores are bold and cliffy, its western low and shelving, with shallow water, and reefs extending a considerable distance off them

In passing Hornby Island, the light on Yellow Island kept in view will clear the Kelp reefs south of the island, while, if the light is obscured, it will indicate that the vessel is in dangerous proximity thereto.

Nash Bank, the outermost of these dangers, is a one fathom rocky patch, which must be carefully avoided. It extends nearly one mile in a southeasterly direction from Dunlop Point. There is a passage ¾ mile wide between it and the eastern side of the bay, but no passage between it and Dunlop Point. Norris Rock kept in line with Yellow

Island, bearing S. 63° W., leads south of it, in 14 fathoms; and when the center of the white sandy beach at the head of the bay bears N. 45° W., steer in for it. Yellow Island well open south of Norris Rock, bearing S. 66° W., leads ½ mile south of the reefs off St. John Point.

Anchorage.—With a leading wind it is recommended to pass the eastern side of the bay within a short ½ mile, and to steer up for the white sandy beach as soon as it is open, anchoring with the eastern bluff of the bay bearing S. 84° E., about 800 yards from the eastern shore, in 9 fathoms, sandy bottom; this berth will be ¼ mile from the white beach at the head, and will enable vessels to leave conveniently on the approach of a SE. wind, which they should always do. There is anchorage, if desired, in 4 fathoms, much closer in.

Cape Lazo is a remarkable salient point about 200 feet high, flat and grassy on its summit, but wooded behind, and falling abruptly to the sea in yellow clay cliffs. Although a bold looking headland, shoal water extends a considerable distance off, a[illegible] vessels should not approach its eastern and southeastern sides ne[illegible]an 2 miles, as only 4½ fathoms uneven bottom is found at the dista[illegible] of 1½ miles. Large bowlder stones dry off for ½ mile at low water. When the pitch of the cape bears S. 68° W. it may be approached to within one mile in 11 or 12 fathoms, and the coast to the westward may safely be passed at that distance.

Oyster Bay.—From Cape Lazo the coast trends NW., is moderately high, and slightly indented with bowlder beaches, which makes boat landing attended with danger unless in very calm weather. At the distance of 15 miles is Kuhushan Point, the southern extreme of a large but not very deep indentation named Oyster Bay; Shelter Point is its northern extreme.

A reef, which affords considerable protection from NW. winds, extends ½ mile eastward from Shelter Point.

Anchorage.—There is fair anchorage in 10 or 12 fathoms water in this bay for vessels waiting wind or tide. A good berth is a little more than ½ mile from the shore with Mitlenatch Island bearing N. 74° E., and the highest part of Cape Mudge bearing N. 11° W.

Cape Mudge is one of those peculiar headlands so frequently met with on this coast, and resembles Roberts Point and Cape Lazo, except that the yellow clay cliff which forms its face is more covered with vegetation. The cape is between 200 and 300 feet high, flat, and wooded on its summit, falling to the westward as it enters Discovery Passage with a low bowlder point; the high land of Valdes Island appears behind it from the southeastward. A bowlder beach extends in a semicircular form from it to the eastward, and at the distance of 2 miles in this direction the depth is not more than 5 fathoms. The edge of this shoal water is fringed with kelp during summer, and is generally well defined by a tidal line, and sometimes heavy tide rips, which it is recommended not to stand into. Between Cape Mudge and Willow

Point the tide rips at flood are dangerous to small craft in blowing weather. The western low part of Cape Mudge should not be brought to bear westward of N. 45° W. when entering or leaving Discovery Passage.

Directions for Georgia Strait.—From the coast of Gabriola Island abreast Nanaimo, to the opposite shore of the continent, about Burrard Inlet, the width of the strait is 14 miles, the navigation free from danger, and the strength of the tide between one and two knots an hour. Coming from the southward, Mt. Shepherd, on the south end of Texada Island, is a very remarkable object, and shows as a solitary peaked island standing in the middle of the strait; it is 2,906 feet high, and is plainly seen in clear weat er more than 30 miles off.

Proceeding westward, the long and comparatively low island of Lasqueti rises above the horizon, its singular bare turret-shaped summit, 1,056 feet high, presenting an unmistakable feature. The Ballinac, and smaller islands westward of them, will now soon be made out. When abreast the former, the width of the channel contracts to 4 miles between them and the small Island of Sangster off the SE. end of Lasqueti, after which it opens out again to 7 miles, and the rather remarkable flat-topped Mt. Geoffrey on the west end of Hornby Island will be plainly seen. The southern coast of Lasqueti is bold, with no dangers off it which are not seen, except Seal Rocks, which cover at half-tide. Off its west end are the small groups of Flat and Bare Islands, but no hidden dangers. False Bay, which indents its west end, is exposed, and not recommended as an anchorage.

The Sisters Islets are the next remarkable objects; they are two small black rocks 17 feet above high water, S. 57° W. of the west point of Lasqueti, with a deep-water channel over one mile wide between them and Flat Islands. They are bold on all sides, but should not be approached too close in calms or light winds, as the tide sets straight past them.

Gillies Bay, on the west side of Texada Island, and 2 miles NW. of the Mouatt Islets, a small group which lie nearly one mile from the shore, is easily recognized by a remarkable white patch on its northern point, which is seen for many miles, and shows as two distinct white spots. An anchor may be dropped at ¼ mile from the beach in 12 fathoms, but it is only a stopping place.

Caution.—When standing to the westward towards the Denman Island shore, Lambert Channel should not be opened out between the SE. end of the island and Shingle Spit, nor should Cape Lazo be approached nearer than 2 miles.

NORTHERN SHORE OF THE STRAIT OF GEORGIA.

Howe Sound, immediately adjoining Burrard Inlet, is an extensive though probably useless sheet of water, the general depth being very great, while there are but few anchorages. It is almost entirely hemmed in by rugged and precipitous mountains rising abruptly from the water's edge. A river of considerable size, the Squawmisht, navigable for boats, flows into its head; it leads by no useful or even practicable route into the interior of the country.

The entrance to the sound is between Atkinson Point and Gower Point The sound penetrates the continent in a northerly direction for 20 miles, and although of such considerable width for nearly 12 miles of its length, yet it is choked by some large and numerous smaller islands, between which are several ship passages

Bowen Island, lying at the entrance, is remarkable, being round, smooth, and partially bare, unmistakably pointing out the entrance from any direction, the island is 7 miles in length in a northerly direction, and more than 3 in width.

Queen Charlotte Channel —Passage Island, only ½ mile long but very prominent from the southward, stands in the center of the channel, and on both sides of it is a deep water passage; that to the west, 1½ miles in width, is the best, the shores of Bowen Island being steep and bold; some small rocky islets lie a short distance off the eastern side of the other passage, but the channel is a good one and one mile wide A tide-rip is frequently met with off Atkinson Point, caused by the meeting of the ebb streams from the sound and Burrard Inlet.

Snug Cove—At 1¾ miles northward of Passage Island, and on the eastern shore, is White Cliff Point, and opposite, on the Bowen Island shore, distant 1½ miles, is a double headed cove. Snug Cove, the southernmost of these, though narrow, affords excellent anchorage to small craft in 9 fathoms, sheltered from all winds.

Deep Cove, the northernmost, is larger, but with a SE. wind, when anchorage would be most required, a swell would set in. After passing White Cliff Point the width of the channel increases to 2½ miles, and 3 miles to the northward is Bowyer Island, with a deep ship passage on both sides of it, that to the westward being the widest

Directions—Vessels bound to Port Graves, which is the principal anchorage in the sound, should pass westward of Bowyer Island between it and Hood Point, the north point of Bowen Island. The latter is a rather remarkable low flat peninsula point, with a small high cliffy island lying off it, connected at low water; both island and point are bold From Hood Point, Hope Point bears N. 72° W., and after rounding it a N. 23° E. course leads into the harbor.

Bound up the sound by Queen Charlotte Channel, a north course leads in mid channel; pass eastward of White Rock, Center Island, and Anvil Island, through Montagu Channel; the depth of water is 140 fathoms; the eastern shore quite bold.

White Rock is a small but remarkable islet 36 feet high; some rocks which cover at high water extend ¼ mile north and south from it.

Center Island lies midway between it and the south point of Anvil Island.

Anvil Island is oval shaped; its summit, Leading Peak, 2,746 feet high, is very remarkable, resembling the horn of an anvil pointed upwards. From almost all parts of the strait of Georgia this peak appears as a most prominent object.

Montagu Channel, between Anvil Island and the eastern shore, is one mile wide and over 100 fathoms in depth, passing out of it the sound takes a northerly direction for 7 miles to Watts Point, when it trends to the northeastward for a further distance of 4 miles, terminating in a low delta, through which flows the Squawmisht River. The sound carries its depth to the head and shoals from 100 fathoms suddenly to 2 fathoms, the latter depth is close to the mud at the head of the sound which is so soft, that supposing a vessel to anchor, she would be certain to drag on shore with any wind up the sound.

Anchorage may be obtained off a waterfall on the eastern side of the sound in 20 fathoms water, about 400 yards from the shore and one mile from the entrance of the Squawmisht River, with Watts Inner Point bearing S. 57° W.

Collingwood Channel, to the westward of Bowen Island, between it and the group of smaller islands which stud the center of the sound, is the most direct route to Port Graves. At the entrance both shores are steep and bold, the channel takes a northerly direction, and is for 4 miles about one mile wide, the general depth varying from 50 to 100 fathoms. The small islands forming the western side have no dangers that are not visible except Passage Rock.

A rock which uncovers at very low spring tides lies $1\frac{1}{4}$ miles S. 46° W of Hutt Island, and one mile S 30° E of Cotton Point, Keats Island.

Worlcombe Island is the outermost of the small islands, $\frac{1}{2}$ mile long east and west, and very narrow.

Passage Rock, which lies almost midway between Worlcombe and Pasley Islands, and covers at half tide, lies 700 yards N. 45° W of the eastern point of Worlcombe Island, and when working in or out, vessels should not stand so far to the westward, between Worlcombe and Pasley Islands, as to shut in the western points of White and Ragged Islands behind the low east point of Pasley Island.

White Island, $1\frac{1}{4}$ miles northward of Worlcombe, is small and round with some white quartz veins showing through the foliage.

Ragged Island is a short distance farther to the northward and has four or five very remarkable bare white rocks lying off its eastern end.

Keats Island forms the western side of the channel, it is moderately high, with a bare clifty summit near its center.

Barfleur Passage lies to the westward of the central group of small islands between them and Keats Island; it is a safe ship channel but not quite so wide as Collingwood Channel.

Working in, it is better not to approach nearer than $\frac{1}{4}$ mile to Popham Island and the two smaller ones north of it, which form the eastern side of the passage. The passages between the small islands are not recommended.

A Rock, on which the sea breaks at low water, extends 300 yards into the channel westward from the second of these islands; otherwise there are no dangers which are not visible.

Shoal Channel, the westernmost entrance to Howe Sound, is between Keats Island and the mainland of Gower Point. It is convenient for vessels coming from the westward, and leads to Plumper Cove, a snug anchorage on the northwestern side of Keats Island; Gower Point, the SW. extreme of the channel, is not very remarkable, but when approaching it a large bowlder rock will be seen at its extreme, and a similar one on the shore ¼ mile to the westward of it; a conspicuous cone 900 feet high also rises immediately over the coast, 3 miles within the point on the west side of the channel, and can be seen a long distance off.

The south point of Keats Island, which forms the eastern point of entrance to the channel, has, lying close off it, Home Island, a small but prominent and thickly wooded island. From a short distance northward from this island a bar of sand and shingle extends quite across the channel to the steep cliffs of the mainland; the depth of water on it varies from 7 to 18 feet; the least water is on a spit extending 500 yards from Keats Island; it then deepens to 2¼ fathoms, but at 100 yards farther to the westward there is a shoal spot of 1½ fathoms, and there is also a similar depth at 300 yards S. 17° W. of Steep Cliff Point; vessels, therefore, when entering Shoal Channel, should keep rather over to the mainland side, about 400 yards from it, which may be increased when Home Island bears S. 33° E.

Observation Point, in line with the north end of South Shelter Island or just showing to the westward of it, bearing N. 47° E., leads over the bar in 2¼ fathoms water, which is here only 250 yards across, but the passage with this depth is very narrow. Observation Point kept just shut in with South Point of North Shelter Island bearing N. 53° E., and when Home Island bears S. 33° E. kept well open of it, leads over the bar in not less than 2 fathoms; but vessels drawing more than 8 feet of water are recommended not to attempt Shoal Channel at low water.

The width of the bar in the center is not over ¼ mile; it does not shoal very suddenly from outside, and a vessel might anchor in 9 or 10 fathoms, sandy bottom, with Home Island bearing S. 62° E.

Two dangerous rocks which uncover at very low water spring tides are reported as lying 600 yards N. 45° E. of Steep Cliff Point.

Plumper Cove.—Immediately after crossing the bar of Shoal Channel the water deepens to 20 fathoms, and two small islets, partially wooded and almost joined at low water, will be seen one mile to the NE.; between them and the shore of Keats Island is Plumper Cove, which is perfectly sheltered from all winds, as, however hard it may be blowing outside, it is generally a calm here. Both shores of the channel are steep, and if wishing to enter, a vessel should pass round the north end of the islets.

[illegible] . There [illegible] mmended [illegible] orth end [illegible] he cove, [illegible] arge ves- [illegible]

[illegible] nel. Its [illegible] after passing Plumper Cove is north, and at the distance of 6 miles is Woolridge Island. The wider channel lies westward of this island, but there is over 100 fathoms of water through Latona Passage to the eastward of it, and a width of ¼ mile. Passing Woolridge Island, the arm turns to the northeastward, and northward of Anvil Island leads to the head of the sound. The depth of water is very great in every part, and there is no anchorage above.

Gambier Island, immediately northward of Bowen Island, is almost square-shaped and 6 miles in extent either way. On its western side rise two very remarkable cone-shaped mountains over 3,000 feet in elevation. The southern face of the island is indented by three very deep bays or inlets, but only in the easternmost is convenient anchorage found. Close off the SW. point of the island are the Twins, two small islets; they are the only part of its coast which may not be approached very close.

Port Graves, the easternmost of the three bays on the south side of Gambier Island, is the principal anchorage in Howe Sound. It is about 8 miles from the entrance and may be reached with great facility by any of the channels already described; its entrance will not, however, be very apparent to strangers until closing Hope Point, which forms its eastern side.

The direction of the port, as also of the two deep bays westward of it, is NNE. and it runs more than 1½ miles in that direction; the width not quite ½ mile.

Hutt Island, scarcely ¼ mile long, but very high and remarkable, lies close off the northwestern side of Bowen Island, and is a good guide to the port when entering by either of the western channels.

Directions.—On the western shore, ¾ mile inside the entrance, a [illegible] extends out for a short distance, which should be given a

(1690) **BRITISH COLUMBIA—Strait of Georgia—Seechelt peninsula—White islet—Light established.**—The Canadian Government has given notice that a *fixed white* light, to be known as Seechelt light, has been established on White islet, lying off Mission point, southeastward from Seechelt peninsula, in the strait of Georgia. The light is unwatched, shown from a Wigham 31-day oil lamp 36 feet above high water, standing on a small white enclosed wooden tower supported on a black wooden framework. It should be visible 6 miles from all points of approach.

This light takes the place of the beacon at present standing on White islet.

Approx. position: Lat. 49° 24′ 50″ N., Long. 123° 42′ 32″ W.

(N. M. 48, 1904.)

ham Island and the two smaller ones north of it, which form the eastern side of the passage. The passages between the small islands are not recommended

(1374) **BRITISH COLUMBIA — Strait of Georgia — Rock Point reef—Buoy established.**—The Government of Canada has given notice that a spar buoy, painted red, has been established off Rock point, which is the point midway between Gower point and Mission point, to show the extent of the reef eastward of Rock point. The buoy is moored in 6 fathoms of water.

Approx. position Lat 49° 24′ 20″ N , Long 123° 37′ 20″ W.

snug anchorage on the northwestern side o **(N. M 38, 1904)**

Point, the SW extreme of the channel, is not very remarkable, but when approaching it a large bowlder rock will be seen at its extreme, and a similar one on the shore ¼ mile to the westward of it; a conspicuous cone 900 feet high also rises immediately over the coast, 3 miles within the point on the west side of the channel, and can be seen a long distance off

The south point of Keats Island, which forms the eastern point of entrance to the channel, has, lying close off it, Home Island, a small but prominent and thickly wooded island. From a short distance northward from this island a bar of sand and shingle extends quite across the channel to the steep cliffs of the mainland; the depth of water on it varies from 7 to 18 feet, the least water is on a spit extending 500 yards from Keats Island; it then deepens to 2¼ fathoms, but at 100 yards farther to the westward there is a shoal spot of 1½ fathoms, and there is also a similar depth at 300 yards S 17° W. of Steep Cliff Point; vessels, therefore, when entering Shoal Channel, should keep rather over to the mainland side, about 400 yards from it, which may be increased when Home Island bears S. 33° E.

Observation Point, in line with the north end of South Shelter Island or just showing to the westward of it, bearing N 47° E , leads over the bar in 2¼ fathoms water, which is here only 250 yards across, but the passage with this depth is very narrow Observation Point kept just shut in with South Point of North Shelter Island bearing N. 53° E., and when Home Island bears S. 33° E. kept well open of it, leads over the bar in not less than 2 fathoms, but vessels drawing more than 8 feet of water are recommended not to attempt Shoal Channel at low water.

The width of the bar in the center is not over ¼ mile, it does not shoal very suddenly from outside, and a vessel might anchor in 9 or 10 fathoms, sandy

Two danger

are reported as

Plumper C

nel the water d

wooded and al

NE.; between

which is perfec

blowing outside, it is generally a calm here. Both shores of the channel are steep, and if wishing to enter, a vessel should pass round the north end of the islets.

Anchorage—Anchor in 8 fathoms in the center of the cove. There is room to lie at single anchor, but a vessel of any size is recommended to moor, dropping her outer anchor in 10 fathoms when the north end of the islets bears N 66° W, and, running up the center of the cove, drop the inner one in 6 fathoms. There is only room for one large vessel, but several small ones could find shelter.

Thornborough Channel is a continuation of Shoal Channel. Its direction after passing Plumper Cove is north, and at the distance of 6 miles is Woolridge Island The wider channel lies westward of this island, but there is over 100 fathoms of water through Latona Passage to the eastward of it, and a width of ¼ mile. Passing Woolridge Island, the arm turns to the northeastward, and northward of Anvil Island leads to the head of the sound. The depth of water is very great in every part, and there is no anchorage above.

Gambier Island, immediately northward of Bowen Island, is almost square shaped and 6 miles in extent either way. On its western side rise two very remarkable cone shaped mountains over 3 000 feet in elevation The southern face of the island is indented by three very deep bays or inlets, but only in the easternmost is convenient anchorage found. Close off the SW. point of the island are the Twins, two small islets; they are the only part of its coast which may not be approached very close.

Port Graves, the easternmost of the three bays on the south side of Gambier Island, is the principal anchorage in Howe Sound It is about 8 miles from the entrance and may be reached with great facility by any of the channels already described, its entrance will not, however, be very apparent to strangers until closing Hope Point, which forms its eastern side.

The direction of the port, as also of the two deep bays westward of it, is NNE and it runs more than 1½ miles in that direction, the width not quite ½ mile.

Hutt Island, scarcely ½ mile long, but very high and remarkable, lies close off the northwestern side of Bowen Island, and is a good guide to the port when entering by either of the western channels.

Directions—On the western shore, ¼ mile inside the entrance, a shingle spit extends out for a short distance, which should be given a berth, as shoal water extends 100 yards off it, when past the spit there is anchorage anywhere in 10 fathoms, but ½ mile or more inside it, in 7 fathoms, is the best berth. Vessels entering by Shoal Channel, and bound for Port Graves, after passing Plumper Cove should steer N. 67° E. until near Hope Point and the harbor opens.

The Coast from Gower Point to the entrance of Malaspina Strait is free from danger White Islet, a bare rock 51 feet high, lies 1½ miles from the shore, 6 miles westward from Gower Point, and is remarkable, always showing very white; there is deep water close to it and inside it.

Trail Bay.—At 4 miles NNW. from White Islet the coast recedes and forms Trail Bay.

Anchorage may be obtained off the village in Trail Bay, abreast a bluff in the northeastern corner, in about 15 fathoms. The Indians (Sechelt) are under the care of the Roman Catholic mission, and their chapel is a conspicuous object from seaward.

Trail Islets, four in number, lie a little more than ½ mile off the western end of this bay, and if necessary small vessels may drop an anchor inside them in 12 or 13 fathoms water.

Texada Island, lying parallel with and on the eastern side of the Strait of Georgia, is 27 miles in length, with an average width of scarcely 4 miles. Throughout its whole length stretches a ridge of rugged trap mountains, wooded generally to their summits; at the southern end Mount Shepherd reaches a height of 2,906 feet. Its shores are steep and bold on all sides, and the land rises abruptly, except at the northern extreme. On the north side, 3 miles from Marshall Point, there is a boat cove.

Gillies Bay, the only anchorage, and that merely a stopping place, is on the southwestern side

Upwood Point, the south extreme of Texada Island, is rugged and precipitous; stunted pines grow between the crevices of the bare trap rock, the land behind more thickly wooded. Almost immediately over it rises Mount Dick, a very remarkable hump shaped hill, and 3 miles inland is Mount Shepherd. A rock which covers lies 400 yards off the point.

Lasqueti Island is separated from Texada by a channel about one mile wide It is 9 miles long, with an average width of over 2 miles; Mount Tremeton, a singular turret shaped summit, rising nearly in its center. On its southern side are several boat coves

Tucker Bay, on the northern side of Lasqueti, and equidistant from either end, is a very fair anchorage. Entering from the westward it will be readily known by a group of small wooded islands which form its eastern side, its western point is sloping and somewhat remarkable, partially bare of trees The water shoals rather suddenly from 30 to 16 fathoms.

Anchorage—The anchorage is in 14 fathoms, with the outermost and westernmost of the small islands bearing N 46° E. and the west point of the bay N 50° W, which will be within ¼ mile of the shore. With a strong NW. wind and flood tide, the bay, though safe, would not be a comfortable anchorage, from the eastward, sailing vessels would find some difficulty in reaching it in consequence of the prevailing NW. winds and the narrowness of the channel at that end

Small vessels may anchor in the southeastern corner, inside the small island on the southern shore, in 6 or 7 fathoms water, sheltered from almost any wind.

Sangster Island, ½ mile long, lies one mile SW. of Young Point. There is a deep passage of 70 fathoms between the two, but a rocky ledge with shoal water on it extends off the western point of Sangster Island.

Seal Rocks, which cover at half tide, lie a little more than one mile N. 61° W of the western point of Sangster Island, and it is not recommended to pass between the island and the rocks.

Jenkins Island lies 3 miles westward of Sangster, and close to the southern shore of Lasqueti

Sea Egg Rocks, always uncovered, lie 600 yards off the west end of

p bight but

would find

ieti, is per-

ild be given

up lying off

the northwestern end of Lasqueti.

Sabine Channel, between Texada and Lasqueti Islands, is a good ship passage with very deep water; it is 3 miles wide at the western end, but several high conical islands lying off the northeastern side of Lasqueti contract the width at the eastern end, in some parts to ¼ mile. Bull Passage, to the southward of these islands, is a narrow but deep channel.

(1659) **BRITISH COLUMBIA—Strait of Georgia—Malaspina strait—Uncharted rock.**—September 10, 1904, Captain A J Bjerre, of the steamer *Active*, found an uncharted rocky shoal, on which a depth of 12 feet was obtained at low water, in Malaspina strait, off Seechelt peninsula, mainland of British Columbia.

From the shoal, which is about 200 feet in extent, point Upwood bears S. 44° W true (S by W ⅝ W. mag.) and Gowlland point S. 38° E. true (SE. by E. ½ E. mag).

Caution must be exercised in navigating deep draft vessels in this neighborhood, as the shoal is nearly in the fairway to Welcome pass.

(N M 47, 1904)

NW. point in a steep clay cliff, off which, at low water, ... point Shoal water extends from this point in a northwesterly direction for about 800 yards, and a bank with not more than 5 fathoms water on it borders the northern side of the western island for a distance of from 600 yards to one mile.

From the north point of the eastern island, Tattenham Ledge extends ½ mile; this ledge uncovers at the inner part and has 4 fathoms water on the outer.

Welcome Pass is a deep but narrow channel, about one mile in length. This passage has not been well sounded, and as sunken rocks exist in its southern entrance, it should be used with great caution

A shoal of some extent is reported to exist in the southern entrance, contracting the passage to about 600 yards.

Buccaneer Bay, formed by the junction of the two Thormanby

from the shore, 6 miles westward from Gower Point, and is remarkable, always showing very white; there is deep water close to it and inside it.

Trail Bay.—At 4 miles NNW. from White Islet the coast recedes and forms Trail Bay.

Anchorage may be obtained off the village in Trail Bay, abreast a bluff in the northeastern corner, in about 15 fathoms. The Indians (Sechelt) are under the care of the Roman Catholic mission, and their chapel is a conspicuous object from seaward.

Trail Islets, four in number, lie a little more than ½ mile off the western end of this bay, and if necessary small vessels may drop an

(1373) **BRITISH COLUMBIA—Malaspina strait—Texada island—North point—Buoy established.**—The Government of Canada has given notice that a spar buoy, painted black, has been established off the north point of Texada island. It is moored in 6 fathoms of water.

Approx position: Lat. 49° 48′ 38″ N., Long. 124° 37′ 55″ W.

This buoy marks a reef which extends from the north point of Texada island for about 400 yards. There is a rock near the end of the reef which dries about 4 feet. (N. M. 88, 1904.)

ern extreme. On the north side, 3 miles from Marshall Point, there is a boat cove.

Gillies Bay, the only anchorage, and that merely a stopping place, is on the southwestern side.

Upwood Point, the south extreme of Texada Island, is rugged and precipitous; stunted pines grow between the crevices of the bare trap rock, the land behind more thickly wooded. Almost immediately over it rises Mo[illegible]

inland is [illegible]

point

Lasque[illegible]

mile wide.

Mount Tre[illegible]

center. O[illegible]

Tucker[illegible]

either end [illegible] ward it

will be rea[illegible] group of small wooded islands which form its eastern side; its western point is sloping and somewhat remarkable, partially bare of trees. The water shoals rather suddenly from 30 to 16 fathoms.

Anchorage.—The anchorage is in 14 fathoms, with the outermost and westernmost of the small islands bearing N. 46° E. and the west point of the bay N. 50° W., which will be within ¼ mile of the shore. With a strong NW. wind and flood tide, the bay, though safe, would not be a comfortable anchorage; from the eastward, sailing vessels would find some difficulty in reaching it in consequence of the prevailing NW. winds and the narrowness of the channel at that end.

Small vessels may anchor in the southeastern corner, inside the small island on the southern shore, in 6 or 7 fathoms water, sheltered from almost any wind.

Sangster Island, ½ mile long, lies one mile SW of Young Point. There is a deep passage of 70 fathoms between the two, but a rocky ledge with shoal water on it extends off the western point of Sangster Island

Seal Rocks, which cover at half tide, lie a little more than one mile N. 61° W of the western point of Sangster Island, and it is not recommended to pass between the island and the rocks.

Jenkins Island lies 3 miles westward of Sangster, and close to the southern shore of Lasqueti.

Sea Egg Rocks, always uncovered, lie 600 yards off the west end of Jenkins Island

False Bay, in the west end of Lasqueti Island, is a deep bight but is not recommended as an anchorage, though small vessels would find shelter in its northwestern corner in 7 fathoms.

Stevens Passage, between the Sisters Islets and Lasqueti, is perfectly safe and clear. Flat Islands, on its eastern side, should be given a berth of ¼ mile, as should also Bare Islands, a small group lying off the northwestern end of Lasqueti.

Sabine Channel, between Texada and Lasqueti Islands, is a good ship passage with very deep water; it is 3 miles wide at the western end, but several high conical islands lying off the northeastern side of Lasqueti contract the width at the eastern end, in some parts to ⅜ mile Bull Passage, to the southward of these islands, is a narrow but deep channel

The Tides through Sabine Channel set at the rate of 2 knots an hour, the flood running to the westward, the ebb to the eastward.

Malaspina Strait is a wide navigable channel. Its general direction is NW The Texada shore is bold, and almost straight for its whole length, fronted by narrow shingle or bowlder beaches.

Thormanby Islands, two in number, are almost joined. They form the southeastern entrance point of Malaspina Strait. Lying close to the mainland, these islands appear as a part of it, terminating at their NW. point in a steep clay cliff, off which, at low water, dries a bowlder point. Shoal water extends from this point in a northwesterly direction for about 800 yards, and a bank with not more than 5 fathoms water on it borders the northern side of the western island for a distance of from 600 yards to one mile.

From the north point of the eastern island, Tattenham Ledge extends ½ mile; this ledge uncovers at the inner part and has 4 fathoms water on the outer

Welcome Pass is a deep but narrow channel, about one mile in length. This passage has not been well sounded, and as sunken rocks exist in its southern entrance, it should be used with great caution.

A shoal of some extent is reported to exist in the southern entrance, contracting the passage to about 600 yards.

Buccaneer Bay, formed by the junction of the two Thormanby

Islands, affords good and sheltered anchorage at its head in 15 fathoms.

Caution must be observed when entering, as shoal water extends for fully ½ mile from the northern shore of both islands on both sides of the entrance. Tattenham Ledge, on the east side of the entrance, will be avoided by keeping the outer of the Surry Islands (lying off the east shore within the harbor) in line with Wolf Point and the center of the beach at the head of the bay, bearing S 89 E

A rock, dry at low-water springs, lies near, but a little to the westward of, the spot marked 2 fathoms on the chart, and on the following bearings Derby Point S 33° E., distant about 700 yards; NW. point of Thormanby West Island S. 71° W.

Secret Cove—At one mile northward of the entrance to the Buccaneer Bay is the entrance to Secret Cove. The channel in, between Point George (the SE. end of Turnagain Island) and Entrance Island to the eastward, is 100 yards wide with depths of from 7 to 11 fathoms in it. One hundred yards S 57° W. of the west end of Entrance Island is a rocky patch which covers at three quarters flood; it will be cleared by keeping White Rock (2 feet high) inside the harbor on its west shore, just open of the northwestern shore of Entrance Island, bearing N 54° E

Anchorage.—When past Entrance Island, anchorage may be taken up as convenient in 7 to 9 fathoms, midway between that island and Echo Island.

Rocky Patch—From Secret Cove the coast, which trends to the northwestward, is bold to for 4 miles, at which distance a rocky patch of considerable extent lies one mile S 33° E of Francis Point, and extends nearly the same distance parallel to the shore. The least water found on this patch was 7 fathoms, but less may probably exist. Several small islets lie north of the patch, between it and the shore.

Bargain Harbor—To the northward of these islets is the entrance to this small harbor, with depths of 5 and 6 fathoms in it The entrance lies between the Whitestone Islands and the islets lying off the shore to the eastward, the largest of which are Flat (the southern) and Green Islets By keeping in mid channel the harbor may be safely entered.

The head of Bargain Harbor communicates with Pender Harbor by a narrow passage, which is available for boats at high water.

Jervis Inlet—The entrances of the inlet are between Francis and Scotch Fir Points. Nelson Island lies immediately in the center, and divides it into two channels, the westernmost being the principal one. Both channels can be made out from Upwood Point Neither from a commercial point of view, as a refuge for shipping, or as a means of communication with the interior of the country, does the inlet appear likely ever to be of any great importance

Agamemnon Channel, the southern entrance to Jervis Inlet, runs between Nelson Island and the main in a general northerly direction for 9 miles, then joins the main channel of the inlet; its average width is little more than ⅙ mile; the tides run from one to 3 knots; the depth of water varies from 50 to 100 fathoms, and it affords no anchorage. The southern entrance is encumbered by a group of small islands, the center and largest of which, Pearson Island, is ¼ mile in extent, wooded, and 250 feet high. Northwestward of Pearson, a little more than ¼ mile, are the Channel Islets, two or three small islets joined by reefs,

(1556) **BRITISH COLUMBIA — Strait of Georgia — Malaspina strait — Nelson rock — Beacon erected.** —A day beacon has been erected by the Government of Canada on Nelson rock, Malaspina strait, 1 mile S. 86° W. true (SW. by W ½ W mag.) from Fearney point, Nelson island.

Approx. position Lat. 49° 38′ 50″ N., Long 124° 08′ 19″ W

The beacon consists of a frustrum of a square pyramid in stone-work, 14 feet square at the bottom, 9 feet at the top, by 16 feet high, surmounted by a wooden staff carrying a lattice work drum 6 feet high by 6 feet in diameter, the whole painted black and showing 26 feet above high water.

Nelson rock dries about 6 feet at low water and extends half a cable in a northeast and southwest direction with a width of 75 feet. The beacon is on the northeast end of the ledge and can be approached on the northeast within 100 yards (N. M. 44, 1904.)

moderate depth of water, to be found at the ...

but its entrance is so encumbered by islands as to render it difficult of access to any but steam or coasting vessels; it immediately adjoins the Agamemnon Channel on the south, and lies ¾ mile east of Pearson Island.

The entrance to Pender Harbor may be approached by three passages between the islands lying off the southern entrance of Agamemnon Channel. When coming from Jervis Inlet by the above named channel, the passage between Channel Islets and Pearson Island to the SW. and Norman Point to the NE., is the most convenient, but coming from any other direction it would be better to use either the one between Pearson Island and Channel Islets or that between the former island and Martin Island; the latter is to be preferred.

Williams and Charles Islands lie immediately across the entrance, forming three channels, that to the northward, between Williams Island and Henry Point, is not 200 yards in width, but it is the best and has a depth of 20 fathoms. A shoal extends about 100 yards from the northwestern side of Williams Island.

Entering the harbor between Williams and Charles Islands the channel is only 100 yards in width, with 7 fathoms water, and a rock which covers at three quarters flood lies a little more than 100 yards north of the eastern point of Charles Island.

Skardon Islands are two in number. Pass on either side of them and steer up the harbor. One mile within the entrance, a peninsula extends to the south from the northern shore; pass between its southern point and Mary Island.

Anchorage.—Anchor in Gerrans Bay, ¼ mile to the southward of the peninsula, in 6 or 7 fathoms; there is also good anchorage in Garden

Islands, affords good and sheltered anchorage at its head in 15 fathoms.

Caution must be observed when entering, as shoal water extends for fully ½ mile from the northern shore of both islands on both sides of the entrance. Tattenham Ledge, on the east side of the entrance, will be avoided by keeping the outer of the Surry Islands (lying off the east shore within the harbor) in line with

beach at [illegible]

A rock, [illegible]
ward of, t[illegible]
bearings [illegible]
of Thormn[illegible]

Secret [illegible]
neer Bay r[illegible]
George (th[illegible]
eastward, [illegible]
One hundr[illegible]
rocky patc[illegible]
keeping W[illegible]
just open [illegible] northwestern shore of Entrance Island, bearing N. 54° E

Anchorage.—When past Entrance Island, anchorage may be taken up as convenient in 7 to 9 fathoms, midway between that island and Echo Island

Rocky Patch.—From Secret Cove the coast, which trends to the northwestward, is bold to for 4 miles, at which distance a rocky patch of considerable extent lies one mile S. 33° E. of Francis Point, and extends nearly the same distance parallel to the shore. The least water found on this patch was 7 fathoms, but less may probably exist Several small islets lie north of the patch, between it and the shore

Bargain Harbor.—To the northward of these islets is the entrance to this small harbor, with depths of 5 and 6 fathoms in it The entrance lies between the Whitestone Islands and the islets lying off the shore to the eastward, the largest of which are Flat (the southern) and Green Islets. By keeping in mid channel the harbor may be safely entered.

The head of Bargain Harbor communicates with Pender Harbor by a narrow passage, which is available for boats at high water

Jervis Inlet.—The entrances of the inlet are between Francis and Scotch Fir Points Nelson Island lies immediately in the center, and divides it into two channels, the westernmost being the principal one. Both channels can be made out from Upwood Point Neither from a commercial point of view, as a refuge for shipping, or as a means of communication with the interior of the country, does the inlet appear likely ever to be of any great importance.

Agamemnon Channel, the southern entrance to Jervis Inlet, runs between Nelson Island and the main in a general northerly direction for 9 miles, then joins the main channel of the inlet; its average width is little more than ½ mile; the tides run from one to 3 knots; the depth of water varies from 50 to 100 fathoms, and it affords no anchorage. The southern entrance is encumbered by a group of small islands, the center and largest of which, Pearson Island, is ¼ mile in extent, wooded, and 256 feet high. Northwestward of Pearson, a little more than ¼ mile, are the Channel Islets, two or three small islets joined by reefs; and southeastward of it at the same distance is Martin Island, also very small. The passages into the channel are about the same width (over ¼ mile), and have deep water. There is also a passage eastward of Martin Island

Nile (Nelson) Rock, which covers at quarter flood, lies one mile S. 85° W. of Fearney Point, and the same distance west of the largest Channel Islet, is steep all round, and is situated ½ mile from the nearest point of Nelson Island, off which a reef extends; unless the rock is visible it is recommended to pass outside or southward of it. The southern Channel Islet in line with the north end of Pearson Island leads on to the rock

Pender Harbor is the only anchorage deserving the name with a moderate depth of water, to be found in the neighborhood of Jervis Inlet, but its entrance is so encumbered by islands as to render it difficult of access to any but steam or coasting vessels; it immediately adjoins the Agamemnon Channel on the south, and lies ¾ mile east of Pearson Island.

The entrance to Pender Harbor may be approached by three passages between the islands lying off the southern entrance of Agamemnon Channel. When coming from Jervis Inlet by the above named channel the passage between Channel Islets and Pearson Island to the SW. and Norman Point to the NE., is the most convenient, but coming from any other direction it would be better to use either the one between Pearson Island and Channel Islets or that between the former island and Martin Island; the latter is to be preferred

Williams and Charles Islands lie immediately across the entrance, forming three channels, that to the northward, between Williams Island and Henry Point, is not 200 yards in width, but it is the best and has a depth of 20 fathoms. A shoal extends about 100 yards from the northwestern side of Williams Island.

Entering the harbor between Williams and Charles Islands the channel is only 100 yards in width, with 7 fathoms water, and a rock which covers at three quarters flood lies a little more than 100 yards north of the eastern point of Charles Island

Skardon Islands are two in number. Pass on either side of them and steer up the harbor. One mile within the entrance, a peninsula extends to the south from the northern shore, pass between its southern point and Mary Island.

Anchorage—Anchor in Gerrans Bay, ¼ mile to the southward of the peninsula, in 6 or 7 fathoms, there is also good anchorage in Garden

Bay, just eastward of the peninsula and abreast an Indian village, in 5 or 6 fathoms. The latter is the more suitable for a large ship. Pender Harbor extends ¾ mile above Garden Bay by a very narrow passage with only 2 fathoms in it, and then opens out with a depth of 7 fathoms. To the eastward of this narrow passage is Gunboat Bay, where small vessels may anchor in 7 fathoms. The space in this anchorage is somewhat confined, as is also the case with both Gerrans and Garden Bays.

The Northern Entrance to Jervis Inlet is between Alexander Point on the east and Scotch Fir Point on the west. The points are not remarkable, but the opening is easily made out; it is nearly 2 miles in width and takes for a short distance a northerly direction. Scotch Fir Point is rocky, and has two small islets lying close to the westward of it, which, like the point itself, are covered with stunted pines. Hardy Island lies close to and is nearly connected with Nelson Island; Blind Bay between them is useless, and its entrance choked by small islands.

Thunder Bay, formed on the western side, is one of the few places in Jervis Inlet where vessels may anchor, and being near the entrance it is likely to prove convenient. The bay is about ½ mile deep, with a sandy beach at its head, off which, at the distance of 400 yards, 17 fathoms water will be found; immediately outside it there are 30 fathoms, and the lead then drops suddenly to a great depth.

One mile within Scotch Fir Point Jervis Inlet takes an easterly direction for 12 miles, when Agamemnon Channel joins it at the northern end of Nelson Island. Just before reaching this point, Hotham Sound, trends to the north, terminating at the distance of 7 miles in a double headed bay, the water in every part of it is too deep for anchorage.

Nelson Island is in the middle of the entrance to Jervis Inlet. Its shores are much broken and indented by several bays, in none of which, however, can anchorage be obtained. Cape Cockburn, its southwestern point, is of white granite, about 80 or 90 feet high, covered with a few dwarf pines; a rock lies 200 yards south of it.

Captain Island, NE of Nelson Island, and separated from it by a narrow passage, is about one mile in extent, rocky, and steep to.

One Tree Islet, 1¼ miles east of Captain Island, is small, and has a single tree on its summit, which is very conspicuous; its height is about 50 feet. A rock awash at low water lies 200 yards off its southeastern side, but the islet may be approached close on the west side. Just within the islet on the east shore of the inlet is a bight where coasting vessels may anchor.

Prince of Wales Reach.—Dark Cove is 2 miles northward of Captain Island. The cove is only about 100 yards in extent, but affords a snug anchorage in 15 fathoms, and is the only place in the inlet deserving of that name. Vessels of considerable size could moor within it. There is a clear deep passage 200 yards wide into this cove on both sides of Sydney Islet.

Vancouver Bay, on the eastern side of the reach, is about ½ mile in extent, and of square shape. From its head, which is low, a considerable valley extends to the eastward, but the shores on both sides are craggy and precipitous, and the bay is too deep to afford anchorage

Princess Royal Reach.—Deserted Bay, on the east side at the termination of Princess Royal Reach, and about 37 miles from the entrance, is small, and affords an indifferent anchorage in its eastern part near the head in about 16 fathoms, exposed to west and southwesterly winds.

Queens Reach —The head of Jervis Inlet terminates in a patch of low swampy land through which flow some small streams, and a bank dries off about 200 yards; it does not afford any anchorage, there being 25 fathoms within 100 yards of the outer edge of the bank. A remarkable peak, Mount Victoria, rises 2 miles north of the head of the reach to a height of 7,452 feet

Princess Louisa Inlet, on the east side of Jervis Inlet, 5 miles below the head, is narrow and about 4 miles long, it is connected by a narrow gorge to the main inlet, which at low tide becomes almost a waterfall, rendering it impossible for boats to enter except at high water; inside, like Jervis Inlet, it is deep, and the mountains on both sides rise to 7,000 and 8,000 feet

Sechelt Arm, the entrance to which is one mile north of Agamemnon Channel, is an extensive arm of the sea, penetrating the land for 17 miles in a southeasterly direction and only separated from the Strait of Georgia by a low neck of land, 1,100 yards wide. On the east side of the arm, at a distance of 7 and 11 miles from its entrance, are two smaller branches, Narrows Arm and Salmon Arm, extending to the northeastward for upwards of 10 miles

Rapids —The arm at three miles within its entrance contracts in breadth to less than ¼ mile, and is partially choked up with rocks and small islands; these cause dangerous rapids, the roar of which may be heard for several miles. The rapids prevent any vessel, or even boat, from entering the arm, except for a short time after high and low water, when the tide slackens for a very limited period; it would, however, be hazardous for any vessel, except a very small one, to attempt to enter at any time.

The shores of the arm, except near its south part or head, are high and rocky, and it is a useless sheet of water, except as regards fishing.

Tides —It is high water at full and change in Jervis Inlet at 6 hours, the rise and fall being about 14 feet; within the Sechelt arm the rise and fall seldom exceeds 6 or 7 feet.

(1375) **BRITISH COLUMBIA—Strait of Georgia—Atrevida reef—Buoy established.**—The Government of Canada has given notice that a spar buoy, painted red, has been established to mark the western extremity of an unsurveyed reef, named Atrevida reef, lying off the mainland coast of British Columbia, northward of Harwood island

Approx. position: Lat. 49° 55′ 05″ N., Long 124° 41′ 48″ W

The buoy is moored in 5½ fathoms of water There is no safe passage eastward of the buoy

(N M 38, 1901.)

Bay, just eastward of the peninsula and abreast an Indian village, in 5 or 6 fathoms. The latter is the more suitable for a large ship. Pender Harbor extends ¾ mile above Garden Bay by a very narrow passage with only 2 fathoms in it, and then opens out with a depth of 7 fathoms. To the eastward of this narrow passage is Gunboat Bay, where small vessels may anchor in 7 fathoms. The space in this anchorage is somewhat confined, as is also the case with both Gerrans and Garden Bays.

The Northern Entrance to Jervis Inlet is between Alexander Point on the east and Scotch Fir Point on the west. The points are not remarkable, but the opening is easily made out; it is nearly 2 miles in width and takes for a short distance a northerly direction. Scotch Fir Point is rocky, and has two small islets lying close to the westward of it, which, like the point itself, are covered with stunted pines. Hardy Island lies close to and is nearly connected with Nelson Island; Blind Bay between them is useless, and its entrance choked by small islands.

Thunder Bay, formed on the western side, is one of the few places in Jervis Inlet where vessels may anchor, and being near the entrance it is likely to prove convenient. The bay is about ½ mile deep, with a sandy beach at its head, off which, at the distance of 400 yards, 17 fathoms water will be found; immediately outside it there are 30 fathoms, and the lead then drops suddenly to a great depth.

One mile within Scotch Fir Point, Jervis Inlet takes an easterly direction for 12 miles, when Agamemnon Channel joins it at the northern end of Nelson Island. Just before reaching this point, Hotham Sound, trends to the north, terminating at the distance of 7 miles in a double headed bay; the water in every part of it is too deep for anchorage.

Nelson Island is in the middle of the entrance to Jervis Inlet. Its shores are much broken and indented by several bays, in none of which, however, can anchorage be obtained. Cape Cockburn, its southwestern point, is of white granite, about 80 or 90 feet high, covered with a few dwarf pines; a rock lies 200 yards south of it.

Captain Island, NE of Nelson Island, and separated from it by a narrow passage, is about one mile in extent, rocky, and steep-to.

One Tree Islet, 1¼ miles east of Captain Island, is small, and has a single tree on its summit, which is very conspicuous; its height is about 50 feet. A rock awash at low water lies 200 yards off its southeastern side; but the islet may be approached close on the west side. Just within the islet on the east shore of the inlet is a bight where coasting vessels may anchor.

Prince of Wales Reach.—Dark Cove is 9 [illegible]
tain Islan[illegible]
snug anc[illegible]
serving c[illegible]
it. Ther[illegible]
sides of S[illegible]

Vancouver Bay, on the eastern side of the reach, is about ½ mile in extent, and of square shape. From its head, which is low, a considerable valley extends to the eastward, but the shores on both sides are craggy and precipitous, and the bay is too deep to afford anchorage.

Princess Royal Reach.—Deserted Bay, on the east side at the termination of Princess Royal Reach, and about 37 miles from the entrance, is small, and affords an indifferent anchorage in its eastern part near the head in about 16 fathoms, exposed to west and southwesterly winds.

Queens Reach.—The head of Jervis Inlet terminates in a patch of low swampy land through which flow some small streams, and a bank dries off about 200 yards; it does not afford any anchorage, there being 25 fathoms within 100 yards of the outer edge of the bank. A remarkable peak, Mount Victoria, rises 2 miles north of the head of the reach to a height of 7,452 feet.

Princess Louisa Inlet, on the east side of Jervis Inlet, 5 miles below the head, is narrow and about 4 miles long; it is connected by a narrow gorge to the main inlet, which at low tide becomes almost a waterfall, rendering it impossible for boats to enter except at high water; inside, like Jervis Inlet, it is deep, and the mountains on both sides rise to 7,000 and 8,000 feet.

Sechelt Arm, the entrance to which is one mile north of Agamemnon Channel, is an extensive arm of the sea, penetrating the land for 17 miles in a southeasterly direction and only separated from the Strait of Georgia by a low neck of land, 1,100 yards wide. On the east side of the arm, at a distance of 7 and 11 miles from its entrance, are two smaller branches, Narrows Arm and Salmon Arm, extending to the northeastward for upwards of 10 miles.

Rapids.—The arm at three miles within its entrance contracts in breadth to less than ¼ mile, and is partially choked up with rocks and small islands; these cause dangerous rapids, the roar of which may be heard for several miles. The rapids prevent any vessel, or even boat, from entering the arm, except for a short time after high and low water, when the tide slackens for a very limited period; it would, however, be hazardous for any vessel, except a very small one, to attempt to enter at any time.

The shores of the arm, except near its south part or head, are high and rocky, and it is a useless sheet of water, except as regards fishing.

Tides.—It is high water at full and change in Jervis Inlet at 0 hours, the rise and fall being about 14 feet; within the Sechelt arm the rise and fall seldom exceeds 6 or 7 feet.

The tidal streams, except near the entrance of Sechelt arm, are weak and irregular and influenced by winds.

Harwood Island, off the northern entrance to Malaspina Strait, 1½ miles from the continental shore and about 3 miles NNW. of Point Marshall, is from 150 to 200 feet high, flat and thickly wooded. It is bordered by a sandy beach, and at its north point is a low, grassy spit. There is deep water between the island and the shore.

Rebecca Islet, lying midway between Point Marshall and Harwood Island, is of small extent and 5 feet above high water.

Bare Islet, one mile west of the south end of Harwood Island, is a bare, yellow, cliffy rock, about 400 yards in extent, and 30 feet above high water.

The Coast.—Westward from Jervis Inlet the north shore of Malaspina Strait takes a westerly direction for 11 miles, terminating at Grief Point; for a considerable distance inland it is low, and bordered by a sandy beach; there are no off-lying dangers that are not seen.

From Grief Point the north or continental shore of the Strait of Georgia trends northwesterly for nearly 20 miles to Sarah Point, the southeastern entrance point of Desolation Sound. Throughout the whole distance the coast is low, not rising to more than 500 or 600 feet and but slightly indented. There is a fresh water stream of considerable size 4 miles north of Grief Point communicating, at about 2 miles from the shore, with a lake which extends some 40 miles northward owards the head of Toba Inlet.

Claamen.—At one mile farther westward vessels may anchor, in fine weather for night or tide, about ¼ mile off shore abreast Harwood Island in 12 to 13 fathoms. Anchorage must be taken up with caution as flats extend a considerable distance off shore. When anchoring do not shut in the eastern point of Savary Island.

Navigating along this coast between Grief and Sarah Points, vessels will avoid danger by keeping about ½ mile off shore as far as Hurtado Point, and passing northward of Harwood and Savary Islands. When past Hurtado Point, a vessel ought to steer more to the westward, and pass southward or westward of the White, Double, and Powell Islets.

Savary Island, one mile from the continental shore, is 4 miles long and less than one mile wide. A sandy beach strewn with huge bowlders surrounds it, and extends a considerable distance off its northern and western sides. These bowlders extend a greater distance from the southern side, and the island should not be closed nearer than ¾ mile.

The height of the island varies from 80 to 120 feet, and the southern side is faced by some remarkable white sandy cliffs, very conspicuous from the southeastward. Its east extreme is a granite cliff, steep-to. There are several clear grassy patches on the island, but the soil is poor and sandy. A sandy bar or ledge of one to 2 fathoms water extends from its west point to Hernando Island.

Hurtado Point, on the main abreast Savary Island, is about 250 feet high, bold and cliffy.

Mystery Rock, 2¾ miles S. 27° E. of the east end of Savary Island, is a patch which uncovers 4 feet at low water. From the rock shoal patches of from one to 3 fathoms extend towards the east end of Savary Island. Vessels, therefore, in navigating this locality should observe great caution when going between Savary and Harwood Islands but by keeping within ½ mile of the continental shore, these dangers will be avoided. Vessels working up or down the Strait of Georgia, when standing to the eastward between Harwood and Savary Islands, should not pass eastward of a line forming the SW. end of Savary and the south end of Hernando Islands.

Ragged Islands, lying close to and parallel with the continental shore, are a rocky group of small islands 2¼ miles long and 600 yards wide; their southeastern part is about 2½ miles NW. of Hurtado Point, and some rocks extend 800 yards from their northwestern extreme.

White Islet, one mile southwestward of the Ragged Islands, is a very remarkable, bare, white granite rock. A rock which uncovers at low water lies 200 yards east of it, but in the middle of the passage between the islet and Ragged Islands is a depth of 37 fathoms.

Double Islets, ½ mile west of the northwestern part of the Ragged group, are small, with a single tree on each of their summits.

Powell Islets, one mile NW. of Double Islets, are two in number, small and covered with a few stunted bushes and trees; the westernmost islet is steep-to on its north and west sides.

Sarah Point may be called the northwestern entrance point of the Strait of Georgia. It is a rounded, rocky point, sloping gradually to sea from a height of about 750 feet, at a short distance within it. The coast here turns sharply round to the eastward into Malaspina Inlet.

Mitlenatch Island lies 3½ miles south of Reef Point. It is ½ mile in extent, 200 feet high, bare and peaked. Between it and the Vancouver Island shore, distant nearly 6 miles, is the fair channel to Cape Mudge and Discovery Passage.

Hernando Island, 2 miles NW. of Savary, is about 2 miles in extent, flat and thickly wooded. A ledge composed of sand and large bowlders extends ¾ miles from its SE. point, and there is only a depth of 1¼ fathoms in the channel between it and Savary Island. From the southwestern side some rocks extend off upwards of 400 yards in many places, and it should not be approached nearer than ¾ mile in passing.

Stag Bay, on the north side of Hernando, affords anchorage in 12 to 15 fathoms at a distance of about 400 yards offshore, and is useful as a stopping place for vessels bound to Bute Inlet or Desolation Sound. There is a small fresh-water stream in the eastern part of the bay.

Tongue Point, the northwestern extreme of Hernando and of Stag Bay, is a low sharp sandy point or spit, covered with a few trees, steep-to, and may be approached to 50 yards.

Anchorage.—Vessels should anchor at about ¾ mile from this point, with the east part of Twins Islands bearing N. 12° E.

Baker Passage, to the northward of Hernando Island and leading from the Strait of Georgia to the entrance of Desolation Sound, is one mile wide in the narrowest part. The only danger is at its northwestern entrance point, off which a bowlder ledge extends upwards of 600 yards in a southeasterly direction.

Twins Islands, about 1½ miles north of Hernando, are two rocky islands connected by a sandy beach at low water. Their southern shore is steep to and may be approached to within a distance of 200 yards. The northernmost Twin is 490 feet high, rising to an almost bare summit in the center; the southern one is about 300 feet. None but small craft should go north of these islands. Some small islets lie a short distance off their northwestern side.

Center Rock, which covers at one quarter flood, is in the middle of the passage, between Twins and Cortes Islands.

To avoid the ledge off Reef Point, when entering Baker Passage from the Strait of Georgia, bring Tongue Point on a N 69° E. bearing, and steer for it, passing about 200 yards off, then keep midway between Hernando and the Twins.

Blind Creek, on the southeastern side of Cortes Island, 1½ miles north of Twins Islands, is a basin of about 800 yards in extent, with from 7 to 9 fathoms water, there is, however, in the entrance, a rock which covers at one-quarter flood, rendering the place useless as an anchorage.

Three Islets, lying ½ mile off the entrance of Blind Creek, are three bare white rocks almost connected at low water; there is a depth of 27 fathoms at a distance of 400 yards eastward of them.

Turn Point, the southwestern entrance point of Lewis Channel and the east extreme of Cortes Island, is about 100 feet high, rocky and covered with a few stunted trees; the coast turns suddenly to the northwestward around it, and close inshore to the northward of the point are two islands forming a small boat cove.

Lewis Channel, between Cortes and Redonda Islands, runs nearly straight upwards of 12 miles in a northwesterly direction, and varies in breadth from one mile to 600 yards; its shores are generally rocky, low in the south part, but rising gradually to the NW., steep to and everywhere free from danger.

Tides.—In Lewis Channel the tides are weak and irregular, seldom exceeding 2 knots, and are influenced by the winds.

Squirrel Cove, 4½ miles from Turn Point, is a small land locked basin of 6 to 7 fathoms water, with room for a vessel of considerable size to lie at single anchor. It is entered by a narrow passage about 130 feet wide, with 5 fathoms water on the west side of Protection Island in the entrance. The shores are moderately high, and though much broken very picturesque and fertile in appearance. To the northward of and connected at high water with the cove is a long narrow lagoon, stretching to the northwestward nearly across Cortes Island.

Squirrel Cove can only be entered by steamers or sailing vessels with a fair wind, and the chart is the best guide. There are no dangers whatever within or near it.

Bowlder Point is low and may be easily known by a large bowlder on its west side; a rock, which covers, lies nearly 200 yards south of it, but the point may be rounded at a distance of 400 yards.

Northward of Squirrel Cove the west side of Lewis Channel becomes more rocky and gradually increases in height. At 3½ miles from Junction Point the depths in the channel shoal to 27 and 30 fathoms, and a vessel may anchor in about 18 fathoms at 200 yards from the west shore.

Malaspina Inlet penetrates the continent 8 miles in a southeasterly direction, forming with the Strait of Georgia a peninsula about 2 miles wide, it has one good harbor, and several arms, at the head of some of which there is anchorage. The inlet at its entrance is 800 yards wide, which is its general width, until abreast Scott Point on the eastern side, a distance of 2 miles, when it is contracted to 400 yards, this portion of the inlet, however, is so studded with islands and rocks as to considerably narrow the navigable channel. The depths in it vary from 30 fathoms to 6 fathoms. At Scott Point the inlet for ⅜ mile takes [illegible] easterly direction, and then between Hillingdon Point and the north [illegible] ...ens out to one mile and again turns to the [illegible] ...of Okeover Arm, con- [illegible] ...dth [illegible] Oke- [illegible] ...s 400 yards from the head of the arm, jus... [illegible] very close to the southwestern shore

Josephine Islands, about ¾ miles within the entrance of Malaspina Inlet, with a passage on both sides, are two in number and almost joining each other; the northwestern one is very small, the other is about 300 yards long in the direction of the inlet, and not more than 100 yards wide. The passage between them and the southwestern shore is 200 yards in width, and that to the northeastward 300 yards, but as the Cavendish Rock lies nearly in the center of the latter, the former, in which the depth of water is not less than 6 fathoms, is to be preferred.

Cavendish Rock, awash and marked by kelp, lies 300 yards S. 78° E. of the SE. end of Josephine Islands.

Cross Islet, distant 300 yards from the eastern shore of the inlet, lies on the northern side of the channel; it is small, not more than 100 yards in extent.

Rosetta Rock, the principal danger in entering Malaspina Inlet, is awash and lies nearly 200 yards S. 35° W. of Cross Islet. The southwestern point of Josephine Islands in line with the extreme of the land near Zephine Head leads nearly on the rock.

Thorp Island lies close to the western shore of the inlet 500 yards S. 7° W. of Josephine Islands; a rock awash lies about 100 yards southeastward of it.

western entrance point, off which a bowlder ledge extends upwards of 600 yards in a southeasterly direction

Twins Islands, about 1½ miles north of Hernando, are two rocky islands connected by a sandy beach at low water. Their southern shore is steep to and may be approached to within a distance of 200 yards The northernmost Twin is 400 feet high, rising to an almost bare summit in the center; the southern one is about 300 feet. None but small craft should go north of these islands. Some small islets lie a short distance off their northwestern side.

Center Rock, which covers at one quarter flood, is in the middle of the passage, between Twins and Cortes Islands.

To avoid the ledge off Reef Point, when entering Baker Passage from the Strait of Georgia, bring Tongue Point on a N. 69° E. bearing, and steer for it, passing about 200 yards off, then keep midway between Hernando and the Twins

Blind Creek, on the southeastern side of Cortes Island, 1½ miles north of Twins Islands, is a basin of about 800 yards in extent, with from

(1376) **BRITISH COLUMBIA — Sutil channel — Cortes island — Whaleton bay—Buoy established.**—The Government of Canada has given notice that a spar buoy, painted red, has been established on the rock lying off the entrance to Whaleton bay, Cortes island. The buoy is moored in 5½ fathoms of water

Approx. position Lat. 50° 06′ 18″ N., Long. 125° 05′ 05″ W.

(N M 38, 1904.)

Turn Point, the southwestern entrance po[...] the east extreme of Cortes Island, is about 100 feet high, rocky and covered with a few stunted trees, the coast turns suddenly to the northwestward around it, and close inshore to the northward of the point are two islands forming a small boat cove

Lewis Channel, between Cortes and Redonda Islands, runs nearly straight upwards of 12 miles in a northwesterly direction, and varies in breadth from one mile to 600 yards; its shores are generally rocky, low in the south part, but rising gradually to the NW., steep to and every where free from danger.

Tides—In Lewis Channel the tides are weak and irregular, seldom exceeding 2 knots, and are influenced by the winds.

Squirrel Cove, 4½ miles from Turn Point, is a small land locked basin of 6 to 7 fathoms water, with room for a vessel of considerable size to lie at single anchor. It is entered by a narrow passage about 130 feet wide, with 5 fathoms water on the west side of Protection Island in the entrance The shores are moderately high, and though much broken very picturesque and fertile in appearance To the northward of and connected at high water with the cove is a long narrow lagoon, stretching to the northwestward nearly across Cortes Island.

Squirrel Cove can only be entered by steamers or sailing vessels with a fair wind, and the chart is the best guide. There are no dangers whatever within or near it.

Bowlder Point is low and may be easily known by a large bowlder on its west side; a rock, which covers, lies nearly 200 yards south of it, but the point may be rounded at a distance of 400 yards.

Northward of Squirrel Cove the west side of Lewis Channel becomes more rocky and gradually increases in height. At 3½ miles from Junction Point the depths in the channel shoal to 27 and 30 fathoms, and a vessel may anchor in about 18 fathoms at 200 yards from the west shore.

Malaspina Inlet penetrates the continent 8 miles in a southeasterly direction, forming with the Strait of Georgia a peninsula about 2 miles wide; it has one good harbor, and several arms, at the head of some of which there is anchorage. The inlet at its entrance is 800 yards wide, which is its general width, until abreast Scott Point on the eastern side, a distance of 2 miles, when it is contracted to 400 yards; this portion of the inlet, however, is so studded with islands and rocks as to considerably narrow the navigable channel. The depths in it vary from 30 fathoms to 6 fathoms. At Scott Point the inlet for ¾ mile takes an easterly direction, and then between Hillingdon Point and the north end of Coode Peninsula widens out to one mile and again turns to the southeastward for 2¼ miles, and, under the name of Okeover Arm, continues in the same direction for a farther distance of 2½ miles, the width gradually decreasing to 700 yards.

Freke Anchorage, in 12 or 14 fathoms water, is at the head of Okeover Arm, about 600 yards from the edge of the flat that extends 400 yards from the head of the arm, just above Lucy Rock, which lies very close to the southwestern shore.

Josephine Islands, about ¾ miles within the entrance of Malaspina Inlet, with a passage on both sides, are two in number and almost joining each other, the northwestern one is very small, the other is about 300 yards long in the direction of the inlet, and not more than 100 yards wide. The passage between them and the southwestern shore is 200 yards in width, and that to the northeastward 300 yards, but as the Cavendish Rock lies nearly in the center of the latter, the former, in which the depth of water is not less than 6 fathoms, is to be preferred.

Cavendish Rock, awash and marked by kelp, lies 300 yards S 78° E of the SE end of Josephine Islands.

Cross Islet, distant 300 yards from the eastern shore of the inlet, lies on the northern side of the channel; it is small, not more than 100 yards in extent.

Rosetta Rock, the principal danger in entering Malaspina Inlet, is awash and lies nearly 200 yards S 35° W of Cross Islet. The southwestern point of Josephine Islands in line with the extreme of the land near Zephine Head leads nearly on the rock.

Thorp Island lies close to the western shore of the inlet 500 yards S 7° W. of Josephine Islands, a rock awash lies about 100 yards southeastward of it.

Neville Islet is very small and lies close to the eastern shore nearly ½ mile SE. of Cross Islet

Cochrane Islands, a group of several small islets, lie 400 yards from the west shore of the inlet, and southward of Neville Islet. These islands should not be approached too closely, and there is a patch with 3 fathoms water on it about 200 yards from their western end

Lion Rock, surrounded by kelp, lies 400 yards S. 21° E. of Selma Point, the southern extreme of Gifford Peninsula, and 400 yards eastward of Coode Peninsula

Trevenon Bay, one of the arms of Malaspina Inlet, indents the land and runs parallel to the Strait of Georgia for 1¼ miles, and at its head is only separated by a narrow neck of land 600 yards broad from Penrose Bay, which branches off at the junction of Malaspina Inlet with Okeover arm Off the SE. extremity of Coode Peninsula, distant 200 yards is Boundary Rock. The entrance to Trevenon Bay is ½ mile SE of Scott Point, the average width of the bay is less than ¼ mile, the depth of water varying from 25 fathoms to 4 fathoms at 400 yards from the head. Off the NW. entrance point of the bay lies the small island of Alton, not 200 yards from the shore

Lancelot Arm branches off at Selma Point, its head is only divided from Portage Cove (Desolation Sound) by a low neck of land not much more than 100 yards across, forming Gifford Peninsula, triangular in shape, rising abruptly over Portage Cove to a height of 1,000 feet

Isabel Bay, on the west shore of Lancelot Arm, is about 400 yards in extent and affords anchorage for coasters in from 10 to 12 fathoms water Mary and Polly islands lie in the entrance

Thors Cove, on the eastern shore of Lancelot Arm, extends in an easterly direction for 600 yards with from 12 to 5 fathoms water. A coaster might drop an anchor in this cove in about 10 fathoms. Off Sebastian Point, the north entrance point of Thors Cove, is Thynne Island.

Theodosia Arm has its entrance at about one mile from the head of Lancelot Arm, but the entrance to it is so very narrow and choked with rocks, as to render it for all practical purposes useless

Anchorage.—Vessels of moderate size may anchor in Wootten Bay, about 200 yards from the head of Lancelot Arm, in 12 fathoms water.

Grace Harbor, on the eastern side of Malaspina Inlet, about 2½ miles from Zephine Head, has its entrance between Scott and Moss Points. The harbor is divided at the head, by a jutting point, into Barlands and Carberry Bays Within the entrance points a small island lies nearly in the middle of the channel; there is a passage on both sides of it, but the western one is only suitable for boats

Directions.—Having entered Malaspina Inlet midway between Georgina Point and Zephine Head, keep over towards Holland Point until the channel on the southern side of Josephine Islands opens out, and then steer boldly through it with Cochrane Islands nearly ahead (the course will be S. 38° E.). Keep the extreme of the land near Zephine Head about midway between the south side of Josephine Islands and the south shore, if anything rather nearer the latter, which will lead between Rosetta Rock and the rock off Thorp Island; when Neville Islet bears S. 76° E. steer towards it for a short distance, to avoid the 3-fathom patch off Cochrane Islands, until the NW. Cochrane Island bears south, when alter course to round Scott Point at the distance of 200 yards and steer up the harbor midchannel, passing to the eastward of the small island lying 400 yards within the entrance. A shoal patch on which, however, the least water is 4 fathoms, lies 400 yards SE. of Scott Point.

Anchorage.—The best anchorage is in about 10 fathoms water, 300 yards to the northward of the small island, abreast Kakaekae village.

Tides.—The tides at the entrance of Malaspina Inlet run about 2 knots. It is high water at full and change at 5h. 0m.; springs rise 12 feet, and neaps 9 feet.

Kinghorn Island, in the southern entrance to Desolation Sound, is about 2 miles in circumference; it is cliffy and steep-to on the southwestern side.

Station Island, lies 450 yards NE. of the north point of Kinghorn Island; two small islets lie between.

Mink Island, in Desolation Sound, nearly midway between Redonda Island and the main, is ¾ mile long and ¼ mile wide; its shores are clear of danger. A short distance from its NE. end are Broken Islands.

The west side of Redonda Island is sterile, rocky, and steep-to, rising in the northern part to Craggy Mountains, upwards of 3,000 feet high At a distance of 6 miles from the south entrance to Lewis Channel the Teakerne Arm penetrates Redonda Island in an easterly direction, but is too deep to afford anchorage, except for small craft near its head, and close to the south side of entrance.

Desolation Sound has too great a depth for anchorage.

At the distance of ½ mile NE. of Mink Island is Otter Island, only separated from the main by a very narrow passage.

Deep Bay.—Bold Head, the western entrance point of Deep Bay, lies one mile from the south point of Otter Island; three small islets lie SW. of it, the outer one, Grey Islet, being distant 800 yards. The entrance to Deep Bay is about 600 yards wide, which width it maintains to its head.

The anchorage space is confined, and but small vessels can anchor in a cove at its northwestern corner in 10 fathoms. When entering from the northward pass between Otter and Broken Islands and westward of Grey Islet; from the westward the channel is clear.

Islands.—To the northward of Otter Island there is a group of small islands lying in pairs, Morgan and Melville and Mary and Eveleigh. Melville is the largest of the group, and the Mary the smallest. At ½ mile N. 51° W. of the south end of Morgan Island there is a rock which is just awash at high water.

Prideaux Haven, 3 miles northeastward of Mink Island, in the north eastern part of Desolation Sound, affords good and sheltered anchorage. The entrance between the east shore of Eveleigh Island and the Oriel Rocks is only 85 yards wide. The anchorage is in the western part of the haven in 7 to 9 fathoms. Melanie Cove, the eastern part of the haven, is entered by a narrow channel about 100 yards wide, opening out inside to 200 yards with 4 to 6 fathoms water.

Homfray and Waddington Channels.—Northeastward of Desolation Sound is Homfray Channel, 15 miles in length, leading to Toba Inlet, and westward through Pryce Channel to Bute Inlet. Homfray Channel appears clear of dangers, with deep water throughout. Waddington Channel, leading from Desolation Sound northwestward between the two Redonda Islands, is about one mile wide at its southern entrance, gradually narrowing to about 200 yards at its northern.

At ¼ mile SSW of Marylebone Point (the SW entrance point of Waddington Channel) there is a remarkable white patch.

Pendril Sound.—At 3 miles NW. of Horace Point, the southeastern entrance point of Waddington Channel, Pendril Sound branches off to the northward; it extends 6 miles with an average width of ½ mile, and nearly divides the east Redonda Island into two parts; it has no anchorage.

Walsh Cove, between the Gorges Islands and the western shore of Waddington Channel, affords anchorage in 12 to 14 fathoms water in mid-channel.

Toba Inlet extends in a general northeasterly direction for 18 miles from the northern end of Homfray Channel. At its entrance lie Channel and Double Islands, leaving a channel of over one mile in width between them. A fair berth is in about 20 fathoms in the northwestern corner of the head of the inlet off the flats. Care must be observed when coming to an anchor, as the water shoals rapidly alongside the flats, the water being of a milky color affords no guide as to its depth. There is a small village (Clahoose Indians) on the banks of the eastern of the two streams which flow into the head of the inlet.

Sutil Channel.—This extensive channel leads from the western part of Strait of Georgia to the entrances of Toba and Bute Inlets. It is 15 miles long in a northerly direction, and at its entrance to the Strait of Georgia is 6 miles wide, decreasing to one mile in the northern part. The soundings in mid-channel are deep, though there are several dangers off both shores near the southern parts, but northward of Mary Island it is quite clear.

There are several good anchorages on both shores, two of which, Drew Harbor (on the west) and Carrington Bay on the east shore of the channel, are easy of access to all vessels, and useful as stopping places.

The Tides in the Sutil Channel are weak, seldom exceeding 2 knots;

the flood stream sets to the northward from the Strait of Georgia, it is high water, full and change, at 6 hours, and the rise and fall is 12 feet.

Cortes Island.—The western side of this island is for the most part low, and indented by several bays and creeks, in many of which good anchorage may be found.

Reef Point, its southern extreme, has a ledge composed of sand and bowlders extending ⅜ mile from it which covers at three quarters flood; off its outer edge are 6 fathoms. The north side of Texada Island, well open south of Savary and Hernando Islands bearing S. 56° E., will lead south of the ledge, and also south of the bowlder reef.

From Reef Point the west coast of Cortes Island trends in a northerly direction, is flat, from 80 to 150 feet high, and bordered by a sandy beach extending upwards of 400 yards off in some parts; it afterwards turns in a westerly direction, becoming rocky and broken, with a few islets a short distance off it in some places.

Gorge Harbor, the entrance to which is on the west side of Cortes Island, is 2 miles long in a westerly direction, and one mile broad at the widest part, affording good anchorage in 9 to 12 fathoms. The entrance to it is through a narrow gorge nearly ½ mile long, bounded on both sides by steep cliffs about 200 feet high, and is less than 40 yards wide in some places, with 6 fathoms in the shoalest part; the tide sets through it at from 3 to 4 knots. At the inner end of the Gorge is Tide Islet, lying nearly in the middle of the channel, the passage is to the westward of it. There are several small islands inside the harbor and the shores are rocky, varying in height from 100 to 300 feet.

Guide Islets just south of the entrance of the harbor, and useful in indicating it, are two small, bare, yellow-topped islets, conspicuous from the southeastward, and are steep-to. There is a clear passage on either side of them into Gorge Harbor.

Bee Islets, within the harbor, are two small bare rocks about 200 yards apart, and 6 feet above high water. They may be approached close to, and the best anchorage is from 200 to 400 yards NW. of them.

Brown Island, in the middle of the harbor, is nearly one mile in circumference, and thickly timbered. The shores are rocky, and it may be approached to within 200 yards.

Ring Island, at about 200 yards east of Brown, is wooded. New Rock, which covers at one quarter flood, lies nearly 200 yards east of it. There are two small islets, Stove and Pill, 600 yards apart, lying close to the shore in the northern part of the harbor. Neck Islet lies off a small cove in the southeastern corner of the harbor.

Anchorage.—The best and most convenient anchorage in Gorge Harbor is in the west part, about ½ mile from the entrance, in 12 fathoms water.

There is also good anchorage between Ring Island and the northeastern part of the harbor in from 7 to 9 fathoms.

Directions.—Entering Gorge Harbor, which can only be done with a favorable tide, unless in a steamer, after passing Guide Islets, steer boldly up the gorge or entrance, and take care, on nearing its north part, to pass between Tide Islet and the west shore, the passage east of the islet being shoal, when haul to the NW., pass on either side of the Bee Islets, and anchor in from 10 to 12 fathoms, muddy bottom, 200 to 400 yards to the westward of them. Proceeding to the eastern part, after passing Tide Islet, keep to the northward, and rounding the west side of Brown Island at 200 yards, haul to the eastward, and passing along the north shore of it and Ring Island at 100 yards, anchor midway between the latter and the NE. end of the harbor in from 7 to 10 fathoms. If requiring to water, this anchorage is more convenient; but to avoid the New Rock vessels should not go to the southward of Ring or Brown Islands.

Mary Island, about 3 miles from Reef Point, is of a round shape, and about 6 miles in circumference. Its shores are bordered by a sandy beach, strewn with large bowlders.

Bowlder Reef, extending upwards of one mile in a southerly direction from its south point, is a ledge about 400 yards, which covers at high water.

When passing west of Mary Island keep the north side of Texada Island open south of Savary and Hernando Islands, bearing S. 56° E. until Camp Island opens west of Mary Island north, which will clear the Bowlder reef on the south and west sides.

Sharp Spit.—From the north part of Mary Island a sand spit extends in a northeasterly direction to within 200 yards of Cortes Island. There are 8 fathoms in the passage between the spit end and Cortes Island.

Camp Island, off the west extreme of Cortes Island and 7 miles from Reef Point, is of small extent, and wooded.

Plunger Pass, between Camp and Cortes Islands, is about 600 yards wide, deep, and clear of danger.

Center Islet, 400 yards west of Camp Island, is bare and about 12 feet above high water.

Carrington Bay, on the NW. side of Cortes, is one mile deep in an easterly direction, about 600 yards wide, and affords anchorage at a distance of 600 yards from its head in from 7 to 11 fathoms water. Along its northern side are some small islets, and a rock which uncovers at low water, but if intending to anchor in the bay, keep at about 200 yards from the southern shore, which will clear all danger. At the head of the bay is a large salt-water lagoon.

Von Donop Creek is long and narrow, penetrating Cortes Island in a southeasterly direction. There is good anchorage in 5 to 6 fathoms near its head, but the entrance being only 30 yards wide in some places, with 3½ fathoms in one spot, vessels should not use it as a stopping place, as Carrington Bay is much more convenient and easy of access.

One mile north from Von Donop Creek the coast of Cortes, which is rocky and steep-to, rising abruptly to 1,141 feet, turns NW. for 3 miles to Bullock Bluff, the termination of the Sutil Channel.

Valdes Island.—From Cape Mudge, the southern extreme of Valdes Island and the SW. entrance point of Sutil Channel, a bank extends in a southeasterly direction for nearly 2 miles, and until well inside the channel the cape should not be approached within that distance. The coast of Valdes turns sharply round the cape to the NNW., and is bordered the whole distance by a beach extending off upwards of 200 yards in many parts. The land is flat, and heavily timbered, but appears very fertile.

Drew Harbor, on the east side of Valdes Island, 6 miles from Cape Mudge, is about one mile deep, and rendered perfectly secure and landlocked by Rebecca Spit, a narrow strip of land 6 to 8 feet high and open wooded, which forms its eastern boundary; its shores are low, and bordered by a sandy beach.

Anchorage.—The anchorage, in 9 to 15 fathoms, sandy bottom, at a distance of ½ mile from its head, is the best in Sutil channel.

Heriot Islet, lying to the NW. of the entrance, is of small extent, and separated from Valdes by a narrow boat-pass. In the bay to the southward of it is fair anchorage, and fresh water may be procured; the depths, however, in the entrance to it are irregular.

Directions.—If intending to anchor in Drew Harbor a vessel may round the north part of Rebecca Spit at a distance of about 200 yards proceed up the harbor in mid-channel, and anchor at about ½ mile from its head in 15 to 9 fathoms. The east side of Rebecca Spit should not be approached within 400 yards.

Hyacinthe Bay, on Valdes Island, 1½ miles NW. of Drew Harbor, is of small extent with from 16 to 20 fathoms water, but affords no anchorage; a small rock 4 feet above high water lies in the middle of the entrance.

Open Bay, ½ mile north of Hyacinthe Bay, and separated from it by a rocky point, is ½ mile in extent, with from 10 to 12 fathoms water, but as the bottom is rocky, and the bay open to the SE., a vessel should not anchor there.

Breton Islets, extending upwards of one mile in a southeasterly direction from the north part of Open Bay, are small, and from the outer one, which is wooded, a reef extends for 600 yards, covering at one quarter flood. The passage between these islets and Rebecca Spit is deep and clear of danger.

Hoskyn Inlet, formed between Read and Valdes Islands, has an average breadth of ⅔ mile; the shores are broken and rocky, with some small islands off the south entrance and along the eastern side; there is no anchorage within it except for small craft. This inlet contracts at its northern end to a very narrow passage leading into Drew Pass, but as it is choked with rocks and dries at low water, connecting Read and Valdes Islands, the only exit is by the southern entrance.

Village Bay, on the western side of this inlet, just within the entrance, is about one mile deep and ½ mile wide, with from 12 to 24 fathoms water, but affords no good anchorage; there is a large village at its head.

Read Island borders the western side of the NW. part of Sutil Channel. Its southern part is low, but rises gradually to the northward to 1,608 feet; the shores are rocky, steep-to, and much indented especially on the eastern side near the middle. Viner Point, its southern extreme, is bare and about 40 feet above high water.

Burdwood Bay, on the eastern side of Read Island, 2 miles from Viner Point, is about one mile wide and contains several small islets. There are 12 fathoms water at a short distance off shore in its north and south parts, where vessels may anchor in fine weather, but the bay is open to the south and east.

Evans Bay, the next inlet on the eastern side of Read Island to the northward of Burdwood Bay, is 1½ miles wide at the entrance, and branches off in two narrow arms near its head; its shores are rocky and much broken and there is no anchorage except in Bird Cove, on the western shore, where small craft may find shelter. Frederic Point, the NE. point of entrance to the bay, is bold and may be approached to within 200 yards.

Hill Island, just outside the entrance to Evans Bay, is of small extent but conspicuous. The shores are rocky, and may be approached to within ¼ mile.

Penn Islands, four in number, near the middle of the Sutil Channel, are rocky, covered with stunted trees, and their greatest elevation is about 270 feet. Vessels should not venture among them, but there is a clear passage on their east and west sides.

A Rock awash lies 80 yards N. 79° E. of the north point of the eastern island.

The east side of Read Island, to the northward of the Penn islands, is rocky but may be approached anywhere to within ¼ mile.

Directions.—Entering the Sutil Channel from the Strait of Georgia, pass within ½ mile on either side of Mitlenatch Island and steer for the entrance, taking care to keep the north side of Texada Island open south of Hernando and Savary Islands bearing S. 56° E., until Camp Island opens west of Mary Island bearing north to clear the reefs extending off the south points of Cortes and Mary Islands; when clear of the latter danger haul more to the northward, and steer to pass about ¼ mile westward of Center Islet, then steer up mid channel, eastward of the Penn Islands.

If entering this channel in thick weather and the above marks be not seen, when past Mitlenatch Island keep it on a S. 33° E. bearing, and steer N. 33° W. till the south part of Mary Island bears S. 57° E.; vessels will then be clear of the Bowlder Reef.

Vessel may beat through this channel, but till past the dangers in the south part it would not be prudent to approach the western sides of Cortes and Mary Islands within 1½ miles when standing to the eastward; and when standing towards Cape Mudge do not approach it within 2 miles, or bring Mitlenatch to the eastward of S. 49° E., until the cape bears S. 69° W., when vessels may stand to within ½ mile of the Valdes shore. If intending to anchor, Drew Harbor and Carrington Bay are easy of access for any class of vessel, and are but little out of the regular track.

Calm Channel, to the north of Lewis and Sutil Channels, leading from them to Bute Inlet, is about one mile broad; its shores rise abruptly to a great height, are everywhere clear of danger, and the tides weak, except in the northwestern part.

Rendezvous Islands, three in number, which lie on the western side of Calm Channel, cover an extent 3 miles long in a northwesterly direction.

Drew Pass is a deep passage between the Rendezvous Islands and the north part of Read Island; and between the middle and southernmost islands is a small spot with from 7 to 15 fathoms water, where a small craft may anchor.

Calm Channel is not well adapted for any vessels except steamers, as there is generally but little wind and no anchorage.

Raza Island, lying at the northern entrance to Sutil Channel, is of a rectangular shape; a portion of its south side, which forms the northern side of Calm Channel, is cliffy.

North Passage.—On the western side of Raza Island is North Passage, communicating with Ramsay Arm, which indents the continent in a northerly direction for 7 miles and has deep water throughout.

Deer Passage, between Raza and Redonda Islands, connects Pryce Channel with Sutil Channel. Both North and Deer Passages are clear of danger.

Stuart Island, at the northern termination of Calm Channel, and in the entrance of Bute Inlet, is of an undulating surface, rising in some parts to 800 and 1,000 feet. Its shores are rocky and clear of danger; the tides set strongly round its north and west sides, but there is a clear passage into Bute Inlet to the eastward of it, nearly one mile wide, in which very little tidal stream is felt.

Bute Inlet penetrates the continent for nearly 40 miles in a winding course to the northward, the general breadth varying from one to 2 miles and the shores on both sides rising abruptly and almost precipitously in many places to high mountains from 5,000 to 8,000 feet high, whose summits are generally covered with snow all the year round. At the head are two extensive valleys, one penetrating to the northwestward and the other to the southeastward, from which flow streams; the one to the northwestward is navigable for a long distance by boats and stern-wheel steamers of light draft. Off these rivers some sand banks extend a short distance, affording indifferent anchorages near their outer edges; but the soundings everywhere else in the inlet are very deep. The water for some distance from the head is nearly fresh and of a milky-white appearance; in the summer months there is a constant outset, varying in strength from one to 2 knots.

Arran Rapids, at the entrance to Bute Inlet, between Stuart Island and the continent, are 200 yards wide in the narrowest part. The tides rush through with great strength (the flood from the westward), and it is very hazardous for a vessel to go through.

Orford Bay, on the eastern side of the inlet, 19 miles from the entrance, is of small extent, with 35 fathoms water close to the edge of the bank, which extends from the head. Small vessels may use it as a stopping place.

Waddington Harbor, at the head of the inlet, is about 2 miles in extent and affords very indifferent anchorage off the edge of the banks (which are constantly changing), and they extend from the Homalko and Southgate Rivers and off the eastern shore. Except in the vicinity of the rivers the land rises almost precipitously, is most sterile, rocky, and covered with stunted pines. The best anchorage is near the north part, about ½ mile offshore, in 15 fathoms, but it is exposed to the southwestward, and strong winds from this quarter would make the anchorage unpleasant if not unsafe.

Homalko River is a stream of considerable extent, winding to the northwestward through a large valley. At the entrance is a bar with only one to 2 feet water over it at low tide but within the water deepens to one and 3 fathoms; the breadth varies from 50 to 200 yards and the river is navigable for boats and small steamers several miles. In summer months the current runs upwards of 5 knots.

Directions.—In navigating Bute Inlet but few directions are required, as the points may be everywhere approached to within 100 yards, and if intending to anchor in Waddinton Harbor, when nearing it steer for its north part. Anchor at about ¾ mile off the head in 15 fathoms and about 600 yards from the high northern shore; the anchor should be dropped immediately 15 fathoms are obtained, as the bottom shoals rapidly.

Sailing vessels entering or leaving the inlet should keep close to the eastern shore or the ebb tide may take them through the Arran Rapids to the westward.

Tides.—It is high water, full and change, in Calm Channel at 7h. 0m.; springs rise 14 feet. In Bute Inlet it is high water at 6h. 0m., and the rise and fall varies from 12 to 14 feet.

Cardero Channel communicates by Nodales Channel with Discovery Passage and Johnstone Strait; it has an average width of one mile at the eastern part but only ¼ mile in the western. The shores, which are much indented, are generally rocky and mountainous and the channel is studded with numerous small islands, and it is not without dangers, the water in most parts, however, being very deep.

Stuart Island lies across the eastern entrance of Cardero Channel, almost blocking it, but leaving narrow passages both to the northward and southward; the former, Arran Rapids, is not navigable; the latter, ½ mile wide, is not recommended, as at its northern end the tide runs directly at right angles to a vessel's course at the rate of from 6 to 7 knots. At 2½ miles within the entrance Dent Island causes further obstruction by contracting the channel to 600 yards, which narrow passage is full of dangerous rapids, overfalls and whirlpools, with the probability of the existence of sunken rocks.

Anchorages.—Cardero Channel has but few places that afford anchorage. Bickley Bay, on the north side of Thurlow Island, and nearly opposite to Philipps Arm, is about 600 yards in extent, with from 16 to 21 fathoms water, and near its head 6 fathoms. Mayne Passage, 3½ miles eastward of Loughborough Inlet, and also on the northern side of Thurlow Island, affords shelter in from 9 to 15 fathoms water. This passage branches off to the southward and westward, probably communicating with Johnstone Strait, but it has only been partially examined. Vessels may also bring up in 15 fathoms in Crawford Anchorage inside the Erasmus Islands on the north shore of Thurlow Island.

Tides.—The tides in Cardero Channel run at the rate of from one to 2 knots in the western part, increasing to 3 and 4 knots to the eastward of Nodales Channel. Between Dent Island and the eastern entrance to the inlet they run with great rapidity, especially in the narrow passage between Dent and Valdes Islands, which, as before observed, is full of whirlpools and overfalls.

Caution.—When bound from Bute Inlet to the northwestward, vessels should proceed to the eastward of Valdes and Read Islands by the Calm and Sutil Channels, round Cape Mudge and through Discovery Passage, and not attempt to shorten the distance by using Cardero Channel.

Frederick Arm branches off to the northward from Cardero Channel opposite Hall Point (the north point of Valdes Island) and extends about 3 miles in that direction, shoaling gradually at its head towards a stream which here enters the inlet, flowing from a sheet of water extending some distance to the northward and known as the Estero Basin. The flats usually found extending a considerable distance from the shore at the head of most of these numerous inlets, and which are invariably steep-to, only extend a very short distance off the shore at the head of Frederick Arm. They are not so steep to, and the arm affords a better anchorage than any of the other inlets on the mainland, being only exposed to the southward. Anchorage may be had at a reasonable distance from the shore.

Philipps Arm, lying immediately westward of Frederick Arm, extends about 5 miles in a northerly direction, shoaling gradually off the flats at its head.

Loughborough Inlet penetrates the continent for 17 miles in a northerly direction; it has much the same characteristics as most of the arms that indent the NW. coast. At the entrance between Styles and Grismond Points the inlet is about ¾ mile wide, which is the average width to within about one mile from the head, when it opens out to 1½ miles It terminates in Fraser and McBride Bays, which are separated by Pan Point jutting out in the center. The latter bay affords anchorage in about 25 fathoms at 600 yards from the shore, in the former the water is very deep until close in

Sidney Bay, 2½ miles south of Cosby Point on the western shore, extends about ¼ mile to the westward and is about 200 yards wide, affording anchorage for coasters near its head in 16 fathoms water.

Beaver Creek, on the western shore of Loughborough Inlet, 4 miles within the entrance, shoals gradually towards its head, where good and sheltered anchorage may be obtained in 7 fathoms; anchorage may also be obtained in about 15 fathoms in mid channel westward of Goat Islands. Vessels must not pass northward of the Goat Islands (lying ½ mile within the entrance), as they are connected to the north shore by a flat which dries at low water Good water may be obtained from a stream at the head of the creek, and firewood (cedar) may be cut for steaming purposes.

Tides —The tides in Loughborough Inlet are not strong, seldom exceeding a rate of from one to 2 knots an hour

CHAPTER VI.

FROM THE STRAIT OF GEORGIA TO CAPE SCOTT AND THE SCOTT ISLANDS.

Discovery Passage, formed between Valdes Island and the Vancouver shore, is the only safe navigable outlet from the northern part of the Strait of Georgia to the northwestward. Its length in a direction from Cape Mudge to Chatham Point is 23½ miles, and its average breadth a little more than one mile; but at Seymour Narrows it contracts to less than ½ mile. Its shores southward of the narrows are moderately high, but northward of them steep, rugged, and mountainous.

Tides.—Southward of Seymour Narrows the streams run with great strength, from 4 to 6 knots at springs, and turn at high and low water by the shore. At the southern entrance, near Cape Mudge and between it and Willow Point, heavy races or tide-rips rage during the flood, which would be dangerous to small vessels in blowing weather.

Northward of Seymour Narrows the tidal streams are comparatively slack; they run from 1½ to 2½ hours after high and low water. At the narrows it is high water, full and change, at 3 hours, and the rise and fall is about 13 feet.

Soundings.—In Discovery Passage, when to the southward of Seymour Narrows, the depths in mid-channel vary from 30 to 60 fathoms, except at one mile N. 33° W. of Cape Mudge, where a shoal patch of 8 fathoms exists. In Seymour Narrows the least water in mid-channel is 2½ fathoms on Ripple Rock; but northward of them the depth increases to 100 and 140 fathoms.

Quathiaski Cove, on the west side of Valdes Island, is a small indentation bordered by a sandy beach. The cove is only fit for steamers or small craft, and affords room for one vessel to moor in its southeastern and another in its northern part; the former is recommended and is about 300 yards SE. of Grouse Island, in 10 fathoms, well sheltered from all winds. The tide sets slightly through the cove, but sweeps strongly past the entrance.

Grouse Island, in the center of the cove, is small and moderately high; a shoal extends for 150 yards off its SE. point. If intending to anchor in Quathiaski Cove, a vessel should enter south of Grouse Island (paying careful attention to the tides) and keep well over towards the southern shore until inside. In the middle of the channel north of Grouse Island is a shoal with only a depth of 3 feet on it.

Anchorage.—Moor midway between the SE. point of Grouse Island and the opposite shore, in from 7 to 10 fathoms. If necessary a vessel may proceed to the north part of the cove inside Grouse Island, and anchor in from 7 to 9 fathoms. Careful attention to the helm is important.

Gowlland Harbor, about 5 miles NW. of Cape Mudge, is of considerable extent, being upwards of 2½ miles long in a NNW. and SSE. direction, and from ¼ to ¾ mile broad. The shores are rugged, and there are several rocks and islands within it.

Steep Island is off the entrance, its western side is cliffy.

Gowlland Island, which protects the southeastern part of the harbor, is about one mile long and ¼ mile wide, high and rugged, with a summit at both ends.

Entrance Bank lies nearly across the entrance to the harbor and partly dries at low water; it is composed of sand, being 800 yards in length and 200 yards broad; there is a clear passage on both sides of it, with not less than 4 fathoms water; its southern end, in 3 fathoms, is 200 yards north of Vigilant Point.

Directions.—If entering Gowlland Harbor from the southward, round Steep Island at a distance of about 200 yards and steer for Vigilant Point which is steep-to, and ought to be rounded at less than 100 yards to avoid Entrance Bank. Having passed the point, anchor in 5 to 7 fathoms, muddy bottom, at about 400 yards east of it, or proceed farther to the SE., where more extended anchorage will be found. The passage south of Gowlland is choked up with rocks.

If coming from the NW., when Vigilant Point bears S. 66° E., steer for it, passing it as before directed.

Anchorage.—The best berth, if stopping for a short time, is in 6 or 7 fathoms at about 400 yards east of Vigilant Point; in the southern part of the harbor the water is deeper and the anchorage more extended.

Maud Island.—From Gowlland Harbor to Seymour Narrows the coast takes a northwesterly direction, being steep-to, high and rugged. Maud Island, the SE. point of the narrows, is small, about 300 feet high, and there is a boat passage between it and Valdes Island. A small islet (Yellow Islet) lies 800 yards east of it.

Willow Point (Vancouver Island), the SW. point of Discovery Passage, is low, covered with willow bushes, and off it a sandstone ledge extends to the northeastward for nearly 600 yards. When passing the point do not approach it within ½ mile. From Willow Point a low coast trends NW., and is bordered the whole distance by a sandy beach.

Orange Point is bare and round, of a reddish color, not unlike the top of an orange. A boulder spit extends 300 yards N. 10° W. from Orange Point, its outer limit being marked by kelp in 4 fathoms.

Campbell River.—About 1½ miles SE. of Orange Point is the entrance of the Campbell River, a large stream of fresh water, navigable for some distance by boats or canoes.

Duncan Bay, of which Orange Point is the east extreme, affords good anchorage in 14 to 7 fathoms, sand, well out of the tide, and sheltered from all except NW. winds. There is a broad sandy beach at the head of the bay, through which a stream of water flows. This bay is easy of access, and is the best anchorage southward of Seymour Narrows.

Anchorage.—A good position to anchor is at from 600 to 1,000 yards N. 72° W. of Orange Point, in from 7 to 14 fathoms.

Race Point, rocky and bare of trees, is bold and steep to. The tide runs past it with great velocity, and, during the flood stream, the over-falls off it are very dangerous for boats.

Menzies Bay, of which Wilfred Point Bluff, rocky and 312 feet high, forms the eastern headland, and immediately SW. of Seymour Narrows, is of considerable extent, running in a northwesterly direction for 1½ miles, and ¾ mile broad, but the center is filled up by a large sand bank, which partly dries at low water; there is, however, a narrow but clear passage on either side, and good, well-sheltered anchorage in 5 to 6 fathoms may be had between this bank and the head of the bay.

The eastern shore of the bay is high and rugged, the western shore low; both are steep, and from the head an extensive valley runs to the northwestward, and a bank extends off for 400 yards.

If intending to anchor in the bay, it is recommended to keep within 200 yards of the eastern shore for ½ mile; when steer to the westward towards the center of the bay, and anchor in about 6 fathoms, muddy bottom, at ¼ mile from the head and 400 yards from the eastern shore.

With the tide running to the southward an eddy sweeps strong into Menzies Bay north from Race Point, but at the head of the bay it is still.

Seymour Narrows is a narrow strait about 1½ miles long, and only from 600 to 1,000 yards wide, the shores on both sides being high, rugged and steep-to.

The southern entrance to the narrows lies between Maud Islet to the east and Wilfred Point to the west.

Ripple Rock, a dangerous rock about 300 yards in extent in a north and south direction, with only a depth of 2¼ fathoms on it, lies nearly in the center of Seymour Narrows, but rather on the western side, between Maud Island and Wilfred Point. Its shoalest part lies 600 yards S. 53° W. of the NW. point of the island, and nearly 400 yards from the nearest land of Wilfred Point; it is near the position of the heaviest tide race. When the tide runs strong the rock is marked by the whirl of water over it.

Tides.—It is high water, full and change, in Seymour Narrows at about 3h. 0m.; springs rise 13 feet. The flood stream (from the northward) commences (at F. and C.) about 10 a. m.; the velocity at springs is from 10 to 12 knots, and at neaps 6 to 8 knots. The flood and ebb streams run for nearly equal intervals of six hours. The average duration of slack water is about 10 minutes.

It is recommended to only enter at or near slack water, and to keep the eastern shore aboard in order to avoid Ripple Rock. The strictest attention to the steerage is essential.

It is stated on good authority that a vessel steaming at the rate of 13 knots has been unable to make headway, and even to be set back, while attempting the narrows during spring tides.

Coming from the southward, Duncan Bay is a convenient anchorage for awaiting slack water at Seymour Narrows.

Northward of the narrows, Discovery Passage takes a northwesterly direction to Chatham Point, the shores becoming more high and rugged than before. On the eastern shore are several bays or openings, but, with the exception of Plumper Bay, too deep to afford anchorage. The western shore is nearly straight, and near Chatham Point are Otter Cove and Elk Bay, both affording anchorage.

Plumper Bay, on the Valdes Island shore, ½ mile north of Seymour Narrows, affords anchorage in from 14 to 9 fathoms, near its southeastern part, easy of access, well sheltered, and out of the tide. If unable to proceed through the narrows in consequence of the tide, Plumper Bay becomes a very convenient stopping place, and no directions are necessary for entering it.

The eddies and tides in Plumper Bay, if anchored far out, are sometimes strong, causing a vessel to surge heavily on her cables.

Deep Water Bay, separated from Plumper Bay by the peninsula of Separation Head, is about one mile deep and ½ mile broad, but too deep for anchorage.

Granite Point is a high white granite bluff on the eastern shore of Discovery Passage, 8 miles from Seymour Narrows. On both sides of the point is an opening, the southern one extending east for nearly 3 miles, and containing several islands: the northern one is smaller, but both are too deep to afford anchorage. At 400 yards N. 21° W. of Granite Point is a rock with only 9 feet water on it.

The coast on the Vancouver side trends nearly straight from Wilfred Point for 9 miles to Otter Point, the SE. point of Elk Bay.

Elk Bay, on the western side of Discovery Passage, affords indifferent anchorage, in 14 to 15 fathoms, about ¼ mile from the head, and is exposed to northerly winds. Otter Point, its southern extreme, slopes gradually to the sea, with a small shingle beach running off.

A Rock which covers at half flood lies off the shore ¾ mile northward of Elk Bay.

Otter Cove, 3½ miles from Otter Point and just south of Chatham Point, is a small but snug anchorage, sheltered from all winds by Limestone Island, in the center of the entrance. Snag Rock, with only 2 feet water on it, lies 200 yards east of Limestone Island.

If intending to anchor in Otter Cove, pass north of Limestone Island, and anchor midway between it and the head of the cove, in from 10 to 6 fathoms; a large vessel should moor. The passage south of the island is choked with kelp, and there is 4 fathoms of water or less in it.

Chatham Point, a low rocky point, is the NW. extreme of Discovery Passage and separates it from Johnstone Strait

Beaver Rock, awash at low water, lies 400 yards N 69° E. of the northern extreme of Chatham point; in rounding the point, the shore should not be approached nearer than ¼ mile. Between the point and Nodales Channel are several strong eddies or tide rips

Rocks extend in a scattered way 600 yards NE. of Beaver Rock The point on Valdes Island, opposite Chatham Point, has a nearly bare, steep rocky face, not much higher than Chatham Point

Directions for Discovery Passage.—Proceeding through Discovery Passage from the southward, if the tide be favorable vessels have only to keep in mid channel till past Seymour Narrows, but if the tide be unfavorable, after passing Cape Mudge keep about ¼ mile off the eastern or Valdes Island shore, which is steep to, and where the tide does not run so strong If unable to get through the narrows, Menzies and Duncan Bays afford good anchorages. The latter is preferable, being quite easy of access.

North of Seymour Narrows, the tides being weaker (3 to 5 knots), vessels may proceed either in mid channel or close to either shore, except in rounding Chatham Point, which should not be approached nearer than ⅓ mile. Plumper Bay, as before mentioned, affords good anchorage to a vessel waiting for the tide to proceed through Seymour Narrows from the northward

(159) **BRITISH COLUMBIA.—Vancouver island —Johnstone strait.—Chatham point.—Sunken rock reported northward of Beaver rock.**—Information has been received from Mr. J. T. Walbran, Commanding the Canadian Pacific Navigation Company's S. S. *Danube*, that, on December 7, 1890, when rounding Chatham point, south shore of Johnstone strait, at the distance of about 800 yards and at low tide, Beaver rock and the kelp patch outside it showing above water, a small patch of kelp was seen farther northward, and the ship passed close outside a rock, visible in clear water, and on which the depth was estimated to be 15 feet. This rock is stated to lie with Beaver rock S 63° W. *true*, (SW. ½ S *mag.*), distant about 400 yards, and the east extreme of Chatham point S. 16° W. *true*, (S ¾ E. *mag.*), or close southeastward of the 18 fathoms heretofore shown on the Admiralty chart.

Approx. position. Lat, 50° 20′ 40″ N, Long, 125° 28′ 25″ W.

Consequent on the foregoing, the danger line has been drawn around Chatham point on the Admiralty chart in a northeasterly direction at the distance of about 800 yards

[illegible] Point in order to avoid the Douglas Rock, lying 100 yards off it It is advisable to keep well outside the kelp when entering

Anchorage sheltered from all winds, in from 8 to 10 fathoms, may be obtained at 400 yards from the head of the harbor. The lead should

IMAGE EVALUATION
TEST TARGET (MT-3)

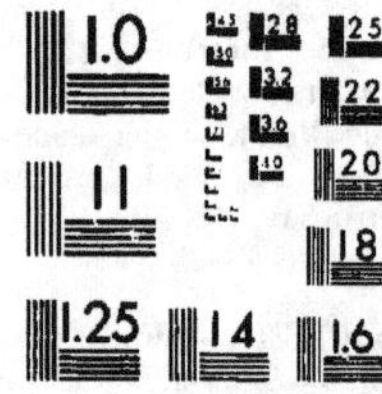

6"

It is recommended to only enter at or near slack water, and to keep the eastern shore aboard in order to avoid Ripple Rock. The strictest attention to the steerage is essential.

It is stated on good authority that a vessel steaming at the rate of 13 knots has been unable to make headway, and even to be set back, while attempting the narrows during spring tides.

Coming from the southward, Duncan Bay is a convenient anchorage for awaiting slack water at Seymour Narrows.

Northward of the narrows, Discovery Passage takes a northwesterly direction to Chatham Point, the shores becoming more high and rugged than before. On the eastern shore are several bays or openings, but, with the exception of Plumper Bay, too deep to afford anchorage. The western shore is nearly straight, and near Chatham Point are Otter Cove and Elk Bay, both affording anchorage

Plumper Bay, on the Valdes Island shore, ½ mile north of Seymour Narrows, affords anchorage in from 14 to 9 fathoms, near its southeastern part, easy of access, well sheltered, and out of the tide If unable to proceed through the narrows in consequence of the tide, Plumper Bay becomes a very convenient stopping place, and no directions are necessary for entering it.

The eddies and tides in Plumper Bay, if anchored far out, are sometimes strong, causing a vessel to surge heavily on her cables.

Deep Water Bay, separated from Plumper Bay by the peninsula of

water on it, lies 200 yards east of Limestone Island.

If intending to anchor in Otter Cove, pass north of Limestone Island, and anchor midway between it and the head of the cove, in from 10 to 6 fathoms; a large vessel should moor. The passage south of the island is choked with kelp, and there is 4 fathoms of water or less in it.

Chatham Point, a low rocky point, is the NW extreme of Discovery Passage and separates it from Johnstone Strait

Beaver Rock, awash at low water, lies 400 yards N. 69° E. of the northern extreme of Chatham point; in rounding the point, the shore should not be approached nearer than ¼ mile. Between the point and Nodales Channel are several strong eddies or tide rips

Rocks extend in a scattered way 600 yards NE of Beaver Rock. The point on Valdes Island, opposite Chatham Point, has a nearly bare, steep rocky face, not much higher than Chatham Point

Directions for Discovery Passage.—Proceeding through Discovery Passage from the southward, if the tide be favorable vessels have only to keep in mid-channel till past Seymour Narrows; but if the tide be unfavorable, after passing Cape Mudge keep about ¼ mile off the eastern or Valdes Island shore, which is steep to, and where the tide does not run so strong. If unable to get through the narrows, Menzies and Duncan Bays afford good anchorages The latter is preferable, being quite easy of access

North of Seymour Narrows, the tides being weaker (3 to 5 knots), vessels may proceed either in mid channel or close to either shore, except in rounding Chatham Point, which should not be approached nearer than ¼ mile. Plumper Bay, as before mentioned, affords good anchorage to a vessel waiting for the tide to proceed through Seymour Narrows from the northward.

Nodales Channel extends 8 miles in a northeasterly direction between Thurlow and Valdes Islands, and leads into Cardero Channel; its western entrance is upwards of one mile wide, with deep water, there are some tide rips off it. No soundings at 40 fathoms could be obtained throughout the channel, and in the fairway of the western entrance the depth was 70 fathoms, sand.

Hardinge Islands, about ¾ mile long and ¼ mile wide, is 1⅛ miles from the entrance to Cameleon Harbor, with a passage on both sides. Young Passage to the southward is ¼ mile wide, and Burgess Passage to the northward ½ mile; there is deep water in both.

Maycock Rock.—Three quarters of a mile N. 68° W. of the south entrance point of Cameleon Harbor, and 1,200 yards N. 76° W. of Bruce Point is Maycock Rock, with one fathom on it. The shore to the eastward of this rock for ½ mile has foul ground marked with kelp extending from it for nearly the distance of 200 yards.

Cameleon Harbor is about one mile deep in a southeasterly direction, and has an average width of 600 yards. The entrance, between Bruce Point on the north shore and a small islet off the south shore, is less than 100 yards wide, and caution must be observed in rounding Bruce Point in order to avoid the Douglas Rock, lying 100 yards off it. It is advisable to keep well outside the kelp when entering.

Anchorage sheltered from all winds, in from 8 to 10 fathoms, may be obtained at 400 yards from the head of the barbor. The lead should be kept going quickly in approaching the head, as the flat, which extends nearly 200 yards from it, is steep-to.

Johnstone Strait, which separates the NE side of Vancouver Island from the mainland, is comprised between Chatham Point and Beaver Cove, being about 55 miles in length in a WNW. and ESE. direction, with a varying breadth of one to 2 miles. The shore on both sides is high and rugged, more especially the southern, which is a continuous mountain range, rising almost abruptly from the sea.

The shores of the strait are nearly everywhere steep to, except a few places along the northern side There are no anchorages whatever along the southern shore, but there are several on the northern, viz, Knox, Blinkinsop, and Forward Bays, as well as Ports Harvey and Neville, all of which, except the latter, are easily accessible to sailing vessels.

At Beaver Cove the high land suddenly terminates, and the shore is indented with a few slight bays, which are too deep to afford anchorage. Banza Cove, one mile east of Beaver Cove, is a small deep bight, and affords no anchorage; some small islets lie in its entrance

Ripple Shoal, on which the least known depth is 7 to 9 fathoms, lies about 1¼ miles west of the west point of Thurlow Island, and ½ mile off the southern shore of the strait.

Tides.—Everywhere in Johnstone Strait it is high water, full and change, at 0h. 30m., and the rise and fall of tide is from 15 to 17 feet. The streams run from 2 to 2½ hours after high and low water by the shore, and except in the vicinity of Helmcken Island and to the eastward of Knox Bay they are not strong. In the former place they run from 3 to 6 knots, and in the latter 2 to 4 knots; but in other parts of the strait they seldom exceed one to 3 knots per hour. Near Helmcken Island are several heavy tide rips, which in blowing weather would be dangerous to boats or small craft; and just west of Chatham Point is an overfall producing a considerable swell at times.

Thurlow Islands.—The southern side, which borders the strait, is rocky and about 13 miles long in a westerly direction, the eastern half is indented by several bays, off which lie some small islands.

The islands are mountainous; Mount Eldon, near the center of the islands, is wooded, square topped and quite isolated.

Pender Islands, between Knox Bay and Nodales Channel, are very rugged and barren; foul ground exists to the east and west of them for nearly ½ mile, and their southern side should not be approached nearer than 400 yards. The tide sets strongly between them.

Knox Bay, on the south side of Thurlow, is ⅜ mile deep and about the same in width, and affords anchorage in from 15 to 17 fathoms at 400 yards from the head, off the edge of the bank, which is steep to. The anchorage is well protected from east or westerly winds, but it ought only to be used as a stopping place for the night or tide, as from the steepness of the bank a vessel would touch if a southerly wind sprang up. Off its SW. point foul ground extends for nearly 200 yards. If intending to anchor, steer for the head of the bay, and anchor immediately 16 fathoms are obtained.

Westward of Knox Bay the shores of Thurlow are high, rugged, and steep-to, and may be approached to within a distance of 200 yards

Eden Point, the southern entrance point of Chancellor Channel and the NW. extreme of Thurlow, is bold and cliffy; ½ mile SE. of it is a small bay, too deep to afford anchorage, except for small craft.

A Rock, covered at high water, lies on a line from Eden Point to Camp Point Peak and close to the Vancouver shore.

Ripple Point, on the Vancouver shore of the strait, 6 miles west from Chatham Point, is steep-to, and between it and Knox Bay are some heavy tide rips in blowing weather The coast between Ripple and Chatham Points is indented by two slight bays, but the water in them is too deep to afford anchorage.

Camp Point slopes gradually to the sea; a rocky beach extends a short distance off it; and ½ mile to the NE. of it is the Ripple Shoal, marked by kelp, about 600 yards in extent, with deep water around it.

Salmon Bay at high water appears of considerable extent, but affords no anchorage, the bank, which runs off ½ mile from its head, being too steep. A river of considerable extent flows into this bay, and is said to be navigable for canoes several miles inland. At this place, is the only break in the mountain range on the southern shore, and a valley of considerable extent stretches away to the SE., in the center of which appears a remarkable bare summit.

Helmcken Island, in the center of the strait, is 1½ miles long east and west, and about ½ mile wide, with a clear channel of the same width on both sides of it. The island has a rugged coast line, and several small islets lie close off its NE. shore.

Speaker Rock, which covers at one quarter flood, lies 500 yards N. 69° E. of its eastern point, and is in the track of vessels using Current Passage

Race Passage, to the southward of Helmcken Island, is ½ mile wide, but deep and clear of danger; the tide sets strongly through it (as much as 6 knots at springs), and there are some heavy tide rips in its eastern part. This is the passage generally used.

Current Passage, to the northward of Helmcken, is about ½ mile wide, and deep, the tide being as strong as in Race Passage

Chancellor Channel connects with Cardero Channel; it lies along the north shore of Thurlow Island, and has its entrance abreast Helmcken Island, at Eden Point; it is ½ mile wide and clear of danger.

Wellbore Channel, along the NE. side of Hardwicke Island, communicates with Forward Harbor, Topaze Harbor and Sunderland Channel. At its entrance is Bulkeley Island, and vessels using the channel should pass east of it, and keep the eastern shore aboard to avoid some rocks which lie off the shore of Hardwicke Island.

Tides.—The tidal streams in Wellbore Channel run with great velocity, often attaining at springs a rate of over 7 knots an hour.

Forward Harbor, the entrance to which between Louisa and Horace Points is only a little over 200 yards wide, extends nearly 3 miles in an easterly direction, and though the entrance is narrow, its freedom from obstruction renders it easily accessible to vessels of moderate size. Its shores are steep to, but the water being of moderate depth over its whole extent, anchorage may be taken up in any part of it, if requisite. At its head a flat dries out 500 yards at low water, and two small streams flow into it.

For ½ mile within the entrance the passage in is from 200 to 400 yards wide, but at that distance the harbor opens. Off Mills Point, where the harbor commences to widen, there is a deep spot of 20 fathoms.

Anchorage may, as already mentioned, be taken up anywhere, but the best position is in Douglas Bay, on the north shore, just round Mills Point, in from 6 to 10 fathoms.

Bessborough Bay, an open indentation on the north shore of Wellbore Channel, affords no anchorage, owing to the great depth of water in it.

Sunderland Channel.—The entrance, which is subject to heavy tide rips, lies between Fanny Reef and the shore near Blinkinsop Bay; the channel is a clear navigable channel extending in a northeasterly direction to the entrance to Topaze Harbor. Seymour and Poyntz Islands lie in midchannel. The depths shoal gradually from 50 fathoms at the entrance, to 22 fathoms north of Poyntz Island; but there is a deep run of water in that locality and along the shore south of the two islands above mentioned.

Tides.—The tidal streams in Sunderland Channel are not strong, attaining a velocity of only from ½ to 1½ knots an hour.

Topaze Harbor is the continuation of Sunderland Channel. Over the whole of this harbor there is an uniform depth until within ½ mile of its head. On the north side, 1½ miles within the entrance, is Jackson Bay, a narrow bight extending 1½ miles in a northwesterly direction, but shoal at nearly a mile from its head.

At the head of Topaze Harbor are Mounts Drummond and Berkeley.

Anchorage may be obtained, well sheltered, in either Jackson Bay or at the head of the harbor.

Hardwicke Island is high and rugged, and the southern shore steep to, except near its SW. extremity, where Earl Ledge runs off for 600 yards, only uncovering at low water.

York Island, high, round and about ½ mile in diameter, and another small low islet ½ mile westward of it, lie off the west point of Hardwicke; and outside them, at the distance of ⅛ mile, is the Fanny Reef, which covers or is awash at high water; between the reef and northern shore there are some heavy tide rips.

Blinkinsop Bay, on the shore of British Columbia, is about 1¼ miles deep and ½ mile wide; its shores are high, and from the head a bank dries out at low water for nearly one mile.

A Shoal marked by kelp, on which there is a depth of 4 fathoms, lies 200 yards N. 35° W. of Tuna Point, the east entrance point of this bay

Anchorage.—This bay affords good anchorage, in 10 to 12 fathoms, about ⅓ mile N. 67° E. of its SW. point, well sheltered and easy of access. The only direction required is to keep in mid channel, avoiding the above mentioned rock, and anchor on obtaining 12 fathoms, as the bank is rather steep.

Jesse Island, lying about 400 yards offshore, nearly ½ mile to the SW. of Blinkinsop Bay, is small and steep to.

Port Neville is of considerable extent, running in a northeasterly direction for 7 miles, and varying from ¼ to one mile in breadth. It affords a spacious and secure anchorage, but in consequence of Channel Rock, lying near the middle of its entrance channel, great caution is required in entering. Its shores, except near the eastern side of entrance and head, are high, sloping gradually to the water's edge

The entrance is between Milly Island and Ransom Point (off which is a small rock), thence the channel into Port Neville is 1¼ miles long and about 600 yards wide, running in a northerly direction; the depths in it vary from 5 fathoms, shoaling to 2¼ fathoms in the north part. The best passage is on the western side of Channel Rock, there being about 17 feet at low water; the passage eastward of it has only 12 feet.

The depth of water when in the port varies from 6 to 9 fathoms; the bottom is muddy.

Channel Rock, of small extent and very dangerous, having only 4 feet over it, lies in the middle of the channel, 700 yards S. 63° W. of Bowlder Point, so that, unless vessels specially require to enter this port, the anchorage of Port Harvey and Blinkinsop Bays, which are at no great distance from its vicinity, ought to be preferred, being both secure and easy of access.

Bowlder Point, the northeastern point of the channel, is low, with a stony beach round it. A shoal extends off it to the northward and eastward for ½ mile, with 1½ fathoms in some parts.

Robbers' Knob is a remarkable low grassy point on the north side of the port, about one mile from Bowlder Point.

Anchorage—To the westward of it is a shoal bay, into which flow some large streams; the best anchorage is about ½ mile SW. of the Knob in 6 or 7 fathoms. Temporary anchorage for a night may also be had at the outer part of the entrance, but the soundings decrease very suddenly when abreast Milly Island.

Shoal Creek, at the head of Port Neville, is about 2 miles long, narrow, and not recommended, as its entrance is only 200 yards wide, with a rock in the middle; from its head a mud flat extends off nearly one mile.

Directions.—Entering Port Neville after rounding Milly Island, which may be approached close to, proceed up mid-channel until Robbers' Knob comes in line with Bowlder Point bearing N. 52° E., when keep well over to the western side of the channel to avoid Channel Rock. When Bowlder Point bears N. 89° E., vessels will be clear to the west of the rock, and may then steer for Robbers' Knob, avoiding a patch of 3 feet which skirts the western shore abreast Bowlder Point, after passing which, steer into the port and anchor in 7 fathoms, about ½ mile S. 79° W. of Robbers' Knob. If necessary, vessels may anchor in the entrance about ½ mile north of Milly Island, in 4½ and 5 fathoms.

Shimpson Reef.—The coast between Ports Neville and Harvey trends in a westerly direction and is slightly indented. Four miles westward of the entrance of Port Neville, and ¼ mile offshore, lies the Shimpson Reef, which covers at half flood.

Port Harvey, the next inlet westward of Port Neville on the northern side, indents the coast in a northerly direction for 4 miles, with a breadth varying from ¼ to ¾ mile, and affords good and well sheltered anchorage in 7 to 9 fathoms, muddy bottom, at ½ mile from its head. There are several small islets (Mist) within it, and the shores are rugged; from its head swampy ground extends to the NE., and to the NW. is a narrow gorge which partly fills at high water and joins Knight Inlet. The depths shoal rapidly towards the head.

Broken Islands, off the east side of the entrance, are low, rugged and of small extent, foul ground extends from them in a northerly direction for ¾ mile; they may be approached, however, to within ¼ mile on the west side, but only a boat passage exists to the eastward of them.

Havannah Channel runs in a northeasterly direction from the east side of Port Harvey, connecting it with Call Creek. The shores are high and much broken, and the depths in mid channel vary from 9 to 30 fathoms. There are several islands within it which lie mostly in mid channel.

Hull Island, the largest, is ¾ mile long and ½ mile broad.

Boughey Bay, in the SE. part of Havannah Channel, is about one mile deep in a southerly direction, and ½ mile broad; a vessel may anchor in this bay at ½ mile from the head, in from 10 to 14 fathoms, but the passage to it has not been sufficiently examined to recommend its being used as an anchorage.

Browning Rock, about ¼ mile north of Hull Island, has only 12 feet over it, and lies nearly in the fairway of the channel to Call Creek; there is an apparently clear passage to the westward of it.

Caution.—As the soundings are uneven and the bottom rocky to the west and NW. of Hull Island, great care should be used in navigating this channel near that neighborhood.

Call Creek is an inlet of considerable extent, its length in a northeasterly direction being 12 miles, and its breadth varying from ½ to 1½ miles, the shores on either side are high and precipitous, rising abruptly to mountains. The head terminates in a low swamp, and a valley extends to the NE. from it.

Anchorage.—The depths in the entrance of Call Creek are about 40 fathoms, but increase to upwards of 120 fathoms towards the head; there is no anchorage whatever except near its entrance, on the north side amongst the Warren Islands, where from 6 to 14 fathoms will be found These islands, four in number and small, are ½ mile from the entrance, they run parallel to the shore from 200 to 400 yards off it. A vessel may anchor between the two southern islands in from 6 to 10 fathoms

Chatham Channel, the east part of which commences at Root Point and trends to the northwestward, connects these waters with Knight Inlet; its breadth as far as surveyed varies from 400 to 600 yards, the depth in mid-channel is 4 fathoms at a distance of ¾ mile west of Root Point It is not recommended to use this channel until further explored.

Directions.—If intending to anchor in Port Harvey, keep in mid-channel till within the Mist Islands, when the anchorage opens out, and anchor in 7 fathoms in the middle of the harbor, at about ½ mile from the head.

Sailing vessels of considerable size can beat in as far as Mist Islands, and may stand anywhere to within 200 yards of the western shore; in making the eastern board, keep outside the line of the Broken Islands, and out of the bight between Transit Point and the Mist Islands

The anchorages in Boughey Bay, Havannah Channel, and among the Warren Islands on the shore of Call Creek, are secure, but the passages to them, though probably deep, have not been sufficiently examined to give directions for entering them.

Escape Reef, lying 2 miles west of the Broken Islands, and ½ mile off the north shore of Johnstone Strait, is about 200 yards in extent, has 4 feet least water on it, and is marked by kelp in the summer. This reef which has deep water around it, is in the track of vessels entering Port Harvey from the westward; to avoid it keep in the middle of the strait till the entrance of the port comes well open, bearing N. 40° E, when steer in for it.

Forward Bay, 3 miles west of Port Harvey, is a slight bend in the coast, about 1¼ miles broad, and ¾ mile deep, with a small islet 30 feet high off its southwestern point; its shores are moderately high, and a bank extends nearly 600 yards from its head

Anchorage—This bay affords good anchorage, in 14 to 10 fathoms, off the edge of the bank, at about ¾ mile N. 69° E. of its SW. point, well sheltered from all except southeasterly winds, and even these send in no sea; it is easy of access for any class of vessels, and a very good stopping place.

Caution.—Entering it from the eastward guard against the Escape Reef.

Boat Harbor, a small cove affording shelter to boats, is 6 miles westward of Forward Bay, the coast between the two places being nearly straight, and may be approached to within ¼ mile.

Cracroft and Hanson Islands.—Between Boat Harbor and Weynton Passage the shores of Cracroft Island are low and rocky. The island is about 15 miles long, and off its southwestern part, at the distance of ½ mile from the shore, are the Sophia Islets, of small extent. Hanson Island is separated from Cracroft by Blakeney Passage, one mile wide, and off the SW. point of the island are some rocks extending 400 or 600 yards to the westward.

Growler Cove indents the western end of Cracroft Island in an easterly direction for ¾ mile, with a width of about 300 yards, and from 20 to 5 fathoms water. At the head a flat runs out for a short distance. The Sophia Islets lie off the southern entrance point.

Directions.—For steamers or sailing vessels with a fair wind, the navigation of Johnstone Strait is perfectly easy, it being only requisite to keep in mid-channel, except when nearing Helmcken Island from the eastward, when a vessel ought, after passing Thurlow Island, to keep within 600 yards of the southern shore, or Camp Point, till past the Ripple Shoal, which, from being marked with kelp, is likely to have less water over it than has been found. In the vicinity of Helmcken the tides are strong, but not enough to stop a steam vessel of moderate power; to the westward of it they have no great strength.

If wishing to anchor for the night, Knox, Blinkinsop and Forward Bays and Port Harvey on the northern side, afford good anchorage, and are, with the present charts, easy of access.

If beating through the strait, when to the eastward of Helmcken Island the shores on both sides may be approached to 200 yards, except for ½ mile on either side of Pender Islands, the southern side of which latter ought not to be approached nearer than 400 yards, as the tide runs strong in their vicinity. Between Thurlow and the west end of Hardwicke Island, it is not advisable to beat, as the tide thereabouts runs strong and irregularly, there being also several dangers in the track, viz, Ripple Shoal, Speaker Rock, and Earl Ledge. From Hardwicke Island to Beaver Cove, the southern shore may be approached to 200 yards; and the only dangers along the northern shore are the Slimpson and Escape Reefs, which can be easily avoided by tacking short of them, and keeping more than ½ mile out when near the latter; elsewhere the northern shore may be approached to within a distance of ¼ mile.

Broughton Strait is upwards of 14 miles in length, east and west, the breadth varying from 4 miles at the eastern to one mile at the western entrance. Both shores, except near Beaver Cove, are low. There are several islands, rocks, and shoals in the eastern part; but there is a clear navigable passage along the southern side ½ mile wide in the narrowest place (abreast Alert Bay in Cormorant Island). There are several anchorages along both sides of the strait, available as stopping places—Alert Bay, on the southern shore of Cormorant Island; Port McNeill on the Vancouver shore; and Mitchell and Rough Bays on the southern side of Malcolm Island. The Nimpkish River, on the southern shore of the strait, is a stream of considerable size, and said to be navigable by canoes for a two days' journey.

Tides.—In the navigable channel the streams run one to 4 knots, but in the Race and Weynton Passages 3 to 6 knots, turning everywhere about two hours after high and low water by the shore.

Beaver Cove is at the SE. extreme of Broughton Strait, its shores are high, and the depth is too great for convenient anchorage. Mount Holdsworth, a remarkable conical peak, and very conspicuous from the eastward, rises 3 miles to the SW. of the cove.

Nimpkish River, which flows into a shallow bay on the southern shore, 5 miles westward of Beaver Cove, is upwards of 200 yards wide at entrance, with 2½ fathoms, but is only navigable by canoes; a bank dries off it for nearly one mile, leaving a narrow winding channel with about 5 feet water into the river.

Green Islet, off the outer edge of this bank, is about 19 feet above low water and is small and bare, a rocky ledge which uncovers at low water extends a distance of ¼ mile ESE. from Green Islet, and there is also an uncovering rock at the same distance west of it. In navigating the strait, this islet should not be approached within a distance of 600 yards.

On the northern bank of the Nimpkish, at the entrance, is a small plateau of grassy land, on which are the ruins of the large native village of Cheslakee.

Port McNeill, about 10 miles west of Beaver Cove, is ⅔ mile broad, and affords a good, well sheltered anchorage in 6 to 9 fathoms. Its shores are low, and bordered by a sandy beach, which extends off ⅔ mile from the head. From Ledge Point, the north point of entrance, a narrow ledge, with from 3 to 5 fathoms on it, extends 1¼ miles east towards Haddington Island; kelp grows over this ledge in summer.

Eel Reef, lying 1,800 yards S. 46° W. of Ledge Point, and about 400 yards off the south shore of the port, covers at three quarters flood.

Directions.—If intending to anchor in Port McNeill keep ½ mile from the southern shore when entering to avoid the ledge off Ledge Point, and anchor when the point bears N. 69° E., about ½ mile distant, in from 5 to 6 fathoms, sandy bottom.

When leaving and bound to the westward, vessels should stand to the eastward until within ½ mile of Haddington Island before hauling to the northward round Ledge Point.

The coast from Port McNeill trends about west 4 miles to the entrance of Queen Charlotte Sound. It is bordered by a sandy beach, and may be approached to within 400 yards.

Blakeney Passage, between Hanson Island on the west and the west extremes of Cracroft and Harbledown Islands on the east, varies in width from one mile to ½ mile. It connects Johnstone Strait with Blackfish Sound. The strength of the tide in it is from 2 to 5 knots.

Weynton Passage, between Hanson and Pearse Islands, is about 1¼ miles wide. The shores on both sides are very much broken; the tide rushes through at the rate of from 5 to 6 knots, and unless wishing to anchor in Mitchell Bay the passage should not be used

Race Passage, between Pearse and Cormorant Islands, is ⅜ mile wide, but a rock lies in mid channel at its south part. The tides set at the rate of from 3 to 6 knots through the passage, and it is dangerous.

Pearse Islands, in the center of Broughton Strait, are a group of small low islands, with some rocks and reefs extending ½ mile NW and nearly one mile SE from them.

Cormorant Island is about 150 feet high, 2¾ miles long, east and west, ¾ mile wide, and bordered by a sandy beach. Gordon Point, its southeastern extreme, is 2½ miles N. 55° W. of Beaver Cove. A small patch of 4 fathoms marked by kelp lies 1¼ miles N. 77° W. of Leonard Point, the NW point of Cormorant Island.

Alert Bay, on the south side of Cormorant Island, is nearly one mile wide and ½ mile deep, affording a good and well-sheltered anchorage in from 6 to 9 fathoms, muddy bottom: it is easy of access, the shores being everywhere clear of danger. There is an establishment here for tinning salmon caught in the Nimpkish River, and a pier, at the extremity of which there is a depth of about 12 feet, extends from the northeastern shore of this bay

There is also a mission established and quite a large Indian village, comprising most of the former inhabitants of Cheslakee. The house marked on the chart is a small one storied house, with three windows towards the water Near it is a very small chapel.

A supply of wood for steaming purposes may be obtained at Alert Bay.

Yellow Bluff, the southwestern point of the bay, may be recognized by a remarkable yellow cliff at the extreme of the point.

Haddington Island is small, its southern and western sides are steep to, but from the northern shore a bar, with as little as 6 feet water in some parts, connects it with Malcolm Island.

Between Haddington Island and the ledge running off from the north point of port McNeill is a passage ¼ mile wide, with not less than 7 fathoms water in mid channel.

Malcolm Island, which forms the northern side of Broughton Strait, is 13¼ miles long east and west; the shores are generally low, a sandy beach extending off a short distance from them. On its southern side are Mitchell and Rough Bays, in which vessels may anchor in 6 or 8 fathoms. Donegal Head, its east point, is high, cliffy, bordered by a beach, and the tide runs strong in its vicinity. Dickenson Point, on the southern side of the island, 7 miles westward of Donegal Head, is

(1755) **BRITISH COLUMBIA—Queen Charlotte sound—Broughton strait—Malcolm island—Graeme point—Light established.**—Referring to Notice to Mariners No 31 (1195) of 1905, the Government of Canada has given notice that on September 12 1905, a *fixed white* dioptric light of the 7th order, elevated 38 feet above high water and visible 11 miles, was established in the lighthouse recently erected on Graeme point, Malcolm island, Queen Charlotte sound. The light is visible over an arc of 230° from N 80° W. true (WSW. ⅝ W. W'ly mag.) to S. 30° E true (SE. ⅞ E. mag.), the light being obscured over the remainder of the horizon by the high land of Malcolm island.

The lighthouse stands on the extremity of the low gravel spit. It is a square wooden building with a square wooden lantern rising from the middle of a cottage roof It is painted white, with red roof, and is 35 feet high from base to vane.

Approx position Lat. 50° 37′ 50″ N., Long. [illegible]° 09′ 50″ W

is a shoal patch of 4½ fathoms, also marked by kelp (N M 44, 1905)

Directions—Passing through Broughton Strait from the eastward, when abreast Beaver Cove, in mid channel, a N 72° W. course, to pass not more than 100 yards south of Cormorant Island, will keep vessels clear to the northward of Nimpkish Bank, and when the west point of Cormorant Island bears N. 55° E they will be westward of it, then steer to round the SW. point of Haddington Island within ¼ mile, to avoid the ledge off Ledge Point, and when the northern shore of Cormorant Island opens off Haddington Island bearing S 80° E., vessels may steer out of the strait in mid channel. None, except small craft, should go to the northward of Haddington Island

Sailing vessels of any size would find it tedious to beat through this strait, and as there are several dangers it is not recommended to do so

Queen Charlotte Sound is an extensive arm of the sea, connecting the inner waters north of Vancouver Island with the Pacific In the north and northeastern parts are innumerable rocks and islands; but along its southern sides are two broad and navigable channels to the Pacific.

Broughton Strait enters this sound at its southeastern part. From thence to Thomas Point the coast of Vancouver is low and is bordered the whole distance by a beach composed of sand and bowlders, and foul ground marked by kelp extends off it, from ¼ to ½ mile.

If intending to enter Beaver Harbor from the eastward, do not approach this shore within a mile till near Thomas Point; and as but

(838) **BRITISH COLUMBIA—Broughton strait—Mitchell bay—Kelp patch reported.**—Captain F. T. [illegible]anders, master of the steamer *Coquitlam*, reports the existence of a patch of kelp, suspected of indicating a shoal, off Donegal head, Malcolm island, in the approach to Mitchell bay.

Approx. position Lat. 50° 36′ 58″ N., Long 126° 51′ 00″ W.

From the patch the south tangent of Donegal head bears N. 57° E. true (NNE. ⅞ E. mag.) and Stubbs island S 59° E. true (E ½ S. mag.), distant 2,200 yards. (N M. 22, 1905.)

about.

There is a coal mine here and a pier.

Blakeney Passage, between Hanson Island on the west and the west extremes of Cracroft and Harbledown Islands ... in width from one mile to ¼ mile ... Blackfish S...

Wey... 1¼ mile... rushes t... anchor i...

Race... wide, bu... the rate...

Pears... small low... nearly one...

Cormo... ...es long, east and west, ¼ m... ...a sandy beach. Gordon Point, its southeaste... ...2½ miles N 55° W of Beaver Cove A small patch of 4 fathoms marked by kelp lies 1¼ miles N 77° W of Leonard Point, the NW. point of Cormorant Island.

Alert Bay, on the south side of Cormorant Island, is nearly one mile wide and ½ mile deep, affording a good and well-sheltered anchorage in from 6 to 9 fathoms, muddy bottom, it is easy of access, the shores being everywhere clear of danger There is an establishment here for tinning salmon caught in the Nimpkish River, and a pier, at the extremity of which there is a depth of about 12 feet, extends from the northeastern shore of this bay

There is also a mission established and quite a large Indian village, comprising most of the former inhabitants of Cheslakee. The house marked on the chart is a small one storied house, with three windows towards the water Near it is a very small chapel.

A supply of wood for steaming purposes may be obtained at Alert Bay.

Yellow Bluff, the southwestern point of the bay, may be recognized by a remarkable yellow cliff at the extreme of the point.

Haddington Island is small; its southern and western sides are steep to, but from the northern shore a bar, with as little as 6 feet water in some parts, connects it with Malcolm Island

Betwee... point of... fathoms...

Malco... is 13½ m... beach ex... are Mitc... fathoms. Donegal Head, its east point, ... beach, and the tide runs strong in its vicinity Dickenson Point, on the southern side of the island, 7 miles westward of Donegal Head, is connected to Haddington Island by a bar, with only 6 feet on it in some parts.

Trinity Bay, on the northern side of Malcolm Island, between Lizard and Bowlder Points, is an open bay 2½ miles wide and one mile deep. Between the points of the bay the water shoals steeply from 40 fathoms to a ledge having 10 fathoms on its outer edge, but which again shoals rapidly, and is covered with kelp.

Anchorage may, with care, be picked up on the outer edge of this ledge in 7 fathoms, with Lizard Point bearing S. 77° E., and Black Bluff S. 80° W., 400 yards outside the kelp; but it is exposed to winds from the westward, between north and SW.

Kelp Patch.—Foul ground marked by kelp extends ¼ mile off the western side of Malcolm Island, and 1¼ miles NW. of Pulteney Point is a shoal patch of 4½ fathoms, also marked by kelp.

Directions.—Passing through Broughton Strait from the eastward, when abreast Beaver Cove, in mid channel, a N. 72° W. course, to pass not more than 400 yards south of Cormorant Island, will keep vessels clear to the northward of Nimpkish Bank, and when the west point of Cormorant Island bears N. 35° E. they will be westward of it; then steer to round the SW. point of Haddington Island within ¼ mile, to avoid the ledge off Ledge Point, and when the northern shore of Cormorant Island opens off Haddington Island bearing S. 80° E., vessels may steer out of the strait in mid-channel. None, except small craft, should go to the northward of Haddington Island.

Sailing vessels of any size would find it tedious to beat through this strait, and as there are several dangers it is not recommended to do so.

Queen Charlotte Sound is an extensive arm of the sea, connecting the inner waters north of Vancouver Island with the Pacific. In the north and northeastern parts are innumerable rocks and islands; but along its southern sides are two broad and navigable channels to the Pacific.

Broughton Strait enters this sound at its southeastern part. From thence to Thomas Point the coast of Vancouver is low and is bordered the whole distance by a beach composed of sand and bowlders, and foul ground marked by kelp extends off it, from ¼ to ½ mile.

If intending to enter Beaver Harbor from the eastward, do not approach this shore within a mile till near Thomas Point; and as but very few soundings have been obtained in this part of Queen Charlotte Sound, if beating to windward, great caution ought to be observed when standing to the northward.

Su Quash Anchorage, at 7 miles west of Pulteney Point, on the southern shore of Queen Charlotte Sound, is bordered by shoal ground extending 800 yards off, and on which anchorage may be had in from 2¼ to 4 fathoms. Care, however, must be observed when anchoring here, as reefs, which dry at low water, and shoal patches lie scattered about.

There is a coal mine here and a pier.

Anchorage.—The best berth is with the pier head bearing S. 77° W., distant 500 yards, in 2½ fathoms water; ½ mile from the pier on the same bearing the depth is 7 fathoms.

Beaver Harbor, 9 miles westward of Broughton Strait, is 3 miles wide at entrance and 2 miles deep. The harbor is protected by several islands lying across and within the entrance. Its shores are low, and from the southern shore a bank extends off nearly ½ mile. A short distance inland from its western side are seven remarkable hills, varying in height from 400 to 640 feet. There is good anchorage in the southern and western parts of the harbor, but northeasterly winds send in a heavy sea, rendering it impossible to land in ships' boats on the southern shore for days together.

On the southern shore is Fort Rupert, formerly a Hudson Bay Company's trading post. In the vicinity of the fort is a large native village Landing here is bad, owing to the beach extending out shoal for some distance, and the bottom is very foul. A strong earthquake shock occurred here on August 25, 1865.

In the vicinity of Beaver Harbor the yellow cypress abounds; it is also found on all parts of the north coast of Vancouver's Island, and at intervals on the main land from Knight Inlet westward.

This tree yields lumber of the finest texture, very hard and durable (good for boats), it is possessed of a peculiarly pleasant odor, and repels the attack or presence of the *teredo navalis*; on this account it is highly prized by the cabinet-makers, and the shipbuilder.

Thomas Point, the southeastern extreme of the harbor, is low and rocky; some rocks lie upwards of 400 yards off it to the westward. The channel between it and Deer Island is about 800 yards wide, with from 13 to 6 fathoms, and clear of danger.

Moffat Rock, 1,600 yards to the westward of Thomas Point, is 600 yards off shore, just at the outer edge of the bank, and uncovers at low water

Deer Island, is about 1½ miles in circumference and wooded; its shores are rocky, and extending nearly 800 yards off its northwestern part is a reef marked by kelp, with only 9 feet water over it. Eagle Island lies close off its southeastern point, with a small rock, 15 feet high, not more than 50 yards from its southern extremity.

Twin Rock lies midway between Round and Peel Islands; a reef extends for more than 200 yards from its east and south ends, the latter being nearly connected with the shoal extending from the north end of Deer Island.

Round Island, is small, but high, and conspicuous from the eastward.

Peel Island is in the northern part of Beaver Harbor. Between it and the western shore of the harbor is a passage 400 yards wide in the narrowest part, with 17 fathoms water. North of Peel are the Charlie Islets, small, and two in number. There is a good channel into the harbor close along the east side of Peel Island, which is steep to, with the exception of a rock and 3 fathom patch close off the NE. end.

Cattle Islands, which lie in the middle of the harbor, are small and connected with each other at low water, and at 350 yards north of the islands, there is a shoal of 3 fathoms.

Shell Islet.—At 350 yards south of them is Shell Islet; the observation spot on its top is in lat. 50° 42′ 36″ N., long. 127° 25′ 07″ W.; a reef awash at high water lies 200 yards south of it.

Cormorant Rock, lying ⅛ mile off the western shore of the harbor, covers at high water, and has from 4 to 6 fathoms close to; midway between this rock and Cattle Islands is a shoal patch of 3¼ fathoms.

Dædalus Passage, leading from the west part of Beaver Harbor to the northward, is 400 yards wide in its narrowest part, and has not less than 17 fathoms in mid channel. The mid channel course should carefully be preserved, especially in the narrowest part west of Peel Island where the deep channel is only about 300 yards wide.

Dillon Point, the NW. extreme of the harbor, and separating it from Hardy Bay, is bold and rocky; some small islets lie to the SE of it close inshore.

Directions.—Beaver Harbor is easy of access to sailing vessels as well as steamers. There are three passages into it, but the southern between Thomas Point and Deer Island is the best, and generally used. This channel is wide enough for a vessel to beat through; and the only caution required in entering it, is not to round Thomas Point nearer than 400 yards in order to avoid the rocks off its NW. part, after passing which steer for Shell Islet.

If entering the harbor by the Dædalus Passage, steer in mid channel, passing between Cormorant Rock and the 3¼-fathom shoal 300 yards eastward of it. A sailing vessel could not easily work through it however, as the breadth abreast Peel Island contracts to about 300 yards.

Anchorage.—Anchor in 10 to 12 fathoms about 400 yards SE. of Shell Islet, with Fort Rupert bearing south, and Thomas Point S. 70° E. Good anchorage in from 6 to 9 fathoms, and better sheltered from all winds, may be obtained westward of the Cattle Islands; but in rounding Shell Islet give it a berth of about 400 yards to avoid the reef south of it.

(323) **BRITISH COLUMBIA—Vancouver island—North coast—Hardy bay—Wharf.**—A wharf has been erected by the Government of Canada at the upper end of Hardy bay, Vancouver island, 600 yards to the northeastward of the entrance to the small inner harbor or bight at the extreme bottom of the bay.

Approx. position. Lat. 50° 43′ 10″ N., Long. 127° 29′ 20″ W.

The wharf, built of piles, consists of an approach 120 feet long with a tee 100 feet long by 40 feet wide at its outer end. Its deck is 5 feet above high watermark. There is a small warehouse on the wharf. The depth along the front of the wharf is 27 feet, deepening rapidly outwards to 40 and 60 feet.

The wharf is easy of approach at all stages of the tide and can be seen in ordinary weather on entering the bay. (N. M. 10, 1904.)

Anchorage.—The best berth is with the pier head bearing S. 77° W., distant 500 yards, in 2½ fathoms water, ½ mile from the pier on the same bearing the depth is 7 fathoms.

Beaver Harbor, 9 miles westward of Broughton Strait, is 3 miles wide at entrance and 2 miles deep. The harbor is protected by several islands lying across and within the entrance. Its shores are low, and from the southern shore a bank extends off nearly ½ mile. A short distance inland from its western side are seven remarkable hills, varying in height from 400 to 640 feet. There is good anchorage in the southern and western parts of the harbor, but northeasterly winds send in a heavy sea, rendering it impossible to land in ships' boats on the southern shore for days together.

On the southern shore is Fort Rupert, formerly a Hudson Bay Company's trading post. In the vicinity of the fort is a large native village. Landing here is bad, owing to the beach extending out shoal for some distance, and the bottom is very foul. A strong earthquake shock occurred here on August 25, 1865.

In the vicinity of Beaver Harbor the yellow cypress abounds; it is also found on all parts of the north coast of Vancouver's Island, and at intervals on the main land from Knight Inlet westward.

This tree yields lumber of the finest texture, very hard and durable (good for boats), it is possessed of a peculiarly pleasant odor, and repels the attack or presence of the *teredo navalis*; on this account it is highly prized by the cabinet makers, and the shipbuilder.

Thomas Point, the southeastern extreme of the harbor, is low and rocky; some rocks lie upwards of 400 yards off it to the westward. The channel between it and Deer Island is about 800 yards wide, with from 13 to 6 fathoms, and clear of danger.

Moffat Rock, 1,600 yards to the westward of Thomas Point, is 600 yards off shore, just at the outer edge of the bank, and uncovers at low water.

Deer Island, is about 1½ miles in circumference and wooded; its shores

part n

Island

high,

Tw

extend

being

Deer

Ro

Pe

and tl

narro

Islets, small, and two in number. There is a good channel into the harbor close along the east side of Peel Island, which is steep to, with the exception of a rock and 3 fathom patch close off the NE. end.

Cattle Islands, which lie in the middle of the harbor, are small and connected with each other at low water, and at 350 yards north of the islands, there is a shoal of 3 fathoms.

Shell Islet.—At 350 yards south of them is Shell Islet; the observation spot on its top is in lat. 50° 42′ 36″ N., long. 127° 25′ 07″ W.; a reef awash at high water lies 200 yards south of it.

Cormorant Rock, lying ¼ mile off the western shore of the harbor, covers at high water, and has from 4 to 6 fathoms close to; midway between this rock and Cattle Islands is a shoal patch of 3½ fathoms.

Dædalus Passage, leading from the west part of Beaver Harbor to the northward, is 400 yards wide in its narrowest part, and has not less than 17 fathoms in mid channel. The mid channel course should carefully be preserved, especially in the narrowest part west of Peel Island where the deep channel is only about 300 yards wide.

Dillon Point, the NW. extreme of the harbor, and separating it from Hardy Bay, is bold and rocky; some small islets lie to the SE. of it close inshore.

Directions.—Beaver Harbor is easy of access to sailing vessels as well as steamers. There are three passages into it, but the southern between Thomas Point and Deer Island is the best, and generally used. This channel is wide enough for a vessel to beat through; and the only caution required in entering it, is not to round Thomas Point nearer than 400 yards in order to avoid the rocks off its NW. part, after passing which steer for Shell Islet.

If entering the harbor by the Dædalus Passage, steer in mid-channel, passing between Cormorant Rock and the 3½-fathom shoal 300 yards eastward of it. A sailing vessel could not easily work through it however, as the breadth abreast Peel Island contracts to about 300 yards.

Anchorage.—Anchor in 10 to 12 fathoms about 400 yards SE. of Shell Islet, with Fort Rupert bearing south, and Thomas Point S 70° E. Good anchorage in from 6 to 9 fathoms, and better sheltered from all winds, may be obtained westward of the Cattle Islands, but in rounding Shell Islet give it a berth of about 400 yards to avoid the reef south of it.

Hardy Bay, separated from Beaver Harbor by Dillon Point, indents the coast in a southerly direction for 4 miles; its breadth at the entrance is 2 miles, narrowing to the head, where it terminates in a narrow creek 1½ miles long, and about ¼ mile broad, with a sand bank extending off its head for ¾ mile. The shores of the bay are rugged, and off the west side, near the head, are some outlying rocks. There is no anchorage, except in the small creek at the head, which is difficult of access, and should not be used by a stranger.

Masterman Islands, off the northeastern point of the bay, are small, moderately high, wooded, and four in number; foul ground exists between them and the shore.

The Eastern Shores of Queen Charlotte Sound consist of an archipelago 12 miles in length, extending from Hanson Island on the south to the entrance to Fife Sound on the north. Between the numerous islands, islets, and rocks which form this archipelago, are many narrow channels leading to the entrances of extensive chasm like inlets, in which the water is of great depth, and whose shores rise in almost sheer precipices.

Baronet Passage.—From Blakeney Passage along the north shore of Cracroft Island, between it and Harbledown Island, is a narrow channel 6 miles long, known as Baronet Passage. At this distance it splits into several small passages, lying between many small islands, islets, and rocks, the navigation of which must be undertaken with considerable caution.

Kelp Rocks lie just within the entrance to Baronet Passage, on the northern shore, and extend over 400 yards offshore in some places, two of them uncovering at low water 8 and 3 feet respectively; they leave a channel 300 yards wide along the southern shore, in which is a depth of 10 fathoms. From here the passage is clear as far as Channel Island, 4 miles from the entrance. The channel on either side of Channel Island is less than 200 yards wide, that to the northward being the deepest. Shoal spots extend both off the east and west ends of the island.

Steamer Passage, between the islands above mentioned as lying 6 miles from the entrance to Baronet Passage, is 200 yards wide, with depths of 10 to 15 fathoms in it. Great care must be observed when passing through Steamer Passage, as a dangerous rock, awash at low water, lies a little over 400 yards north of it.

Clio Channel, the continuation of Baronet Passage and communicating with Knight Inlet, is clear of danger throughout, with the exception of the Negro Rock (awash at low water), lying in the fairway ½ mile S 80° W. of Sambo Head, and to avoid which the SE shore of Turnour Island should be kept aboard at about 500 yards distant. Thence the passage out into Knight Inlet is clear and safe

Lagoon Cove, a small sheltered nook on the NE. side of Double Islands, 2 miles to the SE of the junction of Clio Channel with Knight Inlet, affords anchorage for a small vessel in 10 fathoms. When entering, pass in mid channel between the north shore of Double Islands and a small round island northward of them, but do so with caution.

Harbledown Island forms the northern shore of Baronet Passage.

Parson Bay, on the western side of Harbledown Island, is a spacious bay 1½ miles deep in an easterly direction and ¾ mile wide, shoaling gradually from 30 fathoms just inside the entrance to 12 fathoms at its head.

Anchorage may be obtained in 14 fathoms, mud, at the head of Parson Bay, in the SE. corner, well sheltered from all but westerly winds blowing down Blackfish Sound, in which direction it is open.

Compton Island, ¾ mile long east and west, is triangular in shape. It is separated from Harbledown Island by White Beach Passage. In a bay on the south side is an old village.

Berry Island, to the NE. of Compton Island, is nearly one mile long and forms the east side of Farewell Harbor.

Lewis Island is separated from Berry Island by Village Passage; it forms the north side of Farewell Harbor, and the entrance to Knight inlet lies along its northern shore.

Blackfish Sound, between the north shore of Hanson Island and Swanson Island, has an average width of 1½ miles, and leads into Parson Bay and Blakeney Passage to the SE. and to Farewell Harbor and White Beach Passage to the northward. There is deep water all over the sound, and it is entirely free from dangers.

Swanson Island, forming the northern shore of Blackfish Sound, has regular bold shores and only one or two small indentations. Numerous small islets and reefs lie off the northern shore of the island for the distance of nearly one mile.

Freshwater Bay, on the south side of Swanson Island, about 800 yards to the westward of the southern entrance into Farewell Harbor, affords anchorage for small vessels in 6 fathoms, but it is exposed to southerly winds.

Farewell Harbor, formed between Swanson Island, Lewis Island, Berry Island and Compton Island, is a snug anchorage for a small vessel, ½ mile across in every direction. Its approaches, however, both from the northward and southward, are only 100 yards wide, that to the northward from the main entrance to Knight Inlet (between Swanson and Lewis Islands) being obstructed by the Twilight Reefs and several islets lying ½ mile outside it. Entering through North Passage, Charles Point (the west entrance point), kept touching Maggy Point (the southern point of North Passage on the eastern shore), bearing south, clears the Twilight Reefs, passing eastward of them.

The southern entrance, named West Passage, between Punt Rock and Apples Island (lying close to the shore of Swanson Island), and the Star Islands lying off the NW. shore of Compton Islands, leads out of Blackfish Sound and must be approached with caution, as shoal ground extends 400 yards in a SW. direction from the latter islands, having on its extreme a depth of 4 fathoms, leaving a passage to the east of Punt Rock only 100 yards wide.

Twilight Rock, awash at high water, lies 1,400 yards N. 10° W. of Charles Point, and 400 yards N. 60° W. of it, is Cluck Reef, 200 yards in extent and drying 4 feet. To the westward of the above dangers is a group of small islets and reefs extending along the whole of the northern shore of Swanson Island for a distance of nearly a mile.

Directions.—The southern entrance, which should only be taken by a small vessel, should be approached on a N. 64° E. bearing, passing 50 yards from Bare Rock (10 feet high) at the east side of Freshwater

Bay; on this bearing Stripe Island, a small island in the harbor, should be seen midway between Apples and Star Islands. When abreast of Apples Island haul gradually to the eastward and anchor in 18 fathoms in the middle of the harbor.

If it can be clearly made out, the north extreme of Kamux Island, open a little north of the NW. Star Island, bearing N. 69° E., will clear the shoal ground extending SW. of the Star Islands.

Village Passage, between Lewis and Berry Islands, is a narrow but apparently clear channel 250 yards wide, leading out from the NE. part of Farewell Harbor, north of the Carey group, to Native anchorage.

White Beach Passage, between Compton Island and the NW. point of Harbledown Island, is in its narrowest part only 80 yards across, and must be used with great caution. This passage also leads up through Indian Passage, south of the Carey group, to Native anchorage.

Village Island is 2 miles to the eastward of Lewis Island, and is separated from Tournour Island on the SE. by Canoe Passage. The space between Lewis Island and Village Island is occupied by the Indian Islands A narrow pass, Elliot Passage, leads into Knight Inlet, between the easternmost of these islands and Village Island.

Carey Group are a chain of several small islands lying to the southward of the Indian Islands, and stretch across from Berry Island to Turnour Island

Turnour Island is 9 miles long east and west, and at its center 3 miles wide, narrowing towards its extremities. It is separated from Harbledown Island on the south by Beware Passage, Clio Channel running along its southeastern side, and Knight Inlet along its northern side.

Native Anchorage.—At the SW end of Village Island is Mamalilaculla village, and at the mouth of a small bay to the southeastward of it, at the entrance to Canoe Passage, is Native Anchorage, with from 7 to 8 fathoms water Hail Islands, two small islets, lie to the southward of it, and Chart and Cecil Islets to the westward

Beware Passage, lying between the northeastern shore of Harbledown Island and the southwestern shore of Turnour Island, leads from Native Anchorage eastward into Clio Channel. Though the greater part of it is clear, vessels can not pass through it into Clio Channel, owing to a barrier of islets and rocks which stretch right across it, at one mile from its junction with that channel An Indian village (Karlukwees) is situated on Turnour Island at the eastern entrance to Beware Passage.

Canoe Passage is a narrow pass leading from Native Anchorage along the southeastern shore of Village Island, between it and Turnour Island. At 2 miles up it is completely closed at low water by a stony barrier which dries right across, and it is only available for canoes at high water

Knight Inlet.—**The Main Entrance** to this inlet, which is one of the most extensive of the sea canals of British Columbia, lies northward of Swanson, Lewis, and Village Islands, between them and Midsummer Island and several smaller islands and rocks.

The entrance lies $3\frac{1}{2}$ miles east of Donegal Head, and may be easily recognized by White Cliff Islands, a chain of small islets of a whitish color on the northern side of the passage into the inlet. The entrance between Wedge Island on the north and the northwestern shore of Swanson Island on the south is 700 yards wide and clear of danger, but farther east Twilight Reefs and Clock Rock are dangerous, the former is $1\frac{1}{4}$ miles and the latter 5 miles from Wedge Island. These dangers should be [illegible]

Bay; on this bearing Stripe Island, a small island in the harbor, should be seen midway between Apples and Star Islands. When abreast of Apples Island haul gradually to the eastward and anchor in 18 fathoms in the middle of the harbor.

If it can be clearly made out, the north extreme of Kamux Island, open a little north of the NW. Star Island, bearing N. 69° E., will clear the shoal ground extending SW of the Star Islands.

Village Passage, between Lewis and Berry Islands, is a narrow but

(840) **BRITISH COLUMBIA—Queen Charlotte sound—Knight and Kingcome inlets approaches—Uncharted rocks—Hydrographic notes.**—Captain F. T. Saunders, master of the steamer *Coquitlam*, reports the existence of the following uncharted rocks and suspicious patches of kelp in the vicinity of the approaches to Knight inlet and Kingcome inlet from Queen Charlotte sound. The positions have not been accurately fixed and are to be considered as approximate only

Kelp, between the 14 and 20 fathom soundings southeast of Berry island, 600 yards S. 9° E. true (SE. by S. mag.) from the east tangent of that island. A boat is reported to have struck a rock here.

Latitude 50° 35′ 55″ N., Longitude 126° 39′ 10″ W.

Kelp, where 14 fathoms are marked on the chart, bearing from Cecil islet S. 80° W. true (SW. 7/8 W. mag.), 700 yards, also off the northeast end of Cecil islet.

Kelp, where 13 fathoms are marked on the chart, between the two southernmost islets off Mamalilaculla, 1/2 mile S. 13° W. true (S. by E. E′ly mag.) from the center of the more easterly Indian island.

Kelp, on the west side of Elliott passage off the southeast extremity of the more easterly Indian island, northeast of the 24 fathom sounding.

The rock shown 1,200 yards S. 83° E. true (ENE. 3/8 E. mag.) from the easternmost Ridge islet and that shown off Bare hill cover at high water.

Kelp, where 19 fathoms are shown, between the islets off Bare hill.

Rock off Sail island, Retreat passage, uncovers at low water. Distant 400 yards S. 15° W. true (S. 7/8 E. mag.) from the rock shown off the northwest end of Sail island.

Kelp patch off Saddle hill, immediately south of the rocks west of the 27-fathom sounding.

Kelp close northward of the 20-fathom sounding shown off False cove, northward of Saddle hill.

Rock on which the steamer *Coquitlam* struck off Islet point, Retreat passage, in the entrance to Cramer passage, close southeastward of the 40 fathom sounding shown on the chart.

Latitude 50° 44′ 02″ N., Longitude 126° 34′ 20″ W.

Rock, uncovering at low water, in Penphrase passage, 300 yards off Sir Edmund head bearing from Vigis point South true (SSE. 1/4 E. mag.).

Shoal ground extending 200 yards off the bluff nearly midway between Steep point and Vigis point, Wishart peninsula.

Rock marked with kelp with less than 6 feet over it in the middle of Moore bay, Kingcome inlet, where 55 fathoms are marked on the chart.

Reef reported by Captain Monk of the steamer *Coutli* in the middle of Sharp passage from which the north tangent of Moore point bears N. 73° E. true (NE. 1/4 E. mag.) and the east tangent of Stackhouse island N. 15° E. true (N. 7/8 W. mag.).

Rock awash at high water off Cardale point, Sutlej channel.

(N. M. 22, 1905.)

The entrance lies 3½ miles east of Donegal Head, and may be easily recognized by White Cliff Islands, a chain of small islets of a whitish color on the northern side of the passage into the inlet. The entrance between Wedge Island on the north and the northwestern shore of Swanson Island on the south is 700 yards wide and clear of danger, but farther east Twilight Reefs and Clock Rock are dangerous, the former is 1¼ miles and the latter 5 miles from Wedge Island. These dangers should be passed to the northward, and Jumble Island, lying between them, to the southward, after which a mid channel course should be preserved until east of Lady Islands, when the shores of the inlet may be approached to within a moderate distance. The entrance proper to Knight Inlet is between Warr Bluff on the south and Slope Point on the north. From hence the inlet trends in a general easterly direction for 33 miles, and then turns suddenly to the northward for 26½ miles to its termination, with an average width throughout of 1½ miles. The shores of the inlet are generally bold and formed by high mountains rising precipitously from the water's edge. The water is everywhere deep, except at a spot about 7 miles eastward of Sergeant Passage, where a rocky ridge was found to extend across the inlet, and on which there are heavy overfalls, but no less depth than 23 fathoms was obtained. There are but few places that afford anchorage; Port Elizabeth on the north shore and Glendale Cove on the south being the only two that may be considered available. At 11½ miles east of Slope Point, Tribune Channel branches off to the northward and embracing Gilford Island, connects with Fife Sound and Sutlej Channel, which diverging on either side of Broughton Island lead into Queen Charlotte Sound.

On the southern side, Knight Inlet is connected with Johnstone Strait by two passages, viz, Clio Channel and Baronet Passage and Chatham and Havannah Channels

Tides —The tides at the entrance to Knight Inlet run at the rate of from one to 3 knots.

Wedge Island, a small, round island 400 yards in extent, is clear of danger and may be boldly steered for, passing in mid channel between Wedge Island and the small islets lying close to the shore of Swanson Island

White Cliff Islands.—From Wedge Island a line of small islets, named White Cliff Islands, extends for over a mile in a N. 13° W. direction with patches of shoal water between. A rock awash at high water lies nearly 200 yards northwestward of the northern islet

White Cliff Islands are the key to the entrance to Knight Inlet. The islands, by their color, form a very conspicuous object, and would be most useful for strangers to identify the entrance to the main channel of the inlet

Surge Rocks are a small group of rocky islets lying 600 yards north of Wedge Island.

Midsummer Island, separating Knight Inlet from Spring Passage, is 3 miles long, and one mile wide.

Owl Island, one mile in length, and about ½ mile broad, lies off the west end of Midsummer Island, with a narrow passage (Providence Passage) between them.

Passage Islet is a small, round islet, about midway between the Surge Rocks and the shore of Owl Island. From the northern islet of the White Cliff Islands another channel leads into Knight Inlet on either side of Passage Islet.

Twilight Reefs, which uncover only 4 feet at low water springs, lie about 1½ miles east of the main entrance to Knight Inlet, at from 200 to 250 yards northward of a group of small islets on the south side of channel. To clear them keep Coast Cone (a conical hill on the NW. shore of Village Island) in line with the southern shore of Jumble Island, bearing east.

Jumble Island lies 2 miles east of Wedge Island On its west side is Night Islet, and off its east point lie the three small Bush Islets. When within 400 yards of Night Islet haul to the eastward to pass at that distance southward of it, Jumble Island, and the Bush Islets

Indian Islands lie on the south side of Knight Inlet, between Lewis and Village Islands. Between them are several small channels leading to Native Anchorage, but only the easternmost, Elliot Passage, is navigable, and that only by small vessels.

Clock Rock, which covers at half flood, lies 500 yards north of the easternmost of the Indian Islands, and is especially dangerous to vessels going through Elliot Passage. To clear it keep the coast of Village Island aboard at 400 yards distance.

Leading Mark.—Passing up or down Knight Inlet, the Clock Rock may be safely passed by keeping Leading Point (on the north shore) in line with Ripple Bluff (the north extreme of Village Island) bearing N. 88° E.

Ridge Islands lie on the northern side of Knight Inlet, between the east end of Midsummer Island and the SW. shore of Gilford Island, at the entrance of Spring Passage.

A Rock, which dries 8 feet at low water, lies 600 yards from the shore of Gilford Island; it is, however, out of the fairway of vessels passing up and down Knight Inlet, but is dangerous for those passing through Spring Passage.

Chop Bay is a small bight on the north side of Knight Inlet opposite Ripple Bluff.

Tide Rip.—Heavy tide rips occur off Ripple Bluff, and between it and Leading Point, on the opposite shore, the tidal stream runs at a rate of from 2 to 3 knots an hour.

Lady Islands consist of two islands with deep water on both sides of them, and are 3 miles eastward of Leading Point; the largest is one mile long, but narrow, with several small islets lying off its west extreme.

Port Elizabeth.—Northwestward of the Lady Islands a large bight branches off to the NW., curving round to the SW., and opening out at its head, forming a sheltered anchorage named Port Elizabeth, about one mile in extent; but which is, however, somewhat contracted by two small islands lying in the middle.

Duck Cove, to the SW. of these small islands, forms the termination of the port, a flat dries off its head nearly ½ mile.

Anchorage may be taken up as convenient in the southern part of the port in from 9 to 4 fathoms, the latter depths being found south of the eastern island, midway between it and the shore.

Minstrel Island lies to the eastward of Turnour Island, at the junction of Clio and Chatham Channels with Knight Inlet. Between the south side of Minstrel Island and the opposite shore of Cracroft Island a deep bight is formed, in the center of which is Double Island, two small islets connected at low water with each other, and also with the shore to the eastward, forming to the northward Lagoon Cove.

Chatham Channel has its entrance between White Knob Point (Minstrel Island) and Littleton Point, where it is over ½ mile wide. Thence the channel takes a southeasterly direction, and gradually contracting in width and shoaling, it, at 4 miles from the entrance, joins the head of Havannah Channel.

Cutter Creek, a narrow bight on the east shore of Chatham Channel, 1¾ miles deep, terminating in marshy land bordered by a sandflat, would afford anchorage to a small vessel in 6 fathoms, but caution must be observed when entering, as a small islet (Block Islet) lies in mid-channel at entrance, leaving a passage less than 200 yards wide on each side of it, that to the south being the best.

Shewell Island, on the north side of Knight Inlet, lies at the southern entrance to Tribune Channel, which it divides into Clapp and Nickoll Passages, both being clear of danger.

Tribune Channel, see page 218.

Viscount Island, forming the eastern side of the southern entrance to Tribune Channel, is 3 miles long north and south, and one mile wide.

Sergeaunt Passage (Punish) is a narrow pass on the east side of Viscount Island, 2¾ miles long, and communicates with Tribune Channel.

Tides.—It is high water, full and change, in Sergeaunt Passage at 1h. 0m; springs rise 15½ feet, neaps 12 feet.

Anchorage.—Fair anchorage may be obtained on either side of the passage. It is contracted to 220 yards, where the depth is 11 fathoms at low water. The least water in the kelp patch is 3½ fathoms.

Tsakonu Cove, on the south side of the inlet round Protection Point, is probably too deep for anchorage.

Hoeya Sound, on the north shore of the inlet, 7 miles from Protection Point, is a bight ½ mile wide, indenting the coast in an easterly direction. There are depths of over 40 fathoms over the greater part of the sound, but it shoals suddenly to 5 fathoms at 300 yards from its head.

Prominent Point, on the south shore of Knight Inlet, opposite the entrance to Hoeya Sound, has a rocky ridge of less water than in the center of the inlet, extending northward from it, on which there are heavy overfalls; the least depth obtained during the survey was 23 fathoms.

Glendale Cove (Kiokh), on the south shore of the inlet, immediately eastward of Macdonald Point, is ¾ mile wide at its entrance. It dries about half its length, and the water in the remaining part is deep.

A river flows into the head of Glendale Cove from a sheet of water one mile distant, named Tom Browne Lake, about 5 miles long, which extends nearly to the head of Topaze Harbor.

Anchorage may, with care, be taken up in the southeastern corner in 23 fathoms, with the right extreme of Observation Point in line with Rapid Hill, and a large bowlder on the west side in line with the junction of Flora and Macdonald Ridges, but the bank is very steep to.

Glacier.—On the east shore, at 14 miles from the head, over a gully, under Glacier Peak, there is a remarkable glacier a short distance from the sea. Anchorage was tried for, but no bottom was obtained at 200 yards from the shore with 40 fathoms of line.

From Axe Point the inlet trends nearly straight for a farther distance of 8 miles. At its head it somewhat widens, but maintains its great depth close up to the mud flat, which extends about ½ mile from the shore of the marshy ground at the foot of the valley in which Knight Inlet terminates. In the valley near a stream is Tsauwati village, frequented during the summer months by large numbers of Indians for the purpose of making fish oil. Mount Blair, immediately over the head of the inlet, attains an altitude of 6,550 feet.

Wahshihlas Bay, at 4½ miles from the head of Knight Inlet on the western shore, affords the only place where an anchor could be dropped—securing to the trees by a hawser, in a depth of 30 fathoms close to the south shore, on west side of the bay.

Fire Islands, at the entrance of the inlet, consisting of one large and four small islets, lie close to the west end of Owl Island.

Escape, Canoe, and House Islands.—From the west end of Midsummer Island several small islands extend in a northwesterly direction for 1¼ miles, with rocks between some of them. The largest, Escape Island, lies close off the shore of Midsummer Island. House Island, the NW. of the group, is merely a round rock, but reefs extend over 400 yards east and west from it.

Sedge, Start, and High Islands are the southern and largest of numerous small islands, and rocks lying off the SW. end of Bonwick Island. Several patches of rock lie off and between them, but a clear passage, ½ mile wide, exists between Sedge Islands and House Island, leading into Retreat Passage.

Green Rock, 25 feet high, lies 1$\frac{1}{10}$ miles east of House Island, another small rock lying 300 yards westward of it.

Spring Passage, leading from Retreat Passage into Knight Inlet, is about ½ mile wide, but at the eastern end the channel is contracted by Broken Islands to a width of 600 yards, the passage being to the north of these islands. Ridge Islands lie across the eastern entrance of the passage.

Retreat Passage, an entrance to which lies between House and Sedge Islands, extends in a northeasterly direction, between Bonwick and Gilford Islands. Along the shore of Bonwick Island, which is bold-to, it is a clear navigable passage, but the eastern shore is skirted by several small islands, islets, and rocks, between which a vessel should not pass.

Seabreeze Island is the largest and most southern of the islands on the eastern shore of Retreat Passage. Whale Rock, 3 feet high, lies 800 yards NE. of Seabreeze Island, nearly midway between it and Yellow Rock at the entrance to Health Bay.

Health Bay, a bight one mile deep in a SE. direction, may be safely entered by passing in mid-channel between the south end of Sail Island (which lies off the entrance) and Yellow Rock, 500 yards south of it, or midway between the latter and the shore, when convenient anchorage in 9 to 10 fathoms may be obtained. A narrow passage in the NE. corner of the bay communicates with a lagoon.

Grebe Cove, a narrow bight on the west shore, extends one mile in a westerly direction, shoaling gradually from 18 fathoms off its entrance to 6 fathoms at its head.

Camp Bay, opposite Grebe Cove, is too small, and has too great a depth of water in it, for anchoring in.

Fox Islands.—The north end of Retreat Passage opens out into a space about 2 miles across. In the middle of this space, extending right across from the north end of Bonwick Island to the south shore of Baker Islands, are the Fox Islands. There is a clear channel east of the Fox Islands up to the entrance of Cramer Passage, passing midway between the eastern islet of the chain and Solitary Island.

Cramer Passage, between the southeastern shore of Baker Island and northwestern shore of Gilford Island, is a clear navigable channel, 400 yards wide at its southern entrance, between Steep Island and Islet Point; from thence it extends 2 miles N. 80° E., and then turns suddenly to the N. 12° E. for one mile to its junction with Fife Sound. A sunken rock lies 250 yards west of Powell Point, the NE. entrance point of the passage.

At the northern entrance, at the distance of 300 yards from the western shore is a sand patch, about 400 yards in extent, with from 9 to 16 fathoms water on it. By preserving a mid-channel course the passage may be boldly taken.

Shoal Harbor, on the east shore of Cramer passage, is a narrow inlet 1¼ miles long (east and west), to which access is gained by a channel 150 yards across from shore to shore, in some parts less than 40 yards wide between the 3-fathom lines, and in which there is a depth of only 3¾ fathoms. This channel is 700 yards long in a southerly direction, Mink Point being its southern termination on the eastern side. The western half of the harbor has only from one to 2 fathoms water over it, but over the greater part of the eastern portion there is a depth of 4 fathoms. A bank which dries, and through which flows a small stream, extends more than ¼ mile from the head of the eastern arm. Shoal Harbor is only safely available for small coasting vessels with local knowledge, but in the event of its being necessary to enter, a small vessel may, with care, do so by keeping at 50 to 60 yards from the eastern shore of the passage in, and anchorage may be taken up in 4 fathoms abreast Mouse Island (on the northern shore) about 300 yards eastward of Mink Point.

Tides.—It is high water, full and change, in Shoal Harbor at 1 hr., springs rise 15 feet, neaps 10 feet.

Bonwick Island forms the western shore of Retreat Passage and the eastern shore of Arrow Passage. Off its southwestern end, north of Sedge, Start, and High Islands it is skirted by numerous small islets and rocks, between which, near the shore of Bonwick Island shelter may be found.

Dusky Cove affords anchorage in 6 to 8 fathoms, about 200 yards eastward of Cove Island, the largest of the islets. It is entered by a passage 200 yards wide between the ledges of rock (which extend in patches ½ mile west from Cove Island) and a chain of islets to the southward. Care must be observed when entering to avoid the reefs, which may be cleared by keeping the north point of the small Leading Island at the head of the cove in line with the north extreme of South Island, bearing S. 82° E.

The westernmost of the reefs above mentioned (Evening Rocks) covers at 6 feet rise, and Ledge Rock, the outer of the islets on the south side of the channel, is only 3 feet above high water. Trap and South Islands lie to the eastward of Ledge Rock, the former being 25 feet high.

Fog Islands are a small group lying off the shore of Bonwick Island on the south side of the entrance to Arrow Passage. Evening Rocks and the ledges extending west from Cove Island, lie ½ mile southward of them.

Horse Rock, awash at low water, is a dangerous rock lying off the north side of the entrance to Arrow Passage, 1,600 yards N., 75° W. of the westernmost Fog Island.

Arrow Passage, between Bonwick Island to the SE. and Hudson and Mars Islands on the NW., is a clear navigable channel, in every pa[illegible] of which is deep water. Having passed the Horse Rock, the passage may be boldly passed through in mid-channel, and a vessel may, if necessary, pass westward of the Fox Islands, and rounding the northern islet of that group at 300 yards, pass between it and Steep Island and enter Cramer Passage.

The Coach Islands are a group of several small islands lying on the north side of the entrance to Arrow Passage; they extend over a distance of ¾ mile from the SW. end of Hudson Island.

Hudson Island, on the north side of Arrow Passage, is one mile long.

Mars Island, 2¼ miles long, and ¾ mile wide, lies close to and northeastward of Hudson Island. Spiller Passage, between it and Hudson Island, leads out to the NW. amongst the islets on the SW. side of Eden Island, and into Trainer and Philips passages.

Scrub, Kate, and Triangle Islands, with some other small islets, extend 1¼ miles from the west end of Hudson Island; Scrub Island being the smaller and westernmost of the group.

Sunday Harbor.—Between the above-mentioned islands and Crib Island, to the NW., a small but sheltered anchorage is formed, affording refuge for small vessels. The western entrance is between Scrub Island and Huston Island (a small islet lying 400 yards north of it) and is clear of danger. Half a mile in, the channel contracts to less than 200 yards in width between Narrows Island and Island Point, between which is a ridge with only 4½ fathoms on it, deepening again to 7 fathoms. There is a passage out to the eastward leading into Spiller Passage.

Anchorage should be taken up in mid-channel as convenient, but at not more than 600 yards from the Narrows, in 5 fathoms, with Bush Point bearing N. 29° E., and north point of Kate Island shut in with Island Point.

Crib Island, forming the NW. shore of Sunday Harbor, is 1¼ miles long, and ½ mile wide at its broadest part.

Eden Island, forming the southeastern shore of the entrance to Fife Sound, is about 4 miles long and 1½ miles broad, and has some smaller islands and rocks off its western end. Its southwestern shore is a little more than ½ mile northward of Crib Island, and the passage between them is divided by a group of islets lying in the center into two passages, that to the northward named Trainer, and that to the southward Philips Passage.

Marsden Islands are a group of five islets lying to the eastward of the two passages; southward of them, towards Spiller Passage, are several other islets and rocks; but to the NW. and north of them (along the shore of Eden Island) there is a clear channel to the NE. leading into Joe Cove (Eden Island) and Misty Passage, and thence northward through Blunden and Old Passages, on either side of Insect Island, into Fife Sound, south of the Benjamin group. These passages are, however, very narrow and shoal in places, and are not navigable except by small coasters.

Tracey Island, 1½ miles long and ¾ mile wide in its broadest part, lies between the east ends of Eden and Mars Islands. Between it and Eden Island is Misty Passage.

Monday Anchorage.—Between Tracey Island and Mars Island is Monday Anchorage, a sheltered position affording secure anchorage midway between the shores of the above islands in about 8 fathoms

Baker Island, forming part of the southern shore of Fife Sound, is eastward of Eden Island, the triangular shaped island named Insect lying between them. It is 1½ miles long east and west and 1½ miles broad.

Fife Sound leads from Queen Charlotte Sound to Sutlej and Tribune Channels and Kingcome Inlet, and extends in a general ENE. and east direction for 8 miles, when the Burdwood group divides it into two channels (Raleigh and Hornet Passages) leading into Tribune Channel; it is a clear navigable channel, with deep water throughout. Fife Sound, between Pearse Peninsula and the Burdwood group, turns suddenly to the westward and joins Penphrase Passage, which connects it with Sutlej Channel and Kingcome Inlet.

The entrance from Queen Charlotte Sound, between Duff Island and the entrance to Cullen Harbor, may be boldly steered for, passing at about ½ mile SE. of Gore Rock (4 feet high), which lies about one mile westward of the entrance.

Foster Island, the summit of which forms a remarkable cone about 270 feet high, lies about 5 miles S. 57° W. of the entrance of Fife Sound. Off its south side are the Twin Islets, and off the north side is a patch of kelp, which may possibly overlie a rocky danger. The channel between Foster and Malcolm Islands is called George Passage, and is apparently free from danger

Penfold Island, covered with trees, and small, lies 1½ miles southeastward of Foster Island The channel between Foster and Penfold has not been examined.

Holford Islands, lying 2 miles N. 35° E. of Foster Island, consist of two small islands, covered with trees From the western island, a reef which uncovers 3 feet at low water, extends ¼ mile to the northward and westward, and the islands in this direction should be given a berth of one mile The passage between Foster Island and Holford Islands, known as the Salmon Channel, is clear of danger; a mid channel course should, however, be kept.

Cullen Harbor is on the south side of Broughton Island, at the entrance to Fife Sound. Its entrance between Nelly Island and the shore westward of Gordon Point is less than 200 yards wide, and, when entering, care should be taken to keep exactly in mid channel Inside, the harbor opens out to 600 yards in width, with depths of from 4 to 8 fathoms.

At the head of the harbor, on the west side, a narrow boat passage, through which the tide runs with great strength, leads into Booker Lagoon, an extensive sheet of water about 1½ miles in extent, with depths varying from 12 to more than 45 fathoms. This lagoon has an outlet into Queen Charlotte Sound to the westward of Long Island, which forms the western side of Cullen Harbor.

Anchorage may be had, well sheltered, in 5 fathoms, sandy bottom at 300 yards S. 12° W. of Davidson Island at the head of the harbor.

Tides.—It is high water, full and change, in Cullen Harbor at 12h.; springs rise 16 feet, neaps, 7 feet.

Deep Harbor, on the north side of Fife Sound, 7 miles within the entrance, is formed by a narrow inlet which indents the coast in an easterly direction, forming on its south side Pearse Peninsula. At its entrance is Jumper Island, 400 yards eastward of which, and just north of two small islets, is a reef, leaving a clear passage in along the north shore 100 yards wide. The depths in the harbor vary from 14 to 37 fathoms, but anchorage may be found off a small bight on the south shore, in 18 fathoms, at 600 yards southwestward of the narrow entrance to the bight which forms the head of the harbor.

Benjamin Group, consisting of three islands and several smaller islets and rocks, lie opposite Deep Harbor. Indian Passage, the narrow channel lying between them and the south shore, has a shoal patch of 1½ fathoms in it, and though otherwise apparently clear of danger, should not be attempted.

Ragged Island, lying 1½ miles eastward of Gull Rock (at eastern extreme of the Benjamin Group), has a rocky patch extending 300 yards from its NW. side.

Pym Rock, which uncovers 2 feet at low water, and is steep to, is a dangerous patch lying in the way of vessels entering Cramer Passage.

Viner Sound, on the southeastern shore of Fife Sound, about 3 miles NE. of Ragged Island, gradually narrows from one mile at the entrance to 400 yards in width at the head, from which a bank, drying at low water, exends ½ mile. Anchorage may be had in 10 fathoms at about ¼ mile from its head, abreast an old Indian village.

Burdwood Group, consisting of six large and several small islands, lies off the entrance to Viner Sound. The largest, which is the northwestern one, is 700 feet high. Vessels should not pass between them.

Simoom Sound, the entrance to which is 1¼ miles from the Burdwood Group, between Deep Sea Bluff on the east, and Pollard Point on the west, extends 1½ miles NNE. and then turns suddenly to west, which direction it maintains for nearly 2 miles as far as Curtis Point, where the width decreases from ½ mile to 400 yards, and the inlet bends to the SW., and is separated by a narrow neck of land from Shawl Bay, an indentation on the east side of Sutlej Channel, and forming Wishart Peninsula. The width of Simoom Sound at the entrance is ¼ mile, and on the eastern side, one mile from Deep Sea Bluff, is the small islet of Louisa. The water is deep, but where the sound turns to the westward it shoals to 40 and gradually to 20 fathoms, and to the southwestward of Curtis Point in O'Brien Bay, decreases to 11 fathoms.

Raleigh Passage, to the northward of the Burdwood Group, connects Tribune Channel with Fife Sound and Sutlej Channel; there is also a passage to the southward of the group called Hornet Passage.

There is deep water in both these passages, but the former is the wider and the more direct.

Directions for Fife Sound.—Entering from Queen Charlotte Sound, steer to give Foster Island and the Holford Islands a berth of at least one mile, and pass ½ mile SE. of Gore Rock, which at high water spring tides is only 4 feet above water, whence steer boldly for the entrance, keeping as nearly as possible in mid channel. From abreast the Benjamin Group the northern shore should be kept at about ⅓ mile distant, gradually hauling to the northward, and passing between Nickless Island and Village Point, the west extreme of the southern Burdwood Island. If bound through Sutlej Channel, haul to the northwestward; if through Tribune Channel, steer to round the NW. island of the Burdwood Group at ½ mile distant, and then to the eastward.

Tribune Channel, throughout its greater part, maintains an average width of one mile, but near Kwatsi Bay, where the channel turns to the SE., and again at 2 miles within the southern entrance, it narrows to ⅓ mile in width. The water is deep throughout, the only danger being Humphrey Rock, on which is a depth of 3 fathoms, lying in mid-channel just south of the southern narrows. Tribune Channel has the same characteristics as most of the other deep inlets on this coast.

Kwatsi Bay, on the north shore of Tribune Channel, about 8 miles eastward of the Burdwood Group, indents the coasts for about 2 miles. The water in the southern part is very deep, but shoals at ½ a mile from the head of the bay to 28 fathoms, and gradually to 13 fathoms.

Wahkana Bay, opposite to Kwatsi Bay, indents the shore of Gilford Island in a southwesterly direction for nearly 2 miles, the depth at about one mile within the entrance being 30 fathoms, and near the head 18 fathoms.

Bond Sound, which indents the north shore of Tribune Channel, extends 3 miles in a northerly direction, and has an averaged width of nearly one mile. Bond Sound, owing to the great depth of water, affords no anchorage.

Thompson Sound has its entrance on the east shore opposite Trafford Point. At the head of the sound is Sackville Island, and the Kakweiken River flows into the sound northward of it. Between Sackville Island and the mud flat off the river, the depths shoal, but rather steeply; anchorage, however, might with ease be picked up in the northeastern corner, in 12 fathoms.

Humphrey Rock, with 3 fathoms water on it, lies nearly in the center of the southern part of Tribune Channel, abreast Bamber Point, the west salient point of Viscount Island, and 2 miles to the northward of the NE. point of Shewell Island.

Gilford Island, the largest of the islands forming the archipelago on the eastern shore of Queen Charlotte Sound, is 18½ miles long in a NE. and SW. direction, and 11 miles wide at its NE. end, gradually decreasing to 2 miles near its SW. extreme (Bare Hill). The west side of the island is much indented, and some of the bights thus formed afford anchorage, amongst which are Health Bay and Shoal Harbor Gilford Island is considerably elevated, the highest parts being near the NE. end, where Mount Read rises to a height of 4,820 feet. The SW. part of the island, however, is not so lofty, the hills over Baie Hill Point not being more than 925 feet high, but round its eastern, southern, and northern shores mountains rise almost precipitously from the water's edge.

Broughton Island, which forms the NW. shore of Fife Sound, and the southern and western shore of Sutlej Channel, is 15 miles long in an east and west direction, and 6 miles wide at its western end, gradually tapering to one mile wide at its eastern extreme. The island is much indented, the largest inlet, Greenway Sound, nearly separating the island into two parts, and a canoe passage also leads from Greenway Sound to Carter Bay, at the west point of the Island, thus detaching the northern part of Broughton Island. The hills on Broughton Island are not so lofty as those of the mainland contiguous to it

From the entrance to Cullen harbor, the south shore of Broughton Island trends to the westward for about 8 miles to the entrance to Wells pass, it is steep to and clear of danger at ½ mile distant. Dobbin Bay and Cockatrice Bay afford no anchorage

Polkinghorne Islands, a group consisting of one large and several smaller islets and rocks, lie off the coast at the entrance to Wells pass; the largest island, 190 feet high, is distant from Broughton Island 1½ miles. Foul ground extends for some distance from the east side of this group and it should not be approached within a distance of ½ mile.

Vincent Island lies ½ mile north of the west extreme of the largest of the Polkinghorne Islands, some smaller islands lying between them.

Percy Island lies ¼ mile NW. of Vincent Island, and has several islets and rocks skirting its NW shore and bordering on Wells Pass.

Dickson Island, at the western extreme of Broughton Island, is ½ mile NE. of Percy Island and forms the south shore of Carter Bay; its southern shore is skirted by islets and rocks, some of which extend across to Percy Island.

Caution—Vessels passing between the Polkinghorne Islands, Vincent, and Percy Islands, should do so with great caution, and should not attempt to pass between the latter island and Dickson Island.

Carter Bay is formed between Dickson and Broughton islands, on the eastern shore of Wells Pass; the water in it is deep.

Wells Pass is the entrance to Sutlej Channel from Queen Charlotte Sound. From the entrance between Boyles Point and Percy Island, the pass extends 5 miles in a NE. direction to its junction with Patrick Passage, Grappler Sound, and Drury Inlet. The width at the southern part, between Dickson Island and Popplewell Point, is only ½ mile, widening gradually to one mile at the northern end.

The eastern shore is much broken by bays, including Tracey Harbor, but the west shore is straight and compact.

Ommaney Islet is the westernmost of the islets lying in Wells Pass between Percy and Dickson Islands; its south and SE. sides are surrounded by kelp to a distance of about 400 yards, amongst which are rocks drying at low water. The passage into Wells Pass is to the westward of Ommaney Islet, which narrows the navigable channel to a width of 800 yards. Vessels entering Wells Pass should, when approaching Ommaney Islet, keep the highest peak of Numas Islands (lying off the entrance) just open off Boyles Point until Ommaney Islet is well shut in under Dickson Island, whence steer to pass in mid-channel between the islet and James Point, and hence keep the western shore on board.

Sutlej Channel from its entrance (Wells Pass) takes a NE. direction for nearly 5 miles, varying from ¼ to one mile in breadth, and is clear of danger. At that distance it turns to the eastward through Patrick Passage between Atkinson and Kinnaird Islands, and thence southeastward to the entrance to Greenway Sound, whence it takes a general SE. direction through Pasley and Sharp Passages (on either side of the Stackhouse Island), to its junction with Penphrase Passage and Kingcome Inlet. It is a clear, deep channel throughout, and there is no impediment to safe navigation by maintaining a mid-channel course.

Tracey Harbor, on the western shore of Broughton Island, is at its entrance between Lambert Island and Manve Islet, 800 yards wide, but it soon narrows from 500 to 300 yards, maintaining that width for a little over one mile in an east direction, the harbor then opens out and forms two bights at its head, Napier Bay, the northern, being 500 yards broad. The only danger is the reef skirting Star Rock (which lies on the north shore about half-way through the narrow portion of the harbor), and vessels entering should keep the southern shore aboard at 100 yards distance.

Anchorage, completely sheltered, may be obtained in from 6 to 7 fathoms in Napier Bay, or abreast Freshwater Cove, at about 400 yards S 46° E of the Star Rock, in 10 fathoms, mud bottom.

Lambert Island is on the north side of the entrance to Tracey Harbor. Immediately to the eastward of it is Wolf Cove, extending 800 yards in a northeasterly direction, with a width of 400 yards at the entrance, gradually narrowing to 200 yards; it affords no anchorage.

Atkinson Island lies close off the northwestern shore of Broughton Island; some islets extend off its southwestern point, and vessels should not attempt to pass between it and the shore of Broughton Island.

Surgeon Islands, a group of small islets close together, lie ½ mile west of Atkinson Island, at the entrance of Patrick Passage.

Kinnaird Island, 1¼ miles long, lies with Dunsany Passage on the east and Patrick Passage on the south.

Greenway Sound, on the south shore of Sutlej Channel, is a deep inlet nearly one mile wide at its entrance, extending 6 miles in a westerly and southerly direction, and gradually narrowing towards its head, which approaches within ¼ mile of the head of Dobbin Bay. It has deep water throughout its entire extent, and affords no anchorage; inside its entrance are Cecil and Maude Islets.

Cypress Harbor, in Sharp Passage, 2½ miles eastward of the entrance to Greenway Sound, indents the coast about one mile in a southerly direction; the upper half, however, is both narrow and shallow, and the anchorage is limited to only a small portion of the remainder, owing to the depth of water being too great. The entrance between Donald Head and Woods Point is 400 yards wide, but the navigable channel is only a little over 200 yards wide; the harbor then opens, and is from 400 to 800 yards across, the depth varying from 19 fathoms in mid channel to 6 fathoms abreast Berry Cove.

Fox Rock, 16 feet above low water, lies in the entrance, and is the outer part of a reef which extends 200 yards east from Woods Point. Vessels entering the harbor should, to avoid it, keep Donald Head aboard at a distance of 100 yards.

Anchorage.—Good anchorage may be obtained on the western side in 6 fathoms, mud bottom, off Berry Cove, at 200 yards N. 58° E. of Tree Islet. The land to the southward of the anchorage, between the head of Berry Cove and Rolley Point, is fringed with large cypress trees.

Water.—A stream of fresh water flows into Berry Cove.

Stackhouse Island is about ½ mile in extent, and lies in the middle of Sutlej Channel abreast the entrance to Cypress Harbor. Sharp Passage, to the southward of it, and Pasley Passage, to the northward, are both ½ mile wide.

Magin Islands, three small islands from 120 to 180 feet high, lie one mile to the northward of Stackhouse Island, and ½ mile from the west shore, a small rock, awash at high water, lying between.

Tides.—The tides in Sutlej Channel run at the rate of from one to 3 knots.

Kingcome Inlet takes a northeasterly direction for 6 miles to the entrance to Wakeman Sound (on the north shore), whence it trends easterly for a further distance of 12 miles to its head, maintaining an average width of one mile. Its termination on the northern shore is a low, marshy plain dotted with patches of scrub and stunted trees, and bordered by a flat of soft mud and sand 1¼ miles wide, which extends ½ mile from the shore. This is flat steep to.

The northern shores of this inlet are bordered by snow clad peaks, which are conspicuous from Queen Charlotte Sound; the southern shore is not quite so lofty. Kingcome Mountains rise over the head of this inlet, being 2 miles inland in an easterly direction.

Anchorage.—Kingcome Inlet, in regard to the great depth of water, presents the same features as most of the Inlets on this coast. Anchorage, however, may be obtained in 18 fathoms, off a small cove, near two small bights, at 1½ miles south of the head of the inlet.

Wakeman Sound extends for a distance of 5 miles in a northerly direction, terminating in a low marshy plain dotted with patches of scrub and stunted trees, through which several streams flow, bringing down from the high ranges inland the melting snow, and causing the water for one mile from the head of the sound to be perfectly fresh at low water, and of a dull milky color. At its head is an Indian village. The water is too deep for anchorage.

Belleisle Sound, on the south shore of Kingcome Inlet, has its entrance through a narrow pass which lies south of the small Edmond Islands. The inlet, from its great depth of water, affords no anchorage.

Penphrase Passage connects Sutlej Channel with Fife Sound and Tribune Channel. The west entrance between Hayes and Vigis points is one mile wide, but the width of the passage decreases to 300 yards abreast of Trivett Island. About 200 yards east of Trivett Island is a shoal patch of 3 fathoms, with this exception the passage appears to be clear from dangers. Nicholls Island lies just inside the west entrance on the southern side of the channel.

A rock awash at low water lies 250 yards to the northwestward of the west point of Nicholls Island, but being inside a line joining Hayes Point with the east end of the island, is out of the fairway of the channel.

Drury Inlet at its entrance is only 200 yards wide, with a depth of 15 fathoms; just outside the entrance is Morris Island, which should be passed on the north side, and the northern shore should be closed to avoid a reef (marked by kelp in the season) lying on the southern shore half way between Morris Island and the narrowest part of the entrance channel. Drury Inlet extends in a westerly direction for 12 miles to its head, where another narrower arm (Actæon Sound) branches off on the northern shore for a distance of 4 miles to the northeastward.

Over the greater part of Drury Inlet the depth is less than 25 fathoms, and it is nowhere so deep as most of these inland channels; in width it varies from 200 yards to one mile, the latter being its width throughout the greater part of the inlet; but at one place, Stuart Narrows, 1¼ miles within the entrance, two islets (each connected to the shore by reefs) leave a passage of only 300 yards between them, and this is further obstructed by a dangerous rock, which only uncovers at low water (5 feet), lying directly in the fairway between the two islets. Through these narrows the tidal streams during springs attain a velocity of 5 knots an hour.

Passing up Drury Inlet, at one mile from Stuart Narrows, Leche Island is seen lying in mid-channel, and may be passed on either side; here the inlet opens out to the southward, forming Richmond Bay, in which are several islets. At a little over one mile westward of Leche Island is Ligar Island, 150 feet high, having at 200 yards SE. of its south point a dangerous sunken rock, uncovering only 5 feet at low-water springs.

Voak Rock, another dangerous rock, awash only at low water spring tides, lies 600 yards N. 10° W. of Ligar Island, with deep water between.

Sir Everard Islands, on the southern shore, 1½ miles westward of Ligar Island, form a chain extending in a NW. direction, with rocks between them, a clear channel lying between them and Hooper Island to the northward.

Blount Rock, 3 feet above high water, lies close to the southern shore ½ mile to the westward of Sir Everard Islands.

Jennis Bay, on the north shore, abreast Hooper Island, would afford anchorage for a small vessel, which when entering, should pass eastward of the island and anchor in the center of the bay in 7 to 10 fathoms.

Center Rock, a dangerous sunken rock, uncovering only 8 feet at low-water spring tides, lies in the middle of Drury Inlet 1$\frac{1}{10}$ miles N. 65° W. of the northern of the Sir Everard Islands; it is steep to all round, and vessels will clear it by keeping at 400 yards off either shore.

Muirhead Islands.—At 2¼ miles westward of Center Rock the inlet becomes studded with small islands having deep channels between them, and extending over a distance of 2 miles. The easternmost of these is Wilson Island, 120 feet high; Keith Island, also 120 feet high, lies 400 yards to the westward of it, and the Muirhead Islands, three in number, extending one mile in an east and west direction, are 200 yards westward of the latter. The west Muirhead Island is the largest and 255 feet high, the next in size, the eastern, being 180 feet high. Between this group and the southern shore the space is occupied by numerous small islands, but there is a clear channel along the north side of the group; westward of these, however, the water shoals rapidly, there being only 2 to 3 fathoms in Sutherland Bay at the head of Drury Inlet.

Actæon Sound, which branches off from the north side of Drury Inlet abreast the west Muirhead Island, is so blocked at its entrance by islets and rocks as to render it only available to boats

Grappler Sound.—West of Patrick Passage, between Kinnaird Island and Pandora Head, is the entrance to another inlet which continues in a northerly direction for 4 miles, and is known as Grappler Sound. From it, several smaller bights branch off on both sides, those on the east communicating with Hopetown and Kenneth Passages, north and south of Watson Island. The depths in the Sound range from 20 to 30 fathoms, but shoal in Claydon and Carrden bays on the western shore. At the entrance to the former a reef lies nearly in mid-channel, and a reef also extends 300 yards from Linlithgow Point, on the northern shore of the entrance to the latter.

Buckingham, Hammersley, and Hanbury Islands lie on the north side of Kinnaird Island at the entrance to Hopetown Passage, the first being the largest.

Dunsany Passage, leading from Grappler Sound to the entrance to Hopetown Passage and southeastward into Sutlej Channel, is apparently clear of dangers, with the exception of a reef, which covers at high water springs, lying off the northern shore at the entrance to Hopetown Passage.

Hopetown Passage can only be used by boats which can pass the barrier of rocks that extend right across the passage at 1¾ miles from the entrance.

Kenneth Passage, leading from the head of Grappler Sound round the north side of Watson Island, communicates with Mackenzie Sound. About one mile from its entrance from Grappler Sound it widens considerably, a bight, named Turnbull Cove, extending one mile in a NW. direction; but ½ a mile farther eastward the passage contracts to 600 yards, and thence several islands, islets, and rocks obstruct the passage, rendering its navigation dangerous.

Mackenzie Sound, from the east point of Watson Island, extends 3 miles in an easterly direction, gradually narrowing towards its head at the foot of Mount Stephens, where it becomes a mere chasm, and shoals in the same direction from 25 to 10 fathoms.

Boyles Point, the western entrance point of Wells Pass and the southern point of the peninsula formed by Drury Inlet, has three small islets lying close off it, the outer of which is only 4 feet above high water. Over and on each side of the point are undulating hills of about 500 feet high, rising gradually inland to Mount Wynard.

Lewis Rocks, a small cluster, lie one mile west of Boyles Point, with rocks awash and foul ground extending ½ mile to the southward and westward.

Numas Islands, the largest of which is 1½ miles long in an east and west direction, lie in Queen Charlotte Sound, off the entrance to Wells Pass, and off the western extreme of the largest is Staples Islet, 24 feet high. These form an excellent landmark.

Labouchere Channel, between Numas Islands and the Lewis Rocks is over 2 miles wide. The tidal streams run at the rate of from one to 3 knots through this channel.

The Coast of the mainland from Boyles Point trends nearly WNW. for 20 miles, and to the Rayner Group, a distance of 8 miles, it is steep to.

Rayner Group consists of four or five small islands, lying close to the shore eastward of Blunden Harbor. The southern edge of the group is fringed with sunken rocks, and they should not be approached in that direction nearer than ½ mile. Masses of kelp surround these islands in the season, and skirt the shore towards Blunden Harbor.

Gillot Rock, 2 feet above high water, is the easternmost of the dangers lying to the southward of the Rayner Group.

Black Rock, only 7 feet above high water spring tides, is the westernmost of the dangers in the vicinity of Rayner Group.

Blunden Harbor, on the northern shore of Queen Charlotte Sound, a little more than one mile from Black Rock, is formed between several islands which lie close off an indentation in the coast. The entrance between Shelf Point, the east extreme of Robinson Island and Barren Rock, a small rock 12 feet high, is 500 yards wide; but a reef (marked by kelp) extends 350 yards SSW. from the latter, and another reef extends the same distance east from Burgess Island, a small island lying close to the shore 700 yards SW. of Shelf Point, thus rendering the channel somewhat tortuous.

Inside the harbor, amongst the small islands in its northern part, the depths are shoal and covered with kelp.

Anchorage may be obtained in 4 fathoms, mud bottom, in the western part of the harbor, at 400 yards S. 69° W. of the southern of the two Bonwick Islands, which are joined to the shore and to each other at low water.

Directions.—Vessels entering Blunden Harbor, which is only available for vessels of moderate size, should bring Shelf Point to bear N. 13° W., when it will be just open of Charles Point (on the east shore), and steer in on these marks until Barren Rock bears N. 69° E., when haul to the northward to pass midway between the rock and Shelf Point. When the channel opens, haul to the westward, keeping in mid-channel and steering N. 58° W. with Barren Rock astern, until the passage between the southern Bonwick Island and Bartlett Point bears S. 86° W., when alter course in that direction. As the channel here is only 100 yards wide, very great caution must be observed.

Browning Islands, 2½ miles west of the entrance to Blunden Harbor, are a small group, the largest being 500 yards long. A dangerous rock, which dries only 3 feet at low-water spring tides, lies 600 yards S. 45° E. of the east extreme of the largest of the Browning Islands, and vessels should therefore give those islands a berth of from ½ to one mile when passing.

Stuart Point, 1¾ miles N. 55° W. of the Browning Islands, has some rocky islets off it; and 600 yards S. 60° E. of Stuart Point, in the center of a bay between the point and Browning Islands, is a patch of 2 fathoms.

Leading Hill, 570 feet high, is close over the coast 1¼ miles N. 50° W. of Stuart Point.

Robertson and Jeanette Islands lie close off the shore under Leading Hill.

Round Island, a little over 100 yards in extent, the tops of the trees being 100 feet above the water, lies 1,200 yards S. 35° W. of Jeanette Island; the channel between is clear, there being depths of over 40 fathoms in it.

The Millar Group consists of a chain of small islands extending over a distance of 2 miles in a NW. and SE. direction at 800 yards southward of Round Island, between which and the group vessels should not pass. The tops of the trees on the highest island of the group are from 150 to 200 feet above the sea. At 600 yards N. 50° W. of the western island of the group is David Rock, with 12 feet water on it.

Mary Rock, a dangerous rock lying 1,600 yards S. 38° E of the south end of the Millar Group, is generally visible, it being awash at high water. Vessels passing through the North Channel from the south-eastward should approach it with Round Island bearing N. 55° W., and not bring the island to bear northward of that bearing until the east end of the Millar Group bears west, when alter course for mid channel between Round Island and Jeanette Island.

The Deserters Islands are a group of islands, islets, and rocks, the largest of which is nearly 2 miles in length, lying $1\frac{3}{4}$ miles southward of the Millar Group. The Walker Group lies to the westward of the Deserters, separated from them by Shelter Pass.

Ripple Passage, between the Millar Group and the Deserters Islands, has several dangerous rocks in it, and should therefore not be used except in an emergency, and then only at low water (when nearly all the dangers show) and with the greatest caution

Sun Rock, the most dangerous of these rocks, owing to its locality only being known during bad weather, when the sea breaks on it, lies 1,600 yards S 74° W. of the westernmost islet of the Millar Group.

Twin Rocks, 10 feet above high water, are two small rocks lying 1,200 yards N. 69° E. of McLeod Island. Heavy overfalls are met with northward and westward of the Twins.

Richard Islet, 25 feet above high water, and bare, lies 1,400 yards N. 69° E. of the Twins; it should not be approached within 200 yards.

Barry Islet lies one mile S. 35° E. of Richard Islet; it is bare, and 45 feet above high water.

Echo Islets, a small group lying 1,600 yards to the southward of Barry Islet, extend over $\frac{1}{2}$ mile in a NW. and SE direction At 600 yards off their NW. end is the George reef; it lies $\frac{3}{4}$ mile S 69° W. of Barry Islet.

The North Channel into Queen Charlotte Sound extends close along the shore of the mainland from Bremner Island off Buccleuch Point to between Jeanette Island and the Millar Group, passing between White and Mayor Islands on the north, and North Rock on the south, and at $\frac{1}{2}$ mile southward of Rogers, Dickenson, and Harris Islets; thence past Bold Bluff, and midway between Wentworth Rock and Wallace Islands. To clear the North Rock, passing northward of it, keep Harris Islet just open south of the south extreme of Jeanette Island bearing S. 50° E

Wallace Islands lie close to the shore of the mainland and at the entrance to Shelter Bay; they are steep to at ¼ mile from their southern shore.

Shelter Bay indents the coast in an easterly direction for nearly 2 miles, forming two bights at its head The entrance between the Wallace Islands and the shore to the northward is 800 yards wide, but the bay is incumbered with rocks in its most sheltered part, and could only be made use of as an anchorage by those possessing local knowledge. In a small bay north of Wallace Islands there is good landing for boats, and there is also good landing for boats, in southeasterly winds, in a bight 600 yards west of the point forming the NW. entrance to Shelter Bay.

Wentworth Rock, 10 feet above high water, lies 1½ miles S. 77° W of the Wallace Islands; it should be given a berth of ½ mile in all directions.

Annie Rocks, 16 feet above high water, are bare rocks, lying at 600 yards off the coast, 1¼ miles west of the entrance to Shelter Bay.

Southgate Group, consisting of four larger and several smaller islets, lie close off the coast 3 miles westward of Shelter Bay. Bold Bluff, the SE. island of the group, has rocky patches off its east end. The shore of the mainland abreast Bold Bluff falls back to the northward for a distance of 6 miles, the southern part being skirted by several several small off lying islets and rocks.

Harris Islet, 30 feet above high water, is a small bare islet lying one mile westward of the Southgate Group.

Dickenson Islet, 16 feet above high water, is a small bare islet 1,400 yards N. 52° W. of Harris Islet.

Rogers Islet, a similar small bare islet, 10 feet high, lies 1,200 yards N. 27° W. of Dickenson Islet. Foul ground extends for 400 yards from its north and south ends.

Elizabeth Rocks are a small patch lying 600 yards northwestward of the Southgate Group.

Emily Group, consisting of four small islets, the tops of the trees on which are 90 feet above the sea, lie a mile northward of Rogers Islet.

Eliza Island lies 600 yards from the Emily Group; the tops of the trees on the island are about 240 feet above the sea, and there are some conspicuous white cliffs on its south side.

Frederick Islet is a small islet 90 feet high, lying ½ mile eastward of Eliza Island. From Frederick Islet, towards Elizabeth Rock, there are several rocky patches.

Murray Labyrinth is the name given to the many channels which lie between a group of several islands, islets and rocks lying off the south coast of Branham Island.

Branham Island lies off the coast of the mainland, and together with the Fox Islands forms the southern shore of Slingsby Channel.

Skull Cove, indenting the island to the eastward of Nina Hill on the southern side, affords good shelter for boats

Schooner Passage, between the east shore of Branham Island and the mainland, is a narrow pass having an average width of 200 yards, in a northerly direction for a distance of 2½ miles. It is, however, at one place obstructed by a rock lying in mid-channel, which leaves a passage only 80 yards wide between it and the shore of Branham Island. Schooner Passage communicates with Slingsby Channel, at one mile southward of the Nakwakto Rapids.

The tides in Schooner Passage run at rate of from 2 to 5 knots.

Mayor Island, a small wooded island, lies $1\frac{2}{10}$ miles NW. of the Emily Group. A rock awash at low water lies 400 yards eastward of

White Island, small and bare, lies 1½ miles N 52° W. of Mayor Island.

Morphy Rock, which covers at three quarters flood, lies 1,200 yards N. 86° E of White Island.

Fox Islands, the western of which is 1½ miles long and the eastern ½ mile long, lie off the western end of Branham Island, and form the southern shore of the outer part of Slingsby Channel.

Slingsby Channel, on the northern shore of Queen Charlotte Sound, leading to Seymour and Belize Inlets, is 5 miles in length in an easterly direction, with an average breadth of 600 yards between Outer Narrows and Nakwakto Rapids.

Outer Narrows.—At ¼ mile within the entrance (between Dalkeith and Lascelles Points) the channel contracts to only 200 yards in width, with no bottom at 40 fathoms In these narrows the flood tide runs 2½ hours after high water by the shore, at springs the velocity is from 5 to 9 knots, at neaps from 4 to 6 knots, the change of stream occurring after only about 15 minutes slack water. The ebb tide runs 2½ hours after low water by the shore, attaining at springs a velocity of 10 knots, and at neaps from 5 to 7 knots. With the wind blowing in, *i. e.*, between west and south, the sea breaks across the entrance, and in the narrowest part, even during calms, the water is much agitated.

Nakwakto Rapids (Kahtsisilla), at the eastern end of Slingsby Channel, are 100 yards wide, but in the center of the rapids is Turret Island, 80 feet high, against which the tide rushes with great fury. The channel westward of Turret Islet has a rock in it with only 2 fathoms water on it; that to the eastward has depths of from 6 to 11 fathoms.

The flood tide commences 2½ hours after low water by the shore in Slingsby Channel, and runs (with a velocity at springs of 12 to 15 knots) from 2 to 2¾ hours after high water, or until it is high water at Seymour Inlet, after an interval of 10 minutes slack water the ebb commences and runs until 2 to 3 hours after low water in Slingsby Channel, attended by very heavy and dangerous overfalls, and attaining a velocity at springs of 20 knots.

It is high water, full and change, in Slingsby Channel at 2h. 20m.; springs rise 11 feet, neaps 5 feet.

Directions.—Steam vessels may enter Slingsby Channel from the westward through the Outer Narrows in fine weather, at or near slack water, and proceed to Treadwell Bay, 4 miles within the entrance on the north shore, where anchorage will be found in from 9 to 15 fathoms, avoiding the shoal of 2½ fathoms situated southwards of the center of the bay.

If it be necessary to proceed through Nakwakto Rapids, the turn of the tide should be most carefully watched, so that the vessel may with certainty make the passage during the only 10 minutes of slack water, for at no other time would it be possible to do so with any degree of safety.

These narrows, however, should only be used by a vessel on emergency and after acquiring some practical knowledge, by passing through at slack water in a boat. It is also imperative that the tides should be previously watched from Treadwell Bay.

Small canoes pass from Slingsby Channel into Seymour Inlet at half tide through a very narrow passage on the north shore inside the small island forming the north point of the narrows.

Treadwell Bay, on the north shore of Slingsby Channel, is formed by the channel widening to 1,700 yards and forming a bight in which lie the Anchor Islands (a group consisting of one large and several small islands), leaving a sheltered space 500 yards in extent between the north shore of the large island and the shore. The largest Anchor Island is [illegible] mile long east and west, and 220 feet high. The depth of water in the bay varies from 7 to 12 fathoms, but near the center, rather over to the south side, there is a shoal spot with from 4 to 2½ fathoms on it. The bay affords shelter perfectly free from tide for vessels of any size. Large ships should moor.

Caution Rock, which uncovers (6 feet) only at low-water spring tides, is a dangerous rock lying in the fairway channel southeastward of the Anchor Islands and 300 yards from the southern shore of Slingsby Channel. To avoid it, keep the southern shore aboard at less than 200 yards.

Directions.—Entering Treadwell Bay, give the southeastern Anchor Islands (Current Point) a berth of 300 yards, and having rounded them keep the shore of the mainland aboard.

Anchorage.—Anchor as convenient in 10 to 12 fathoms northward of the 2½ fathoms patch.

Tide.—It is high water, full and change, in Treadwell Bay at 0h. 30m.; springs rise 11 feet, neaps 5 feet.

Schooner Passage, North Entrance.—One mile southward of the Nakwakto rapids is the north entrance to Schooner Passage; it may be approached on either side of Buttress Island (210 feet high), which lies on the south shore of Slingsby Channel, fronting the passage.

Nugent Sound.—From the Nakwakto rapids a branch $\frac{1}{2}$ mile wide takes a SE. direction for about one mile; here it divides into two, one branch continuing in a SE. direction and the other (Nugent Sound) an easterly direction for 11 miles. Nugent Sound in some places is only 400 yards across, but it has deep water throughout and is navigable, though there is no anchorage in it. A very narrow passage leads from the head of Nugent Sound into a sheet of water taking an easterly direction for [illegible] mile, from which there is communication overland by Schwartzenber[illegible]e with Seymour Inlet.

Seymour Inl[illegible] The other branch, from Margaret Point at the entrance to Nugent Sound, takes a SE. direction for 6 miles, with deep water in mid-channel. On the northern shore is Charlotte Bay and on the southern Ellis Bay, both, however, unavailable as an anchorage. At the above distance, on the north shore, is the entrance to Seymour Inlet, several islets lying just within it. A narrow pass of shallower water, with depths of 4 and 10 fathoms, continues for 3 miles to the SE., communicating with a large sheet of water extending to the foot of Mount Adams, and only one mile from Actæon Sound. Wawattle Bay lies between the entrances to these two arms, and extends one mile in an easterly direction.

Seymour Inlet maintains a depth of over 40 fathoms throughout to within $\frac{1}{4}$ mile of the shore at its head. There are several indentations on both shores, the largest being Maunsell Bay on the northern shore; none, however, afford an anchorage. At 3 miles eastward of Maunsell Bay are the Eclipse Narrows, where the tides run with great strength, and no bottom could be obtained at 12 fathoms; these narrows lead to Salmon Arm and Frederick Sound. Frederick sound terminates at the foot of Mount Stephens, a conspicuous mountain with a pointed overhanging peak close to it, overlooking Mackenzie Sound.

Salmon Arm terminates at the foot of Perpendicular Mountain, 5,000 feet high. Taaltz, a winter Indian village, is on the shore at its head.

The continuation of Seymour Inlet northward of Eclipse Narrows terminates at 6 miles, a river flowing into it at its head, on which is situated a winter village of the Wawatl Indians.

Belize Inlet.—From the Nakwakto rapids another branch takes a westerly direction for 3 miles to Mignon Point, where it suddenly turns back to the eastward, continuing in that direction almost in a straight line for 24 miles, with an average width of $\frac{1}{2}$ mile and with deep water throughout. From the head of Belize Inlet to Maunsell Bay, on the northern side of Seymour Inlet, there is, according to Indian reports, a portage about $2\frac{1}{2}$ miles long.

Lassiter Bay, at the head of the continuation of the inlet, between Harvell and Mignon Points in a westerly direction, forms two small bights with some few islets and rocks in it, but the water is inconveniently deep for anchorage.

Mereworth Sound.—At 5 miles to the eastward of Mignon Point, on the north shore, is the entrance to Mereworth Sound, another similar inlet branching off to the northward, in which direction it continues for 4 miles and then suddenly turning to the eastward for 6 miles, maintaining deep water throughout.

Flat Rock, Square and Round Islands lie on the western shore at the entrance to Mereworth Sound, with deep water around.

Strachan Bay, at 1½ miles from the entrance to Mereworth Sound, is the entrance to a small inlet, which takes a westerly direction for 1½ miles and has depths of 40 to 16 fathoms.

Village Bay, on the opposite shore abreast Strachan Bay, is a small bay with two islets off its north point, and depths of 19 to 22 fathoms in it.

Westerman Bay is a small bight 1½ miles long in a northerly direction with from 30 to 20 fathoms water, except at its head, where it suddenly shoals to 3½ fathoms at 800 yards from the shore. The entrance to Westerman Bay is 2 miles westward of the entrance to Mereworth Sound.

Allison Sound.—At about 10 miles from the entrance to Mereworth Sound, on the northern shore of Belize Inlet, is the entrance to Allison Sound, another narrow branch which, like Mereworth Sound, first takes a northerly direction (for 3 miles) and then suddenly turns to the eastward for 3 miles, finally turning again to the northward for a further distance of 2 miles, to its head. At about 2 miles from the entrance Allison Sound is only about 350 yards wide; here, in the middle of the passage, is a small islet (Obstruction Islet) having a passage on either side of it 150 yards wide, with a depth of 10 fathoms in it.

The Coast from Lascelles Point, the north entrance point to Slingsby Channel, trends 7 miles NW. to Cape Caution, and is clear of danger.

Bremner Islet, covered with grass, lies 1½ miles N. 60° W. of Lascelles Point, and ½ mile distant from the shore.

Goletas Channel runs along the northern shore of Vancouver Island to the Pacific. Its shores are high, rugged, and steep-to, except in the western part, and may be generally approached to within ¼ mile; the northern side is composed of a group of islands (the principal of which are Galiano and Hope Islands), mostly small, through which are several navigable passages. There are four anchorages in the channel, viz, Shushartie Bay on the southern side; Port Alexander, Shadwell Passage, and Bull Harbor on the northern side; and all, with the exception of the latter, are easily accessible to sailing vessels.

The depths throughout the channel up the western entrance are very deep, but there the bottom suddenly rises from 40 to 7 and 9, and in one part to less than 3 fathoms, forming Nahwhitti Bar, stretching completely across the channel, and in a great measure preventing any heavy sea rising inside it during westerly gales.

Tides—It is high water, full and change, in the Goletas Channel at 0h. and 30m., and the rise and fall varies from 12 to 14 feet. The tidal streams in the eastern part of the channel run from one to 3 knots, but near the west entrance, in the vicinity of the Nahwhitti Bar, they are much stronger (2 to 5 knots), turning shortly after high and low water by the shore.

Shushartie Bay.—From Duval Point the southern shore of Goletas Channel runs in a WNW. direction to Shushartie Bay; it is everywhere steep-to. Shushartie Bay is about ½ mile in extent, and its shores are high, except at the head, from which a sand-bank extends off more than 400 yards. There is a very limited but fairly sheltered anchorage just inside the NE. point of the bay in about 13 fathoms, at the distance of 200 yards offshore, but from the steepness of the bank it should only be considered as a stopping place. Less water than charted was found in this bay in 1885 by the U. S. Coast Survey Steamer *Patterson*, the bank at the head of the bay having extended.

Dillon Rock, which covers at one quarter flood, lies 300 yards N. 66° W. of Halstead Island, which lies close off the eastern point of bay, and is in the way of vessels entering from the eastward.

Directions.—If entering Shushartie Bay from the eastward and the Dillon Rock be covered, do not steer in for the anchorage till the easternmost peak of the Shushartie saddle is seen in the center of the bay bearing S. 15° W., then proceed in with that mark on, which leads west of Dillon Rock; when the NE. point of the bay bears S. 83° E., the vessel will be close south of it, and should steer for the eastern shore.

Entering from the westward keep the westward shore aboard till Halstead Island bears S. 83° E., when steer in as before directed.

Anchorage.—Anchor immediately 14 fathoms are obtained, as the bank is steep, which will be at about 200 yards off it with the extremes of the bay bearing N. 69° E. and N. 32° W.

Shingle Point, 2 miles west of Shushartie Bay, is low; a beach runs off it a short distance; westward of this point it is difficult to land, except in fair weather.

Cape Commerell is the northernmost point of Vancouver Island. The cape is low, and some rocks extend off it for nearly 400 yards; to the eastward of it the coast forms a large bay 3 miles wide and about one mile deep, with from 2½ to 6 fathoms rocky bottom, and not in any way adapted for anchoring. The shoal part of Nahwhitti Bar, on which there is as little as 2½ fathoms, extends to the northwestward from the east point of this bay; it is marked by kelp and named Tatnall Reefs. Weser Islet, 8 feet high, lies in the western part of the bay, distant ¼ mile from the shore. There is an Indian village on the east side of the cape.

Gordon Group consists of a number of small islands, and border the north part of the east entrance of Goletas Channel. They are high and steep-to, and on the eastern or Doyle Island is Miles Cone, a remarkable summit 380 feet high.

Duncan Island, one mile south of the Gordon Group, is about one mile in circumference.

Noble Islets lie 1½ miles west of Duncan Island, between which and the group it is not advisable for a large vessel to go.

Blyth Island lies ¾ mile S. 79° E. of the SE. of the Noble Islets, and 600 yards north of it is Mouat Rock, with 1¼ fathoms of water over it.

(94) **BRITISH COLUMBIA—Queen Charlotte sound—New channel—Christie passage—Balaklava island—Scarlett point—Temporary light.**—Pending the completion of a lighthouse on Scarlett point, Balaklava island, northwest point of entrance to Christie passage, a temporary *fixed white* light will be shown near the site of the new lighthouse.

Approx. position Lat. 50° 51′ 50″ N., Long. 127° 37′ 30″ W.

(N. M. 3, 1905.)

Balaklava Island, has a ledge extending from it for 40

(841) **BRITISH COLUMBIA—Queen Charlotte sound—New channel—Christie passage—Balaklava island—Scarlett point—Lighthouse established.**—A lighthouse has been erected by the Government of Canada on Scarlett point, Balaklava island, northwest point of the entrance to Christie passage, and the light was put in operation on April 12, 1905, when the temporary light described in Notice to Mariners No. 3 (94) of 1905, was discontinued.

Approx. position: Lat. 50° 51′ 50″ N., Long. 127° 37′ 30″ W.

The lighthouse stands 100 feet back from the water's edge at the small depression in the eastern extremity of the point. It is a rectangular wooden building with a hip roof, surmounted by a square wooden lantern rising from the middle of the roof. The sides of the building and lantern are painted white and the roofs red. The lighthouse is 37 feet high from its base to the ventilator on the lantern.

The light is a *fixed red* light, elevated 90 feet above high-water mark and should be visible 10 miles from all points of approach by water. The illuminating apparatus is dioptric of the 7th order.

(N. M. 22, 1905.)

from the SW. entrance point of the channel. A reef of ... ground marked by kelp extends 300 yards from Balaklava Island, just opposite the above-mentioned rock, and this is the narrowest part of the channel, which is deep; a mid channel course through is free from danger. The tide is very weak in this channel.

Galiano Island, the largest of the islands on the northern side of Goletas Channel, is of triangular shape, the base fronting to the southward. The shores are very much broken along the northern and eastern sides. Port Alexander is formed at its southeastern extreme.

The southern side of Galiano Island is high, steep-to, and cliffy, trending in a straight direction to the westward; at 4½ miles west of Boxer point is a small cove, which would afford shelter to small craft from westerly winds.

Port Alexander indents the coast of Galiano Island for 1½ miles, with a general breadth of about 800 yards; there is a small islet in the middle of it, ½ mile from the entrance, and another close off Boxer Point, on the west side of entrance. This port is easy of access to steamers and sailing vessels with a fair wind, and affords good anchorage in 12 to 13 fathoms at ½ mile from its head, well sheltered from all except southeasterly winds.

but near the west e ... Nahwhitti Bar, they are much stronge ... high and low water by the shore ...

Shushartie Ba ... Channel runs in a ... where steep to. Shushartie Bay ... are high, except at the head, from which a s... than 400 yards There is a very limited but fairly she... just inside the NE point of the bay in about 13 fathoms, distance of 200 yards offshore, but from the steepness of the bank it should only be considered as a stopping place. Less water than charted was found in this bay in 1885 by the U S Coast Survey Steamer *Patterson*, the banl ...

Dillon Ro ... W of Halste ... is in the way ...

Direction ... Dillon Rock ... ernmost pea ... bearing S. 1 ... of Dillon R ... vessel will l ...

Entering ... Halstead I ...

Anchor ... bank is ste ... of the bay ... and N. 52° W ...

Shingle Point, 2 miles west of Shushartie Bay, is low; a beach runs off it a short distance; westward of this point it is difficult to land, except in fair weather.

Cape Commerell is the northernmost point of Vancouver Island. The cape is low, and some rocks extend off it for nearly 400 yards; to the eastward of it the coast forms a large bay 3 miles wide and about one mile deep, with from 2½ to 6 fathoms rocky bottom, and not in any way adapted for anchoring. The shoal part of Nahwhitti Bar, on which there is as little as 2½ fathoms, extends to the northwestward from the east point of this bay; it is marked by kelp and named Tatnall Reefs. Weser Islet, 8 feet high, lies in the western part of the bay, distant ¼ mile from the shore. There is an Indian village on the east side of the cape.

Gordon Group consists of a number of small islands, and border the north part of the east entrance of Goletas Channel. They are high and steep to, and on the eastern or Doyle Island is Miles Cone, a remarkable summit 380 feet high.

Duncan Island, one mile south of the Gordon Group, is about one mile in circumference.

Noble Islets lie 1½ miles west of Duncan Island, between which and the group it is not advisable for a large vessel to go.

Blyth Island lies ¾ mile S. 79° E. of the SE. of the Noble Islets, and 600 yards north of it is Monat Rock, with 1¼ fathoms of water over it.

Balaklava Island, ragged and irregular, with three peaks, lies between the Gordon group and Galiano Island, forming Christie and Browning Passages. A small rock 4 feet high, surrounded by kelp, lies 200 yards south of the southeastern Lucan Islands, a group of three small islets lying parallel with the southwestern shore of Balaklava Island at the distance of 250 yards. Raglan Point, the NW. point of Balaklava Island, has a ledge extending from it for 450 yards, and ½ mile N. 21° W. of the point are the Cardigan Rocks, 6 feet high, with Croker Rock 300 yards N. 69° E. of them. These rocks are surrounded by kelp.

Christie Passage is ½ mile wide; some shoal patches, with from one to 3 fathoms water on them, lie 350 yards from the eastern shore of Balaklava Island, and 1,200 to 1,400 yards S. 10° E. of Scarlett Point; between them and the island is George Island. With these exceptions the shores of the passage are free from danger. The tide runs from one to 3 knots through it, the flood to the southward.

If intending to go through this passage from Goletas Channel, a large vessel should enter it west of the Noble Islets.

Browning Passage is to the west of Balaklava Island. There are some small rocks and islets off its southeastern and northeastern points; and a rock which covers at three-quarters flood lies on the western side of the channel about 150 yards from Galiano Island, and 1,600 yards from the SW. entrance point of the channel. A reef of rocks and foul ground marked by kelp extends 300 yards from Balaklava Island, just opposite the above-mentioned rock, and this is the narrowest part of the channel, which is deep; a mid-channel course through is free from danger. The tide is very weak in this channel.

Galiano Island, the largest of the islands on the northern side of Goletas Channel, is of triangular shape, the base fronting to the southward. The shores are very much broken along the northern and eastern sides. Port Alexander is formed at its southeastern extreme.

The southern side of Galiano Island is high, steep-to, and cliffy, trending in a straight direction to the westward; at 4½ miles west of Boxer point is a small cove, which would afford shelter to small craft from westerly winds.

Port Alexander indents the coast of Galiano Island for 1½ miles, with a general breadth of about 800 yards; there is a small islet in the middle of it, ½ mile from the entrance, and another close off Boxer Point, on the west side of entrance. This port is easy of access to steamers and sailing vessels with a fair wind, and affords good anchorage in 12 to 13 fathoms at ½ mile from its head, well sheltered from all except southeasterly winds.

Shadwell Passage is between Galiano and Hope Islands; the eastern shore is straight, in a northeasterly direction, but the western is indented into several small bays, with some rocks and islets off them, and foul ground extending nearly ½ mile from the shore between Turn Point and Cape James.

The depths in the southern part of this passage are from 80 to 100 fathoms, decreasing rapidly to 9 and 13 fathoms to the northward; a vessel may anchor about 400 to 600 yards NW. of Center Island, sheltered from all except northerly winds. The tidal streams set with considerable strength (4 knots) between Center Island and Turn Point.

Vansittart Island is one mile long and ¼ mile wide, west of it are some rocks and small islets extending 1,200 yards off it; and ½ mile from the north point are two wooded islets called Nicolas Islands.

Willes Island, in the southeastern part of the passage, close to Galiano Island, is steep to, and may be approached to within a distance of 200 yards; ¼ mile to the SE. of it is a small low islet named Slave Island.

Center Island, in the middle of the passage, and ½ mile from Vansittart Island, is small; west of it some kelp extends a short distance, but there is a passage on either side of it; that to the westward, however, is much obstructed by Suwanee Rock, and it should therefore not be used.

Suwanee Rock, which dries 4 feet at low water spring tides, lies 200 yards west of the high-water mark of Center Island, rendering the passage west of that island unsafe.

One Tree Islet, 800 yards west of Vansittart, is small, and has a single tree on its summit, which is very conspicuous when seen from the northward, and of great use in identifying the passage, this islet may be approached close to on the western side, but between it and Vansittart are rocks and foul ground. A dry rock lies about 100 yards west of the islet.

Breaker Reef, the outer of the dangers extending to the NW. from Vansittart Island, lies ½ mile N. 4° E. of One Tree Islet.

Turn Point—The southwestern headland of the passage, Heath Point, is rocky, fringed with kelp, and presents a cliffy appearance. Turn Point lies 2 miles NE. of Heath Point, about midway between it and Cape James, it is backed by a summit 300 feet high. Halfway between Heath and Turn Points is Quoin Islet, about 300 yards offshore.

Cape James is a rocky bluff 90 feet high; some rocks extend off it to the southward for a short distance, and foul ground, marked by kelp, exists between it and Turn Point. The cape should at all times be given a berth of at least ½ mile.

Tides.—The flood tide runs to the southward through Shadwell Passage at the rate of about 4½ knots, whilst the ebb, in the northern part, sets 2 knots in the contrary direction: to the southward of Center

Island, however, it runs as strong as the flood. Tide rips exist between Center and Vansittart Islands.

Directions.—Bound through Shadwell Passage to the northward, round Willes Island at about 100 or 400 yards distance, when abreast Turn Point, steer to pass about 200 yards off the east side of Center Island and 400 yards west of One Tree Islet, keeping the south peak of Magin Saddle (on the west end of Galiano Island) in line with the east end of Center Island bearing south, which leads through the northern entrance of Shadwell Passage.

Shadwell Passage may be used by steamers or sailing vessels with a fair wind; it would hardly be prudent to beat a large vessel through it, as there is generally a heavy swell and strong tide in the northern part.

Bate Passage, to the eastward of Vansittart Island, is deeper and nearly straight; if proceeding through it, keep in mid channel. Vessels that do not steer well are recommended to use Bate Passage instead of Shadwell Passage.

Anchorage.—The best anchorage in Shadwell Passage is near the middle, with One Tree Islet bearing N 58° E, and Center Island south.

Hope Island is moderately high, and its shores are very much broken, the sea breaks heavily along its northern and western sides, and off Mexicana Point, the western extreme, a reef extends 600 yards; the southern shore is steep, and may be approached to ¼ mile.

Bull Harbor has its entrance 2 miles from the western entrance of Goletas Channel. Though small, this harbor affords a very secure landlocked anchorage. It runs in a northerly direction for 1½ miles across Hope Island. The harbor ½ mile wide at the entrance, is contracted to 200 yards at half the distance from the head, after which it increases to nearly 400 yards.

Indian Island, 300 yards north of the narrowest part of the entrance, is small, but completely shuts in the harbor to the southward, leaving a passage to it on the eastern side 200 yards wide; between the island and the west shore there is only a depth of 11 feet.

Directions.—If intending to enter Bull Harbor, steer up in mid-channel, passing east of Indian Island, and moor immediately the vessel is north of it, anchors north and south. Only steamers or small sailing vessels should use this anchorage, as from its narrow and tortuous entrance it is rather difficult of access to long vessels.

Anchorage.—The anchorage is to the northward of Indian Island, in about 4 fathoms water, but there is only room for one or two vessels of moderate size to lie moored.

Westward of Bull Harbor the coast of Hope Island is rocky and edged by kelp; the sea in westerly winds breaks heavily along it.

Nahwhitti Bar, or ledge, stretching across the west entrance of the Goletas Channel, is of sandstone formation, and on the eastern edge rises suddenly from 40 to 9 fathoms, the depth increasing very grad nally to the westward. Its breadth within the 10 fathom line is from one to nearly 3 miles, it being broadest at the south part, where are several shoal spots. On the western edge of the bar the tide runs from 2 to 5 knots.

Tatnall Reefs, with 2½ and 3½ fathoms on them, lie on the bar 1¼ miles from the south shore; northward of these patches the depths vary from 6 to 9 fathoms. In heavy westerly gales the sea breaks right across the Goletas Channel at this bar.

Leading Mark.—Boxer Point (the SE. point of Galiano Island), open north of Shingle Point (Vancouver Island), bearing S. 74° E. leads over the Nahwhitti Bar in the deepest water well to the northward of Tatnall Reefs.

Directions.—Bound to the westward through Goletas Channel, steer in mid channel, or within ½ mile of either shore, until west of Bull Harbor, after which keep Boxer Point open north of Shingle Point bearing S. 74° E, until Mexicana Point bears N 21° E., when a vessel will be to the westward of the Nahwhitti Bar. A sailing ship, if beating through the channel, should keep south of Duncan and Noble Islands elsewhere, until west of Bull Harbor, the shores on both sides may be approached to within ¼ mile; when standing to the southward, west of Bull Harbor, tack when Shingle and Lemon Points are in line, and do not approach nearer than ½ mile towards Mexicana Point, as there is generally a heavy swell setting in on it, and the ground is uneven.

When crossing the bar in the deepest water, if the weather be clear, Mount Lemon, a high conical peak, should appear nearly midway between Shingle Point and Heath Point on the opposite shore, or nothing to the southward of midway between them

If obliged to anchor for the night or tide, Shushartie Bay, though small, is easy of access, the only danger being the Dillon Rock off its east point. Port Alexander and Shadwell Passage are also, with a fair wind, easy of access to sailing vessels, and the latter is preferable, being more roomy with better holding ground.

New Channel is an extensive clear passage to the Pacific Ocean. Its depth in the shoalest part is 55 fathoms, near the eastern entrance, and its shores, except near the western part of the Gordon Group, may be approached to within nearly ½ mile, the northern limit of the channel is formed by Walker Group to the eastward, and a few low rocks and islets to the NW

Generally a heavy swell sets through New Channel from the westward, and with the exception that there is more room for a large vessel to work in or out than in Goletas Channel, there is no reason to use it in preference to the latter, unless, if running in before a heavy westerly gale, the sea were breaking across the west entrance of Goletas Channel at the Nahwhitti Bar

Doyle Island, the southeasternmost of the Gordon Group and at the SE. point of New Channel, is ¾ mile long There are some small islets off its east point. The northern side of the Gordon Group to Crane Islets is steep-to, and may be approached to ¼ mile.

Crane Islets are small and steep to, there being 100 fathoms water at 200 yards' distance. They lie about 600 yards north of Gordon Group.

Boyle Island, ½ mile north of Hurst Island, is small.

Grey Rock, which covers at one quarter flood, lies ½ mile NW. of Boyle Island, and is dangerous to vessels beating through this channel. The best mark to clear this rock, is to keep the Crane Islets just touching the north side of Gordon group bearing S 46° E. which leads nearly ¼ mile north of it; when Boyle Island bears S. 21° W. a vessel will be clear east of it, and when the SW. and NE. points of Christie passage come open bearing S. 27° W., she will be clear to the NW. of it.

The Coast.—The north shore of Balaklava Island is rugged, and ½ mile N. 21° W. from its NW. point are three low islets (Cardigan Rocks), 6 feet above high water, at the north entrance to Browning channel.

The north shore of Galiano Island is also rugged; some outlying rocks lie a short distance off it, but it may be approached to ¼ mile.

Westward of Cape James, the NE. point of Hope Island, the shore is generally rocky, and the sea breaks heavily along it, do not approach it within ½ mile.

Walker Group is composed of two large islands and several small islets and rocks; among them are several small creeks and bights, which would afford shelter to boats, or even small craft; along their south side some rocks extend a short distance off.

Castle Point, at the east extreme of the group, is bold, cliffy, and steep to.

White Rock lies 2 miles west of Castle Point, it is 4 feet above high water, and there are 10 fathoms 100 yards south of it. Between White Rock and Boyle Island a strong tide race usually prevails.

Ragged Reef, a cluster of rocks 4 feet high, lies 1,200 yards to the northward of the west end of Kent Island.

Nye Rock, off the south end of Schooner Passage, at the west part of the group, covers at high water; it lies 2¼ miles N. 60° W of White Rock, and may be approached to within a distance of 400 yards on the south side, but large vessels should not stand inside it to the northward.

Redfern Island, is the southwestern of the Walker group; ½ mile SE. of it are some rocks just above high water, as also to the NW.

Hedley Islands are a group of small rocks lying in mid channel between Kent and Staples Islands and Redfern Island; a reef which covers at high water lies 800 yards to the eastward of them, and 1,200 yards from the south side of Kent Island. Schooner Passage, not recommended, lies between Hedley and Kent Islands.

Prosser Rock, two miles N. 46° W. of Redfern Island, is small, about two feet above high water, and may be approached to within a distance of 400 yards

Bright Islet, nearly one mile farther in the same direction, is 100 feet high; ½ mile N. 58° E of it is a reef which covers at high water, and one mile S 83° E. lies Herbert Island, with a reef lying between.

Pine Island, at the NW. part of New Channel, about one mile in circumference, bold, wooded, and about 250 feet high, is conspicuous from the westward.

Tree Islets, some small islets, which are also wooded, lie ½ mile N 69° E. of Pine Island

Storm Islands, in the center of Queen Charlotte Sound, 2½ miles northward of Pine Island, are a narrow chain of islets, and form a most useful landmark when crossing Queen Charlotte Sound. The tops of the trees are about 150 to 200 feet above high water. and on the western part is a single tree which is conspicuous. There are no off lying dangers beyond 600 yards. An Indian fishing village is situated on one of the group, near the east end. Water may be obtained here.

Reid Island, the easternmost of the Storm Islands, on the north side of Sealed Passage, is about 300 yards long east and west, 150 yards broad, having a rock above water 100 yards off its west end.

Naiad Islet is bare, it lies ½ mile northward of Reid Island

Sunken Rock, on which the sea breaks in bad weather, lies about 5 miles N 69° E of Shadwell Passage; from the center of the Rock, Bright Island bears S. 32° E, 1½ miles, and Pine Island N. 66° W., 1½ miles

Sealed Passage, 5 miles to the northward of Shadwell Passage, between Pine Island and the Storm Islands, is about 2½ miles wide. This passage should not be attempted

Blind Reef, on which the sea breaks in heavy weather, extends nearly across Sealed Passage, and closes it to navigation; close to the western edge of Blind Reef there are 17 to 40 fathoms, rocky bottom.

South Rock, awash at low water, lies about 1¼ miles northeastward of Blind Reef; from the center of this rock Pine Island bears S. 58° W., 3¼ miles nearly, and Reid Island N. 63° W., 1¾ miles

Middle Rock, on which the sea nearly always breaks, is covered at three quarters flood, and lies one mile N. 13° E of South Rock.

North Rock, on which the sea nearly always breaks, is awash at high water, and lies N. 69° E., ¾ mile nearly from Middle Rock Harris Islet, a little open south of Jeanette Island, bearing S 49° E, leads ½ mile to the northward of North Rock.

Directions—If using the new channel, and the wind be fair, a mid-channel course about N. 55° W will take vessels clear. If working through, when between the Walker and Gordon Group, keep ¼ to ½ mile south of the southern shores of the former, and on nearing the Grey Rock, when standing towards the southern shore, avoid opening the southern part of Crane Islets north of the Gordon group S. 46° E., until the eastern and western points of Christie Passage come open bearing S. 27° W., or the eastern edge of Redfern bears N. 4° W., when a vessel will be clear to the westward of the rock; and if going east, when Boyle Islet bears S. 24° W., she will be east of it. In the vicinity of the Galiano and Hope Islands, tack about ½ mile off shore, and keep outside Shadwell Passage and Roller Bay; when west of Pine Island, do not bring it to bear east of S. 77° E.

The Coast from Cape Commerell takes a southwesterly direction for 16 miles to Cape Scott. It is rather low, but rises at a distance inland to hills 800 and 1,000 feet high; it is indented by several bays, which, however, are too open to afford any shelter, except in southerly winds; foul ground extends off in some places more than one mile.

Hecate Rock, lying 1½ miles N. 77° W. of Cape Commerell, and ¾ of a mile off shore, covers at three-quarters flood, and the sea breaks heavily over it. Lemon Point (Galiano Island), just open of or touching Shingle Point (Vancouver Island), bearing S. 77° E., leads north of it.

Cape Scott, the extreme NW. point of Vancouver Island, is a small promontory about 500 feet high, connected to the island by a low sandy neck about 200 yards wide; some rocks extend west from it for more than ½ mile.

Shelter.—There is a bay on both sides of the neck, which would afford anchorage to boats or small craft in fine weather only; close to its SW. extreme is a small creek among the rocks, difficult of access, but, once within it, boats may obtain shelter in southerly gales; unless acquainted with the locality, it would not be prudent to make for it in bad weather.

At Cape Scott the flood comes from the southward, and rounding the cape sets into the Goletas Channel, its strength varying from one to 3 knots.

When navigating between Cape Commerell and Cape Scott, do not approach the shore within 1½ miles, at which distance there are depths of from 16 to 20 fathoms.

Scott Channel, between Cape Scott and Cox Island, is a safe navigable channel for any class of vessel, the only known dangers in it being the rocks extending nearly one mile west from Cape Scott; the tide runs through from one to 3 knots, the flood from the southward. There are some heavy tide rips near its east and west sides, but a large vessel may beat through with safety, tacking when upwards of one mile off Cape Scott, or ½ mile of Cox Island.

Scott Islands, 5 in number, with some adjacent smaller islets, extend nearly 20 miles in a westerly direction from Cape Scott. There are wide passages between the western islands, but as no soundings have been obtained in them, and strong tide rips and overfalls have invariably been observed raging there, no vessel should venture among or through them, unless compelled to do so.

Westward of Cape Scott the tides set with considerable strength to the north and south across the entrance to Goletas Channel, and a vessel passing out northward of the Scott Islands must beware that she is not set down too near them with the ebb stream.

Cox Island, the easternmost and largest of the group, has iron-bound rocky shores and several off-lying dangers.

Lanz Island is separated from Cox Island by a passage ½ mile wide; its shores, like Cox Island, are rocky, and it rises near the center to a summit 1,177 feet above the sea; both the islands are wooded.

There are 17 fathoms in the passage between Cox and Lanz Islands, and in fine weather with southerly winds a vessel may drop an anchor northward of the former island in 14 fathoms, but at all times it is a neighborhood to be avoided.

East Haycock, a small islet, has a rugged outline, and is covered with a few stunted trees. Some small islets extend a short distance NW. of it.

West Haycock, is small and rocky. Some small islets extend upwards of one mile southwestward of it; foul ground existing around them for ½ a mile.

Triangle Island, the westernmost of the group, 25 miles N. 77° W. of cape Scott, is about one mile in extent, and differs from the other islands in being very precipitous and bare of trees, and has a remarkable gap in its summit; a ledge or reef extends one mile NW. from it; to the eastward are three low islets, the outermost of which, 40 feet high, is 1¾ miles from Triangle Island.

When navigating near the Scott Islands, it is recommended to give them a good offing, especially in a sailing vessel, as the tides set very strongly through the passages between them.

Navigation.—For steamers, the navigation of the inner waters between Cape Mudge and the Pacific is very simple, the only caution required being to steer mid-channel; if the weather be fine, except in the vicinity of the Nimpkish River, Helmcken Island, and Seymour Narrows, these waters may be navigated as well by night as during the day, the shores being so high on either side as to be easily defined.

If in a sailing vessel, unless the wind be fair and likely to remain so, it would be preferable to anchor for the night, as the wind usually falls after sunset, especially during summer months.

Inner passage to Alaska.—Steamers running on summer excursions through the inland waters of Alaska as far as Glacier Bay always use the main channel of Haro Strait to reach the Gulf of Georgia. Seymour Narrows, in Discovery Passage, should not be attempted except at slack water. Broughton Strait is generally used, and is recommended as the safest. After passing through this strait keep the Vancouver shore aboard, follow Goletas Channel, and enter Queen Charlotte Sound by way of Christie Pass, which is said to be safe at all times and at all stages of the tide. Issuing from Christie Pass a straight course is laid for Pine Island, which is left to the eastward, thence for Egg Island, which is also left to the eastward, and thence the course is laid for Cape Calvert.

The inner passage is always to be preferred, for the reason that in winter there is less inconvenience from SE and SW. gales, and in summer the fogs and high NW. winds are partly avoided.

Water is generally so plentiful that at every valley or beach a stream will be found.

Supplies.—The natives will generally bring alongside deer, grouse, salmon, rock, cod and other fish in moderate quantities, selling them at reasonable prices. Blankets, shirts of the most common description, knives, beads, powder, shot, tobacco and red paint are very useful to barter with. To men-of-war they are usually very civil, but crews of coasters and merchant vessels should watch them vigilantly, as they are cunning and treacherous (especially near the northern parts of Vancouver Island), and have captured several small coasters.

CHAPTER VII.

WEST COAST OF VANCOUVER ISLAND, FROM THE STRAIT OF JUAN DE FUCA TO CAPE SCOTT.

General description of the outer or western coast.—The general direction is NW. and SE., but the coast is broken into deep inlets, the principal of which, Barclay, Clayoqnot, Nootka, Kyuquot and Quatsino Sounds, are large sheets of water, with features similar to the other great inlets on this part of the American continent.

Making the land.—When first making the land an unbroken range of mountains will be seen; on a nearer approach it appears thickly wooded and apparently fertile, intersected with many deep openings and valleys. The coast is mostly low and rocky, but rises immediately to mountains of considerable height. It is fringed by numerous rocks and hidden dangers, especially near the entrances of the sounds, and the exercise of great caution and vigilance will be necessary on the part of the navigator to avoid them. Strangers should not attempt to enter any of the harbors or anchorages during night or thick weather, but rather keep a good offing until circumstances are favorable; and when about to make the coast, it can not be too strongly impressed on the mariner to take every opportunity of ascertaining his vessel's position by astronomical observations, as fogs and thick weather come on very suddenly at all times of the year, more especially in summer and autumn months. The current generally sets to the SE. across the entrance to Juan de Fuca Strait. The use of the lead is strictly enjoined.

Tides.—All along the outer or west coast of Vancouver Island it may be said to be high water at full and change when the moon crosses the meridian, viz, at noon and midnight, the tide showing considerable regularity as compared with the inner waters, the greatest rise and fall being everywhere about 12 feet. There are two high and low waters in the 24 hours all the year round. In summer months the superior high water is at midnight, and in winter months at noon.

The flood stream appears to set along the coast to the NW., and the ebb to the SE.; neither are of great strength, except in the vicinity of Fuca Strait and the Scott Islands. In summer months a set is generally found to the southward and in winter in the opposite direction, but as a rule the currents are irregular, and apparently influenced by prevailing winds.

Soundings.—At the entrance of Fuca Strait the 100 fathom edge of the bank extends 40 miles offshore; it then runs in nearly a straight direction, gradually nearing the coast, and abreast Cape Cook or Woody Point the depth of 100 fathoms will be obtained within 4 miles of the shore; to the NW. of Woody Point the 100-fathom edge does not extend more than 10 miles offshore, and to the southward and westward of the Scott Islands even less.

The nature of the bottom, when under 100 fathoms, appears to be generally composed of sand and gravel, and does not differ in one part from another sufficiently to afford any guide for ascertaining a vessel's exact position on the coast; the bank, however, extends far enough offshore to the SE. of Cape Cook to enable the mariner making the coast in thick weather, by sounding in time, to get due notice of his approach to the land, as the edge of 100 fathoms does not come within 18 miles of it, and the bank shoals very gradually.

Climate and Winds—The seasons, wet and dry, generally take the following course After the gales with rain, which usually occur about the time of the equinox, fine clear weather sets in, and continues until about the middle of November. At this period rain begins to fall continuously for days, and gales of wind are frequent on the coast.

The barometer ranges from 29 50 to 30 10 and falls rapidly on the approach of a southerly gale. Rising gradually to 30.20 and 30.50, a northerly wind springs up, and 3 days of fine clear weather with hoar frost generally follow. After the third day the barometer slowly falls, and again the gale with rain springs up, to be succeeded after a few days by a rising barometer and frosty weather, which, as the season advances, occasionally becomes intense, and is accompanied by hail and snow; the latter seldom lasts for any length of time. The summer is dry, with a most scorching sun. Little or no rain falls from the middle of April until the equinox The prevailing winds during these summer months are from SW. to NW., blowing freshly during the day, the nights are calm and clear. Northerly winds occasionally prevail, and in the southern parts of the island are hot and dry

Natives.—The west coast of the island is very thinly populated, the highest estimate of the natives not exceeding 4,000, divided into a number of very small tribes. As a rule they are harmless and inoffensive, though in a few cases the crews of vessels wrecked on their coasts have been plundered and ill treated. They are addicted to pilfering, especially in the vicinity of Nootka Sound, and ought to be carefully watched.

The tribes speak different dialects, and the Chinook jargon, which is used at Victoria in transactions with the settlers and natives, will not be generally understood on the west coast.

Supplies.—The natives live principally on fish, potatoes, and berries. Fish, salmon, halibut, rock cod, herring, and hoolican, the latter somewhat resembling a sardine, are found in great abundance. Deer, grouse, and wild fowl are also to be had, but they are not by any means so plentiful as along the northeastern coast of the island.

Trade.—Furs and fish oil are the only articles of trade with the natives, and the quantity small.

At the Alberni Inlet in Barclay Sound a large sawmill was established in 1860 by an English company, and a considerable lumber trade was carried on.

At Forward Inlet and Coal Harbor, in Quatsino Sound, seams of coal of considerable thickness have been seen, and there is no doubt that a quantity of that valuable article is to be met with in the northwestern part of the island.

Indications of copper and iron are also plentiful, especially in Barclay Sound. In Port San Juan, and in the Muchalat or Guaguma arm of Nootka Sound, some traces of gold have been met with.

The Coast from Port San Juan trends 10 miles in a westerly direction to Bonilla Point, rising gradually to elevations from 1,000 to 2,000 feet. Bonilla Point slopes gradually to the sea, is not in anyway remarkable, and may be approached within one mile; to the westward of it the coast becomes more broken, still keeping a westerly direction, being high a short distance inland.

Nitinat Lake, the entrance to which is narrow and shoal, is of considerable size, extending to the northward. There are only one to 2 fathoms in the entrance, and the sea generally breaks heavily across it in bad weather. Four miles to the westward of the entrance is a remarkable waterfall, called by the natives Tsusiat, which may be seen at a good distance, even in thick weather, when it would help to identify a vessel's position, being the only waterfall on this part of the coast.

Pachena Bay is nearly 2 miles deep and ½ mile wide, with from 5 to 6 fathoms water, but as it is open to the southwestward, and there is usually a heavy swell setting into it, no vessel should anchor there. At its head, on the west side, is a stream where boats can get in and find shelter in bad weather.

Sea-Bird Islet, off the entrance of the bay, is bare, about 10 feet above water, and of small extent.

A rock which does not uncover lies ½ mile S. 68° W. of Sea-Bird Islet, also at ¼ mile S. 50° E. of the islet there is a similar rock that breaks at very low tides. Sea-Bird Islet should not be approached within 1½ miles.

The coast between Pachena Bay and the SE. point of entrance of Barclay Sound, a distance of 3 miles, is rocky, forming an open bay that affords no shelter.

The soundings between Port San Juan and Barclay Sound, at a distance of 2 miles offshore, vary from 50 to 18 fathoms, shoaling when to the westward of Nitinat Lake, 10 miles to the southward of which will be found less than 50 fathoms.

Barclay Sound is upwards of 14 miles wide at its entrance, and [illegible] dth for lets or e, and slands, e used in the d, and mountainous.

Soundings —A bank of sand and gravel, with depths from 25 to 45 fathoms, extends 40 or 45 miles to the southward and westward of the entrance of Barclay Sound. In the middle of this bank is a deep hole the east part of which is 5 miles SW. of the entrance; from thence the hole extends 19 miles in a westerly direction, with depths varying from 60 to 100 fathoms, so that if steering for Barclay Sound from the SW., and the weather be thick, by attention to soundings a vessel might ascertain her position within a few miles. To the SE. of the entrance the water becomes deeper, and at a distance of 10 miles offshore there are 60 to 70 fathoms, sand and mud.

The Eastern Channel is on the southeastern side of the sound, between the main shore and Deer Islands. Its shores are low and rugged, except in the northern part, where they become high. There are several dangers within it, viz, the rocks off Cape Beale and Channel Rocks at the southern part, and the Fog Rock off Tzaartoos Island.

Cape Beale, the southeastern entrance point of Barclay Sound and of the Eastern Channel, is a bold rocky point, 120 feet high (the tops of the trees being 300 feet above high water), and some rocks extend off it from 400 to 800 yards

Light —On a small islet at the extremity of Cape Beale is a square light-house.

Caution —The light house should not be brought to bear eastward of S. 73° E. so as to avoid the foul ground which extends off the entrances to Barclay Sound.

Bamfield Creek —At 4 miles from Cape Beale, on the east side of the channel, is the entrance to two creeks. the southern of which is Bamfield. There is room for a vessel to moor at a short distance from its head in 6 fathoms. A narrow passage, 30 yards wide, with 6 feet at low water, runs from the head to an inner basin, which is one mile long, and has from 2 to 4 fathoms.

Grappler Creek, the northern arm, extends ⅔ mile to the southeastward, it is about 40 yards wide, with from 8 to 10 fathoms; it then takes a northerly direction and becomes very shoal. Both these creeks afford good sheltered anchorage to small craft

Kelp Bay, 5¾ miles from Cape Beale, affords a fairly sheltered anchorage in from 6 to 14 fathoms. Its shores are low, and a rock which covers at one-third flood lies 200 yards north of its southern entrance

and wild fowl are also to be had, but they are not by any means so plen-

(2006) **BRITISH COLUMBIA—Vancouver Island—South coast—Clo-oose village—Information.**—The village and Methodist mission of Clo-oose is situated in the small cove between the mouth of Chuck-wear river and the outlet of Nitinat lake, in (approximately) latitude 48° 40′ 22″ N., longitude 124° 50′ 00″ W.

The village is connected with the Government telegraph line to Victoria and by telephone with Carmanah lighthouse Shipwrecked mariners can get shelter and assistance here (N M 49, 1905)

of considerable thickness have been seen, and there is no doubt that a quantity of that valuable article is to be met with in the northwestern part of the island.

Indications of copper and iron are also plentiful, especially in Barclay Sound. In Port San Juan, and in the Muchalat or Guaguma arm of Nootka Sound, some traces of gold have been met with.

The Coast from Port San Juan trends 10 miles in a westerly direction to Bonilla Point, rising gradually to elevations from 1,000 to 2,000 feet. Bonilla Point slopes gradually to the sea, is not in anyway remarkable, and may be approached within one mile; to the westward of it the coast becomes more broken, still keeping a westerly direction, being high a short distance inland.

Nitinat Lake, the entrance to which is narrow and shoal, is of considerable size, extending to the northward. There are only one to 2 fathoms in the entrance, and the sea generally breaks heavily across it in bad weather. Four miles to the westward of the entrance is a remarkable waterfall, called by the natives Tsusiat, which may be seen at a good distance, even in thick weather, when it would help to identify a vessel's position, being the only waterfall on this part of the coast

Pachena Bay is nearly 2 miles deep and ½ mile wide, with from 5 to 6 fathoms water, but as it is open to the southwestward, and there is usually a heavy swell setting into it, no vessel should anchor there. At its head, on the west side, is a stream where boats can get in and find shelter in bad weather.

Sea-Bird Islet, off the entrance of the bay, is bare, about 10 feet above water, and of small extent.

A rock which does not uncover lies ½ mile S. 68° W. of Sea-Bird Islet, also at ⅛ mile S 50° E. of the islet there is a similar rock that breaks at very low tides. Sea-Bird Islet should not be approached within 1½ miles

The coast between Pachena Bay and the SE. point of entrance of Barclay Sound, a distance of 3 miles, is rocky, forming an open bay that affords no shelter.

The soundings between Port San Juan and Barclay Sound, at a distance of 2 miles offshore, vary from 50 to 18 fathoms, shoaling when to the westward of Nitinat Lake, 10 miles to the southward of which will be found less than 50 fathoms.

Barclay Sound is upwards of 14 miles wide at its entrance, and though encumbered by numerous islands it maintains this breadth for nearly 12 miles inland, when it separates into several narrow inlets or canals, the principal of which is Alberni Inlet. Off the entrance, and in the southern parts of the sound, are innumerable rocks and islands, with several navigable channels between them, which ought to be used with great caution by strangers. The shores are low, except in the northern part among the canals, where they become high, rugged, and mountainous.

Soundings.—A bank of sand and gravel, with depths from 25 to 45 fathoms, extends 40 or 45 miles to the southward and westward of the entrance of Barclay Sound. In the middle of this bank is a deep hole the east part of which is 5 miles SW. of the entrance; from thence the hole extends 19 miles in a westerly direction, with depths varying from 60 to 100 fathoms, so that if steering for Barclay Sound from the SW., and the weather be thick, by attention to soundings a vessel might ascertain her position within a few miles. To the SE. of the entrance the water becomes deeper, and at a distance of 10 miles offshore there are 60 to 70 fathoms, sand and mud.

The Eastern Channel is on the southeastern side of the sound, between the main shore and Deer Islands. Its shores are low and rugged, except in the northern part, where they become high. There are several dangers within it, viz, the rocks off Cape Beale and Channel Rocks at the southern part, and the Fog Rock off Tzaartoos Island.

Cape Beale, the southeastern entrance point of Barclay Sound and of the Eastern Channel, is a bold rocky point, 120 feet high (the tops of the trees being 300 feet above high water), and some rocks extend off it from 400 to 800 yards.

Light.—On a small islet at the extremity of Cape Beale is a square light-house.

Caution.—The light-house should not be brought to bear eastward of S. 73° E. so as to avoid the foul ground which extends off the entrances to Barclay Sound.

Bamfield Creek.—At 4 miles from Cape Beale, on the east side of the channel, is the entrance to two creeks, the southern of which is Bamfield. There is room for a vessel to moor at a short distance from its head in 6 fathoms. A narrow passage, 30 yards wide, with 6 feet at low water, runs from the head to an inner basin, which is one mile long, and has from 2 to 4 fathoms.

Grappler Creek, the northern arm, extends $\frac{3}{8}$ mile to the southeastward; it is about 40 yards wide, with from 8 to 10 fathoms; it then takes a northerly direction and becomes very shoal. Both these creeks afford good sheltered anchorage to small craft.

Kelp Bay, $5\frac{3}{4}$ miles from Cape Beale, affords a fairly sheltered anchorage in from 6 to 14 fathoms. Its shores are low, and a rock which covers at one-third flood lies 200 yards north of its southern entrance point, and there is a small islet at its north point, which shows a conspicuous white mark; foul ground, marked by kelp, exists in the northern part of the bay.

If intending to anchor in this bay give the entrance points a berth of 400 yards, and anchor in its southern part in 6 to 11 fathoms, with the entrance points bearing S. 70° W. and N. 34° E. This anchorage is easy of access, but the bottom is irregular.

Mark Islet, 8 miles from Cape Beale, and 200 yards off the eastern side of the channel, is small and wooded, and conspicuous from the entrance of the Middle Channel; the shore between it and Kelp Bay runs nearly straight, and may be approached to within a distance of 400 yards.

Numukamis Bay, in the northeastern part of the Eastern Channel, is of an oblong shape; its shores rise gradually to mountains. From the center of its head the Sarita Valley extends away to the eastward, a stream of considerable size flowing from it into the bay. In the center of the bay are the San Jose and Reef Islets, of small extent, and low; from the south point of the latter islet a reef extends 200 yards.

The depths in Numukamis Bay are great, and there is no anchorage except in Christie Bay. The shores are steep-to, except off Sarita Valley, where a sand bank extends out ½ mile

Poett Nook, in the southern part of this bay, is a landlocked basin. The entrance to it is nearly straight, 200 yards long and 150 feet wide, with 7 fathoms in the shoalest part; it is difficult for large vessels to enter unless they warp in.

There are three small creeks on the north side of Numukamis Bay, but the water is too deep for anchorage.

Turn Island, at the northeastern point of the Eastern Channel, is small and wooded, and separated by a narrow boat pass from the east shore. At ½ mile south of it is a narrow creek, with from 9 to 12 fathoms, available for small craft.

Ship Islet, at the southwestern point of the Eastern Channel, is rocky, with a few remarkable trees on its northern part, which at some distance seaward give the islet the appearance of a ship under sail, forming a good mark for identifying the channel; there are depths of from 23 to 24 fathoms at 400 yards from it.

Deer Islands extend in a NE. and SW. direction for 10 miles They are low, and of inconsiderable size, except Tzaartoos Island There is only one navigable passage through them, the Satellite Pass, between Helby and Hill Islands.

King Island, the southernmost, is rugged and broken, with rocks extending from 200 to 400 yards off. This island is separated from Ship Islet by a passage ¼ mile wide, but there is a rock in the middle of it, which is awash at high water.

Channel Rocks, on the western side of the channel, 600 yards east of King Island, are about 200 yards in extent, and cover at half flood;

there are 10 to 12 fathoms 200 yards to the eastward of them, and upon them the sea generally breaks.

Leading Mark—Turn Island, at the northeastern point of the Eastern Channel, shut in by Leading Bluff of Tzaartoos Island bearing N. 43° E., leads east of the Channel Rocks, and west of the rocks off Cape Beale.

Diana Island, separated from King Island by a passage full of rocks, is of triangular shape; its shores are rocky. Taylor Islet lies 600 yards S. 51° W. of its SE point

Todd Rock lies 400 yards from the eastern side of Diana Island. The rock is awash at high water, with 16 fathoms close to it.

Helby Island, Entrance Anchorage The next island northward of Diana, has off its northern side a small but well sheltered anchorage in from 6 to 9 fathoms, easy of access from either the Eastern or Middle Channels, and very convenient as a stopping place for vessels entering or leaving Barclay Sound.

Wizard Islet, northeastward of the anchorage, is small, about 8 feet high and bare It is about 800 yards from Helby Island, and vessels intending to anchor should do so about 200 yards SW. of the islet in 6 fathoms.

Hill Island, separated from Helby Island by the Satellite Pass, is small, with a summit of moderate height at its southern end. At ¼ mile southward of it is a patch of 3½ fathoms, marked by kelp, and there are several small islets and rocks off its eastern and western sides.

Robbers Island, separated from Hill Island by a passage full of rocks, is one mile broad at its widest part. It is low, and steep to on the eastern side, and between it and Tzaartoos Island is a small landlocked basin of 5 to 7 fathoms water, but almost inaccessible in consequence of the many rocks at its entrance.

Tzaartoos or Copper Island is higher than the other islands, its eastern side, except in the vicinity of Sproat Bay, is steep to, and may be approached to within a distance of 400 yards Limestone of a fine quality is to be found in its northern part, and there are several indications of copper and iron ores.

Sproat Bay, on the southeastern side of Tzaartoos Island, is about ½ mile wide and 400 yards deep. In its center are two small islets. and between them and the southern side of the bay a vessel may anchor in from 11 to 15 fathoms.

Leading Bluff, just south of the bay, is a steep point and conspicuous from the entrance of the Eastern Channel.

Fog Rock, lying about 400 yards east of Sproat Bay, is of small extent, with only 9 feet over it, and steep to all round. This danger is in the track of vessels using Sproat Bay, and requires caution to avoid it, not being marked by kelp in the spring.

The east side of Robbers Island open of Leading Bluff bearing S.

62° W. leads SE of Fog Rock, and the west side of Knob Point well open east of Limestone Point N. 20° E. leads east of it.

Knob Point, the southwestern entrance point of Alberni Inlet, is about ½ mile to the northward of Tzaartoos Island. It is a remarkably cliffy projecting point, steep to on its southern and eastern sides.

Alberni Inlet runs in a winding northerly direction for 22 miles, with a breadth varying from 400 yards to one mile, and terminates in a fine capacious anchorage at its head; the shores on either side are rocky and rugged, rising abruptly from the sea to mountains 2,000 and 3,000 feet high; at the head, however, the land becomes low and fertile, a large extent being fit for cultivation. A settlement and large sawmills are established there, and quantities of timber exported. There is also a salmon fishery.

The depths to within one mile of the head vary from 160 to 40 fathoms, and the shores of the inlet are everywhere free from danger.

San Maeto Bay is on the east side of the inlet, just within the entrance; its shores are high, and it is too deep for anchorage.

Mutine Point, midway between this bay and Turn Island, is rocky, and as at a short distance off it a rock is said to exist, a berth of 400 yards should be given in passing. Just south of this point is a small bay with irregular soundings.

Uchucklesit Harbor, on the west side of Alberni Inlet, 3 miles within Knob Point, is 3 miles long in a northwesterly direction, and its average breadth is about ½ mile; the north shore is high, rising gradually to mountains, but the south shores and head are low; all are free from danger at a distance of 200 yards There are two secure anchorages, Green Cove at the entrance, and Snug Basin at the head Limestone of a very fine quality is to be procured at the head of the harbor.

Green Cove, just within the entrance, affords a snug, well sheltered anchorage. Harbor Island, off its south side, and completely landlocking the anchorage in that direction, is of small extent, with a clear deep passage on each side into the anchorage, a rock lies 100 yards off its southeastern point.

This anchorage is convenient as a stopping place for vessels bound to or from Stamp Harbor at the head of Alberni Inlet, and the entrances to it, on either side of Harbor Island, make it available for sailing vessels or steamers

Steamer Passage, on the east side of Harbor Island, is 400 yards long and about 150 yards wide in the narrowest part, with not less than 9 fathoms, but it should only be used by steam vessels, or sailing ships with a fair wind.

Ship Passage, north of Harbor Island, is 800 yards long, and 400 yards wide, and is clear of danger.

Snug Basin, at the head of Uchucklesit Harbor, is ½ mile long and about 400 yards broad, is well adapted for refitting or repairing a ship, and affords anchorage in 12 to 14 fathoms; but the entrance, though deep, is only 150 feet wide.

Water.—On the north shore, one mile from Green Cove, is a large stream of fresh water, with a bank extending a short distance off it.

Nahmint Bay, on the west side of Alberni Inlet, 10 miles within its entrance, is about ½ mile in extent and deep.

The First Narrows are 600 yards wide at low water and are steep to on the western side. If passing through them at high water, keep well over to the western shore

The Second Narrows are 400 yards wide at low water, steep to on the eastern side; the western side dries out 200 yards at low water. In going through them a vessel should keep well over on the eastern side.

Stamp Harbor, at the head of the inlet, is a large and secure anchorage Its western shore is high and rocky, but the eastern side and head are low and fertile, with a quantity of clear level land. The Somass River, a stream of considerable size, flows into the head of the harbor and is navigable for canoes several miles; it has its source in a chain of extensive lakes in the interior of Vancouver Island, and the quantity of water discharged from it is so great that there is a constant current out of the inlet, often exceeding one knot in strength There is a settlment about 1½ miles up the river, which is increasing.

Great quantities of the finest timber in the world for spars are exported from this place, and vessels of considerable size may lie close to the saw mill.

A steam tug is attached to the sawmill establishment for the purpose of towing vessels through the Eastern Channel; when a vessel is expected the tug generally lies in Dodger Cove, at the entrance of Middle Channel, where a good lookout can be kept. It is believed that this establishment has since been abandoned.

Observatory Islet, in the center of the harbor, is a small bare rock about 6 feet above high water, some rocks extend 100 yards north of it, but it may be approached within 200 yards.

Sheep Islet, in the northwestern part of harbor, is wooded, and connected to the head of the harbor at low water by a sand bank.

Anchorage—The anchorage in the harbor is in 8 to 12 fathoms, at the distance of ¼ mile from the head, with Observatory Islet S. 68° W.

Supplies.—Game is plentiful, and there is excellent fishing in the river and lakes. Fresh beef, vegetables, and fruit are plentiful and cheap.

Directions for Barclay Sound.—Entering Barclay Sound through the Eastern Channel Cape Beale may be easily recognized from the SE. by the light house and by the islands west of it, Ship Islet being also very conspicuous from the trees on its north part. When approaching or rounding the cape, do not come nearer that ½ mile, to avoid the rocks off it, until Turn Island, at the northeastern part of Eastern Channel is well shut in by Leading Bluff, bearing N 43° E, when steer up the Eastern Channel with that mark on, which will lead clear of the rocks off the western side of Cape Beale and east of Channel Rocks.

On nearing Leading Bluff keep the east side of Robbers Island open south of it, bearing S. 62° W., to pass east of the Fog Rock, until the west side of Knob Point comes open east of Limestone Point, bearing N. 20° E., when steer up within 400 yards of either shore, or in mid channel. If bound to Stamp Harbor, after entering Alberni Inlet keep in mid-channel, except when passing through the First and Second Narrows, and anchor on the eastern side of the harbor with the bearings already given.

After entering Alberni Inlet a strong southerly wind will generally be experienced, blowing home to the head, it, however, usually falls a little during the night.

If beating into the Eastern Channel (which should only be done by small or quick-working vessels), when standing towards Cape Beale, tack before the passage between Turn Island and the main comes open of Leading Bluff, bearing N. 15° E. Ship Islet may be approached to within ¼ mile; when nearing King Island, or the Channel Rocks, tack when Turn Island becomes shut in with Leading Bluff. As a rule, in standing towards the east shore, do not approach within 400 yards, and after passing the Channel Rocks keep outside of the lines of Deer Islands. On nearing Leading Bluff use above mentioned precautions for clearing Fog Rock, when standing into Numukamis Bay give Reef and San José Islands a berth of about 400 yards, after which the shore on either side may be approached to about 200 yards, except near the center of Numukamis Bay, which should not be approached closer than ½ mile.

Anchorages.—If necessary to anchor, Entrance Anchorage, in the Deer group, just north of Helby Island, is recommended, being secure and easy of access from either Eastern or Middle Channels. Kelp, Sproat, Christie and Nahmint Bays, also Green Cove, are easy of access, and may be used as stopping places.

Middle Channel, the largest passage into Barclay Sound, is adjacent to the Eastern Channel, and separated from it by the Deer Islands. On either side are numerous small islands and rocks. Off its entrance are three dangers, viz. Danger Rock, Channel Reef and Western Reef, which only break in heavy weather and require great caution to avoid. In southerly or southwesterly gales there is generally a very heavy sea in this channel.

Danger Rock, in the southeastern part of entrance to Middle Channel, 3½ miles N. 62° W. of Cape Beale, is of small extent, and the sea only breaks on it in heavy weather. There are from 22 to 40 fathoms around it at a distance of 400 yards.

Leading Marks.—Swiss Boy Island just open west of Entrance Island, bearing N. 15° E. (northerly), leads east of Danger Rock; Mark Islet open north of Ragged Islet, bearing N. 08° E., leads west of it and east of Channel Reef, and Sail Rock in sight west of Storm Island, bearing N. 39° W., leads south of it and Channel Reef.

Channel Reef lies near the center of the entrance to Middle Channel. It is about 200 yards in extent, uncovers at low water, and has 27 fathoms close to on the eastern side; there are from 19 to 50 fathoms in the channel between it and Danger Rock, and the same marks clear both of them.

Western Reef lies in the southwestern part of entrance to Middle Channel, and one mile south of the Broken group. It is about 200 yards in extent, awash at low water, and should not be approached within ½ mile.

In bad weather the sea breaks heavily over all these reefs.

Entrance Island, at the southeastern point of Middle Channel, and nearly one mile NW. of Ship Islet, is of small extent, and wooded, the tops of the trees being 350 feet above high water. It is steep to and clifty on the southern and western sides; ¼ mile NE. of it is a small islet and some off lying rocks.

Hecate Passage, leading into the middle channel between Entrance Island and Danger Rock, is 2 miles wide, and is the best way to enter Middle Channel in thick weather, or from the southward or eastward.

Shark Pass, between Entrance and Ship Islands, is ¾ mile wide, and may be used by steamers, or sailing vessels with a fair wind.

Dodger Cove—Between Diana and King Islands are two small islands (Hains and Seppings) connected to each other by a reef. Dodger Cove is between these islands and Diana Island, and is a narrow creek about ⅜ mile long and 200 yards wide, with several rocks and small islets off its entrance. It affords good shelter to coasters or small craft at its head, where there are from 2½ to 3 fathoms water, but it should not be attempted by strangers, as the entrance along the south side of Diana Island is rather intricate.

Ragged Islet, ¼ mile west of Helby Island, is rocky and of small extent, with a few trees on its summit; the western side may be approached to within a distance of about 400 yards, but it is connected to Helby Island by a ridge of rocks, and no vessel should attempt to go between them.

Satellite Pass, between Helby and Hill Islands, is about one mile long and ½ mile wide; the southern side is clear of danger; but 600 yards southward of Hill Island, on the north side of the pass, is a shoal patch of 3½ fathoms, marked by kelp; Leading Bluff open of east side of Hill Island, bearing N. 57° E., leads to the SE of this shoal

Vessels bound to Alberni Inlet, after having entered Middle Channel, should proceed through this pass into the Eastern Channel and on to the inlet through the latter, keeping about 400 yards north of Ragged, Helby, and Wizard Islands.

Village Rocks, lying ¼ mile from the northwestern point of Robbers Island, are nearly awash at low water, and the sea usually breaks on them in heavy weather, they should not be approached within ¼ mile. Between Robbers and Tzaartoos Islands is a small landlocked basin with from 5 to 7 fathoms, but the entrance to it from the Middle Channel, though deep, is very intricate

Chain Islands, on the east side of Middle Channel, are a chain of small islets and rocks nearly 4 miles long in a northeasterly direction. They lie parallel to the western side of Tzaartoos Island, being separated from it by a passage ¼ mile wide, filled with rocks, and through which vessels should not attempt to pass.

Swiss Boy Island, the southernmost of this group, is small and cliffy Bull Rock, 400 yards N. 18° W. of its southern end, is of small extent, and has less than 2 fathoms water on it, which breaks in bad weather.

Caution—Vessels should not approach the western side of these islands within ½ mile, except when rounding their north part

Junction Passage connects Middle Channel with Alberni Inlet and Eastern Channel, it is north of the Chain and Tzaartoos Islands, and between them and the main. Its shores are clear of danger. On the northern side of the passage is Rainy Bay, about 1½ miles in extent; but there are several rocks and small islets within it; the shores are rugged and broken, and the water too deep for anchorage. Northward of this bay, and connected to it by a very narrow boat pass, is Useless Arm, a large sheet of water not accessible to vessels

Broken group, which forms the boundary of Middle Channel along the west side, is composed of a number of small islands and rocks, covering a space upwards of 6 miles long and 4 wide They are low and the principal ones wooded, the largest being about one mile in extent; there are several passages through them, and a good anchorage (Island Harbor) in their northeastern part, but strangers should not venture among them or approach them within ½ mile, as the depths are irregular, and other rocks besides those known may exist.

Redonda Island lies at the southwestern entrance point of Middle Channel It is small, wooded, and of a round shape; some rocks extend 600 yards off its southeastern point, and ½ mile east of it is a reef which covers at half-flood. Between Redonda Island and Channel Reef is a passage one mile wide, but it should not be attempted by strangers.

Village Island, the largest of the group, is upwards of one mile in extent; the eastern side is bold and cliffy, with 24 fathoms at 200 yards distance. On its northern side is a village of considerable size, where landing may be effected in almost all weather. Off its western side are several rocks and a small bay, where a vessel may anchor in from 7 to 10 fathoms, but it is difficult of access.

Coaster Channel, which runs in a westerly direction through Broken Group, north of Village Island, is about 4 miles long and from ½ mile to one mile wide, but as there are several rocks in it, this channel should not be attempted by strangers.

A sunken rock lies 600 yards N. 10° W. of the north end of Grassy Island

Village Reef, in the eastern part of Coaster Channel, ½ mile north of Village Island, is small and 4 feet above high water; there is a depth of 34 fathoms at 600 yards east of it.

Island Harbor, formed by several rocks and islands, in the northeastern part of Broken Group, viz, Protection Island on the east, Puzzle and Gibraltar Islands on the north, and Mullins and Keith Islands on the west, is 5 miles from the entrance to Middle Channel; it is a good, well-sheltered anchorage, about ½ mile in extent, with from 10 to 14 fathoms water, and there are two good passages into it from Middle Channel.

Protection Island, off its eastern side, protecting it in that direction, is ⅝ mile long, narrow, and its shore is rugged and broken, but it may be approached to within 200 yards. There are two small, bare islets 200 yards from its southern shore and almost connected to it at low water.

Observation Islet, 30 feet high, and another small islet to the south of it, lie 100 yards from the middle of the southern side of Protection Island.

Elbow Island, 600 yards S. 45° W. of Protection Islands, is small and rugged, with a notch in the center; there are a few trees on it, and the island is conspicuous from the southward.

Elbow Rocks, which cover at two-thirds flood, lie 300 yards N. 45° E. of Elbow Island, and are steep-to on all sides.

Several small islets and reefs, some above water and some covering at one-third flood, lie in almost a straight line between Elbow Island and the northeastern point of Keith Island; these, with Elbow Rocks, form the western limit of the South Entrance Channel to the harbor.

Pinnace Rock, 600 yards east of Elbow Island, almost in the fairway of the south entrance, only breaks in heavy weather, and is dangerous to vessels entering the harbor by that passage.

Channel Rock, in the middle of harbor entrance, 800 yards from its eastern end, is of small extent, with only 9 feet on it at low water.

Directions.—Island Harbor may be entered either by the south or by the harbor entrance. The south entrance, between the Elbow Rocks and Protection Island, is 300 yards wide at its southern part, with from 8 to 14 fathoms water. Harbor entrance, along the north side of Protection Island, between it and Gibraltar Island, is nearly one mile long, with an average breadth of about 400 yards; the depths within it vary from 15 to 18 fathoms.

Entering the harbor by the south entrance, steer for the southeastern point of Protection Island on a N. 55° W. bearing, to avoid Pinnace Rock; if the Elbow Rocks are covered, keep along the southern side of Protection Island, about 100 yards distant, till past them, when steer for the anchorage, passing about 200 yards south of the islets off Protection Island. Coming in through Harbor entrance, after entering it in mid-channel keep about 100 yards from the north side of Protection Island till clear of Channel Rock.

No one should attempt to enter this harbor without the chart, unless thoroughly acquainted with the place; and it should only be entered by sailing vessels with a fair wind.

Anchorage.—The best anchorage is near the center of the harbor, about 400 yards NW. of the NW. end of Protection Island, in from 10 to 12 fathoms, protected from the northward and from the westward by Puzzle, Keith and Mullins Islands.

Nettle Island, the NE. island of Broken Group, is nearly one mile in extent, steep-to off its northern side, but east and west of it islets and rocks extend out ½ mile.

Swale Rock, at ½ mile east of the east point of Nettle Island, is a small bare rock 8 feet above high water, which is very conspicuous from the Middle Channel, and marks the east entrance of Sechart Channel.

Sechart Channel, north of Broken Group, between it and the main, connects the Western and Middle Channels. It is a winding channel, 5 miles long in a westerly direction and about ½ mile wide; a mid-channel course through is free of danger.

A rock that only uncovers at low-water spring tides lies 500 yards S. 60° W. of Sechart Village, and 300 yards N. 14° W. of the westernmost of the Hundred Islands.

Capstan Island, nearly in the middle of this channel, is small, and the southernmost of a number of small islands extending nearly one mile from the northern shore; a rock lies 100 yards south of it, but the island may be rounded at ¼ mile. Westward of these islets is the extensive village of Sechart, off which a vessel may anchor ¼ mile from the shore in 14 fathoms, open however to the SW.

Northward of Sechart Channel the western side of Middle Channel is bounded by two narrow islands about 2 miles in length, and separated from the mainland by a narrow boat pass; they should not be approached nearer than ½ mile.

Birch Islets, two small, bare, conspicuous rocks, lie almost in the center of the northern part of Middle Channel; some rocks which cover extend 200 yards north and east of them.

Effingham Inlet, the entrance to which is in the NW. part of Middle Channel, is narrow, and about 8 miles long in a curved direction to the northwestward, terminating in a low swamp; its shores on both sides are high and rocky, the western being indented by several bays. The depths in it vary from 35 to more than 70 fathoms, and there is no anchorage; off its south entrance point are some small islets and rocks extending one mile to the eastward. Twin Islets, George Islet, and several sunken rocks lie off the entrance to the inlet.

A sunken rock lies 700 yards N. 70° E. of the north end of Webster Island, and nearly 200 yards distant from the eastern shore of Effingham Inlet.

Vernon Bay, one mile east of Effingham Inlet, is upwards of one mile in extent, open to the southward, and too deep to afford anchorage; its shores are high and rocky.

Edward Rock.—At 600 yards S. 22° E. of Palmer Point, the SW. extreme of Vernon Bay, is Edward Rock, 3 feet above high water; just within the entrance is a reef awash at high water.

The northern shore of Middle Channel is rocky and bold, rising in some places to mountains upwards of 3,000 feet high; it is steep-to and clear of danger; in southerly winds the sea breaks violently along it.

Directions.—Entering Barclay Sound by the Middle Channel with a fair wind, and coming from the west or SW., keep well clear of the western part of the sound and 3 miles south of Broken Group. Steer towards Ship Islet on an east bearing until Mark Islet comes open north of Ragged Islet bearing N. 68° E., when haul into the Middle Channel with that mark on, which will lead midway between Channel Reef and Danger Rock; when Ship Islet bears S. 67° E. the vessel will be north of these reefs, and may then steer up in mid-channel. If bound to Alberni Inlet, a sailing vessel should proceed through Satellite Pass into the Eastern Channel. Should it be necessary to go through Junction Passage, give the Chain Islands a berth of nearly ½ mile to avoid the rocks off them, and proceed in mid-channel through the passage into Alberni Inlet.

Unless intending to go through Satellite Pass, do not approach the Deer Islands within ½ mile.

If entering Middle Channel from the eastward or in thick weather, and not able to see the marks for clearing the reefs, keep well out until Entrance Island bears N. 23° E., when steer through Hecate Passage so as to pass ¼ mile west of the island, which will lead well eastward of all danger, then proceed as above directed.

Beating into Middle Channel, when south of Danger Rock and Channel Reef, keep Sail Rock open south of Storm Island, the southernmost of the group, bearing N. 40° W. until Mark Islet comes nearly in line with the SE. point of Hill Island N. 70° E., when, if standing to the westward, tack; in standing to the eastward avoid shutting in the passage between Hill Island and Ragged Islet, which should be kept well open; tacking when these latter marks are on will lead between Danger and Channel Reefs, and clear of them; when Ship Islet bears S. 67° E. vessels will be northward of them, and may stand over to within about ½ mile of the Deer Islands and one mile of Broken Group. If bound to Alberni Inlet, when able to lay through the Satellite Pass do so, keeping nearer to its southern shore, and beat up to the former through the Eastern Channel. Vessels should not attempt to beat through Middle Channel unless the weather be clear and the marks well made out.

Vessels may go between Entrance Island and Danger Rock, to the northward of the latter and Channel Reef, by keeping Sea-bird Islet at the entrance of Pachena Bay well shut in by Cape Beale, bearing S. 47° E.

Western Channel is westward of the Broken Group, between it and Great Bank, and except in the vicinity of Broken Group it is clear of danger.

Sail Rock, lying off the southwestern part of Broken Group, is a bare rock like a sail, rising 100 feet above the sea and very conspicuous; to the northward of it are some low islets and rocks extending from the SW. island of the group, and on the eastern side of the Western Channel foul ground projects in some places as far as ½ mile off the western side of the group

Black Rock, at the southwestern entrance point of the Western Channel, is 10 feet above high water and small; some rocks which break extend 400 yards east of it.

Great Bear Islet lies 1½ miles N. 45° E. of Black Rock; about 100 yards off its east end there is a rock awash.

Channel Rock, at the southeastern extreme of the Great Bank, is bare and steep to on its eastern side.

Great Bank is, within the 10 fathom edge, 2½ miles long, and its greatest breadth is 1½ miles; on the shoalest parts, near the north and SW. ends, are from 3 to 4 fathoms, marked by kelp, over which in heavy gales the sea breaks.

Shag Rock, on the eastern side of the channel, 2¾ miles N. 15° E. of Sail Rock and ½ mile west of the Broken Group, is small and bare, and foul ground exists 200 yards from it.

Round Island, near the middle of the northern part of the channel, is small and but 200 feet high.

Beacon—A beacon has been erected near the summit of Round Island. The structure is conical in shape, 40 feet high, and whitewashed, and is surmounted by a mast and spire 15 feet high and 155 feet above high-water mark.

Gowlland, Table, and Castle Islets, at the northern termination of Western Channel, are small, but steep to on their southern sides At 400 yards NW. of Table Islet is a rock, awash at high water, and ½ mile ENE. of it is a patch 600 yards in extent, with from 4 to 7 fathoms, the best passage into Toquart Harbor appears to be to the eastward of these islets. A rock which dries 9 feet lies about 150 yards eastward of Gowlland Islet, and another, awash at low water, lies 400 yards north of the islet.

Beacon.—A beacon consisting of a whitewashed wooden conical shaped structure 40 feet high, surmounted by a mast and triangle 10 feet high, stands on the summit of Castle Islet. The beacon is 94 feet above high water mark.

Directions.—The Western Channel, though clear of danger and wide, should only be used by steamers, or sailing vessels with a fair wind, and not then unless bound to Toquart Harbor, in the northwestern part of Barclay Sound. When entering, give the Sail and Black Rocks a berth of ½ mile, and steer up in mid channel, passing ½ mile west of Round Island

Leading mark.—Keep the beacon on Castle Islet well open to westward of that on Round Island, bearing N. 23° E., which will lead between the reefs, ¾ mile clear of all danger.

Peacock Channel lies through the northwestern part of Broken group in a NE. direction from the Western to Sechart Channel.

A rock lies nearly in the center of the channel midway between Dodd and Pender Islands. It has 4 feet water on it, and lies 900 yards S. 43° W. of south end of Pender Island.

Galley Rock, on the eastern side of Peacock Channel, 1⅝ miles within the west entrance, uncovers at low water, and has 22 fathoms 200 yards SW. of it. Peacock Channel is fit for steamers, or sailing vessels with a fair wind; the only caution required in navigating it is to keep the northern shore aboard till past Galley Rock.

Hand Island, the northwestern island of the Broken group, is small and rugged; foul ground exists off its eastern and western sides, which should not be approached within 600 yards.

Lyall Point, at the northwestern extreme of Sechart Channel on the mainland, is a low, sharp point, with a sandy beach round it; there is a depth of 18 fathoms within 200 yards of it.

Mayne Bay, northward of Lyall Point, is of an oblong shape. Its shores, except near the northern part, are low and steep to; there is no anchorage except in its southeastern corner, where there is a limited area with 14 fathoms at about 400 yards offshore.

The Sisters, a group of small islets extending ½ miles southward of the NW. point of Mayne Bay, may be approached to 200 yards.

Stopper Islands, lying off Mayne Bay, are wooded, and 200 feet high; the rocks extend from 400 to 600 yards off their eastern and western sides.

Larkins Island lies close off their west side; a reef awash at high water extends 500 yards north from its northern end.

St. Innes Island lies to the southward of Stopper Islands, 1¼ miles west of Lyall Point.

David Channel leads into Toquart Harbor.

Richard Rock, on its western side, 800 yards from the Stopper Islands, is steep to on the east side, and may be approached to within 200 yards; vessels should not pass between this rock and the islands.

Hermit Islet, north of the Stopper Islands, is low, with 20 fathoms close to; at 400 yards N. 33° W. of it is a small rock, 2 feet above high water.

Toquart Harbor is about 1½ miles in extent, and well sheltered from all winds by the Stopper Islands. Its shores are low and steep to, except at the head, where Black Patch, a shoal with 9 feet on its outer part, extends out nearly ½ mile.

Image Island is small, and may be approached pretty close, to the northwestward of it is an excellent anchorage in from 11 to 12 fathoms. A rock lies close to its NW. end, and a reef near its southern point.

Village Passage leads into the harbor westward of Stopper Islands; it is upwards of one mile long, and 600 yards wide in its narrowest part, and is clear in mid-channel; some rocks awash at high water lie on its eastern side, extending from the north end of Larkins Island.

Pipestem Inlet, a long narrow inlet extends nearly straight in a ENE. direction from Toquart Harbor, but affords no anchorage; its shores are rocky and rise abruptly; at its head is a small patch of swampy ground, some fresh water streams flowing through it.

Directions.—Entering Toquart Harbor by David Channel, after passing Lyall Point steer well into Mayne Bay to avoid Richard Rock; when Hermit Islet comes open of the Stopper Islands bearing N. 28° W vessels will be clear eastward of it, and may steer for the harbor, passing midway between the Sisters and Stopper Islands and eastward of Hermit Islet; anchor in 14 fathoms, with Image Island bearing N. 57° E. and Hermit Islet S 22° E, or proceed farther north, keeping 200 yards off the west side of Image Island, and anchor NW. of it in 11 or 12 fathoms. Entering by Village Passage, keep in mid channel, or well over to the west shore, to avoid the rocks off the Stopper Islands.

Anchorage.—The anchorage is of considerble extent, in from 12 to 14 fathoms, muddy bottom.

The west coast of Barclay Sound from Toquart Harbor to Ucluelet Arm trends nearly straight to the SW and rises gradually to high land 2,000 feet above the sea.

Forbes Island.—For 2½ miles from the Stopper Islands a chain of small islands lie parallel to the coast at a distance of about ¾ mile, with from 5 to 11 fathoms between them and the shore. Forbes Island, the southernmost of them, is moderately high, steep-to on its southern side; nearly one mile SW. of it, and extending from the opposite shore, are a number of rocks above high water.

Ship Channel is between the Vancouver Shore and the Great Bank. It is 4 miles long NE. and SW, ¾ mile broad in its narrowest part.

Double Island, at its southeastern point is of small extent, steep to on the western side, but from the southern and eastern sides foul ground extends upwards of ½ mile.

Kelp Islet, on the opposite side of the channel, is low and bare, kelp extends 400 yards south from it.

Ugly Channel, connects Ship Channel with the ocean. It is bounded on both sides by rocks and reefs, and though probably deep, it has not been sufficiently examined to recommend its being used by strangers.

Starlight Reefs, at its southeastern part, are a cluster of rocks about ¼ mile in extent, some above high water, in bad weather the sea breaks heavily over them.

Heddington, and Sykes Reefs lie between Starlight Reefs and Double Islands.

Look-out Island, on the west side of Ugly Channel, is well wooded and of small extent; at 600 yards southward of it is Humphries Reef, a patch of rocks 400 yards in extent, and 1,200 yards northward of it lies a bare rock 6 feet above high water.

Ucluelet Arm, just within the SW entrance point of Barclay Sound, is a narrow inlet parallel to the outer coast, and separated from it only by a narrow peninsula. Its western shore is low, and indented by several small creeks and bays; the eastern shore is nearly straight, and, at a short distance inland, rises gradually to a flat top range of considerable height, the SE. shoulder of which, Mount Ozzard, is conspicuous from the southeastward.

The depths in this arm vary from 4 to 8 fathoms, and there is secure and well sheltered anchorage from one mile inside the entrance to the head.

Shelter Islands, upwards of ½ mile SE. of the entrance of the Ucluelet Arm, are an irregular cluster of small islets and rocks, about one mile long in a northwesterly direction and 600 yards wide, and completely shelter the arm from the sea.

Center Reef, 600 yards westward of their northern part, is of small extent, and about 3 feet above high water.

Alpha Passage, between Center Reef and Shelter Islands, is 400 yards wide in its narrowest part. There is, however, said to be a sunken rock in this passage, and it should therefore not be used by

(1189) **BRITISH COLUMBIA — Vancouver island — Barkley sound — Carolina channel — Amphitrite point — Whistling buoy established.**—The Canadian Government has given notice that an automatic whistling buoy, on the Courtenay principle, has been established off Amphitrite point, Carolina channel, western entrance to Ucluelet, Vancouver island.

The buoy is painted red and is moored in 25 fathoms of water

Approx. position Lat 48° 54′ 57″ N., Long 125° 33′ 23″ W.

(N. M. 31, 1905.)

an unbroken line of surf.

Round Island, at the north part of this channel, is the south... entrance point to the Ucluelet Arm, it is high and is connected by a sandy beach at low water to the mainland; the eastern side is steep to, and may be approached to within 200 yards; on the opposite side of the entrance rocks awash at high water extend 200 yards off the eastern shore.

Leading Point, on the western side of Ucluelet Arm, is bold, steep to, and may be approached to within a distance of 50 yards; between it and Round Island is a narrow creek, with 2 fathoms water, but the entrance is blocked up by kelp. At Leading Point the breadth of the inlet contracts to 200 yards.

Stewart Bay, ½ mile within the entrance, is 400 yards deep and ½ mile wide. In its center is a rock awash at high water, and the bay is too shallow to afford anchorage except to coasters; there is a native village of considerable size in its western part, off which some small rocks extend about 100 yards.

Village Passage leads into the harbor westward of Stopper Islands; it is upwards o. one mile long, and 600 yards wide in its narrowest part, and is clear in mid channel; some rocks awash at high water lie on its eastern side, extending from the north end of Larkins Island.

Pipestem Inlet, a long narrow inlet extends nearly straight in a ENE. direction from Toquart Harbor, but affords no anchorage, its shores are rocky and rise abruptly; at its head is a small patch of swampy ground, some fresh water streams flowing through it

Directions.—Entering Toquart Harbor by David Channel, after passing Lyall Point steer well into Mayne Bay to avoid Richard Rock; when Hermit Islet comes open of the Stopper Islands bearing N. 28° W. vessels will be clear eastward of it, and may steer for the harbor, passing midway between the Sisters and Stopper Islands and eastward of Hermit Islet; anchor in 14 fathoms, with Image Island bearing N. 57° E. and Hermit Islet S. 22° E., or proceed farther north, keeping 200 yards off the west side of Image Island, and anchor NW. of it in 11 or 12 fathoms Entering by Village Passage, keep in mid-channel, or well over to the west shore, to avoid the rocks off the Stopper Islands.

Anchor[illegible] [illegible] anchorage is of considerble extent, in from 12 to 14 fathoms

The west [illegible]

Arm trend [illegible]

2,000 feet [illegible]

Forbes [illegible]

small islan[illegible]

with from [illegible]

the southernmost [illegible], is moderately [illegible] side; nearly one mile SW. of it, and extending from the [illegible] shore, are a number of rocks above high water.

Ship Channel is between the Vancouver Shore and the Great Bank. It is 4 miles long NE. and SW., ¾ mile broad in its narrowest part.

Double Island, at its southeastern point is of small extent, steep to on the western side, but from the southern and eastern sides foul ground extends upwards of ½ mile.

Kelp Islet, on the opposite side of the channel, is low and bare; kelp extends 400 yards south from it.

Ugly Channel, connects Ship Channel with the ocean. It is bounded on both sides by rocks and reefs, and though probably deep, it has not been sufficiently examined to recommend its being used by strangers

Starlight Reefs, at its southeastern part, are a cluster of rocks about ¾ mile in extent, some above high water; in bad weather the sea breaks heavily over them.

Heddington, and Sykes Reefs lie between Starlight Reefs and Double Islands.

Look-out Island, on the west side of Ugly Channel, is well wooded and of small extent; at 600 yards southward of it is Humphries Reef, a patch of rocks 400 yards in extent, and 1,200 yards northward of it lies a bare rock 6 feet above high water.

Ucluelet Arm, just within the SW. entrance point of Barclay Sound, is a narrow inlet parallel to the outer coast, and separated from it only by a narrow peninsula. Its western shore is low, and indented by several small creeks and bays; the eastern shore is nearly straight, and, at a short distance inland, rises gradually to a flat-top range of considerable height, the SE. shoulder of which, Mount Ozzard, is conspicuous from the southeastward.

The depths in this arm vary from 4 to 8 fathoms, and there is secure and well-sheltered anchorage from one mile inside the entrance to the head.

Shelter Islands, upwards of ½ mile SE. of the entrance of the Ucluelet Arm, are an irregular cluster of small islets and rocks, about one mile long in a northwesterly direction and 600 yards wide, and completely shelter the arm from the sea.

Center Reef, 600 yards westward of their northern part, is of small extent, and about 3 feet above high water.

Alpha Passage, between Center Reef and Shelter Islands, is 400 yards wide in its narrowest part. There is, however, said to be a sunken rock in this passage, and it should therefore not be used by steamers or coasting vessels bound to the Ucluelet Arm, except from necessity.

Carolina Channel is west of Center Reef, between it and Amphitrite Point. It is nearly straight, and ¼ mile wide in its narrowest part. This channel appears to be the best for strangers to use if entering the Ucluelet Arm from seaward, but in heavy weather, when there is a long swell from seaward rolling in, the entrance often appears to be an unbroken line of surf.

Round Island, at the north part of this channel, is the south entrance point to the Ucluelet Arm; it is high and is connected by a sandy beach at low water to the mainland; the eastern side is steep-to, and may be approached to within 200 yards; on the opposite side of the entrance rocks awash at high water extend 200 yards off the eastern shore.

Leading Point, on the western side of Ucluelet Arm, is bold, steep-to, and may be approached to within a distance of 50 yards; between it and Round Island is a narrow creek, with 2 fathoms water, but the entrance is blocked up by kelp. At Leading Point the breadth of the inlet contracts to 200 yards.

Stewart Bay, ½ mile within the entrance, is 400 yards deep and ½ mile wide. In its center is a rock awash at high water, and the bay is too shallow to afford anchorage except to coasters; there is a native village of considerable size in its western part, off which some small rocks extend about 100 yards.

Channel Islet, in the middle of the arm about 2 miles within the entrance, is small. There is a clear passage east of the islet with 6 fathoms water, but only 2 fathoms on its western side; at 400 yards N 33° W. of the islet lies a small rock above high water, steep-to on all sides, except the southeastern, from which a shoal with 2¾ fathoms water extends for 200 yards

Anchorage.—To the northwestward of Channel Islet the arm becomes wider, affording good anchorage in 4 to 7 fathoms, over a space one mile long and ½ mile wide

Staples Island, ½ mile from the head on the southern side of the arm, and connected to the latter at low water, is about one mile in circumference, and low.

A sandy beach borders the eastern shore of Ucluelet Arm from its head to Stewart Bay.

Directions.—Several channels lead into Ucluelet Arm, with apparently deep water through them, but there are so many rocks and dangers in their vicinity that great vigilance is recommended, and it would hardly be advisable to enter without a pilot; should it, however, be necessary to do so, a vessel should steer for Amphitrite Point, and when about 400 yards from it, proceed to the eastward through the Carolina Channel, keeping about 400 yards off its western shore to avoid Center Reef. Pass Round Island at the distance of 200 yards, and rounding it sharply steer about NW up the arm, keeping well over to the western shore; pass Leading Point within 100 yards to avoid the rocks abreast of it on the eastern side, and anchor midway between it and Channel Islet, in 6 to 9 fathoms; or proceed farther to the westward, where a more extended anchorage will be found, taking care to pass east of Channel Islet

Channel Islet kept open between the sides of the inlet bearing N. 42° W. leads to the entrance of Ucluelet Arm from off the entrance of the Western Channel, to the northward of the Shelter Islands, and between the Great Bear and Sykes Reef to the eastward and Black Rocks, Starlight and Heddington Reefs to the westward, but as this channel has not been closely examined, it should be used with great caution.

Entering the arm from the northward through Ship Channel, keep about ½ mile off the western shore, and passing about 400 yards north of Shelter Islands, steer up the arm as before directed.

The Coast from Amphitrite Point takes a NW. by W. direction to Point Cox; it is low and indented by two large sandy bays, which afford no shelter; at a distance of 4 miles from it are depths of from 20 to 27 fathoms.

Wreck Bay is nearly 3 miles wide and one mile deep, with a small islet in the center, there are several rocks in the bay, and it is totally unfit for anchorage.

Long Bay is 7 miles wide, and [illegible] yards of one mile deep, with from 8 to 11 fathoms between the ent[illegible]ce points; there are several rocks in it, and vessels should not anchor here; at its SE. point, just within the reefs, good shelter for boats will be found in all weather.

Schooner Cove, in the northwestern part of the bay, is of small extent, with 2 fathoms water inside; it would afford good shelter to small vessels.

Portland Point, the northwestern extreme of Long Bay, is high and abrupt, with some small rocks and islets around it, at a distance of ½ mile.

Gowlland Rocks, 1½ miles west of Portland Point, are of small extent, bare, and from 10 to 15 feet above high water; they should not

(1658) **BRITISH COLUMBIA—Vancouver Island—Clayoquot sound—Templar channel—Lennard island—Light established.**—A lighthouse established by the Government of Canada on Lennard island at the entrance to Templar channel, the southernmost approach to Clayoquot, on the Pacific coast of Vancouver island, will be put in operation on November 1, 1904.

The lighthouse stands on the summit of the southwest point of the island, where the rock rises about 35 feet above high watermark. It is an octagonal wooden building with sloping sides, painted white, surmounted by a metal lantern, circular in plan, painted red, and is 80 feet high from its base to the vane on the lantern. A white wooden light keeper's dwelling and outbuildings have also been erected on the island.

The light is a *flashing white* light, giving *1 flash every 11¼ seconds*. It is elevated 115 feet above high watermark and should be visible 16 miles from all points of approach, except where obscured by trees on Lennard island. The illuminating apparatus is dioptric, of the first order, and the illuminant petroleum vapor burned under an incandescent mantle.

Approx. position Lat. 49° 06′ 40″ N., Long. 125° 55′ 45″ W.

mile, Vargas Cone, a remarkable summit, rises just wit. (N. M. 47, 1904.) and is very conspicuous from the westward.

Templar Channel, the eastern entrance to the sound, is a winding passage about 4 miles long in a northerly direction, with an average breadth of ⅓ mile. The soundings vary from 8 to 10 fathoms in its entrance to 3½ fathoms in its shoalest part near the northern end, and a shoal bank lies in the middle abreast Wakennenish Island; in heavy weather the sea breaks right across the channel. Vessels drawing more than 12 feet water should not attempt to enter the sound by this channel, and never without a pilot, as it is very intricate, and no directions can be given, coasters, however, generally use it.

False Bay, just northward of Cox Point, is about ½ mile in extent, with from 3 to 4 fathoms water, but open to the SW., and unfit for anchorage, its shores are low and sandy.

Lennard Island, 1½ miles N. 55° W. of Cox Point, is of small extent and wooded, steep-to on the eastern side, but west of it are some rocks and small islets.

Wakennenish Island, on the western side of the channel, has on its southern point Echachets, a large Indian village, generally occupied by the natives during the summer season when fishing.

Channel Islet, in the middle of the arm about 2 miles within the entrance, is small. There is a clear passage east of the islet with 6 fathoms water, but only 2 fathoms on its western side; at 400 yards N. 33° W. of the islet lies a small rock above high water, steep-to on all sides, except the southeastern, from which a shoal with 2¼ fathoms water extends for 200 yards.

Anchorage.—To the northwestward of Channel Islet the arm becomes wider, affording good anchorage in 4 to 7 fathoms, over a space one mile long and ½ mile wide.

Staples Island, ½ mile from the head on the southern side of the arm, and connected to the latter at low water [illegible] cumferen[illegible]

A sand, [illegible] head to S[illegible]

Directi[illegible] ently dee[illegible] dangers i[illegible] would ha[illegible] be necess[illegible] when abo[illegible] Carolina C[illegible] Center R[illegible] rounding [illegible] the weste[illegible] rocks abr[illegible] and Chan[illegible] ward, wh[illegible] pass east [illegible]

Channe[illegible] between the sides of the inlet bearing N. 42° W. leads to the entrance of Ucluelet Arm from off the entrance of the Western Channel, to the northward of the Shelter Islands, and between the Great Bear and Sykes Reef to the eastward and Black Rocks, Starlight and Heddington Reefs to the westward; but as this channel has not been closely examined, it should be used with great caution.

Entering the arm from the northward through Ship Channel, keep about ¼ mile off the western shore, and passing about 400 yards north of Shelter Islands, steer up the arm as before directed.

The Coast from Amphitrite Point takes a NW. by W. direction to Point Cox; it is low and indented by two large sandy bays, which afford no shelter; at a distance of 4 miles from it are depths of from 20 to 27 fathoms.

Wreck Bay is nearly 3 miles wide and one mile deep, with a small islet in the center; there are several rocks in the bay, and it is totally unfit for anchorage.

Long Bay is 7 miles wide, and upwards of one mile deep, with from 8 to 11 fathoms between the entrance points; there are several rocks in it, and vessels should not anchor here; at its SE. point, just within the reefs, good shelter for boats will be found in all weather.

Schooner Cove, in the northwestern part of the bay, is of small extent, with 2 fathoms water inside; it would afford good shelter to small vessels.

Portland Point, the northwestern extreme of Long Bay, is high and abrupt, with some small rocks and islets around it, at a distance of ½ mile.

Gowlland Rocks, 1½ miles west of Portland Point, are of small extent, bare, and from 10 to 15 feet above high water; they should not be approached nearer than one mile.

Caution.—When navigating between Barclay and Clayoquot Sounds do not approach the shore within 2 miles, nor stand within one mile of the entrance to Wreck and Long Bays.

Clayoquot Sound comprises a number of inlets, islands and rocks, covering an area 30 miles long in a westerly direction and 16 broad. The entrance to it is fringed by numerous dangerous rocks, which require due caution to avoid.

There are several channels into the inner waters of this sound, but with the exception of Ship Channel they should not be attempted by strangers.

The soundings at a distance of one mile outside the outer rocks vary from 20 to 30 fathoms, but in the channels and inside the bottom is irregular.

Tides.—It is high water, full and change, in Clayoquot Sound at 12 hours, the rise and fall being about 12 feet.

Point Cox is rocky, and may be approached to within a distance of ½ mile; Vargas Cone, a remarkable summit, rises just within the point, and is very conspicuous from the westward.

Templar Channel, the eastern entrance to the sound, is a winding passage about 4 miles long in a northerly direction, with an average breadth of ½ mile. The soundings vary from 8 to 10 fathoms in its entrance to 3¼ fathoms in its shoalest part near the northern end, and a shoal bank lies in the middle abreast Wakennenish Island; in heavy weather the sea breaks right across the channel. Vessels drawing more than 12 feet water should not attempt to enter the sound by this channel, and never without a pilot, as it is very intricate, and no directions can be given; coasters, however, generally use it.

False Bay, just northward of Cox Point, is about ¾ mile in extent, with from 3 to 4 fathoms water, but open to the SW., and unfit for anchorage; its shores are low and sandy.

Lennard Island, 1½ miles N. 55° W. of Cox Point, is of small extent and wooded, steep-to on the eastern side, but west of it are some rocks and small islets.

Wakennenish Island, on the western side of the channel, has on its southern point Echachets, a large Indian village, generally occupied by the natives during the summer season when fishing.

Round Island, at the northern part of the channel, is small, but with a clear but narrow passage on either side of it; a bank, dry at low water, extends ⅔ mile northward from it.

Stubbs Island, west of Round Island, has a sand bank, which dries at low water, extending one mile north from it.

Broken Channel, between Wakennenish and Vargas Islands, is ½ mile wide in its narrowest part, with from 6 to 15 fathoms water; several rocks lie off its entrance and on both sides; the tide runs through from 2 to 5 knots, and vessels should not attempt it without a pilot.

McKay Reef, lying off the entrance, is of small extent, 5 to 10 feet above high water, and the sea generally breaks heavily over it.

Passage Rock, which covers at high water, lies ⅔ mile N. 23° E. of McKay Reef.

Vargas Island, on the western side of Broken Channel, is 4½ miles long, and 4¼ miles wide at its broadest part, and its surface is low and undulating; on the eastern side near the middle is Kelsemart, a native village.

The Rugged Group, at ½ mile from the southern shore, running parallel to it, is a chain of small islets and rocks.

Open Bay, on the western side of Vargas, is about one mile in extent, and has apparently a clear passage into it from the NW., but it has not been examined.

Blunden and Bare Islands, to the westward of Open Bay, are of small size; numerous reefs are scattered about this locality.

Ship Channel, to the westward of Vargas Island, between it and a number of small islands and rocks, is the only passage into Clayoquot Sound which should be attempted by strangers. The depths in the south part vary from 20 to 22 fathoms, decreasing to 5½ fathoms in the shoalest part near the northern end; the tide sets through it at from one to 2 knots.

Bare Island, at the southeastern entrance point of the channel, is small, and forms a good mark for identifying Ship Channel; a rock on which the sea breaks lies ½ mile S. 56° E. of it, and there are 20 fathoms within ½ mile of its southwestern side.

Plover Reefs, on the eastern side of the channel, are of considerable extent, stretching one mile from the west side of Blunden Island; some parts are 6 feet above high water, and there are 5 fathoms at 400 yards west of them.

Hobbs and Burgess Islets lie 400 yards from the northwestern side of Vargas Island, and nearly connected with it at low water; they are small, and may be approached to within a distance of 400 yards.

Sea Otter Rock lies at the southwestern entrance point of Ship Channel; it is very small, only 6 feet above high water, and there are 5 fathoms close to.

Shark Reefs, some of which cover, others 6 and 10 feet above high water, lie on the western side; they are about 600 yards in extent, and should not be approached nearer than 400 yards on their southern and eastern sides.

Lawrence Islands, on the western side, are small, low and wooded, but steep-to on the eastern side.

Bartlett Island, ½ mile to the westward of the Lawrence Islands, is

(1853) **BRITISH COLUMBIA—Vancouver island—West coast—Clayoquot sound—Hecate passage—Buoys established.**—A platform buoy carrying a wooden slatwork pyramid surmounted by a drum, the whole painted black, has been established off the south extreme of North bank, Hecate passage, Clayoquot sound. The buoy is moored in 5 fathoms of water.

Approx. position: Lat. 49° 13′ 22″ N., Long. 126° 00′ 00″ W.

A platform buoy carrying a wooden slatwork pyramid surmounted by a ball, the whole painted red, has been established at the eastern entrance of Hecate passage to mark the rock that dries. The buoy is moored in 5 fathoms of water. The rock dries about 1 foot at an extreme low water and is marked by kelp.

Approx. position: Lat. 49° 12′ 55″ N., Long. 125° 57′ 20″ W.

(N. M. 52, 1904.)

side. Hobbs Islet open west of Burgess Islet, bearing S. 37° W., leads west of it; and the Twins, in line with the NW. Whaler Island bearing N. 77° W., leads north of it and south of North Bank.

North Bank, lying in the center of the passage, is of considerable extent, composed of sand, and has 5 feet water on its shoalest part; there are 4 to 5 fathoms north of it, but the passage south is the better.

White Islet, to the NW. of the North Bank, is small, bare, and conspicuous from the entrance of Ship Channel; there are several rocks between it and the northern shore.

The Cat Face Mountains, rising on the main shore of Vancouver Island, and fronting Ship Channel, are a remarkable flat-top range nearly 3,000 feet high, with some patches of cliff and white bare rock in about the middle of their south side. They are very conspicuous from seaward.

Deep Pass, between two islands at the northeastern part of Hecate Passage, is about 600 yards long and 300 yards wide, with 9 fathoms water, and is the best channel leading from Hecate Passage into the inner waters. The tide sets at the rate of from 2 to 3 knots through it.

Hecate Bay, 2 miles northward of Deep Pass, on the western shore, is clear of danger, and one of the best anchorages within the sound, being easy of access and well sheltered. There is a stream of fresh water in the middle of the bay, very convenient for watering.

Observatory Islet, at its north point, is 35 feet high and bare; 400 yards NE. of it is a small rock 2 feet above high water.

Cypress Bay, 4 miles north from Deep Pass, is nearly 2 miles in extent. On the eastern and western sides the shores are low, but are high on the north. There is a large stream, with some swampy land, on its western side; on the east is Calm Creek with a narrow entrance, to the southward of which are some offlying rocks and small islands.

Round Island, at the northern part of the channel, is small, but with a clear but narrow passage on either side of it; a bank, dry at low water, extends ⅔ mile northward from it.

Stubbs Island, west of Round Island, has a sand bank, which dries at low water [illegible] mile north from it.

Broken Cl [illegible]
wide in its [illegible]
rocks lie off [illegible]
from 2 to 5 k [illegible]

McKay I [illegible]
above high [illegible]

Passage [illegible]
of McKay I [illegible]

Vargas I [illegible]
long, and 4 [illegible]
undulating [illegible]
village.

The Rugged Group, at ½ mile from the southern shore, running parallel to it, is a chain of small islets and rocks.

Open Bay, on the western side of Vargas, is about one mile in extent, and has apparently a clear passage into it from the NW., but it has not been examined.

Blunden and Bare Islands, to the westward of Open Bay, are of small size; numerous reefs are scattered about this locality.

Ship Channel, to the westward of Vargas Island, between it and a number of small islands and rocks, is the only passage into Clayoquot Sound which should be attempted by strangers. The depths in the south part vary from 20 to 22 fathoms, decreasing to 5½ fathoms in the shoalest part near the northern end; the tide sets through it at from one to 2 knots.

Bare Island, at the southeastern entrance point of the channel, is small, and forms a good mark for identifying Ship Channel; a rock on which the sea breaks lies ½ mile S. 50° E. of it, and there are 20 fathoms within ½ mile of its southwestern side.

Plover Reefs, on the eastern side of the channel, are of considerable extent, stretching one mile from the west side of Blunden Island; some parts are 6 feet above high water, and there are 5 fathoms at 400 yards west of them.

Hobbs and Burgess Islets lie 400 yards from the northwestern side of Vargas Island, and nearly connected with it at low water; they are small, and may be approached to within a distance of 100 yards.

Sea Otter Rock lies at the southwestern entrance point of Ship Channel; it is very small, only 6 feet above high water, and there are 5 fathoms close to.

Shark Reefs, some of which cover, others 6 and 10 feet above high water, lie on the western side; they are about 600 yards in extent, and should not be approached nearer than 400 yards on their southern and eastern sides.

Lawrence Islands, on the western side, are small, low and wooded, but steep-to on the eastern side.

Bartlett Island, ½ mile to the westward of the Lawrence Islands, is low and wooded; its shores are much broken, and a number of rocks extend from ¼ to ½ miles on all sides of it; the island should not be approached within the latter distance.

Twin Islets, 4 miles from Sea Otter Rock, are low, but wooded, and connected at low water; kelp extends 200 yards south of them.

Hecate Passage connects Ship Channel with the inner waters of Clayoquot Sound; there are several rocks on both its shores and a sand bank in its center, but to the southward of the bank, along the northern shore of Vargas, is a clear passage with not less than 5½ fathoms.

Half-tide Rock, 400 yards from Vargas Island, is of small extent, covers at half flood, and may be approached to 200 yards on the outside. Hobbs Islet open west of Burgess Islet, bearing S. 37° W., leads west of it; and the Twins, in line with the NW. Whaler Island bearing N. 77° W., leads north of it and south of North Bank.

North Bank, lying in the center of the passage, is of considerable extent, composed of sand, and has 5 feet water on its shoalest part; there are 4 to 5 fathoms north of it, but the passage south is the better.

White Islet, to the NW. of the North Bank, is small, bare, and conspicuous from the entrance of Ship Channel; there are several rocks between it and the northern shore.

The Cat Face Mountains, rising on the main shore of Vancouver Island, and fronting Ship Channel, are a remarkable flat-top range nearly 3,000 feet high, with some patches of cliff and white bare rock in about the middle of their south side. They are very conspicuous from seaward.

Deep Pass, between two islands at the northeastern part of Hecate Passage, is about 600 yards long and 300 yards wide, with 9 fathoms water, and is the best channel leading from Hecate Passage into the inner waters. The tide sets at the rate of from 2 to 3 knots through it.

Hecate Bay, 2 miles northward of Deep Pass, on the western shore, is clear of danger, and one of the best anchorages within the sound, being easy of access and well sheltered. There is a stream of fresh water in the middle of the bay, very convenient for watering.

Observatory Islet, at its north point, is 35 feet high and bare; 400 yards NE. of it is a small rock 2 feet above high water.

Cypress Bay, 4 miles north from Deep Pass, is nearly 2 miles in extent. On the eastern and western sides the shores are low, but are high on the north. There is a large stream, with some swampy land, on its western side; on the east is Calm Creek with a narrow entrance, to the southward of which are some outlying rocks and small islands.

Mussel Rock lies 800 yards off the eastern shore of the bay and ½ mile N. 8° W. of the east extreme. It is of small extent, and covers at half flood.

Calm Creek is in the northeastern part of Cypress Bay; the entrance to it is narrow, with only 2 fathoms water, it is useless for anchorage, except to small craft.

Anchorage.—There is good anchorage in Cypress Bay in 12 fathoms near its northern part at ½ mile from the shore; and though it is open to the southward, no sea rises.

Meares Island, adjacent to and east of Vargas Island, is 6 miles in extent in a northerly and 7 miles in an easterly direction. Its shores, except on the northern side, are high and rugged, and there are several summits on the east and west sides upwards of 2,000 feet above the sea. An extensive inlet (Disappointment Inlet) runs nearly through the island from the south side to north, and there are several other bights and bays.

Deception Channel is a continuation of Broken Channel to the northward, between Meares and Vargas Islands. There are several rocks in its northwestern part, and a large sand bank, which partly dries at low water, extends from Vargas Island along its western side for nearly 2 miles, reducing the deep part of the passage to about 600 yards. The tide sets at from 2 to 5 knots through this channel, and strangers should not attempt its navigation.

Ritchie Bay, on the northwestern side of Meares Island, affords anchorage in 5½ to 10 fathoms at 400 yards off its eastern shore. The shores of the bay are rocky, but have no outlying dangers; Robert Point, its southwestern extreme, slopes gradually to the sea, and may be approached to within a distance of 200 yards.

Yellow Bank, which lies almost athwart the entrance of Ritchie Bay, is about ¾ mile in extent and has 3 feet on the shoalest part; there is deep water around it, and the channel between it and Robert Point is 400 yards wide, with from 6 to 10 fathoms.

Saranac Island, near the north part of Ritchie Bay, is wooded, steep-to on the eastern side; some small islets extend 600 yards off its western side and there is a narrow but deep passage between it and Yellow Bank.

Directions.—If wishing to anchor in Ritchie Bay, and coming from Deep Pass, proceed to the eastward so as to pass about 200 yards north of Robert Point, and keeping the same distance off the south shore, steer into the bay, anchoring in 5 or 7 fathoms about 400 yards from its eastern side, with the extremes bearing N. 23° E. and S. 70° W.; entering from the northward, steer midway between Saranac Island and the north point of the bay.

The north shore of Meares Island is low, nearly straight, and steep-to for nearly 4 miles, and then turns sharply to the south.

Bedwell Sound is one mile broad till within 2 miles of its head, when it contracts to 600 yards; the shores are high and rugged, rising on the east side to sharp jagged peaks. At its head is a small patch of low swampy land and a valley from which the Bear River, a stream of considerable size, flows into the sound. There is no anchorage.

Race Narrows, between the northern side of Meares Island and the main, are 1½ miles long, and about 400 yards wide in the narrowest part; the tides set through them at the rate of from 3 to 4 knots, the flood from the westward, and there are 10 fathoms in the shoalest part of mid-channel.

Ripple Islets, off the eastern entrance to Race Narrows, are small and covered with bushes; there are some strong tide rips around them, but they may be approached to within about 200 yards.

Warn Bay is one mile from the northeastern part of Meares Island. The shores on both sides are high, but low at the head, from whence issue several streams, and a sand bank dries out upwards of 200 yards. The depths in the bay are irregular, but vessels may anchor about 600 yards off shore near the western side of the head of the bay in 14 to 16 fathoms.

Fortune Channel, between the east side of Meares Island and the main, varies in breadth from 600 yards to 1¼ miles; its shores are high, and there are several off-lying rocks on its western side near the middle.

The eastern shore of the channel from Warn Bay to Deception Pass is rocky and indented by several small bays which afford no anchorage.

Mosquito Harbor, on the northeastern side of Meares Island, is narrow, and about 2 miles long in a northwesterly direction; there are several rocks and small islets off its entrance, but it affords good anchorage inside in from 4 to 7 fathoms; the entrance is 300 yards wide, with 11 fathoms, and the harbor may easily be entered by steamers.

Plover Point, at the SE. side of the entrance to Mosquito Harbor, is rocky, with some small islets a short distance off it.

Hankin Rock lies 500 yards SW. of Plover Point, and in the track of vessels entering Mosquito Harbor; it is marked by kelp, and there are 23 fathoms midway between it and the point.

Wood Islands, in the middle of the entrance, nearly ¼ mile west of Plover Point, are small and extend in a northerly direction for ½ mile; some rocks lie a short distance off their south part, but there is a clear passage into the harbor on both sides of them.

Blackberry Islets, in the center of the harbor and ¾ mile from the entrance, are small but steep-to, there being 4 fathoms within 200 yards of them.

Directions.—When entering Mosquito Harbor, round Plover Point at 200 yards' distance to avoid the Hankin Rock, and keep midway between Wood Islands and the eastern shore, anchoring in about 7 fathoms ¼ mile south of the Blackberry Islets; a vessel may enter westward of the Wood Islands by keeping midway between them and the shore.

Anchorage.—The best anchorage is a short distance to the southward of the Blackberry Islets, in from 5 to 7 fathoms, northward of them are from 3 to 4 fathoms.

Dark Island, 1,400 yards south of Plover Point, is small; some rocks extend a short distance off its west side, but there is a clear passage between it and the western shore.

Double Island, south of Dark Island, is small and steep to.

Deception Pass, at the southern extreme of Fortune Channel and connecting it with Tofino Inlet and Browning Passage, is a winding passage to the southward; it is free from danger in mid channel, and the tide sets with considerable strength through it. On its western side is a narrow creek ½ mile long with from 8 to 9 fathoms, and in the middle of the pass is a small islet.

Tofino Inlet is in the eastern part of Clayoquot Sound, its shores are high and rocky, indented on the western side by some large creeks; there are several islands in the inlet and along both shores, but none of any considerable size. There is no anchorage, except near the entrance on the western side.

Indian Island, in the entrance, is about one mile in extent, and steep to on the northern side, a bank extends 400 yards from its western point, with 3½ fathoms close to the edge.

Warn Island, north of Indian Island, just within the entrance, is upwards of ½ mile in extent, and steep to on all sides.

Island Cove, west of Warn Island, is of small extent, with from 8 to 10 fathoms in the middle, and completely landlocked, a small island lies off the entrance, with a clear passage 200 yards wide on either side of it into the cove.

Gunner Harbor, just north of Warn Island, is narrow; a small islet lies in its center, about ½ mile north of the entrance, and between them a vessel may find good anchorage in about 10 fathoms, the harbor becomes shoal towards the head.

Tranquil Creek, on the west side of the inlet is narrow, and upwards of one mile long; its shores are high and rocky, and the creek is too deep for anchorage.

Between Tranquil Creek and Warn Island, along the west shore, are several small rocky islets, extending off from 400 to 600 yards.

Flat Top Islets, 5 miles from the entrance of the inlet, are steep to on the eastern side. Northward of these islets Tofino Inlet takes a winding direction to the northward, narrowing gradually towards the head, and terminating in Deer Creek, one mile long and ¼ mile broad, but it is too deep for anchorage.

On the east side of Tofino Inlet, 4 miles from the entrance, is a stream of considerable size, said to communicate with an extensive lake.

Browning Passage, on the southern side of Meares Island, connects Tofino Inlet with Templar Channel. Its east end is only 300 yards wide, and off the west entrance there are several rocks, and strangers should not attempt it. The tide sets through at a rate of 2 to 4 knots, the flood stream from the westward.

North Channel, to the westward of Ship Channel, and separated from it by a number of small islands and rocks, lies along the southeastern side of Flores Island. Both sides of the channel are bordered by innumerable rocks; strangers should not use it, as it has not been closely examined; the sea generally breaks heavily along both sides of its outer part.

North Arm, between the east side of Flores Island and the main, is nearly one mile broad. Its western shores are high, but decrease gradually to the southward; the depths are very great in the north part, but they shoal rapidly to the southward, where vessels may anchor in from 5 to 8 fathoms abreast Base Point.

Matilda Creek, on the western side of North Arm, abreast the entrance to Herbert Arm, is very narrow and useless as an anchorage.

Base Point, the southwestern entrance to North Arm, is low and sandy, and there are from 2 to 3 fathoms at 200 yards distance from it. Vessels may anchor in from 5 to 8 fathoms midway between this point and the eastern shore.

Herbert Arm, the entrance to which is on the east side of North Arm, about 2 miles from the south entrance of the latter, has an average breadth of about one mile. The shores are high, mountainous and much broken; and there is no anchorage except at the southern part of its entrance.

Cone Island, lying at the entrance of this arm, is steep to on the southern and western sides, but the passage into Herbert Arm, north of it, is blocked up by rocks and small islets.

Bawden Bay, on the southeastern side of entrance to Herbert Arm, is of small extent and affords anchorage in 15 fathoms near the center; enter it in mid channel.

White Pine Cove, on the eastern side of Herbert Arm, is small, with a bank extending from the head; small vessels may anchor close to the edge of this bank in about 10 fathoms; care, however, should be taken to avoid a shoal of 3 fathoms lying almost in mid channel.

Directions.—Entering Clayoquot Sound by Ship Channel, round either Bare Island or Sea Otter Rock at the distance of ¼ mile, and steer up the channel [illegible] l the

tains

him ½

west

f 600

clear

ng S.

bear

tern,

[illegible] Rock and south of the North Bank.

Anchorage.—The best anchorage is a short distance to the southward of the Blackberry Islets, in from 5 to 7 fathoms; northward of them are from 3 to 4 fathoms.

Dark Island, 1,400 yards south of Plover Point, is small, some rocks extend a short distance off its west side, but there is a clear passage between it and the western shore.

Double Island, south of Dark Island, is small and steep to.

Deception Pass, at the southern extreme of Fortune Channel and connecting it with Tofino Inlet and Browning Passage, is a winding passage to the southward; it is free from danger in mid channel, and the tide sets with considerable strength through it. On its western side is a narrow creek ½ mile long with from 8 to 9 fathoms, and in the middle of the pass is a small islet

Tofino Inlet is in the eastern part of Clayoquot Sound, its shores are high and rocky, indented on the western side by some large creeks; there are several islands in the inlet and along both shores, but none of any considerable size. There is no anchorage, except near the entrance on the western side

Indian Island, in the entrance, is about one mile in extent, and steep to on the northern side, a bank extends 400 yards from its western point, with 3¼ fathoms close to the edge.

Warn Island, north of Indian Island, just within the entrance, is upwards of ½ mile in extent, and steep to on all sides

Island Cove, west of Warn Island, is of small extent, with from 8 to 10 fathoms in the middle, and completely landlocked; a small island lies off the entrance, with a clear passage 200 yards wide on either side of it into the cove.

Gunner Harbor, just north of Warn Island, is narrow; a small islet lies in its center, about ½ mile north of the entrance, and between them a vessel may find good anchorage in about 10 fathoms, the harbor becomes shoal towards the head

Tranquil Creek, on the west side of the inlet is narrow, and upwards of one mile long, its shores are high and rocky, and the creek is too deep for anchorage.

Between Tranquil Creek and Warn Island, along the west shore, are several small rocky islets, extending off from 400 to 600 yards

Flat Top Islets, 5 miles from the entrance of the inlet, are steep-to

(1852) **BRITISH COLUMBIA—Vancouver island—West coast—Clayoquot sound - Browning passage—Buoys established.**—A black spar buoy has been established on the north side of Browning passage, to show the extent of the shoal ground The buoy is moored in 5 fathoms of water.

Approx. position· Lat 49° 08′ 05″ N, Long. 125° 51′ 14″ W

A red spar buoy has been established on the south side of Browning passage, to show the northerly extent of the shoal referred to in Notice to Mariners No 40 (1480) of 1902 It is moored in 5 fathoms

Approx. position. Lat 49° 07′ 50″ N, Long. 125° 51′ 50″ W.

(N. M 52, 1904)

should not attempt it. The tide sets through at a rate of 2 to 4 knots, the flood stream from the westward.

North Channel, to the westward of Ship Channel, and separated from it by a number of small islands and rocks, lies along the south eastern side of Flores Island. Both sides of the channel are bordered by innumerable rocks; strangers should not use it, as it has not been closely examined; the sea generally breaks heavily along both sides of its outer part.

North Arm, between the east side of Flores Island and the main, is nearly one mile broad. Its western shores are high, but decrease gradually to the southward; the depths are very great in the north part, but they shoal rapidly to the southward, where vessels may anchor in from 5 to 8 fathoms abreast Base Point.

Matilda Creek, on the western side of North Arm, abreast the entrance to Herbert Arm, is very narrow and useless as an anchorage.

Base Point, the southwestern entrance to North Arm, is low and sandy, and there are from 2 to 3 fathoms at 200 yards distance from it. Vessels may anchor in from 5 to 8 fathoms midway between this point and the eastern shore.

Herbert Arm, the entrance to which is on the east side of North Arm, about 2 miles from the south entrance of the latter, has an average breadth of about one mile. The shores are high, mountainous and much broken, and there is no anchorage except at the southern part of its entrance.

Cone Island, lying at the entrance of this arm, is steep to on the southern and western sides, but the passage into Herbert Arm, north of it, is blocked up by rocks and small islets.

Bawden Bay, on the southeastern side of entrance to Herbert Arm, is of small extent and affords anchorage in 15 fathoms near the center; enter it in mid channel.

White Pine Cove, on the eastern side of Herbert Arm, is small, with a bank extending from the head; small vessels may anchor close to the edge of this bank in about 10 fathoms; care, however, should be taken to avoid a shoal of 3 fathoms lying almost in mid channel.

Directions.—Entering Clayoquot Sound by Ship Channel, round either Bare Island or Sea Otter Rock at the distance of ½ mile, and steer up the channel with the south point of Lawrence Island and the Twins Islets in line with the north summit of the Cat Face Mountains bearing N. 48° E. Keep the above-mentioned mark on till within ½ mile of the Shark Reefs, when haul more to the eastward for the west extreme of Vargas Island, which may be rounded at a distance of 600 yards. If going on through Hecate Passage into Hecate Bay, to clear Half tide Rock keep Hobbs Islet open west of Burgess Islet bearing S. 37° W. until the Twins come in line with the west Whaler island bearing N. 77° W., when steer up the passage with that mark on astern, which will lead north of Half tide Rock and south of the North Bank.

When past the latter, steer through Deep Pass and anchor in Hecate Bay midway between its entrance points in 9 or 10 fathoms.

During heavy southwesterly gales the sea is said to break right across Ship Channel, between Lawrence and Hobbs Islands.

Although there are several apparently deep channels into Clayoqnot Sound, they are, with the exception of Ship Channel, so tortuous and filled with rocks that strangers should not attempt to enter by any except the latter, and not by it unless having the latest chart of the sound. If the weather be clear it will be easy to recognize Ship Channel, but if in doubt there will be little difficulty found in procuring a native off the entrance of sufficient intelligence to pilot a vessel in.

Intending to navigate the inner waters of the sound, which can only be done by steamers or small craft, the chart will be found the best guide.

Flores Island, in the western part of Clayoqnot Sound, is nearly 7 miles in extent and of a square shape; it is low on the southern and eastern sides, but high on the north and west; the shores are rugged and broken, and there are several off-lying rocks along its southern and western sides; as a rule its southern side should not be approached nearer than 2 miles.

Rafael Point, the southwestern extreme of Flores, is cliffy and of moderate height; some rocks extend 400 yards from it, and the point should not be rounded within ½ mile. From thence the west coast of the island turns suddenly to the north, and continues in that direction for 7 miles, being indented by several small bays; some rocks and small islets extend 400 or 600 yards off in many parts.

Sydney Inlet, at the west end of Clayoquot Sound, varies in breadth from ½ to one mile. Four miles from the head are two small branches about 2 miles in length, one extending north the other SW.; the shores are high and rugged, rising abruptly from the sea. The depth is great and there is no anchorage.

Sharp Point, the SW. extreme of Clayoquot Sound, is low and rocky, but may be approached to 200 yards.

Refuge Cove, just west of Sharp Point, is from 200 to 400 yards wide, and affords good anchorage in 4 to 5 fathoms at ½ mile within the entrance, well sheltered and secure from all winds.

Sunken Rock.—The entrance is narrow, and at 400 yards inside Sharp Point and about 200 yards from the eastern shore is a rock having only 9 feet on it at low water. This rock lies slightly eastward of the fairway, and a good lookout is necessary, as it is not always marked by kelp.

Canoe Reef, lying just SW. of the entrance, is 2 feet above high water, but steep to on the southern and western sides.

Directions.—Entering Refuge Cove from seaward, bring the entrance or Sharp Point to bear N. 50° W., and steer for it, so as to pass 200 yards west of the point; then keep in mid channel, or rather nearer the western shore, to avoid the 9 foot rock, having passed which keep close to the eastern shore and anchor in 4½ or 5 fathoms, about ¼ mile within the entrance.

Shelter Arm branches off from the eastern side of Sydney Inlet, along the northern side of Flores Island, and then indents the mainland and terminates in a narrow creek at the head. It is upward of ½ mile wide, 10 miles long, and the depths vary from 40 to 90 fathoms in the southern part.

The shores of Shelter Arm are high, precipitous, and steep-to, the tide runs from one to 2 knots through it, the flood stream from the westward.

Steamer Cove is the only anchorage (indifferent) in it, just 2 miles within the entrance on the northern side of Flores Island; it is a small bight where a vessel may anchor in 17 to 19 fathoms, passing on either side of the islet at its entrance.

Obstruction Island is on the eastern side of Shelter Arm and separated from the north point of Flores Island by a narrow pass. Its shores are rocky and broken, and the passages along its southern and eastern sides are blocked up with rocks.

Rocky Pass, on its southern side, is narrow and filled with rocks, so that no vessel could get through it; the tide runs irregularly through, but seldom exceeds 4 knots.

Hesquiat Harbor, 8 miles northwestward of Clayoquot Sound, is formed at the bottom of the bay on the eastern side of Estevan Point. It is 4 miles long in a northerly direction, and upwards of 2 miles wide at the entrance, opening out a little inside, but on nearing the head it contracts to less than one mile.

The Bar.—Across the entrance, between Hesquiat Bluff and Estevan Point, is a bar or ledge, with from 3 to 5 fathoms water over it, which in a great measure prevents the sea from setting home into the harbor. Kelp grows more or less all over the anchorage in a depth of 5 fathoms.

Hesquiat Bluff is a remarkable low, wooded point, with a shingle beach around it; a reef, which covers at a quarter flood, lies ½ mile southwest of it.

Boat Basin is a small cove at the head of the harbor, there is a large fresh-water stream here, and vessels may obtain wood and water with great facility.

The shores of the harbor are mostly low and wooded, and within the entrance, at a distance of 400 yards, clear of danger. On the western side of the bay, near Estevan Point, are several indications of coal, and the land is apparently fertile.

Tides.—It is high water, full and change, in Hesquiat Harbor at 12h. 0m.; springs rise 12 feet.

Directions.—Hesquiat Harbor is easy of access to sailing vessels, even with a foul wind. The notch of Leading Mountain in line with the east entrance point, bearing north, leads over the bar in 4½ fathoms at low water Entering either from the east or west, give the outer shores of the harbor a berth of more than ½ mile, till past the bar, after which they may be approached to 400 yards; anchor in 7 or 8 fathoms near the center of the harbor, about ½ mile from its head.

In strong south or southwesterly gales the sea breaks heavily over the bar, but the anchorage is always safe, and landing is at all times practicable in Boat Basin.

The natives, though friendly, are much inclined to pilfering, and should be carefully watched.

Estevan Point is a low, wooded, and projecting point, bordered by a sandy beach, strewed with huge bowlders A ledge a mile wide extends nearly one mile off its southwestern side. Hole in the Wall, the southwestern part of the point, may be easily known by a remarkable gap in the trees at its extreme, which is conspicuous from the SW.

Sunday Rock lies nearly 3 miles N. 64° W. of Hole in the Wall; within the ledge good shelter will be found for boats in all weathers.

In rounding the western part of Estevan Point, it would not be prudent to approach the shore within 2 miles.

From this point the coast takes a northerly direction to Escalante Point at the entrance of Nootka Sound, and is low, foul ground existing off it for some distance.

Nootka Sound is a large sheet of water upwards of 6 miles in extent, containing several islands, and from its northern side three long, narrow arms penetrate the land for distances of 18, 7, and 14 miles, respectively. Its entrance is 4½ miles wide between Maquinna and Escalante Points. At the entrance the shores are low, and have several off lying dangers, but inside the sound they become high, rugged, and precipitous, and are everywhere free from danger.

In fine weather the natives will be met with in canoes in considerable numbers fishing for halibut, which are very plentiful along this coast.

There are four anchorages in the sound, two of which, Friendly Cove and Plumper Harbor, on the eastern side of Nootka Island, are small, though easy of access to steamers; the former is one and the latter 7 miles within the entrance; the others are in the Tlupana Arm.

Aspect.—From seaward the appearance of the land near the entrance of the sound offers to the navigator many striking features which in fine weather render it almost impossible to be mistaken; the low land of Estevan and Maquinna Points at the entrance, with the breakers off them; the Nootka Cone at the eastern point of Nootka Island, and if coming from the south or SSW., Conuma Peak, a remarkable steeple shaped mountain 4,889 feet high, is a most conspicuous feature.

Tides.—The tidal streams are everywhere inconsiderable.

Escalante Point is low and rocky; some small islets, and rocks generally above high water, extend off it in a westerly direction for upwards of one mile, but they are steep to on their outer edge. At their outer end is a rock only uncovering at low water.

From Escalante Point to Burdwood Point, at the narrowest part of entrance on the east side, the coast, is bordered by several off-lying rocks, and should not be approached within one mile until close to the latter point, which is steep to, and may be approached to within 200 yards.

Maquinna Point is low and wooded, and at its extreme is a remarkable bare-topped conical rock about 60 or 70 feet high; some rocks extend 600 yards off it in a southeasterly direction, also along the coast from it to the eastward nearly as far as the entrance of Friendly Cove, and the shore should not be approached nearer than ¾ mile till near the latter place.

Bajo Reef, 6 miles S. 86° W. of Maquinna Point, is about 400 yards in extent, and the sea only breaks on it in heavy weather. This reef is the only hidden danger outside the sound, and is dangerous to vessels entering it from the westward. Yuquot Point, kept open east of Maquinna Point, bearing N. 72° E., leads SE of it; and Bight Cone (a remarkable summit on the southern side of Nootka Island) kept well open west of Bajo Point, bearing N. 12° E., leads west of the reef.

Friendly Cove, just within the narrowest part of the entrance to the sound, is about 400 yards in extent and sheltered from the sea by several small rocky islets on its southeastern side. The entrance, 200 yards wide, is from the NE. The shores on both sides of the cove are rocky, and about 60 feet high on the north side, but at the head, is a small space of clear cultivated flat land, around which in the summer the natives build an extensive village.

Anchorage in Friendly Cove is of small extent, affording only room for one vessel of moderate size to lie moored in the middle, though several small ones would find shelter.

Directions.—If desiring to anchor in Friendly Cove, round Observatory Islet, the east entrance point, close to, and if in a large vessel, moor with anchors SW. and NE., letting go the first immediately on entering the cove. Sailing vessels, unless with a fair wind, would find some difficulty in entering; and if unable to shoot in, it would be preferable to warp or proceed farther up the sound to Plumper Harbor.

Supplies.—No fresh water in any quantity can be procured at Friendly Cove or nearer than Marvinas Bay; but fish and deer may generally be obtained in large quantities from the natives.

Marvinas Bay.—The west shore of Nootka Sound from Friendly Cove is rocky, and near the southern part some islets lie parallel to it, extending for nearly 2 miles, distant about 600 yards from the shore. There are two small creeks with entrances too narrow for vessels to enter; the northernmost of them, named by the Spaniards Boca del Infierno, lies abreast the northern part of the above-mentioned islands. Marvinas Bay, 4 miles north of Friendly cove, is of small extent and open to the southward; it only affords anchorage to coasters.

Water.—There are large fresh-water streams at the head of Marvinas Bay, and just south of it, convenient for watering.

Kendrick Arm, between Nootka and Narrow Islands, is about 5 miles long and ½ mile wide, connected at the northern part by a narrow boat pass to the Tahsis Canal; on the western side, 2 miles from its entrance, is Plumper Harbor, easy of access and well sheltered. Northward of this harbor the shores of the arm on both sides are rocky, terminating in two narrow creeks at the head, useless for purposes of navigation.

Plumper Harbor is a small bay indenting the eastern side of Nootka Island, about 600 yards in extent, and affords good anchorage in 12 fathoms. It is protected on the eastern side by two small wooded islets from 30 to 40 feet high; on the western side the shore is rather swampy, and there are several fresh water streams.

Anchorage.—There is a clear passage into the harbor between the two islets, or to the northward of the north one, which may be rounded at the distance of 200 yards, and there is room for a vessel to lie at single anchor inside; it is the best anchorage in the sound, the only drawback being its distance from the entrance.

Tahsis Canal, the entrance to which is about 6 miles from Friendly Cove, is a long narrow arm of the sea, nearly straight, and 14 miles long; the shores are mountainous, rocky and steep to, and there is no anchorage in it. In many parts this canal is only 400 yards wide, but it becomes gradually broader at the head, where is a large stream, and also a considerable village, to which the natives resort during the season for salmon, which are caught here in great plenty.

At 10½ miles from the entrance of the canal on the western side, and separating the north point of Nootka Island from the main of Vancouver Island, are the Tahsis Narrows, 200 yards wide, with 28 fathoms in the center; they connect Esperanza Inlet with the Tahsis Canal; the tide runs weakly through them, the flood from the westward.

At the entrance of Tahsis Canal is a small island with a clear passage about 200 yards wide on both sides of it.

Bligh Island, lying in the center of Nootka Sound, is the largest island in it, being about 4½ miles long in a northerly direction and 2 miles wide in the northern part, its shores are rocky, and indented by creeks on the southern side. Its southern extreme is a long, narrow point, and off its southern and western sides are a number of islands extending upwards of one mile from it, all steep-to on their outer edges, but among which no vessel should venture. The south part of the island is rather low, but it rises in the northern and western parts to 1,030 and 1,200 feet.

Resolution Cove, at the SE. point of this island, just within the entrance of the Zuciarte Channel, is only a slight bend in the coast, with a deep and rocky bottom, and inconvenient for an anchorage, being also open to the SW.

Junction Island, lying about midway between the SE. point of Narrow Island and west side of Bligh Island, is about ½ mile long; a small islet lies close off its NW. side and another on the opposite side. The channel lies to the west and north of Junction Island, and vessels should not pass between the latter and Bligh Island.

Zuciarte Channel is between the eastern shore of Nootka Sound and Bligh Island; its shores are high and clear of danger; the depths within the channel are great.

Guaquina, or Muchalat Arm, extends in an easterly direction from the eastern part of Nootka Sound, and varies in breadth from ¼ to upwards of one mile. It is bounded on both sides by mountains, and presents similar features to the inlets before described along this coast, terminating in low land at the head, through which a small stream flows into the inlet; there is no anchorage whatever within this arm except for coasters.

One and a half miles within the entrance is Gore Island; there is a clear deep passage on either side of it, the southern one being less than 200 yards wide at the eastern part. The island rises in the center to 1,200 feet, sloping gradually to each end; its shores are rocky.

On the northern side of this arm, 14 miles within the entrance, is an extensive valley, through which flows a large stream, named the Gold River, indications of that metal having been discovered there.

The Muchalat Indians have a village at the mouth of Gold River.

Tlupana Arm, the entrance to which is in the northern part of Nootka Sound, branches off at the head in two smaller arms extending to the NW. and NE., each terminating in low land. Its shores are high and rocky; there are two anchorages, one at Deserted Creek, on the western side, and the other at Head Bay, the termination of the northwestern branch.

The mountains at the northern part of this arm are the highest in the sound; Conuma Peak, rising 7 miles NE of the head, is 4,889 feet high, and of a steeple shape.

Deserted Creek, 3 miles within the entrance, is 2 miles long in a northwesterly direction and about ¼ mile wide, vessels may anchor in 12 to 14 fathoms at ¼ mile from its head. Island Bay, a small cove on its northeastern side, just within the entrance, has an islet in the center, to the westward of which is room for a vessel to anchor in 12 fathoms.

At the southern extreme of the promontory separating the two branches at the head of Tlupana Arm is Perpendicular Bluff, a remarkable precipice of considerable height.

Head Bay, the termination of the western branch of the Tlupana Arm, affords anchorage in from 14 to 16 fathoms at the distance of 600 or 800 yards from its head. At the entrance on the north side, are three small islets about 3 or 4 feet above high water, the inner one connected to the shore by a beach at low water, between these islands and Perpendicular Bluff is a small bay, where a vessel may anchor in from 16 to 18 fathoms.

Directions.—Entering Nootka sound from the southward, after rounding Estevan Point steer about north for the entrance, which will be easily made out by the rocks off Escalante and Maquinna Points; keep about 2 miles off the eastern shore till past Escalante Point, when steer up mid-channel into the sound. If bound to Friendly Cove, haul over to the western side of entrance for Yuquot Point, which may be approached within a distance of 200 yards, and rounding it sharply, anchor or moor, as most convenient, in Friendly Cove.

If bound to Plumper Harbor, after passing Yuquot Point keep about ½ mile from the eastern side of Nootka Island to the entrance of the Kendrick Arm, when steer up the latter in mid-channel till abreast Plumper Harbor, which may be entered by passing between Bold and Pass Islets on its east side, or going to the northward of the former.

Should it be desired to anchor in any of the anchorages within the Tlupana Arm, steer as before directed till within ½ mile of the entrance to the Kendrick arm, when haul to the NE., pass to the westward of Junction and Bligh Islands, and steer up the Tlupana Arm in mid-channel, or close to on either shore. Deserted Creek and Head Bay are clear of danger and may be entered without difficulty.

Entering Nootka Sound from the westward, on nearing Bajo Point do not approach the south shore of Nootka Island within 4 miles, or shut in Bight Cone with Bajo Point bearing N. 12° E. until Yuquot point opens east of Maquinna Point bearing N. 72° E., which will clear the Bajo Reef; a vessel may then steer for the entrance of the sound, about N. 80° E., not approaching the shore between Maquinna and Yuquot Points nearer than one mile until abreast the latter, which may be rounded close to; after which proceed up the sound as before directed.

If beating into Nootka Sound, when standing to the westward, keep Yuquot Point open east of Maquinna Point bearing N. 72° E., which will keep a vessel well clear to the eastward of Bajo Reef; in standing to the eastward do not approach Escalante Point within 1½ miles, nor bring Burdwood Point to bear northward of N. 35° E. until abreast it, when the shore may be approached close to; when standing towards Maquinna and Yuquot Points on the western side avoid bringing the latter to bear to the eastward of N. 46° E. until abreast it, when it may be approached close to.

Nootka Sound is easier of access than any other place on the whole of the western coast of Vancouver Island. the entrance being nearly 2 miles wide in the narrowest part, and by attending to the above directions any sailing vessel may beat in or out of the sound. If the night be clear, and provided with a chart, it may be entered without risk by bringing the entrance to bear N. 46° E., and in a steamer but little difficulty would be experienced in picking up the anchorages of Friendly Cove and Plumper Harbor.

Nootka Island is of considerable extent, being 15 miles long in a northerly and 20 miles in a westerly direction. Its southern or outer shore is low, rising gradually inland, and it has a beautiful and fertile appearance; it is bordered by a sandy beach nearly the whole distance, and the sea breaks heavily along it.

Bajo Point is low and rocky. A ledge named the Inner Bajo Reef extends 1½ miles from it in a southerly direction, and the Bajo Reef lies 2¾ miles south of it.

Westward of Bajo Point the coast takes a NW. direction and is slightly indented. Bight Cone, a remarkable summit, 340 feet high, rises 3 miles N. 4° W. of Bajo Point, and is about one mile inland.

When navigating along the south side of Nootka Island west of the Bajo Reef it would not be prudent to approach the shore within 2 miles, until near Ferrer Point, though there are no known outlying dangers.

Nuchatlitz Inlet, on the northwestern side of Nootka Island, is 6 miles long in a northeasterly direction and 3 miles wide at entrance, narrowing towards the head; its shores are high and rocky, and much broken into creeks and small bays; off the entrance and within are several dangers. There are two good anchorages, Port Langford on the northern side and Mary Basin at the head; but owing to the dangers off the entrance of the inlet they are both rather difficult of access.

Ferrer Point, the southern entrance point of the inlet, is low and rocky; there is a depth of 14 fathoms at a distance of 400 yards from it, and ½ mile eastward of the point is Northwest Cone, a very remarkable conical summit 350 feet high, which proves a very useful guide to this locality from the westward.

Danger Rock, about one mile N. 27° W. of Ferrer Point, is the worst danger in entering, as it is of very small extent, and the sea only breaks on it in heavy weather; it is steep to on all sides, there being 11 fathoms close to it. The best passage into the inlet is between this rock and Ferrer Point.

Leading Mark.—Mark Hill, at the head of inlet, in line with the north part of Fitz Island bearing N. 74° E., leads south of this rock midway between it and Ferrer Point, and through the fairway into the inlet north of South Reef.

Nuchatlitz Reef, in the center of the entrance and ¼ mile northward of Danger Rock, is about ¾ mile long in an east and west direction and 200 yards wide. The sea generally breaks on this reef, and at its eastern extremity is a small rock awash at high water; there is a clear deep passage between it and Danger Rock, and also apparently to the northward of it, but neither should be attempted by strangers, as no leading marks can be given for going through them.

South Reef, nearly 400 yards in extent and covering at three-quarters flood, lies just within the entrance on the south side, one mile N. 58° E. of Ferrer Point, and about 600 yards from the shore.

Louie Creek, just inside South Reef, is shoal and nearly a mile in extent; there are several rocks off its entrance and vessels should not enter it, to the eastward of the creek the south shore of Nuchatlitz Inlet is rocky, but appears to be clear of danger at the distance of 200 yards.

Fitz Island, in the center of the inlet, is of small extent, low, rugged, and covered with a few stunted pine trees, the tops of which are about 100 feet above the sea. At ½ mile WNW. of it is a small bare island 20 feet high, and steep to on the western side, but between the rock and Fitz Island foul ground exists.

Bare Rock, of small extent, lies ¾ mile to the SW of Fitz Island, and there is a clear passage between them.

Mary Basin, the termination of the inlet, is of considerable extent, and completely land locked by Lord Island, which lies across the inlet at the southwestern part of the basin. The depths inside the basin vary from 5 to 9 fathoms, and the entrance on the north side of Lord Island appears clear of danger, but it has not been sufficiently examined to recommend its use by strangers.

To the eastward of Mary Basin and connected to it by a narrow pass 50 yards wide, with from 7 to 9 fathoms, is Inner Basin, a sheet of water upwards of 3 miles long in an easterly direction, with from 20 to 39 fathoms, and apparently useless as an anchorage.

Port Langford, on the northern side of the inlet, is about 1¾ miles long in a northwesterly direction, and varies in breadth from ¼ to ½ mile. The depths in it vary from 5 to 8 fathoms, and it affords a secure and well sheltered anchorage in about 6 fathoms, muddy bottom, at the distance of ½ mile from the head. The eastern shore of the port is high, rising to a summit, Mount Rosa, but the western shore is much lower; both are rocky, but within the entrance clear of danger.

Colwood Islet, at the southwestern extreme of the entrance, is small and bare, and nearly ½ mile offshore; it may be approached to within 200 yards on the east side, but inside it and to the westward round the western entrance point of Nuchatlitz Inlet are innumerable rocks and small islets, among which vessels should not venture.

Belmont Point, the eastern entrance point into Port Langford, is low, and a rock uncovers 200 yards west of it.

Directions.—Entering Nuchatlitz Inlet from the southward, bring Ferrer Point on a N. 13° E bearing, and steer to pass ½ mile west of it; and when Mark Hill comes in line with the north part of Fitz Island N. 74° E., haul in for the entrance on that mark, which will lead in clear of Danger Rock and South Reef. When Ferrer Point bears S. 24° W., vessels will be inside the rock and may steer for the entrance to Port Langford, pass midway between Colwood Islet and Belmont Point, and proceed up the port in mid channel, anchoring in 5 or 6 fathoms at a distance of ½ mile from the head.

Approaching the port from the westward, keep an offing of 4 or 5 miles till Ferrer Point bears S. 66° E., when steer for it on that bearing till the leading mark for the channel comes on, when proceed as before directed to the anchorage in Port Langford.

Intending to enter Mary Basin, not recommended, when past Ferrer Point keep the leading mark on till abreast Louie Creek, then steer a little to the eastward, passing about 200 yards south of Fitz Island and Bare Rock; when past the former steer N. 86° E. until the western point of Lord Island bears N. 35° E., which will clear the shoal extending ½ mile to the southward from Benson Point, and then, on approaching Lord Island, borrow a little towards the northern shore, and enter Mary Basin to the westward of the island and the small islet NW. of it; when abreast the latter haul more to the eastward, and anchor in from 5 to 6 fathoms near the middle of the basin

Vessels of any size should not attempt to beat into this inlet, as there is generally a heavy sea at the entrance, and strangers should not attempt to enter unless the leading mark is easily distinguished.

Esperanza Inlet, the entrance to which lies between the northwestern side of Nootka Island and the mainland of Vancouver Island, is about 16 miles long in a winding northeasterly direction, with an average breadth of about one mile, narrowing at the head, and connected by a narrow pass (Tahsis Narrows) to the Tahsis Canal, in Nootka Sound.

The entrance, though wide, contains several dangers; but inside the shores are nearly everywhere steep to, rising on both sides to mountains of considerable height. The southern shore is indented by three bays of moderate extent, which afford no anchorage; and from the northern one three arms of considerable length penetrate the Vancouver shore for several miles. Port Eliza, in the western arm, is the only anchorage in the inlet.

Middle Channel, the widest and best into Esperanza Inlet, lies 3 miles NW. of Ferrer Point, between Blind Reef, Needle Rock, and a number of small islets extending off the northwestern point of Nootka Island on the east, and Middle Reef and Black Rock on the west, a part of the former is always above water.

Blind Reef, at the southeastern extreme of the channel, 3 miles N 27° W. of Ferrer Point, is about 400 yards in extent, and the sea only breaks on it in bad weather; 200 yards northward of it is a small rock, and at a distance of 400 yards from its south and west sides are depths of 13 to 19 fathoms.

Pin Rock, of small extent, awash at low water, lies ⅜ mile S. 66° E. of Blind Reef.

Needle Rock, of small extent, lies ⅓ mile northward of the Blind Reef, and has from 14 to 15 fathoms at a distance of 400 yards west of it.

Middle Reef, at the southwestern entrance point of Middle Channel and separating it from the North Channel, is about 600 yards long in a northeasterly direction and 200 yards wide. The sea generally breaks on this reef, and at its southern extreme is a small rock 4 feet above high water; there are from 5 to 20 fathoms at the distance of 200 yards on all sides of it.

Leading Mark.—Leading Hill, in line with Black Rock, bearing N. 13° E., leads through the fairway of Middle Channel west of Blind Reef and Needle Rock, and east of Middle Reef.

North Channel leads into the inlet west of Middle Reef, between it and the dangers off the southeastern point of Catala Island. It is about ⅓ mile wide, merging at the north part into Middle Channel. The depths in it vary from 17 to 22 fathoms, and the dangers on its western side are all above water.

Leading Mark.—Black Rock, in line with Double Island, bearing N. 43° E., leads in through the fairway of North Channel clear of all danger.

Catala Island, on the western side of the entrance to Esperanza Inlet, is wooded; its shores are rocky, and several dangers exist at a considerable distance off it on all sides; its northern side is separated from the Vancouver shore by a passage ½ mile wide, named Rolling Roadstead, and vessels may find a tolerably secure anchorage there in from 4 to 6 fathoms, though generally a swell prevails.

The Twins, two small islets connected with each other at low water, lie off the south point of Catala Island, and foul ground extends nearly 1½ miles south from them, terminating in Low Rock, which forms the southwestern entrance point to the North Channel.

Black Rock, which lies 800 yards S. 21° E. of the east point of Catala, is a small, bare rock. Foul ground exists between it and Catala, and also 200 yards south of it. Vessels should not approach its eastern side nearer than 400 yards, nor attempt to pass west of it.

Rolling Roadstead.—Entrance Reef, about 600 yards north of the east point of Catala Island at the eastern part of Rolling Roadstead, is of small extent, and covers at half flood.

Arnold Rock, ½ mile from Entrance Reef, and about 400 yards from the opposite shore, is awash at high water; midway between these rocks are 6½ fathoms, and in the roadstead from 4 to 6 fathoms. The outer rocks off the NW. part of Catala Island, open north of the low grassy point at the north side of the latter, bearing N. 77° W., leads into Rolling Roadstead, midway between the Arnold Rock and Entrance Reef.

Half a mile inshore, and overlooking the NE. part of Rolling Roadstead, is Leading Hill. It is of conical shape, and conspicuous from the entrance to the Middle Channel.

Double Island lies ½ mile from the western shore at the inner and narrowest part of the entrance to Esperanza Inlet. It is of small extent, and wooded. A number of rocks exist between it and the shore, but 400 yards from its east side are depths of 25 to 45 fathoms

Flower Islet, on the opposite shore, ½ mile from the NW. point of Nootka Island, is small and bare. At 400 yards SW. of it is a small rock 2 feet above high water.

Eastward of Flower Islet the southern shore of Esperanza Inlet takes a winding irregular outline to the eastward. It is everywhere steep to, and rises gradually to summits 2,000 and 3,000 feet high. There are three bays, all too deep for anchorage. In the western one, which is just within the entrance, are several small islets.

Center Island, ½ mile off the southern shore, is about ¾ mile long in an east and west direction, and of moderate height; its shores are rocky, and may be approached to 200 yards.

Hecate Channel, near the head of the inlet, is 4¾ miles long and has an average breadth of about 1,200 yards. The eastern end, Tahsis Narrows, is about 200 yards wide; the shores are high and rocky, and may be approached close to.

Port Eliza, the entrance to which is one mile NE. of Double Island, is a narrow arm; its breadth varying from 400 to 800 yards; the shores are high, and there are some rocks and small islands in the entrance, and along the eastern shore. There is good anchorage in from 14 to 15 fathoms at ½ mile from the head, and also in Queen's Cove, which is upwards of one mile within the entrance on the east side.

The head terminates in a small patch of low swampy land, through which flow two fresh water streams, and off it a bank dries 200 yards at low water.

Harbor Island, in the center of the entrance, is wooded and of moderate height. The passage into Port Eliza on its east side, through Birthday Channel, is 400 yards wide in the narrowest part, and clear of danger. Between Harbor Island and the western shore lies False Channel, which has irregular soundings, and in its southern part are two rocks which cover at half flood.

Fairway Island, on the east side of Birthday Channel, is of small extent, and covered with a few stunted trees; some rocks extend a short distance off around it, the eastern ones being about 6 feet above high water.

Channel Reef, ½ mile north of Harbor Island, in the middle of Port Eliza, is about 200 yards in extent, and covers at three quarters flood; at 200 yards from its eastern side, are from 16 to 26 fathoms; beyond this reef there are no dangers in the port at more than 200 yards from the shore.

Queen's Cove, on the eastern side of the port, about 1½ miles from the entrance, is ½ mile long and 400 yards wide, but at the entrance the width is contracted to 100 yards by a small island, which at low water, is connected to the eastern side of the cove.

The cove affords room for a large vessel to lie moored in the center. Its shores are high and rocky, and it is completely land-locked, but it is easy of access for steamers; most likely large sailing vessels would be obliged to warp in; there is a fresh-water stream of considerable size on the west side of its head, very convenient for watering.

Espinoza Arm, the entrance to which is 2 miles NE. of port Eliza, is 8 miles long in a northerly direction, and its average breadth is ½ mile. The soundings within it are deep, and it affords no anchorage; at the entrance, on the west side, are some small islets, and a rock which uncovers. This inlet is bounded by high, rocky, rugged shores, and terminates in low land at the head. At the distance of 4 miles within the entrance, on the eastern side, is a narrow branch or fork extending to the NE. Its head is separated by a narrow neck from the Zeballos Arm. The entrance to this narrow branch is choked up with rocks.

Zeballos Arm, at the west end of Hecate channel, is about 6 miles long in a winding direction to the NW., and about ⅔ mile wide; similar to Espinoza Arm, it offers no anchorage whatever, and is of no use to the navigator.

Directions.—A stranger entering Esperanza Inlet from the southward through the Middle Channel, and intending to anchor in Port Eliza, should pass Ferrer Point at a distance of about 3 miles, and keep on a northerly course till nearing the entrance to Middle Channel, when steer to bring Leading Hill in line with Black Rock bearing N. 13° E., which will lead through the fairway, and clear of the dangers on both sides of the channel. When the southern point of Catala Island bears N. 44° W., vessels will be inside the dangers at entrance and should steer about N. 45° E. for the entrance to Port Eliza, passing ¼ mile east of Double Island. When entering the port steer through Birthday Channel, passing 200 yards east of Harbor Island; when past the east point of the latter, keep about N. 10° W. for the entrance to Queen's Cove, or further over to the eastern shore, to avoid Channel Reef; in entering the cove, pass to the west of the island at its entrance, and moor immediately the vessel is inside, anchors NNE. and SSW.

If going to the head of Port Eliza, keep on as before directed till within 200 yards of Queen's Cove, when haul sharply to the westward, keeping about 200 yards from the eastern shore till Fairway Island comes in line with the eastern point of Harbor Island bearing S. 32° E., when the vessel will be west of Channel Reef, and may steer up the port in mid channel, anchoring near the center, about ½ mile from the head, in 15 or 16 fathoms.

Sailing vessels of any size should not attempt to enter Port Eliza unless with a steady fair wind.

If bound to Rolling Roadstead, enter the Middle Channel as before directed, but instead of steering for the entrance of Port Eliza, keep on a N. 12° E. course (passing about ¼ mile east of Black Rock) until the outer extreme of the islets off the northwestern part of Catala Island come open north of the low grassy point on its northern side bearing N. 77° W., when haul in for the roadstead on that mark, which will lead midway between Arnold and Entrance Reefs; anchor in 6 fathoms, with the extremes of Catala Island bearing west and S. 10° E.

Entering Esperanza Inlet from the westward, keep an offing of 2½ or 3 miles from Catala Island till Double Island comes in line with Black Rock bearing N. 43° E., and enter the Inlet through the North Channel with this mark on, which will lead in clear of danger. When the Twins Islets bear N. 32° W. haul more to the eastward, passing ¼ mile outside the Mid and Black Rocks, and steer for Rolling Roadstead or Port Eliza as before directed.

If the weather be clear and the marks can be made out, both North and Middle Channels are equally good, the latter being wide enough for a vessel to beat through, though it would be hazardous for strangers to attempt, as no turning marks can be given.

Generally a heavy swell prevails off the entrance to Nuchatlitz and Esperanza Inlets, and sailing vessels should not attempt to enter or leave either of them unless with a steady fair or leading wind.

The Coast, westward of Catala Island to Tatchu Point, takes a westerly direction for upwards of 3 miles, is indented by two small sandy bays, and bordered by a number of rocks, some of which extend nearly 2 miles offshore. Tatchu Point is cliffy; some rocks lie a short distance to the southward of it, and there is a native village of considerable size at ½ mile east of it. Eliza Dome, a remarkable summit, rises 1½ miles north of the point, and is very conspicuous from seaward.

From Tatchu Point the coast turns to the NW. to the entrance of Kyuquot Sound, and is indented by several small bays, in some parts of which boats may find shelter.

Barrier Islands.—At 2 miles northwestward of Tatchu Point is the commencement of a chain of small islands and reefs bordering the coast of Vancouver Island for nearly 20 miles in a westerly direction to the entrance Ououkinsh Inlet. They extend in some parts as far as 5 miles offshore, and through them are two known navigable channels, the Kyuquot and Halibut, leading to anchorages; the former channel leads into Kyuquot Sound, and the latter into Clanninick Harbor, but as a rule strangers should not venture in the channels among these islands, unless the weather be clear, or without a pilot.

Highest Island, one of the Barrier Group, lying 2 miles southwestward of Union Island, is a remarkable bare rock 98 feet high, and useful in identifying the Kyuquot Channel.

In thick weather vessels should stand no nearer the Barrier Islands than into a depth of 40 fathoms.

Kyuquot Sound is a large broken sheet of water penetrating from the coast to a distance of 14 or 15 miles inland in two large arms and several smaller ones. Union Island, a large island lying at the entrance, forms on either side of it a channel into the sound, the eastern one only being fit for large vessels; there are also several islands within, mostly small.

There are three anchorages, Narrowgut and Easy Creeks and Fair Harbor, the two latter being of considerable size, but at a distance of 13 and 10 miles from the entrance; the former, though very small, is only 5 miles within the sound.

Kyuquot Channel leads into the sound through the Barrier Islands and to the eastward of Union Island. It is nearly straight, about 5 miles long in a NE. direction and about ¾ mile wide; a mid-channel course through is clear of danger.

East Entrance Reef, one of the Barrier group lying at the southeastern extreme of the channel, is about 100 yards in extent and 4 feet above high water; vessels should not stand inside it, nor, when entering the channel, round the reef nearer than ½ mile.

Rugged Point, the southeastern entrance point to Kyuquot Sound, is rugged and rocky, but steep to on the western side; between it and East Entrance Reef are a number of rocks, among which vessels should not venture. The eastern side of the channel to the northward of this point is formed by the Vancouver shore, and is slightly indented and steep to, to the termination of the channel.

West Rocks, at the southwestern extreme of Kyuquot channel, are two in number; some rocks which cover at a quarter flood extend ½ mile SE. from them, with 20 fathoms close to their outer edge. When navigating the channel do not approach West Rocks within ⅜ mile.

White Cliff Head, the southern extreme of Union Island, is about 70 feet high, faced to the southward by a remarkable white cliff; there are 35 fathoms within 200 yards of it. Half a mile north of the head is Kyuquot Hill, a remarkable summit 740 feet high, bare of trees on its eastern side, and very conspicuous from seaward.

Northward of White Cliff Head, the east coast of Union Island trends in an irregular outline to Chat Channel Point; it is generally rocky, and rises gradually.

Chat Channel Point, the eastern point of Union Island, is a low rocky point with a remarkable knob just inside it; a rock which covers at a quarter flood lies 400 yards east of it, and the point should not be rounded nearer than ½ mile.

Leading Island, just northward of Kyuquot Channel, is about 1½ miles long in an east and west direction, and ½ mile wide: its shores are steep to, and the island rises near the center to a summit 489 feet high, which, when kept midway between White Cliff Head and Rugged Point, leads into the sound through the fairway of Kyuquot Channel.

Union Island, at the entrance to the sound, and protecting it from the ocean, is of square shape; the shores are rocky and much broken on the southern and western sides.

Blind Entrance leads into Kyuquot Sound westward of Union Island, it is a narrow tortuous channel with some rocks in the outer part and should not be entered by strangers, coasters often enter the sound by this channel, but no directions can be given for navigating it.

Narrowgut Creek, in the southeastern part of the sound is one mile long in an easterly direction, but is less than 200 yards wide just inside the entrance. The depths in it vary from 16 to 8 fathoms, and there is only just room for a vessel to moor; the shores are high, the entrance is clear of danger, and the creek easy of access to steamers. A stream of considerable size empties at the head of the creek, from which a bank extends off 600 yards.

Shingle Point, at the entrance to the creek on the north side, is bordered by a sandy beach, and has 9 fathoms close to.

Deep Inlet, northward of Narrowgut Creek, is about 3 miles long in a easterly direction, but affords no anchorage; on its northern side, at the entrance, is a remarkable high precipice.

Hohoae Island is nearly in the center of the sound, ½ mile north of Union Island, its shores are rocky and steep to. On its eastern side is Dixie Cove, where a small craft may anchor in 6 fathoms completely landlocked.

Pinnace Channel, between Hohoae Island and the eastern shore of the sound is clear of danger.

Tahsish Arm is in the northern part of the sound. It is 6 miles long in a winding direction to the northward, and its shores, except at the head, are high, rugged, and mostly steep to, the head terminates in low swampy land, through which flows a considerable stream off which a bank dries 200 yards; there is a small village at the mouth of the stream; on the eastern side, 2 miles below the head, is a similar stream, off which a bank extends about 400 yards.

Fair Harbor, on the east side of Tahsish Arm, is of an oblong shape, and affords anchorage near either end in from 13 to 11 fathoms; its shores, generally, are high and steep; at its head a bank dries off for 200 yards. The western end of the harbor is formed by a low, narrow neck, about 200 yards wide at low water, connecting an island to the mainland of Vancouver, and separating the harbor from Pinnace Channel. The entrance lies on the northern side of this island, and has some small islets on its northern side; when entering keep the southern shore pretty close aboard, but take care to avoid a rock which lies on that shore about half way in. A patch of 9 feet lies abreast it, and therefore considerable caution must be observed. This harbor can be entered by steamers, or sailing vessels with a fair wind.

Some rocks, the outer one of which covers, lie 600 yards west of the entrance to Fair Harbor, about 200 yards from the shore

Moketas Island, in the northern part of the sound, is rocky, its eastern and western sides being steep to At 200 yards from its northern shore, near the center, is a sunken rock, and on its southeastern side lie the Channel Rocks, a small patch, about 3 feet above high water; they, however, are steep to.

The passage between Moketas Island and the northern shore of the sound is 600 yards wide in the narrowest part: if using it, vessels ought to keep well over to the northern side.

Kokshittle Arm, the entrance of which is in the northwestern part of the sound, is upwards of 8 miles long and about one mile wide at the entrance, narrowing gradually towards the head; its shores are rocky, and of a broken outline, with several small islets off them. It shoals gradually towards the head, and there are no dangers; a very good anchorage, the best in the sound, is on its western side at 4 miles from the entrance. The head of the arm terminates in low, swampy land, through which flows a small stream, and a bank extends off for the distance of about 400 yards.

Just within the entrance, on the eastern side, is a small cove with 4 fathoms in the center, available for small craft.

Easy Creek, the anchorage before referred to on the western side of Kokshittle Arm, is about 2 miles long in a southeasterly direction, turning sharply round from its entrance and running in this direction parallel to the inlet, being separated from it by a narrow rocky peninsula. It is 800 yards wide at the entrance, narrowing gradually to the head; the depths in it vary from 12 to 20 fathoms, and there is good anchorage from ½ mile within the entrance to the head. The shores are rocky, of moderate height, steep to on the eastern side, but from the western a sand-bank dries off in some parts for the distance of nearly 200 yards. The best anchorage is one mile within the entrance, in from 13 to 16 fathoms, about 200 or 400 yards from the eastern shore; when entering keep near the east shore.

On the opposite side of the arm, abreast Easy Cr[illegible], is a village and a stream of considerable size, off which a bank dries out about 400 yards.

Chamiss Bay, on the western side of Kyuquot Sound, about one mile from the north part of Blind Entrance, is nearly ½ mile in extent, but affords no anchorage.

Directions.—Sailing vessels should not attempt to enter Kyuquot Sound, unless with a steady, fair, or leading wind, as generally a heavy swell prevails outside, which in a light wind would render t[illegible] position critical; and strangers should not attempt to venture in unless the weather is clear and the leading mark for the channel can be easily made out.

Entering the sound by the Kyuquot Channel, which is the only one strangers should use, keep a good offing till the entrance of the channel is made out, when bring the summit of Leading Island midway between Chat Channel and Rugged Points bearing N. 42° E. and steer up the channel with that mark on; when nearing Chat Channel Point, give it a berth of at least 800 yards to avoid the rock which lies off it. If bound to Narrowgut Creek pass eastward of Leading Island, and keeping about 200 yards from the southern shore, enter the creek in mid-channel, and moor, if in a large vessel, when inside.

If bound to Fair Harbor, keep as before directed till near Leading Island, pass to the westward of this island, and proceed up to the northward through Pinnace Channel, keeping about 200 yards or so from either shore, on to the entrance of Tahsish arm On nearing Fair Harbor keep from 400 to 600 yards from the eastern side of the arm till the entrance bears SE, when steer for it on that bearing, keeping close over to the southern shore till inside, and anchor in the middle, about ½ mile from the east end, in 11 fathoms.

Bound to Easy Creek, pass to the westward of Leading, Hohoae and Moketas Islands; enter the Kokshittle arm in mid channel, and proceeding up it for a distance of 4 miles will bring a vessel abreast the creek, which may be entered in mid-channel; anchor in from 13 to 16 fathoms, about one mile within the entrance and from 200 to 400 yards from the shore.

Clanninick Harbor, on the Vancouver shore, 3 miles to the westward of Kyuquot Sound, is about one mile long in a westerly direction, ½ mile wide, and affords good anchorage in from 7 to 10 fathoms, at the distance of ½ mile from the head, from which a sand bank extends 400 yards; its shores are mostly low, and there are some rocks on either side of the entrance.

The harbor is protected by Village, Table, and other islands of the Barrier group, from the ocean, and there is only one channel, the Halibut, into it through them, which, though clear of danger, should not, except under unavoidable circumstances, be attempted by strangers.

Halibut Channel, through the Barrier group from the ocean to the entrance of Clanninick Harbor, lies westward of Table and Village Islands and east of Look out Island. It is about 3 miles long in a northerly direction, and ½ mile wide in the narrowest part; the depths in are somewhat irregular, but a mid channel course through, except in the northern part, is clear of danger.

Table Island, on the eastern side of the channel, is the largest of the Barrier group, being nearly ½ mile in extent. some rocks, mostly above water, extend ½ mile from its southern side, the outer one being 50 feet high, with 15 fathoms 400 yards west of it. Trap Bluff on the western side of the island is conspicuous.

Anchorage—Half a mile eastward of Table Island is an anchorage with from 4 to 6 fathoms, tolerably sheltered by some islands from seaward, and much used by coasters in summer months, the entrance to it is rather intricate, and strangers or any except in a small vessel should not attempt to enter

Village Island, on the east side of Halibut Channel, just north of Table Island, is small, on its eastern side is a large native village, much frequented in summer; off it a bank dries nearly 600 yards. To the eastward of this island among the Barrier Islands is a small cove, (Barter Cove), with from one to 3 fathoms; it is well sheltered in all weather, and much frequented by coasters when fur trading, the entrance to it is very narrow, and almost choked up with rocks.

Rock.—North of Village Island 400 yards is a rock awash at high water springs, but there is a depth of 5 to 6 fathoms at a distance of 200 yards from the western side.

Lookout Island, at the southern entrance point of Halibut Channel, is small, covered with a few trees, and about 150 feet high; its eastern side may be approached to 400 yards, but ½ mile SW. of it are some rocks, on which the sea always breaks.

Granite Island, which forms the southern side of Clanninick Harbor, is about ½ mile in extent, and joined by a sandy beach at low water to the Vancouver shore.

Chief Rock, 600 yards from its eastern point, is a very dangerous rock, which lies at the termination of the Halibut Channel, and only uncovers at low-water springs.

A sunken rock is said to exist nearly midway in the entrance to the harbor, 400 yards north of Chief Rock.

Directions—Bound into Clanninick Harbor by the Halibut Channel, keep about 2 miles off the Barrier Islands till Lookout Island bears N. 10° W., when steer for the entrance of the channel, passing about 400 yards east of Lookout Island. When the NW. end of Table Island bears N. 69° E, steer about N. 46° E, or more easterly, so as to pass about ¼ mile NW. of Trap Bluff on its western side; on nearing Granite Island, bring Trap Bluff in line with the east high-water part of Lookout Island S. 52° W., and steer N. 52° E. for the entrance of the harbor, with the above-mentioned mark on astern, till the northern side of Granite Island bears N. 52° W., or the harbor comes well open, when a vessel will be clear of the Chief Rock, and may haul into the northwestward for the anchorage, passing about 200 yards to the southward of a small rock 2 feet above water lying on the northern side of the harbor 300 yards within the entrance.

As before mentioned, strangers should not attempt to enter this harbor without a pilot, unless from absolute necessity, and if in a sailing vessel, only with a steady fair wind.

Anchorage.—Anchor in from 7 to 10 fathoms, with the extremes of the harbor bearing S. 66° E. and S. 20° E

Ououkinsh Inlet is 7 miles long in a northeasterly direction, and 1,600 yards wide at the entrance, narrowing gradually towards the head; the shores within are high.

There is only one indifferent anchorage, Battle Bay, just within the entrance on the western side.

Clara Islet, at the southeastern extreme of the entrance, is small and bare; vessels should not go eastward of, or approach it within ½ mile. This island is the westernmost of the Barrier Islands, and lies 21½ miles N. 55° W. of Tatchu Point, where they may be almost said to commence.

Rock.—A rock, awash at low water and not indicated on the charts has been reported as situated off the mouth of Ououkinsh Inlet, and near the fairway of vessels entering that inlet. The rock lies on the following bearings: Clara Islet N. 69° E. Outermost of the Barrier Islands S 55° E.

Bunsby Islands are on the eastern side of entrance, close in shore; the passages between them and the shore are choked up with rocks, but their western side is steep to; Pinnacle Point and Green Head at their southwestern extreme are remarkable. To the northeastward of these islands is Malksope Inlet, 4 miles long in a northeasterly direction, but the entrance is intricate, and there is no anchorage within it.

Cuttle Group, lying at the southwestern entrance point of Ououkinsh Inlet, comprises a number of small islets and rocks, some of the former being wooded; nearly one mile SW. of them is a rock on which the sea breaks in fine weather. On the Vancouver shore, just NW. of them, is Low Cone, a remarkable summit, and useful in identifying the entrance.

Vessels should not go to the westward of these islets, or approach their east side nearer than 400 yards.

Sulivan Reefs are a very dangerous patch of rocks lying nearly 3 miles outside the entrance of Ououkinsh Inlet, 2½ miles N. 77° W. Clara Islet; they are about ½ mile in extent, and the sea only breaks occasionally on them.

The entrance of Ououkinsh Inlet open N. 46° E. leads east of these reefs; Solander Island, off Cape Cook, just open or shut in by the land east of the cape, bearing N. 68° W., leads south; Hat Island, in the entrance of Nasparti Inlet, in line with a summit on the west shore of the inlet, bearing N. 24° E., leads west; and Hat Island seen between the Haystacks, bearing N. 13° W., leads NE. of them.

Battle Bay, just within the entrance of Ououkinsh Inlet on the western side, is upwards of a mile wide, and ½ mile deep, with several islets and sunken rocks inside it, near the middle; near the northern part there is anchorage in from 6 to 9 fathoms, which may be used in fine weather.

Directions.—A vessel intending to enter Ououkinsh Inlet, and anchor in Battle Bay, should keep an offing of 4 or 5 miles from the main, till Clara Islet at the western extreme of the Barrier Islands is made out, when steer for it on a N. 58° E. bearing, passing about ¾ mile west of the islet to avoid the rock previously mentioned off Clara Island. When abreast the islet steer for the center of the entrance about N. 46° E., round the Skirmish Islets, which lie in the middle of Battle Bay, at a distance of 400 yards, and anchor in 7 fathoms, midway between them and the north side of the bay.

It is not recommended to use this anchorage, unless embayed, as it affords but indifferent shelter in southerly gales, and sailing vessels should not attempt to enter unless with a steady fair wind.

Nasparti Inlet, west of Ououkinsh Inlet, is about 4 miles long, in a northerly direction, and about ½ mile wide at the entrance, decreasing in some places to less than 600 yards Its shores are high and rocky, indented by some slight bays; there is a fresh-water stream at the head, from which a bank extends about 600 yards. There is a secure though rather limited anchorage, in from 13 to 16 fathoms, at the distance of ½ mile from the head. Outside the entrance are several dangers, but none within, and the projecting points may be approached to a distance of 200 yards.

Haystacks, off the eastern side of the entrance, and 1⅝ miles northward of the Sulivan Reefs, are two bare, sharp topped, clifty rocks, about 600 yards apart, there is a clear, deep passage between them and the Sulivan Reefs; northward of them, rocks and foul ground exist.

East Rock, 600 yards from the eastern entrance point, is of small extent, has 17 fathoms at a distance of 200 yards to the westward of it, and covers at half flood; the Haystacks open south of Yule Islet bearing S. 32° E., lead west of it.

Yule Islet lies midway between the Haystacks and East Rock

Mile Rock Breaker lies 2 miles N. 49° W. of Sulivan Reefs. It is very dangerous to vessels entering the inlet, as it is of small extent and the sea only breaks on it in heavy weather; the depths around it are irregular, there being from 13 to 32 fathoms at 400 yards from it.

Hat Island, in the entrance of inlet, in line with a summit on the west side bearing N. 24° E., leads east of it, and well clear of the Sulivan Reefs, into the inlet. Vessels should not stand to the westward of this danger.

Mile Rock, nearly one mile northward of the above-mentioned danger, is a small bare rock, 12 feet above high water; there are 29 fathoms 200 yards east of it, and a deep clear passage between it and the western shore. A ledge, however, extends fully 200 yards from its northern side.

Hat Island, lying in the center of the inlet just within the entrance, is small, and has a few stunted trees on the summit; from the southward it is very conspicuous, and appears somewhat like a hat. It is steep to on the eastern side, but nearly midway between it and the western shore is a shoal patch of 2½ fathoms, marked by kelp. When entering Nasparti Inlet pass eastward of the island.

Directions.—Nasparti Inlet should not be used by strangers unless from necessity, as in thick or cloudy weather it might be difficult to make out the leading marks, and no one should attempt to enter unless they are well made out, especially as the sea only breaks on the outlying dangers in heavy weather, and they are seldom seen. Sailing vessels should, in passing the entrance of this and Ououkinsh Inlet, keep Solander Island open south of the land east of Cape Cook, bearing N 66° W.

If entering Nasparti Inlet, keep Solander Island (off Cape Cook) in line with the land eastward of it bearing N. 69° W., until Hat Island comes in line with a summit on the west side of the inlet bearing N. 24°

E., then steer in for the entrance on that bearing, which will lead east of the Mile Rock Breaker, well clear of the Sulivan Reefs, and west of East Rock; pass 200 or 400 yards east of Hat Island and steer up the inlet in mid-channel, anchoring in 13 fathoms, about ⅓ mile from the head.

Brooks Peninsula.—To the westward of Nasparti Inlet is a peninsula of an oblong shape, projecting into the ocean in a SW. direction, its shores are for the most part very rocky, and rise almost abruptly from the sea to upwards of 2,000 feet; there are several off lying dangers around it, some of which extend upwards of one mile from the shore.

Cape Cook or Woody Point, the southwestern extreme of this peninsula, is the most projecting point of the outer coast of Vancouver Island. The cape rises abruptly from the sea to a summit 1,200 feet high.

At a distance of 2 miles from Cape Cook and the southern side of the peninsula the depths are from 20 to 90 fathoms, and as a rule vessels should not approach nearer.

Banks Reef, which covers at three quarters flood, and on which the sea breaks heavily, lies 3 miles S. 44° E. of Cape Cook, and ⅝ mile distant from the south shore of the peninsula.

Solander Island, nearly one mile off Cape Cook, is bare, and has two sharp summits; between it and the cape the passage is choked up with rocks, and vessels or boats should not go inside the island.

Brooks Bay, on the western side of Brooks Peninsula, is a large open bay about 12 miles wide, and 6 miles deep; there are several dangers within it, and two inlets, Klaskish and Klaskino, which afford anchorage but are very difficult of access, and vessels should not attempt to enter either unless embayed and unable to get out of Brooks Bay.

Clerke Reefs lie in the southeastern part of the bay, 5 miles northward of Cape Cook, their outer extreme being 2½ miles off the eastern shore of the bay. They cover an extent of upwards of 2 miles, some are under water, others uncover and vessels should not venture among them.

Cape Cook kept on S. 4° E. bearing leads 2 miles west of these reefs, and Small Islet, at the entrance of Klaskish Inlet, in the line with Leading Cone at its head, bearing N. 84° E., leads 1½ miles north.

Klaskish Inlet is about 3 miles long in a easterly direction, and one mile wide at entrance; at its head is a long narrow basin, the entrance of which is too contracted for vessels to enter. There is an anchorage just within the entrance to the inlet on the southern side to the eastward of Shelter Island, but it is difficult of access to sailing vessels.

Surge Islets, on the southern side of the entrance, about ½ mile from the shore, are small and rocky; foul ground exists among them, and in entering the inlet vessels should not approach their western side nearer than 800 yards.

Shelter Island, just within the entrance of the inlet, has a summit at each end covered with a few stunted trees; some rocks extend a short distance from its eastern and western sides, but the northern shore is steep to. The anchorage on its eastern side is about ½ mile in extent, with from 10 to 13 fathoms, well sheltered, but the bottom is irregular; the entrance to it, round the northeastern side of the island, is less than 200 yards wide in the narrowest part. About 200 yards from the northeastern point of Shelter is Bare Islet, which on entering the anchorage should be passed close to on its east side.

Between Shelter Island and the north entrance point of the inlet is a heavy confused sea, which is dangerous for sailing vessels, as the wind generally falls there.

Directions.—Entering Klaskish Inlet from the eastward and intending to anchor in the anchorage on the east side of Shelter Island, do not bring cape Cook to the southward of S. 4° E., till Leading Cone comes in line with Small Islet, which mark will lead into the inlet well north of the Clerke Reefs and Surge Islets, when abreast the latter haul a little to the eastward, so as to enter midway between Small Islet and Shelter Island; pass within 200 yards east of Bare Islet, and anchor in 13 fathoms with the extremes of Shelter bearing N. 38° W. and S. 74° W.

Caution.—The entrance to this anchorage is intricate and narrow; and unless necessary vessels larger than coasters should not attempt it, as a heavy sea rages all around the outer parts.

Ship Rock, lying 7½ miles N. 13° E. of cape Cook, in the center of Brooks Bay, and midway between Klaskish and Klaskino Inlets, is of small extent, and has from 17 to 20 fathoms close on its south and east sides; the sea generally breaks very heavily over it.

Leading Mark.—Small Islet, in line with Leading Cone, N. 84° E., leads south of it; and Twenty-foot Rock, at the entrance of Klaskino Inlet, in line with lower part of the stripe on Red Stripe Mountain on the north shore of that inlet, bearing N. 54° E., leads NW. of it.

Klaskino Inlet, the entrance to which is in the northern part of Brooks Bay, is nearly 6 miles long in a winding direction to the eastward. Numerous rocks lie off the entrance, but there is a safe though intricate passage through them; and there is also a good anchorage on the southern side 2 miles within the inlet. The inlet becomes narrow towards the head, with high and rocky shores, terminating in low land at the head.

Knob Point, the southern entrance point of the inlet, is rocky, and covered with a few stunted trees, and close to its outer part is a rocky knob about 100 feet high. From Knob Point a line of reefs above and below water, with deep water between them, extends fully 1½ miles in a NW. direction.

Twenty-foot Rock, 800 yards N. 44° W. of Knob Point, is bare. It is conspicuous from the outside, and there are 19 fathoms close to its north and west sides, but between it and Knob Point the passage is choked up with rocks; the only channel into the inlet being to the westward of the rock, between it and the Channel Reefs.

Two rocks on which the sea breaks at low water lie to the southward of the Channel Reefs and one mile distant from Knob Point. The southernmost lies ¾ mile S. 71° W. of Twenty foot Rock.

Channel Reefs, the southeastern part of which is 700 yards N. 77° W. of Twenty foot Rock, are an irregular cluster of rocks, mostly under water, extending in a northwesterly direction to the northwestern shore of Brooks Bay. There is deep water between them in many places, but the only safe passage into Klaskino Inlet, upwards of 600 yards wide, with deep water, is between their southeastern part and Twenty-foot Rock.

Anchorage Island, in the middle of the inlet, about 2 miles within the entrance, is of small extent and rocky; some small islets extend 200 yards from its northwestern and southeastern points. The anchorage between the eastern side of this island and the shore is from 600 to 800 yards in extent and well sheltered The entrance to it, round the southeastern point of Anchorage Island, is about 200 yards wide in the narrowest part.

Between Twenty-foot Rock and the entrance to the anchorage are several dangers; a rock 3 feet high, and another 2 feet high, lie in the southern part of the inlet SW of Anchorage Island, and there is a reef which covers 200 yards, N. 83° W of the latter rock.

Above Anchorage Island some rocks extend nearly across the inlet, rendering it almost impossible for a vessel to go beyond them

Red Stripe Mountain, rising on the northern side of entrance, abreast Anchorage Island, is a remarkable conical-shaped summit 2,200 feet high, with a valley on either side of it; on its south part facing seaward is a conspicuous red cliffy stripe or landslip, easily distinguished from the outside.

Directions.—Bound for Klaskino Inlet, when outside Ship Rock, bring Twenty-foot Rock in line with the lower part of the red stripe on Red Stripe Mountain bearing N 55° E., and run boldly for the entrance with that mark on, which will lead east of the eastern patches of the Channel Reefs; keep on this course till within 400 yards of Twenty-foot Rock, when haul a little to the northward, and pass it on its north side at 200 yards distance, after which steer about N. 85° E. for the center or southern part of Anchorage Island, passing 200 yards north of the rocks off the southern side of the inlet; when abreast the southwestern point of the island, haul quickly to the southward and eastward, round the rocks off its southeastern point within 100 yards, and anchor in from 9 to 10 fathoms midway between the eastern side of the island and the main, with the extremes of the former bearing N. 21° W. and S. 80° W., a large vessel should moor.

The entrance to Klaskino Anchorage is even more intricate than that of Klaskish, and should not be attempted by strangers unless absolutely necessary for safety.

Water.—Fresh water may be procured at both these anchorages

Three miles from Klaskino, in the northwestern part of Brooks Bay, is a large rivulet where boats may enter and find shelter in bad weather.

Lawn Point, the northwestern extreme of Brooks Bay is low, and some rocks extend more than ½ mile in an easterly direction from it, inside of which a boat may find shelter. The sea breaks violently about this point, and everywhere along the shores of Brooks Bay.

The land in the vicinity of Lawn Point appears very fertile, and lightly timbered; it rises gradually from the sea to a height of 1,900 feet. At a distance of 3 miles from the point are from 24 to 30 fathoms, and a vessel should keep a good offing.

Boat Shelter.—Between the entrance to Klaskino Inlet and Lawn Point is a deep bay, in which are several islets and reefs, it is unfit for anchorage, being open to seaward, but at its head, north of May day Island, there is good shelter for boats.

Quatsino Sound, the northwesternmost of the deep inlets on the outer coast of Vancouver Island, penetrates the island in a northeasterly direction for upwards of 25 miles. At the entrance it is nearly 6 miles wide, narrowing to less than one mile at a distance of 5 miles within; the sound then takes a northeasterly direction for 13 miles, when it branches off in two arms, one extending to the SE. for 12 miles, and terminating in low land. The other lies to the northward, and is connected with the sound by a straight narrow pass about 2 miles long; it is 24 miles long, and the eastern extreme, Rupert arm, is only 6 miles distant from Hardy Bay on the northeastern side of Vancouver Island. Just within the entrance of the sound on the northern side is Forward Inlet, a much smaller arm, about 6 miles long in a northerly direction, in which are the best anchorages in the sound.

The shores of Quatsino Sound are mostly high, and near the entrance very much broken; there are several small islands within and along its shores.

There are several dangers along the southern shore at the entrance; in the fairway are two very dangerous rocks, on which the sea only breaks in heavy weather, and it requires great caution on the part of the navigator to avoid them.

Reef Point, the southeastern entrance point of the sound is low and rocky, but rises gradually to a well defined summit; the coast between it and Lawn Point forms a slight bay filled with a number of rocks extending a considerable distance from the shore.

Boat Cove, into which flows a small stream (Culleet River) in which a boat can enter, and find shelter in bad weather, is a small bight on the eastern shore of the sound, 5½ miles north of Reef Point; the coast between the two places is indented by several bays, and fringed by a barrier of reefs, which extend in many places nearly one mile from the shore, and over which the sea usually breaks very heavily.

Bold Bluff, a bold, rocky, salient bluff rising suddenly to upwards of 200 feet, when it slopes gradually to a summit 1,609 feet high; it may be safely approached to within a distance of 200 yards. At this spot the sound contracts to less than one mile in breadth.

The shore between Boat Cove and Bold Bluff is rocky, but apparently steep to, and clear of danger.

Surf Islands, 1½ miles S. 46° W. of Bold Bluff, are a chain of small islands, nearly one mile long in a NNW. and SSE. direction, some of which are covered with a few stunted trees, and are about 40 feet above high water; a short distance from them are a number of rocks on which the sea breaks, but 600 yards from their south and west sides there are from 10 to 30 fathoms. Although there appears to be deep water between these islands and the eastern side of the sound, it is not advisable to use that passage, as it has not been sufficiently examined.

Entrance Island, at the northwestern entrance point of the sound, is small and rocky, and covered with a few stunted trees. It is steep to on its southeastern side, which may be approached to 400 yards; to the northward of it is a narrow boat pass into the sound, about 200 yards wide, but filled with rocks.

Danger Rocks, nearly in the fairway, are two very dangerous pinnacle rocks, of small extent, steep to on all sides. The south Danger Rock is awash at low water, and lies one mile S 60° E. of the southern extreme of Entrance Island; the north Danger Rock is 1,400 yards distant from the same island, and breaks at low water; there is deep water between the rocks. The sea very seldom breaks on these rocks; great caution is therefore required, when entering or leaving the sound, to avoid them.

Leading Marks.—Pinnacle Islet in line with the east point of Low Islets, in Forward Inlet, bearing N. 7° W., leads west of Danger Rocks, and midway between the north rock and Entrance Island.

Robson Island, in Forward Inlet, open north of Entrance Mount Point bearing N. 38° W., leads east of Danger Rocks; and Village Islet, on the east side of Forward Inlet, just touching Brown Point bearing N. 21° W. leads about ⅜ mile east of them, and midway between them and the Surf Islands.

Bold Bluff in line with the gap in the center of Surf Islands, bearing N 44° E., leads SE. of the south Danger.

Between the Danger Rocks and Surf Islands, the passage is 1½ miles wide; and clear of danger.

Forward Inlet becomes shoal at the head, and terminates in large salt water lagoons; in the upper part it contracts to less than ¼ mile in width in some places. There are two anchorages within it, North and Winter Harbors, the former easy of access to sailing vessels, and both are very secure and well sheltered.

Entrance and Flattop Mountains, on the west side of Forward Inlet, near the entrance, are very conspicuous objects from seaward.

Pinnacle Islet, ¾ mile north of Entrance Island, is a small, jagged rock about 40 feet high, with a few trees on its summit. There are 15 fathoms at 200 yards from its eastern side.

A shoal patch of 8 fathoms lies in the fairway to the inlet, 1,200 yards east of Pinnacle Islet.

Robson Island, $1\frac{1}{2}$ miles from Pinnacle Islet, is about $\frac{1}{2}$ mile in extent, its shores are rocky, but at a distance of 200 yards, free from danger on its northern and eastern sides. Between it and the west shore is a narrow passage of 2 to 3 fathoms water.

Low Islets, SE. of Robson Island are small wooded islands which are steep-to on all sides.

Village Islet—A small village is situated on the eastern side of Forward Inlet, abreast Robson Island, and close off it is Village Islet, a small, bare islet about 40 feet high, which is rather conspicuous

North Harbor, NW. of Robson Island, is a snug and secure anchorage. The entrance is 600 yards wide, rendering the harbor easy of access to sailing vessels; it is perhaps the best anchorage within the sound, and from being only 4 miles within the entrance, is very convenient. Browning Creek, in its western part, extends $1\frac{1}{4}$ miles to the westward, and is very narrow, with from 2 to 5 fathoms water in it, terminating in a shallow basin, dry at low water

Observatory Rock, which lies on the northern side of the entrance to North Harbor, is a small, bare rock, connected at low water to the mainland

Winter Harbor comprises that part of Forward Inlet which runs in a NE. direction, and is a capacious anchorage. Its shores are low, and bordered by a sandy beach, and the harbor becomes shoal at a distance of one mile from the head.

Log Point, just outside the entrance to this harbor on the eastern side, is low, and bordered by a sandy beach; to the southward of it, and extending 800 yards from the shore, is the New Bank, with $3\frac{1}{2}$ fathoms on the shoalest part, and contracting the breadth of the entrance passage to the harbor to less than 200 yards between it and a shoal spit extending from the opposite shore; but by keeping a little over to the western side when abreast North Harbor, vessels may avoid this bank and enter Winter Harbor without danger.

At the narrowest part of the entrance to Winter Harbor, above Log Point, on the western side, is a low, grassy point, bordered by a sandy beach, which is steep to, there being 16 fathoms within 100 yards of it.

Burnt Hill, just over Brown's Point, the northeastern entrance point of Forward Inlet, is remarkable from the southward, being bare of trees and cliffy on its southern side; one mile NE. of it is Nose Peak, another conspicuous summit, with a bare, rocky top.

Bare Islet, lying off the northeastern entrance point to Forward Inlet, is about 12 feet high, and steep to on the outside; it is 300 yards from the shore, but the passage inside is only fit for a boat.

Pilley Shoal of 3 fathoms, on the northern side of Quatsino Sound, is of small extent, steep to on the outside, and marked by kelp. It lies 300 yards from the shore and one mile westward of Bold Bluff.

Boat Cove, on the northern side of the sound, is of small extent, with 5 fathoms inside, it would afford good shelter for a small craft; the northern shore of Quatsino Sound between it and Bare Islet is rocky and very much broken.

Bedwell Islets, lying 5½ miles within the entrance, off a projecting point on the northern side of the sound, are of small extent, wooded, and separated from the shore by a very narrow boat pass, which is conspicuous from the entrance.

Monday Shoal, at 600 yards NE. of them, has 4 fathoms on it, is marked by kelp, and steep-to on the outside; eastward of Bedwell Islets no sea is ever experienced in the sound.

Koprino Harbor, in the center of a bay on the northern side of Quatsino Sound, is a perfectly landlocked but small anchorage, affording room for one or two ships to lie moored within. It lies to the northward of Plumper Island, which is about ½ mile in extent, low, wooded, and steep to on all sides, there being a good passage on either side of it into the harbor.

Dockyard Island, in the western part of the harbor, midway between Plumper Island and the northern shore, is small, but may be approached close to, a ledge, the greatest depth on which is 4 fathoms, connects it with Plumper Island.

Mud Bank, about 300 yards east of Dockyard Island, in the middle of the harbor, is a small patch of 15 feet, there is good anchorage 200 yards SW. of Dockyard Island, in 14 fathoms.

Wedge Island lies at the eastern limit of the anchorage, about 200 yards from Plumper Island; it is very small, and covered with a few bushes; a ledge extends a short distance from it to the westward; there is a deep passage close to on either side of it into the harbor

Obsevatory Islet, at the northeastern extreme of the harbor, is bare about 12 feet high and 600 yards from the northern shore, connected to the latter by a bank which dries at low water.

East Passage, leading into Koprino Harbor, eastward of Plumper Island, is ½ mile wide at entrance, narrowing to 400 yards at its termination, is clear of danger.

East Cove, the head of the bight between Observatory Islet and Prideaux Point, in the northeastern part of East Passage, appears to afford a good anchorage in 6 to 10 fathoms; but the entrance to it has hardly been sufficiently examined to recommend its being used by a large vessel

Prideaux Point is low, bordered by a sandy beach, and may be approached to a distance of 200 yards. The northern shore of the sound from Prideaux Point takes a general northeasterly direction for 9 miles to Coffin Islet, at the entrance of Hecate Cove. It is bordered by a sandy beach, and is clear of danger at the distance of 200 yards, except in the vicinity of the Percy Ledge, which lies 6 miles from Prideaux Point, is 400 yards from the shore, and has 4 fathoms on its outer edge.

From Bold Bluff the southern shore of the sound runs nearly parallel to the northern for 13 miles It is high and indented by two bays of considerable size and some small creeks, none of which afford anchorage. In Koskeemo Bay, at 2 miles within Bold Bluff, is a native village of considerable size

Village Islands, at the east extreme of Koskeemo Bay, are of small extent and low, their outer part is steep to

Brockton Island, lying 400 yards from a projecting point on the southern side of the sound, is nearly ½ mile long, but narrow; its western side is steep to.

Limestone Island, in the center of the sound, is the largest island in the sound and shaped somewhat like a crescent. Its shores are rocky, but clear of danger, and the island is of moderate height; Quiet Cove, on its northwestern side, is small, and affords anchorage for small craft.

Foul Islets, lying midway between Holloway Point, the southwestern extreme of Limestone Island and the southern shore of the sound, are small, and about 600 yards in extent in an east and west direction. There is a clear deep passage about 400 yards wide on either side of them, the southern passage is to be preferred.

Single Islet, ½ mile eastward of Holloway Point, is low and bare, but may be approached to the distance of 200 yards.

Kultus Cove, abreast Limestone Island, on the southern side of the sound, is about ½ mile in extent, with irregular soundings, of from 12 to 25 fathoms, it affords no anchorage except for small craft.

Southeast Arm varies in breadth from 600 yards to one mile. Its shores are generally high and rugged, but terminate in low land at the head; the depths are great, and there is no anchorage, except for small craft; a bank dries off 400 yards from the head, and close to its edge is 15 fathoms.

Mist Rock, 5 miles within the entrance, and 800 yards from the eastern shore, is of small extent, and covers at half flood; it is the only danger in the Southeast Arm, but by keeping in mid-channel or well over to the western shore vessels will clear it

Atkins Cove, on the eastern side of entrance to the Southeast Arm, is 200 yards wide, with from 5 to 7 fathoms; there is room for a small vessel to anchor in it, but the cove is open to the southeastward.

Whitestone Point, at the separation of the two arms at the head of Quatsino Sound, is a rocky point of moderate height. Bull Rock, which covers, and is marked by kelp, lies 600 yards off Whitestone Point, and 400 yards from the shore. Between Atkins Cove and Whitestone Point the coast is rocky, and should not be approached nearer than 600 yards.

Hecate Cove, on the northern shore, indents the shore about ⅜ mile in a northerly direction, is from 400 to 600 yards wide, and affords good anchorage near the center in 9 to 11 fathoms. The entrance is clear of danger, but in the inner part of the cove, near the northern side, are some shoal patches marked by kelp, with only 11 feet water in some parts; the shores of the cove are moderately high, and bordered by a sandy beach.

This cove is convenient for steamers or small craft, and vessels ought to anchor in about 11 fathoms, with the entrance points bearing S 24° W. and S 21° E ; large vessels should moor.

Kitten Island, at the eastern side of entrance, is steep to on the outside.

Round Island (Quatishe,) nearly in mid channel, just south of Quatsino Narrows, is small, and of moderate height; there is a clear passage between it and the northern shore, but the one south of it is filled with rocks. At 600 yards SE. of it is Bight Cove, of moderate extent, with from 8 to 10 fathoms inside, but as the tide runs strong off the entrance, and there are also some rocks, it is only recommended for small craft.

Quatsino Narrows connects the sound with the Rupert and West Arms. They are 300 yards wide in the narrowest part; the depths in it vary from 12 to 20 fathoms, its shores are high and rocky, but at 100 yards distance are clear of danger. Turn Point, at the southwestern extreme of the narrows, is bold and cliffy, the coast turning sharply round it to the northward; a short distance off it are some strong tide rips. Between this point and Hecate Cove the coast is broken, but clear of danger at the distance of 200 yards.

Tides.—The tide runs through these narrows at a rate of from 4 to 6 knots, and the streams turn shortly after high and low water.

Philip and James Points, at the northern extreme of the narrows, are bold and steep to; off the latter, which lies on the east side, is a small island.

Rupert Arm.—The shores are high and clear of danger, its head terminates in low land, and a bank dries off it for 400 yards. The depths in this arm vary from 80 to 30 fathoms, shoaling gradually to the head, off which a vessel may anchor, in 14 to 17 fathoms, a short distance from the edge of the bank.

Marble Creek, which lies at the entrance of Rupert Arm, is of small extent, and affords anchorage in from 5 to 6 fathoms; off its head a sand bank extends 800 yards, and midway up the creek are some small islets on either side; if intending to anchor, pass between and go just inside them.

Hankin Point, abreast Quatsino Narrows on the northern side, is bold and rocky; it separates the Rupert from the West Arm.

West Arm trends in a westerly direction, and varies in breadth from 400 yards to one mile. Its shores are mostly high and rocky; the northern one is indented by several small bays, and off it are some rocks and small islands. It shoals gradually to the head, and there are two anchorages, one at Coal Harbor on the northern side, and the other at the edge of the bank extending from the head; the former is of moderate extent, and the best anchorage northward of the narrows.

Coal Harbor, 2 miles from the narrows, is of square shape, and affords good anchorage near the middle in from 12 to 14 fathoms. The shore is bordered by a sandy beach, and at the head are some fresh-water streams. This anchorage is easy of access for any vessel. Indications of coal have been met with in this vicinity; it was at one time worked to a small extent.

Pot Rocks, 2 miles west of Coal Harbor, are of small extent, and cover at three quarters flood.

Straggling Islands, about 5 miles from the narrows, are an irregular group of small islands and rocks extending upwards of ½ mile from the northern shore, the depths among them and to the northward are irregular, and a vessel in passing should not approach their southern side nearer than 400 yards; just west of them on the northern shore is a small patch of swampy ground, through which flow some fresh water streams, and a bank extends 200 yards from it.

The West Arm gradually decreases in breadth to the westward of the Straggling Islands, and the shores on both sides at the distance of 200 yards are clear of danger. The head terminates in low land, and a bank extends upwards of 400 yards from it. Close to the outer edge of the latter are from 12 to 14 fathoms, where a vessel may anchor.

Directions.—Entering Quatsino Sound from the southward, give Reef Point an offing of about 2 miles, and steer N 24° E till Bold Bluff comes in line with the gap in the center of the Surf Islands, bearing N. 44° E. Keep this course until the western side of Robson Island comes open north of Entrance Mount Point, bearing N. 38° W., or Village Islet, on the east side of that inlet, is just touching Brown Point, bearing N 21° W. Vessels will be well east of Danger Rocks. If bound up the sound, round the north end of Surf Islands at a distance of about ½ mile, or if going to Forward Inlet, steer about N 32° W., taking care not to shut in the south side of Robson Island with Entrance Mount Point, until Bedwell Islets come open north of Bold Bluff, bearing N. 69° E, when she will be well north of the Danger Rocks. Pass from 200 to 400 yards off the eastern sides of the Low Islets and Robson Island, and rounding the northern point of the latter, at the same distance, enter North Harbor, and anchor in from 4 to 6 fathoms near its center.

If intending to anchor in Winter Harbor, when abreast the north part of Robson Island, steer north, keeping well over to the western shore to avoid the New Bank, and when past it enter the harbor in mid-channel, anchoring in 11 fathoms about ½ mile north of Grass Point. Winter and North Harbors are easily available for sailing vessels, and they could beat into the latter

Bound to Koprino Harbor, which can only be entered by steamers or sailing vessels with a fair wind, round the NW point of Surf Islands at about ½ mile distance, and steer up the sound in mid channel until abreast the harbor. If in a large vessel, go through the East passage, keeping from 200 to 400 yards from Plumper Island; enter the anchor age close to on either side of Wedge Island, and moor immediately the vessel is west of it (with anchors north and south); vessels may also enter by West Passage, and anchor in 14 fathoms south of Dockyard Island.

When navigating the sound to the eastward of Koprino Harbor the chart is indispensable, but a mid channel course is everywhere free of danger; sailing vessels of any size should not, however, go eastward of that harbor, as the anchorages beyond are rather difficult of access for them. If wishing to anchor in Hecate Cove, enter it in mid channel, passing north of Limestone Island, and moor immediately the vessel is inside the entrance points, the tide runs from one to 3 knots abreast the entrance, and should be guarded against.

Going through the Quatsino Narrows, keep well over to the northern shore, pass north of Round Island, round Turn Point close to, and guarding against tide, steer up the narrows in mid channel, these narrows should only be attempted at slack water or with a favorable tide, unless in a full powered steamer. The best anchorage north of the narrows is Coal Harbor, vessels may anchor near the center in from 12 to 14 fathoms. In navigating the West Arm keep well over to the southern shore, when in the vicinity of the Pot Rock and Straggling Islands

From Westward—Entering Quatsino Sound from the westward, keep an offing of about 2 miles till Entrance Island bears N 69° E., when steer to pass about 400 yards east of it, but not further off. When abreast it haul to the northward, bringing Pinnacle Islet in line with the east side of Low Islets, bearing N. 7° W., and steer up with that mark on till Bedwell Islets come well open north of Bold Bluff, bearing N. 69° E., when enter Forward Inlet, or proceed further up the sound, as before directed.

If, when coming from the southward, Pinnacle and Low Islets can be well made out, vessels by keeping the former in line with the east part of the latter, bearing N 7° W., will pass west of the Danger Rocks; but as a rule it would be more prudent to pass eastward of them

If the weather be so thick that the marks for clearing the Danger Rocks can not be distinguished, a vessel, if able to distinguish Entrance Island, may enter the sound by steering for it on a N. 36° E. bearing; pass close to its eastern side, and haul to the northward when abreast it, by keeping ½ mile on that course, she will be well clear NW. of the Danger Rocks, and may proceed anywhere up the sound On a clear night in fine weather a vessel may also enter in the above manner.

There is room, with a steady breeze, for smart working vessels to beat into the sound to the southward and eastward of Danger Rocks, though without previous knowledge of the place it would be rather hazardous to attempt it. If obliged to do so, when standing to the northward towards the Danger Rocks, tack when Bold Bluff comes in line with the center of the northernmost (wooded) Surf Island, bearing N. 52° E.; and in standing to the southern shore, tack when Bold Bluff comes in line with the SE. extreme of the Surf Islands bearing N. 35° E. When the south side of Robson Island comes open north of Entrance Mount Point, N. 38° W., she will be eastward of the Danger Rocks, and may stand further to the northward.

Beating between Surf Islands and Danger Rocks, tack at about 600 yards of the former; and in standing towards the latter keep Robson Island open as before directed, till Bedwell Islets comes open north of Bold Bluff, N. 69° E.; if going to North Harbor, when inside Forward Inlet, guard against the New Bank.

The Coast of Vancouver Island from Quatsino Sound to Cape Scott, the NW. extreme of the island, takes a general NW. direction; it is mostly rocky and iron bound, indented by several bays, most of which are small, and from the projecting points some rocks extend in some places nearly one mile from the shore.

Caution.—When navigating between Cape Scott and Quatsino Sound do not approach the shore nearer than 2 miles.

Rugged Point, 3 miles from the northern entrance point of Quatsino Sound, is a rocky, rugged point, of moderate height, with 12 fathoms at ½ mile outside it. Open bay, which lies just inside it, affords landing for boats in fine weather on its east side.

The coast between Open Bay and the entrance to Quatsino Sound is high and cliffy, some rocks extend nearly one mile from it.

Top-knot Point, 5 miles from Rugged Point, is low, with a summit 300 feet high, shaped like a top knot, just within it; some rocks extend ½ mile to the southward from it.

Raft Cove, 8 miles from Rugged Point, is an open bight about one mile in extent, and affords no shelter whatever

Cape Palmerston is a bold rocky point rising to a summit 1,422 feet high; some rocks extend ½ mile from it.

San Josef Bay is an extensive open bay, 3 miles deep in a north-easterly direction; the breadth at the entrance is nearly 2 miles, narrowing gradually towards the head. Its shores are high, and off the southern side are several off lying rocks; the depths vary from 11 to 4 fathoms, but the bay affords no shelter except with northerly winds, and should only be used as a stopping place in fine weather; generally a heavy sea sets into it, and a vessel caught there with a southwesterly gale would inevitably go on shore. At the head of the bay is a fresh-water stream of considerable size, which boats can enter at high water and find shelter in.

Directions.—Intending to anchor in the bay, bring the entrance to bear N 69° E., and steer for it, anchoring in 7 or 9 fathoms near the middle, with the entrance points bearing S. 24° W. and N. 66° W.

Sea Otter Cove, just west of San Josef Bay, is about one mile long in a northerly direction, and from 400 to 600 yards wide. There are 5 fathoms in the entrance, and from one to 3 fathoms inside it, the shelter within is very indifferent, there are several rocks, and the place is only fit for coasters Off its southeastern entrance point, and separating the cove from San Josef Bay, are some small islets extending nearly one mile from the shore; they are bare and yellow topped, about 40 feet high, and conspicuous from the NW.

Cape Russell, immediately westward of Sea Otter Cove, is a remarkable headland 870 feet high, and the outer part of a peninsula formed by Sea Otter Cove and a small bay NW of it; some rocks, on which the sea breaks very heavily, extend nearly one mile south from the cape.

Between Cape Russell and Cape Scott the coast is indented by three open bays which are nearly one mile deep, but afford no shelter whatever.

Cape Scott.—(See page 239.)

CHAPTER VIII.

INNER CHANNELS OF BRITISH COLUMBIA—QUEEN CHARLOTTE SOUND TO MILBANK SOUND.

The Inner Channels, herein described, of the seaboard of British Columbia afford smooth water, together with anchorages at suitable distances, for vessels of moderate length.

These channels offer facilities to steam vessels for avoiding the strong gales and thick weather so frequently met with in Hecate Strait. They are also available for fore-and-aft schooners, when navigating between Vancouver Island and Alaska.

Unless directed to the contrary, the mid-channel course is recommended to be kept when navigating these inner waters

Proceeding northward from Cape Calvert, pass through Fitzhugh Sound, Lama Channel, Seaforth Channel, Milbank Sound, Finlayson Channel, and Grenville Channel, to Chatham Sound. These channels, which are fairly well charted, with the anchorages on a large scale, offer no difficulties for the largest ships with an experienced pilot.

The usual track of steam vessels through the inner channels of Alaska is from Chatham Sound, British Columbia, to westward of Cape Fox, then through Tongass Narrows, Clarence Strait, Stikine Strait, and Sumner Strait, to Cape Decision.

Tongass Narrows is a perfectly safe passage for the largest steamers with a competent pilot.

Sumner Strait, the best channel for large vessels, has some hidden dangers, notably McArthur's Ledge, the Eye Opener, and Helen Rock, (off Point Baker).

Wrangel Narrows is the passage commonly used by mail steamers of 1,000 tons burden, or 230 feet in length, but is not a safe channel for larger vessels or those exceeding 17 feet draft of water, and its passage should only be attempted at high water slack.

From Cape Decision to Juneau, through Chatham Straits, Frederick Sound, and Stephens Passage, is open, clear navigation, for which the charts are sufficiently reliable, and with an experienced pilot offers no difficulty.

Large steam vessels bound to Sitka should take the sea passage via Cape Ommaney, but if required to touch at Juneau, may proceed to sea from there by way of Cross Sound.

Cross Sound presents no difficulties to navigation, except at times great quantities of ice floes, drifting with the strong currents, render the passage somewhat dangerous, and only to be undertaken in clear weather or daylight Anchorages may be found at Hoonah, Willoughby Cove, Bartlett Bay, and along the SE. shore of Gustavus Point, towards Pleasant Island. The passage inside Pleasant Island, to the northward, also affords fair anchorage, but in the absence of surveys, should not be attempted without a local pilot.

Cape Caution (Kakleesla), the northern entrance point of Queen Charlotte Sound, is of moderate height and level, the tops of the trees being about 200 feet above the sea; the shore is white, and of granite formation, with a few rocks off it; the land NE of the cape rises gradually in a distance of 5 miles to Coast Nipple, 1,350 feet high.

Sea Otter Group, consisting of several dangerous rocks, islets, and shoals which cover a space of about 12 miles in extent north and south and 10 miles in an east and west direction, lies at a distance of 6 or 7 miles from the seaboard of British Co umbia, fronting the coast between Capes Caution and Calvert.

Danger Shoals, on which the sea is reported to break in heavy weather, is the southernmost outlying danger of Sea Otter Group, and lies N. 82° W., 10½ miles from Cape Caution; near the center of this shoal a depth of 9 fathoms, rocks and stones, was obtained, with 23 fathoms close around. Shoaler water probably exists.

Virgin Rocks, near the western limit of the group, consists of three white rocks, the largest of which lies N. 37° W., 7½ miles from Danger Shoal. Rounding the rocks a vessel should not stand into less than 30 fathoms.

Watch Rock, 74 feet high and black, lies near the northern limit of the group, 7¼ miles N. 33° E. of Virgin Rocks. The rock is steep to.

Pearl Rocks comprise several rocks above and below water, extending 1½ miles in a NW. and SE direction, the largest rock (15 feet high) lies S. 76° E., 3 miles from Watch Rock, and the southeastern rock, on which the sea always breaks, lies one mile S 31° E. of the largest rock.

Devil Rock, the NE. outlying danger, lies 1¼ miles N. 76° E. of the largest Pearl Rock, and nearly 3 miles S. 51° W. of Sorrow Islands. The sea seldom breaks on Devil Rock, and there is apparently deep water close around. There are from 80 to 40 fathoms between the rock and Cape Calvert.

New Patch, on which the sea generally breaks, is nearly 2 miles in extent, and lies 4½ miles S. 14° W of the largest Pearl Rock.

Channel Reef, the easternmost danger of Sea Otter Group, has about 6 feet over it at low water; from the center of this reef Table Island, at the entrance of Smith Sound, bears S. 82° E, 4⅝ miles distant. The sea seldom breaks on Channel Reef. and there are 60 fathoms close eastward of it.

Hannah Rock, the southeasternmost outlying danger, on which the sea nearly always breaks, is situated about 2¼ miles S. 25° W. of Channel Reef; the rock is awash at high water, and from its center Cape Caution bears S. 59° E., distant 8 miles.

Clearing mark.—The south extremes of Egg and Table Islands in line, bearing N. 62° E., leads clear to the southeastward of Danger Shoal and all other dangers on the southeastern side of Sea Otter Group.

Caution.—Dangerous rocks have been reported as lying in a S. 59° W. direction, 5 miles from Danger Shoal, and occupying a space of 2½ miles in diameter, but their existence is doubtful.

South Passage, leading to Smith and Fitzhugh Sounds from the southward, lies between Cape Caution and the southeastern limit of Sea Otter Group, where it is about 7 miles broad, with irregular depths. False Egg Island, its own breadth open west of Egg island, bearing N. 19° E., leads through South Passage, nearly in mid-channel.

Blunden Bay, a slight bend in the coast between Cape Caution and Neck Point, is about one mile wide at its entrance, and nearly one mile deep. Indian Cove, which lies in the northern part of this bay, affords good shelter for boats; it is the rendezvous for Indians on their canoe voyages.

Hoop Reef.—Midway between Neck Point and Good Shelter Cove is Hoop Reef, about ⅓ mile from the shore; this reef is ¾ mile in extent NNW. and SSE., and ¼ mile broad.

South Iron Rock, on which the sea seldom breaks, lies ¾ mile to the westward of Hoop Reef; there are 35 fathoms close to, on the northern side of the rock, and 25 fathoms in the channel between it and Hoop Reef.

North Iron Rock, which dries 7 feet, lies nearly in the fairway of Alexandra Passage, ¾ mile north of South Iron Rock; there are 7 to 9 fathoms close to, and no bottom at 40 fathoms within ¼ mile of North Iron Rock.

Clearing marks.—False Egg Island in line with West Rock off Table Island, bearing N. 10° E., leads west of South and North Iron Rocks.

Egg Island, immediately fronting Smith Sound, and standing boldly out from the coast, is the prominent landmark between Goletas Channel and Fitzhugh Sound. The island is covered with trees, and is remarkable for its egg like shape. From the southwestern side of the island rocks extend about 200 yards, and on the eastern side is a small island, which is separated from Egg Island by a narrow gully, giving the appearance of a split in the island itself, when seen from north or south.

Egg Rocks, on the westernside of Alexandra Passage, are a cluster of rocks lying nearly ¾ mile NW. of North Iron Rock, and about 400 yards south of Egg Island; these rocks extend about ¼ mile north and south, the northernmost being 30 feet high.

Denny Rock, a sunken danger on which the sea seldom breaks, and a source of danger in thick weather, lies ¼ mile west of the southernmost Egg Rock. The west extreme of Ann Island open west of Egg Island bearing N. 36° E. leads west of Denny Rock.

Smith Sound is about 8 miles long ENE. and WSW., with an average breadth of 3½ miles; the entrance between Jones and Long Points is 1½ miles across. At 6 miles within the entrance, on either side of a cluster of islands, is a channel leading into Smith Inlet. In almost every part of the sound the depths are over 40 fathoms, and there is generally a heavy swell.

The southern shore of Smith Sound, for a distance of 4 or 5 miles from the entrance, is skirted by several small islands and rocks having deep water close to; good shelter for boats will be obtained in a small cove about ¼ mile NE. of Jones Point; also in a cove one mile south of Jones Point, abreast Egg Rocks.

The entrance to the sound is protected by a rocky plateau (Cluster Reefs) and several islands, islets, and rocks; some above, and many under water, prominent amongst them being Egg and Table Islands. Access to Smith Sound may be had on either side of these islands.

Alexandra Passage lies between Egg Island and the southeastern point of entrance, the narrowest part, between Egg Rocks and North Iron Rock being 1,200 yards; here as elsewhere, the dangers are so steep to that the *quickest* use of the lead is enjoined. A general leading mark through Alexandra Passage (making allowance for heave of swell and tide) is the west extreme of Surf Islet in line with the islets near the south point of Shower Island bearing N. 59° E.

Beaver Passage.—The northern channel into Smith Sound lies between the islands skirting the northern point of the sound and Wood and White Rocks. In Beaver Passage the bottom is irregular, 20 fathoms being the least depth obtained. The course through the passage is S. 61° E., the east extreme of Search Islands just open of the west end of Surf Islet on that bearing, leads in midway between John Reef and False Egg Island, where the width is 1,200 yards. The western entrance to this passage is the narrowest part; with the usual amount of sea or swell, good steerage and vigilant attention are required.

White Rocks, very conspicuous, lie in the western entrance of Beaver Passage, nearly one mile NW. of Cluster Reefs.

John Reef is 600 yards north of White Rocks; it dries 3 feet at low water, with 9 to 20 fathoms close around, forming the northwestern danger on the southern side of Beaver Passage.

False Egg Island, resembling Egg Island in shape, but smaller, lies on the northern side of Beaver Passage and is the outlying landmark for the northern entrance to Smith Sound.

James Rock.—At about 600 yards N. 62° W. of False Egg Island lies James Rock, the exact position of which is somewhat doubtful; the sea breaks on this rock at low water, and between it and False Egg Island the bottom is foul.

Clearing Mark.—The west part of the large Canoe Rock bearing N. 25° E., or in line with Quoin Hill (on Penrose Island) passes ¼ mile westward of James and John Rocks, and leads clear (westward) of all dangers at the entrance of Smith Sound.

Table Island, the largest of the group of islands occupying the entrance to Smith Sound, is about one mile long north and south and ½ mile broad, with the tops of the trees 120 feet above the sea, nearly flat. Table Island, when seen from abreast Cape Caution, appears to have two summits.

A cluster of rocks, several of which are covered at low water, extend ½ mile from the western side of Table Island, having 21 fathoms close to the outer rock.

Ann Island, about ½ mile in extent, is separated from the north end of Table Island by a channel (200 yards wide in some parts) in which shelter will be found for boats.

Cluster Reefs, consisting of several rocky heads and shoal patches, extend from Table Island in a northerly and northeasterly direction into the entrance of Smith Sound.

George Rock, on which the sea breaks at low water, is the northwesternmost of the reefs, and lies one mile N. 5° E. of Ann Island.

Edward Reef dries 7 feet, and lies east nearly ⅓ mile from George Rock.

Wood Rocks, which are awash at low water, are nearly ¼ mile S. 76° E. of Edward Reef, consist of three rocky heads, and are the northeasternmost of Cluster Reefs.

Bertie Rock, with 3½ fathoms water on it, lies near the eastern edge of Cluster Reefs, from the center of this rock the northwestern extreme of Ann Island bears S. 62° W. distant nearly ¾ mile.

Leading Marks.—The west extreme of False Egg Island in line with Kelp Head, bearing N. 16° E., leads to the westward, and Limit Point, midway between Long and Shower Islands, bearing S. 85° E. leads to the northward of Cluster Reefs.

Long Point is the northwestern point of Smith Sound. Tie Island, which is nearly ¼ mile in extent, lies close westward of Long Point, and is separated from it by a boat passage, in which there is a depth of 4 fathoms. Ada Rock, which is awash at low water, lies 400 yards south of Tie Island.

Brown Island lies ½ mile S. 15° E. of Long Point; the island is nearly ½ mile long and ¼ mile broad, with 17 to 23 fathoms close to its southern point.

Surprise Patch, on the northern side of Smith Sound, has a depth of 5 fathoms, and 7 to 17 fathoms close around, with no bottom at 40 fathoms 400 yards to the northward.

Judd Rock, with less than 6 feet water on it, lies ¼ mile eastward of Surprise Patch. There is no bottom at 40 fathoms in the vicinity of this rock.

Barrier Islands, at the head of Smith Sound, consists of two large and several small islands, covering a space of about 5 miles in extent. Blakeney Passage on the north and Browning Passage on the south side of these islands, leading to Smith Inlet, are each about one mile wide, with no bottom at a depth of 40 fathoms.

Takush Harbor, on the southern shore of Smith Sound, 6 miles within the entrance, is the only anchorage to which a ship can resort for shelter when crossing Queen Charlotte Sound. Vessels of large size can lie secure here.

Petrel Shoal, on which there is a depth of only 15 feet, lies 200 yards S. 6° E. from the easternmost Gnarled Island, and is the principal danger in rounding into Anchor Bight.

Fly Basin, at the head of Takush Harbor, perfectly land-locked, is about one mile long east and west, with 2½ to 3 fathoms in the western and 6 to 8 fathoms in the eastern part of the basin. The entrance to Fly Basin, which is about 200 yards wide, is contracted 50 yards by a shoal extending from the eastern entrance point, with a rock (dry 2 feet at low water) and a patch of 9 feet on its western edge. Between this shoal and the western entrance point there is a depth of 9 fathoms. If required, small vessels could be taken into Fly Basin

Anchorage in Takush Harbor will be found in 10 or 11 fathoms mud, in Anchor Bight, midway between Ship Rock and Steep Point, with the north extreme of Bull Point in line with Anchor Islands, bearing N. 87° E, and east extreme of Bloxham Point N 12° E

Directions—When bound to Takush Harbor, it is recommended to pass through Browning Passage, and, after passing North Point, keep the north extreme of Bright Island a little open north of that point bearing N. 79° W, until Berry Point (south side of Fly Basin) appears midway between the entrance points of Fly Basin, S. 20° E., which will lead through Ship Passage; and when Steep Point is well open of the southernmost Gnarled Island bearing west, a course may be steered for the anchorage in Anchor Bight, taking care to avoid the shoal ground south of Gnarled Island, passing midway between Anchor and Gnarled Islands. Good steerage is required here, speed should be proportionately slow, the leads kept quickly going, and the water not shoaled to less than 7 fathoms.

Smith Inlet (Quascillah), the continuation of Smith Sound, is about 3 miles wide at its entrance, between eastern part of Takush Harbor and Doolish Bay; it is said to extend nearly 25 miles in an easterly direction, and at about 9 miles from its entrance contracts to a general width of ½ mile, the shores being formed of high, rocky precipices covered with wood. The inlet has not been surveyed.

A good sized stream flows into Smith Inlet up which the salmon run in large numbers, and several canneries have been established in the neighborhood.

Fitzhugh Sound is 30 miles long in a general north and south direction, having an average breadth of 3 miles, with no known hidden dangers throughout. The shores are mostly bold and rocky, the slopes are wooded and steep, and the elevation of the peaks from 1,000 to 3,400 feet. The flood tide runs to the northward. The southern entrance to Fitzhugh Sound lies between Cranstown Point and Cape Calvert, the southern extremity of Calvert Island

The sound at 4 miles north of Safety Cove is contracted to 1½ miles in width by Addenbrooke and adjacent islands, which lie on the eastern side; the shores on both sides are steep to and the depths in the channel great.

Canoe, Spur, and Paddle Rocks lie about one mile off Kelp Head, and occupy a space of 1½ miles in a north and south direction, the space thus inclosed being foul, and more or less covered with growing kelp. Canoe Rock, the center and most prominent of these rocks, is bare, 25 feet high, and stands boldly out from the coast, making a good point for identification.

Open Bay, on the northeastern side of Cranstown Point, affords anchorage in 7 fathoms, about 400 yards from the shore during summer or with offshore winds, but there is generally a swell in the bay, and it is only used by local craft as a temporary anchorage.

Cape Calvert is the southern termination of Cape Range; it presents a broad face of rocky shore extending in a ENE. and WSW. direction, about 350 feet high, and covered with a thick growth of hemlock and pine trees At 2 miles north of the cape is Entry Cone, which is conspicuous, and forms a good mark for recognizing Fitzhugh Sound from the southward and westward; Cape Calvert is fronted by the Sorrow Islands, which are steep to, of granite formation, and covered with gnarled and stunted trees; between these islands and the cape, fair shelter may be found for boats in Grief Bay (Telakwas), but during SE. or SW gales, a swell is more or less experienced, rendering landing difficult and sometimes dangerous.

Directions for Fitzhugh Sound from the Southward.—After passing Cape James (Shadwell Passage), a N. 6° W. course should be steered (or for Entry Cone) until past the Storm Islands; when, Addenbrooke Island open of, and the east shore of Fitzhugh Sound (beyond) shut in by, Cape Calvert bearing north., will lead midway between Channel Reef and Egg Island, and up to the entrance of Fitzhugh Sound Allowance should be made for tidal streams, the flood sets to the eastward into Queen Charlotte and Smith Sounds with a velocity at spring of nearly 2 knots.

From the Westward.—Vessels from the westward bound for Fitzhugh Sound, should use North Passage, between Sea Otter group and Calvert Island, this passage is about 3 miles wide. Hedley Patch, with 9 fathoms water (possibly less) lies in the western entrance to North Passage, at 3½ miles N. 22° E. of Watch Rock.

Schooner Retreat (Kapilish), on the eastern side of Fitzhugh Sound, is the name given to the anchorages among a cluster of islands at the southwestern end of Penrose Island, which here separates Fitzhugh Sound from Rivers Inlet. The Retreat affords a secure stopping place, and with care may be safely entered by steam vessels. Karslake Point (Joachim Island) is its southeastern entrance point. The entrance to Schooner Retreat trends in a NE. direction from Karslake Point, where it is about ½ mile wide, contracting to 200 yards between Sea Bluff and Grey Islets; inside the narrows to the eastward it expands into Frigate Bay.

Penrose Island, which forms the northern protection to Schooner Retreat, lies in the mouth of Rivers Inlet, a branch of the inlet passing on either side of it. Quoin Hill is situated near its southern end about ¾ mile inland.

Joachim Island, the southeasternmost and largest of the cluster of islands at the SW. end of Penrose Island, is 400 feet high, 1¼ miles long north and south, with an average breadth of ½ mile; the northern extreme of this island is separated from Penrose Island by a boat passage.

Ironside Island is the next in size and is separated from Sea Bluff, the northwestern point of Joachim Island, by the channel into Schooner Retreat. Grey Islets on the western side of the channel into Schooner Retreat, lie close off the southeastern extreme of Ironside Island.

Safe Entrance, between Joachim and Ironside Islands, is ¼ mile wide. On the west side of Safe Entrance, about 50 yards from Grey Islets, lies a rock awash; from it shoal ground extends 300 yards in a northerly direction, with 2 to 3 fathoms on it and 4 to 10 fathoms close-to.

Comber Rock, on which the sea often breaks, is at the northern side of Safe Entrance; the rock covers at three quarters flood, and lies 150 yards S. 36° W. of Surf Point, the southwestern extreme of Ironside Island.

Frigate Bay, the southernmost anchorage in Schooner Retreat, is formed by the junction of Joachim and Penrose Islands on the south, east and north, and is protected on the west by Ironside and Maze Islands. Center Islet in the northern part of the bay is of small extent; a shoal with from 2 to 3 fathoms on it extends for more than 200 yards from its eastern end in a northeasterly direction toward Penrose Island. There are several other islets and rocks in the eastern part of the bay, from which a boat passage leads into Rivers Inlet.

The best anchorage in Frigate Bay will be found just within Safe Entrance, off a clean sandy beach, in 13 fathoms water, with the north eastern extreme of Ironside Island bearing N. 71° W. and the northwestern extreme of Sea Bluff S. 28° W. Vessels should moor.

Maze Islands are a cluster of small islands on an extensive shoal projecting in a northerly direction from the northeastern end of Ironside Island; the NE. prong of this shoal extends nearly across to Penrose Island, leaving a narrow channel with 5½ to 9 fathoms water, which leads from Frigate Bay to Secure Anchorage.

Secure Anchorage, NW. of Frigate Bay, is protected from seaward by Ironside, Bird and Highway Islands. Verney Passage, leading to Secure Anchorage from the westward, between Ironside and Bird Islands, is nearly 100 yards wide with 7 fathoms water in mid-channel, but it is contracted to about 30 yards by the shoals on either side, and is only suitable for small coasting vessels. [illegible] Rock, at the entrance between Folly and Stunted Islands, rend[illegible] passage dangerous.

Gales.—During SE. and SW. gales, the gusts are furious but with good ground tackle and care there is no danger in Schooner Retreat.

Directions.—Vessels bound to Schooner Retreat should at all times use Safe Entrance; from the southward, Quoin Hill at the south part of Penrose Island, should be brought in line with the hill 200 feet high, on the east end of Ironside Island bearing N. 47° E., this will lead to abreast Karslake Point, when Safe Entrance will be open. After passing Karslake Point steer very carefully and proceed at a moderate speed towards Bluff Point until Quoin Hill is in line with Center Island bearing N. 32° E., which will lead through Safe Entrance in mid channel, and to the anchorage in Frigate Bay.

Rivers Inlet, the shores of which have not been surveyed, has an entrance on either side of Penrose Island, but it is not known whether they are clear of danger. The inlet takes a northerly direction for about 8 miles, and then suddenly turns to the eastward and again to the northward for nearly 4 miles, terminating in three [illegible] about 5 miles long.

At the head of Rivers Inlet is a settlement of Bella [illegible] Indians numbering about 150, and a canning establishment named Owikino.

Addenbrooke Island.—At about 8 miles NNW. of Karslake Point lies a group of islands off the eastern shore of the sound abreast an unexplored opening. Addenbrooke, the most western of these islands, extends westward into the sound narrowing the width of the passage between it and Calvert Island to about 1¾ miles.

Safety Cove (Catsoalis), on the western shore of Fitzhugh Sound, 7 miles to the northward of Cape Calvert, is about one mile long west and east and nearly ½ mile wide at its entrance, to the westward of which the shores of the cove extend parallel to each other at a distance of 400 yards apart; there are depths of 9 to 17 fathoms within 100 yards of its shores, and 14 to 19 fathoms, soft mud, in the middle of the cove; a bank of sand and mud which dries extends 600 yards from the head with 7 fathoms close to its edge. The shores, except near the head, are high, rocky, and steep-to. There is a conical peak at the head of the cove which bears N. 71° W. from the middle of the entrance. The north entrance point of Safety Cove has two small islets lying off it which are useful in identifying the entrance, especially when coming from the northward.

Anchorage.—Good anchorage will be obtained in 13 fathoms, mud bottom, in the middle of Safety Cove abreast a waterfall on the northern shore. Entering at night, a vessel should keep in the middle of the cove and keeping the lead going, anchor as soon as 17 fathoms are struck. During SE. or SW. gales, strong gusts blow across the valley at the head of this cove.

Fresh Water.—The stream which flows into the head of Safety Cove affords excellent water but is difficult to obtain by boats. The waterfall on the northern shore, unless in exceptionally dry weather (August and September), will afford a good supply.

Kwakshua Passage, between Calvert and Hecate Islands, leads to the sea; this passage is only partially examined; it has been used by coasting vessels.

Hakai Channel, between Hecate Island and the smaller islands lying off the southern side of Hunter Island, is an unexplored channel leading to sea.

Goldstream Harbor, at the southeastern entrance point of Hakai Channel, affords good accommodation for small vessels; it is about 400 yards long and 400 yards broad, with depths of 6 to 15 fathoms, sand and mud. The entrance to this harbor from Fitzhugh Sound is through an intricate passage little over 100 yards wide, between the northern extreme of Hecate Island which forms the southern shore, and an island about one mile in extent which forms the northern side of the harbor. Foul ground marked by kelp, extends 200 yards from Kelp Point, the northern entrance point of the harbor. Evening Rock, which dries 3 feet at low water springs, lies near the middle of the passage about 400 yards within the entrance on the northern side of the channel, it would be advisable, in the absence of good local knowledge, to place a boat near this rock (when covered) before entering or leaving the harbor, and proceeding at slow speed, keep in mid channel, where there is a general depth of 6 fathoms.

Nalau Island lies between Hunter and Hecate Islands.

Nalau Passage, 4 miles northwestward of Hakai, is an unexplored channel leading to sea.

Namu Harbor is at the southern entrance of Burke Channel and one mile south of Edmund Point. This harbor is included between Cliff and Kiwash Islands to the west, and Plover Island and the mainland in other directions. At its entrance lies Kiwash, a round island, ¼ mile in diameter, and covered with trees. South Passage, between Kiwash and Plover Islands, is nearly ½ mile wide; North Passage, between Kiwash and Cliff Islands, is 600 yards wide. Namu Harbor may be entered by either passage.

From the eastern side of Namu Harbor two inlets indent the land for the distance of about one mile, the more northern is named Harlequin Basin, the other, which is choked with rocks, is called Rock Creek. At the mouth of the latter is Whirlwind Bay, its entrance being marked by two small islands, Sunday Island to the northward and Clam Island to the southward, ¼ mile apart. Two or 3 miles to the eastward of the harbor a chain of mountains extends in a NE. and SW. direction for 6 miles

Anchorage.—Large vessels should anchor in 20 fathoms, in the center of Namu Harbor, with the northern extreme of Kiwash Island bearing N. 65° W., and the western extreme of Plover Island S. 14° W. Small vessels may anchor in Whirlwind Bay in 12 fathoms, clay, with the northern extreme of Kiwash Island bearing N. 76° W., and the center of Clam Island (a small island south of the bay) S. 25° W. During the autumn and winter months the anchorage in Whirlwind Bay is not recommended, as furious gusts blow over the mountains in its vicinity. This anchorage is moreover confined by Loo Rock, on which there is only 3 feet water, lying nearly in the middle of the bay, S. 79° E., 400 yards from the southern extreme of Sunday Island. It is recommended not to bring Sunday Island to bear to the westward of NW. when entering Whirlwind Bay.

There is a large stream and an old Indian camp in Whirlwind Bay.

Burke Channel, an inlet on the eastern side of Fitzhugh Sound, leads to Belakula anchorage at the head of North Bentinck Arm, a distance of 55 miles in a general northeasterly direction from its junction with Fitzhugh Sound. Burke Channel lies between high, precipitous rocky mountains, the sides of which are covered with stunted pine trees, and mostly snowcapped, becoming more lofty as the head of the inlet is approached. Burke Channel and Bentinck Arm, though not surveyed in detail, have been frequently traversed both by day and night and may be safely navigated.

Edmund Point, the southern entrance point of Burke Channel, is low and wooded, and has several small islands south of it, lying off an indentation, which has the appearance of affording sheltered anchorage. Some small islets also lie in the channel eastward of Edmund Point.

Walker Point, the northern entrance point to the channel, is formed by an island 2 miles NW. of Edmund Point; this island is steep to, but at a distance of 400 yards the water is not deeper than 26 fathoms, mud bottom, deepening quickly a short distance further. This position might be used in a fog for anchoring.

Temporary anchorage north of Walker Point might, in an emergency, with care and sending a boat ahead, be taken up, but there are many covering reefs.

The first reach of Burke Channel takes a N. 53° E. direction for 5 miles, and thence N. 78° E. for 3½ miles, the first part being a little over one mile wide, but the latter part only ¾ mile across. The tides are strong in this reach, and several heavy tide rips are met with, but for the remainder of the distance to Belakula the tidal streams are not much felt. Immediately facing the eastern end of this reach is a bay which might possibly afford anchorage. The water here is brackish

Restoration Cove, at 4 miles from the NE. point of the first reach, is immediately under a high, conical mountain, and has a sandy beach at its head, off which, at ½ mile, is a depth of 10 fathoms shoaling gradually to 3 fathoms close to the shore. Several small streams enter the cove.

Anchorage may be taken up in 18 fathoms at about 300 yards from low water mark; the shore should be approached very slowly when coming to an anchor, as the bank is extremely steep to and the water shoals very suddenly.

The second reach of Burke Channel trends N. 14° E. for 10½ miles, ending abreast a low, wooded point at the foot of a high mountain; thence the channel takes a N. 56° E. direction for 12 miles, another arm (Kwatna) branching off to the SE. At 200 yards from the SW. point of entrance to this arm is a rock which uncovers at low water; it is the only known danger in Burke Channel, and may be avoided by keeping the northern shore aboard

Hence the channel takes a N. 67° E. direction for 4 miles along the base of a remarkably bare, stony mountain on the southern shore, which is almost entirely devoid of vegetation. Thence the channel trends north for 6 miles, at which distance Dean Channel (or canal) branches off to the NW., Burke Channel continuing for 7 miles east to Menzies Point, in latitude 52° 18′ 30″ N., where it divides into the north and south Bentinck Arms, the former taking an ENE. and the latter an ESE. direction.

North Bentinck Arm is 8 miles long, and just within the entrance on the northern shore is a small bay, affording anchorage for small craft. The head terminates in a sand and mud flat fronting low swampy ground covered with grass, which is submerged at high water. The inlet is here $1\frac{3}{10}$ miles wide

Belakula, at the head of North Bentinck Arm, affords indifferent anchorage to vessels close to the mud flat at the mouth of the river east of Sutlej Point. In taking up a berth great care is required against getting too near the edge of the flat, which is quite steep to. Large vessels should moor in 45 to 50 fathoms, as the bank is very steep to, deepening from one to 18 fathoms in a distance of 200 feet; a stern anchor may also be required, or a hawser laid out to the shore will be useful for keeping the hawse clear. Small vessels may find shelter during summer on the northern shore under Custom house Point. The country abounds in fur-bearing animals.

Belakula or Nookhalk River is a stream of considerable size and velocity, the deposit from which has formed the steep bank at the head of the inlet. The water at Belakula is quite fresh alongside, and if pumped in at low water is fit for drinking There are also several good places for watering on the northern shore, opposite the anchorage, a boat being able to go right underneath the waterfalls.

Tides—It is high water, full and change, at 12 hrs., springs rise 13 feet.

Winds—The prevailing wind in Bentinck Arm in summer is from SW.; the westerly winds of the ocean blowing across Fitzhugh Sound being led up the inlet as through a funnel, following the direction of the different bends. The breeze generally sets in about 10 o'clock in the forenoon and blows fresh until sunset, when it usually falls calm.

South Bentinck Arm.—From Menzies Point the South Bentinck Arm branches off the southeastward about a mile in breadth, with high land on both sides, for about 20 miles. At 9 miles from Menzies Point an island lies on the eastern shore. The head of the arm is reported to be shallow, 5 and 12 fathoms, but it has not been surveyed, and is seldom visited

Kiltik.—From Nalau Passage the coast of Hunter Island extends 12 miles in a northerly direction with only two openings, the northernmost of these, named Kiltik, opposite Edmund Point, is a narrow creek extending nearly a mile in a westerly direction, with an average depth of 20 fathoms in the center, but shoal for ½ mile from its head. This creek might be used by moderate sized vessels, but has not been examined in detail.

The Trap, 13 miles from the southeastern point of Hunter Island a small islet lies off an indentation of the coast, forming what has been termed the Trap. Strangers might be tempted to enter this opening, it is extremely contracted, not affording room for a steamer to turn, and dangers are supposed to exist in the passage round the island.

Fisher Channel, the continuation of Fitzhugh Sound northward, leads to Lama and Gunboat Passages on the west, and to Port John and Evans Arm on the east. It is a clear navigable channel, possessing, with the exception of the Fog Rocks, no known danger. At 15 miles from Walker Point the channel divides into two, Johnson Channel taking a NNW. and Cousins Inlet a NNE direction; the former at a distance of 9 miles splitting into several arms (Roscoe and Sisters Inlets on either side of Florence Peninsula, and Bullock and Ellerslie Channels on either side of Yeo Island) Bullock and Ellerslie Channels communicate with Seaforth Channel, and from the north point of Yeo Island, at their northern junction, the main inlet continues northward for a further distance of 10 miles to about lat 52° 37′ N. These channels northward of Gunboat Passage have not been surveyed in detail, and should therefore be navigated with caution.

Fog Rocks, lying rather on the east side of Fisher Channel and 3 miles north of Walker Point, consist of six rocks above water, flat and of a whitish color, the highest of which is 25 feet high, with a few shrubs on it; close to the southernmost rock, several small black rocks uncover at low water. These rocks (which appear nearly in mid channel from the southward) may be passed on either side, but the main route lies to the westward of them, passing them at about ½ mile There is a depth of 103 fathoms, mud, between Fog Rocks and the eastern shore of Fitz hugh Sound.

Port John is in the northern part of an indentation, 9 miles northward of Fog Rocks, and immediately under Remarkable Cone, a mountain 2,302 feet high. Southward of Port John is Evans Arm, into which there are two passages on either side of Matthew Island, which lies at the entrance to the arm. The south passage is ½ mile wide and clear of danger. The north passage is only ¼ mile wide, and this near the east end is contracted to 300 yards by a rock lying in the center.

Port John affords anchorage in 20 fathoms, but is much confined by Mark Rock nearly in the middle, covering at half flood, and by a flat extending off the stream at its head. There is also anchorage at the head of Evans Arm in 20 fathoms, which may be reached through South Passage, but the immediate approach to it north of Boot Island is foul, and a vessel of size should be preceded by a boat. North Passage should only be used after temporarily buoying Peril Rock, which has only 12 feet water on it, and lies nearly in the middle of the east entrance to the passage

Dean Canal leads out of Cousins Inlet to the NE., in which direction it extends for about 12 miles, and there divides into three branches; one (Cascade Inlet) taking a northwestern direction; another (Labouchere Channel) to the SE. and communicating with Burke Channel; the other, main inlet, extending in a north and NE. direction, with an average width of one mile, for a distance of 18 miles, when it turns to the NNW. for 9 miles, terminating in low marshy land in about latitude 52° 30′ N. into which the Kimswit River discharges itself. Anchorage [illegible] near the [illegible] tends in [illegible] f ¾ mile. [illegible] not been [illegible] precipices, [illegible] ains that overlook it.

Lama Passage, between Hunter and Denny Islands, is the main passage connecting Fisher Channel with Seaforth Channel and Milbank Sound; its eastern entrance, on the west side of Fisher Channel, may be recognized by a conical mountain 1,000 feet high, on the northeastern point of Hunter Island, and by Pointer Island, on the southern side of this entrance, where it is nearly one mile wide

The entrance to Plumper Channel, which is one mile wide, lies opposite Twilight Point, from which Lama Passage turns to the northward between Denny and Campbell Islands, for 4 miles to Grave Point, which

pumped in at low water is fit for drinking. There are also several good places for watering on the northern shore, opposite the anchorage, a boat being able to go right underneath the waterfalls.

Tides.—It is high water, full and change, at 12 hrs.; springs rise 13 feet.

Winds.—The prevailing wind in Bentinck Arm in summer is from SW.; the westerly winds of the ocean blowing across Fitzhugh Sound being led up the inlet as through a funnel, following the direction of the different bends. The breeze generally sets in about 10 o'clock in the forenoon and blows fresh until sunset, when it usually falls calm.

South Bentinck Arm.—From Menzies Point the South Bentinck Arm branches off the southeastward about a mile in breadth, with high land on both sides, for about 20 miles. At 9 miles from Menzies Point an island lies on the eastern shore. The head of the arm is reported to be shallow, 5 and 12 fathoms, but it has not been surveyed, and is seldom visited.

Kiltik.—From Nalau Passage the coast of Hunter Island extends 12 miles in a northerly direction with only two openings, the northernmost of these, named Kiltik, opposite Edmund Point, is a narrow creek extending nearly a mile in a westerly direction, with an average depth of 20 fathoms in the center, but shoal for ⅛ mile from its head. This creek might be used by moderate-sized vessels, but has not been examined in detail.

The Trap, 13 miles from the southeastern point of Hunter Island a small islet lies off an indentation of the coast, forming what has been termed the Trap. Strangers might be tempted to enter this opening; it is extremely contracted, not affording room for a steamer to turn, and dangers are supposed to exist in the passage round the island.

(374) **BRITISH COLUMBIA—Fisher channel—Walbran rock—Buoy established.**—A wooden spar buoy, painted red, has been established off Walbran rock, Fisher channel

Approx position Lat. 52° 03′ 28″ N., Long 127° 57′ 30″ E.

The buoy is moored in 5 fathoms of water.

From the buoy Pointer Island lighthouse bears N 48° W. true (WNW. ⅝ W mag), distant 600 yards, and the islet off Nob point N 80° E. true (NE. ¾ E. mag)

(N M 11, 1905)

either side of Florence Peninsula, and Bullock and Ellerslie Channels on either side of Yeo Island). Bullock and Ellerslie Channels communicate with Seaforth Channel, and from the north point of Yeo Island, at their northern junction, the main inlet continues northward for a further distance of 10 miles to about lat. 52° 37′ N. These channels northward of Gunboat Passage have not been surveyed in detail, and should therefore be navigated with caution

Fog Rocks, lying rather on the east side of Fisher Channel and 3 miles north of Walker Point, consist of six rocks above water, flat and of a whitish color, the highest of which is 25 feet high, with a few shrubs on it: close to the southernmost rock, several small black rocks uncover at low water. These rocks (which appear nearly in mid channel from the southward) may be passed on either side, but the main route lies to the westward of them, passing them at about ½ mile. There is a depth of 103 fathoms, mud, between Fog Rocks and the eastern shore of Fitz hugh Sound.

Port John is in the northern part of an indentation, 9 miles northward of Fog Rocks, and immediately under Remarkable Cone, a mountain 2,302 feet high. Southward of Port John is Evans Arm, into which there are two passages on either side of Matthew Island, which lies at the entrance to the arm. The south passage is ½ mile wide, and clear of danger. The north passage is only ¼ mile wide, and this near the east end is contracted to 300 yards by a rock lying in the center.

Port John affords anchorage in 20 fathoms, but is much confined by Mark Rock nearly in the middle, covering at half flood, and by a flat extending off the stream at its head. There is also anchorage at the head of Evans Arm in 20 fathoms, which may be reached through South Passage, but the immediate approach to it north of Boot Island is foul, and a vessel of size should be preceded by a boat North Passage should only be used after temporarily buoying Peril Rock, which has only 12 feet water on it, and lies nearly in the middle of the east entrance to the passage.

Dean Canal leads out of Cousins Inlet to the NE., in which direction it extends for about 12 miles, and there divides into three branches; one (Cascade Inlet) taking a northwestern direction, another (Labouchere Channel) to the SE. and communicating with Burke Channel; the other, main inlet, extending in a north and NE. direction, with an average width of one mile, for a distance of 18 miles, when it turns to the NNW. for 9 miles, terminating in low marshy land in about latitude 52° 52′ N., into which the Kimswit River discharges itself. Anchorage is reported on a spit, off a small stream on the west shore, near the head.

Cascade Inlet, so named from the number of water-falls, extends in a NW. direction for about 11 miles, with an average width of ¾ mile It, in common with the other branches of Dean Channel, has not been surveyed in detail; its shores are composed of perpendicular precipices, and several large cascades come down from the high mountains that overlook it.

Lama Passage, between Hunter and Denny Islands, is the main passage connecting Fisher Channel with Seaforth Channel and Milbank Sound; its eastern entrance, on the west side of Fisher Channel, may be recognized by a conical mountain 1,000 feet high, on the northeastern point of Hunter Island, and by Pointer Island, on the southern side of this entrance, where it is nearly one mile wide.

The entrance to Plumper Channel, which is one mile wide, lies opposite Twilight Point, from which Lama Passage turns to the northward between Denny and Campbell Islands, for 4 miles to Grave Point, which has several Indian graves on it, from 2½ miles north of Twilight Point to Grave Point the passage is contracted to 400 yards, with uniform depths of 25 to 30 fathoms.

The northern shore of Lama Passage is bold and but slightly indented, but the southern, after the first 3 miles, is penetrated by a number of indentations, some of which afford shelter.

Tides.—About midway between Fog Rocks and Lama Passage the flood tide from the northward meets that from the southward.

Cooper Inlet, on the southern shore of Lama Passage, 5 miles from the eastern entrance, is deep, and contains several small creeks, the indentations already mentioned, off which lie a number of islets and rocks In fine weather anchorage may be obtained in 14 fathoms water under Westminster Point, the northwestern point of the inlet, by bringing it to bear NW., and Harbormaster Point, the northeastern point of the inlet, just open of the reefs off Charles Point bearing east.

Jane Creek, in the southeastern corner of Cooper Inlet, may be used by small vessels. Charles Point, its north point, has two reefs extending 200 yards from it in a northwesterly direction, the outer of which dries 9 feet.

Anchorage.—Good anchorage may be had in this creek in 9 fathoms water, with Charles Point in line with the east point of Canoe Bight (on the opposite shore of the passage) bearing N. 23° W., and George Point, the southern entrance point of Jane Creek, bearing S. 81° W. Large vessels may anchor in about 18 fathoms, midway between Charles and George Points, the bottom in this creek is mostly rocky.

Camp Island, lying close to the southwestern extremity of Denny Island, and the turning point into the northern part of Lama Passage, should not be rounded nearer than ½ mile, as the bottom is foul for a distance of 600 yards in a southeasterly direction from it, with patches that uncover 2 feet at low water springs.

McLaughlin Bay, on the western shore of Lama Passage, ½ mile south of Grave Point, is a good stopping place; it is about 800 yards wide and 300 yards deep, with 8 to 14 fathoms water. The south point of the bay has a bare summit 150 feet high, which in thick weather is a useful guide to strangers. The anchorage is in 11 fathoms off the center of the beach about 200 yards from the shore, with Grave Point open east of SW. point of Narrows Island bearing N. 22° E. A spit runs off with Bare Hill bearing N. 65° W. Anchorage should be taken up well to the southward of the church.

In this bay is the site of an old Hudson Bay trading post; there is a small quantity of cleared ground at the foot of a rocky hill 200 feet high, ¼ mile from the beach, on the west side of which there is a lake. This is the only Indian winter residence between Queen Charlotte Sound and Seaforth Channel.

The Bella Bella natives migrated here from Bella Bella Islands in 1868; an American missionary now resides in the bay, and a small church and schoolhouse have been recently erected.

A rock is said, from Indian report, to exist in Lama Passage abreast McLaughlin Bay, and to lie 100 yards from the eastern shore, with Napier Point bearing south distant nearly 1,200 yards. This rock has been searched for without success. The passage was frequently used during the survey, and though not then found the rock may exist, and consequently the western shore should be favored

Bella Bella Islands, northward of Grave Point, are bare and about 15 feet high; these islands were formerly inhabited during the summer months by the Indians of the once powerful Bella Bella tribe. In 1884 there was an Indian population of 250 Temporary anchorage may be had to the eastward of Bella Bella Islands off a green bushy flat, the old winter residence of these natives.

Klicktsoath Harbor, on the northern side of Denny Island, is about one mile in extent, with depths of 9 to 13 fathoms, and affords excellent shelter for vessels of any size. Harbor Island, off the northwestern point of Klicktsoath, has a reef extending 200 yards from its eastern end.

Steamer Passage.—The channel south of Harbor Island is 200 yards wide, with a depth of 7 fathoms, and is suitable for small vessels, large vessels are recommended to pass north of Harbor Island and through Wheelock Pass, which lies between a 3 fathom patch near the center of the channel and Noble Point, the northeastern entrance point of the harbor, from which a 3 fathom shoal extends 150 yards in a southwesterly direction.

The west extreme of Cypress Island in line with the east extreme of Meadow Island bearing N. 6° W. leads through Wheelock Pass in 11 to 19 fathoms water, and when Harbor Island bears N. 65° W., vessels may anchor in 12 fathoms.

Large vessels not wishing to enter Klicktsoath Harbor may obtain secure anchorage in 15 fathoms, with Harbor Island bearing south, distant 600 yards

Kakooshdish Creek, just north of Noble Point, and extending 1¾ miles in an easterly direction, is suitable for small craft, but is barred across by kelp, having 3½ fathoms.

There is an Indian fishing station at the head of this creek.

Main Passage, leading from Lama Passage to Seaforth Channel, between the northeastern extreme of Campbell and Narrows Islands, is ¾ mile long and about ¼ mile wide, with depths of 20 to 30 fathoms in it. Care should be taken to maintain a mid channel course, and in thick weather much caution must be observed, as the tides are very strong

Narrows Island is ¾ mile long and nearly ½ mile broad; at 200 yards from the southern side of Narrows Island there is a ledge of rocks awash at high water, with 5 fathoms close to.

Pole and Tree Islets, east of Narrows Island, are two small islets 400 yards apart; Tree Islet, the northernmost is 120 feet high, with a detached rock close to its northeastern side. There are two rocky ledges between these islets and Narrows Island.

Hodges Reef, which dries 2 feet at low water springs, with 6 and 7 fathoms close to, lies nearly in mid channel between between Tree Islet and Deer Island. From this reef the center of Tree Islet bears N. 65° W., 400 yards, and the east extreme of Pole Islet S. 62° W., 600 yards.

Meadow Island, lies 100 yards SE. of Pole Islet. In the channel between them are depths of 5 to 15 fathoms, and a reef lies 100 yards off the north point of Meadow Island.

Deer and Cypress Islands lie to the eastward of the above islands, and are joined at low water.

Gunboat Passage, between Denny and Cunningham Islands, is narrow and intricate, containing many rocks and kelp patches; in some places the channel is not more than 100 yards wide. From its western entrance it trends about easterly for 6 miles, thence northerly 2 miles to its eastern entrance, which is at the junction of Fisher and Dean Channels.

Gunboat Passage should not be attempte' unless in small handy steam coasting vessels and with good local ' ledge.

Seaforth Channel, the main channel co g Lama Passage with Milbank Sound, is 14 miles long, with an average breadth of one mile; the land on both sides is much broken by islands with channels between leading north and south; the water is generally deep, and with the charts there should be no difficulty in navigating, in ordinary weather.

On the northern side three arms branch off to the northward: Deer Passage, the eastern, between Cunningham and Chatfield islands, is about 7 miles long, and communicates with Johnson Channel; Return Channel, the middle one, between Chatfield and Yeo Islands, is about 3 miles in length and joins Bullock Channel, and Spiller Channel, the west rn, between Yeo and Don Islands, extends 4 miles and connects with Ellerslie. These channels have not been more than casually examined, and their entrances are fronted by innumerable small islands, rocks and reefs. On the southern si le of Seaforth Channel, at 9½ miles to the eastward of Sound Point, is the entrance to Hecate Channel. This passage is about 10 miles long in a general southerly direction, with an average width of one mile, and leads into Queen's Sound.

Ormidale Harbor, at the northern extreme of Campbell Island, is about one mile deep, and is protecte from the NE. by Thorburne and Nevoy Islands, which lie across i's entrance The channel in lies westward of Nevoy Island, it is about 600 yards wide, with from 14 to 16 fathoms water, and is clear of danger it a mid channel course is steered. Inside the wat r is deep, the depth over the greater part being from 15 to 20 fathoms Anchorage may be had in 17 fathoms about 400 yards south of Nevoy Island.

The passage in is longer, but the berth is more convenient than in Kynumpt Harbor, directly west of it

Kynumpt Harbor, immediately west of Ormidale Harbor, may be recognized by Grassy Islet, 20 feet high, and Regatta Reefs, both of which are conspicuous, lying in the middle of the channel, 1¼ miles eastward of the harbor, and also by White Stone, a conspicuous bare rock 12 feet high, lying 400 yards west of the entrance.

The harbor, the entrance to which is between Shelf Point and Low Island, is 800 yards long and averages 400 yards in breadth, with 6 to 10 fathoms, mud bottom; the best anchorage is in 7 to 9 fathoms, with the north extreme of Berry Point bearing east and the west extreme of Low Island N. 41° E. A shoal patch with 1¼ fathoms on it lies on the western side of the harbor, 450 yards S. 3° E. of Shelf Point, distant 200 yards from the shore.

A rock with 10 feet water over it has been reported to lie 400 yards S. 70° W. of Low Island, but though searched for in 1883, it was not found.

Hecate Channel leads into Queen Sound; its southern entrance is obstructed by rocks.

Grassy Islet, small, 20 feet high, covered with long grass and bushes, and with only two trees on it, lies nearly one mile N. 59° E. of the entrance to Ormidale Harbor.

Regatta Rock, awash at high water, 200 yards in extent, lies ½ mile N. 48° W. of Grassy Island.

Dall Patch, a shoal with less than 6 feet water on it, lies ½ mile N. 48° E. of the entrance to Kynumpt Harbor; from the center of the patch Defeat Point bears S. 30° W., distant 800 yards, and White Stone S. 84° W., 1,300 yards; a shoal of 3 fathoms extends 250 yards to the westward of Dall Patch.

Caution.—To avoid Dall Patch, it is recommended to keep the southern shore aboard, which in this vicinity may be approached to within 300 yards; or if wishing to go northward of the patch, Grassy Islet, in line with the south extreme of Handyside Island bearing S. 71° E., leads nearly midway between Dall Patch and Regatta Rock.

Dundivan Inlet, on the northern shore of Dufferin Island, about 3 miles westward of Kynumpt Harbor, indents the coast about 1¾ miles in a southerly direction. It branches off into several creeks, of which Lockhart and Rait are the largest, and there are several small islets just within the entrance. The water is too deep to afford convenient anchorage. The southern shore of Seaforth Channel, westward of Dundivan Inlet, trends in nearly a straight line to Sound Point, the south point of entrance. At 2½ miles eastward of Sound Point, Gale Creek branches off in a southerly direction, and is supposed to connect with Boddy Creek from the SE. thus separating Dufferin Island from the remainder of the Bardswell group.

Edge Reef, on which there is a depth of 4½ fathoms, lies nearly 800 yards distant from the southern shore, at 2 miles eastward of Sound Point. Several patches lie between it and the shore.

Cod Bank, on which the least depth found was 27 fathoms, sand, lies in the middle of the western entrance to Seaforth Channel; there are

58 fathoms on the southern side, and 163 fathoms, rock, close to on the northern side of the bank.

Anchorage.—Two and one-half miles to the eastward of Sound Point, a bank extends about ⅝ mile from the south shore of Seaforth Channel, on its outer edge, which is steep-to, there are depths of 28 and 30 fathoms, decreasing to 18 and 10 fathoms close to the shore, for a distance of one mile east of Sound Point. During foggy weather, temporary anchorage may, with careful use of lead, be obtained on this bank

Hyndman Reefs, the outer of several islets and reefs lying on the western shore at the entrance to Spiller Channel, is nearly in the middle of that channel, and has a small rock only 3 feet above water on its south end.

Midge Reefs, on the northern side of Seaforth Channel, cover at 10 feet rise, and extend 800 yards in a southerly direction from Bush Point (Don Island), and are 3¾ miles within the western entrance to the channel. The Mark Rock lies 200 yards distant from the SE. point of Don Island, and one mile east of Midge Reefs; between them is Sunk Reef with 4 fathoms water on it. Bare Rock, black and low, kept just open to the southward of Surf Islet, bearing N. 68° W., leads ½ mile to the southward of Midge Reefs; the northern shore of Seaforth Channel should not be approached within this distance.

Berry Creek.—The southern shore of Don island is broken and rocky, and has numerous islets and rocks skirting it. Berry Creek is nearly 2 miles long and has its entrance blocked by small islets; it is useless as an anchorage.

Blair Inlet, 3 miles westward of Berry Creek, is another indentation useless as an anchorage on account of the numerous rocks with which it is studded. Ivory and Watch Islands form its south side.

Mouse Rock, on which the sea sometimes breaks, lies ½ mile west of Ivory Island off the entrance to Blair Inlet. Idol Point kept open of Surf Islet, bearing S 71° E. leads south of Mouse Rock.

CHAPTER IX.

MILBANK SOUND TO CHATHAM SOUND—INNER AND OUTER CHANNELS.

Milbank Sound is the main opening from seaward leading to Seaforth, Finlayson, and Mathieson Channels.

At its entrance, between Cape Swain and Day Point, the sound is nearly 9 miles wide, which breadth it maintains in a northeasterly direction for 5 miles, thence it trends more northerly, and takes a north direction for 10 miles, leading in that direction into Finlayson Channel.

Landmarks.—Approaching Milbank Sound from the southwestward, Helmet Peak on Lake Island, at the eastern shore of the sound, is conspicuous. This remarkable peak is 1,032 feet high, and bears a striking resemblance to a helmet, with the sloping side towards the west.

Stripe Mountain, on the north side of Dowager Island, at the entrance of Finlayson Channel, is 2,020 feet high, pyramidal in shape, with a remarkable landslip down its southwestern side, destitute of timber and soil, but otherwise wooded to its summit; at its base is a comparatively level space scantily covered with vegetation, which is remarkable in such a thickly timbered country.

Nearing the sound the low wooded shores of Cape Swain, in the SW. entrance point to the sound, will be recognized. The shore northward of it is much broken, and the tops of the trees are about 120 feet high.

Fogs.—Vessels meeting with a fog in this portion of Milbank Sound would find Beaver Bank of service, not only as indicating her position, but as affording temporary anchorage.

Soundings.—A run of deep water 8 miles broad, with depths of over 100 fathoms, mud, extends southwestward of Milbank Sound. Northwestward of this channel the depths decrease to 50 fathoms, and less, off the entrance to Laredo Sound, with a bottom of fine sand. Southeastward the depths are 70 and 80 fathoms, with a bottom consisting of sand, mud, and rock at intervals.

In thick weather, therefore, or if overtaken by fog, when approaching Milbank Sound from the southwestward, with average precautions, a vessel's position can be indicated by the deep sea lead.

Kelp grows on nearly every danger with a bottom of rock or stones and is generally seen on the surface of the water during the summer and autumn months.

Day Point, the southern point of Price Island, has a group of wooded islets, and rocks awash at high water, and sunken rocks extending 2 miles SW. from it; the western island of the group (Outer Island) being round, wooded, and conspicuous. The outer edge of these dangers lies $2\frac{1}{10}$ miles SW. of Day Point and 1,600 yards S. 14° E. of Outer Island.

White Rock (Kamasik), lying about 5 miles within the sound, is 59 feet high, and ½ mile N. 37° E. of it is a smaller rock (Bare Rock) 6 feet above high water. Both rocks are conspicuous, as, lying well out in the sound, they show out against the dark background of pine and cedar, which line the shores of Milbank Sound.

From White Rock, a rocky ridge (on which the sea sometimes breaks) extends ¼ mile to the southwestward, and a patch of 2 fathoms lies 500 yards eastward of the same rock.

There are depths of 50 fathoms, rock, at one mile eastward, and 34 fathoms close-to, westward of this rock.

The south extreme of Cliff Island, seen just open of Bowlder Head, bearing N. 2° W., leads eastward of this rock.

Discovery Rocks, off Cape Swain, are two dangerous rocks lying 1,600 yards N. 34° E. and S. 34° W. of each other. The southern danger, over which the sea seldom breaks, lies one mile N. 71° W. of Cape Swain. The northern rock, which is usually indicated by breakers, lies N. 23° W. distant $1\frac{1}{10}$ miles from Cape Swain.

West Rock, on the eastern shore of the sound, is of small extent, 8 feet above high water, and lies ½ mile S. 68° W. of Sound Point.

Several patches which uncover at low water lie between Sound Point and West Rock.

Mouse Rock is a dangerous sunken rock on which the sea generally breaks, lying at the northwestern entrance to Seaforth Channel.

Bush Point (north side of Seaforth Channel) seen just open south of Surf Islet, bearing S. 81° E., leads southward; and Helmet Peak, seen just open of the west extreme of Mary Island, bearing N. 34° E., leads westward of Mouse Rock.

Vancouver Rock, a dangerous rock which uncovers 12 feet at low water and is steep-to on all sides (there being depths of 13 and 14 fathoms within 200 yards of the rock), lies 1½ miles N. 36° W. of Bowlder Head. When visible this rock presents the appearance of a large whale, and is conspicuous.

Cross Point (southeastern extreme of Lady Island), in line with Bowlder Head, bearing S. 56° E., leads southward; and Low Point seen just open westward of the North Island Group, bearing N. 26° E., leads westward of Vancouver Rock.

Cross Ledge extends 1,600 yards to the southward and westward of Cross Point, and partially uncovers. There is a depth of 20 fathoms close southward of Cross Ledge.

Surf Islet, bearing S. 53° E., leads southward of Cross Ledge, in mid-channel between Cross Point and White Rock.

Bowlder Ledge, of sunken rocks with depths of 1½ and 5 fathoms, extends about one mile in a southeasterly direction from Bowlder Head.

Bowlder Bank, with 18 fathoms, rock, lies ¾ mile S. 48° W. of Bowlder Head.

Surf Islet, bearing S. 53° E., leads southward of the dangers off Bowlder Head.

North Ledges, which uncover at low water, lie northward of the North Island Group. The north extreme of these ledges lies 1,200 yards N. 9° E. of North Island, and the south extreme 400 yards N. 71° E. of that island.

Beaver Bank has 27 fathoms water (least depth found) on it, over a bottom of sand and shells. The center of this bank lies $2\frac{2}{10}$ miles N. 53° W. of Low Point.

Sandstone Reef, situated close to the shore in the northwestern portion of Milbank Sound, is a conspicuous narrow ridge, of sandstone formation, about one mile long in nearly an east and west direction. The highest portion of this ridge is 4 feet above high water.

The western extreme of Sandstone Reef lies ½ mile from the shore of Swindle Island, and 1½ miles from the eastern side of Price Island.

The Coast.—Between Cape Swain and Sound Point the land is low, wooded and broken into creeks and bays.

Price Island, forming the western shore of Milbank Sound, has a conspicuous ridge of hills (Jocelyn Range) along its eastern shore. The cluster of islets off Day Point are wooded and conspicuous; and from Day Point the eastern shore of Price Island to Aldrich Point is much broken into small exposed bays.

Boat Cove, which affords shelter to boats, is situated ½ mile northward of Aldrich Point. With this exception the coast of Price Island, north of Aldrich Point, is almost straight and unbroken for 8 miles, to the entrance of Schooner Passage.

The Eastern Shores of Milbank Sound are comparatively low and wooded, with pine and cedar trees predominating. In that portion of

Moss

north-

ooded

w and

...heastern extreme of an island contiguous to Lady Island terminates in a high bold cliff (Bowlder Head). Cliff Island which lies off the SW. side of Dowager Island at the entrance to Moss Passage is small, 225 feet high and its SE. extreme terminates in high, conspicuous white cliffs.

North Island is rocky, about 150 feet high, with some stunted trees growing on its summit.

Low Point, the western extreme of Dowager Island, and the southeastern entrance point of Finlayson Channel, is low and wooded.

Day Point, the southern point of Price Island, has a group of wooded islets, and rocks awash at high water, and sunken rocks extending 2 miles SW. from it; the western island of the group (Outer Island) being round, wooded, and conspicuous. The outer edge of these dangers lies $2\frac{1}{10}$ miles SW of Day Point and 1,600 yards S. 14° E of Outer Island.

White Rock (Kamasik), lying about 5 miles within the sound, is 50 feet high, and ½ mile N. 37° E. of it is a smaller rock (Bare Rock) 6 feet above high water. Both rocks are conspicuous, as, lying well out in the sound, they show out against the dark background of pine and cedar, which line the shores of Milbank Sound.

From White Rock, a rocky ridge (on which the sea sometimes breaks) extends ½ mile to the southwestward, and a patch of 2 fathoms lies 500 yards eastward of the same rock.

There are depths of 50 fathoms, rock, at one mile eastward, and 34 fathoms close to, westward of this rock.

The south extreme of Cliff Island, seen just open of Bowlder Head, bearing N. 2° W., leads eastward of this rock.

Discovery Rocks, off Cape Swain, are two dangerous rocks lying 1,600 yards N. 34° E. and S. 34° W. of each other. The southern danger, over which the sea seldom breaks, lies one mile N. 71° W. of Cape Swain. The northern rock, which is usually indicated by breakers, lies N. 23° W distant $1\frac{1}{10}$ miles from Cape Swain.

West Rock, on the eastern shore of the sound, is of small extent, 8 feet above high water, and lies ½ mile S. 68° W. of Sound Point

Several patches which uncover at low water lie between Sound Point and West Rock

Mouse Rock is a dangerous sunken rock on which the sea generally breaks, lying at the northwestern entrance to Seaforth Channel.

Bush Point (north side of Seaforth Channel) seen just open south of Surf Islet, bearing S. 81° E , leads southward; and Helmet Peak, seen just open of the west extreme of Mary Island, bearing N. 34° E., leads westward of Mouse Rock.

Vancouver Rock ...

(1347) **BRITISH COLUMBIA—Milbank sound—Vancouver rock—Whistling buoy established.**—The Canadian Government gives notice that an automatic whistling buoy, on the Courtenay principle, has been established off Vancouver rock, Milbank sound, in (approximately) latitude 52° 21′ 18″ N., longitude 128° 31′ 20″ W.

The buoy is painted red and is moored in about 38 fathoms of water.

(N. M. 34, 1905.)

der Head, bearing S. 56° E , leads southward; and Low Point seen just open westward of the North Island Group, bearing N. 26° E , leads westward of Vancouver Rock.

Cross Ledge extends 1,600 yards to the southward and westward of Cross Point, and partially uncovers. There is a depth of 20 fathoms close southward of Cross Ledge.

Surf Islet, bearing S. 53° E., leads southward of Cross Ledge, in mid-channel between Cross Point and White Rock.

Bowlder Ledge, of sunken rocks with depths of $1\frac{1}{2}$ and 5 fathoms, extends about one mile in a southeasterly direction from Bowlder Head.

Bowlder Bank, with 18 fathoms, rock, lies $\frac{3}{4}$ mile S. 48° W. of Bowlder Head.

Surf Islet, bearing S. 53° E., leads southward of the dangers off Bowlder Head.

North Ledges, which uncover at low water, lie northward of the North Island Group. The north extreme of these ledges lies 1,200 yards N. 9° E. of North Island, and the south extreme 400 yards N. 71° E. of that island.

Beaver Bank has 27 fathoms water (least depth found) on it, over a bottom of sand and shells. The center of this bank lies $2\frac{2}{10}$ miles N. 53° W. of Low Point.

Sandstone Reef, situated close to the shore in the northwestern portion of Milbank Sound, is a conspicuous narrow ridge, of sandstone formation, about one mile long in nearly an east and west direction. The highest portion of this ridge is 4 feet above high water.

The western extreme of Sandstone Reef lies $\frac{1}{2}$ mile from the shore of Swindle Island, and $1\frac{1}{2}$ miles from the eastern side of Price Island.

The Coast.—Between Cape Swain and Sound Point the land is low, wooded and broken into creeks and bays.

Price Island, forming the western shore of Milbank Sound, has a conspicuous ridge of hills (Jocelyn Range) along its eastern shore. The cluster of islets off Day Point are wooded and conspicuous; and from Day Point the eastern shore of Price Island to Aldrich Point is much broken into small exposed bays.

Boat Cove, which affords shelter to boats, is situated $\frac{1}{2}$ mile northward of Aldrich Point. With this exception the coast of Price Island, north of Aldrich Point, is almost straight and unbroken for 8 miles, to the entrance of Schooner Passage.

The Eastern Shores of Milbank Sound are comparatively low and wooded, with pine and cedar trees predominating. In that portion of the sound lie two extensive channels (Mathieson Channel and Moss Passage), which branch off from Milbank Sound eastward and northward of Lady Island, respectively. Lady Island is low and wooded throughout. The western shores of Dowager Island are also low and wooded, but are flanked by high mountains.

The southeastern extreme of an island contiguous to Lady Island terminates in a high bold cliff (Bowlder Head). Cliff Island which lies off the SW. side of Dowager Island at the entrance to Moss Passage is small, 225 feet high and its SE. extreme terminates in high, conspicuous white cliffs.

North Island is rocky, about 150 feet high, with some stunted trees growing on its summit.

Low Point, the western extreme of Dowager Island, and the southeastern entrance point of Finlayson Channel, is low and wooded.

The Northern Shore of Milbank Sound (Swindle Island) is high and bold, with mountains rising immediately over it.

Directions.—Approaching Milbank Sound from the southwestward in clear weather, Helmet Peak should be kept in line with White Rock, bearing N. 56° E., which mark will lead nearly in mid channel up the sound. When within $2\frac{1}{2}$ miles of White Rock, on that line, a vessel bound eastward may steer S. 84° E. towards Seaforth Channel, with Day Point astern bearing N 84° W., or if bound to the northward a N 15° E course may be steered towards Finlayson Channel.

In thick weather, as before mentioned, with average precautions and attention to the deep sea lead, the soundings will indicate the vessel's position.

Bound from Seaforth Channel into Finlayson Channel, keep Idol Point well open to the southward of Surf Islet, bearing S. 70° E., until Helmet Peak comes open of the west extreme of Mary Island bearing N. 34° E., and then Surf Islet should be kept astern bearing S. 53° E for 3 miles, which will lead in mid channel, $1\frac{1}{2}$ miles northward of White Rock From this position Cliff Island should be seen open westward of Bowlder Head. bearing N 2° W., and a vessel may steer N 36° W. for 3 miles, or until Low Point is seen open westward of the North Island group bearing N. 26° E.; thence steer N. 4° E. for 3 miles, or until Stripe Mountain bears N. 60° E., when it may be steered for on that bearing, and the course gradually altered northward into Finlayson Channel.

Mathieson Channel is an extensive arm of the sea, leading many miles northward from Milbank Sound, eastward of Lady and Dowager Islands At the distance of $2\frac{1}{2}$ miles within its southern entrance this channel is obstructed by islands, islets and rocks, and strangers should not proceed farther. From the eastern entrance of Oscar Passage, by which it communicates with Finlayson Channel, Mathieson Channel extends in a northerly direction along the east side of Roderick Island for over 25 miles to its junction with Mussel Inlet, one arm, about 5 miles long, branching off to the eastward at about 5 miles south of the junction.

Northward of Oscar Pass, Mathieson Channel has not been surveyed in detail

Tides.—The flood stream sets to the northward and divides near the middle of Milbank Sound, one portion running towards Finlayson Channel, another towards Mathieson Channel, and another towards Seaforth Channel. The reverse takes place on the ebb.

The strength of tide is variable, but it seldom exceeds one knot an hour in Milbank Sound, but increases within the channels to 2 and 3 knots an hour

St. John Harbor (Cheeksquintz) lies nearly midway between Cape Swain and Sound Point, and, though somewhat confined, affords good anchorage for small vessels.

The harbor is protected at its entrance by a reef of rocks awash and sunken rocks, which form a natural breakwater, and breaks the ocean swell. Eastward of this reef at the entrance there is a clear channel, 400 yards wide, with depths of 10 to 30 fathoms.

At ½ mile within the entrance are two small islands, the eastern and smaller one (Wood Island) being round, wooded, and conspicuous. The channel eastward of these islands is barely 200 yards wide abreast Wood Island, and leads into Anchor Bay, which is the usual anchorage for small vessels. Westward of these islands the channel is wider and leads into Deep Bay, which forms the SW arm of St. John Harbor.

There are depths of 9 to 20 fathoms in Deep Bay, and 11 to 14 fathoms in Anchor Bay

Rage Reef extends ¾ mile northward from the western point of St. John Harbor, and is about 400 yards wide. This dangerous reef consists of ledges which uncover, and rocks awash at high water; the northern extreme uncovering 4 feet at low water

Mark Islet, 6 feet above high water, lies about midway on the eastern side of Rage Reef.

Ledges, which uncover, extend 200 yards from the eastern shore of the channel leading into St John Harbor

Directions—Approaching St. John Harbor, Cape Swain should be kept well open of the conspicuous quoin-shaped point situated 2 miles northward of the cape, bearing S. 32° W. On no account should Rage Reef be approached inside that line, until Wood Island is distinctly seen, and North Point bears S. 64° E. When Wood Island is recognized, it should be brought to bear south and steered for Wood Island on that bearing should be seen in line with a black high-water rock on the southern shore of Anchor Bay, with a sandy bay immediately east of the rock.

Anchorage.—Pass 100 yards eastward of Wood Island and anchor in 10 to 11 fathoms, sandy bottom, in Anchor Bay, with the eastern side of Wood Island seen in line with the north extreme of Rage Reef, bearing N. 25° W., distant 600 yards.

Caution.—At high water, when Rage Reef is nearly covered, it is difficult to distinguish the entrance into St. John Harbor At half tide and at low water, the northern end of that reef and also the dangers on the eastern side of the channel are visible, and a vessel can be guided clear of them by the eye.

Port Blakeney, formed between Mary and Don Islands, on the southern side of Mathieson Channel, about 3 miles within the entrance, is easy of access, and, lying immediately at the head of Milbank Sound, may be approached from the southwestward with the swell astern.

At its entrance, between Promise and Rain Points, the port is 500 yards wide; thence it takes a southerly direction for about one mile, terminating in a small creek leading into Seaforth Channel.

Cod Reefs are a cluster of rocks awash, and sunken rocks, at the entrance to Port Blakeney. The southern rock of this cluster is 4 feet above high water, and the northern rock, with 24 feet water over it, lies 600 yards N. 48° E. of Promise Point, with a clear channel northward of it 300 yards wide.

Oke Reefs, about 400 yards northward of Cod Reefs, extend 400 yards from the southern side of Oke Island. The outer detached rock is 3 feet above high water, and between it and Oke Island several patches of rock uncover at high water.

Clearing marks.—White Rocks, off the south end of Lake Island, seen in line (astern) with the north end of Passage Island (between Lake and Lady Islands) bearing N. 58° W. will lead between Oke and Cod Reefs. Mark Islet, seen in line with Oke Island, bearing N. 8° W., will lead eastward of those dangers.

Sand Patch, with 24 feet of water upon it, is of small extent, and lies nearly in mid-channel about ½ mile within Port Blakeney. Helmet Peak, seen in line with Promise Point, bearing N. 9° E., will lead westward of Sand Patch.

Anchorage in 10 to 12 fathoms, sandy bottom, will be found about ½ mile within Port Blakeney, with Helmet Peak seen just open of Promise Point bearing N 9° E., and Observation Point on the north shore of East Bay bearing S. 81° E.

Supplies.—Wood and water may be obtained in Port Blakeney. Rock cod and other fish may be caught in abundance on Cod Reefs, and clams and cockles in the sandy bays They are readily obtained at low water by digging in the mud and sandy ground, especially in those places over which a fresh-water stream runs. Wild fowl are also plentiful in the season.

Directions.—Approaching Port Blakeney from the southward, Helmet Peak should be kept just open of the eastern point of Lady Island (Long Point) bearing N. 43° E., and when within ½ mile of the latter a N. 65° E. course should be steered towards Oke Island. The clearing mark before mentioned for leading between the Oke and Cod Reefs should be brought on astern, and when Mark and Oke Islands are seen in line bearing N. 8° W, a vessel will be eastward of Cod Reefs, and may then haul into the harbor with the south extreme of William Island astern, bearing N. 26° E, and anchor in the depth and position before mentioned

Moss Passage (Toowitl) leads northward of Lady Island into Mathieson Channel. At its western entrance this passage is over one mile wide; but at 3 miles within this entrance, and one mile from its junction with Mathieson Channel, it is contracted by Squaw Island to barely 200 yards. Beyond that position, therefore, it should not be attempted by strangers

Bird Rock, at the western entrance of Moss Passage, is 3 feet above high water, with foul ground extending from it 400 yards to the east ward. The south extreme of the North Island Group seen just open southward of the south extreme of Cliff Island, bearing N. 47° W., leads southward of Bird Rock.

Morris Bay, on the southern side of Moss Passage, about one mile within its western entrance, is ½ mile wide and extends in a southerly direction, terminating in a cul de sac which dries at low water. Westerly winds send a swell into the anchorage; but the bay possesses the great advantage of permitting the state of the weather in Milbank Sound being ascertained when at anchor, and if fog be prevalent (as is often the case) it can be seen from Morris Bay.

Kitty Patch lies at the eastern entrance to Morris Bay, 200 yards from the eastern shore. This bank is 200 yards in extent north and south, with depths of 4 and 5 fathoms, sand.

Directions.—Approaching Morris Bay, a mid channel course should be kept between Bird Rock and Salal Point; and if Vancouver Rock be uncovered, it should be kept astern bearing S. 82° W. (westerly). When the southern extreme of Cliff Island is seen open northward of Bird Rock bearing N. 58° W., that mark kept on astern will lead to the entrance to Morris Bay.

Anchorage will be found in 12 to 14 fathoms, sandy bottom, at 200 yards from the western shore, with Salal Point shut in by the western entrance point of Morris Bay, bearing N. 81° W., and Detached Island (north side of Moss Passage) bearing N. 4° E.

Supplies.—Good water may be obtained in Morris Bay. Clams and cockles can be gathered in abundance. Plover and other birds frequent Bird Rock. Berries grow in abundance on Salal Point.

Alexandra Passage lies eastward of Vancouver Rock and the North Island Group. Small steam vessels, possessing local knowledge, make use of Alexandra Passage, especially when coming from the northward and wishing to anchor in Morris Bay, but this passage is only 1,200 yards wide in its narrowest part, and in the event of an accident to the machinery a vessel using it would be in a dangerous position.

Cliff Island is nearly steep to, but the small islet close northward of it has foul ground extending from it 200 yards to the westward.

Soundings.—The depths in Alexandra Passage are 14 to 42 fathoms, rocky at the former, and mud at the latter depth.

Directions.—A vessel compelled by circumstances to make use of Alexandra Passage should keep the western shore of Finlayson Channel north of Jorkins Point in line with Low Point, bearing N. 6° E. which is the general leading mark through this passage. It is, however, recommended alternately to open and close those points, especially when nearing North Island Group, so as to keep in mid channel.

Schooner Passage, leading from Laredo Sound into the northwestern corner of Milbank Sound, is obstructed by islands, islets, rocks, and sunken dangers, and no specific directions can be given for it. It is occasionally made use of by small coasting craft.

Finlayson Channel, the entrance to which is between Jorkins and Low Points, extends from Milbank Sound in a general northerly direction to the head of Carter Bay, with an average width of one to 2 miles. The land on both sides is high, the peaks closely approaching the shores and rising in a precipitous manner from the water's edge. Unless where the vegetation has been denuded from the mountain sides by landslips, both shores are thickly wooded, the pine and cedar predominating; occasionally their dark green foliage is relieved by the bright light green leaf of the maple.

Landmarks.—Stripe Mountain lies at the southeastern entrance to Finlayson Channel. The summit of Cone Island (Bell Peak), together with two high waterfalls which fall into the sea on the SE. side of Sarah Island, are the principal landmarks of importance.

Oscar Passage, 1¼ miles north of Low Point, leads eastward out of Finlayson Channel, between Dowager and Roderick Islands, and is about one mile wide and 6 miles long to its junction with Mathieson Channel.

Bulley Bay, on the southern shore of Oscar Passage, though small, affords temporary anchorage in 15 fathoms, at 200 yards from the shore, and is occasionally used by coasting vessels.

The Sisters, two small islets, lying 400 yards from the eastern shore of Finlayson Channel, 3¼ miles northward of Oscar Passage, are wooded and about 90 feet high. They lie 800 yards from each other, and are joined by ledges which uncover at low water.

Nowish (Otter Cove) is ½ mile from the Sisters Islets, between Indian and Susan Islands. The entrance, northward of Indian Island, is 400 yards wide; the cove then extends in a SE direction, narrowing near its head to 200 yards, and having on its northern shore, about 800 yards within the cove, a small bay, which affords anchorage for small vessels in 10 to 14 fathoms, sandy bottom, in the middle of the bay.

Jackson Passage, an unexplored arm on the eastern shore of the channel, is 400 yards wide, and extends in an easterly direction from its entrance.

Mary Cove, on the eastern shore, 3½ miles northward of the Sisters Islets, is barely 200 yards wide at its entrance, and extends in a northerly direction for ½ mile, terminating in a sandy beach. There are depths of 24 and 7 fathoms in mid-channel within this cove.

Cone Island, on the western shore of Finlayson Channel, is 3½ miles long and about ½ mile broad. The summit of this island, situated about one mile from its south extreme, is conical in shape, 1,280 feet high; the eastern and western sides are abrupt and precipitous, but the land slopes gently to the northward, terminating in Wedge Point.

Klemtoo Passage, between Cone and Swindle Islands, is about 3½ miles long in a NNW. and SSE. direction, and in some parts barely 200 yards wide. The depths in mid channel are 10 and 30 fathoms, sand and shells, with rock at intervals. Though narrow, this passage is safe (provided a mid-channel course be kept), and affords anchorage almost throughout.

Anchorage, suitable to vessels of moderate length, will be found north of Star Islet, nearly in mid channel, 200 yards from the shore of Cone Island.

Tides.—The tidal streams are comparatively weak. The flood stream is but little felt, the great body of water passing into Finlayson Channel. The ebb seldom exceeds the rate of one mile an hour.

South Passage, between Cone and Jane Islands, is ½ mile wide, with depths of 18 and 37 fathoms, rock.

Kelp Patch, with only 5 to 12 feet over it, lies 200 yards to the southward and westward of Jane Island, and is about 200 yards in extent.

Berry Point (Swindle Island), seen just open of Leggo Point (Cone Island) bearing S 5° E, will lead westward of Kelp Patch.

Wedge Rock uncovers at low water, and lies 50 yards from the northern extreme of Cone Island.

Ripple Bank, with 11 fathoms rocky bottom, lies nearly in mid channel of South Passage.

North Passage, between Jane and Sarah Islands, is ½ mile wide.

Danger Patch, with one to 3 fathoms water over it, lies 200 yards northward of Jane Island.

Directions.—When proceeding through South Passage, the southern shore should be kept aboard, passing 400 yards northward of Cone Island. North Passage is to be preferred to South Passage when communicating between Finlayson and Tolmie Channels. Keep nearer the northern shore, and pass 400 yards south of Sarah Island.

Jane Island, ½ mile north of Cone Island, is about one mile long and ½ mile broad. It is low and wooded, the tops of trees being 200 feet high.

Sarah Island, the south point of which is 1,200 yards northward of Jane Island, is 15 miles long in a north and south direction, and from one to 2½ miles broad. This island reaches its greatest elevation of 2,000 feet at 4 miles from its southern extreme. On the eastern side of the island, at 7 miles from the southern extreme, an unexplored bay faces southward, and at 3½ miles from the southern extreme, on its eastern shore, there are two high waterfalls.

Watson Bay lies on the eastern side of Finlayson Channel, 9 miles northward of Sisters Islets. This unexplored bay is one mile wide at its entrance, and extends in an easterly direction.

Wallace Bight lies 2½ miles northward of Watson Bay. It is one mile wide at its entrance, and takes a northerly direction for one mile. There is no bottom at 106 fathoms, between its entrance points.

Goat Cove, 4 miles northward of Wallace Bight, is ½ mile wide, and extends in an easterly direction for ½ mile, terminating in a sandy beach.

There are depths of 23 to 34 fathoms within this cove, the former being close to the head.

Sheep Passage is nearly one mile wide, and leads eastward from Finlayson Channel, just south of Carter Bay. At 3 miles within its western entrance it trends northward until its junction with Mussel Inlet.

Mussel Inlet takes a northerly direction for about 5 miles, when it suddenly turns to the eastward for about the same distance, terminating in Poison Cove. It is stated to have the same general characteristics as the other inlets.

Carter Bay.—This excellent stopping place lies at the head of Finlayson Channel, 26 miles within its entrance, and is easily recognized by the high cliffs on its western shore. The bay is 800 yards wide at its entrance, abreast the anchorage ground, and about 1,200 yards deep in a northerly direction, the head terminating in a large stream, fronted by an extensive flat. This stream takes a northeasterly direction for about one mile to the foot of a waterfall at the entrance of a lake.

Anchorage will be found in 14 to 15 fathoms, mud bottom, at 300 yards from the eastern shore and 400 yards from the sand flat at the head of the bay, with the entrance points of the bay bearing S. 11° E and S. 54° W., respectively.

Supplies.—Water can be obtained from the large stream at the head of the bay, which is probably one of the best watering places along the coast. Trout abound in the fresh water stream. Wild fowl frequent Carter Bay. Shell fish, of whatever kind, should not be eaten.

Tides.—It is high water, full and change, in Carter Bay at noon; springs rise 13 feet.

Hiekish Narrows lie northward of Sarah Island, and lead from Finlayson Channel into Graham Reach. They are about 5½ miles long, and from ¼ to one mile wide. The depths in the narrows are 31 and 73 fathoms in mid-channel, with a bottom of sand and shells.

Hewitt Rock, a dangerous sunken rock with only 10 feet over it, and deep water close to, lies at the northern entrance of the narrows nearly in mid channel.

The eastern shore of the channel should be kept aboard when navigating the northern portion of the narrows.

Tolmie Channel, between Princess Royal and Sarah Islands, is about 15 miles long in a general north and south direction, and from ½ to one mile wide.

On the west shore, 2½ miles northward of southern point of Sarah Island, an extensive arm takes a southerly direction, and is reported to communicate with Laredo Sound. Abreast the northeastern point of this inlet, a small islet lies close to the shore of Sarah Island. About ¼ mile NNW. of this island is a sunken rock.

Caution.—The northern reach of Tolmie Channel looks directly into this arm, care is therefore necessary when approaching from the northward not to mistake this unexplored arm for the reach leading to Klemtoo Passage.

At 2 miles northward of the above-mentioned inlet, on the west shore of Tolmie Channel, lies another unexplored passage, facing the south east.

Tolmie Rock, on which is only 4 feet water, lies 100 yards from the shore of Sarah Island, at ½ mile within the northern entrance of the Tolmie Channel.

Directions.—Tolmie Channel, though not so wide as Finlayson Channel, is preferable in some respects, especially if compelled to be under way at night. A mid channel course should be steered through out except when navigating the northern part of the channel, when the western shore should be neared to avoid Tolmie Rock. Avoid the rock near the small island towards the southern entrance.

Tides.—The flood stream sets to the northward, and is stronger in Finlayson than in Tolmie Channel. The ebb, however, is stronger in Tolmie Channel, and runs for 1½ hours after the ebb has ceased in Finlayson Channel. In the narrow parts of these channels both flood and ebb streams attain a velocity of 3 knots an hour at springs.

Graham Reach, northward of the junction of Tolmie Channel with Hiekish Narrows, is about 17 miles long, and from ½ to one mile broad, with depths of 38 fathoms, rock, and 130 fathoms, sand and shells. In general features this reach resembles Finlayson Channel.

Green Inlet lies on the eastern shore, 2 miles northward of Sarah Island. This unexplored arm takes an easterly direction at its entrance.

Flat Point lies on the western shore, 3 miles westward of Green Inlet This point is wooded, flat, and comparatively low. Abreast Flat Point on the south shore of the channel is a remarkable large bowlder rock.

Dangers.—There are no known dangers at 200 yards from the shore in this reach.

Swanson Bay lies on the eastern shore, 7 miles from Sarah Island. There is a conspicuous waterfall on the western shore of the channel abreast Swanson Bay In very dry weather this fall is small and sometimes ceases altogether.

Anchorage may be obtained in 19 fathoms, sandy bottom, in the northern part of Swanson Bay, with the conspicuous waterfall shut in with the northern entrance point, and Flat Point shut in with the southern entrance point of the bay.

Khutze is an unexplored arm, on the north shore, 6 miles northward of Swanson Bay

Anchorage is reported by Indians at the head of this inlet.

Aaltanhash is another inlet on the eastern shore, unexamined, 3 miles northward of Khutze. In size and direction it is similar to Khutze, and is reported by Indians to afford anchorage.

Tides.—The tides meet abreast Aaltanhash Inlet

Red Cliff Point, the turning point into Fraser Reach, lies on the western shore, 17½ miles from Sarah Island. This point terminates in a conspicuous cliff of a reddish brown color; and is a good landmark.

Fraser Reach, the channel northwestward of Graham Reach, is 12½ miles long and from ½ to 1½ miles wide, with depths of 62 fathoms, rock, to no bottom at 145 fathoms. In features it resembles Finlayson channel.

Warke Island is 1½ miles long and ½ mile broad. The channel on both sides of the island is deep, but that to the south is slightly the wider There is a bay on the southern shore of the channel, abreast Warke Island, at the head of which is a fine trout stream, communicating with a large lake

Klekane, an unexamined arm on the northern shore, abreast Warke Island, is ½ mile wide, and takes a NNW. direction from its entrance. Approaching from the southeastward this arm appears as the continuation of Graham Reach

Anchorage may, from Indian report, be obtained at the head of Klekane Inlet.

Landslip Point lies on the northern shore, 4 miles from Warke Island. Over this point is a remarkable landslip.

Kingcombe Point, the turning point into McKay Reach, lies on the southern shore 12 miles from Red Cliff Point. This point is long, sharp and conspicuous

McKay Reach leads westward from Fraser Reach into Wright Sound, there is no bottom in mid channel at 139 and 225 fathoms, the latter depth being found at 400 yards southward of Cumming Point.

From mid channel abreast Kingcombe Point, the reach takes a westerly direction for 4 miles to abreast Trivett Point, thence a W. by S. direction for 4 miles to abreast Cumming Point. Westward of Kingcombe Point, a deep bay lies on the southern shore, between Kingcombe and Trivett Points

The land on the northern shore of the channel is high and bold, with mountains 3,000 feet high. The land on the southern shore is not so high; and near the summits of the mountains are some extensive bare patches of slate color.

Gribbell Island, the shores of which have not been surveyed in detail, is of somewhat rectangular form, about 11 miles long (north and south), and 7 miles wide

Ursula Channel.—Between Pilot Point, the southeastern point of Gribbell Island, and Fisherman Cove, on the opposite shore, is the entrance to Ursula Channel which skirts the eastern side of Gribbell Island for about 7 miles. Its shores are composed of steep, lofty mountains rising abruptly from the sea, and covered with pines and forest trees.

Fisherman Cove, on the eastern shore at the entrance to Ursula Channel, affords a very indifferent anchorage with barely room for the ship to swing in 30 fathoms, with the south point of the bay (a clump which is connected to the shore by a sandy neck covered at high water) bearing S 29° W Vessels anchoring here must feel their way with the deep sea lead as the water shoals very suddenly from 30 fathoms to 12 fathoms, the latter depth being at about 25 yards from the shore A small stream flows into the head of the cove, off which a shoal extends some distance, its edge being very steep.

Boxer Reach, the continuation of Ursula Channel in a NW. direction along the northeastern side of Gribbell Island, is about 6 miles long On its northern shore good anchorage may be found in the northwestern part of Bishop Cove in from 15 to 20 fathoms.

Bishop Cove is a very good anchorage, and is formed by a narrow neck of sand running out from the land terminated by a clump covered with trees, similar to that at Fisherman's Cove The water shoals gradually up to the sandy neck and a vessel might go into 15 fathoms.

There appears to be anchorage on the southeastern side of the sandy neck, but the beach runs out shoal a long way on that side

Verney Passage, along the western shore of Gribbell Island, communicates with Boxer Reach; its shores have not been surveyed.

Devastation Channel.—From the junction of Verney Passage and Boxer Reach at the northern point of Gribbell Island, the channel continues northward along the eastern side of Hawkesbury Island for a distance of 20 miles, and is known as Devastation Channel, its shores have not been surveyed.

Gardner Canal, the entrance to which is on the eastern side of Devastation Channel, about midway along it, turns off at Staniforth Point to the eastward, in which direction it continues, with many bends, for upwards of 45 miles The land is an entirely barren waste, nearly destitute of wood and verdure, appearing as a mass of almost naked rocks rising to rugged mountains. Its shores have not been surveyed in detail, but there is reported to be anchorage on either side of Richardson Point, on the southern shore, about 6 miles from the entrance, in from 18 to 5 fathoms; and also at Kemano Bay on the northern shore, 20 miles farther up, but here the anchorage is said to be indifferent, as the water is deep and shoals very rapidly from no bottom at 25 fathoms, to 3 fathoms. A vessel may anchor in Kemano Bay in 15 fathoms with Green Point bearing S 38° W and Entrance Bluff S 16° E, but great caution is required in picking up a berth, and when entering vessels should keep over towards the eastern entrance point (Entrance Bluff), as shoal water extends for some distance from the opposite point

The Kemano River flows through an extensive valley into the head of Kemano Bay, and is a stream of some size, navigable in the summer by canoes for a distance of 8 miles from its mouth. Kemano Bay is frequented by the Kitlup Indians during the hoolican fishing season; their village, however, is at the head of the inlet Firewood can be obtained from the Indians at a moderate price.

In the winter months ice forms at 25 miles from the head of Gardner Canal.

Tides.—It is said to be high water, at full and change, in Kemano Bay at 1 h. p. m. (June) springs rise about 9 feet.

Kitimat Arm.—From the north end of Hawkesbury Island, Devastation Channel continues in to a northerly direction for a further distance of about 17 miles to about latitude 54° 2′ N., where it is terminated by a border of low land with a shallow flat extending from side to side, through which a small rivulet discharges itself at the eastern corner, navigable only for canoes. This termination differs in some respects from many of the others; its shores are not very abrupt, but are bounded on each side by a range of lofty mountains, which continue apparently in a direction parallel to each other. The valley between them, which is 3 or 4 miles wide, being covered with trees, mostly of the pine tribe. Two Indian villages of the Kitimat tribe are situated near the head of this arm.

Clio Bay, on the eastern shore of the Kitimat Arm, affords anchorage in 17 fathoms.

Kildala Arm extends in an easterly direction for about 10 miles, branching off from the east side of Kitimat Arm at about 11 miles from its head.

Douglas Channel, which extends along the western shore of Hawkesbury Island, leads into the Kitimat Arm at its junction with Devastation Channel; it has not been surveyed. "It is about 3 miles broad and the shores are very high." Kitkiatah, an unexplored inlet, branches off from the western side of Douglas Channel in a southwesterly direction at 6 miles from Money Point, its SE entrance point. Small vessels may anchor in 5 fathoms ½ mile within Kitkiatah Inlet.

Wright Sound lies between Gribbell and Gil Islands, with no bottom at 110 and 220 fathoms.

It communicates eastward with McKay Reach and westward with Grenville Channel. Whale Channel and Lewis Passage lead southward, and Douglas Channel and Verney Passage lead northward from Wright Sound.

Landmarks.—Gil Island on the southern side of the sound culminates in a well defined snow clad peak 3 000 feet high.

The mountains northeastward of Holmes Bay have bare patches down their sides.

Directions.—In thick weather, when the shores are almost obscured to the water's edge, Wright Sound, with its different openings, north and south, makes a very perplexing picture to strangers. Under such circumstances it is well to remember that a N. 64° W. course leads across the sound from McKay Reach to Grenville Channel; the distance from Point Cumming to Yolk Point being just 7¼ miles.

Holmes Bay, on the eastern shore of Wright Sound at the entrance of Whale Channel, is 1,600 yards wide at its entrance, and terminates in a sand flat, which extends 200 yards from the head of the bay.

The northern entrance point is high and bold, and a small islet lies off the southern entrance point of the bay.

Anchorage will be found in 14 fathoms, sand, with the southern extreme of Promise Island in line with the north point of the bay, bearing N. 47° W.; and Gil Mountain in line with the south entrance point, S. 83° W.

Fisherman Cove is the name of an anchorage one mile eastward of Turtle Point, close to the shore of Gil Island. The water is deep, and the anchorage reported indifferent.

Promise Island, at the southern end of Douglas Channel, is covered with pine and cedar, and culminates in two peaks of dome-shape. Cape Farewell, the southeastern extreme of the island, terminates in a high, bold cliff. A conspicuous white cliff lies on the southern shore, midway between Cape Farewell and Thom Point.

The eastern shore of the island is high, with an occasional bay with a sandy beach at its head. Dawson Point, the northern extreme, is low and wooded.

Farewell Ledge uncovers at low water, and extends 400 yards from Cape Farewell. This ledge is nearly steep-to, there being no bottom at 40 fathoms at 30 yards from it. Ledges extend 200 yards from the eastern shore of Promise Island.

Dawson Ledge extends 400 yards northward from Dawson Point,

, is

and

s to

ion

Point.

Harbor Rock is a dangerous rock of small extent, which uncovers 6 feet at low water, and lies nearly in mid-channel near the head of the harbor. This rock is nearly steep-to, there being depths of 10 and 18 fathoms at 100 feet from the rock.

Gil Mountain seen in line with Thom Point, bearing S. 22° E., will lead NE.; and Camp Point, seen just open of Observation Point, bearing S. 16° E., will lead westward of Harbor Rock.

Otter Shoal extends 100 yards from the western shore at the head of the anchorage, with depths of 3 fathoms and less upon it.

Soundings.—Southward of Observation Point there are depths of 24 to 40 fathoms; northward of that point 19 to 7 fathoms, sand.

Anchorage in 6 to 7 fathoms, sand, will be found near the head of Coghlan Anchorage, with Gil Mountain just shut in with Thom Point, bearing S. 19° E., and Stephens Point just open of Letitia Point (Stewart Narrows) bearing N. 60° E. Or, for a long vessel, not wishing to go

In the winter months ice forms at 25 miles from the head of Gardner Canal.

Tides.—It is said to be high water, at full and change, in Kemano Bay at 1 h. p. m. (June), springs rise about 9 feet.

Kitimat Arm.—From the north end of Hawkesbury Island, Devastation Channel continues in to a northerly direction for a further distance of about 17 miles to about latitude 54° 2′ N., where it is terminated by a border of low land with a shallow flat extending from side to side, through which a small rivulet discharges itself at the eastern corner, navigable only for canoes. This termination differs in some respects from many of the others, its shores are not very abrupt. but are bounded on each side by a range of lofty mountains, which continue apparently in a direction parallel to each other. The valley between them, which is 3 or 4 miles wide, being covered with trees, mostly of the pine tribe. Two Indian villages of the Kitimat tribe are situated near the head of this arm.

Clio Bay, on the eastern shore of the Kitimat Arm, affords anchorage in 17 fathoms.

Kildala Arm extends in an easterly direction for about 10 miles, branching off from the east side of Kitimat Arm at about 11 miles from its head.

Douglas Channel, which extends along the western shore of Hawkes-

(843) **BRITISH COLUMBIA—Douglas channel—Uncharted rocks.**—Captain Hughes, master of the steamer *Princess Beatrice*, reports the existence of two uncharted rocks in Douglas channel, the one immediately west of a line drawn between Halsey point and the extreme west tangent of Hawkesbury island, in latitude 53° 30′ 00″ N., longitude 129° 13′ 30″ W., ½ mile offshore, marked by kelp, the other halfway between this rock and the shore on a bearing N 24° W true (NW ½ W. mag.) The latter dries at extreme low water. Positions are approximate. (N. M. 22, 1905.)

It communicates eastward with McKay Reach and westward with Grenville Channel. Whale Channel and Lewis Passage lead southward, and Douglas Channel and Verney Passage lead northward from Wright Sound.

Landmarks.—Gil Island on the southern side of the sound culminates in a well defined snow-clad peak 3,000 feet high.

The mountains northeastward of Holmes Bay have bare patches down their sides.

Directions.—In thick weather, when the shores are almost obscured to the water's edge, Wright Sound, with its different openings, north and south, makes a very perplexing picture to strangers. Under such circumstances it is well to remember that a N. 64° W. course leads across the sound from McKay Reach to Grenville Channel; the distance from Point Cumming to York Point being just 7½ miles.

Holmes Bay, on the eastern shore of Wright Sound at the entrance of Whale Channel, is 1,600 yards wide at its entrance, and terminates in a sand flat, which extends 200 yards from the head of the bay.

The northern entrance point is high and bold, and a small islet lies off the southern entrance point of the bay.

Anchorage will be found in 14 fathoms, sand, with the southern extreme of Promise Island in line with the north point of the bay, bearing N. 47° W.; and Gil Mountain in line with the south entrance point, S. 83° W.

Fisherman Cove is the name of an anchorage one mile eastward of Turtle Point, close to the shore of Gil Island. The water is deep, and the anchorage reported indifferent.

Promise Island, at the southern end of Douglas Channel, is covered with pine and cedar, and culminates in two peaks of dome-shape. Cape Farewell, the southeastern extreme of the island, terminates in a high, bold cliff. A conspicuous white cliff lies on the southern shore, midway between Cape Farewell and Thom Point.

The eastern shore of the island is high, with an occasional bay with a sandy beach at its head. Dawson Point, the northern extreme, is low and wooded.

Farewell Ledge uncovers at low water, and extends 400 yards from Cape Farewell. This ledge is nearly steep to, there being no bottom at 40 fathoms at 30 yards from it. Ledges extend 200 yards from the eastern shore of Promise Island.

Dawson Ledge extends 400 yards northward from Dawson Point, and uncovers at half ebb.

Coghlan Anchorage, between the mainland and Promise Island, is 600 yards wide at its entrance between Camp and Thom Points, and extends in a NW. direction for 2 miles, widening within the entrance to 800 yards.

Thom Ledge extends 100 yards SW. of Thom Point.

Promise Ledge extends 50 yards from Promise Point.

Observatory Ledge extends 100 yards eastward of Observation Point.

Harbor Rock is a dangerous rock of small extent, which uncovers 6 feet at low water, and lies nearly in mid channel near the head of the harbor. This rock is nearly steep to, there being depths of 10 and 18 fathoms at 100 feet from the rock.

Gil Mountain seen in line with Thom Point, bearing S. 22° E., will lead NE.; and Camp Point, seen just open of Observation Point, bearing S. 16° E., will lead westward of Harbor Rock.

Otter Shoal extends 100 yards from the western shore at the head of the anchorage, with depths of 3 fathoms and less upon it.

Soundings.—Southward of Observation Point there are depths of 24 to 40 fathoms; northward of that point 19 to 7 fathoms, sand.

Anchorage in 6 to 7 fathoms, sand, will be found near the head of Coghlan Anchorage, with Gil Mountain just shut in with Thom Point, bearing S. 19° E., and Stephens Point just open of Letitia Point (Stewart Narrows) bearing N. 60° E. Or, for a long vessel, not wishing to go beyond Harbor Rock, a berth, in 24 fathoms, mid-channel, at ½ mile off Observation Point, may be found.

Directions.—When entering keep in mid-channel, to avoid the ledge which uncovers off Thom Point, and proceed to the anchorage with the leading mark above given for clearing Harbor Rock on astern; and anchor as before directed.

Stewart Narrows lead northward of Promise Island into Douglas Channel The tides in this passage are strong, and the channel confined; it is therefore not recommended.

Tidal Streams.—The flood stream which enters Campania Sound from the southward divides off Passage Island, and the main body of water passes up Squally Channel. The lesser body, passing into Whale Channel, skirts the north shore of Gil Island, and unites, at one mile northward of Turtle Point, with the main body of water which has entered Wright Sound by Lewis Passage. The flood stream from that position sets directly across Wright Sound, and impinging on Camp Point causes very strong eddies off that point, and is then deflected towards Grenville Channel.

A portion of the flood stream by Whale Channel turns into McKay Reach and meets, abreast of Aaltanhash Inlet, the flood stream from the Finlayson Channel. Another portion proceeds into Douglas Channel and Verney Passage. On the ebb the reverse takes place, the main body of water from Wright Sound obtaining an exit by Whale Channel.

The ebb streams from Wright Sound, Douglas Channel, and McKay Reach unite nearly midway between Maple Point and Holmes Bay, setting directly towards the latter, producing strong eddies at the mouth of Holmes Bay. Thence the stream sets fairly through Whale Channel, and passing north and south of Passage Island unites with the stream of Squally Channel and united they pass out into Campania Sound.

Both flood and ebb streams attain the velocity of 3 knots an hour, at springs, in the contracted portions of the channels

Grenville Channel leads northwestward out of Wright Sound, and is the usual channel taken by steam vessels when proceeding to the northern waters of British Columbia.

At its southeastern end Grenville Channel abreast Yolk Point is 1,600 yards wide; thence it extends in a NW. direction for 4 miles to abreast Davenport Point, with an average width of one mile. From this point the channel continues in about the same direction for 11 miles, and narrows to 600 yards as Lowe Inlet is approached, seldom exceeding 800 yards in width until northwestward of Evening Point (Klewnuggit), thence it widens out to one and 3 miles, and extends for 23 miles to abreast Ogden Channel. The depths in Grenville Channel are 48 to 133 fathoms, rock

The land on both sides is high, reaching an elevation of 3,500 feet on the northern and from 1,000 to 2,000 feet on the southern shore; and for the most part is densely wooded with pine and cedar.

The channel is comparatively free from danger at 100 yards from either shore, with the following exception

Morning Reefs extend for nearly one mile off Evening Point. The western shore of Grenville Channel must be kept on board when passing Morning Reefs.

Bare Islet (north side of Klewnuggit Inlet) kept open of Camp Point (south side of that inlet), bearing N. 80° E. will lead northward of Morning Reefs

Tides.—The tides in Grenville Channel are weak, in most parts not exceeding one knot, the flood stream from the northward meeting that from the southward abreast Nabanhah Bay.

Directions—The only directions necessary for navigating Grenville Channel are to keep in mid channel, except when passing Nabanhah Bay, and then the west, or Pitt Island, shore should be kept aboard.

Lowe Inlet is a little over ¼ mile wide at its entrance between James and Hepburn Points.

Nettle Basin is nearly circular in shape, and is ½ mile across, but between its entrance points the basin is barely 200 yards wide.

In the NE. corner of Nettle Basin is a large stream, with a waterfall close to its mouth, and several others within (Verney Falls) This stream is reported to be connected by a chain of lakes with Douglas' Channel.

Landmarks.—On the west shore, at 2 miles southward of Lowe Inlet, there is a remarkable bare hill 400 feet high.

Tom Islet, a small and wooded islet, lies close to the eastern shore of the channel at 400 yards westward of Lowe Inlet.

On the east side of the inlet a remarkable mountain, with a conical summit (Anchor Cone), rises to the height of 2,010 feet. From its summit the land slopes northward and southwestward. The latter spur terminates in the eastern entrance point of Lowe Inlet; and when seen from the eastward appears as a long, low, wooded projection. Over the northwestern shore of the inlet mountains with bare summits rise to the height of 2,000 feet

High-water Rocks, 200 yards from the western shore, at 800 yards within Lowe Inlet, are awash at high water, and lie close to each other in a north and south direction. There is a depth of 23 fathoms at 100 feet eastward of the rocks.

Don Flat, with depths of 3 fathoms and less upon it, extends 200 yards from the head of the bay south of Don Point.

Whiting Bank, at 100 yards within the mouth of Lowe Inlet, has depths of 10 fathoms and less on it extending across the entrance. Northward of that position the water deepens to 19 and 20 fathoms, mud. Within Nettle Basin the general depths are 15 to 17 fathoms, mud.

Anchorage for vessels of moderate length will be found, in mid-channel, on Whiting Bank, in 8 and 10 fathoms, sand and shells. In this position, Anchor Cone Mountain should bear S. 75° E. and Hepburn Point S. 8° E. For a long vessel more convenient anchorage will be found higher up, in mid-channel, in 20 fathoms, mud bottom, with Anchor Cone Mountain bearing S. 30° E.

Supplies.—Good water can be procured in Lowe Inlet, from the stream in Nettle Basin. Trout may be caught in the stream. Whiting, in abundance, may be caught on Whiting Bank.

Edible nettles grow on the shores of the basin, and are useful when cooked as an antiscorbutic.

Klewnuggit Inlet has its entrance between Camp Point and Leading Island; it is 800 yards wide, and thence the inlet takes an easterly direction for 800 yards, and there divides; the longer arm (Exposed Arm) extends in a southeasterly direction for 3 miles, and terminates in a swamp fronted by a sand flat. The shorter arm takes a northwesterly direction for 1¼ miles, passing eastward of Leading Island, and is ¼ mile wide.

With the exception of Morning Reefs, Klewnuggit Inlet has no dangers beyond 200 yards from the shore.

Anchorage may be obtained in the NW. arm (Ship Anchorage) in 15 to 20 fathoms, mud bottom, in mid channel, at 200 yards from either shore.

Directions.—Entering Klewnuggit Inlet, having cleared Morning Reefs, keep in mid channel between Camp Point and Leading Island. Pass 400 yards SE. of the latter, and anchor on its eastern side in Ship Anchorage. In this position the southeastern extreme of Leading Island should be seen in line with a conspicuous cliff of purple color, on the south shore of Exposed Arm, bearing S. 26° W.

Kxngeal, an unexplored inlet on the eastern shore, ½ mile northwestward of Evening Point, is ½ mile wide at its entrance, and takes a northwesterly direction.

A rock which uncovers lies 400 yards SE. of the northwestern entrance point of Kxngeal Inlet.

At the distance of 6 miles NW. of Kxngeal is Baker Inlet with a narrow opening, but apparently quite extensive within, and in an easterly direction; a small islet or rock lies in the entrance. From this, in a westerly direction nearly 3 miles, is a narrow but deep opening, which from Grenville Channel appears to cut Pitt Island in two, and may join the eastern arm of Petrel Channel.

Kumealon, an unexplored inlet on the eastern shore, abreast of False Stuart Anchorage, has an entrance 400 yards wide, and takes a northerly direction. Some small islets lie near the northern shore of Grenville Channel westward of Kumealon Inlet.

Stuart Anchorage, on the western shore of Grenville Channel just within its western entrance, is ½ mile westward of a long, low, wooded projection, which serves to distinguish it.

Stag Rock uncovers 13 feet at low water, and lies 800 yards N. 46° W. of the above mentioned point. This rock has foul ground extending from it 800 yards in a N. 41° W. direction, and a small patch, which uncovers at low water, lies 200 yards S. 27° W. of the rock.

The whole of this foul ground is indicated by kelp during summer and autumn.

Anchorage will be found in 10 to 15 fathoms, rock, N. 72° W., 400 yards from Stag Rock, with the south extreme of Gibson Island seen touching Culvert Point bearing N. 41° W. northerly.

Directions.—Proceeding for this anchorage, especially at high water, care is necessary. Pass 400 yards westward of the foul ground extending from the Stag Rock, and anchor when at 200 yards to the southward.

Tides.—It is high water, full and change, at Stuart Anchorage at 0h. 30m.; springs rise 17 feet.

The tidal streams meet abreast Evening Point, eastward of that point the flood approaches from the eastward, and westward of the point from the westward.

At springs the flood stream in the narrow portions of Grenville Channel attains the velocity of 2 knots, and the ebb 4 knots an hour. The latter stream continues to run for $1\frac{1}{2}$ hours after low water by the shore. Abreast Lowe Inlet, strong eddies will be felt on the ebb.

False Stuart Anchorage lies on the southern shore 3 miles southeastward of Stuart Anchorage. On its northwestern side there is a high, bold projection. This point should serve to distinguish False Stuart Anchorage from Stuart Anchorage, as the latter has a long, low, projection on its southeastern side. The water is deep close to the shore.

Gibson Islands, a group in the western portion of Grenville Channel, at its junction with Ogden Channel, consists of one large island 160 feet high, about one mile in extent and wooded, and several smaller islets and rocks; the shores of the larger island are broken into several bays. On the eastern side of the large island is Bloxham Island, of small extent, and Lamb Islet lies 200 yards from the northeastern shore.

Watson Rock uncovers 18 feet at low-water springs, and lies 400 yards from the southwestern shore of the large Gibson Island. There is a depth of 47 fathoms, rock, at 200 yards south of Watson Rock.

Bloxham Shoal extends 1,200 yards eastward from the southeastern extreme of Bloxham Island, and passes eastward of Gibson Islands at that distance, with depths of one to 3 fathoms water over it.

Gunboat Harbor, between Gibson and Bloxham Islands, is a small harbor which faces the SE., affording temporary anchorage to small vessels, in 4 to 10 fathoms, 200 yards within the entrance, in midchannel.

Bedford Island, of small extent, lies ½ mile north of the larger Gibson Island.

Bedford Spit extends 600 yards westward from Bedford Island. The channel between Bedford and Gibson Islands has depths of 4 fathoms and less in it; this passage is not recommended.

Marrack Island lies ½ mile north of Bedford Island and is one mile in extent

Marrack Rock, which uncovers, lies nearly in mid channel between Bedford and Marrack Islands

Port Fleming, between Marrack, Bedford, and Gibson Islands and the mainland eastward of them is a good, well sheltered harbor, of even soundings, from 3 to 7 fathoms, with muddy bottom, and very little current or tide.

The approach to Port Fleming from the north is by Arthur Passage.

Kennedy Island is wooded, rising gradually, and culminates near the middle in two conspicuous peaks. The western and southern shores of Kennedy Island are bold and little broken; the northern shores have not been examined in detail.

Cardena Bay is an open bay on the southern side of Kennedy Island, and is skirted by a mud bank, which extends over ½ mile from the shore, with depths of 5 to 10 fathoms upon it

In May, 1880, there were three houses, a wharf, and an Indian summer village, and also a supply of wood for steamers at this place, which is called Inverness or Aberdeen fishery

It is a good temporary stopping place in case of fogs or darkness on reaching Chatham Sound.

Anchorage may be found on the bank, in 7 to 8 fathoms good holding-ground at 600 yards from the shore of Kennedy Island; and it is the best anchorage in the vicinity of Skeena River, sheltered from north and SE

Lewis Island, one mile westward of Kennedy Island, is low, wooded, narrow, and 2½ miles long.

Arthur Passage, between Kennedy and Lewis Islands, is about 5 miles long, in a general NNW. and SSE. direction, and about one mile wide, with depths of 18 to 63 fathoms, mud.

Herbert Reefs lie on the western side of Arthur Passage, about 800 yards from the northeastern extreme of Lewis Island, and 1,200 yards from Kennedy Island. This dangerous reef consists of two rocks which uncover at low water, with depths of 7 and 9 fathoms between them lying NNW. and SSE., distant ¼ mile from each other. There are depths of 37 fathoms and over, at 200 yards northward, and of 20 fathoms at 200 yards southward of Herbert Reefs.

The eastern and smaller Genn Island seen in line with the west extreme of White Cliff Island, bearing N. 24° W., leads eastward of Herbert Reefs

Lawson Harbor, on the northwestern side of Lewis Island, is about ½ mile long and ¼ mile wide.

Anchorage for small vessels may be found in 4 fathoms water, in mid channel, about 200 yards within Lawson Harbor.

Elliott Island, NW. of Lewis Island, is low and wooded, with a greatest breadth of ¾ mile.

Bloxam Passage, between Lewis and Elliott Islands, and connecting Arthur and Chismore Passages, is about 400 yards wide, with a depth of 21 fathoms in mid-channel.

Elizabeth Island is nearly 3 miles long in a NW. and SE. direction, with an average breadth of ¾ mile. With the exception of a hill, 334 feet high, near its southeastern end, this island is low and wooded.

Bamfield Islands, a group of small islets, lie about ¼ mile from the northeastern shore of Elizabeth Island; 600 yards eastward of these islands are some reefs. A deep but narrow passage exists between Bamfield Islands and the reefs.

Chismore Passage, between Porcher Island and Lewis, Elliott and Elizabeth Islands, is about 4 miles long in a NW. and SE. direction, and from 400 to 1,000 yards wide, with depths of 4 to 21 fathoms, mud. It is obstructed by foul ground at its southeastern end, and is only accessible for ships by Bloxham Passage.

Kelp Passage, between Lewis and Porcher Islands, is available only for boats.

Elizabeth Rock, which uncovers at low water, lies 200 yards from the western shore of Elizabeth Island, at one mile within the northern entrance of Chismore Passage.

Anchorage may be obtained in mid-channel, in 7 to 10 fathoms, 400 yards distant from the western shore of Elliott Island; with Genn Islands seen midway between Elliott and Elizabeth Islands, bearing N. 4° W. Good holding-ground and excellent shelter.

Chalmers Anchorage on the northern side of Elliott Island is formed at the junction of that island with Elizabeth Island.

Anchorage may be found in 13 to 14 fathoms, at 400 yards from the northwestern extreme of Elliott Island; with that extreme seen in line with south extreme of White Cliff Island, bearing N. 55° E.

White Cliff Island, 260 feet high, is about ½ mile long in a north and south direction; its southern extreme terminating in high, bold, white cliffs. A ledge extends 400 yards southward from White Cliff Island. There is a depth of 30 fathoms, mud and shell, at 200 yards southward of this ledge.

Cecil Patch, seldom marked by kelp, has 4 fathoms upon it, and lies one mile west of White Cliff Island. There are depths of 7 and 18 fathoms at 100 yards from the patch.

The summit of Kennedy Island (Elizabeth Peak), seen in line with the southern extreme of White Cliff Island, bearing S. 52° E., will lead northward of Cecil Patch.

Genn Islands consist of two small wooded islands, lying close together. The eastern and smaller island lies 2¼ miles N. 24° W. of the west extreme of White Cliff Island.

Bribery Island, small and wooded, lies 1,600 yards N. 74° W. of the western Genn Island. It consists of rocks very little above high-water.

Lawyer Group consist of two principal islands and several smaller ones, about one mile in extent.

Cruice Rock, of small extent, covers at three-quarters flood, and lies 450 yards N 57° W. of the western Lawyer Island

Hunt Point, the northern extreme of Porcher Island, is about 3 miles northwestward of Chismore Passage. Temporary anchorage in off-shore winds may be had under the point in about 10 fathoms.

Malacca Passage, between Porcher Island and the Genn and Lawyer Groups, is about 6 miles long, and about 1¾ miles wide, with depths of 21 to 81 fathoms, mud, the latter depth being found in the western portion of the channel.

Directions.—The summit of Kennedy Island, Elizabeth Peak (bare patches on the northwestern side), seen in line with the south extreme of White Cliff Island, bearing S. 52° E., will lead through Malacca Passage.

Skeena River, the largest river on the coast of British Columbia, northward of Fraser River, takes its rise in Lake Babine, near the village of Naas Glee, about 200 miles beyond Port Essington At 120 miles from Port Essington the river divides into three branches, known as the Forks of the Skeena, the principal branch taking a northerly direction, the others a NW and SE. direction, respectively For about 20 miles above Port Essington the Skeena River is available for vessels drawing 4 feet water; beyond that distance it is only navigable for canoes. The head of navigation for vessels drawing over 6 feet may be said to terminate 6 miles beyond Port Essington, and 21 miles from the mouth of Skeena River.

The river is navigable for light draught steamers as far as Mumford Landing, 60 miles inland, and 200 miles further for canoes. There are two missionary stations on the river.

The water, as far as Port Essington, is stated to be of light blue color, similar to that of Fraser River. The shores of the Skeena are said to be low, and covered with small hard wood and cotton trees; also good sized white oak, similar to those found on the banks of the Fraser River. The shores at the entrance are densely wooded, chiefly cedar and hemlock, and bear evidence of a remarkably wet climate. The Skeena is stated to freeze over during the winter months at 6 miles below Port Essington.

The entrance to the Skeena River is divided into three channels by Smith and Kennedy Islands They are designated North, Middle, and Telegraph Channels or Passages North Channel is suitable only for small craft. Middle Channel is obstructed by shifting sandbanks, and is in some places very narrow. Steamers coming from the north often take this channel in order to touch at Port Essington. It is dangerous for sailing vessels, or without a pilot Telegraph Channel is the main passa, . The north channel of the Skeena River is blocked with ice nearly all the winter, but it seldom reaches down as far as Kennedy Island. Port Fleming is free from ice.

The head of tide water in Skeena inlet and where the river proper appears to commence is about 18 miles above port Essington. The river is navigable with difficulty for small stern wheelers about 38 miles above tide water to Kitsumgallum, where there is a trail up the valley of the Kitsumgallum River, to the head waters of Nass River.

Supplies.—Potatoes of large size and good quality are plentiful; also berries, which are dried by the Indians for their winter food. The Skeena is a prolific salmon stream, and fish of the finest quality are procured here. Good timber is plentiful and of large size, especially spruce and yellow Alaska cedar.

Telegraph Passage, the southern and principal channel of the Skeena River, is about 8 miles long, with an average width of 1½ miles. The western side of the channel is rendered dangerous by sand flats,

(160) **BRITISH COLUMBIA.—Skeena river.—Sunken rocks in port Essington.—North Skeena passage entrance.—Shoal ground southeast of Kitson island.**—Information has been received from Mr. J. T. Walbran, Commanding the Canadian Pacific Navigation Company's S. S. *Danube*, of the existence of the three under-mentioned sunken rocks lying in and near the fairway in port Essington, and which are described as dangerous, being sharp and jagged:

(1) The northern sunken rock in port Essington, which dries 2 feet at ordinary low water, lies with Veitch point bearing S. 61° W. *true*, (SW. by S. *mag.*), distant $2\frac{4}{10}$ miles, and the north extreme of a small island (Village island) at the entrance to Ecstall river S. 26° E. *true*, (SE. ¾ E. *mag.*).

(2) The center sunken rock in port Essington, which is the most dangerous as it so seldom shows, dries 1 foot at low water spring tides, and lies with Veitch point bearing S. 68° W. *true*, (SW. ¾ S. *mag.*), distant $2\frac{6}{10}$ miles, and the north extreme of Village island S. 10° W. *true*, (S. by E. ½ E. *mag.*).

(3) The southern sunken rock in port Essington, awash at ordinary low water, lies with Veitch point bearing S. 72° W. *true*, (SW. *mag.*), distant $2\frac{4}{10}$ miles, and the north extreme of Village island S. 26° E. *true*, (SE. ¾ E. *mag.*), distant 50 yards.

Also, that shoal ground, with 6 to 8 feet on it at ordinary low water, extends about 1,200 yards in a southeasterly direction from the south end of Kitson island, at the entrance to North Skeena passage. Near the outer end of this shoal ground the water deepens to 3 fathoms.

Approx. position. Lat., 54° 10′ 30″ N., Long., 130° 18′ W.

NOTE.—The passage between Kitson island and Leer point is only navigable for boats.

Lawyer Group consist of two principal islands and several smaller ones, about one mile in extent.

Cruice Rock, of small extent, covers at three quarters flood, and lies 450 yards N. 57° W. of the western Lawyer Island.

Hunt Point, the northern extreme of Porcher Island, is about 3 miles northwestward of Chismore Passage. Temporary anchorage in off-shore winds may be had under the point in about 10 fathoms.

Malacca Passage, between Porcher Island and the Genn and Lawyer Groups, is about 6 miles long, and about 1½ miles wide, with depths of 21 to 81 fathoms, mud, the latter depth being found in the western portion of the channel.

Directions.—The summit of Kennedy Island, Elizabeth Peak (bare patches on the northwestern side), seen in line with the south extreme of White Cliff Island, bearing S. 52° E., will lead through Malacca Passage.

Skeena River, the largest

nearly all the winter, but it seldom reaches down as far as Kennedy Island. Port Fleming is free from ice.

The head of tide water in Skeena inlet and where the river proper appears to commence is about 18 miles above port Essington. The river is navigable with difficulty for small stern-wheelers about 38 miles above tide water to Kitsumgallum, where there is a trail up the valley of the Kitsumgallum River, to the head waters of Nass River.

Supplies.—Potatoes of large size and good quality are plentiful; also berries, which are dried by the Indians for their winter food. The Skeena is a prolific salmon stream, and fish of the finest quality are procured here. Good timber is plentiful and of large size, especially spruce and yellow Alaska cedar.

Telegraph Passage, the southern and principal channel of the Skeena River, is about 8 miles long, with an average width of 1½ miles.

The western side of the channel is rendered dangerous by sand flats, some of which dry, extending from the eastern side of Kennedy Island, but the eastern side has depths of 4½ to 17 fathoms.

Caution.—Unless under the guidance of a pilot, as the channels of the Skeena are subject to periodical changes, it is recommended, before attempting them, to buoy the channel by boats or other means.

North Passage, between Tsimpsean Peninsula and Smith and De Horsey Islands, has a depth of about 3 fathoms in some parts, and is not recommended. Mount McGrath on Smith Island is conspicuous, 2,200 feet high. At the entrance to this passage several dangers lie nearly in mid-channel; the navigable channel lies on the southern shore, and is barely 200 yards wide in some parts.

Near the entrance of North Skeena Passage there is a considerable mining camp called Willaclagh.

From Woodcock landing, on the northern shore of North Skeena Passage, a narrow inlet extends to the westward of north, cutting off Tree Point from the mainland, sending a branch to join the sea, near Coast Islet, the inlet itself continuing northwesterly joins the large basin in which Oldfield Island (containing Mount Oldfield 2,300 feet high) is situated. This basin enters Malacca Passage between Lima Point and Coast Islet, and connects with Metlah Catlah Bay through Venn Creek at its NW. angle. The large mass of land west of Oldfield Basin, SE. of Metlah Catlah, and of which Lima Point appears to be the SE. entrance, has been named Digby Island.

Anchorage will be found at one mile within the passage, off Woodcock Landing on the northern shore, nearly in mid-channel, in 8 to 10 fathoms, but the anchorage is limited though it is more sheltered than Port Essington. Vessels should moor. Anchorage is also reported off the western side of Smith Island under Mount McGrath.

Soundings.—The depths in the navigable channels of the Skeena, from the entrances to abreast Port Essington, are from 4 to 20 fathoms.

Tides.—The night tides rise higher than those of the day. It is high water at full and change in Port Essington at 1h. 0m.; springs rise 24 feet, neaps 15 feet. The flood stream at the entrance attains the velocity of 4, and the ebb 5 knots an hour at springs.

Winds.—During September easterly and southeasterly winds, accompanied by almost continuous rain, with frequent squalls, have been experienced.

Port Essington (Spuksūt) lies on the southern shore of the Skeena River, about 11 miles from its mouth, and affords extensive anchorage for vessels of any size. The village is situated on the western side of a point forming the angle between the Skeena and Ecstall Inlet. The latter is a long channel extending in a southeasterly direction from its junction with the Skeena. From this channel come the greater part of the ice-floes which encumber the Skeena in the cold season. Behind the flat on which the village stands is a ridge which rises in one place to a rather remarkable conical mountain. Strong NE. gales in winter interrupt communication with the shore, and though not frozen over there is much loose ice, as also quantities of heavy driftwood. Ships could not remain at Port Essington during the months of December, January, February, and March, and well into April. The snowfall has been about 6 feet on the level.

Three canneries have been established in the vicinity of Port Essington, and a temporary church has been erected.

Anchorage with good holding ground will be found in mid-channel abreast Port Essington, in 4 to 7 fathoms, mud.

A heavy cross-sea is caused by strong winds from NW. to SE., and vessels riding at anchor in the current during a gale of wind would be very liable to foul and trip their anchors.

Raspberry Islands, eastward of Port Essington, consist of three wooded islets, lying close to the eastern shore.

De Horsey Island lies about one mile northward of Kennedy Island, leaving a passage between choked with sandbanks, and only available for boats.

Middle Passage, situated between Kennedy and De Horsey Islands, is obstructed at its western entrance by sand-flats, some of which uncover. It should not be attempted by a stranger.

LAREDO SOUND, OGDEN CHANNEL, TO GRENVILLE CHANNEL.

Laredo Sound, between Price and Aristazable Islands, and connecting Hecate Strait with Laredo Channel, is nearly 20 miles long in a general north and south direction and from 3 to 14 miles wide.

Landmarks.—Kitistu Hill, on the northeastern shore of the sound, is of triangular shape, with a well-defined summit 760 feet high. Over the north shore of the sound rise three remarkable mountains, the summits of the two northern having sharp pinnacles, North and South

Needle Peaks. The summit of the southern and lowest of the three peaks, Cone Mountain, is of conical shape. At 4 miles from the southern extreme of Aristazable Island, two conspicuous hills, forming a saddle, rise to the height of 610 feet.

Coast.—The eastern shore of Laredo Sound is low, wooded, much broken into bays and creeks, and fringed by numerous islets, rocks awash, and sunken rocks to the distance of 2 miles from the west coast of Price Island. Outer Island, which lies off Day Point, when seen from Laredo Sound, appears round and well defined.

At the western entrance of the sound a group of islands and islets extend from Aristazable Island for a distance of more than 5 miles in a southerly direction.

Entrance Island, $\frac{3}{4}$ mile long in a north and south direction, is the outer of a chain of islands lying off the southern extreme of Aristazable Island.

Nab Rock, a dangerous sunken rock, over which the sea only breaks at long intervals, lies $3\frac{8}{10}$ miles S. 30° E. of the summit of Entrance Island.

The ground is foul to the distance of one mile SE. from the rock, and several ledges uncover at low water between Nab Rock and Entrance Island.

Don Point, situated on the western shore of Laredo Sound, is a peninsula 150 feet high, and when first seen appears as an island. Close northward of Don Point is a small cove, which affords shelter to boats.

Double Island, on the eastern shore of the sound, abreast of Don Point, is wooded, about 100 feet high, and divided near the center by a cleft, which causes it to appear as two islands, when seen from the southward and northward.

Low Point, wooded and flat, lies $2\frac{1}{2}$ miles north of the summit of Double Island.

Low Rock, which uncovers at low water, lies 800 yards north of Low

and lies
Island,

ls north-

ad of La-
h.
, of small
miles N.

nce point

ing across
sound, in

Tides.—The night tides rise higher than those of the day. It is high water at full and change in Port Essington at 1 h. 0m.; springs rise 24 feet, neaps 15 feet. The flood stream at the entrance attains the velocity of 4, and the ebb 5 knots an hour at springs.

Winds.—During September easterly and southeasterly winds, accompanied by almost continuous rain, with frequent squalls, have been experienced.

Port Essington (Spuksut) lies on the southern shore of the Skeena River, about 11 miles from its mouth, and affords extensive anchorage for vessels of any size. The village is situated on the western side of a point forming the angle between the Skeena and Ecstall Inlet. The latter is a long channel extending in a southeasterly direction from its junction with the Skeena. From this channel come the greater part of the ice floes which encumber the Skeena in the cold season. Behind the flat on which the village stands is a ridge which rises in one place to a rather remarkable conical mountain. Strong NE. gales in winter interrupt communication with the shore, and though not frozen over there is much loose ice, as also quantities of heavy driftwood. Ships could not remain at Port Essington during the months of December, January, February, and March, and well into April. The snowfall has been about 6 feet on the level.

Three canneries have been established in the vicinity of Port Essington, and a temporary church has been erected.

Anchorage with good holding ground will be found in mid-channel abreast Port Essington, in 4 to 7 fathoms, mud.

A heavy cross-sea is caused by strong winds from NW. to SE., and vessels riding at anchor in the current during a gale of wind would be very liable to foul and trip their anchors.

Raspberry Islands, eastward of Port Essington, consist of three wooded islets, lying close to the eastern shore.

De Horsey Island [illegible]

(839) **BRITISH COLUMBIA—Laredo channel—Uncharted rocks—Directions.**—Captain Holmes Newcomb, master of D. G. steamer *Kestrel*, reports the existence of an uncharted rock in the middle of Laredo channel, between Aristazable and Princess Royal islands. The rock carries 8 feet and is covered with kelp.

Approx. position: Lat. 52° 47′ 10″ N., Long. 129° 05′ 37″ W.

A reef is also reported extending 1 mile due east from Channel rock in the same channel, covered with kelp and drying in patches, where the chart shows 40 fathoms, no bottom.

Captain Hughes, master of the steamer *Princess Beatrice*, reports the existence of a sunken rock, covered with kelp, between Spray point and Surf inlet. From the rock Spray point bears S. 8° E. true (SE. by S. mag.), and the westernmost Surf island N. 42° W. true (WNW. mag.).

Mariners navigating this channel from the southward are advised, after passing Schooner point, to immediately haul over to the northeast shore and keep it close aboard until Spray point is passed, as the middle and southwest side of Laredo channel are reported full of dangers.

(N. M. 23. 1908.)

Needle Peaks. The summit of the southern and lowest of the three peaks, Cone Mountain, is of conical shape. At 4 miles from the southern extreme of Aristazable Island, two conspicuous hills, forming a saddle, rise to the height of 640 feet.

Coast.—The eastern shore of Laredo Sound is low, wooded, much broken into bays and creeks, and fringed by numerous islets, rocks awash, and sunken rocks to the distance of 2 miles from the west coast of Price Island. Outer Island, which lies off Day Point, when seen from Laredo Sound, appears round and well defined.

At the western entrance of the sound a group of islands and islets extend from Aristazable Island for a distance of more than 5 miles in a southerly direction.

Entrance Island, $\frac{3}{4}$ mile long in a north and south direction, is the outer of a chain of islands lying off the southern extreme of Aristazable Island.

Nab Rock, a dangerous sunken rock, over which the sea only breaks at long intervals, lies $3\frac{8}{10}$ miles S. 30° E. of the summit of Entrance Island.

The ground is foul to the distance of one mile SE. from the rock, and several ledges uncover at low water between Nab Rock and Entrance Island.

Don Point, situated on the western shore of Laredo Sound, is a peninsula 150 feet high, and when first seen appears as an island. Close northward of Don Point is a small cove, which affords shelter to boats.

Double Island, on the eastern shore of the sound, abreast of Don Point, is wooded, about 100 feet high, and divided near the center by a cleft, which causes it to appear as two islands, when seen from the southward and northward.

Low Point, wooded and flat, lies $2\frac{1}{2}$ miles north of the summit of Double Island.

Low Rock, which uncovers at low water, lies 800 yards north of Low Point.

Schooner Point is the turning point into Laredo Channel, and lies 7 miles N. 15° E. of Don Point. The coast of Aristazable Island, between Schooner and Don Points, is bold and rocky.

Schooner Ledge, which uncovers at low water, lies 600 yards northward of Schooner Point.

South Bay Islands, a group of small extent, lie at the head of Laredo Sound. The larger islands are wooded, and 250 feet high.

North Bay Islands consist of three principal wooded islets, of small extent, 250 feet high. The center island of the group lies $1\frac{1}{2}$ miles N. 10° W. from the center island of the South Bay group.

Steep Point, high and bold, forms the northeastern entrance point of Laredo Channel.

Soundings.—The bank of comparatively shoal water stretching across the mouth of Laredo Sound, should serve to distinguish that sound, in thick or foggy weather, from Milbank Sound, there being depths of over 120 fathoms at the entrance of the latter.

Directions.—Small sailing coasting vessels, to avoid the light winds and calms which frequently prevail in the inmost channels, make use of Laredo Sound and the channels leading northward from it, as the wind seldom fails them there.

In clear weather, if Outer Island be not brought to bear southward of S. 64° E., a vessel will pass south of Nab Rock. Kititstu Hill steered for on a N. 32° E. bearing will lead eastward, and Schooner Point bearing N. 4° E. leads northward of Nab Rock. Pass one mile off Schooner Point and proceed through Laredo Channel as herein-after directed.

Laredo Channel, between Princess Royal and Aristazable Islands, is about 20 miles long, and from 2 to 5 miles wide.

At 6 miles within the eastern entrance Laredo Channel is obstructed by a group of islands and islets, which contracts the navigable channel to barely 1,400 yards. Westward of that group the channel again widens out, and attains a width of 5 miles at its western end.

Fury Point on the western shore, terminates in black, smooth rocks. A small bay, with a sandy beach at its head, and an islet at its entrance, lies close southward of Fury Point.

Beaver Ledge uncovers at low water, and lies ½ mile from the western shore, at 1 3/10 miles northward of Schooner Point. There is deep water close northward of this ledge.

Islet Rock lies close southward of a small islet on the eastern shore, at 1½ miles north-westward of Steep Point.

South Channel Islands, consisting of five principal wooded islands, 150 feet high, and about one mile in extent, lie nearly in mid-channel, 6 miles from Schooner Point.

North Channel Islands consist of two principal wooded islands of small extent. The eastern island of the group lies 1½ miles N. 30° W. of the western island of the South Channel Group.

Channel Rock is a dangerous sunken rock, lying nearly in mid-channel, 1,200 yards S. 30° E. of the eastern islet of the South Channel Group.

Bluff Point, on the western shore, is high and bold, with a hill 400 feet high rising immediately over it. On the eastern shore of Laredo Channel, abreast Bluff Point, is an islet at the mouth of a creek.

Seal Rocks, which cover at high water, and are of small extent, lie ½ mile from the south shore, 2 miles NW. of Bluff Point. There is deep water at 400 yards northward of Seal Rocks.

Sandspit Point, on the western shore, is white and conspicuous, with a ridge of bare hills, 700 to 950 feet high, immediately over it.

Sandspit Shoal extends ½ mile off from Sandspit Point.

Devil's Point is the western entrance point of Laredo Channel. Over this point is a bare hill with a conspicuous bowlder or knob on its summit.

Spray Point, the northeastern entrance point of Laredo Channel, is bold and high. At one mile southward of Spray Point a small islet lies close to the eastern shore.

Tides.—The flood stream which approaches from Laredo Sound increases in strength as the Channel Island Group is approached, attaining a velocity of 6 knots an hour at springs, in the channel east of that group (Surge Narrows).

In the wider portions of Laredo Channel both streams attain a velocity of 3 knots an hour at springs.

Midway between Devil's and Spray Points, the flood stream by Laredo Channel is met by the stream passing round the northwestern end of Aristazable Island, causing at springs dangerous tidal races in that locality.

The ebb stream having divided in mid-channel off Devil's Point, one portion sets round the northwestern end of Aristazable Island. The other sets fairly down Laredo Channel, and attains a velocity of 6 knots an hour, at springs, in Surge Narrows. From Surge Narrows the ebb stream sets directly towards Fury Point, and thence sweeps along the southern shore of the channel, passing across Laredo Sound to Low Point, whence it is deflected and sets fairly to the southward.

It is high water, full and change, in Surge Narrows at 6 h. 0 m.; springs rise 12 feet.

Directions.—Having rounded Schooner Point at a distance of one mile, a N. 30° W. course for 6 miles should lead into Surge Narrows, taking care, especially if the ebb stream be running, to avoid Channel Rock.

Northward of Surge Narrows, a general course of N. 30° W. will lead through Laredo Channel to the entrance of Estevan Sound.

Campania Sound, between Princess Royal and Campania Islands, is 5 miles long in a general north and south direction, and 3 miles wide.

On the eastern shore of the sound, a conspicuous ridge of hills, with rounded summits, rise to the height of 900 feet, and the coast is slightly broken into by a few useless bays and creeks.

On the western shore, the coast off Campania Island is indented with a few rocky bays. At the southwestern entrance of the sound, 600 yards from the southeastern extreme of Campania Island, lies Eclipse Island, a small wooded islet, 100 feet high.

The western shore of the sound, for one mile northward of Eclipse Island, has ledges which uncover to the distance of ½ mile. Northward of that position, the western shore has no known danger beyond 400 yards from it.

The eastern shore of the sound has ledges extending from it to a distance of ¼ mile.

South Surf Islands, at the southeastern entrance of Campania Sound, consist of three wooded islands 250 feet high, with several small rocky islets close to.

North Surf Islands, 250 feet high, lying ½ mile N. 46° W. of South Surf Islands, consist of three wooded islands one mile in extent north and south.

Squally Channel, between Gil and Campania Islands, is 10 miles long and from 2½ to 4½ miles wide.

Gil Island, which forms the eastern side of Squally Channel, is 15 miles long and 6 miles broad. Turtle Point, the northern extreme of the island, is a peninsula, with small bays east and west of it. The eastern shore has a few indentations along it, scarcely deep enough to be called bays.

Mount Gil is situated near the northeastern end of the island, the summit being well defined, and always clad with snow on the north side, from Mount Gil the land slopes gradually towards the northern extreme of the island.

A ridge of mountains extends in a southerly direction from Mount Gil, curving gradually to the southeastward, and terminating at about 3 miles from the south end of the island.

The southeastern extreme of Gil Island is wooded, flat and low.

Channel Reef uncovers at low water, and extends ½ mile from the SW. extreme of Gil Island (Ledge Point), and fringes the shore of that island, at the same distance, for 1½ miles northwestward of Ledge Point.

Windy Islets are a group of three islets, the outer of which lies ½ mile from the southwestern shore of Gil Island.

Windy Rock uncovers at low water, and lies ½ mile S. 40° E. of the outer or south Windy Islet. There is a depth of 20 fathoms at 200 yards south of the rock.

Black Rock, 400 yards from the western extreme of Gil Island (Blackrock Point), the turning point into Lewis Passage, covers at high water, is small, and nearly steep-to.

Soundings.—The depths in Squally Channel are from 15 fathoms to no bottom at 40 fathoms. The southern side of Squally Channel has no known danger beyond 200 yards from the shore.

Weather.—Violent squalls will often be experienced in Squally Channel, descending from the high land of Campania Island, when calms or light winds and smooth water will be found in Whale Channel.

Lewis Passage is between Gil and Fin Islands, and leads into Wright Sound.

The eastern shore of Lewis Passage has no known danger beyond 100 yards from the shore.

Fin Island is westward of Gil Island. Plover Point, the northern extreme of Fin Island, has a deep bay close southward of it, with several islets lying off the entrance to the bay, which dries throughout at low water. Four bare rocky islets fringe the northern shore of Fin Island, at the distance of 200 yards.

Fin Rock, awash at high water, lies on the western shore of the channel, 400 yards from the southern extreme of Fin Island.

Cridge Passage, between Fin and Farrant Islands, is 3 miles long and one mile wide. There is no bottom at 40 fathoms in mid channel in Cridge Passage.

Farrant Island lies at the southeastern entrance of Grenville Channel. The land on the southwestern side of Farrant Island reaches an elevation of 1,700 feet.

Blossom Point, the southern extreme of the island, has a small islet lying close to, with a ledge extending 200 yards westward from it.

Block Head, terminates in a high, bold, white cliff. The coast between Block Head and Yolk Point is broken into several bays, the largest lies close under the latter point, and has two patches of rock which uncover, lying 400 yards off shore.

Yolk Point is smooth, bare and rocky, and is nearly steep to.

Davenport Point, the northern extreme of Farrant Island, is bold, and lies 3 miles NW. of Yolk Point.

Union Passage (Mathksimtas), between Farrant and Pitt Islands, enters Grenville Channel about 4 miles westward of Yolk Point. This passage has not been explored.

Whale Channel, between Princess Royal and Gil Islands, is 12 miles long in a general north and south direction, and from 2 to 3 miles wide. There is no known danger in this channel beyond 100 yards from the shore. There is no bottom at 40 fathoms in Whale Channel.

Leading Point, on the eastern shore, 5 miles southward of Holmes Bay, has immediately over it a conspicuous hill, of triangular shape, 700 feet high.

River Bight, between Holmes Bay and Leading Point, is a deep indentation with a large river at its head.

Maple Point, on the western shore, abreast of Holmes Bay, is comparatively low, and wooded, with many maple trees growing.

At one mile south of Maple Point is a sandy bay, with a conspicuous sandy beach at its head.

Shrub Point, on the western shore, 5 miles southward of Maple Point, is comparatively low, flat, and wooded.

Camp Islet, a small, conspicuous, wooded islet, lying 400 yards from the western shore, at 9 miles southward of Maple Point, is connected with the eastern shore of Gil Island at low water.

South of Camp Islet there is a comparatively deep bay, one mile wide at its entrance; but which at low water is blocked by a ledge of rocks which uncover.

Molly Point, on the western shore, is the turning point of Whale Channel into Campania Sound.

Trouble Island, a small, narrow, low island, lies 200 yards from the eastern shore, at the southern entrance to Whale Channel.

Barnard Cove, SE. of Trouble Island, affords shelter to boats and small craft. Pass in mid-channel between Trouble Island and the eastern shore of Whale Channel, and anchor in 20 fathoms, mud, in the eastern part of the cove, at 400 yards from the eastern shore.

Passage Island, at the junction of Whale Channel and Campania Sound, is 2 miles long in a north and south direction, and one mile broad. It is wooded, the tops of the trees being about 250 feet above high water. Off the southeastern side of Passage Island, a group of islets, rocks, and sunken dangers extend ½ mile in a southeasterly direction.

The passage east and west of Passage Island are deep and 1,200 yards wide. On the eastern shore of the eastern channel, several rocky islands extend from 200 to 400 yards from the shore, off the entrance to a bay.

Campania Island has at one mile from its southeastern extreme an elevation of 1,000 feet, increasing westward until it culminates in two bare mountains, with dome-shaped summits, 2,000 feet high. These mountains are of granite formation, and furnish an excellent landmark when seen from seaward. From their summits the land slopes to the westward, the western end of Campania Island being comparatively low and wooded.

The northern shore of the island is bold, with a few rocky bays along it. The northeastern extreme terminates in a high, bold, white cliff.

The western shore is low, wooded, and broken into bays and creeks, fringed by islets, rocks awash at high water, and at low water, to the distance of one mile.

The northwestern shore is bold, and little broken. Marble rock, a small, white rock, 6 feet above high water, lies ¼ mile from it.

Estevan Sound, between Estevan and Campania Islands, is about 15 miles long in a general NW. and SE. direction, and from 2½ to 5 miles wide. At the southeastern entrance of the sound there are several islets, rocks, and sunken rocks, nearly in mid channel. Estevan Sound is not recommended to strangers.

If, however, circumstances should necessitate its being made use of, a course should be steered to pass ¾ mile northward of South Watcher Islet. Thence a general course of NW., cautiously, for 15 miles, should take a vessel into Nepean Sound, keeping nearer the western shore of the channel to avoid the dangerous ledges which extend to the distance of one mile from the western side of Campania Island.

Guano Rocks, on the eastern shore of Estevan Sound, consist of a cluster of three white rocks, lying one mile distant from the western side of Campania Island at 6 miles northwestward of Eclipse Island. The highest rock is 30 feet above high water, and the group is surrounded by rocks awash and sunken rocks to the distance of from ½ to ¾ mile.

Between Guano Rocks and Eclipse Island ledges, which uncover at low water, extend from 1,000 to 1,200 yards from the shore.

Marble Rock, $\frac{1}{4}$ mile northward of the western extreme of Campania Island, is a bare rock 6 feet above high water, small, white, and conspicuous; it is nearly steep to on all sides, and may be approached to 100 yards.

South Watcher is a small wooded islet, 100 feet high, lying nearly in mid channel at the eastern entrance of Estevan Sound

The South Watcher has ledges which uncover at low water, extending from it NW. and SE. to the distance of $\frac{1}{2}$ mile.

North Watcher Islet, 60 feet high, is small, wooded and conspicuous; it lies $1\frac{8}{10}$ miles N. 53° W. of South Watcher Islet

The North Watcher has ledges which uncover, and sunken dangers surrounding it to the distance of nearly a mile.

Blinder Rock, over which the sea breaks occasionally, lies one mile S. 83° W. of the summit of South Watcher Islet, and a little more than one mile S. 18° E. of North Watcher Islet.

Estevan Ledge, which uncovers at low water, is 200 yards in extent, and lies 1,600 yards N. 63° W. of the summit of North Watcher Islet.

Breaker Point, the southeastern extreme of Estevan Island, is low and wooded; from this point the coast trends northward for about 4 miles, and is broken into bays and creeks, with several islets and rocks lying close to the shore. Thence it trends NW. for about 5 miles, at which point lie two conspicuous small islets 200 yards from the shore, and then takes a westerly direction for about 6 miles, with a deep curve to the southward, until terminating at the mouth of Otter Passage

Don Ledge, which uncovers at low water, extends 1,200 yards east from Breaker Point

Breaker Reef consists of three rocks awash, surrounded by sunken rocks over which the sea nearly always breaks; the outer rock lies $2\frac{1}{2}$ miles S. 72° W of Breaker Point, and nearly $1\frac{1}{2}$ miles from the nearest part of Estevan Island

Trap Rocks, some of which are awash at high water, extends 1,600 yards northward from the northern point of Estevan Island, and thence front the northern side of the island at the distance of from 400 to 1,200 yards

Soundings—The depth of 40 fathoms was obtained in Estevan Sound, at 400 yards from the dangers fronting the shore of Campania Island, depths of 7 and 20 fathoms were found close alongside of the rocks.

Nepean Sound connects Estevan Sound and Principe Channel.

Otter Channel, between Pitt Island and Campania Island, connects Nepean Sound with Squally Channel. There is no known danger beyond 200 yards from the shores The water in Otter Channel is deep, there being no bottom at 40 fathoms at $\frac{1}{4}$ mile from the shore on both sides.

Steep Point, the northeastern entrance point of Otter Channel, terminates in a high, bold, white cliff

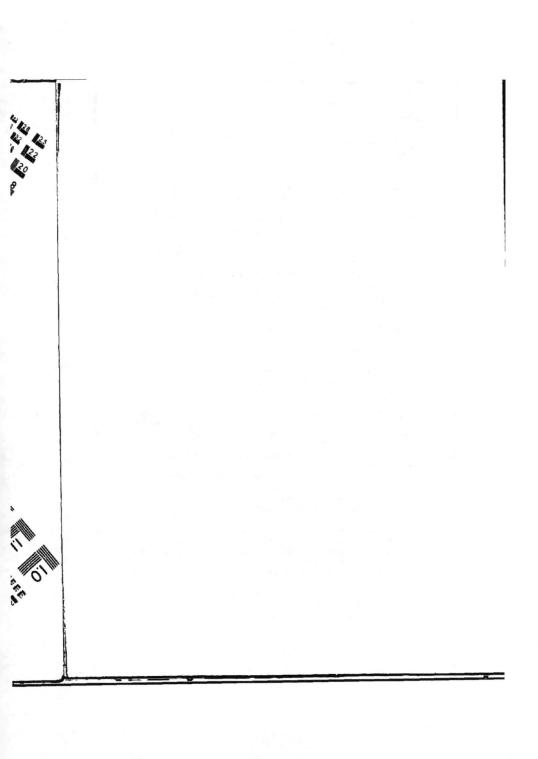

Otter Passage leads southwestward from Nepean Sound, between Estevan and Banks Islands. This passage, though nearly 1½ miles wide, is obstructed on its northwestern shore by a group of islands, islets, and rocks (Block islets), which contract the navigable channel to ⅝ mile.

The narrow channel is rendered more dangerous by the strong tides experienced in it, the greater portion of the ebb stream finding its way out of Nepean Sound by Otter Passage, at the rate of more than 6 knots an hour at springs, which meeting the ocean swell at the western entrance of Otter Passage produces a most turbulent breaking sea, dangerous to small vessels.

Otter Passage should not be attempted, except at slack water and with local knowledge.

Principe Channel, between Pitt and Banks Islands, is about 42 miles long, and from 2 to 7 miles wide.

The western shore of the channel is bold, with mountains from 1,200 to 1,700 feet rising over it.

The eastern shore is much broken into bays, especially about midway, in two of which ports Stephens and Canaveral, anchorage may be found.

The mountains on Pitt Island, at about 3 miles from the shore, rise to a height of 1,000 to 3,000 feet.

Deer Point, at 4 miles westward of Block Islets, is a small peninsula on the western shore, which when first seen appears to be an islet.

Gale Point is prominent, bold and high. A remarkable bare mountain, 1,250 feet high, is situated close to the shore at 4 miles northwestward of Gale Point. The coast immediately under this mountain is broken into several narrow creeks, with some small rocky islets at their mouths. With the exception of these bays the western shore of Principe Channel is unbroken.

Despair Point, at 11 miles northwestward of Gale Point, is bold, and nearly steep-to

Headwind Point lies 5½ miles northwestward of Despair Point; thence the coast is bold and unbroken.

Deadman Islet, a small wooded islet, lies close to the shore off the northeastern extreme of Banks Island.

End hill, an oval shaped hill 450 feet high, lies close to the west shore of Principe Channel at 2 miles southeastward of Deadman Islet.

Wolf Point, the southeastern entrance point of Principe Channel, and the south point of Pitt Island, is high, bold and conspicuous, with several small islets close to.

Brodie Rock, a dangerous sunken rock, lies one mile west of Wolf Point. Between Brodie Rock and the shore the ground is foul to 2 miles northwestward of Wolf Point. A depth of 66 fathoms was found at 400 yards south of Brodie Rock.

Port Stephens, on the eastern shore, at about 8 miles within the southern end of Principe Channel, is 800 yards wide at its entrance, and extends in a general northeasterly direction, terminating in two bays, with a large stream at the head of the southern bay

Guide Islet, a small bare islet, lies one mile southeastward of the port, with two small islets (the Sisters) lying nearly midway between it and Port Stephens.

Directions—Keep midway between the entrance points (Bluff and Center Points), and steer N. 38° E. for ½ mile; thence N. 72° E. for ½ mile, keeping mid channel. Haul gradually to the eastward as the harbor opens out, and anchor in mid channel in about 12 fathoms, with Bluff Point shut in with the south shore, the latter distant 400 yards.

Bluff Point forms the western entrance point of Port Stephens, and terminates in a high, white cliff.

Oar Point lies NW. of Bluff Point, the coast between those points being bold and unbroken. Immediately northward of Oar Point the coast recedes, terminating in two narrow arms (Mink Trap Bay).

Canoe Islet, a small bare islet, not unlike a canoe in appearance when first seen, lies off the mouth of Mink Trap Bay.

Green Top Islet, ¾ mile N. 35° W. of Canoe Islet, is small, with a patch of grass and shrub on its summit.

Mink Trap Bay consists of two long narrow creeks, separated by a peninsula; this bay has deep water in it, but it is useless as an anchorage for other than small vessels and boats.

At the head of the eastern arm is an Indian village, to which a tribe of the Kitkatlah Indians resort in summer for salmon fishing.

Anger Island, on the eastern shore, is about 4 miles long and 2 miles broad, with shoals extending from its south and east sides from ½ to ¾ mile.

Trade and Storm Islands are clusters of islets which extend from ½ mile to 1½ miles from the south and eastern shores of Anger Island.

Petrel Channel is an unexamined passage between Pitt and McCauley Islands; its southern entrance is about 3 miles wide; thence the channel takes a northwesterly direction for nearly 8 miles, when it divides, one passage going northward, the other southward of Lofty Island, and again joining at 2 miles eastward of Ogden Channel.

Lofty Island in Petrel Channel has not been surveyed in detail, but it is about 8 miles long and 2¾ miles wide near its SE. end, gradually narrowing to the northwestward, near the south shore Noble Mountain rises to a height of 2,874 feet.

Wheeler Islet is a small wooded islet, distant 5 miles N. 57° W of Foul Point, the western extreme of Anger Island.

Cliff Islets extend east of Wheeler Islet to the entrance of Petrel Channel. These islets are bare and rocky, with foul ground between them and the shore of McCauley Island.

McCauley Island, on the northern shore, is wooded nearly throughout. The island near its center rises to the height of 1,100 feet. Almost midway, on its south side, a bare hill (Tablo Hill) with a flat top, 400 feet high, lies close to the shore.

Port Canaveral, near the southeastern extreme of McCauley Island, is an inlet trending to the eastward for about ¾ mile with an average breadth of about 600 yards, and depths of 6 to 18 fathoms over it.

Dixon Island lies on the western side of the port, with several islands and islets lying off its south and eastern sides to the distance of 400 yards.

Squall Point, the southeastern entrance point of Port Canaveral, is the termination of the spur from Hat Hill, and is bold and conspicuous.

Red Point, on the northern shore, opposite Squall Point, has a cliff of red-brown color over it.

Alarm Rock, with 8 and 10 fathoms close-to, is a dangerous sunken rock lying nearly in mid-channel at the entrance to Port Canaveral, at 300 yards N. 41° W. of Squall Point.

Harbor Bank, with 6 fathoms over it (probably less), lies 300 yards eastward of Alarm Rock, and midway between Squall and Red Points.

Clown Rock is the outer danger extending SE. of Dixon Island. This rock, which dries 3 feet, lies 550 yards S. 29° E of Tonkin Point, the south extreme of Dixon Island, with foul ground between it and the shore.

Stephen Rock, 3 feet above high water, lies on the western shore at 300 yards from Dixon Island. The outer portion of Stephen rock, which uncovers at low water, lies 400 yards S. 24° E. of Dimple Point.

Directions—Entering Port Canaveral, Dimple Point may be steered for when in line with Stephen Rock, bearing N. 10° W., until Bush Islet (off SW extreme of Dixon Island) is just shut in with Tonkin Point bearing N. 85° W. The latter mark kept on astern will lead to the anchorage ground, when anchor in 14 to 15 fathoms, sandy bottom, at 300 yards SE. of Red Point.

Bush and Dark Islets are small, wooded islets which lie close to the shore of McCauley Island, off the entrance to Port Canaveral.

Hankin Ledges consist of rocks awash, and sunken dangers, which extend nearly one mile from Hankin Point (western extreme of McCauley Island)

Directions.—A mid-channel course should be kept when navigating Principe Channel, until nearing Anger Island, when the western shore should be closed to avoid the dangers which extend off that island.

Tides—The flood tide setting to the NW. approaches principally by Estevan Sound, being joined in Nepean Sound by the stream which enters through Otter Passage. At the western end of Principe Channel this stream is met by the flood which has passed up outside Banks Island. The ebb stream runs out principally by the Otter Passage. Both streams attain a velocity of 3 knots an hour at springs.

Browning Entrance is the common approach to Ogden and Principe Channels. It is included between the SW. side of Goschen Island and the northwestern extreme of Banks Island, and between Cape George and White Rocks is 14 miles wide.

Ogden Channel, between Pitt and Porcher Islands, is about 16 miles long and from 800 yards to $1\frac{1}{2}$ miles wide, and affords the shortest means of communication between Queen Charlotte Island's (Skidegate) and the inner waters. At its southern end Ogden Channel is divided by Spicer Island into two passages (Schooner and Beaver), and at one mile northward of Spicer Island the channel is obstructed by a group of islands (Channel Islands) which reduce the navigable channel to 600 yards.

The water in Ogden Channel is deep, and the dangers, with one exception, are visible, except at high water.

Landmarks.—On Dolphin Island a mountain with an irregular broken summit rises to the height of 1,400 feet. Southeast of that mountain, and close to the shore, is False Cone Hill—a hill with a conical summit. Off the southern shore of Dolphin Island, in the vicinity of False Cone Hill, are two small islets, the western of which lies close to the shore and is bare. Sentinel Island, the eastern islet, lies about one mile distant from the shore, is wooded, and about 100 feet high.

On the eastern side of Dolphin Island, close to the shore, Passage Cone, a hill with a conical summit, rises to the height of 454 feet, and is a useful mark for indicating Schooner Passage. On the NW. side of Spicer Island a saddle-shaped hill rises to the height of 800 feet.

Northward of the Channel Group of islands the land becomes higher.

On the eastern shore, close northward of Alpha Bay, is Anchor Mountain. At one mile south of Alpha Bay there is a remarkable white patch on the rocky eastern shore.

On the western shore, abreast of Alpha Bay, an extensive valley extends inland. At 3 miles northward of the valley is a mountain 1,645 feet high, on the sides of which are several landslips.

Long Island consists of two low wooded islets, lying close together at $1\frac{1}{2}$ miles southwestward of Spicer Island.

Channel Island is a small wooded islet, lying nearly midway between Long and Spicer Islands.

Spicer Island is of a triangular shape, the base being to the north, and $2\frac{1}{2}$ miles long. The island near its center attains an elevation of 827 feet. On its southeastern side two small narrow bays indent the shore in a northwesterly direction; and off its southwestern side, at $\frac{1}{2}$ mile from the shore, are Christie Islands, a cluster of islets and rocks, some wooded and others bare.

Channel Group lies northward of Spicer Island. The large islands are wooded, and the eastern islet of the group is small, bare, and conspicuous. Half a mile northward of the Channel Group are some small islets, one bare (White Rock), and another covered with vegetation (False Grassy Islet).

South Twin Islet is a small wooded islet on the eastern shore, ½ mile from the eastern islet of the channel group and one mile from Spicer Island. This islet, and the eastern bare islet of the Channel Group, indicate the navigable channel, which lies between them.

North Twin Islet resembles South Twin Islet from which it lies N. 4° E. distant ½ mile. The tops of the trees on North Twin Islet are about 130 feet high. Several small islets lie between the North and South Twins and McCauley Island.

Beaver Passage, between McCauley and Spicer Islands, is the wider and better of the two passages leading into Ogden Channel.

At its western entrance Beaver Passage is about ½ mile wide, and takes a northeasterly direction for about 4½ miles, thence turning sharply to the NW., towards the Channel Group, for 2½ miles.

North Rock is always visible and lies nearly in mid-channel at the southern entrance of Beaver Passage, ½ mile SE. of Long Island.

Connis Rocks lie on the western shore (marked by kelp in the season) 600 yards from the east extreme of Spicer Island. The outer of these rocks only covers at high water.

On the eastern shore, abreast Connis Rocks, is a small bare islet off a sandy bay.

Directions.—Having passed through in mid-channel between Long Island and North Rock, steer N. 58° E. for about 4 miles; thence N. 29° W. for about 1½ miles, and pass midway between South Twin Islet and the Eastern (bare) Islet of the Channel Group; taking care not to shut in the western point of Channel Island with the southeastern extreme of Spicer Island until the Bare Islet (Channel Group) bears N. 29° W. to clear Connis Rock. The east side of Long Island touching the west side of Channel Island bearing S. 58° W. also leads eastward of Connis Rock.

Northward of the Channel Group, Ogden Channel widens to nearly 2 miles. The shore on both sides has no known danger beyond 400 yards from it.

Schooner Passage, between Spicer and Dolphin Islands, is barely 400 yards wide in its narrowest part, and is about 3 miles long in a general north and south direction.

Boys Rock, a dangerous sunken rock, lies at the southern end of Schooner Passage, 400 yards from the southeastern extreme of Dolphin Island. There is a depth of 49 fathoms, rock, at 100 yards south of Boys Rock.

Sentinel Island, bearing N. 74° W., will lead southward, and Passage Cone Hill, bearing N. 16° E., will lead eastward of Boys Rock.

Directions.—Having brought the clearing marks on for Boys Rock, pass 200 yards westward of the two small rocky islets which lie ½ mile NE. of that rock. Thence mid-channel should be kept, and when abreast of the northern end of Spicer Island steer to pass midway between that island and the south islet of the Channel Group. Pass eastward of the latter at a distance of 400 yards, and proceed as before directed for Beaver Passage.

Tides.—The flood stream sets to the northward, and near the north end of Ogden Channel divides, one part turning to the eastward into Grenville Channel, the other continuing northward towards Skeena River. The ebb stream from Grenville Channel, Chatham Sound, and Skeena River unite off the north end of Ogden Channel and pass out by it. The muddy water of Skeena River is usually clearly defined against the blue water of Ogden Channel.

Both flood and ebb streams, in the narrow portions of Ogden Channel, attain a velocity of 4 knots an hour at springs.

An unexplored canoe passage lies between Goschen and Porcher Islands; it is about 15 miles long, and leads from Ogden Channel into Edye Passage.

Alpha Bay, on the eastern shore, 4 miles within the northern entrance of Ogden Channel, faces the west, and is nearly one mile wide, but only 600 yards deep. Near its northern end a deep valley extends inland, and through it flows a fine trout stream. From the south entrance point of this stream a sandspit extends 400 yards towards the north point of Alpha Bay.

Anchorage may be obtained in 10 and 11 fathoms, at 300 yards from the nearest shore (Fish Point), with the south entrance point of the trout stream bearing N. 72° E. distant ¼ mile and Anchor Mountain over the north shore of the bay N. 68° E.

Tides.—It is high water, full and change, in Alpha Bay at noon; springs rise 18 to 19 feet.

Peninsula Point, the northwestern entrance point of Ogden Channel, is prominent, with a hill near its eastern extreme. Northward of the point, at the mouth of the River Oona, is Oona Bay, about ½ mile wide, and one mile deep in a westerly direction. In this vicinity the surface water has a dirty white appearance

[illegible] is said to be anchorage in 8 or 10 fathoms water on the north- [illegible] near the mouth of the river Oona.

South Twin Islet is a small wooded islet on the eastern shore, ½ mile from the eastern islet of the channel group and one mile from Spicer Island. This islet, and the eastern bare islet of the Channel Group, indicate the navigable channel, which lies between them.

North Twin Islet resembles South Twin Islet from which it lies N. 1° E. distant ½ mile. The tops of the trees on North Twin Islet are about 130 feet high. Several small islets lie between the North and South Twins and McCauley Island.

Beaver Passage, between McCauley and Spicer Islands, is the wider and better of the two passages leading into Ogden Channel.

At its western entrance Beaver Passage is about ½ mile wide, and takes a northeasterly direction for about 4½ miles, thence turning sharply to the NW., towards the Channel Group, for 2½ miles.

North Rock is always visible, and lies nearly in mid-channel at the southern entrance of Beaver Passage, ½ mile SE. of Long Island.

Connis Rocks lie on the western shore (marked by kelp in the season) 600 yards from the east extreme of Spicer Island. The outer of these rocks only covers at high water.

On the eastern shore, abreast Connis Rocks, is a small bare islet off a sandy bay.

Directions.—Having passed through in mid-channel between Long Island and North Rock, steer N. 58° E. for about 4 miles; thence N. 29° W. for about 1½ miles, and pass midway between South Twin Islet and the Eastern (bare) Islet of the Channel Group; taking care not to shut in the western point of Channel Island with the southeastern extreme of Spicer Island until the Bare Islet (Channel Group) bears N. 29° W. to clear Connis Rock. The east side of Long Island touching the west side of Channel Island bearing S. 58° W. also leads eastward of Connis Rock.

Northward of the Channel Group, Ogden Channel widens to nearly

(842) **BRITISH COLUMBIA—Schooner passage—Uncharted rock.**—Captain Hughes, master of the steamer *Princess Beatrice*, reports having struck a pinnacle rock in Schooner passage between Dolphin and Spicer islands where the chart shows 29 fathoms

Approx. position Lat. 53° 45′ 52″ N., Long 130° 23′ 53″ W.

This rock carries 12 feet and from it the extreme south end of Dolphin island bears S. 61° W. true (SW. by S. mag.) and the south end of Spicer island in line with small island bears S 13° E. true (SE ½ S. mag.). (N. M 22, 1905)

Rock.

Sentinel Island, bearing N. 74° W., will lead southward, and Passage Cone Hill, bearing N. 16° E, will lead eastward of Boys Rock.

Directions.—Having brought the clearing marks on for Boys Rock, pass 200 yards westward of the two small rocky islets which lie ½ mile NE of that rock. Thence mid-channel should be kept, and when abreast of the northern end of Spicer Island steer to pass midway between that island and the south islet of the Channel Group. Pass eastward of the latter at a distance of 400 yards, and proceed as before directed for Beaver Passage.

Tides.—The flood stream sets to the northward, and near the north end of Ogden Channel divides, one part turning to the eastward into Grenville Channel, the other continuing northward towards Skeena River. The ebb stream from Grenville Channel, Chatham Sound, and Skeena River unite off the north end of Ogden Channel and pass out by it. The muddy water of Skeena River is usually clearly defined against the blue water of Ogden Channel.

Both flood and ebb streams, in the narrow portions of Ogden Channel, attain a velocity of 4 knots an hour at springs.

An unexplored canoe passage lies between Goschen and Porcher Islands; it is about 15 miles long, and leads from Ogden Channel into Edye Passage.

Alpha Bay, on the eastern shore, 4 miles within the northern entrance of Ogden Channel, faces the west, and is nearly one mile wide, but only 600 yards deep. Near its northern end a deep valley extends inland, and through it flows a fine trout stream. From the south entrance point of this stream a sandspit extends 400 yards towards the north point of Alpha Bay.

Anchorage may be obtained in 10 and 11 fathoms, at 300 yards from the nearest shore (Fish Point), with the south entrance point of the trout stream bearing N. 72° E. distant ¼ mile and Anchor Mountain over the north shore of the bay N. 68° E.

Tides.—It is high water, full and change, in Alpha Bay at noon; springs rise 18 to 19 feet.

Peninsula Point, the northwestern entrance point of Ogden Channel, is prominent, with a hill near its eastern extreme. Northward of the point, at the mouth of the River Oona, is Oona Bay, about ½ mile wide, and one mile deep in a westerly direction. In this vicinity the surface water has a dirty white appearance.

There is said to be anchorage in 8 or 10 fathoms water on the northern side of Peninsula Point, near the mouth of the river Oona.

CHAPTER X.

OUTER COAST.—CAPE CALVERT TO OGDEN CHANNEL.

Calvert Island, the southern island at the entrance to Fitzhugh Sound, is 13 miles long and 8 miles across at its broadest part. The southern and western shores of Calvert Island are but little broken, comparatively low, and thickly wooded.

Sorrow Island lies at the pitch of Cape Calvert; is conspicuous and an excellent thick weather mark, from its cliffy formation and by being covered with stunted, weather-beaten trees.

Mark Nipple, an isolated hill, 350 feet high, at the southwestern extreme of Calvert Island, is a very useful landmark when approaching Fitzhugh Sound.

Landing, with fine weather and off shore winds, may be effected in Grief Bay (north of Sorrow Island) and in other bights westward to Herbert Point.

Hedley Patch, with 9 fathoms on it, and probably shoaler, is of small extent, and lies 3¼ miles S 26° E. of Blakeney Island; at nearly ½ mile NE of it there is a depth of 19 fathoms.

Blakeney Islet, 150 feet high, ½ mile from the SW. extreme of Calvert Island, is small, wooded and about ½ mile long.

Fitz Roy Reef, the most outlying danger off the western shore of Calvert Island, uncovers at low water, dries one foot, and is about ½ mile in extent in an east and west direction. Its outer or western edge lies 1½ miles N. 54° W. of Blakeney Island, and 1½ miles from the nearest shore of Calvert Island.

Carrington Reefs are a cluster of sunken rocks, the outer edge of which lies ½ mile from the western shore of Calvert Island.

The coast of Calvert Island, northward of the Carrington Reefs, is foul to the distance of ½ mile

Kwakshua is an unexamined channel lying between Calvert and Hecate Islands. At its western entrance this passage is ½ mile wide, and takes a northeasterly direction.

Kwakshua Rock lies nearly in mid channel, at the western entrance of Kwakshua Channel. The sea only breaks at intervals over this dangerous sunken rock

Hecate Reefs fringe the western shore of Hecate Island for nearly a mile.

lo
hi
tı
fe
lie
1½
th
sh
gr
na
fr
Gi
ne
25
te
bo
fat
Ro
lin
wi
le
st
y
Tl
w
a
tl
a
cl
is

Hakai Channel between Hecate and Nalau Islands, is about 7 miles long in a general northeasterly direction, and from one to 1½ miles wide.

Sugar Loaf Hill, on the western side of Hecate Island, is 500 feet high.

Leading Peak, about 1½ miles southward of Sugar Loaf Hill, is of triangular shape, with a sharp, well defined summit.

South Pointers are a cluster of bare black rocks, of small extent, 2 feet above high water, surrounded by sunken dangers for ¼ mile; they lie on the southern shore, at the western entrance of Hakai Channel, 1½ miles westward of the Starfish Group.

North Pointers are a cluster of bare rocks, of light color, lying on the northern shore at the western entrance of Hakai Channel.

Starfish Group, wooded, from 70 to 150 feet high, lie on the southern shore, and extend about 1½ miles in a NE. and SW. direction. The group consists of three principal islands, much broken into long rocky, narrow creeks with shores of white cliffs.

Starfish Ledge, over which the sea usually breaks, lies 400 yards from the NW. shore of Long Island, the northernmost of the Starfish Group.

Breaker Group, on the northern shore in the middle of Hakai Channel, is about one mile in extent, the larger islands being wooded, about 250 feet high, and the smaller bare.

Breaker Ledge uncovers at half ebb, and lies ½ mile SE. of the center island of the Breaker Group.

East Rock, on the southern shore, off the entrance to Welcome Harbor, is awash at low water, and lies ½ mile off shore.

There are depths of 23 and 25 fathoms close to East Rock, and 30 fathoms between that rock and Port Reef.

Port Reef, awash at high water, lies 400 yards S. 60° E. of East Rock.

Clearing Marks.—Leading Peak (head of Welcome Harbor) seen in line with Bluff Point (north side of Welcome Harbor) bearing S. 6° W. will lead westward; and South Pointers rocks bearing S. 49° W. will lead northward of these rocks.

Choked Passage lies southward of the Starfish Group, it is obstructed by rocks awash, reefs, and sandbanks.

Welcome Harbor, near the western end of Hakai Channel, is 600 yards wide at its entrance, and 1½ miles long in a southerly direction. Though somewhat confined, it affords good shelter to small vessels, and within the harbor, on the eastern shore, there is a sandy beach where a vessel might be beached. Strong westerly winds send a swell into this harbor.

Fairway Rock, with 24 feet water over it, lies nearly in mid channel at the entrance to Welcome Harbor. There is a depth of 20 fathoms close westward, and of 9 fathoms close eastward of the rock. The rock is marked by kelp in summer.

Leading Peak seen just northward of Bluff Point bearing S. 6° W. will lead eastward; and Sugar Loaf Hill, seen in line with Leading Island (a small, round, wooded island within the harbor), will lead close westward of Fairway Rock.

Harbor Ledge, situated 200 yards from the western shore of Harbor Island, is of small extent, and dries 3 feet at low water.

Codfish Rock, with 12 feet water over it, lies 100 yards off the southern shore of Harbor Island.

Wolf Rock, awash at high water, lies close to the eastern shore, at nearly 400 yards northward of Sandspit Point

Sanspit Point has a sandspit extending 290 yards from it

Directions.—Having passed not less than ½ mile northward of Starfish Group, the leading mark before given for clearing East Rock should be brought on and steered for. Especial care will be necessary if the flood stream be making.

Having cleared East Rock, pass east or west of Fairway Rock as requisite, and anchor in 7 to 9 fathoms in mid-channel between Leading Island and Wolf Rock, with the former bearing N. 41° W. distant 200 yards.

Exposed Bay, just eastward of Welcome Harbor, has a dangerous cluster of sunken rocks near the middle of the bay.

Tides—The flood sets to the northeastward. Both streams attain a velocity of 4 knots an hour at springs.

Directions.—Hakai Channel is not recommended to strangers. If using it, steer midway between North and South Pointers Rocks, and thence a mid channel course towards a conspicuous mountain on the eastern shore of Fitzhugh Sound, which will lead through into that sound.

Nalau Passage, between the Nalau Group and Hunter Island, is obstructed by islands, islets, rocks awash, and sunken dangers, and is useless for navigation.

White Cliff Island, situated 4 miles N. 46° W. of the western or North Pointer Rock, is of small extent, bare, and 250 feet in height; its shores, consisting of high white cliffs, render it conspicuous when seen from the south and west.

A reef, on which the sea breaks at low water, lies midway between White Cliff Island and the North Pointers

Queen's Sound is between Goose and Hunter Islands. At its northern end is a mass of islands and islets, which render that portion of the sound intricate and dangerous.

Spider Island, 250 feet high, on the eastern shore, at the entrance to Queen's Sound, 3 miles northward of White Cliff Island, is connected with Hunter Island by a ledge of rocks awash, through which there are boat passages, and its north extreme terminates in high, bold, white cliffs. The shores of Spider Island are broken into numerous narrow rocky creeks.

Superstition Point, on the eastern shore of Queen's Sound, 2 miles northward of Spider Island, is the southwestern extreme of a small island, which is connected with Hunter Island by a narrow neck, awash at high water.

Superstition Ledge consists of high rocks, connected by rocks awash and sunken dangers, the outer extreme of which lies S. 72° W., distant 1¼ miles from Superstition Point. Strong tide races will be met with in the vicinity of this ledge, and the sea breaks upon it heavily at times.

Purple Bluff, the southwestern extreme of a group of islands, on the eastern shore of Queen's Sound, at the entrance to Plumper Channel, terminates in high, bold, basaltic cliffs of a purple tint. The group consists of numerous islands, islets (wooded and bare), rocks awash, and sunken rocks, extending over a space of nearly 5 miles.

Goose Islands, on the western shore of Queen's Sound, consist of four principal islands, connected at low water, the largest and northernmost being about 200 feet high, and wooded; its northeastern extreme terminates in conspicuous, high, white cliffs.

Yellocki, an Indian fishing village, is on the eastern side of the westernmost Goose Island.

Gosling Rocks consist of numerous rocks, awash at high water, and sunken dangers, the outer extreme of which lies nearly 4 miles S. 4° W. of the southernmost Goose Island.

West Rock, awash at high water, lies one mile westward of the westernmost Goose Island.

Plumper Channel, between Hunter and Campbell Islands, leads from Queen's Sound into Lama Passage; its southern end is obstructed by numerous islets and rocks, and no specific directions can be given for entering it.

Hecate Channel, between Campbell Island and the Bardswell Group, leads from Queen's Sound into Seaforth Channel. It is also obstructed at its southern end by numerous islets and rocks. The two principal passages are Codfish Passage and Brown Narrows; no directions, however, can be given for entering them.

Broken Group (Qualaqute), 2 miles northward of the Goose Island Group, extend 2 miles in a north and south direction, and consist of several islets and rocks, connected throughout by ledges which uncover at low water.

Fingal Island is a small, wooded island, lying one mile N. 51° W. of the northernmost island of the Broken Group.

Fingal Ledges extend one mile in a southerly direction from Fingal Island, and consist of rock awash, and ledges which uncover at low water.

Peveril Rock lies 1½ miles N. 49° E. of the northernmost Goose Island, and is awash at high water.

Middle Rock, 6 feet high, lies 2½ miles N. 74° W. of the south island of the Broken Group. There is a depth of 29 fathoms, rock, at ½ mile southward of the rock.

North Breaker, a dangerous sunken rock, lies one mile N. 4° E. of Middle Rock. There is a depth of 27 fathoms, rock, at one mile westward of the North Breaker.

Limit Island is a small wooded island, with foul ground extending ½ mile SW. from it.

Rempstone Rocks consist of two patches awash at high water, one mile apart The western or outer rock lies $1\frac{1}{10}$ miles south of Cape Swain.

Bardswell Group, forming the eastern side of Milbank Sound, consist of low, wooded islands, extending over a space of 7 miles square, the largest of which, Dufferin Island, forms the western shore of Hecate Channel. Among the group are several boat channels, communicating between Milbank Sound and Seaforth and Hecate Channels.

Milbank Sound —(See page 321.)

Laredo Sound —(See page 344.)

Aristazable Island forms the western shore of Laredo Sound. At about 8 miles from its southeastern extreme there is a conspicuous, saddle-shaped hill 640 feet high. Near the northern end of the island a bare ridge of hills, with four conspicuous peaks, rises to the height of 950 feet.

Over the southwestern extreme of the island there are some bare hills 350 feet high, and at the extreme western end of the island there is a remarkable bowlder or knob lying on the summit of a bare hill. The western shores are broken into bays and creeks, obstructed by islets and sunken rocks; and there are several off lying groups of islands.

Entrance Island, 1½ miles from the southern extreme of Aristazable Island, has a small islet lying close south of it, and is the outer island of a group which extends from the SE point of Aristazable Island. The larger islets of the group are wooded, the smaller bare.

White Rock, 100 feet high, bare and conspicuous, is 5 miles N. 39° W. of Entrance Island and is the outer rock of a group extending 2 miles from the shore of Aristazable Island.

Sentinel Island, 250 feet high, small, round wooded, and conspicuous, lies off the southwestern point of Aristazable Island, at 1½ miles from the shore. Between Sentinel Island and the nearest island of the group east of it, distant ½ mile, there is no bottom at a depth of 40 fathoms.

Several rocks awash and sunken rocks lie northward of Sentinel Island, fringing the western shore of Aristazable Island.

The two most outlying rocks, which are from one to 2 feet above high water, lie respectively one mile N. 52° W. and 4½ miles N. 41° W. of Sentinel Island.

Gander Islands (Chachekwas) are a group of islands, islets and rocks, extending over a space 11 miles long in a north and south direction, and 4 miles broad, at about 6 miles from the western shore of

Aristazable Island. The larger islands of the group are wooded, the smaller ones bare, and the tops of the trees are from 70 to 150 feet above high water.

Large Gander Island is the northernmost and largest of the group.

Middle Gander Islands are two small, wooded islands, lying close together, the northern island 5 miles south of the south extreme of the Large Gander Island. A bare rock, with sunken rocks surrounding it, lies N. 7° W. distant 2 miles from the Middle Gander Islands.

South Gander Island, one mile south of the Middle Gander Islands, is 70 feet high, and wooded.

Southeast Gander Islands are two small wooded islands 100 feet high, lying close together, 3 miles S. 30° E. of South Gander Island. Two small, bare, rocky islets lie 1½ miles northward of Southeast Gander Islands.

Goose Ledge, which uncovers at low water, lies 3 miles S 43° W. of Southeast Gander Islands.

Sparrowhawk Breakers lie, respectively, 4 and 6½ miles S. 15° W. of Southeast Gander Islands. There is a depth of 21 fathoms between these dangers.

Tide Rip Islands consist of two groups lying north and south, distant 2 miles from each other; the southern group lying 2 miles north of the Gander Group. These islands, which extend over a space of about 12 miles, are wooded, and about 200 feet high, the northern and largest island terminating at its NW. extreme in high, white conspicuous cliffs, 2½ miles to the northwestward of Devils Point

Tides.—The flood sets to the northward, both flood and ebb streams attaining at springs, among these islands, a rate of 4 knots an hour.

Soundings.—Westward of Laredo Sound no soundings have been taken beyond the distance of one mile from the western shore of Aristazable Island. The depths obtained at that distance were 23 fathoms, and no bottom at 40 fathoms

Caution.—As an extended examination has not been made of the Gander and Tide Rip Groups and their vicinity, and the tides being strong, the channels between them, though deep, should not be attempted by strangers. When approaching these groups of islands the lead and lookout should be attended to.

Estevan Island is 6 miles northwestward of the Tide Rip Group, the western shores being comparatively low, wooded, and much broken into bays and creeks. Near the center, the land attains an elevation of 1,500 to 1,700 feet, forming a saddle shaped mountain with the highest part to the westward.

Haycock Island, small, bare, and 60 feet high, lies 4½ miles S. 25° E. of Curtis Point.

Haycock Rocks are three rocks awash, which lie about one mile from Haycock Island.

The passage between Haycock Island and Estevan Island should not be attempted.

Curtis Point, on the western shore of Estevan Island, is low and wooded, with some rocky islets close to.

Curtis Rock, a dangerous sunken rock, over which the sea breaks occasionally, lies one mile S. 49° W. of Curtis Point.

Cox Point is the northwestern extreme of Estevan Island. With the exception of a small bay at one mile northward of Curtis Point, the shore between Curtis and Cox Points is but little broken

Marchant Rock, over which the sea breaks at low water, lies 2 miles S. 26° W. of Cox Point, and 1¼ miles from the nearest shore of Estevan Island.

Cone Islet, small, wooded, 250 feet high, and conical, is the southernmost of the Block Islets, and lies at the southern entrance of Otter Passage, and on the western side of that channel, at 2 miles from the shore of Banks Island

Breaker Islets, one mile westward of Cone Islet, consist of a group of islets and rocks awash, the highest islet being about 70 feet high and wooded.

Banks Island is about 41 miles long, and from 5 to 10 miles broad. The western shore is wooded and comparatively low, seldom exceeding 150 feet in height, and is broken into bays and creeks, rendered useless as anchorages by numerous rocks awash, and sunken dangers.

The eastern shore is high and bold, with a mountain range of 1,000 to 1,760 feet over it, the latter elevation being attained about midway between the north and south extremes of the island. At about 10 miles from the northwestern end of Banks Island the land becomes low and flat, and is intersected by many creeks.

Calamity Bay, at the southern extreme of Banks Island, is 3 miles wide at its entrance, and extends 3 miles in a northerly direction; it consists of iron bound shores, with rocky islets and sunken dangers occupying the bay nearly throughout.

Terror Point, the southwestern extreme of Banks Island, is high and bold, 200 feet above high water. From its outer extreme this point slopes inland, and when first seen appears as an island

Terror Rocks consist of rocks awash and sunken rocks, over which the sea breaks heavily, extending one mile southward from Terror Point.

Shrub Islet, of small extent, 80 feet high, with a conspicuous patch of bush upon its summit, lies 3 miles S. 77° W. of Terror Point, and has sunken rocks surrounding it to the distance of 600 yards.

Grief Point, 8 miles from Terror Point, is low and wooded. A ledge, consisting of rocks awash and sunken dangers, extends 1½ miles southwestward from Grief Point.

The coast between Terror and Grief Points has foul ground extending off it to the distance of one mile.

Foul Bay, between Grief and Wreck Points, is 5 miles wide, and 2 miles deep, it is, however, useless as an anchorage, being obstructed by islets, rocks and sunken dangers.

Wreck Point, a conspicuous projection, is low and wooded.

Junk Ledge, consisting of rocks awash, and ledges which uncover at low water, extends nearly 2 miles southeastward from Wreck Point.

North Danger Rocks, 7 miles southwestward of Wreck Point, are a dangerous cluster of five bare rocks of small extent, 10 feet above high water, and surrounded by rocks awash and sunken rocks to the distance of $\frac{1}{2}$ mile.

The center of the cluster lies 18 miles S. 36° E. of the summit of Bonila Island. Vessels should keep southward of the line joining Shrub Islet and North Danger Rocks, and not pass between those dangers and Banks Island

Kelp Point lies 8 miles from Wreck Point.

Kelp Ledge extends $1\frac{1}{2}$ miles southeastward from Kelp Point. Between Wreck and Kelp Points the shore of Banks Island is foul to the distance of one mile.

Halibut Rocks consist of two dangerous clusters (covered at high water) about $\frac{1}{2}$ mile each in extent, lying NW and SE, distant $1\frac{1}{2}$ miles from each other. The center of the eastern cluster lies 8 miles S. 44° E. of the summit of Bonila Island.

Cliff Point terminates in high, bold white cliffs Three small rocky islets lie near the shore close eastward of the point.

South Rocks, lying to the southward of Bonila Island, consist of two clusters of rocks awash at high water, of small extent, lying north and south, distant one mile from each other. The south or outer group, over which the sea usually breaks heavily, lies $3\frac{1}{10}$ miles S. 4° W. of the summit of Bonila Island.

High Water Rocks, lying nearly midway between Bonila Island and Cliff Point, consist of six rocks, awash at high water, about 400 yards in extent.

Bonila Island, 9 miles south of the northwestern point of Banks Island, and 4 miles from the south shore of the island, forms an excellent landmark. The island is about 2 miles long and one mile broad, having on its southeastern shore two small bays, with some rocky islets lying off them at 400 yards from the shore. Near the center the island reaches an elevation of 550 feet, the summit being dome shaped, falling almost perpendicularly on its north and south sides, but sloping gradually to the westward. During the summer months, the sides of Bonila Peak are clothed with purple-tinted heather.

Landing may be effected at the head of the southern small bay on the southeastern side of Bonila Island.

North West Rocks are a cluster, $\frac{1}{2}$ mile in extent, lying 2 miles N. 30° W. of the summit of Bonila Island, the highest rock is 3 feet above high water.

North Rocks, a cluster about $\frac{1}{2}$ mile in extent, and awash at high water, are 2 miles northward of the Summit of Bonila Island.

Middle Rocks, two clusters, awash at low water, lie respectively $1\frac{1}{2}$ miles N. 41° W. and 2 miles N. 49° E. of the summit of Bonila Island.

White Rocks lie close to the shore at the northwestern extreme of Banks Island, the two largest rocks are about 30 feet above high water, bare and conspicuous, with several smaller rocks surrounding them, and they form an excellent landmark when making Ogden Channel from Hecate Strait.

The coast between White Rocks and Clift Point, and between those rocks and Deadman Islet, is much broken, with several creeks running inland.

Anchorage for small craft in fine weather is stated to be obtainable close northward of White Rocks at the mouth of a creek.

Supplies.—Game abounds on all the off-lying islands. Notwithstanding the presence of wolves, deer are in great numbers, especially on the southern shores, which appear to be their favorite resort. Water is plentiful at all seasons, the source apparently being springs. Trout may be procured in the streams.

Berries, especially the whortleberry, cranberry, and wild raspberry, were found in abundance during July and August (1869).

Cedar and pitch pine are the principal woods met with.

Browning Entrance, between Banks and Goshen Islands, leads into Principe and Ogden Channels. It is 14 miles wide between White Rocks and Cape George.

CHAPTER XI.

CHATHAM SOUND, EDYE AND BROWN PASSAGES, AND DIXON ENTRANCE.

Chatham Sound is an extensive sheet of water about 38 miles long, and from 7 to 14 miles wide, lying between the Tsimpsean Peninsula and Stephens and Dundas Islands, the northwestern portion of the sound washing the southern shores of Alaska.

In the middle of the southern portion are the Rachel and Lucy Islands, together with other detached islets and rocks.

At the northern end of Chatham Sound, nearly abreast Port Simpson, there are some clusters of low rocky islets (Connis and Pointers Rocks), which render that portion of the sound dangerous to navigation under certain conditions, and divide the sound into two navigable channels (Main and Oriflamme Passages)

Chatham Sound communicates with Hecate Strait by three channels, Edye Passage, in the southwestern corner of the sound, being the channel usually taken. Brown Passage, south of Dundas Islands, though comparatively wide, has strong and irregular tides near its western end; and a patch of rocks awash at high water lies nearly in mid channel.

Dixon Entrance, the principal channel north of Dundas Islands, is about 5 miles wide, and is the channel usually taken by vessels proceeding northward along the coast of Alaska.

Landmarks.—On the eastern shore, in the southeastern portion of Chatham Sound, Mount Oldfield and Mount McGrath are conspicuous.

With the exception of a cluster of bare rocks (Gull Rocks) off the mouth of Edye Passage, the islets in that portion of the sound are wooded, and of a conspicuous dark color.

On the South Dundas Island there are four conspicuous peaks, the eastern and highest of which is 1,400 feet high. Northward of Metlah Catlah, Mission Mountain and Deer Mound of rounded form, will be seen rising from comparatively low land to the height of 1.310 and 2,230 feet respectively

At 2 miles southward of Port Simpson, Mount Griffin (Waverly Peak), a mountain of triangular shape with a sharp summit, rises to 1,410 feet. Southeast of Mount Griffin, the ridge has several conspicuous peaks, amongst which are Leading Peak and Basil Lump.

Mount McNeil, on the northern side of Work Channel, has a snow-clad summit, of conical shape, 4,300 feet high.

On the western shore of the sound Coast Mound, a conspicuous hill of oval shape, 750 feet high, will be seen on Middle Dundas Island, with a chain of wooded islets, of a peculiarly dark color, fringing the shore.

Near the northeastern extreme of North Dundas Island, Table Hill with a flat summit rises to the height of 700 feet, and is conspicuous Southward of Table Hill, Thumb Peak rises to the height of 2,300 feet. With the exception of one small islet (Grassy Islet), the islets and rocks in the northern portion of Chatham Sound are bare and conspicuous.

Dangers—The southern portion of Chatham Sound is comparatively free from danger, the rocky clusters being of considerable elevation above high water and moderately steep-to Northward of Metlah Catlah Bay, however, ledges which uncover at low water extend in many places to the distance of 2 miles from the eastern shore. On the western side of the sound, also, there are several off lying detached sunken rocks, with deep water close to them. Abreast Port Simpson two clusters of rocks lie in the fairway of the sound; and being but little elevated above high water, render that portion of the sound dangerous by night or in thick weather.

Caution.—Northward of Metlah Catlah Bay, during a fog, or if uncertain of the position, the eastern shores of Chatham Sound should not be approached under 70 fathoms; nor the western shores under 40 fathoms.

Soundings.—The general depths in the southern portion of Chatham Sound are from 10 to 66 fathoms, the former depth being obtained upon Alexandra Bank nearly in the middle of the sound, northward of Rachel Islands Northward of Metlah Catlah Bay the water deepens The deep water commences near the southern extreme of South Dundas Island, and extends towards the mouth of Big Bay, skirting the dangerous ledges which front the eastern shores of the sound.

From abreast of Big Bay the deep water extends toward the northern extreme of North Dundas Island and widens in extent, occupying nearly the whole of the northern portion of the sound, with depths from 58 to 214 fathoms, mud bottom, with occasional patches of rock.

Anchorages.—Anchorage will be found off the northern entrance of Skeena River, in Metlah Catlah Bay, Duncan Bay, Big Bay, Pearl Harbor, and Port Simpson, on the eastern side of Chatham Sound. Also in Refuge Bay, at mouth of Edye Passage, and in Qlawdzeet, north end of Stephen Island, on the western side of the sound.

Gull Rocks, consisting of three principal bare rocks, about ½ mile in extent, the highest rock being about 30 feet above high water, lie off the eastern entrance of Edye Passage.

Ettrick Rock, a dangerous patch of small extent, which uncovers 3 feet at low water, lies 1½ miles S. 29° E of the center of the Gull Rocks.

Havelock Rock, of small extent and uncovering 6 feet at low water, lies 2½ miles S 29° E. of the center of Gull Rocks. Both Ettrick and Havelock Rocks have deep water close to.

Green Top Island, 15 feet high, is small with a patch of shrub on its summit, and lies 4¼ miles N. 32° W. of the western island of the Lawyer Group.

Holland Island, small, wooded, and 10 feet high, lies 1¾ miles S. 83° E. of Green Top Islet.

Kitson Island, off the mouth of North Skeena Passage, is about 400 yards in extent.

Kinnahan Islands, two in number, and about ½ mile long, lie close [illegible] the shore of Tsimpsean Peninsula; they

[illegible]

of the group, and is marked by kelp.

Metlah Catlah Bay is formed between the shore of the Tsimpsean Peninsula and the NW. coast of Digby Island, and is protected from the westward by Tugwell Island and the reefs which join that island to the shore of the peninsula. The bay from its entrance takes a general northeasterly direction, gradually narrowing as the settlement is approached, it then turns sharply to the east and SE., the latter part being known as Venn Creek.

Metlah Catlah Village, an Indian settlement, founded as a missionary station, is situated upon Mission Point. The houses forming the mission are built upon an elevated bank, about 100 feet above high-water mark, and are mostly whitewashed. The most conspicuous buildings being the church, schoolhouse and mission house. Patches of

On the western shore of the sound Coast Mound, a conspicuous hill of oval shape, 750 feet high, will be seen on Middle Dundas Island, with a chain of wooded islets, of a peculiarly dark color, fringing the shore.

Near the northeastern extreme of North Dundas Island, Table Hill with a flat summit rises to the height of 700 feet, and is conspicuous. Southward of Table Hill, Thumb Peak rises to the height of 2,500 feet. With the exception of one small islet (Grassy Islet), the islets and rocks

(254) **BRITISH COLUMBIA—Chatham sound—Rocks located.**—Captain H. Newcomb, master D. G. S. *Kestrel*, reports the existence of the following uncharted dangers in Chatham sound

A shoal 200 yards in extent, marked by kelp in summer, carrying 18 feet, with 7 to 9 fathoms all around it and 9 fathoms between it and the rock 600 yards northwestward from Green Top rock

From the shoal the summit of Green Top rock bears S 27° E true (SE ¾ E. E'ly mag), distant 600 yards, the north tangent of Rachel islands N. 70° W true (W. ⅝ N. mag.), and the summit of Coast island N. 57° E. true (NNE. ⅝ E. mag.).

Two shoals west of Holland island, each 200 yards in extent, marked by kelp in summer, carrying 9 feet, with 5 to 7 fathoms all around them and 8½ fathoms between them and Holland island From the more easterly shoal the summit of Holland island bears S. 64° E true (E ⅛ N. mag.), distant 966 yards, the east tangent of Kinnahan islands N. 15° W. true (NW. ¼ N. mag.), and the summit of Coast island N. 31° E. true (N. ⅜ E mag), distant 2.6 miles From the middle of the more westerly shoal Lawyer Island lighthouse bears S 18° E. true (SE mag.), distant $4\frac{1}{18}$ miles, the west tangent of Kienahan islands N. 37° W. true (NW by W ⅝ W. W'ly mag.), and the summit of Coast island N. 38° E true (N. by E. mag.), distant 2.7 miles.

A pinnacle rock off Island point, Porcher island, which carries 6 feet, and is marked by kelp

From the rock Island point bears S. 32° E. true (SE. by E ¼ E mag.), distant 900 yards, and the north tangent of Creak point S 42° W. true (S by W ⅜ W. mag). This position must be considered as approximate only, until it can be checked

(N. M 7, 1905.)

58 to 214 fathoms, mud bottom, with occasional patches of rock

Anchorages.—Anchorage will be found off the northern entrance of Skeena River, in Metlah Catlah Bay, Duncan Bay, Big Bay, Pearl Harbor, and Port Simpson, on the eastern side of Chatham Sound. Also in Refuge Bay, at mouth of Edye Passage, and in Qlawdzeet, north end of Stephen Island, on the western side of the sound.

Gull Rocks, consisting of three principal bare rocks, about ½ mile in extent, the highest rock being about 30 feet above high water, lie off the eastern entrance of Edye Passage.

Ettrick Rock, a dangerous patch of small extent, which uncovers 3 feet at low water, lies 1½ miles S. 29° E. of the center of the Gull Rocks.

Havelock Rock, of small extent and uncovering 6 feet at low water, lies 2¼ miles S 29° E. of the center of Gull Rocks. Both Ettrick and Havelock Rocks have deep water close to.

Green Top Island, 15 feet high, is small with a patch of shrub on its summit, and lies 4¼ miles N. 32° W. of the western island of the Lawyer Group.

Holland Island, small, wooded, and 10 feet high, lies 1⅜ miles S. 83° E. of Green Top Islet.

Kitson Island, off the mouth of North Skeena Passage, is about 400 yards in extent.

Kinnahan Islands, two in number, and about ½ mile long, lie close together about one mile from the shore of Tsimpsean Peninsula; they are wooded, about 200 feet high.

Rachel Islands (Lakōhwitz), two in number, about one mile in extent, wooded and about 200 feet high, lie nearly midway between Tsimpsean Peninsula and Stephen Island. The southeastern extreme of the SE. Rachel Island lies 5¼ miles S. 86° W. of the south extreme of south Kinnahan Island.

Alexandra Patch is nearly circular, one mile in diameter, within the depth of 20 fathoms. This bank has depths of 10 to 17 fathoms, over a bottom of mud and sand.

The eastern edge of Alexandra Patch lies one mile N. 27° E. of the North Rachel Island. There are depths of 46 and 50 fathoms, mud, at ½ mile eastward and northward of Alexandra Patch.

Lucy Islands, a group of islands and high-water rocks, the large islands being wooded and the small bare, lie nearly in the middle of the sound abreast Metlah Catlah Bay, and are about one mile in extent in an east and west direction. This group is of great use when making Metlah Catlah during thick weather, as being comparatively free from danger it may be approached (except on the southern side), and, when made, the easternmost island of the group kept astern bearing S. 80° W. will lead to the entrance of Metlah Catlah Bay.

A Ledge of Rocks, which partially uncover, extends along the southwestern side of the Lucy Group, the outer rock lying 1,800 yards S. 27° W. of the summit of the eastern island of the group The northwestern rock dries 3 feet and lies ¼ mile S 77° W. of the nearest island of the group, and is marked by kelp.

Metlah Catlah Bay is formed between the shore of the Tsimpsean Peninsula and the NW. coast of Digby Island, and is protected from the westward by Tugwell Island and the reefs which join that island to the shore of the peninsula. The bay from its entrance takes a general northeasterly direction, gradually narrowing as the settlement is approached; it then turns sharply to the east and SE., the latter part being known as Venn Creek.

Metlah Catlah Village, an Indian settlement, founded as a missionary station, is situated upon Mission Point. The houses forming the mission are built upon an elevated bank, about 100 feet above high-water mark, and are mostly whitewashed. The most conspicuous buildings being the church, schoolhouse and mission house. Patches of ground are cultivated, and potatoes of large size and good quality grown.

Tugwell Island lies southwestward of Metlah Catlah Village, and vessels desirous of communicating with that place usually anchor off the eastern side of the island, or off its northern side in Duncan Bay, according to circumstances. The island is fringed by dangerous rocky ground, marked by kelp, especially on its southeastern side. It is wooded and connected at low water with Mission Point upon which Metlah Catlah Village stands

Dawes Rock, awash at low water, lies 800 yards S. 55° W. of Dawes Point.' Between Dawes Rock and Dawes Point, large bowlder rocks uncover at low water, and extend along the western side of Tugwell Island, generally marked by kelp.

Enfield Rock has 5 fathoms water upon it, and lies one mile S. 55° W. of the same point with foul ground between.

Caution.—Vessels should pass westward of Enfield Rock, in not less than 10 fathoms, at low water.

Leading Marks.—To enter, Knight Island kept midway between Shrub and Pike Islands bearing N. 52° E. leads safely in to the bay, between Tugwell Island and Alford Reefs, in 25 fathoms.

Carr Islet, just shut in with the western extreme of Devastation Island bearing N 38° E. northerly, will lead eastward of the foul ground off the southeastern part of Tugwell Island. The south extreme of the large Cridge Island seen in line with Quartermaster Rock, and touching the north extreme of the small Cridge Island bearing S 74° E, will lead southward of Alford Reefs and the dangers off Tugwell Island. The flagstaff on Mission Point (Metlah Catlah Village) in line with the western extreme of Pike Island bearing N 38° E., will lead eastward of Alford Reefs.

Alford Reefs are a dangerous cluster of rocks, about 600 yards, lying at the entrance of Metlah Catlah Bay. The northern rock, which uncovers 2 feet at low water, lies 1,200 yards N. 29° W. of Quartermaster Rock.

Quartermaster Rock, a small black rock, 2 feet above high water, lies 800 yards N. 74° W. of the southern extreme of the large Cridge Island, and 300 yards from the small Cridge Island, on the same bearing.

A Rock, which uncovers one foot at low water, lies 300 yards S. 27° W. of Quartermaster Rock.

Cridge Islands are two in number. The eastern and larger island lies 400 yards off the eastern shore of Digby Islands. The western island is small. Both islands are wooded.

Midge Rock, a patch of small extent, which uncovers at low water, lies ½ mile north of the Small Bridge Island, and about the same distance eastward of the nearest part of Alford Reefs.

Devastation Island lies almost in the center of the bay ½ mile eastward of Tugwell Island The island is wooded, and two rocky islets lie close to its southern extreme.

The western shore of Devastation Island has no danger off it beyond 100 yards, but from the northern extreme of this island a shoal, portions of which uncover at low water, extends ½ mile towards Pike Island.

Carr Islet, small, lies ½ mile N. 38° E. of the northern extreme of Devastation Island. A small islet lies 400 yards N. 18° W. of Carr Islet. Carr Islet is connected at low water with the spit which joins Tugwell Island and Observation Point.

Knight Island, barely 10 feet high, small, with stunted scrub upon it, lies 800 yards S 55° E. of the northern extreme of Devastation Island.

Armour Rock, with 9 feet water over it, lies S. 7° E., distant 200 yards from Knight Island.

Pike Island, 100 feet high, is wooded.

Shrub Islet lies 300 yards north of Pike Island, and is of small extent, low, and easily recognizable from its having three peculiar trees on it, the only ones on the island.

Pike, Carr, and Shrub Islands are not easily distinguished by strangers making for Metlah Catlah; and Carr Islet appears as part of Devastation Island.

A Shoal, the outer portion of which uncovers at low water, extends nearly 400 yards from the northern side of Shrub Islet, and is the outer portion of a bank of sand with patches of rock upon it, which connects Pike Island, Shrub Islet, Gribbell and Isabel Islands at low water

A Ledge of Rocks, which uncovers at low water, extends 300 yards southward from Observation Point.

Kelp Rock, a dangerous sunken rock, lies nearly midway between Shrub Islet and Observation Point. The navigable channel between Shrub Islet and Observation Point is contracted by Kelp Rock to barely 100 yards in width at low water. Another rock lies 250 yards N. 72° E. of Kelp Rock.

A small iron buoy is moored on Kelp Rock; but this buoy is often washed away, therefore its being in position can not be depended on.

Gribbell Island, on the southern side of the channel leading into Venn Creek, is about the same size as Shrub Islet, from which it is distant ½ mile in a northeasterly direction. A small rocky islet lies about 100 yards off the north side of Gribbell Island.

Isabel Island lies 300 yards NE. of the summit of Gribbell Island.

A dangerous sunken rock lies 100 yards westward of Isabel Island, and reduces the navigable channel at low water to barely 60 yards in width.

Venn Creek takes a southeasterly direction from Mission Point, but is only suitable for small vessels. There are several fishing stations upon the shores of this creek, in which the Indians obtain salmon The creek at its head connects with the unexplored Oldfield Basin, east of Digby Island, which extends southward and eastward, connecting with Malacca and North Skeena Passages. The best time for entering Venn Creek for a ship of moderate draft is at half tide, or between that and low water.

Anchorage will be found in 11 to 12 fathoms, mud bottom, 600 yards off the western side of Devastation Island, with the southern extreme of Devastation Island seen in line with the smaller Cridge Island, and the southern extreme of Carr Islet bearing N. 69° E. Small vessels occasionally proceed into Venn Creek and anchor off Metlah Catlah Village, in 10 to 12 fathoms, with the flagstaff on Mission Point bearing N. 74° W., distant 600 to 800 yards.

The channel into this anchorage is barely 60 yards wide at low water, when the dangers on either side indicate themselves, but the passage should only be attempted by short vessels, of light draft; and at all times it would be well to place boats upon the outer edge of the shoal off Shrub Islet, and also upon the rock which lies westward of Isabel Island, and likewise on Kelp Rock, should the buoy marking that danger be not in position.

Auriol Point, just open north of Shrub Islet bearing N. 78° E., leads between the foul ground southward of Carr Island and the ledge extending from the north extreme of Devastation Island, and when Ryan Point comes open east of Carr Island bearing N. 12° W. a course may be steered to round the boat moored upon the outer edge of the shoal off Shrub Islet.

For all ordinary purposes, however, the anchorage off Devastation Island is within easy distance for communicating by boat with Metlah Catlah Mission.

Duncan Bay affords anchorage when desirous of communicating with Metlah Catlah during the prevalence of southeasterly winds.

The entrance to this bay is about 1¾ miles wide, and takes a southeasterly direction for about 1½ miles, terminating in the sandspit which connects Tugwell Island and Tsimpsean Peninsula.

Dangers.—A shoal with 3 fathoms (and probably less) water upon it extends ½ mile northward of Tugwell Island. Ledges, which uncover, and sunken rocks extend nearly ¼ mile from the northern shore of Duncan Bay.

Hecate Rock, with only 10 feet water on it, lies near the head of Duncan Bay, ½ mile N. 52° W. of Observation Point.

Directions.—If desirous of anchoring in Duncan Bay, pass one mile northwestward of Tugwell Island, and when the south extreme of Gribbell Island is seen just open of Observation Point, bearing S. 57° W. that mark should be steered for, a berth should be taken up on that bearing, in 8 to 10 fathoms, mud, with Chapman Point, the NW. extreme of Tugwell Island, bearing S. 83° W.

Approaching Metlah Catlah from the southeastward, if the Lawyer Group of islands be kept in line with Green Top Island bearing S. 35° E., that mark astern will lead directly to the entrance of Metlah Catlah Bay; and having brought Carr Islet in line with the western side of Devastation Island bearing N. 38° E. northerly, a vessel may steer in on that mark, and proceed as before directed to the anchorage off the

NW. side of Devastation Island Or, if bound into Duncan Bay, pass one mile westward of Tugwell Island, and proceed as before directed. During a fog or in thick weather, when approaching Metlah Catlah from the southeastward, do not shoal to less than 40 fathoms, and on such occasions the Lucy Islands should be cautiously steered for and sighted, taking care to avoid the reefs which extend from the S. and SW. side of the group. The large or eastern Lucy Island should be brought to bear S. 80° W. astern, and a N. 80° E. course should take a vessel to the entrance of Metlah Catlah Bay. The bank of 10 fathoms (and less water) extends nearly one mile to the southward of Tugwell Island, and the hand lead, if proceeding slowly, should indicate the position. During summer and autumn large quantities of kelp mark this bank.

Tree Bluff, the southern entrance point of Big Bay, lies 5 miles north of Ryan Point. The shore northward of Ryan Point is low and wooded to the distance of 3 miles back from the coast, where it rises into high land; the two most conspicuous mountains being Mission Mountain and Deer Mound. Two streams enter the sound on this part of the coast, and there are two islets lying close to the shore, respectively one and 2 miles northward of Ryan Point. The former (Swamp Islet) is covered with low grass, and lies about ½ mile from the shore. The latter islet is bare (Slippery Rock), about 800 yards from the shore.

Immediately eastward of Tree Bluff there is a wooded hill, close to the shore, 250 feet high.

Dangers.—Between Metlah Catlah and Big Bays, dangerous ledges extend off shore in many places to the distance of 2 miles. These edges uncover at low water, and are steep to.

Hodgson Reefs, a dangerous cluster, lie northward of Duncan Bay, their south part covers at half flood, and lies 2 miles N. 18° W of the NW. extreme of Tugwell Island. From that position dangerous sunken rocks extend in a northerly direction for 2 miles.

Abreast Tree Bluff the edge of the bank, which dries at low water, lies 1½ miles from the shore.

Leading Marks—The southern side of Kinnahan Islands, just showing clear of the south end of Tugwell Island, bearing S. 26° E, leads, westward of Hodgson Reefs; and the eastern island of the Lucy Group should not be brought to bear south of S. 16° W. (astern) until Mount Griffin (over Port Simpson) is seen in line with the north end of Burntcliff Island N. 42° E., this mark leads westward of all dangers off the entrance of Big Bay.

Big Bay (Lakhou), the entrance to which between Tree Bluff and South Island is 2½ miles wide. At its head, which is skirted by a sand flat, which dries one mile from the shore at low water, several streams flow into the bay, this part being known as Salmon River Bight.

South Island is small and wooded, with a sharp summit 150 feet high, and connected with the mainland by a space of foul ground, dry at low water, and one mile in width.

A Ledge of Sunken Rocks, with depths of 6 and 12 feet, extends ½ mile S. 33° W. from the southwestern side of South Island.

Haycock Island lies 600 yards S 63° E of the summit of South Island.

White Cliff Island lies about a mile S. 37° E of Haycock Island; it is small, and terminates in high, white, conspicuous cliffs.

Shattock Point, 600 yards east of White Cliff Island, is the northwestern entrance point of Salmon River Bight.

Swallow Island lies one mile S. 55° E. of White Cliff Island, and 200 yards off the north shore.

Curlew Rock is small, about 2 feet above high water, and lies ½ mile S. 27° W. of Swallow Island

Ripple Bank, at the entrance to Big Bay, is about 400 yards in extent in an ESE and WNW. direction, the shoalest spot near the eastern end, having 12 feet water over it, sandy bottom, lies 1 $\frac{1}{10}$ miles S 47° W. of the summit of South Island. This bank usually indicates itself by a tide rip but no kelp.

A Sandbank, about 200 yards in extent, with 3 fathoms water, lies S. 21° W. 600 yards from Haycock Island.

Escape Reefs are a dangerous cluster at the entrance to Big Bay, SE of Ripple Bank The outer or western reef has 4 feet water over it, and lies 1 $\frac{4}{10}$ miles S. 35° W. of the summit of South Island. The eastern reef has 5 feet water over it, and lies ½ mile east of the western one. There are depths of 16 and 17 fathoms between these reefs During the season of kelp growth, that weed is found in great quantities upon Escape Reefs, and near the head of Big Bay. Both reefs have small lumps dry at low water

Anchorage will be found in Big Bay, in 11 and 12 fathoms, mud, with Haycock Island in line with the north extreme of South Island, and White Cliff Island in line with Mount Griffin

Directions—Approaching Big Bay from the southward, Mount Griffin should be kept in line with the north extreme of Burnt cliff Island N. 42° E until Sharp Peak on the ridge SE of Mount Griffin is in line with the south end of Swallow Island bearing S. 75° E. the latter mark will lead directly into Big Bay; anchor with Sharp Peak open south of Swallow Island, in the position and depth above given

Burnt-cliff Island, northward of South Island, is wooded, its highest point near its north end being 200 feet high The northern extreme of this island terminates in high red-brown cliffs; the northeastern extreme is cultivated, and from that point a long bank of shingle, awash at high water, extends 600 yards in an easterly direction. The whole space inshore of South and Burnt cliff Islands uncovers at low water.

A Ledge, which uncovers at low water, extends 600 yards in a northerly direction from the NW. extreme of Burnt cliff Island. The channel between Burnt cliff and One Tree Islands is available only for boats.

One Tree Island is of small extent, with a sharp wooded summit A low grassy point extends 100 yards in a northerly direction from the northern extreme of One Tree Island. One Tree Island forms the southern point of entrance to Cunningham Passage, and the western shelter of Pearl Harbor.

A Ledge, which uncovers at low water, surrounds One Tree Island; its greatest distance from the shore being ¼ mile.

Flat-top Islands, northward of Pearl Harbor, consist of three wooded islands. The middle and longest island of the group is connected by a narrow grassy neck with the northern island, and the latter has a flat summit, covered in July with long grass.

Ledges, which uncover at low water, and foul ground surround the Flat top Group to the distance of 300 yards

Finlayson Island, the largest in this locality, is 2¾ miles long in a north and south direction, one mile broad, and is wooded The southern extreme of the island terminates in cliffs, but the northern extreme (Gordon Point) is long and comparatively low, with ledges which uncover extending 400 yards to the northward; and on the NW. side of the island, about ½ mile from the northwestern extreme, is a large stream

Red Cliff Point, on the eastern side of Cunningham Passage, is rendered conspicuous by the high red brown cliffs over it, and the small islet close to. Immediately SE. of the point there is a bay, with a sandy beach, and stream at its head.

Pearl Harbor, eastward of One Tree Island, is nearly circular in shape and ½ mile across, its eastern side being formed by a bay, which dries nearly throughout at low water On its southeastern side the high bank of shingle which extends from the northeastern point of Burnt-cliff Island effectually shelters the harbor from southeasterly winds

Anchorage.—Good anchorage will be found in 9 to 10 fathoms, mud bottom, near the middle of Pearl Harbor.

Otter Anchorage, at the south end of Cunningham Passage near the eastern shore, northward of Flat top Islands, is useful if communicating with the wood-cutting establishment abreast it.

Anchorage in 15 to 17 fathoms, sand, will be found with the center of the Wood cutting Establishment in line with Leading Peak, bearing S. 77° E., and the northernmost Flat top Island (Green Mound) S 16° W., distant 300 yards.

Wood-cutting Establishment, from which the principal supplies for Port Simpson are obtained, is near the middle of a sandy bay, the northern point of the bay terminating in cliffs. The bay dries nearly throughout at low water.

From Otter Anchorage there is a passage eastward of Flat-top Islands into Pearl Harbor, but this is not recommended to strangers.

Sparrowhawk Rock, a dangerous, sunken, pinnacle rock, on which is only 5 feet water, lies nearly ½ mile N. 12° W. of One Tree Island

and nearly in midchannel between One Tree and Finlayson Islands, it is steep to, there being depths of 10 and 12 fathoms at a distance of 50 feet from it

Leading Peak, a well defined peak of triangular shape, in line with northern extreme of the northernmost islet of the Flat-top Group, bearing S. 80° E., or that peak seen just open southward of the Wood cutting Establishment abreast Otter Anchorage, S. 77° E., will lead northward of Sparrowhawk Rock and southward of Dodd Rock.

Dodd Rock is the most outlying danger extending from the southern side of Finlayson Island, and lies a little over 400 yards S. 27° W. of Fortune Point, ledges which dry connect it with that point. Dodd Rock only covers at the highest equinoctial tides, and is therefore a useful mark when entering Cunningham Passage, as there is deep water a short distance southward of the rock.

Directions.—Approaching Cunningham Passage, Red Cliff Point should be steered for in line with Fortune Point, bearing N. 72° E., until Leading Peak is seen in line with the north Flat top Island (Green Mound), bearing S. 80° E., when the latter mark should be steered for. When the western side of Burnt-cliff Island is seen open eastward of One Tree Islet, bearing south, vessels will be eastward of Sparrowhawk Rock; and if bound to Port Simpson, may haul to the northward into Cunningham Passage.

If bound into Pearl Harbor, a midchannel course from the above mentioned position should be shaped between One Tree Islet and the southernmost Flat-top Island. Belletti and Shattock Points, two conspicuous wooded points on the eastern shore, should be kept in line, bearing S. 29° E., when entering Pearl Harbor.

Cunningham Passage is eastward of Finlayson Island, between it and the Tsimpsean Peninsula. The southern portion of this channel is barely 700 yards wide; but northward of Sarah Point the passage widens, attaining, between One Tree Islet and Gordon Point, a width of 1¼ miles. The depths in midchannel are from 16 to 36 fathoms, with no danger beyond 200 yards from the shore, until nearing Village Island.

Village Island, at the southwestern entrance of port Simpson, at about 200 yards from the shore, with which it is connected at half tide, is about ¼ mile long in a NW. and SE. direction; its southern side forms a bay. Village Island near its NW. extreme is about 50 feet high, having on it a high pole.

One Tree Islet, covered with stunted trees, lies close to the north western extreme of Village Island. Near the western end stands a conspicuous decayed tree from which the name of the islet is given.

Birnie Island lies at the northern entrance of Port Simpson. The shores of this island are comparatively bold and unbroken. Knox Point is the southern extreme. Ledges which uncover at low water extend 200 yards from Knox Point.

... harbor on this part of the coast, ... easterly ... is ap- ... n Bay ..., where ... with a ... nd The ... ch dry at ... gh water ... 1 to 20 ... free from ... no strong tidal currents, ... st, which here seldom blows. The prevailing winds ... SW., from which the harbor is perfectly protected

Supplies.—Wood, water, poultry, potatoes, and crabs may be obtained

Landmark.—The villages on Village Island, the decayed tree on One Tree Islet, Fort Simpson, and Mount Griffin, with its triangular summit, are all conspicuous objects at the SW. entrance of Port Simpson On the northern shore George and Lizzie Hills, of nearly the same height, are wooded and easily recognized. The mouth of a lagoon, on that shore, is also conspicuous. Ben Hill, over the southern entrance point of Stamaun Bay, is wooded, 130 feet high, and conspicuous amid the adjacent low land.

Fort Simpson.—The trading post or fort stands near the southwestern entrance point of the bay, close to the beach, and consists of a stockade of oblong shape, 250 feet long and 100 feet deep, with high bastions. A large entry gate faces the beach with a landing jetty of stones in front of it. Excellent potatoes, lettuces, and radishes are grown. Raspberries and strawberries grow in abundance.

The village contains a population of about 800 Indians.

Good wood ready cut for steaming purposes may be obtained at $3 a cord.

The land at the back of the fort is about 130 feet high, and has been cleared to the distance of about one mile.

The Hudson Bay Company's trading steam vessel calls periodically at Port Simpson, bringing supplies and returning with the furs There is a good pier with a depth of over 4 fathoms alongside it at low water.

Temperature.—From observations taken in 1868 the maximum and minimum registrations of temperature were as follows June, 65°, 50°; July, 74°, 48°; August, 70°, 54°, September, 64°, 44°

Anchorage.—The usual anchorage is off the fort, in about 10 fathoms, mud bottom; a good berth being with Parkin Island, seen just open northward of Birnie Island, bearing N. 18° W. (westerly), and Gordon Point in line with the decayed tree on One Tree Islet, N. 85° W.

(255) **BRITISH COLUMBIA—Chatham sound—Inskip passage—Port Simpson entrance - Birnie Island light—Corrections.**—Referring to Notice to Mariners No. 53 (1878) of 1904, describing the new beacon light on Birnie island, later information received from British Columbia corrects the particulars therein contained as follows:

The light is situated on a bluff between the south and southwest points of the island.

Approx position: Lat. 54° 35′ 30″ N., Long. 130° 27′ 20″ W

The following sextant angles fix its position:

End of Port Simpson wharf, 0°

East tangent, Finlayson island, 27°

Pointer rocks, middle rock, 87°.

The Wigham lamp stands on a small white enclosed wooden tower and the light should be visible over an arc of 172° from N. 37° W. true (NW. by W ⅞ W mag), through north and east, to S. 45° E. true (ESE ½ E E'ly mag). (N. M 7, 1905)

a short distance southward of the rock.

Directions.—Approaching Cunningham Passage, Red Cliff Point should be steered for in line with Fortune Point, bearing N. 72° E , until Leading Peak is seen in line with the north Flat top Island (Green Mound), bearing S. 80° E., when the latter mark should be steered for. When the western side of Burnt cliff Island is seen open eastward of One Tree Islet, bearing south, vessels will be eastward of Sparrowhawk Rock; and if bound to Port Simpson, may haul to the northward into Cunningham Passage.

If bound into Pearl Harbor, a midchannel course from the abovementioned position should be shaped between One Tree Islet and the southernmost Flat-top Island Belletti and Shattock Points, two conspicuous wooded points on the eastern shore, should be kept in line, bearing S. 29° E., when entering Pearl Harbor

Cunningham Passage is eastward of Finlayson Island, between it and the Tsimpsean Peninsula. The southern portion of this channel is barely 700 yards wide, but northward of Sarah Point the passage widens, attaining, between One Tree Islet and Gordon Point, a width of 1¼ miles. The depths in midchannel are from 16 to 36 fathoms, with no danger beyond 200 yards from the shore, until nearing Village Island.

Village Island, at the southwestern entrance of port Simpson, at about 200 yards from the shore, with which it is connected at half tide, is about ¼ mile long in a NW. and SE. direction; its southern side forms a bay. Village Island near its NW. extreme is about 50 feet high, having on it a high pole.

One Tree Islet, covered with stunted trees, lies close to the northwestern extreme of Village Island. Near the western end stands a conspicuous decayed tree from which the name of the islet is given.

Birnie Island lies at the northern entrance of Port Simpson. The shores of this island are comparatively bold and unbroken. Knox Point is the southern extreme Ledges which uncover at low water extend 200 yards from Knox Point.

Port Simpson, the most spacious harbor on this part of the coast, is nearly 1¼ miles wide at its entrance; thence it takes a southeasterly direction for about 3½ miles, contracting gradually as the head is approached, and terminating in a narrow bight named Stumaun Bay, which dries across at low water. At its head are several streams, where salmon are caught. The northern shore of the port is fringed with a rocky beach, compact and backed by rapidly rising high land. The southern shore is not so regular nor so steep to, the rocks which dry at low water near the eastern part of the bay extending from high water mark in some places for the distance of nearly ¼ mile.

Port Simpson embraces over 4 square miles of water, from 1 to 20 fathoms deep, with muddy bottom, good holding ground, and free from rocks and shoals. It is easy of access from the sea, having no strong tidal currents, and well sheltered from all winds except the west, which here seldom blows. The prevailing winds are SW. and NW., from which the harbor is perfectly protected.

Supplies.—Wood, water, poultry, potatoes, and crabs may be obtained.

Landmark.—The villages on Village Island, the decayed tree on One Tree Islet, Fort Simpson, and Mount Griffin, with its triangular summit, are all conspicuous objects at the SW. entrance of Port Simpson. On the northern shore George and Lizzie Hills, of nearly the same height, are wooded and easily recognized. The mouth of a lagoon, on that shore, is also conspicuous. Ben Hill, over the southern entrance point of Stumaun Bay, is wooded, 130 feet high, and conspicuous amid the adjacent lowland.

Fort Simpson.—The trading post or fort stands near the southwestern entrance point of the bay, close to the beach, and consists of a stockade of oblong shape, 250 feet long and 100 feet deep, with high bastions. A large entry gate faces the beach with a landing jetty of stones in front of it. Excellent potatoes, lettuces, and radishes are grown. Raspberries and strawberries grow in abundance.

The village contains a population of about 800 Indians.

Good wood ready cut for steaming purposes may be obtained at $3 a cord.

The land at the back of the fort is about 130 feet high, and has been cleared to the distance of about one mile.

The Hudson Bay Company's trading steam vessel calls periodically at Port Simpson, bringing supplies and returning with the furs. There is a good pier with a depth of over 4 fathoms alongside it at low water.

Temperature.—From observations taken in 1868 the maximum and minimum registrations of temperature were as follows: June, 65°, 50°; July, 74°, 48°; August, 70°, 54°; September, 64°, 44°.

Anchorage.—The usual anchorage is off the fort, in about 10 fathoms, mud bottom; a good berth being with Parkin Island, seen just open northward of Birnie Island, bearing N. 18° W. (westerly), and Gordon Point in line with the decayed tree on One Tree Islet N. 85° W.

Hankin Reefs are a dangerous cluster of reefs which partially uncover, situated SW. of Village Island. The southwestern extreme of these reefs uncovers 6 feet at low water, and lies a little over 600 yards S 61° W. of the northwestern extreme of Village Island There is deep water between these reefs and Village Island.

Fortune Point, just shut in with Sarah Point bearing S. 10° W., leads westward of the reefs

Harbor Reefs are an extensive plateau of rocks, awash at high water, forming a natural breakwater at the entrance to Port Simpson, protecting the anchorage from NW winds This sunken plateau is nearly square in shape, and about one mile in extent, within the depth of 5 fathoms The southeastern portion of these reefs only covers at the highest tides.

Dodd Passage lies between One Tree Islet and Harbor Reefs, and is 400 yards wide, with depths of 6 and 8 fathoms in it This is available for steam vessels, but local knowledge is necessary.

Anchorage Patch, with 18 feet water, sandy bottom, lies in the western portion of the anchorage ground off Fort Simpson, with the fort gate bearing S 24° E, and the pole on the NW. extreme of Village Island, S. 72° W., distant 300 yards.

Choked Passage, northward of Birnie Island, has several ledges which uncover, and sunken dangers with deep water between them This passage should not be attempted except in boats, and when using it keep near the eastern shore

Directions.—Approaching Port Simpson from the southward by Cunningham Passage, the cliffs on the NW. extreme of Burnt cliff Island kept in line with the southernmost Flat-top Island, bearing S. 13° W. (astern) will lead through until abreast Sarah Point. Thence the mark for leading westward of Hankin Reefs should be brought on astern, and when the lagoon mouth on north shore of Port Simpson opens westward of the decayed tree on One-Tree Islet, bearing N. 72° E., a course should be steered to pass 200 yards northwestward of One-Tree Islet, and anchor in the position before mentioned.

Vessels not wishing to enter by Dodd Passage, should, when abreast Sarah Point, bring that point in line with the south point of a bay on the eastern shore of Cunningham Passage, bearing S 21° E (astern), which mark will lead southward of the Harbor Reefs, midway between that danger and Finlayson Island.

Inskip Passage, the northern and principal entrance into Port Simpson, is a little over ½ mile wide, and should invariably be used by strangers.

Entering Port Simpson by Inskip Passage, Lizzie Hill (on the north shore) well open southward of Birnie Island, bearing N. 72° E., will lead 400 yards south of that island and 600 yards north of the Harbor Reefs. When Ben Hill comes open of Bath Point, bearing S. 52° E., a S. 74° E. course may be steered, until Parkin Island is seen just open northward of Birnie Island, bearing N. 18° W. (westerly), that mark kept on astern will lead up to the anchorage, in the depth and position before mentioned.

Repairs.—The great rise and fall of tide at Port Simpson permits a vessel to be beached. A good site will be found for this purpose just westward of the fort. The bottom consists of hard sand, with a covering of weeds.

Tides.—Chatham Sound has very little current, not more than one knot, as far as the Pointers. A strong current sets out of Nass and Work Channels in Chatham Sound and then flows out through Dixon Entrance between Dundas Islands and Alaska, at the rate of about 2½ knots an hour.

Deviation.—For swinging to ascertain the deviation of the compass in Port Simpson, Table Hill on Dundas Island, 12 miles distant, is conspicuous. The bearing of the knob at the north end of Table Hill, from the anchorage in Port Simpson, is N. 76° 00′ W.

Parkin Islands consist of two islands lying close together, about 200 yards in extent; though small, they are 250 feet high, wooded and conspicuous. The south extreme of Parkin Islands lies about 1½ miles N. 15° W. of the northern extreme of Birnie Island, and 1,200 yards from the nearest shore (Black Point).

Maskelyne Point is the southwestern entrance point of Portland Inlet, and the northwestern entrance point of Work Channel. Deep water was found within 200 yards of that point.

Work Channel, the entrance to which lies close northward of Point Maskelyne, takes a southeasterly direction for about 35 miles; near its termination it divides into two arms, one branching off to the NW. for 5 miles, and then turning suddenly to the NE. for the same distance, the other arm continuing to the SE., and approaching within one mile of the Skeena river; this channel has not been examined in detail. At its entrance Work Channel is barely 800 yards wide, which width it preserves for about 7 miles, when it widens to 1½ miles, and afterwards to 2 miles; its shores are stated to be "straight and compact." A rock just visible at low water is reported to lie in the middle of this channel just abreast of Mount McNeil. It is described as having a very small top with a depth of 130 fathoms close to it.

WEST COAST OF CHATHAM SOUND

Prescott and Stephens Islands lie in the southwestern part of Chatham Sound, and are separated by a narrow passage available only for boats. These islands together are about 12 miles long, of triangular shape; the base of the triangle, the northwestern side of Stephens Island, is 4 miles long.

Stephens Island attains an elevation of 1,340 feet near its east end; its southern shores are comparatively low, with some white cliffs near the center.

Tree Knob Groups are a mass of islands, islets, and rocks awash at low water, which extend 6 miles in a northwesterly direction from the NW. side of Stephens Island. The larger islets are wooded and the smaller bare

Edye Passage lies on the southern side of Prescott and Stephens Islands, and is the channel usually taken when communicating between Chatham Sound and Hecate Strait, as, by using it, vessels avoid the strong and irregular tides met with in Brown Passage. It is comparatively free from danger, and at its eastern end possesses an excellent anchorage (Refuge Bay), in which a vessel may await a favorable opportunity for proceeding.

Goschen Island—Approaching Edye Passage from the southward, the oval-shaped hill, 630 feet high, near the western extreme of Goschen Island is conspicuous, and at 2 miles northward of that hill lies another, with a flat summit, 170 feet high. At 3 miles southward of the latter, the western shore of Goschen Island terminates in high white cliffs.

The western side of Goschen Island has several rocks awash, and sunken rocks extending one mile off it in a westerly direction.

Bass Rock, 30 feet high, close to the shore of Goschen Island under Oval Hill is small and bare.

A Rocky Ledge, with depths of 4 to 8 fathoms upon it, extends westward nearly 4 miles from Goschen Island, in the vicinity of the Bass Rock.

Clearing Mark.—The conspicuous white cliffs on the south side of Stephens Island should not be brought to bear westward of N. 27° E. approaching the western shore of Goschen Island.

Seal Rocks, a cluster of bare rocks of small extent, 10 feet above high water, the center of which lies 5 miles N. 38° W. of the summit of Oval Hill, have depths of 12 to 31 fathoms at 400 yards from them.

Warrior Rocks, two bare rocks 30 feet above high water, lie SE. and NW. distant 1,600 yards from each other. The eastern rock lies 3¾ miles N. 24° W. of the center of the Seal Rock Cluster.

Deep Patch, at the western entrance of Edye Passage, is stated to have 19 fathoms upon it; there is, however, probably less water on this patch, as kelp was observed growing upon it in August

The patch is of small extent, and lies one mile N. 49° E. of Cape Ibbetson.

Clearing Mark—The south extreme of Arthur Island (View Point) seen in line with the SE. extreme of that island, bearing S. 83° E, will lead northward of Deep Patch.

Truscott Patch, with 16 feet water upon it, lies 1¾ miles S. 86° E. of Cape Ibbetson, and 1,200 yards from the nearest shore of Henry Island

Foul Ground extends off the southeastern side of Arthur Island to the distance of 600 yards.

Tides.—The flood approaches from the westward, and both streams set fairly through Edye Passage, with an average rate of 2 knots an hour.

Directions.—Approaching Edye Passage from the southwestward, the eastern portion of the high white cliffs on the south side of Stephens Island should not be brought to bear westward of N. 27° E. until Oval Hill, on Goschen Island, is seen in line with Seal Rocks bearing S. 38° E. Thence a N. 66° E. course may be steered for the entrance to Edye Passage, taking care not to shut in Oval Hill with Cape Ibbetson until the south and SE. points of Arthur Island are seen in line. The latter mark may then be steered for, bearing S. 83° E., until Seal Rocks are seen in line with Cape Ibbetson bearing S. 47° W., when a more southerly course may be steered to pass ½ mile southward of the south extreme of Arthur Island. When the entrance points of Refuge Bay are seen in line, that mark may be steered for, bearing N. 61° E., taking care to avoid the small patch, which uncovers at low water, 600 yards from the south point of Useless Bay. Pass ¼ mile westward of the south entrance point of Refuge Bay (Pearce Point), and if not desirous of anchoring in that bay, a N. 7° W. course should be steered towards Rachel Islands, passing midway between that group and Gull Rocks, whence steer as requisite for destination.

Refuge Bay, at the northwestern extreme of Porcher Island, is an excellent stopping place during southeasterly winds, or if desirous of proceeding to sea from Chatham Sound by the Edye Passage, the state of the weather in Hecate Strait can be ascertained. The bay is 1,100 yards wide between its entrance points, and takes a southeasterly direction for about one mile, terminating in a sand-flat which extends nearly ½ mile from its head.

The depths in the middle of the bay are from 11 to 23 fathoms, sand, shoaling gradually towards either shore.

Anchorage will be found in 12 to 14 fathoms, sand and mud, near the middle of the bay, about 400 yards from the north and south shores, with the north entrance point (Table Point) bearing N. 4° E., and Pearce Point bearing N. 80° W.

Brown Passage, between Tree Knob Islands and South Dundas Islands, is about 5 miles long and 5 miles wide.

Nearly in mid channel, however, lies a cluster of rocks, awash at high water, which divides Brown Passage into two channels.

Butterworth Rocks, are a dangerous cluster of rocks, the southernmost of which is 10 feet above high water, with several patches which uncover at low water extending from it in a northerly direction for ¾ mile. This rock lies 3½ miles S. 52° W. of Bare Island, the southwestern island of the Tree Knob Group, with that island in line with some wooded islands forming the N.W. cluster of Tree Knob Group (Osborne Islands).

There is deep water between Butterworth Rocks and Tree Knob Islands.

Stenhouse Shoal, a dangerous patch, with 7 feet least water upon it, and reported to be 50 yards in extent, lies at the western entrance of Brown Passage, 6½ miles S. 80° W. of Cape Islet, the southern extreme of South Dundas Island, and 5 miles N. 46° W of the outer Osborne Island.

North Breaker, over which the sea usually breaks, is the outer known danger extending NW. from the Tree Knob Group, and lies one mile N. 40° W. of the outer Osborne Island.

Hanmer Rock, a dangerous rock, nearly in mid-channel, 2½ miles N. 38° E of the outer Osborne Island, and 2½ miles S. 35° W of Cape Islet, is awash at high water, with depths of 12 and 32 fathoms close to; there are several patches which uncover, extending from Hanmer rock in a NW direction to the distance of ¼ mile.

Simpson Rock lies on the northern side of Brown Passage ¾ mile S. 38° W. of Cape Islet; this rock is 6 feet above high water, with rocks awash extending ½ mile northward and westward, and a depth of 17 fathoms at 800 yards southward of it; there is a patch which uncovers 3 feet at low water, at 600 yards S. 18° E. of Simpson Rock

Beaver Rock, with 12 feet water on it, lies 1¼ miles S. 4° W. of the SE. extreme of South Dundas Island; several patches of rock lie between Beaver Rock and the shore of South Dundas Island. There are depths of 13 and 17 fathoms at 800 yards southward of Beaver Rock.

Tides—In Brown Passage the tides set fairly through at an average rate of 2 knots an hour. The flood stream sets to the eastward, and off the western entrance to this passage the tides are strong and complicated.

Directions—Brown Passage is not recommended to strangers, but should circumstances compel, the eastern peak of the four peak range, on South Dundas Islands, should be steered for, bearing N. 61° E., until the eastern and highest Lucy Island bears S. 85° E, which will lead through Brown Passage south of Hanmer Rock, or bearing S 71° E, will lead through, northward of this rock.

Qlawdzeet Anchorage lies on the northern side of Stephens Island. It is ¼ mile wide at its entrance, and one mile deep in a southerly direction.

Entrance Reef, awash at high water, lies 400 yards N 18° W of the eastern entrance point of Qlawdzeet Bay.

Directions.—The entrance to Qlawdzeet Bay will be made if the north extreme of Tugwell Island is kept in line (astern) with the eastern island of the Lucy Group, bearing N. 55° E

Keep in mid channel when entering, and anchor at 600 yards within the bay and 300 yards off the south shore, in 12 to 14 fathoms, mud bottom, with the eastern entrance point of the bay bearing N. 66° E, distant 800 yards and the western entrance point bearing N. 49° W., distant 1,200 yards.

Bay Islands, on the southern side of South Dundas Island, are reported to afford anchorage off their northwestern side.

The examination of this locality has shown the existence of many sunken rocks, the anchorage under Bay Islands should therefore not be attempted.

Dundas Islands consist of three islands, the northernmost being the largest and highest. A number of smaller islands (Moffat Islands) lie close to the eastern shores of South and Middle Dundas Islands. The western shores of the group have not been thoroughly examined, but they are much broken into bays and inlets, with several small off lying islets.

South Dundas Island is about 3 miles long and 5 miles broad, its shores being comparatively low, wooded, and broken into bays on the south and western sides. Near the middle of the island a mountain range rises to the height of 1,400 feet, with four conspicuous peaks. The eastern and highest peak of this range is 1,400 feet high, the western and lowest 1,100 feet high.

Middle Dundas Island lies about 2 miles from South Dundas Island, the passage between being obstructed by numerous low, wooded islets, and sunken dangers. The island is nearly 5 miles long, with a greatest breadth of 5 miles, it is mostly low and wooded, with numerous creeks and bays on its shores. Near the southern end of the island the land suddenly rises in an oval shaped hill (Coast Mound) 750 feet high, which is a useful land-mark.

Connel Islands, a group of small wooded islands, lie off the western side of Middle Dundas Island. The outer or southwestern island of the group lies off the entrance to the passage between South and Middle Dundas Islands, about 2 miles from the western shores of the latter.

North Dundas Island is about 12 miles long and about 7 miles broad near its north end. This island, the highest and largest of the group, culminates in a mountain with a thumb-shaped summit, 2,500 feet high, about 4 miles from the southern end of the island. Near the northern extreme of North Dundas Island there is a hill 700 feet high, with a flat top, and a knob near its north end (Table Hill), a most conspicuous and useful mark. The eastern shore of North Dundas Island is but little broken; bold, with a range of coast hills rising immediately above it. On the northern side, nearly midway between Whitley Point and White Islands, there is a deep bay, though useless as an anchorage, at the entrance to which lies a group of small, wooded islets (Gnarled Islands). Off the northwestern extreme of the island, close to the shore, are two conspicuous rocks (White Rocks).

The western shore of North Dundas Island has not been examined in detail. Several islands lie off that shore to the distance of 2 miles.

Zayas Island is the largest of the islands which lie off the western shore of North Dundas Island. The extent of this island has not been ascertained. A ledge of rocks, which uncover at low water, was observed to extend nearly one mile from the NW. extreme of Zayas Island. From the west side of the island rocks are said to extend 3 miles.

Zayas Island appeared flat and heavily timbered and probably 3 or 4 miles in extent. The following dangers have been reported in the neighborhood of Zayas Island: An uncovering rock in mid channel between Zayas and North Dundas Islands; two rocks close in on the north side of the island; three small islets less than a mile from its NW. extreme. Besides these, dangers are shown as lying 3 miles west of the NW. point of North Dundas and 2 miles north of the NW. extreme of Zayas.

Channel Islands are a group of wooded islands, about 100 feet high, extending across the channel between Middle and North Dundas Islands. This group renders that channel useless for any but the smallest class of sailing vessels.

Moffat Islands consist of six principal wooded islands and several lesser ones, the highest being about 250 feet in height. This group, which lies close to the eastern shore of the Dundas Islands, extends over a distance of 6 miles. When abreast these islands show out well, being covered with pine trees of a peculiar deep green foliage.

Ducie Island is a small, wooded islet, 350 feet high, lying one mile northward of the Moffat Group. Two conspicuous white rocks, 30 feet high, lie 600 yards from Ducie Island.

Whitesand Islet, a small, sandy islet, about 10 feet above high water, lies eastward of Ducie Island. A ledge of rocks, which uncover, extends north and south from Whitesand Islet, to the distance of 800 yards.

Hammond Rock, of small extent, with 9 feet water over it, lies nearly a mile eastward of the southeastern extreme of the SE. Moffat Island. This rock has 34 fathoms close northward of it.

Coghlan Rock, with 3 feet water and 6 and 7 fathoms close around, lies 2 miles N. 15° W. of Hammond Rock. There are depths of 43 and 46 fathoms, mud bottom, at one mile northward of this rock.

Brodie Rock lies 3¾ miles N. 18° W. of Coghlan Rock. This dangerous pinnacle rock has only 3 feet water over it at low water, with depths of 26 and 33 fathoms at a distance of 100 feet.

The Rachel Group of islands, kept open of the Lucy Group, bearing S. 12° E., will lead eastward of the above mentioned dangers; but during a fog, or in thick weather, the western shore of Chatham Sound must not be approached under the depth of 40 fathoms.

Pointers Rocks are a dangerous cluster of bare rocks, 3 feet above high water, about 400 yards in extent. The southernmost and highest rock lies 3 miles N. 41° W. of the northern extreme of Finlayson Island. There are depths of 40 fathoms, no bottom, at 100 yards westward; and 12 fathoms, rocky bottom, at 200 yards eastward of Pointers Rocks.

Connis Rocks consist of one large and several small rocks, nearly in the middle of Main Passage into Chatham Sound, abreast Port Simpson.

The southernmost and highest rock, 15 feet above high water, is bare, and from it rocks extend 400 yards in a northerly direction. The summit of this rock lies 5 miles N. 86° W. of the north extreme of Finlayson Island.

Green Islet, on the western shore of Chatham Sound, about 1½ miles from North Dundas Island, is covered with long grass during the summer. It is small, 40 feet above high water, and has a small bare rock lying close northward, and another close southward.

Grey Islet is a small bare rock of a greyish color, 30 feet above high water, 1,800 yards N. 21° E. of Green Islet.

A Sunken Rock with 6 feet water upon it, lies one mile N. 41° W. of Grey Islet. There are depths of 19 and 27 fathoms at 200 yards from this rock.

A Sunken Rock, with 4 feet water upon it, lies between Grey and Green Islets.

Main Passage is between Pointers and Connis Rocks, and is 3½ miles wide. Both Connis and Pointers Rocks may be approached to within a distance of ½ mile.

Oriflamme Passage lies westward of Connis Rocks, between that cluster and Green and Grey Islets It is nearly 3 miles wide.

The passage between Dundas Island and the Green and Grey Islets is nearly 1½ miles wide. The tides in this passage are strong, and the channel is not recommended to strangers.

Gnarled Islands, a group of wooded islands, about one mile in extent, lying off the northern side of the North Dundas Island, are from 150 to 250 feet in height.

The channel between Dundas and Gnarled Islands is obstructed by ledges which uncover, and sunken rocks.

White Islands are two bare rocks, about 30 feet high, lying ½ mile from the northwestern extreme of North Dundas Island.

Dixon Entrance is the channel between Prince of Wales and Queen Charlotte Islands, passing northward of Dundas Islands Several sunken rocks, of doubtful position, are reported to lie in the western part of this passage, on or near a line joining the north end of the Dundas Group and the south end of the Prince of Wales Group.

Various positions have been assigned to the East Devil Rock (one of the dangers lying in Dixon Entrance); it is situated about 4 miles northwestward of Zayas Island, in latitude 54° 40′ N., longitude 131° 6′ W. According to the report of the commander of the Hudson Bay Company's steamer *Otter*, Devil Rock is marked by a breaker, and is awash at low water. West Devil Rock is approximately 18½ miles S. 84° W. of East Devil Rock; a breaker (Chacon) is reported as lying 7 miles S. 27° E. of Cape Chacon and Núnez Reef as lying 6 miles S. 13° W. of the same cape.

McCullough Rock, on which the sea breaks, is said to have been discovered by Captain McCullough. From it the NW. end of Zayas Island bears N. 78° E., whilst the western shore of Zayas Island is distant about 3 miles in a SE. direction.

Cape Fox lies about 7 miles northward of the Gnarled Island group, and terminates in remarkable high, white cliffs, with a conspicuous saddle-shaped mountain 2,060 feet high, immediately over it.

Lord Islands, a group of about one mile in extent, lying 2½ miles southeastward of Cape Fox, are wooded and about 250 feet high.

Lord Rock, which uncovers 3 feet at low water, lies 1,600 yards S. 61° W. of the SW. island of the Lord Group.

Nakat Inlet has its entrance between Cape Fox and Tongass Island, and extends about 11 miles in a northerly direction. The entrance has several dangers. In the inlet, in the farther bight inside the group of islands, is a well-sheltered anchorage in less than 15 fathoms

Tongass Island is about 3 miles eastward of Cape Fox The settlement is dreary, and the almost constant rain and soft soil produce mud of a most tenacious nature.

Anchorage—The approaches to Tongass settlement are intricate and require local knowledge; the anchorage abreast the fort is bad, with deep water and limited accommodation even for a vessel of moderate length.

Tlekhonsiti Harbor is one of the southeastern approaches to Tongass from Chatham Sound. This passage is intricate and contracted

Boston Islands, lying off Wales Island, at the southeastern approach to Tongass, are about one mile in extent The larger islands are wooded, about 150 feet high; the smaller ones are bare, 50 feet high. The western island is 450 feet high, round, wooded and conspicuous.

A Ledge, which uncovers at low water, lies one mile SE. of the easternmost of the Boston Islands, and one mile from the nearest shore of Wales Island.

Wales Island, on the northwestern side of the entrance to Portland Inlet, is about 7 miles long in an east and west direction, its northeastern side being about 4 miles long. The northeastern shore is bold, with some conspicuous cliffs of red brown color, nearly midway between the north and south extremes of the island A small islet lies close to the shore arm at the north extreme. On the southern side, a deep bay faces south, and within it are some patches which uncover, and rocks awash. A wooded islet, about ½ mile long, lies off the entrance to this bay. A smaller islet lies one mile southwestward of the larger one.

Entry Peak, about ½ mile NW of Wales Point, is of triangular shape, with a sharp conspicuous summit. A mountain, with a flat summit, is situated near the middle of Wales Island.

Cod Bank, with depths of 33 and 47 fathoms, mud and shells, lies between Pointers Rocks and Parkin Island, extending from the latter within the 50 fathom line, to the distance of 1½ miles.

There is a depth of 109 fathoms, mud bottom, at $\frac{1}{2}$ mile south, and 99 fathoms, rock, at $\frac{1}{2}$ mile north of Cod Bank. Codfish of large size are caught upon this bank.

Tides.—The tides in Dixon Entrance and Brown Passage, especially in the western part of those channels, are variable and complicated. The flood stream approaching from the southward up Hecate Strait is met by the stream passing westward and northward of Queen Charlotte Islands at about 15 miles eastward of Rose Point, or about midway between the northeastern extreme of Queen Charlotte Islands and the Tree Knob Group. Northward of that position this meeting of the streams produces tidal irregularities, and at spring tides or during bad weather the turmoil caused by the meeting of the streams is so great as to convey an appearance of broken waters to that portion of them which lies between Queen Charlotte Islands, Brown Passage, and Dixon Entrance. In Chatham Sound the tides set fairly through.

CHAPTER XII.

QUEEN CHARLOTTE ISLANDS.

Queen Charlotte Islands consists of three principal islands, together with several smaller islands and form a compact archipelago.

The general character of these islands is mountainous and heavily timbered, and the mining resources are very extensive. The only industry at present is the manufacture of oil from the dogfish. The chief item of trade is in the fur seals, value of which is about $10,000 annually.

Climate—The climate of these islands and of the off-lying islands of the coast is influenced by the warm body of water which washes their shores. The climate is milder and the winters less severe than in the inlets. The vapor arising from this body of warm water is condensed upon the mountains forming the shores of the mainland and causes an almost constant drizzling rain.

Winds—Southeast winds are prevalent and are generally accompanied with thick rain. Winds from the opposite quarter bring fine weather. No dependence can be placed on the weather for 24 hours at a time.

The heaviest rainfall takes place on the western mountains and often while it is raining heavily on the mountains, it is clear over the strait to the eastward. Snow occasionally falls in winter.

Prevost Island is the southernmost island of the group. The land gradually rises northward from Cape St James (its southern point) till near Houston Stewart Channel, where it has in places an elevation of about 2,000 feet, which heights, if the weather is clear, will be the first land seen on approaching Queen Charlotte Islands from the southward

The east coast of Prevost Island is bold, and in many places bordered by steep cliffs. This part of the coast, between Cape St. James and the East Point, a distance of 12 miles, is indented by two bays or inlets, the southern apparently inconsiderable, while Luxana Bay, the northern, is probably 3 or 4 miles in depth From East Point the shore trends northwestward 6 or 7 miles to Moore Head, the southeastern entrance point of Houston Stewart Channel. The shore is much broken, being penetrated by inlets which extend back among the high hills. Several small islands lie off it, one of which is bold, densely covered with trees, and has a height of 150 feet.

The western side of Prevost Island, between Cape St. James and the western entrance of Houston Stewart Channel, for about 12 miles is apparently bold, but it is less known than the opposite side. The land near Cape St. James is not as thickly wooded as that to the northward.

Cape St. James appears to be the southern extremity of an island one mile in diameter. The southern point of Cape St. James is a vertical cliff about the same height as the larger of the islets lying off it. The cape slopes gradually from a summit 1,000 feet high to the sea, low at its extreme, with the Hummock Islets lying off it (two apparently detached hummock islets), about 180 feet high; outside these again lie three others, nearly 100 feet high, bare and whitish; the western side of the cape is also whitish.

Kerouart Islets consist of a chain of rocky islets and rocks which run off from Cape St. James 3½ miles in a southeasterly direction. A sunken ledge is reported to extend 1½ miles further in the same direction. As seen at a distance of some miles to the northeast, Kerouart islets appear to form three groups, the first lying close to Cape St James, consisting of two large rocks (Hummock Islets), the second of one large and several smaller rocks, and the third and furthest southward, of two or three rocks of some size and a number of lesser ones. These islets are remarkable, standing boldly up with rounded tops, and vertical cliffs on all sides; the smaller rocks having the same pillar like form

(1215) **BRITISH COLUMBIA**—**Grenville channel**—**Western entrance**—**Watson rock**—**Beacon rebuilt.**—A new beacon has been erected on Watson rock, to replace the beacon which was destroyed in November, 1903.

The new beacon is placed on a stone foundation 12 feet square and 3 feet above high water It is a pyramidal structure painted white, surmounted by a latticework drum painted red, and shows 22 feet above high water

Approx position: Lat. 53° 55′ 15″ N, Long 130° 10′ 40″ W

(See Notice to Mariners No. 3 (91) of 1904.) (N M 33, 1904)

stunted and show much dead wood, the roots holding to the almost naked rock.

... **Westward.**—This entrance may be known by its ... At about 4 miles ... gradually ... nce off, the ... ver a series ... ce, which is about one mile ... Point there are 20 fathoms water, with a rocky bottom ... lies close off Moore Head.

Raspberry Cove.—Within Forsyth Point, on the northern side, is a snug bay, bordered by a sandy beach, in which, at about ⅜ mile from Forsyth Point, and at ¼ mile from the beach, is a secure and convenient anchorage in 16 fathoms. In the northwestern part of the bay is Raspberry Cove, into which a stream of water flows.

CHAPTER XII.

QUEEN CHARLOTTE ISLANDS.

Queen Charlotte Islands consists of three principal islands, together with several smaller islands and form a compact archipelago. The general character of these islands is mountainous and heavily timbered, and the mining resources are very extensive. The only industry at present is the manufacture of oil from the dogfish. The chief item of trade is in the fur seals, value of which is about $10,000 annually

Climate.—The climate of these islands and of the off-lying islands of the coast is influenced by the warm body of water which washes their shores. The climate is milder and the winters less severe than in the inl

up

alu

pa

we

a t

while it is raining heavily on the mountains, . . .

to the eastward. Snow occasionally falls in winter.

Prevost Island is the southernmost island of the group. The land

(1877) **BRITISH COLUMBIA—Queen Charlotte islands—Name of southernmost island (Prevost island) changed to Kunghit island.**—To prevent confusion, the Geographic Board of Canada has decided to change the name of the southernmost large island of the Queen Charlotte group from Prevost island to Kunghit island, the former name being better known as that of an island off the east coast of Vancouver island. (N. M. 58, 1904.)

East Point, a distance of 12 miles, is indented by two bays or inlets, the southern apparently inconsiderable, while Luxana Bay, the northern, is probably 3 or 4 miles in depth. From East Point the shore trends northwestward 6 or 7 miles to Moore Head, the southeastern entrance point of Houston Stewart Channel. The shore is much broken, being penetrated by inlets which extend back among the high hills Several small islands lie off it, one of which is bold, densely covered with trees, and has a height of 150 feet.

The western side of Prevost Island, between Cape St. James and the western entrance of Houston Stewart Channel, for about 12 miles is apparently bold, but it is less known than the opposite side. The land near Cape St. James is not as thickly wooded as that to the northward.

Cape St. James appears to be the southern extremity of an island one mile in diameter. The southern point of Cape St. James is a vertical cliff about the same height as the larger of the islets lying off it. The cape slopes gradually from a summit 1,000 feet high to the sea, low at its extreme, with the Hummock Islets lying off it (two apparently detached hummock islets), about 180 feet high; outside these again lie three others, nearly 100 feet high, bare and whitish; the western side of the cape is also whitish.

Kerouart Islets consist of a chain of rocky islets and rocks which run off from Cape St. James 3½ miles in a southeasterly direction. A sunken ledge is reported to extend 1½ miles further in the same direction. As seen at a distance of some miles to the northeast, Kerouart islets appear to form three groups, the first lying close to Cape St. James, consisting of two large rocks (Hummock Islets), the second of one large and several smaller rocks, and the third and furthest southward, of two or three rocks of some size and a number of lesser ones. These islets are remarkable, standing boldly up with rounded tops, and vertical cliffs on all sides; the smaller rocks having the same pillar-like form so frequently found where a rocky coast is exposed to the full sweep of a great ocean.

Houston Stewart Channel trends from Moore Head westerly 2½ miles to Hornby Point, thence SW. 3 miles to the entrance from the Pacific Ocean. Opposite the bend formed by Hornby Point is Rose Harbor. Lonscoone, at the west entrance of the channel and just within Anthony Island, is said to be a good harbor similar to Rose Harbor. The country round this locality is mountainous, mostly rising steeply from the shore, and thickly wooded; the trees, however, are stunted and show much dead wood, the roots holding to the almost naked rock.

Entering from the Eastward.—This entrance may be known by its bold south point, and the round, thickly wooded islet. At about 4 miles from the entrance there are 90 fathoms water, and the depths gradually shoals to 20 fathoms to within one mile of it; from this distance off, the soundings are very irregular, varying from 30 to 7 fathoms over a series of ridges or bars of rock, sand, shell, and mud. In the entrance, which is about one mile wide, between Moore Head and Langford Point there are 20 fathoms water, with a rocky bottom. Haydon Rock lies close off Moore Head.

Raspberry Cove.—Within Forsyth Point, on the northern side, is a snug bay, bordered by a sandy beach, in which, at about ¾ mile from Forsyth Point, and at ¼ mile from the beach, is a secure and convenient anchorage in 16 fathoms. In the northwestern part of the bay is Raspberry Cove, into which a stream of water flows.

Rock.—At ¼ mile inside Forsyth Point, and a little to the northward of the line of the direction of the channel, is a rocky patch with kelp on it which dries at low-water springs; vessels should not haul to the northward too soon after entering.

On the southern side of the channel are some small wooded islands, here and there fringed with outlying patches of kelp, which latter should always be avoided.

Trevan Rock, 1¼ miles, nearly west of Forsyth Point, lies almost in mid-channel, and contracts the passage on its northern side to rather less than ½ mile; patches of kelp and Ellen Island, the largest of the islands before mentioned, reduce the channel on the southern side of it to about 200 yards in width. Trevan Rock is covered at high water, close to the north side of it the depth is 7 fathoms.

Anchorage.—There is a good anchorage to the eastward of Ellen Island, in a bay formed by the island and a rocky patch which covers at half tide, at nearly ½ mile to the eastward of the island. The anchorage is in 14 fathoms, mud, and the tide is not felt.

Rose Harbor.—This secure and capacious harbor takes a northerly direction between Catherine Point on the west and Ross Island on the east, for 3 miles from its junction with the channel, and is a continuation in nearly a straight line with the western portion of it. For the first 2 miles the average breadth of the harbor is ¾ mile, the western shore rising boldly with deep water close to, the eastern shore, although high, has kelp along it, with shoal water, extending for a distance of from 200 to 300 yards. The harbor then contracts to ½ mile in width between two low points forming its head, beyond which is a basin, about 2 miles in circumference, filled with rocks and wooded islets, having on its western side Sedmond River, a small stream abounding in the season with geese and ducks. The land on its northern and western sides is high and mountainous, whilst that on its eastern side is low. Pincher Rocks lie nearly 400 yards S. 15° W. of the east entrance point of the basin.

Danger Rocks.—About 3 miles to the northward of the eastern entrance to Houston Stewart Channel, and at about 2 miles off the low and densely wooded point between the eastern entrance of Houston Stewart Channel and Carpenter Bay, is a ledge of rocks, lying a little above water, on which the sea breaks violently, and for a considerable distance around; other rocks encircle these, but they are under water. Approaching Houston Stewart Channel from the northward, these rocks should be given a wide berth. On the northern side of the low wooded point is a little cove full of kelp and protected by rocks.

Entering from Westward.—Vessels from the southward bound in by this entrance, when abreast Cape St. James, should close the land to 1½ miles, and after coasting it for about 12 miles, the entrance will open out. Two remarkable white stripes down the mountains, 6 or 7 miles to the northwestward, are excellent landmarks. After passing at a convenient distance to the southward of Anthony Island, the largest and outer island at the entrance, which is 200 feet high, with white cliffs (off the southern end of which an extensive ledge of rocks projects ½ mile in a SW. direction), the channel will show itself Flat Rock, 50 feet high, bare and resembling a haystack, lies much nearer the western than the eastern side, and which should be kept on the port hand, will be a good guide. There is an Indian village known as Nin stints, of the Shangoi tribe, on the inner side of Anthony Island, the natives are very wild, and persons visiting or trading with them should be on their guard.

Moresby Island, the center of the three principal islands of the Queen Charlotte Group, is 72 miles long, but explorations on its east coast have resulted (by tracing out of the channels) in leaving it a mere skeleton, in places varying from only 1½ to 2 miles in breadth. The highest and most rugged part of the island is probably in about latitude 52° 30′, where many peaks bear patches of perennial snow. Also on Louise Island, and about the head of Cumshewa, the land is very rugged, with many summits of over 3,000 and 4,000 feet in height

Carpenter Bay, the southernmost bay on the east side of Moresby Island, is between Iron and Islet Points, a little over 2 miles wide, extending westward about 5 miles It is not quite landlocked, but is sheltered from the only direction otherwise exposed, by a little rocky reef which extends out from its east side On its southern side are two small bays, the western of which, South Cove, approaches near to the head of Rose Harbor. At its head is good anchorage for a small vessel in from 6 to 10 fathoms.

Carpenter Bay ends westward in a narrow arm, which receives two streams of some size. It resembles the head of Rose Harbor in being filled with small rocky islands and rocks, making it unsafe for even a small craft.

Collison Bay, between Carpenter Bay and Skincuttle Inlet, is about 1¼ miles wide between Bluff Point and the northwest point, and has a probable depth of 2 miles. It runs up into a narrow arm, which has not been examined. Several small islands and rocks lie off its entrance, and it does not appear to be serviceable as a harbor.

Gull Rock, 10 feet high, bears N. 82° E. 1¼ miles from Deluge Point, and is ½ mile off Moresby Island, between Collison Bay and Skincuttle Inlet. Inner Low Rock lies S 4° W. of Gull Rock, and midway between it and the shore.

Skincuttle Inlet is 5½ miles deep in a southwesterly direction, with a width of 4 miles between Deluge and Granite Points. The northern side of the inlet is formed by Burnaby Island, and from the northwestern angle Burnaby Strait runs northward to Juan Perez Sound, and separates Burnaby Island from the east shore of Moresby Island. The shores of Skincuttle Inlet resemble those of other parts of the islands already described. Near the northwestern angle of the inlet the mountains rise steeply to a height of 3,000 feet or more.

The entrance to Skincuttle Inlet is south of a chain of islands called the Copper Islands. It is 1½ miles wide, but should be used with caution as there is reason to believe that a rock, sometimes bare, lies in it. The passage to the north of the Copper Islands is contracted, and with one or more rocks in its narrowest part.

Granite Point is a rather remarkable whitish crag, separated from the main shore by a narrow neck of low land.

The Bolkus Islands, five in number, with many small rocks and reefs, form a chain about 2 miles long, lying east and west in the center of Skincuttle Inlet. The land is low, and on the western and largest of the islands the soil appears to be good, though covered with dense forest.

A rock awash at high water lies midway between the Bolkus Islands and the southern shore, and at equal distances from the entrances to Harriet Harbor and Huston Inlet. Bush Rock lies at the distance of 200 yards northwest of the eastern entrance point of Huston Inlet, and 1,600 yards N. 67° W. of it is Low Black Rock.

Harriet Harbor is the first opening on the southern shore of Skincuttle Inlet. It should be entered by the channel on the western side of Harriet Island, which lies at its entrance, and a vessel should be kept near the western side of the channel (as several small rocks covered at high water lie along Harriet Island), and run some distance beyond the inner end of the island before anchoring, to avoid the shoal bank which lies off its point. The depth is about 8 fathoms, with good holding ground, and the harbor is well sheltered from most directions, though subject to heavy squalls from the valley at its head when a southerly gale is blowing.

Huston Inlet, 1½ miles west of Harriet Harbor, is a wide inlet which runs southeastward about 4 miles, and then turns to the west, in which direction its extremity was not visited, but it approaches the western side of Moresby Island to within about 1½ miles.

Tangle Cove.—At the western end of Skincuttle Inlet are three indentations of the coast, of which the southern is George Harbor. The northern, lying at the entrance of Burnaby Strait, is Tangle Cove, a well sheltered anchorage for a small vessel, but a shoal, the extent of which is unknown, lies off its entrance. The entrance is between a small island, at its southern side, and two other little islets to the north, and in it is a rock which uncovers at low water. The mountains at the head of Tangle Cove are steep, and probably reach 3,000 feet in height; part of their upper slopes are bare of trees, but apparently covered with moss, where not composed of rock.

North Side.—On the south shore of Burnaby Island is a bay, with several small islands across the mouth of it, which may be a good harbor, but it has not been examined. Farther east, in the vicinity of an abandoned copper mine, are Blue Jay and Kingfisher Coves.

Burnaby Strait is 9 miles in length between Skincuttle Inlet and Juan Perez Sound, the southern portion for a distance of about 4 miles being narrow, but gaining at the northern end an average width of 1¼ miles. All parts of Burnaby Strait must be navigated with great caution, as there are many rocks, and a large portion of them are covered at high water.

Dolomite Narrows, at 2½ miles north of Skincuttle Inlet, are not more than ¼ mile wide, and here the channel is crooked, and obstructed by rocks and shoals, having from 6 to 8 feet at low water. The tides, however, are not strong, but it can not be recommended as a passage for any craft larger than a boat or canoe. Just south of Dolomite Narrows, from the west side of the strait, opens Bag Harbor, expanding within to a basin nearly one mile in diameter

The Twins.—Nearly abreast of Dolomite Narrows, on Burnaby Island, are 2 conspicuous mountains estimated at 1,500 feet in height.

Island Bay, at 1½ miles north of the narrows, extends westward, and is 2 miles deep. It was so named from the number of small islands in it, abont 17, and is probably too rocky for a safe harbor.

Skaat Harbor, at the north end of Burnaby Strait, is a bay 2¾ miles wide, with a depth of about 3 miles. Wanderer Island and several smaller islets lie off the entrance. The harbor turns into a narrow inlet in its upper part, and terminates among high mountains. Skaat Harbor has not been carefully examined, but from the character of its shores it would be likely to afford good anchorage, especially westward of Wanderer Island, and if so, it is the best for large vessels in this vicinity. The harbor will probably be found deepest on the Wanderer Island side, as there is an extensive field of kelp off the opposite shore. All Alone Stone and Monument Rock form good marks to the northern entrance of Burnaby Strait, near which lies the entrance to the harbor. The entrance to Skaat Harbor on the southern side of Wanderer Island is very narrow, at the angle formed between it and the shore of Burnaby Strait are two small coves affording anchorage for a small vessel, but with wide tidal flats at their head, which a short distance beyond low water mark fall away rapidly into deep water.

Limestone Rock is a dangerous reef, dry only at low water, but not extensive, though a second rock, also only dry at low water, lies a short distance southeast of it. The eastern point of Wanderer Island, in line with that of Center Island, leads clear of Limestone Rock, one mile to the southward of the second rock.

Huxley Island, at the northern entrance of Burnaby Strait, is nearly 2 miles long north and south, and about 1¼ miles broad; it is bold and remarkable, rising rapidly from the beach to a height of 1,500 feet. Abreast the NW. point of the island, in mid-channel, a cast of 70 fathoms was obtained, with a fine sandy bottom.

Burnaby Island.—The north shore of Burnaby Island, 5¾ miles in length, is nearly straight, though it has a few shallow bays, one of which is called Section Cove.

Alder Island lies about the center of this stretch of coast, it is about ½ mile in diameter, nearly flat, with probably a good anchorage behind it, which should be approached from the north, as Saw Reef runs out from the shore of Burnaby Island to the eastward, and this part of the coast is broken and rocky, with large fields of kelp extending from it.

Scudder Point.—From Scudder Point, the northeastern point of Burnaby Island, the eastern side of the island trends southwestward, allowing the outer of the Copper Islands to be seen. A considerable width of low land stretches back from Scudder Point, covered with an open growth of large but gnarled spruces. Little beaches of coarse gravel fill the spaces between the low shattered rock masses, apparently caused by the action of a heavy surf. In a cove on the north side is a strongly built but abandoned Indian house. North of Granite Point is a deep bay with a high island lying in the mouth of it.

Juan Perez Sound has at its entrance between the north of Burnaby Island and Ramsay Island, a width of 8 miles. The sound extends westward, a number of smaller inlets and bays branching off from it, and is continued in a more northerly direction by Darwin Sound, by which it communicates with the upper ends of the long inlets which extend westward from Laskeek Bay.

On its southwestern side are Werner Bay, Hutton Inlet, and De la Beche Inlet, which terminate in narrow channels or fiords, extending among the mountains, and which have not been examined to their heads. From Werner Bay two small inlets branch. Hutton Inlet appears to be about 3 miles long, De la Beche nearly 6 miles, with a low valley, hemmed in by hills on either side running northwestward from its extremity. None of these openings seem to be well adapted for harbors, as the shores are bold and rocky, seldom showing beaches, and the water to all appearances too deep for anchorage.

Bischoff Islands, lying in the northwestern part of Juan Perez Sound off the southern side of Lyell Island, are low, but densely wooded. There is sheltered anchorage for small craft between the two larger islands, but it must be entered from the westward, and with much caution, owing to the number of rocks and sunken reefs which surround it.

Sedgwick Bay, about 3 miles deep, on the southern shore of Lyell Island, is too much exposed for a harbor, as southerly winds draw directly up Juan Perez Sound.

Ramsay, Murchison, and Faraday Islands are the largest of a group of islands forming the northeastern side of Juan Perez Sound.

Ramsay Island is 2½ miles in length east and west, has bold hills rising in the center, and is densely wooded. Its southern shore is high, with some rocky cliffs; two small islets lie off the northeastern side, which is rugged and composed of solid rock. The NW. shore has several coves, but none suited for anchorage.

Murchison Island is 2½ miles long, and Faraday Island nearly 2 miles; both are low.

Between Ramsay and Murchison Islands is a small group composed of Hot Spring, House, and a few smaller islets and rocks. On the southern side of Hot Spring Island is the spring from which it has its name. Its situation is easily recognized by a patch of green, mossy, sward which can be seen from a considerable distance, steam also generally hovers over it. The temperature is so high that the hand can scarcely bear it with comfort. The water has a slight smell of sulphuretted hydrogen, and a barely perceptible saline taste. The Indians bathe in a natural pool in which the waters of one of the streams collect

Anchorage.—Between Hot Spring and House Islands is a good anchorage for small craft, sheltered on all sides but the north

Tar Islands.—Extending northward from the end of Murchison Island is a chain of small islands about 4 miles long, named the Tar Islands, as the Indians report that on one of them bituminous matter is found, oozing out among the stones on the beach. Agglomerate Island, the southernmost, has apparently been burnt over, and is covered with standing dead trees These islands are only approximately placed on the chart. Northward of them lies a single low island with a few trees on it, named Tuft Island.

Rocks dry at low water lie between Faraday and Murchison Islands, and there are several small rocky islets and low water rocks in the vicinity of Hot Spring and House Islands

Entering Juan Perez Sound.—Vessels entering the sound had best do so to the southward of Ramsay Island No bottom was reached with 94 fathoms of line in the center of the sound south of Ramsay Island, nor at about one mile SE. of the extremity of Bischoff Island. The water is apparently deep throughout, but it has not been sounded

Lyell Island, about 15 miles in diameter east and west, and 9 miles north and south, is separated from Moresby Island by Darwin Sound. The island is composed of hilly land. It is densely wooded, and on the low land has some fine timber. The east coast has not been surveyed. Atli Inlet, on the northern side of Lyell Island, has not been examined: it is about 3 miles deep, with two main arms, and does not appear to be a good harbor

Halibut Bank.—About 3 to 4 miles east of the NE point of Lyell Island is Halibut Bank, with 23 fathoms water on it.

Darwin Sound lies between Lyell and Moresby Islands, and from its southern entrance to White Point is 12 miles in length, in width it is irregular, but it is a fine navigable channel. In the south entrance no bottom was found at 94 fathoms When entering from the southward, Shuttle Island appears to be nearly round. The channel on its eastern side should be followed, as this seems to be quite free from impediments. Abreast the northern end of Shuttle Island in this channel a cast of 18 fathoms was obtained. A mile beyond this point, and in mid-channel, is a low rock which is not readily seen, with a second, uncovered only at low water, a short distance to the north of it.

Tides.—The flood sets up Darwin Sound from the southward into the various inlets, and then eastward to the open sea again by Richardson and Logan Inlets. The ebb in like manner draws through from end to end in the opposite direction. The tidal stream runs at the rate of 2 knots at the strongest.

Bigsby Inlet.—The southwestern side of Darwin Sound for 5 miles from the south entrance is rocky and broken, with several coves and inlets. At that distance is Bigsby Inlet, extending 2½ miles in a westerly direction. It is a gloomy chasm, scarcely ½ mile in width, and surrounded by mountains probably as high as any in the islands. The inlet is almost void of anything like a beach.

Shuttle Island, though low, is rocky. The channel to the west of it is probably deep enough for vessels of any class, but should not be used until surveyed. There is a rock, covered at high water, on the west side of its northern entrance.

Echo Harbor.—At 1½ miles northward of Shuttle Island, and opposite the inner end of Richardson Inlet, is Echo Harbor. The passage into the harbor runs southward about one mile, and is surrounded by high hills, which, toward its head, rise to rugged mountains. The outer part of the entrance has a depth of 10 fathoms in it, the sides then approach, leaving a channel scarcely 300 yards wide between abrupt rocky shores.

In the harbor proper the depth is everywhere about 15 fathoms, decreasing gradually toward the head for a short distance, and then running steeply up to a flat which is partly dry at low water, and above high-water mark forms a narrow, grassy beach. The bottom is soft mud, and excellent holding ground. A very narrow passage leads westward from the bottom of the harbor into a secluded basin, scarcely ¼ mile in diameter, which, with the exception of a channel in the middle, is nearly dry at low water. Into its head flows a large brook, coming from the mountains to the southwestward.

Klunkwoi Bay.—At 2 miles west of the entrance to Echo Harbor, the shore line falls back in Klunkwoi Bay. The bay runs up in several arms, which have not been carefully examined, among the bases of rugged snow clad mountains, which rise steeply from the shores. The mountains of Moresby Island appear to culminate here, and are not such a prominent feature further southward.

Crescent Inlet may be considered as forming the extension of Darwin Sound northward. It turns gradually through nearly half a circle from a northwest bearing to a direction nearly southwest, and is over 4 miles in length. It is a fiord, with steep mountains and wooded sides, but probably not so deep as most similar inlets, as there are stretches of beach of some length. Red top mountain, partly bare, is the most conspicuous peak in the vicinity, rising on the northern side of the inlet, at the angle of the bend.

Laskeek Bay is the name given to the wide indentation of the coast between the northeastern extreme of Lyell Island and Vertical Point, the southeast point of Louise Island, and 10 miles apart. From Laskeek Bay 4 large inlets extend westward; of these the 2 southern, Richardson and Logan Inlets, open into the head of Darwin Sound.

The two northern inlets, Dana and Selwyn, communicate at their heads with the head of Cumshewa Inlet to the northward.

Richardson Inlet is about 11 miles in length in an east and west direction, with an average breadth of 1½ miles, and is straight, with moderately bold shores. Atli Inlet is just within the entrance, and Dog Island about 5 miles within it; Kunga, Tanoo, and Inner Islands, from east to west, form the northern side. Kunga Island is about 1,500 feet high, and forms a good mark for the entrance; there is a low, rocky reef some distance eastward of the outer point of Kunga, and a second off the south shore of the same island. Near Dog Island there are several small islets and rocks; and at about 3½ miles west of it, on the southern side of the inlet, is a cove, where a small vessel can find a convenient anchorage, probably the nearest stopping place to Laskeek village. The channels between Kunga and Tanoo and the latter and Inner Islands are probably deep, though the first should be navigated with caution, and care taken to avoid the east end of Tanoo Island, as several rocks and patches of kelp lie off it.

Laskeek or Klue Indian village is on the eastern extremity of Tanoo Island. It is one of the most populous still remaining in the Queen Charlotte Islands. The village, extending round a rocky point, faces two ways, which prevents its being wholly seen from any one point of view. The western end of Richardson Inlet is contracted to a width of about ¼ mile, and obstructed by a small island and several rocks.

Anchorage has been obtained in 11 fathoms, about 400 yards east of the village. This anchorage is not a good one, being exposed to NW. and SE winds, and is steep close-to. On anchoring the houses should not be brought to bear south of N. 64° W., as patches of rock stretch out two thirds the distance across to the opposite shore from Laskeek Point, so that going or coming from the north the east shore should be kept well on aboard, it being steep-to and quite safe. In the season, kelp marks the patches.

The Tide runs through this passage with considerable strength, and it is unsuited as an approach to Echo Harbor, though the most direct way in from the sea.

Logan Inlet is nearly parallel to Richardson Inlet, with Flower Pot Island, a small bold rock covered with trees, off its mouth. One other small island lies close to the shore on its southern side, but it is otherwise free from obstructions, and constitutes a fine navigable channel, the best approach to Echo Harbor.

Vessels should enter to the north of Flower Pot Island and keep in the center of the channel. Kunga Island, as already mentioned, is high. Tatul Island, small and with low limestone cliffs, lies northward of it. Tanoo and Inner Islands are also bold, rising to rounded hills of nearly uniform height of about 800 feet. They have some good gravelly beaches, though mostly rocky.

Dana Inlet, with bold shores, has at its entrance Helmet Island, small, rocky, high, and of rounded form. A second small island is near it, and from most points of view the channel between the two is not seen, and care is necessary not to mistake this island for Flower Pot Island, at the entrance to Logan Inlet. At its western extremity Dana Inlet turns northward, communicating by a narrow but apparently deep passage with Selwyn Inlet.

Talunkwan Island is 8 miles long, and 2 miles broad, the hills are rounded in form, and from 800 to 900 feet high.

Selwyn Inlet is nearly parallel to Dana Inlet, and near its head turns northward, forming at high water a passage for canoes into the upper part of Cumshewa Inlet. The passage is narrow and walled in on both sides by mountains which rise very steeply from it Entrance Island is small and lies off the northern entrance point with a low rock about one mile eastward of it. With the exception of a small rock about the middle of Talunkwan Island and near the southern shore, the inlet appears to be free from dangers.

After giving the islets off the north entrance a wide berth, a vessel should keep the northern shore for a distance of 5 miles until the entrance of Rock fish Harbor is reached.

Rock-fish Harbor is formed by a boot shaped projection of low land at the angle of Selwyn Inlet, and extends in a westerly direction for about $1\frac{1}{2}$ miles, with a width of $\frac{1}{2}$ mile, and an average depth of 15 fathoms It is a secure and well sheltered anchorage, more easily entered than Cumshewa.

At about 3 miles from the entrance of the passage leading to Cumshewa is the opening to an inlet about 3 miles deep in a southwesterly direction, approaching to within $4\frac{1}{2}$ miles of Mitchell Harbor. These upper arms of Selwyn Inlet are environed by high and rugged mountains.

Reef and Low Islands lie in the outer part of Laskeek Bay. The southern and first named is steep along the water's edge, and a reef runs off about half a mile to the southward from it. Their exact position is not known.

Louise Island is about 15 miles long east and west, and 8 miles broad, with high mountains, and doubtless the snow on them lasts throughout the summer. From Selwyn Inlet the east coast of the island trends northeastward 8 miles, with several small bays, fully open to the sea, and mostly rocky.

Vertical Point projects at about half-way along this stretch of shore, and is remarkable from the shape of the beds of gray limestone of which it is composed, aggregating at least 400 feet in thickness. North of the point are two small limestone islands, behind which the tide, running southward along the coast, forms a race on the ebb.

Skedans Bay, about 2 miles from the entrance to Cumshewa, is strewn with sunken rocks and fully open, and should not be entered by vessels. A large stream enters its head, which can be seen at some distance inland forming a high waterfall, and which, according to the Indians, flows out of a lake of some size, high among the mountains. Skedans Village forms a semi-circle round the head of a small bay or cove, very rocky, which indents the south side of a narrow isthmus, connecting two remarkable nipple-shaped hills with the main shore. This peninsula is situated at the southern entrance point to Cumshewa Inlet, and between it and the Skedans Islands the tide forms a race. Skedans Islands, distant 3½ miles from the shore, are low and covered with trees.

Cumshewa Inlet is a long inlet extending about 15 miles westward, with a prolongation southward connecting it with Selwyn Inlet. It differs in the low character of the land on its northern shore from the inlets to the south, and marks the junction, on the east coast of the islands, of the mountain region and flat country. There is more beach along the shores than in the southern inlets, and wide tide-flats, indicating shoaler water, which is not only found in the inlet itself, but extends off the coast. Towards the head of the inlet, the shores are quite bold in some places, and the water probably deep.

In the entrance of Cumshewa Inlet, to the north of Skedans Islands, are depths of 20 fathoms, with a shell and gravel bottom. Off the north point of entrance, Cumshewa Island, a small barren rock, and the Cumshewa Rocks, extend in a southeasterly direction nearly 1½ miles. Vessels coming from the north should keep well off the shore till the rocks are passed, and then stand in to the entrance in a northwesterly direction. On the outer point, near Cumshewa Island, are the ruins of an abandoned village.

Kingui Island, just within the north entrance point, on the northern side of the inlet, is covered with dead trees, and can be recognized easily. At about one mile within the entrance, an extensive shoal, on which the sea breaks heavily, runs off from the south shore, leaving a channel about ½ mile wide between it and the north shore of the inlet. The passage in is through this channel, in which it is reported there are depths of 7 and 8 fathoms. The southern point of a peninsula which projects from the northern shore of the inlet, bearing N. 66° W., just clears the northern edge of the shoal. A few patches of the shoal dry at low water, but the greater part is indicated only by the kelp which grows thickly on it during the summer. The tides run strongly in the mouth of the inlet.

McKay Cove.—Within the narrows, on the northern shore, is a cove, where a small house for the purpose of trade was built, but is now abandoned. The shore dries out for some distance at low water, but off it a small vessel may find a pretty secure anchorage, though the tide sweeps round the cove.

Cumshewa Village is also on the northern side of the inlet, about one mile westward of McKay Cove, the houses being built along the shore of a bay facing southeastward, 3½ miles within the entrance. A small rocky islet, connected with the main at low water, lies off it.

Anchorage.—The best anchorage for a large vessel is probably to be found on the southern side, nearly opposite the peninsula before alluded to, and abreast a stretch of low land, eastward of a stream.

The Coast—From the entrance to Cumshewa Inlet, the coast runs northwestward to Spit Point, the south point of Skidegate Inlet, a distance of 17 miles. It is indented by two considerable bays. Copper Bay—the northern—about 5 miles from Spit Point, received its name from some copper works which were carried on there at one time The land is low, and very different in appearance from that of the coast southward. The projecting points are mostly low and flat, and formed of gravel deposits. With the change in the character of the land, the beach becomes flat, and shoal water extends far off shore, the depth shoaling from 10 fathoms at 3 miles off Cumshewa Island, to 6 and 7 fathoms at 7 miles off Spit Point. Near Cumshewa the beaches are almost entirely composed of bowlders, but show more gravel and sand toward Skidegate. The surface of the country is densely wooded with trees of large size.

Cape Chroustcheff, 2 miles to the southward of Spit Point, should not be passed nearer than 5 miles; the cape is low and dark-looking. Coming from the southward, it shows very conspicuous; when abreast of it, Spit Point, the low southern point of Skidegate, becomes visible.

Skidegate Inlet, separating Moresby from Graham Island, forms a spacious harbor communicating with the Pacific at Buck Point, south of Cartwright Sound, by an intricate channel, only navigable for canoes a portion of the way. Skidegate Inlet from its entrance extends in a southwesterly direction for about 9 miles from the Bar Rocks, where it contracts to a width of 1¼ miles between Image Point and Flowery Islet. Within these points it opens again, forming two expansions, separated by Maude Island. That part of the northern expansion eastward of Lina Island forms Bear Skin Bay; the part westward of the island has several islands in it, with Anchor Cove in the western end. Beyond Anchor Cove it turns northwestward, forming Long Arm. The southern expansion forms South Bay, in which is South Island, its western side passing into Skidegate Channel and thence to the Pacific.

The shores of Skidegate Inlet are not so bold as those of the fiords to the south, and are mostly fringed with a beach of greater or less width. The surrounding country is densely wooded, and where the land is flat, timber of magnificent growth is found.

Spit Point is low and wooded and composed of sand deposits, which, extending northward, form the bar which stretches across the entrance to Skidegate Inlet.

The Bar or spit, with from one to 3 fathoms water on it, extends in a northwesterly direction for about 9¼ miles to within nearly 1½ miles of Lawn Point, the northern point of entrance. The Spit slopes off very gradually seaward, while toward the inlet it rapidly deepens to 20 or 30 fathoms.

Bar Rocks, on the outer edge of the Spit, 2½ miles from its extremity, are two in number; the western one dries 5 feet, and lies 6¾ miles N. 12° W. of Spit Point; the outer or eastern rock dries one foot at low water and bears N. 9° W. the same distance from Spit Point; 800 yards N. 82° E. of the inner rock; and 3 miles N. 77° E. of Dead Tree Point. The sea does not always break on these rocks. Lawn Point, bearing N. 56° W., leads to the northward of Bar Rocks.

Lawn Point is generally green, with a small sand cliff and a large bowlder in front of it; a hill 500 feet high rises immediately to the westward of the point. The coast southward of Lawn Point is flat for 10 miles to Village Bay, and is covered with standing dead trees. The point is not easily distinguished when the grass is dried up.

Dead Tree Point, 3¾ miles to the southward of Lawn Point, is a projecting part of the coast, but otherwise is not conspicuous. It can only be seen as a tangent when on a north and south bearing.

Village Islands, in front of Village Bay, form good marks for Skidegate Inlet; the northern one (Bare Islet) is almost bare, and the other (Tree Islet), has trees upon it.

The village of Skidegate, nearly ½ mile in length, is in the bay, off which are the Village Islands, and consists of many houses, with the usual carved posts, fronting the beach.

Village Bay is a good stopping place; anchorage may be taken up between Bare Islet and the beach in 14 fathoms. It is exposed to SE. winds. Should one of these gales spring up, good shelter will be found in Alliford Bay.

Image Point.—In the cove at Image Point some rude buildings have been erected in connection with the dog-fish fishery.

Alliford Bay is an excellent anchorage, with good holding ground, in about 9 fathoms. The passage between Flowery Islet and the northern point of the bay, should not be used. Wood and water may be obtained.

Anchor Cove, in the western part of the inlet, affords anchorage in 5 fathoms. This is the place of export for the anthracite coal, found on both shores of the inlet, but principally on the sides of mount Seymour, one mile to the northward of the cove. The coal has been mined, a small railway being laid to Anchor Cove.

Slate Chuck Brook is the largest stream in Skidegate Inlet, its mouth being about one mile north of Anchor Cove. The brook receives its name from a quarry a few miles up its course, where the Indians obtain the dark shaly material from which they make carvings.

Leading Island forms the western part of Allıford Bay, is 400 feet high, and appears round

Maude Island is nearly 4 miles long, WSW. and ENE., 1½ miles broad, and 1,260 feet high On the western end of the island the Indians belonging to Gold Harbor (on the west coast) have established a village.

Skidegate Channel extends from South Bay for 15 miles to the Pacific. From South Bay to Log Point, a distance of 8½ miles, the channel is contracted, particularly in the East and West Narrows, the former in one part being only 200 feet wide, and the latter 400 yards The tides from east and west meet about the East Narrows, running through the channel with great strength, probably 5 knots in several places. The narrows must be passed at slack water of high tide, which lasts for a very short time, so that both narrows can not be got through in one tide.

Directions.—From the northeastward Lawn Point makes like a bluff sloping towards the north. Large ships should bring Lawn Point to bear S. 71° W and steer for it, the water will gradually shoal from 10 and 12 fathoms at 4 miles off, to 5 and 4½ fathoms at about one mile from the point, when it suddenly deepens to 12 and 20 fathoms. From this position, Welcome Point, which appears as a low and grassy patch under Table Mountain (but is difficult to distinguish), should bear S. 6° W. If it does not, bring it on that bearing and exactly in line with the left tangent of the highest part of Table Mountain. This will lead in between the Bar Rock spit and the shoal extending from Lawn Point to Dead Tree Point, and up to the leading marks. This course will lead very close to the northwestern point of the Bar Rock Spit, if not over the extremity of it in 3 fathoms at low water. The deep portion of the channel from opposite Lawn Point till past the northwestern point of Bar Rock Spit (or until the bowlder at Lawn Point bears N. 53° W.) is only ⅓ mile wide; attention to the lead and steering, with a sharp look out, is therefore necessary, for, as previously remarked, Welcome Point is not readily distinguished.

The west side of Leading Island, in line with the east side of Bare Island bearing S. 26° W., leads over the Bar Rock Spit, to the northward of the rocks, in 15 feet at low water, from whence the depth is from 20 to 30 fathoms to Village Island, passing to the southward of these Islands anchorage may be found in the northeastern side of Bear Skin Bay in 12 fathoms, or, to gain shelter from a SE. gale, Allıford Bay is recommended.

Coasting vessels with local knowledge use a passage with 3½ fathoms over the spit, about one mile south of the Bar Rocks (when they are visible), by keeping Dead Tree Point bearing N. 88° W. until the leading mark comes on.

Approaching Skidegate Inlet the water should not be shoaled under 6 fathoms at low water until Lawn Point bears S. 71° W. or the leading marks are on.

The Coast.—From Lawn Hill, near Lawn Point at the entrance of Skidegate, to Rose Point, the northeastern extreme of Graham Island, the distance is about 48 miles. The coast line is straight and open, with no harbor, and scarcely a creek or protected cove for canoes or boats for long distances The beach is gravelly and sometimes stony to the Tlell River, beyond this it is mostly sandy to Rose Point. For many miles northward cliffs of clay and sand are found alongshore, and for about 17 miles northward of Tlell River these frequently rise into cliffs 50 to 100 feet in height. North of the range of cliffs the shore is almost everywhere bordered by sand hills, which are covered with coarse grass, beach pea, etc Behind these are woods, in some places burnt, and the trees generally scrubby. This part of the coast is also characterized by lagoons, and is evidently extending seaward, by the banking up of the sand under the action of the sea. The largest lagoon opens out at Cape Fife about 6 miles to the southward of Rose Point, extending southward for some miles, and is reported by the Indians to communicate with a second further inland. The mouth of this lagoon forms a safe harbor for boats or canoes at high water, but is nearly dry at low water

The coast between Skidegate and Rose Point having dangerous flats extending off it, which have not been examined, should be given a berth of 6 or 7 miles, and the lead kept constantly going whilst running along it, the depths varying from 9 to 11 fathoms.

Tlell River enters the sea at 10½ miles north of Lawn Point, and is a stream of some size. For about 3 miles above its mouth it runs nearly parallel to the shore, separated from the sea by a low swampy strip of land only about half a mile in breadth A ruined Indian house stands about 3 miles south of the mouth of the river. The water of the river is of a dark coffee or amber color.

Cape Ball (Kultowsis) is very conspicuous, having a remarkable white cliff on it, with lower cliffs on both sides; it can not be mistaken. The Indians report that at very low tides patches of clay dry a long way off from the cape. In the bay north of Cape Ball are the remains of an Indian village.

Rock.—A rock with 2 fathoms on it, lies about 6 miles ESE. of Cape Ball.

Cape Fife.—Near this cape on some parts of the shore magnetic iron sand is abundant, with numerous colors of gold in it. There is anchorage off the cape with offshore winds; in this neighborhood the lead must be most carefully attended to.

Rose Point is known to the Haida Indians as Naikoon, or long nose. It is a remarkable low promontory, apparently formed by the meeting of the currents and waves from the southward and westward round this corner of the island. The inner part of Rose Point, near Cape Fife, does not differ from the low wooded coast to the south; the Indians say there are many lakes and swamps inland. Further out, where the point is narrower and more exposed, it is clothed with small stunted wood, which in turn give place to waving grass-covered sand hills. Beyond this the narrow gravelly point is covered above high water mark with heaps of drifting sand, and great quantities of bleached timber, logs, and stumps piled promiscuously together. The apex of the point is a narrow, steep sided, gravelly bank, which extends for a long distance at low water.

A dangerous spit extends off Rose Point in a northeasterly direction, for, it is said, a distance of nearly 5 miles, but its exact extent has not been ascertained The point should, therefore, especially in dark or thick weather, be given a wide berth Several vessels have been lost on Rose Point, which is a dangerous and treacherous point to round at any time, except in fine clear weather.

Hecate Strait, is 75 miles wide at its southern entrance, gradually narrowing to 25 miles between Rose Spit (Graham Island), and the Butterworth Rocks on the eastern side of the strait. In the fairway of the southeastern part of Hecate Strait the water is deep. From Skidegate across to within 10 miles of the mainland, in a NE. direction, the depths are from 8 to 25 fathoms, in some cases, growing kelp has been seen in 8 and 13 fathoms.

With the center of Zayas Island bearing N. 9° E., and the north extreme of Stephens Island N. 84° E., the depth is 15 fathoms. This bank of soundings may be found useful in thick weather for temporary anchorage.

From the vicinity of Masset a bank of sand not exceeding 20 fathoms extends to the north and east, trending with Rose Spit, and on the east side of the island extending towards Cumshewa, its eastern margin reaching the middle part of Hecate Strait The average depth of water is from 7 to 10 fathoms, but there are much shoaler parts. This bank was named Dogfish Bank by Ingraham in 1791. Near its eastern edge he places, in latitude 53° 50′ and about 30 miles SE. of Invisible Point, a rock or shoal on which the ship *Margaret* struck in 1792 drawing 13 feet. Near the spot he notes 3 fathoms, deepening to 5, 7, and 12 fathoms eastward

Shoal.—In latitude 53° 26′ N., long 131° 6′ W., approximate, a shoal has been reported, but its position is doubtful

Tides—In Hecate Strait, the flood tide sets to the northward In Dixon Entrance, the flood coming from the westward round North Island, sets along the Masset shore, across Hecate Strait for Brown Passage, spreading for about 15 miles round Rose Point, towards Cape Ibbetson (Edye Passage), where it meets the flood from the southward; consequently between Rose Point, Cape Ball, Cape Ibbetson, and thence southeastward 15 or 20 miles, the tides are irregular.

The direction and rate of the tidal streams are not regular, being greatly influenced by the winds. At full and change they run with great strength. Time of high water over the strait generally is about 0h. 30m.

Between Cape Murray, Percy Point, and Zayas Island the tides are the strongest and most irregular, causing a heavy and confused sea, so much so, that in bad weather it has the appearance of breakers.

Rose Point to Masset Sound.—The shore between these two places forms a bay 22 miles in width. With the exception of a few small rocky points, the beach is smooth and regular, and almost altogether composed of sand with gravel in some places, sloping steeply above the ordinary high-water mark. Low sand hills generally form a border to the woods which densely cover the land. The water is shoal far off the shore, especially at 15 miles from Rose Point, and on approaching Masset Sound, where kelp forms wide fields at a great distance from the beach. In the northeastern part of the bay there is anchorage with off shore winds.

Hiellen River, at 9 miles southwestward of Rose point, is a stream of some size, which is frequented by great numbers of salmon in the autumn Its mouth forms a good boat harbor On its east bank are the ruins of an Indian village, and on its west, Tow Hill, an eminence remarkable in this low country, facing the sea with a steep cliff 200 feet high.

Masset Harbor should be approached with caution, the entrance is between a low point with a ledge of rocks covered with kelp, extending ½ mile from it on the western side, and the point of a long spit partly dry (the surf usually breaking the whole length of it) on the eastern, the passage between having an extensive bar.

Just inside and around the eastern point of inner entrance is a pretty bay, with a beach, containing the principal village (Uttewas), off the center of which there is anchorage in 10 fathoms. At this part the width of the harbor is nearly 2 miles, a large sand bank filling up its western side. The ebb tide runs very strong, making this by no means a good anchorage.

In 1878 the Hudson Bay Company had a post at Uttewas, the only one on the islands, the Church Missionary Society also had a station here which had been established 2 years About one mile south of this place, also on the east shore, is a second village, and on the opposite side a third. They are all decaying, and have comparatively few inhabitants.

Directions—With the outer western point bearing N. 53° W one mile, the depth is 5 fathoms at low water; from this position the course in is about S 9° W., the depths over the bar varying from 5 to 3 fathoms, for about 3 miles, to abreast a village on the western shore a little more than one mile from what may be termed the inner or proper entrance to the harbor; the water then suddenly deepens to 9 and 11 fathoms, the channel lying in the direction of the eastern point of what has been called the inner entrance, and the depth, at about 400 yards from the beach that forms it, being from 10 to 13 fathoms A safe mark for going in to the outer anchorage is a small islet inside the channel in line with the outer eastern point bearing S. 25° E, or if the islet can not be seen, a point will be seen open on that bearing. With winds from seaward the outer anchorage is uncomfortable owing to the tide keeping the ship swung across the swell. The plan of this harbor has been reported defective and should be used with caution.

Masset Sound, from its seaward entrance to the point at which it expands to Masset Inlet, is 19 miles long, and about one mile in average width, and, though slightly tortuous, preserves nearly the parallelism of its sides. The depth, ascertained in a few places, varies from 10 to 12 fathoms. A number of small streams flow into it, most of which, according to Indian reports, have their sources in small lakes. At 3 miles up the sound a lagoon or arm runs off on the eastern side. Nearly opposite this place, on the west side is Maast Island. It lies across a bay which seems at first sight to offer better anchorage than that already referred to. The island is low and sandy, and a great part of the bay or passage behind it is dry at low water. On the eastern side at 4½ miles from the southern or inner end of the sound, where its trend is nearly SW. and NE a narrow passage runs off southward, joining the expanded portion of Masset Inlet, and forming a large island, which is mostly lower than the surrounding country. This passage is partly dry at low water, and is occasionally used by the Indians in canoes.

At its southern end, the narrow part of the inlet, which has been called the sound, expands suddenly to a large sheet of inland water. The western half of the inlet is studded with islands, and it is rather irregular in outline, forming four large bays or inlets, with intervening mountainous points. The shores are steep, with narrow bowlder beaches sloping down at once into deep water. About the heads of the inlets and near the mouths of streams only are small areas of flat ground found. Of these inlets, that which reaches farthest southward is called by the Indians Tinlnowe

Tsooskatli —On the southern side of the inlet is a narrow passage, the mouth of which is partly blocked by islands, but which leads into a second great inlet known by the Indians as Tsooskatli, or "the belly of the rapid." The largest of the islands in this passage is named Shpatia. Kelp grows abundantly in the channel on both sides of the islands, which, therefore, can not be very deep. The tide runs through them with great velocity, especially at ebb, when in the western channel it forms a true rapid, with much broken water.

Its eastern side is formed of low land, while its southwestern extremity is a long, fiord-like inlet. In this inlet are many islands; the largest, Hasheions, is nearly one mile in diameter and about 200 feet high The eastern portion of the southern shore is rocky, with many small islets off it. On the eastern side of Tsooskatli, 2½ miles from its extremity, is Towustasin, a remarkable hill, with a steep cliff on one side. The northeastern part of Tsooskatli has a depth of from 10 to 16 fathoms. The depth of the northwestern part, about the center between the large island and the mainland, was 23 fathoms in one place

Yakoun River.—Many streams flow into these inlets; the largest is probably that which is known as Yakoun, and enters the southeastern corner of Masset Inlet, in the bottom of a shoal bay. About the mouth of the Yakoun are large sandy flats, dry at low water. It was formerly navigable for small canoes a long way up, and is reported to head in a large lake On the western side of the bay at the mouth of this river are a few small houses, used during the salmon season.

The Mamin River joins the Tsooskatli Inlet at its eastern end, and has a wide delta flat about its mouth. It is navigable by small canoes for several miles, but is much obstructed by logs

The Awun River, west of the entrance to Tsooskatli, is said to rise in a lake.

Ain River, entering Masset Inlet from the northwestward, is an important stream. There are several Indian houses which are occupied in the summer above its mouth It is said to flow out of a very large fresh water lake of the same name, the river itself being short. The lake is filled with islands, and in the winter is frozen completely over.

Tides.—The rise of a spring tide at the entrance of Masset Sound was estimated at about 14 feet, but, owing to the length of the narrow sound, Masset Inlet has a tide of from 8 to 10 feet only; and the second or Tsooskatli still less, about 6 feet On one occasion, it was high water at the entrance of Masset Sound at 1h. 15m. p. m., while in the narrow entrance to Tsooskatli, 23½ miles distant, the flood had just caused a reversal of the current at 0h. 20m Owing to the great expansion of the upper part of Masset Inlet the tide continues to run up opposite Masset for about 2½ hours after it is falling by the shore, whilst the ebb runs out for about 3 hours after the water has begun to rise on the beach.

Masset to Virago Sound.—The coast between these two places is everywhere low and wooded, with occasional open grassy spaces, differing from the coast east of Masset in being rocky or covered with bowlders. No wide sandy bays occur, and the points are mostly of dark low rocks. The trees along the shore are not of great size and are interspersed with occasional grassy spaces

The water is shoal far offshore, with wide fields of kelp. The shore should be approached with caution, with the lead constantly going

In a N. 54° E. direction from the eastern point of Virago Sound there are soundings for several miles; at 8 miles the depth was 52 fathoms, sand; at 5 miles off, the depths were about the same, at 2 miles there were 28 fathoms, sand, and the water then gradually shoaled in to the shore. Great quantities of drift kelp have been seen.

Anchorages—Between Masset Harbor and Virago Sound there are some good anchorages, in which a vessel might remain a night instead of keeping under way or cruising about with a SE wind and thick weather.

Virago Sound, constituting the entrance to Naden Harbor, is 3½ miles wide between its outer points, Capes Edensaw and Naden; and 2½ miles deep to the narrow passage leading into the harbor.

To the northward of the narrows the western shore between Mary Point and Jorey Point is bordered by a flat extending to a distance of about ½ mile, and on the opposite shore from Cape Edensaw to Inskip Point, a shoal also extends about the same distance; from the latter point a spit runs off to the westward for ⅜ mile, with a depth of 2½ fathoms, contracting the channel, in which the least water is 3¼ fathoms, to a width of 800 yards. From Inskip Point to George Point, the eastern shore is clear of danger

With two small wooded islets on the west side of the entrance, bearing west one mile, Cape Edensaw east 2 miles, and the opening to the inner harbor S 32° W about 2½ miles, the depth is 5½ fathoms water, sand and shells; the shores are low and fringed with kelp, but the lead will be a safe guide, as the water shoals gradually towards the land.

Vessels can always get a pilot by firing a gun and anchoring for a short time. The Indian fishermen will come off and point out any danger that may be in the way for a small recompense.

The inner anchorage, opposite Kung village on the western side, just within the narrows, is in 10 fathoms, at about ¼ mile from shore This village has been nearly abandoned for the new Yatza village on the coast at about 4½ miles NW. of Virago Sound. There is a rather prominent hill behind Klaskwun Point. Above Kung village a bank extends off the eastern side of the narrows nearly half way across, leaving a channel along the western shore, with 7 to 10 fathoms water in it.

Naden Harbor is about 4 miles in greatest length north and south, and 2 miles in width, with depths of 8 to 12 fathoms in it Low land, densely wooded with spruce and hemlock of fine growth, borders the whole harbor Rock appears on the shore only near the bottom of the harbor, and at Kung village in the narrows. The southeastern shore of the harbor is low, with wide tide-flats; the northwestern comparatively bold.

Naden River enters the harbor at its southeastern corner, and is probably the largest river on Queen Charlotte Islands It flows from a large lake, which, according to Indian account, must be 10 miles or more in diameter, but is much encumbered by fallen trees, and its banks, except in a few swampy flats, are densely wooded At high water a boat can proceed about 2 miles up. Stanley (Teka) River, in the southwestern corner of the harbor, is reported to be navigable for boats, and several smaller streams also enter the harbor.

Tides.—The rise and fall is about 13 feet.

Virago Sound to Cape Knox.—From Cape Nadeu the general trend of the shore is westward for about 17 miles to Cape Knox, the northwestern extreme of Graham Island. The shore and country behind it are mostly low, though with some rocky cliffs of no great height, and the points are rocky, but wide gravelly or sandy bays intervene. Some rocks occur at a little distance offshore, but there is no appearance of a wide shoal belt like that found eastward of Masset. Klaskwun Point, 4½ miles from Cape Nadeu, is a remarkable promontory, rising in the center to a hill about 200 feet in height, which, owing to the flat character of other parts of the shore, is visible for a long distance. In a rocky bay to the east of the point, and open to the northeastward, is Yatza village before described.

Jalun River—Half way from Klaskwun Point to the eastern entrance of Parry Passage is Jalun River. This stream is of no great size, but its mouth, in the bottom of a small bay, forms an excellent canoe or boat harbor at high water, and appears to be a favorite stopping place for traveling Indians. At 3 miles further westward is a small promontory, on the east side of which is another excellent boat harbor.

Pillar Bay is so called from a very remarkable columnar mass of sandstone and conglomerate rock which stands near the eastern side, about 25 feet in diameter and 95 feet high. The summit is sloping and covered with some small bushes. It is separated at high water from the main shore, but rises from a sandy and stony flat at low water

Parry Passage separates North Island from Graham Island. The western entrance at the SE. angle of Cloak Bay is ¾ mile wide, but is contracted to less than 600 yards by foul ground which extends in a northerly direction from a point on the southern side of the entrance. The passage proper is about 2 miles in length, with an average width of ¼ mile This channel, between the ledges of rock which extend off the southern side for about one mile and North Island, is clear, but the tide rushes through it, forming a race. The flood runs eastward, leaving the east end of the passage with a northeasterly direction. Two deserted Indian villages (Kakoh and Kioosta) are situated on the southern side of the passage, near its western entrance.

Parry Passage towards its eastern end is separated into two arms by Lucy Island, somewhat less than ¾ mile long and ¼ mile broad. The northern arm is not much over 200 yards wide, the southern or main channel is more than ½ mile wide. The soundings in the main passage are 30 fathoms, with a rocky bottom The shores, except in the narrow western entrance, seem to be clear of dangers. The northern arm, while extremely narrow, is still farther obstructed by foul ground extending off to the northeastward from the eastern shore of Lucy Island less than ½ mile, and a similar bank from the opposite shore of North Island There is a narrow channel having from 4 to 6 fathoms, hard bottom, at the eastern end, and this increases to 15 fathoms in the western part of the arm.

A small islet lies about one mile to the eastward from the eastern entrance to this arm, and a rock awash is reported 2¼ miles N. 71° E. of the same locality, and about 1¼ miles from the southern shore of North Island.

Bruin Bay.—Just without the eastern entrance of Parry Passage, and on the southern side, abreast of Lucy Island, is a bay affording anchorage in from 12 to 14 fathoms, sand. A line of kelp fringes the shore which is studded with rocky patches and stones. This is not a good anchorage except for a temporary stopping place during thick weather, as the flood sets into it from the passage, forming a number of eddies, and rendering it difficult to lie at a single anchor without fouling it. The country at the back is low and covered with trees, with here and there grassy spots.

North Island is about 5 miles in length, between North Point and its southern extreme, and composed of low land It is densely wooded. On the eastern side of North Island there is said to be a good anchorage in a bay which was formerly often used by the vessels belonging to the old Northwest Company. A small round high island situated close to Point North, a prominent object in approaching, is named Thrumb Cape.

Cloak Bay forms the western entrance to Parry Passage. It is about 2½ miles wide, and the same deep; the depths in the middle of the bay vary from 30 to 17 fathoms, sand, gravel and shells. Some rocks, on which the sea breaks only in heavy weather, lie some distance from the North Island shore, and there are also a couple of remarkable pointed islands on this side.

Henslung.—On the southern side of North Island, in Parry Passage, is a snug cove named Henslung, in which whalers used occasionally to anchor At the head of the cove is a sandy beach, with a stream of water running through it

Tides.—It is high water at full and change at Henslung, at 0h 20m., and the rise 16 feet. The night tides are 2 feet higher than the day.

Lucy Island is separated from the south side of North Island by a narrow channel, on the northern shore of which is a small Indian village, called Tartanne. A reef runs off the eastern end of Lucy Island, and a wide shoal with kelp stretches eastward from the shore of the southern extremity of North Island. Between these lies the channel with 8 to 11 fathoms water. Abreast the Indian village the depth in the channel is 6 fathoms

Cape Knox is a long narrow tongue of land, on which are a few low hills. Its southern side is bold, and off it lie several rocks in a westerly direction, the farthest out at a distance of about 3½ miles from the cape. On these the swell of the Pacific seldom ceases to break with great violence.

Directions.—On leaving Bruin Bay or Henslung Cove for the westward, a vessel may pass close to the cliffs forming the southern side of

North Island, and keeping at about ½ mile outside the reefs that extend off the southern shore (Graham Island), get a good offing before hauling to the southward, to clear the rocks off Cape Knox. When well out, the projecting point of Frederick Island will be seen about 18 miles to the southeastward. At 2 or 3 miles to the southward of Parry Passage is an indentation of the shore, which might be taken as its entrance by a vessel coming from the southward—a mistake that might lead to serious consequences, as the whole coast as far as Frederick Island appears to contain several open bays, with outlying rocks off each of them. The Indians, in their sketches of this part of the coast, do not draw any harbors, but merely exposed bays.

Frederick Island is stated to have behind it a commodious harbor. The northern entrance is formed by two high bluffs with some small islets between them. Northward of the entrance on the coast is a large reef of rocks, and westward and southward of the southern point of entrance along the shore of Frederick Island is a large number of sunken rocks. The port extends about 6 miles from the entrance in an easterly direction; is about 2 miles wide, with four small islets near the head. In the vicinity of the islets is some kelp. At the head is a beach and 9 or 10 fathoms water. Towards the head the port curves more to the eastward. The passage eastward of Frederick Island has several islets in it and 6 fathoms water. Some kelp is found in the channel.

Hippa Island appears, from a position 1½ miles seaward of Frederick Island, as high and bold; but from the south, its outer end appears as a low point, and the inner end bold. This portion of the coast is higher and more broken than the former, the openings appearing deeper, neither does it seem to have so many rocks lying off it. The Indians show some good harbors towards Hippa.

Buck Point, on the northern side of Skidegate Channel, is rather low and rugged, jutting out from the high land at the back. It has a large high island just to the northward of it, and there is another, much smaller and peaked, standing out clear of the land at about 3 or 4 miles farther to the northward, and lying in the entrance of Cartwright Sound

Skidegate Channel is a little more than one mile in width, extends in an easterly direction for 6 or 7 miles to Log Point, where it is one mile wide This part of the channel affords no sheltered anchorage At Log Point the West Narrows commence, which lead to Skidegate Inlet. About one mile west of Log Point a branch turns off to the southward for one mile, and then westward to the Pacific, which it enters at about 3 miles to the southward of the main channel, forming an island.

This passage is only adapted for canoes or boats, as it is blocked by a bank at its eastern end, with not more than 4 feet on it at high water.

A vessel entering the main channel from the west might find anchorage in the entrance of this passage where it unites with the main channel.

Inskip Channel, leading round the north side of Kuper Island, is about 8½ miles long, and ½ mile wide. A short distance outside it, there are some small islands on both sides, but there will be no difficulty in discovering the passage in. At a short distance inside the islands on the northern side of the entrance, is a village belonging to the Kilkite tribes. Further in, on the same side, and about 3½ miles up, is a deep opening, and where this and Moore Channel meet are two other openings to harbors with some small islands lying near them.

Moore Channel, on the southern side of Kuper Island, is 5 miles long in an east and west direction, and ½ mile wide, the shore on each side being bold of approach, high, and covered with trees nearly down to the water's edge On the northern side, just without the entrance, are some small rocky islets, named Moresby Islands, and on the southern side, a few rocks close in shore.

Mitchell or Gold Harbor, about 2½ miles deep and ½ mile wide, is surrounded by precipitous and densely wooded hills, from 700 to 800 feet in height, and at its head in Thetis Cove is a sandy beach and a stream of water. At 1¼ miles up the harbor is Sansum Island, a small spot covered with trees, and the ruins of a number of huts. The anchorage lies ½ mile further on, in Thetis Cove, keeping Sansum Island on the port hand, the passage being 200 yards wide, with deep water. This cove is completely landlocked, but squalls, frequently accompanied by rain, come over the hills with considerable violence.

Thorn Rock lies a good ½ mile from the mouth of the harbor on the starboard hand going in, and has only 3 feet on it at low water; it lies about 200 yards from the shore; and on the opposite side, at not quite so great a distance from the land, but a little further out, is another rock.

Douglas Harbor.—At one mile to the westward of Mitchell Harbor, is the entrance to Douglas Harbor, apparently very similar to the former, from which it is separated by Josling Peninsula

Directions.—The land being very high on both sides of the channels leading into the above harbors, influences the direction of the wind which is either right in or out. Winds with any westing blow in, and those with easting the contrary. A sailing vessel leaving Moore Channel with a SE wind should keep well over towards Hewlett Bay, to enable her to fetch clear of the Moresby Islands, as the wind will be very unsteady until well clear of the high land to windward

Tasoo Harbor—Cape Henry, lying 3 miles from the entrance to Moore Channel, terminates in a steep slope with a hummock at the extremity; 17 miles to the southward of this is the entrance to Tasoo Harbor, the intermediate coast being high, and rising abruptly from the sea. The entrance is short and narrow, but the harbor itself is extensive, with deep water in many places, the anchorage being near some small islands on the port hand going in, it has only been visited by a few of the Hudson Bay Company's officers.

Between Tasoo Harbor and Cape St James are other openings, which, according to Indian report, lead into good harbors, the southernmost of which is that leading into Houston Stewart Channel and Rose Harbor. Inside Anthony Island, and close to Houston Stewart Channel, is an opening called by the natives Louscoone, and reported to be a good harbor, not unlike Rose Harbor. This coast, excepting off Anthony Island, is also apparently bold. The land near Cape St. James has fewer trees on it than that to the northward

The Natives (Haida Indians) of the Queen Charlotte Islands are fond of traveling, and make voyages of several hundred miles in their canoes, visiting Sitka on the north, Port Simpson to the northeastward, and Victoria Harbor on the south. They excel in the construction of their canoes.

Supplies.—The banks in and near Hecate Strait, swept by strong currents, with the shore line of inlets and fiords, constitute the feeding grounds of the halibut and other fish, which abound in the vicinity of the islands The halibut is the most important, and is largely consumed by the natives, the dog-fish is also very abundant, and is taken for the manufacture of oil; salmon run up most of the streams in large numbers, especially in the autumn; herring are plentiful in some places, especially about Skidegate, at certain seasons; pollock or coal fish are caught on the northern and western coast, and supplies an edible oil; flounders and plaice abound in some localities; cod and mackerel are also caught, and probably are abundant on certain banks at some seasons, while smaller fish and shell fish, oysters excepted, form an important item in the native dietary From April to October the shell fish are said by the natives to be poisonous Immense flocks of wild geese and duck visit the northern shores of the islands in the autumn. Potatoes grow in abundance in most parts, and thrive exceedingly well, forming an important article of food. These are all to be bought either for money, strong cotton shirts, cotton dresses, plain cotton, knives, tobacco, mother of pearl jacket buttons for ornamenting their blankets, or any of the articles commonly bartered among aborigines The blanket is now, however, a recognized currency.

Bears are numerous, also martens, sea and land otters, which are caught for their furs, and mostly taken to the Hudson Bay Company's establishment at Fort Simpson.

CHAPTER XIII

PORTLAND AND OBSERVATORY INLETS AND PORTLAND CANAL.

Portland Inlet extends from the northeastern part of Chatham Sound in a general northeasterly direction for 20 miles, thence it divides, one arm continuing to the head of Observatory Inlet and the other taking a northerly direction to the head of Portland Canal. At its southern entrance, between Wales and Maskelyne Points, the inlet is about 3 miles wide, and its shores are comparatively free from danger beyond the distance of 400 yards.

Landmarks.—The shores of Portland Inlet are high and bold, especially the eastern Needle Peak, on the SE side of Nasoga Gulf, is a remarkable mountain terminating in a sharp snow clad pinnacle Northward of Nasoga Gulf the shores of Mylor Peninsula are high, bold, and precipitous, rising almost perpendicularly from the sea. On the western shore Entry Peak on Wales Island has been already described. The mountains on Pearse Island lie in ridges nearly parallel to the shore, and the land is lower than on the eastern shore of the inlet. Northward of Lizard Point the western shore becomes low and wooded, flanked by mountains.

York Island lies nearly in midchannel, between Wales and Pearse Islands, it is small, wooded, and 100 feet high.

Abreast York Island a narrow channel leads westward communicating with Pearse Channel and Portland Canal, but it is obstructed by several islands and islets, which render the passage intricate.

Compton Island, at the north entrance of Work Channel, is of triangular shape, with a base 2 miles long to the southward, the northern extreme of the island terminating in a long, low point. There is a boat passage into Work Channel eastward of Compton Island.

Emma Passage, northward of Compton Island, is ½ mile wide, and takes a SE. direction for 3 miles, thence NE 3 miles, and terminating in a sandy bay. The depths throughout the latter arm are from 23 to 36 fathoms.

Union Bay, at the head of the SE arm, affords anchorage for small vessels in 20 fathoms at 200 yards from either shore.

Somerville Island on the eastern side of the inlet, is 8½ miles long and 3 miles broad. The shores of this island are wooded and bold, the land on its western side rising almost perpendicularly from the sea. The island is but little broken, except on its northern side, where there is a bay, with deep water in it, ½ mile wide and one mile in extent, in a southerly direction.

Elliott Point is the southern extreme of Somerville Island.

Truro Island, off the SW. side of Somerville Island, is wooded with bold shores, and culminates in two hills 800 feet high.

Anchorage has been found off a small bay on the west side of Truro Island, in "35 fathoms, soft bottom."

Knob Islet is a small, round, wooded islet, 30 feet high, lying close to the western shore of Somerville Island. There is a remarkable white cliff just southward of Knob Islet.

Start Point, the north extreme of Somerville Island, lies abreast Lizard Point; it is high and bold, with a deep bay close eastward of it.

Cliff Point, on the western shore, terminates in high cliffs. Immediately south of the point is a narrow creek, which extends some distance inland in a NW. direction.

Lizard Point is a prominent point on the western shore. There are sandy bays close north and south of this point, extending back a considerable distance, giving to Lizard Point the shape of a peninsula, and when first seen from the westward it appears to be an island. At 2½ miles northward of Lizard Point there are some conspicuous red-brown earthy cliffs.

Flat Point lies 5½ miles from Lizard Point. The shore between these points is wooded and comparatively low, and a similar conformation exists 1½ miles northward of Flat Point.

Portland Point, lies 3 miles from Flat Point. This point, which forms the turning point into the SE. arm of Portland Canal, is high, bold and nearly steep-to.

Ramsden Point divides Observatory Inlet from Portland Canal.

A dangerous cluster of rocks (awash and sunken) extend 800 yards southward from Ramsden Point.

Steamer Passage, eastward of Somerville Island, has an average width of ¼ mile, and is deep.

Khutzeymateen Inlet is an unexamined arm, 5 miles within Steamer Passage. It is ½ mile wide at its entrance, and takes an easterly direction.

Quinamass Bay, abreast the northern end of Somerville Island, is ½ mile wide at its entrance, and takes an easterly direction. At low water it is almost completely filled by a sand flat, rendering the bay useless as an anchorage.

Nasoga Gulf, eastward of Mylor Peninsula, extends in a northeasterly direction for 5 miles, is one mile wide, and terminates in comparatively high land. There is no bottom at 39 fathoms in this gulf, except near the head.

Anchorage will be found near the head of Nasoga Gulf, in 10 to 12 fathoms, sand, in midchannel, at 400 yards from the north shore.

Mylor Peninsula is a high and comparatively narrow strip of land on the eastern side of Portland Inlet. A small islet (Ranger Islet) lies off its southern extreme and there the land is comparately low (450 feet); but it rises quickly to the height of 2,900 feet, and forms high, bold, precipitous shores. About one mile from the north extreme of the peninsula the land again begins to fall, and terminates in Low Point, the low wooded point which forms the southwestern entrance of Nass Bay.

Trefusis Point, the southern extreme of the peninsula, terminates in high white cliffs.

Nass Bay is 2 miles wide at its entrance, and the bay preserves this width in an easterly direction for 3 miles, where it divides, one branch taking a northeasterly direction to the mouth of Nass River, and the other a southwesterly direction, forming Iceberg Bay.

An extensive sand flat occupies nearly the whole of the eastern portion of the bay at low water. And the entrance into Nass River is obstructed by a bar upon which there is only 9 feet at low water.

The western portion of Nass Bay is deep, but as the northern shore is approached, it shoals suddenly from 45 to 15 and then 2 fathoms water.

North Point, the northern entrance point of the bay, terminates in a bold cliff, and one mile eastward is Mission Valley, a deep valley extending to the northward, on the western side of which, one mile back from the coast, is Mount Tomlinson, a conspicuous mountain. Through the valley a large stream runs, dividing near its mouth into two branches. Fort Point, the northwestern entrance point of Nass River, terminates in white cliffs. Mud Islands, low and dark, will be seen on the eastern side of the bay.

Kincolith, a mission station situated east of the stream at the mouth of the valley, is fronted by a sand flat (Canoe Flat), which renders communication by boat, except at high water, almost impossible. There are two sawmills here, one owned and worked by Indians. Gold is found here in small quantities, and also coal. The temperature is very severe, the thermometer in some winters falling to from 40° to 50° below zero for weeks in succession.

Observation Spot, at the east side of Mission Valley, is in latitude 54° 59′ 26″ N., longitude 129° 57′ 36″ W.

Canoe Flat.—An extensive sand flat commences at Fort Point, and taking a southwesterly direction forms a triangle, the apex of which lies 1,200 yards off shore south of the mission station, thence it takes a northwesterly direction, and meets the shore ½ mile westward of Kincolith.

Anchorage in fine weather may be had off Kincolith, nearly in the middle of Nass Bay on the line adjoining the mission station and Landslip Mountains, in 10 fathoms mud bottom, at about 1,600 yards from the northern shore; with the mission flagstaff seen in line with the center of Mission Valley, bearing N. 39° E., and Leading Point (south side of Nass River) seen just open of Fort Point, bearing east.

Caution.—A strong ebb tide will be felt in this position, and care must be exercised in taking up a berth, as Canoe Flat is very steep to and it is recommended to use the deep sea lead in approaching it.

Iceberg Bay terminates in a low, swampy flat, fronted by a sand flat.

At the entrance of Iceberg Bay the depth of 10 fathoms and less will be found, but as the head of the bay is approached the water will deepen to over 40 fathoms.

Anchorage may be obtained at the entrance to Iceberg Bay, in 7 to 8 fathoms, mud, with North Point seen in line with Double Islet Point bearing N. 31° W.; distant 1,200 yards from the latter.

Directions—If taking up this anchorage, having rounded Low Point at a distance of 600 yards, keep the southern shore of the bay aboard, pass 200 yards northward of Double Islet Point, and anchor as above directed.

Mud Islands consist of two small islands parallel to the eastern shore, at 1,200 yards from it.

Nass River.—The mouth of the river is obstructed by a sand flat, which dries at low water, and extends towards Iceberg Bay Ripple Tongue, the SW. extreme of this extensive flat, lies ¼ mile N 28° E. of Double Islet Point.

Within the river the navigation is difficult and dangerous, the channel at low water being barely available for large canoes, local steamers, however, from Victoria, drawing 6 feet water, venture up, though they frequently run aground.

Two salmon canneries, a sawmill, store, two missionary stations, and several Indian villages are situated along the stream. The climate is favorable to the growth of fruit, cereals, and root crops near the coast.

Nass Villages—The lower Nass villages, three in number, are situated 16 miles from the entrance, the north and south villages being situated on islands, and separated from the middle village at high water. The south, middle, and north villages are known, respectively, by the names of Kitminnook, Kitlahkunkadah, and Kitakauze. The population of the three villages amounted in 1868 to about 500

Tides—The time of high water at the lower Nass villages is uncertain, depending apparently upon the freshets down the river. There was no slack at high water, the water beginning to fall immediately it had ceased to rise (August, 1868). At low water there was slack for one hour and a half. In the month of August the flood stream was not felt above the Middle Bank, and from Indian report this is the case at all seasons.

Ice—The river is reported to freeze over down to its mouth during severe winters.

Fish.—The Houlican, from which the nutritious oil is obtained, the principal sustenance of the Indians, are caught in great numbers during the spring, as also are salmon. For this purpose, numerous fishing weirs are erected along the banks of the river, especially on the southern shore; and about 13 miles up, near Stony Point, there is an establishment where the fish are salted down and shipped off to Victoria.

Directions.—The Nass River is used by small coasting vessels after half flood. The navigable channel is tortuous, and it is recommended not to attempt the river until the strength of the flood tide has slackened. The channel is liable after freshets to change.

Observatory Inlet, northward of Nass Bay, and called by the Indians Kitsahwatl, is, generally speaking, similar to the other inlets; in some parts, however, the shores are low and wooded, the land rising at a few miles back to 4,000 and 5,000 feet high. The low, wooded shore has an undergrowth of thick moss, overlying rock, and saturated with moisture, which renders traveling difficult.

Abreast the NW. entrance point of Nass Bay, Observatory Inlet is 1¼ miles wide, having a general northerly direction for about 16 miles, and widening to 3 miles abreast Salmon Cove. Northward of Salmon Cove the inlet widens to 4 miles, and at 6 miles from the cove is obstructed by several islands, islets and rocks. At 10 miles from Salmon Cove the inlet divides into two arms, one taking a northeasterly direction for 12 miles, the other a northwesterly direction for 15 miles, both arms terminating in low, wooded swamps, fronted by mud flats.

Salmon Cove lies on the western shore.

Richard Point, the northern point of Salmon Cove, is a long, wooded, conspicuous projection. From its NE. extreme the land trends in a southwesterly direction, for 1¾ miles, to the head of Salmon Cove, which is barely 600 yards wide in that position.

A sand flat extends 400 yards from the southern shore at the entrance to Salmon Cove.

Anchorage has been obtained in Salmon Cove "in 31 and 35 fathoms water, muddy and small stony bottom."

Anchorage was also obtained in 30 fathoms, on the eastern shore, one mile northward of Salmon Cove.

Soundings.—The water in the reach south of Salmon Cove is deep, there being over 100 fathoms in mid channel. The shores are compact and steep, with no known danger beyond 400 yards from the shore.

Brooke Island, 2¾ miles long and ½ mile broad at its northern end, is low and wooded. Several patches of rock, which uncover at low water, extend ½ mile northward from Brooke Island.

Paddy Passage is ½ mile wide, between Brooke Island and the eastern shore, but near its northern end it is barely 400 yards wide, the navigable channel being reduced to that width by the ledges which extend northward from Brooke Island.

Frank Point, northward of Richard Point, is low and wooded; between it and Richard Point the land trends considerably to the westward, and forms near the latter point a bight nearly 2 miles deep. Northward of Frank Point the western shores are much broken, with several deep bays, which take a southerly direction.

Xschwan is the name of a salmon fishery which lies at the head of a small bay on the western shore, 4 miles northward of Frank Point.

Larcom Island, situated nearly in mid-channel, at the mouth of Hastings Arm, is about 5 miles long, in a north and south direction, with an average breadth of ½ mile. The island is flat, wooded, and ... nsive

... north

... e for

... gen-

... imi-

... —a wooded swamp fronted by a mud flat

Directions—The water in Hastings Arm is deep, with no known anchorage ground. If proceeding into this channel pass between Brooke and Larcom Islands, taking care to avoid the foul ground which extends ½ mile northward from the former; a mid-channel course is clear of danger.

Alice Arm, the eastern branch of Observatory Inlet, from its junction with Hastings Arm, runs in a northeasterly direction for 13 miles and terminates in the usual manner. This arm is obstructed at its entrance by a small wooded island (Liddle Island), which divides it into two channels 600 yards wide. There is a depth of 23 fathoms in mid channel in the southern and 16 fathoms in the northern of these passages.

Alice Arm varies in width from ½ mile to 2 miles, the latter being at the head of the inlet. The flat at the head is extensive, and through it a large stream flows, flanked on its eastern side by mountains over 5,000 feet high.

Perry Bay, situated on the eastern shore, at the entrance to Alice Arm, is ¼ mile wide, and takes a southerly direction for nearly one mile, with depths of 14 and 18 fathoms, mud bottom, in mid channel.

Off its western entrance point lies a small islet (Sophy Islet). At the head of the bay there is a salmon fishery (Muckshwanne).

Tides—The strength of tide in Observatory Inlet depends upon the freshets caused by the melting snow. Abreast Nass Bay the ebb runs with great strength, the blue water being clearly defined when meeting the muddy waters of the Nass River.

It is high water, full and change, in Observatory Inlet at 1h 5m.; springs rise 23 feet, neaps 12 feet.

Portland Canal—At about 20 miles from Wales Point an arm branches off NW 6 miles, with an average breadth of 1½ miles. Here a channel (now named Pearse Channel) stretches to the SW., which was not examined in the survey of 1868. From this the canal trends in a general northerly direction for about 55 miles. Throughout

are erected along the banks of the river, especially on the southern shore; and about 13 miles up, near Stony Point, there is an establishment where the fish are salted down and shipped off to Victoria.

Directions.—The Nass River is used by small coasting vessels after half flood. The navigable channel is tortuous, and it is recommended not to attempt the river until the strength of the flood tide has slack-

(1760) **BRITISH COLUMBIA—Northern mainland—Observatory inlet — Rock reported — Note.** — Captain Hughes, master of the steamer *Tees*, reports the existence of a dangerous rock in mid-channel between the islet north of Frank point and Larcom island, Observatory inlet

Approx position: Lat 55° 22′ 48″ N. Long 129° 45′ 55″ W.

The rock has about 5 feet over it at low water and is not marked by kelp.

In the bay north of this, marked Xschwan fishery and locally known as Goose bay, there is a mining establishment

(N. M. 50, 1904.)

1¼ miles wide, having a general northerly direc[illegible], and widening to 3 miles abreast Salmon Cove. Northward of Salmon Cove the inlet widens to 4 miles, and at 6 miles from the cove is obstructed by several islands, islets and rocks. At 10 miles from Salmon Cove the inlet divides into two arms, one taking a northeasterly direction for 12 miles, the other a northwesterly direction for 15 miles, both arms terminating in low, wooded swamps, fronted by mud flats.

Salmon Cove lies on the western shore.

Richard Point, the northern point of Salmon Cove, is a long, wooded, conspicuous projection. From its NE. extreme the land trends in a southwesterly direction, for 1¾ miles, to the head of Salmon Cove, which is barely 600 yards wide in that position.

A sand flat extends 400 yards from the southern shore at the entrance to Salmon Cove.

Anchorage has been obtained in Salmon Cove "in 31 and 35 fathoms water, muddy and small stony bottom."

Anchorage was also obtained in 30 fathoms, on the eastern shore, one mile northward of Salmon Cove.

Soundings.—The water in the reach south of Salmon Cove is deep, there being over 100 fathoms in mid channel. The shores are compact and steep, with no known danger beyond 400 yards from the shore.

Brooke Island, 2¾ miles long and ½ mile broad at its northern end, is low and wooded. Several patches of rock, which uncover at low water, extend ½ mile northward from Brooke Island.

Paddy Passage is ½ mile wide, between Brooke Island and the eastern shore, but near its northern end it is barely 400 yards wide, the navigable channel being reduced to that width by the ledges which extend northward from Brooke Island.

Frank Point, northward of Richard Point, is low and wooded, between it and Richard Point the land trends considerably to the westward, and forms near the latter point a bight nearly 2 miles deep. Northward of Frank Point the western shores are much broken, with several deep bays, which take a southerly direction.

Xschwan is the name of a salmon fishery which lies at the head of a small bay on the western shore, 4 miles northward of Frank Point.

Larcom Island, situated nearly in mid channel, at the mouth of Hastings Arm, is about 5 miles long, in a north and south direction, with an average breadth of ½ mile. The island is flat, wooded, and comparatively low. At its southwestern end there is an extensive lagoon.

The channel westward of Larcom Island is obstructed near the north end of that island by several islets and rocks, and is only available for boats.

Hastings Arm passes eastward of Larcom Island and takes a general northerly direction for 13 miles.

This branch of Observatory Inlet is from ½ to one mile wide, terminating in the usual manner—a wooded swamp fronted by a mud flat.

Directions.—The water in Hastings Arm is deep, with no known anchorage ground. If proceeding into this channel pass between Brooke and Larcom Islands, taking care to avoid the foul ground which extends ½ mile northward from the former; a mid channel course is clear of danger.

Alice Arm, the eastern branch of Observatory Inlet, from its junction with Hastings Arm, runs in a northeasterly direction for 13 miles and terminates in the usual manner. This arm is obstructed at its entrance by a small wooded island (Liddle Island), which divides it into two channels 600 yards wide. There is a depth of 23 fathoms in mid-channel in the southern and 16 fathoms in the northern of these passages.

Alice Arm varies in width from ½ mile to 2 miles, the latter being at the head of the inlet. The flat at the head is extensive, and through it a large stream flows, flanked on its eastern side by mountains over 5,000 feet high.

Perry Bay, situated on the eastern shore, at the entrance to Alice Arm, is ¼ mile wide, and takes a southerly direction for nearly one mile, with depths of 14 and 18 fathoms, mud bottom, in mid channel.

Off its western entrance point lies a small islet (Sophy Islet). At the head of the bay there is a salmon fishery (Muckshwanne).

Tides.—The strength of tide in Observatory Inlet depends upon the freshets caused by the melting snow. Abreast Nass Bay the ebb runs with great strength, the blue water being clearly defined when meeting the muddy waters of the Nass River.

It is high water, full and change, in Observatory Inlet at 1h. 5m.; springs rise 23 feet, neaps 12 feet.

Portland Canal.—At about 20 miles from Wales Point an arm branches off NW. 6 miles, with an average breadth of 1½ miles. Here a channel (now named Pearse Channel) stretches to the SW., which was not examined in the survey of 1868. From this the canal trends in a general northerly direction for about 55 miles. Throughout the canal no soundings were obtained at 40 fathoms. It possesses the general characteristics of the other fiords on the coast of British Columbia, viz, high land on both shores, terminating in low, swampy land at the head, and deep water, with few and indifferent anchorages.

The head of Portland Canal terminates in low, woody, swampy land, through which two rivers flow into it.

The two rivers (Bear and Salmon) at the head of Portland Canal are separated by a high ridge of bare mountains. On the east side of the valley of Bear River a mountain range extends in an east and west direction, Mount Disraeli, the highest peak of the range, being a snow-clad pinnacle 7,000 feet high. The delta of the Bear and Salmon Rivers consists of a mud flat, which covers at high water, and extends over one mile from the mouth of the former river. This deposit of mud is nearly steep to, breaking down suddenly to no bottom at 40 fathoms.

Current.—During the month of August, 1868, a current of about 1½ knots an hour was observed setting down Portland Canal, to the distance of 25 miles below the mouth of Bear River.

Climate.—The sun's rays in August, between 9 a. m and 3 p m, were very powerful, and, reflected from the snow, caused occasionally intense heat. When the sun was obscured by the mountains the atmosphere at once conveyed a sensation of chilliness. During that month, just before sunrise, the thermometer registered 32° F., water left in basins within the tent being frozen during the night. The vapor developed by the heat of the sun during the early portion of the day, becoming condensed on the mountainous shores of the inlet, usually fell as a drizzling rain from 3 p. m. to about midnight.

Temperature of the surface water, within 20 miles of the head of the canal, was 33°. At that distance from the mouth of the Bear River the water on the surface was fresh.

Supplies.—Salmon, mountain sheep, bears, and berries abound at the head of Portland Canal.

Natives.—A party consisting of about 200 natives were met with fishing at the mouth of Salmon River; they annually visit the head of the Portland Canal.

Dogfish Bay, on the eastern shore, about 3½ miles northwestward of Ramsden Point, is about 1½ miles wide, ½ mile deep, and faces the SW.; it is, however, filled by a sand flat at low water, rendering it useless as an anchorage.

Windy Islet is small, and lies close to the shore at the northern entrance point of Dogfish Bay.

Tree Point, on the western shore, 4½ miles from Portland Point is low, wooded, and conspicuous, with high land at about one mile south of it.

Tree Point Reef extends ½ mile in a northerly direction from Tree Point, and is nearly steep-to.

Spit Point, on the eastern shore, is the turning point into the northern reach. Between Spit Point and Dogfish Bay several small wooded islets lie close to the eastern shore, and are connected with it at low water. A tongue of sand, which uncovers at low water, extends 600 yards SW. from Spit Point.

Reef Island is a small island lying on the western shore abreast Spit Point.

Two small bays, with sandy beaches, lie under Reef Island, in which a boat may find shelter. A reef with rocks awash at high water, and sunken rocks, extends 400 yards SE. from Reef Island.

Leading Point, a high bold point, on the western shore, lies 2½ miles north of Reef Island.

Dickens Point is on the eastern shore, 4 miles from Spit Point, the coast between them having a considerable curve to the eastward.

A small black rock, 8 feet above high water, lies close south of Dickens Point, and a ledge of rocks which uncover, extends 400 yards from the point.

Sandfly Bay, on the western shore, abreast Dickens Point, is ½ mile wide, and ¾ mile deep in a northwesterly direction, terminating in a swamp with streams in the NW. and NE. corners. At the north point of the bay, 2 small islets lie close to the shore.

Sandfly Bay is nearly filled up at low water by a sand flat, with deep water close-to, and is therefore useless as an anchorage.

Stopford Point, bold and conspicuous, lies on the eastern shore.

Halibut Bay, on the western shore, 4 miles from Sandfly Bay, is ½ mile wide at its entrance, and extends back 1½ miles, having an extensive swamp at its head, through which three large streams flow. Off the southern point of this bay lie a cluster of small, black, rocky islets.

Anchorage.—The only known anchorage in Portland Canal is in Halibut Bay, in mid-channel, at 600 yards within the entrance, in 6 to 10 fathoms, mud bottom.

Cross Islet, a small wooded islet, connected at low water with the shore, lies close northward of Halibut Bay.

Logan Point lies on the eastern shore. At 3 miles SE. of Logan Point, is a conspicuous saddle-shaped mountain 5,057 feet high.

Camp Point, on the western shore, is the turning point of the northern arm; it is wooded, bold, and precipitous.

Center Island, nearly in mid-channel, abreast Camp Point, is 400 yards long in a north and south direction, with some stunted brush growing upon it.

A ledge of rocks awash, and sunken rocks, extend 400 yards northward from Center Island. The water is deep on either side of the island, beyond the distance of 400 yards, but the channel westward of the island is recommended.

Barclay valley lies on the eastern shore, abreast Center Island; a large stream flows through it, and the neck of land separating Portland Canal and Salmon Cove (Observatory Inlet) is here about 4 miles across.

Landslip Point lies on the eastern shore, 2 miles northward of Center Island. Three conspicuous landslips are seen on the mountains south of Landslip Point.

Bluff Point terminates in a high bold cliff, and lies on the eastern shore, 2 miles from Landslip Point. The channel abreast Bluff Point is one mile wide.

Breezy Point, on the western shore, 3½ miles from Camp Point, is conspicuous, and the land recedes to the southward between Camp and Breezy Points.

Tombstone Bay lies on the western shore. At its entrance the bay is 600 yards wide, and takes a southerly direction, narrowing rapidly, until it terminates one mile within the entrance at the mouth of a river.

An extensive well-wooded valley lies at the head of the bay, and on the northern side of the valley a remarkable mountain, with a snow-clad summit of dome shape, rises to the height of 6,500 feet. Trout are plentiful in the river, flowing into this bay. Berries are found in abundance, especially salmon berries and the wild raspberry.

Maple Point lies on the eastern shore. Maple trees grow upon this point, and when in leaf render it conspicuous. Immediately northward of Maple Point is a bay, with a large stream flowing into it, fronted by a sand flat.

Swamp Point, a low, marshy, wooded point, through which a river flows, lies northward of Maple Point. A sandspit extends ½ mile to the southward from Swamp Point.

Pirie Point is high, bold, and conspicuous. A sandspit extends 400 yards from the eastern shore midway between Swamp and Pirie Points.

White Point lies on the eastern shore, 4 miles from Pirie Point.

Turn Point lies on the western shore, 1½ miles from Tombstone Bay, and is high, bold, and conspicuous.

Steep Point, on the western shore, is bold and steep to. Two large streams flow into the sea, midway between Turn and Steep Points.

Foggy Point lies on the western shore, 6 miles from Steep Point. The coast between Steep and Foggy Points trends considerably to the southward in a deep curve, and at 2½ miles southward of the point is an extensive valley lying in a southerly direction, between mountains from 3,500 and 4,000 feet high. The valley is thickly wooded, and a large stream flows through it.

Bay Islet, on the eastern shore abreast of Foggy Point, is small and wooded, and lies 200 yards off a point which divides two sandy bays, being connected with the point at low water.

Green Islets are two small, wooded islets, on the eastern shore, 2 miles from Bay Islet. Close northward of these islets there is a considerable tract of comparatively low land, thickly wooded, through which a large stream flows.

Slab Point, terminating in a high, smooth, slate colored cliff, lies on the western shore, 2 miles from Foggy Point.

Blue Point, on the eastern shore, 5½ miles from Green Islet, and 1¼ miles from Cliff Point (on the western shore), terminates in high, bold cliffs, of purple blue color, and basaltic formation. Close south of the point, an extensive wooded valley extends to the northeastward, through which two large streams flow. A sandspit extends off their mouths to the distance of 400 yards.

Cliff Point terminates in high white cliffs, and is steep-to.

Verdure Point, on the western shore, is 4 miles from Cliff Point. The maple trees growing upon this point, when in leaf, render it conspicuous.

Midway between Cliff and Verdure Points there is an extensive wooded valley, through which a large stream flows in a southwesterly direction. Close northward of Verdure Point is a bay, with a conspicuous sandy beach at its head.

Landslip Point, one mile from Verdure Point, is conspicuous, it having high landslip over it.

Round Point is the turning point, on the eastern shore, into the northern and last reach of Portland Canal. With the exception of a small bay, which dries throughout at low water, the eastern shore northward of Blue Point, for 6 miles, is high, bold, and almost inaccessible. The northern extreme of Round Point lies 6 miles from Blue Point.

Seal Rocks, on the western shore, at the entrance of the north reach of the canal, are of small extent, and lie 100 yards from the western shore. The highest rock is 6 feet above high water. Between Verdure Point and the point off which Seal Rocks lie, the coast curves considerably to the westward. At one mile to the southward of the latter point an extensive wooded valley takes a westerly direction, between high mountains, and a large stream flows through it.

Marmot River, on the eastern shore, 2½ miles from the mouth of Bear River, flows through an extensive valley which lies in an easterly direction. A sandspit extends 600 yards off the mouth of Marmot River, and is steep-to. At the head of the valley is a mountain range with three conspicuous peaks.

Salmon River, on the western shore, is a stream of considerable size, and the valley through which it flows is ½ mile wide at its mouth; the river then takes a northwesterly direction, widening to one and 2 miles, and is flanked by high mountains.

Bear River flows through an extensive wooded flat, at the head of the Portland Canal, and divides near its mouth into several streams, from which, during the summer months, when the snow is melting, a considerable body of water passes out into the inlet. The valley through which this river flows extends 10 miles from the mouth of Bear river, and is thickly wooded, and flanked by the Gladstone Mountains, it terminates at the foot of the Disraeli Mountains, a range which extends in an east and west direction. The Bear and Salmon Rivers have a mud flat extending across their mouths, rendering communication even by canoes, difficult at low water Commencing at about 600 yards south of Salmon River Valley, this deposit of mud extends across the canal in a northeasterly direction, passing over one mile from the mouth of Bear River. The edge of the bank is steep, breaking down almost suddenly to no bottom at 40 fathoms.

Anchorage was unsuccessfully searched for off the above mentioned delta of the Salmon and Bear Rivers. The depth of 24 fathoms was found alongside the edge of the mud at low water; and at the distance of 50 yards from it no bottom could be obtained at 40 fathoms.

Tides—It is high water, full and change, at the head of Portland Canal at 1h 30m; springs rise from 23 to 27 feet, and occasionally 30 feet; neaps 15 to 20 feet. In August, 1868, it was noticed that the night tides rose considerably higher than the day tides.

Observation Spot, at the wooded high water mark of the point near the center of the mouth of Bear River, was found, by observations taken in August, 1868, to be situated in latitude 55° 56′ 03″ N., longitude 130° 03′ 27″ W., depending on Duntze Head, Esquimalt Harbor being in longitude 123° 26′ 45″ W.

ADDENDA

ADDENDA.

LIST OF LIGHTS INCLUDED IN LIMITS OF THIS WORK.

UNITED STATES—WASHINGTON.

Name.	Location.	No. of lights.	Character of light.	Height of light above sea level.	Distance visible, in nautical miles.	Character of light-house or vessel.	Remarks.
Cape Flattery	On Tatoosh Island, ½ mile NW. of Cape Flattery, entrance to the Strait of Fuca.	1	F., with red sector.	162	19	Conical brick tower; white; rising from keeper's house; lantern black.	The red sector embraces an arc of 7° 02′ between the bearings S. 7° 36′ E. and S. 14° 38′ E., covering Duncan and Duntze Rocks, which lie in the axis of the sector. Fog-signal: a 12-inch steam whistle, giving blasts of 8 seconds at intervals of 52 seconds. Red whistling buoy ½ mile from Waaddah Island. Red whistling buoy lettered "Umatilla Reef," 1½ miles S. 74° W. of the reef.
Ediz Hook	80 feet from extremity of Ediz Hook, the northern side of the bay of Port Angeles, in the Strait of Fuca.	1	F.	42	12	White square wooden tower on keeper's house; lantern black.	Fog-signal: a bell struck a single blow every 15 seconds.
Cattle Point	S. end of San Juan Island.	1	F.	100		Stake	
New Dungeness	On outer end of sand spit of that name, in Strait of Fuca.	1	F.	100	16	Conical brick tower; rising from keeper's house; upper part of tower black; lower part white; lantern red.	Fog signal: a 12-inch steam whistle, giving blasts of 6 and 3 seconds at alternate intervals of 12 and 39 seconds.
Fidalgo Island, Deception Pass	SW. end of island	1	F.	45		Stake	Bell buoy, marks Belle Rock.
Burrows Bay	On sand spit N. side of bay W. coast of island.	1	F.	20		do	
Smith's or Blunt's Island.	About 13 miles NNE. of New Dungeness and 11 miles NW. of entrance to Admiralty inlet.	1	Fl. every ½ min.	90	15	Low conical brick tower, rising from keeper's house; lantern black	
Peavine Pass	W. entrance to pass on SW. end of Obstruction Island.	1	F. red.	30		Stake	About 20 feet from end of point and serves as guide through the pass.

List of lights included in limits of this work—Continued.

UNITED STATES—WASHINGTON—Continued.

Name.	Location.	No. of lights.	Character of light.	Height of light above sea level.	Distance visible, in nautical miles.	Character of light-house or vessel.	Remarks.
Admiralty Head	On Red Bluff, Whidbey Island, entrance to Puget Sound.	1	F.	10[illegible]	15	Low square white tower, rising from end of keeper's house; lantern black.	
Oak Harbor	At the butt of Maylor's Spit, entrance to the harbor, Whidbey Island.	1	F.	15	......	White stakes	
	On the end of Maylor's Spit	1	F. red.	25	......	White stakes	
La Conner	On point abreast of Small Island about 2 miles from La Conner.	1	F. red.	25	......	White stake	
Hole-in-the-Wall	On a rocky point east side of narrow channel known as Hole in the Wall, about one mile from La Conner.	1	F. red.	15	......	do	The channel is very narrow. The light is close to the water's edge about midway and at a sharp turn of the passage.
Point Pleasant	On a low point inside of Hole in the Wall, about ½ mile from La Conner.	1	F. red.	6	......	do	The point is covered at high water. The light should be left to the eastward.
Gallagher's Point	On low point, about ½ mile from La Conner.	1	F. red.	6	......	do	The point is covered at high water. The light is about 10 feet from edge of channel, and should be left to the northward.
Fidalgo Bay	On Crandall Spit, E. side of entrance to the bay.	1	F.	20	......	do	About 50 yards from low-water end of spit.
	On Weaverling Spit, W. side of entrance to the bay.	1	F. red.	20	......	do	About 50 yards from end of spit.
Pole Pass	On a rocky point, N. side of the pass, S. side of Orcas Island near Wasp Passage.	1	F. red.	15	......	do	
Bellingham Bay: William Point	S. entrance to Bellingham Bay, [illegible] feet from edge of bluff and 163 yards N. 87° W. from N. end of point.	1	F.	36	......	do	
Taylor's Spit	About 80 yards from low-water end of spit, E. side of Lummi Island, Hale's	1	F.	27	......	do	Serves to guide through Hale's Passage.

	Bay; 8 feet from edge of bluff and 100 yards N. 67° W. from N. end of point.	1	F.	35		do	
Tayler's Spit	About 60 yards from low-water end of spit, E. side of Lummi Island, Hale's Passage.	1	F.	27		do	Serves to guide through Hale's Passage.
Skagit River	On E. side of channel, ½ mile from mouth of South Fork of the river.	1	F.	15		Arm on cluster of three piles.	Guide for mouth of river.
Stanwood	300 feet east of channel, at mouth of West Pass, Stillaquamish River.	1	F. red.	15		White stake	Guide for entering West Pass.
Port Susan	On east bank of South Fork of Stillaquamish River, one mile S. 11° 25′ W. of Stanwood.	1	F.	15		do	Guide over the flats in Port Susan.
Sandy Point (also Brown Spit).	On east side of Whidbey Island, 100 feet from high-water end of the spit at Sandy Point, entrance to Saratoga Passage.	1	F.	24		do	
Point Wilson	On spit 2 miles NW. of Port Townsend.	1	F.	[illegible]	13	Square white tower, top of keeper's dwelling; lantern black.	Fog signal: a 12-inch steam whistle; blasts 8 seconds, interval 52 seconds.
Point Hudson	On the point 1½ miles S. 57° 30′ E. of Point Wilson light.	1	F. red	12		Stake	
Marrowstone Point	On point at eastern entrance to Port Townsend, Admiralty Inlet.	1	F. red	15		do	
Point no Point	Puget Sound, 3½ miles S. of entrance to Hood's Canal.	1	F.	27	10	Tower white; lantern and dome black.	Fog signal: a bell struck every 10 seconds.
Point Monroe	About 150 yards from low-water end of the spit.	1	F. red.	25	4	White stake	
West Point (Ranny Point).	Puget Sound, E. side, 7 miles N.W. of Seattle.	1	Fl. red and white, every 10 sec., alternate red and white	27	10	Tower white; lantern black.	Fog signal: a trumpet, giving blasts of 5 seconds' duration, with intervals of 25 seconds.

List of lights included in limits of this work—Continued.

UNITED STATES—WASHINGTON—Continued.

Name.	Location.	No. of lights.	Character of light.	Height of light above sea level.	Distance visible, in nautical miles.	Character of light-house or vessel.	Remarks.
Battery Point	On point	1	F.	15		Stake	About 50 yards from low-water end of spit.
Point Robinson	On low point, 150 yards from wooded bluff.			30		Dwelling, stake, and signal-house white; roofs brown; 700 feet apart.	Fog-signal; a 12-inch steam whistle, giving blasts of 6 seconds every 54 seconds.
Point Brown	On point	1	F.	12		Stake	About 50 yards from low-water end of spit.
Eagle Island	South end of island, Balch's Passage.	1	F.	25		do	
Johnson's Point	About 30 feet from high-water end of the spit.	1	F.	25		White stake	
Doffiemyer's Point	On point	1	F.	20		Stake	
Olympia	South end of Budd's Inlet at a turn in the channel near the steamboat landing at Olympia.	1	F. red.			do	Vessels entering should leave this light to the westward.
West Olympia	Small wharf at West Olympia.	1	F. red.	20		Arm on pile	

BRITISH COLUMBIA.

Name.	Location.	No. of lights.	Character of light.	Height of light above sea level.	Distance visible, in nautical miles.	Character of light-house or vessel.	Remarks.
Vancouver Island: Race Islands	On largest rock; Juan de Fuca Strait.	1	Fl. every 10 secs.	118	18	Stone tower, with 5 alternate horizontal bands, black and white.	Fog-signal: A whistle; blasts of 5 seconds, intervals of 72 seconds.
Discovery Island	Near Sea Bird Point, the most easterly extremity of the island.	1	F.	91	15	Square; wood; white; keeper's dwelling attached.	Visible between S. 20° E. and N. 53° E., over an arc of 253°. Fog-signal, blasts of 8 seconds every minute.
Victoria	[illegible] Island, [illegible] side of harbor entrance.	1	F. [illegible]	44	6	do	Harbor light: A fixed red light is shown during the autumn and summer months from the beacon buoy which marks the outer end of spit off Shoal Point. Fog-signal: A bell rung by hand only in

Victoria	Berens Island west side of harbor entrance	1	F. blue.	41	6	....do	Harbor light: A fixed red light is shown during the autumn and summer months from the beacon buoy which marks the outer end of spit off Shoal Point. Fog-signal: A bell rung by hand only in answer to steamers blowing their whistles on entering in thick weather.
Esquimalt	Summit of Fog Island, S. point	1	F. with red sector	76	10	Circular; brick; white; lantern red.	White, from N. 19° E. to N. 37° W.; red, from N. 37° W. through west to S. 13° W.; white, from S. 13° W. to S. 28° E.; and eclipsed from S. 28° E., landward to the white limit.
Carmanah	....		....			....	In course of construction.
Cape Beale	SE. point of entrance to Barclay Sound.	1	Rev., every 30 sec.	164	19	Square; light stone color	Do not bring the light to bear southward of S. 72° E.
Saturna Island ...	Extremity of East Point	1	Rev. Fl. attaining greatest brilliancy every 30 secs.	140	18	Wooden tower; square; white; iron lantern red; keeper's dwelling attached.	Illuminates an arc of 274° 26' between the bearings N. 62° 22' E. and S. 36° 94' E. The light should not be approached within 1 miles from northerly or westerly directions, in order to avoid the dangerous ground in that locality.
Georgina Point ...	N. extreme of Mayne Island	1	F.	55	12	Square; wooden tower, white, keeper's dwelling attached.	Fog signal: A bell, one stroke every 15 seconds. Indicates east extreme of Active Pass. Visible between N. 73° W. and N. 62° E. through N.
Entrance Island	S. point, entrance to Nanaimo Harbor, Georgia Strait.	1	F.	63	14	Square; wood; white; keeper's dwelling attached.	Indicates entrance to Nanaimo Harbor and Departure Bay.
Yellow Island	Summit of island at SE. entrance to Baynes sound	1	Rev., every minute, 3 flashes in succession, with intervals of 15 seconds between points of greatest brilliancy.	120	17	Square wooden building, with dwelling attached; all white, iron lantern red.	Visible between the bearings S. 65° W. and S. 78° E. over an arc of 217°. Coming down Baynes sound, do not bring the light to bear eastward of S. 84° E. in order to clear Maple bank. Vessels passing south of Hornby Island should not lose sight of the light.
Fraser River, North Sand Heads	On SW. end of Sturgeon Bank.	1	F.	52	12	Hexagonal wooden tower on iron piles.	Indicates entrance to river channel through Sand Heads. Fog-signal: A bell.

List of lights included in limits of this work—Continued.

BRITISH COLUMBIA—Continued.

Name.	Location.	No. of lights.	Character of light.	Height of light above sea level.	Distance visible, in nautical miles.	Character of light-house or vessel.	Remarks.
Brockton Point	On point	1	F. with red sector.	48	8	Mast, red	Shows red over an arc of 29° 30′ between the bearings N. 44° 20′ W. and N. 73° 50′ W., covering Burnaby Shoal; and white from all other points of approach. Fog-signal: A bell struck by machinery, a single blow every 20 seconds.
Point Atkinson	Burrard Inlet, N. point of entrance.	1	Rev. every minute.	110	11	Square; white; attached to keeper's dwelling.	Vessels in the Strait of Georgia should not bring the light to bear to the northward of N. 25° E., in order to clear the Sturgeon Bank off Frazer River. Fog-signal: Horn, blasts of 8 seconds' duration, at intervals of one minute, from wooden building, painted white with brown roof, 200 feet from lighthouse.

COALING AND REPAIRING FACILITIES.

Machine shops at

Coaling and Repairing Facilities.

Name of port.	Kind of coal.	Cost per ton.	Manner of coaling, rapid or slow, etc.	Next nearest coaling port.	Number and size of dry docks.	Machine shops at which steamers can repair.
Mare Island, Cal.			At navy-yard, coal at wharf by wheelbarrows.	San Francisco	Dock will take vessel 460 by 79 by 27½; one wooden sectional for vessels 347 by 92 by 16.	Machine shops for all kind of repairs.
San Francisco	Coos Bay	[illegible]	Men-of-war usually coal at anchorage in bay, by large lighters and hoists; only liable to temporary interruption from heavy winds.	Coos Bay, Oregon.	Two wooden floating docks 108 by 40 by 9; 210 by 60 by 15; one stone dry dock at Hunter's Point will take vessel 448 by 90 by 24; hydraulic dock, Union works, 450 by 66 by —.	Extensive and numerous.
	Wellington	16.50				
	Seattle	[illegible]				
	Australian	[illegible]				
	West Hartley	[illegible]				
	Cardiff	[illegible]				
	Anthracite	15.00				
	Cumberland	[illegible]				
Coos Bay, Oregon	Native bituminous	$4 delivered; 10 cents for stowing.	Alongside wharf, rapid, two wharves at Empire City, one at Marshfield.	Portland, Oregon	None	None.
Portland, Oregon	do	$5		Tacoma	do	Do.
Olympia, Wash				do	do	Do.
Tacoma, Wash	Native bituminous "Roslyn."	$3.25 at mines; 10 cents for stowing	Alongside wharf; chutes, rapid	Seattle	do	A good one.
Seattle, Wash	Native bituminous	$[illegible].25	do	Tacoma	do	Do.
Port Townsend, Wash				Esquimalt	do	One quite small.
Esquimalt, Vancouver Island.	Nanaimo			Victoria	One, take vessel 450 by 65 by 27.	
Victoria, Vancouver Island.	do	$7; stowing 10 cents; $3 to $4 at mines.	From coal yards with wheelbarrows; rapid.	Esquimalt	None	Several.
Nanaimo, Vancouver Island.	Native bituminous	$3.75 at mines; 10 cents for stowing	Alongside wharves; chutes; rapid	Victoria	do	None.

COALING AND REPAIRING FACILITIES—Continued

Name of port	Kind of coal	Cost per ton	Manner of coaling, rapid or slow, etc	Next nearest coaling port	Number and size of dry docks.	Machine shops at which steamers can repair
Departure Bay, Vancouver Island	Native bituminous, Wellington best	$4 at mines, 10 cents for stowing	Alongside wharves, chutes, rapid	Nanaimo	None	None
Port Augusta, Vancouver Island	Comax mine				do	Do
Sitka, Alaska	Wellington	$10	At wharf by lighters, moderately fast.	Departure Bay	do	Do.
Cook's Inlet, Alaska	Cannel		By boats, slow	Ounalaska	do	Do
Unga Island, Alaska	Bituminous			do	do	Do
Ounalaska, Alaska	Nanaimo	$16 to $20	At wharf by wheelbarrows, fast	Sitka	do	Do
Port Clarence, Alaska			From alongside of vessel that brings coal to whaling fleet.		do	Do
Cape Sabine, Alaska	Semi bituminous		Moved from cliff, dangerous, possible in good weather	Ounalaska	do	Do
Cape Lisburne, Alaska	Native lignite, good			do	do	Do

INDEX.

IMAGE EVALUATION
TEST TARGET (MT-3)

6"

C.

E

G

H.

K.

L.

N.

O.

X.

Y.

Z.

BOOKS FOR THE PURPOSE OF NAVIGATION PUBLISHED BY THE HYDROGRAPHIC OFFICE, NAVY DEPARTMENT.

No.	Title.	Price
	ATLANTIC OCEAN	
22	Atlantic Ocean, General Examination of 1870	$2.00
	Supplement. 1886	.10
45	Atlantic Ocean, the Navigation of Second edition. 1887	2 00
73	Newfoundland and Labrador 1881	2 00
78	Newfoundland and Labrador. Supplement 1886	.62
65	Caribbean Sea and Gulf of Mexico Vol I The West India Islands, including the Bahama Banks and the Bermuda Islands Second edition 1887	1 00
	Supplements 1889 and 1890	10
64	Caribbean Sea and Gulf of Mexico Vol II Coast from the Rio Grande del Norte to Cape Orange, with adjacent islands and dangers Second edition. 1890	1.50
	Supplement. 1891	10
88	South America East coast of Coast of, from Cape Orange to Cape Virgins, including the Falkland, South Georgia, Sandwich, and South Shetland Islands 1889	1.00
	Supplement 1891	10
61	The Rio de la Plata 1875	1 50
	Supplement 1886	.10
70	Kattegat, Sound, and the Great and Little Belts to the Baltic Sea. 1881	.75
	Supplement. 1886	10
34	English Channel Part I. South Coast of England, 1886	1 50
	Supplement. Second edition 1889	10
35	English Channel Part II North Coast of France and Channel Islands 1877	2 50
	Supplement Second edition. 1889	10
60	Biscay, Bay of, coasts and ports of 1876	2 50
	Supplement Second edition 1890	10
23	Cadiz, Gulf of The Western Coast of the Spanish Peninsula, and the Strait of Gibraltar, Winds, Currents, and Navigation of 1870	1.00
52	Spain, Northwest, West and South Coast of, and the Coast of Portugal Point Estaca to Cape Trafalgar 1874	1 50
	Supplement Second edition 1890	10
25	Mediterranean Sea, General examination of 1870	2 00
37	Mediterranean Sea. Part I South and Southeast Coasts of Spain from Mala Bahia to Cape Creux. Balearic Islands and the North Coast of Africa from Ceuta to La Cala. 1875	2 50
	Supplement. Second edition 1890	10
38	Mediterranean Sea Part II South Coast of France; West Coast of Italy; Tuscan Archipelago; Corsica and Sardinia. 1878	2.50
	Supplement. Second edition. 1890	.10
42	Mediterranean Sea Part III Coast of Tunis, Sardinia, Sicily, and Malta Channels, Lipari Islands, Sicily, Strait of Messina; Coast of Tripoli; Coast of Egypt, Syria 1879	2 35
	Supplement. Second edition. 1890	.10
68	Mediterranean Sea Part IV. Gulf of Gioja to Cape Santa Maria de Leuca; South Coast of Italy; Adriatic Sea; Ionian Islands; the Coasts of Albania and Greece to Cape Malea, with Cerigo Island, including the Gulfs of Patras and Corinth. 1883	2.35
	Supplement. Second edition. 1890	.10

No	Title	Price.
	ATLANTIC OCEAN—continued.	
53	Azores, Madeiras, Canaries, and Cape Verde Islands. 1874.	$2.00
	Supplement 1886	.10
46	Africa, West Coast of Part I. Cape Spartel to Sierra Leone. 1873	2.00
	Supplement. 1886	.10
47	Africa, West Coast of Part II. From Sierra Leone to Cape Lopez 1875	2 00
	Supplement 1886	.10
48	Africa, West Coast of Part III From Cape Lopez to Cape of Good Hope, including the Islands in the Bight of Biafra, and Ascension and St Helena Islands First edition. 1877	1.50
	Supplement 1886	.10
15	Atlantic, North Memoir of the Dangers and Ice 1868	.25
	PACIFIC OCEAN.	
96	The Coast of British Columbia, including the Strait of Juan de Fuca Puget Sound, Vancouver, and Queen Charlotte Islands 1891	
5	Pacific Ocean, General examination of 1867	1 50
	Supplement. 1886	.10
58	Pacific Ocean, Navigation of. 1874	2.00
20	Alaska, Coast of, and Bering Sea Directory for 1869	1.00
	Supplement 1886	.10
84	Mexico and Central America, From Panama to the United States. 1887	.60
89	South America, Coast of West coast of. Including Magellan Strait, Tierra del Fuego, and outlying islands 1890	1.28
	Supplement. 1890	.10
41	Pacific, North Reported Dangers to Navigation in. 1871	1 00
41b	Pacific, North Supplement. 1880	1.00
	Supplement. 1887	.10
41a	Pacific, South Reported Dangers to Navigation in 1879	1 00
	Supplement 1887	.10
	INDIAN OCEAN	
85	Indian Ocean Including the Java Sea, Sulu Sea, Afuera Sea, and the Philippine Islands 1887	1.00
	Supplement 1889, and No 2, 1890	.10
24	Indian Ocean, General Examination of, with directions for the navigation of Torres Strait, etc 1870	2.00
	Supplement 1886	.10
39	Red Sea, Physical Geography of 1872	.25
	LIGHT-LISTS.	
30	List of Lights (No. 1) of North and South America (East and West Coasts), including the West Indies and Pacific Islands. Hydrographic Office	.25
	Supplement 1890	.15
74	List of Lights (No. 5) of the North, Baltic, and White Seas, including the Coast of Denmark, Prussia, Russia, Sweeden, and Norway. 8vo. Hydrographic Office	.25
75	List of Lights (No 6) of the British Islands 8vo Hydrographic Office	.25
33	List of Lights (No 4) of the Atlantic Coast of Europe, including Spain, Portugal, France, Belgium, and Holland. 8vo. Hydrographic Office	25
	Supplement 1890	.15
32	List of Lights (No 3) of the West Coast of Africa and the Mediterranean Sea, including the West and North Coasts of Africa, the Mediterranean, the Adriatic, the Black Sea, and the Sea of Azof 8vo Hydrographic Office	.25
	Supplement 1890	.15
31	List of Lights (No. 2) of South and East Coasts of Africa, and the East Indies, including the East India Islands, China, Japan, Australia, Tasmania, and New Zealand. 8vo. Hydrographic Office	.25
	Supplement 1890	.15

No.	Title	Price.
	MISCELLANEOUS PUBLICATIONS.	
93	Report of the International Meteorological Congress at Paris, France, 1889	$0.25
94	Ice and Ice Movements in the North Atlantic Ocean. 1890	.25
92	Ice and Ice Movements in Bering Sea and the Arctic Basin 1890	.25
91	Table of Meridional Parts for the Terrestrial Spheroid 1889	1.28
90	The Development of Great Circle Sailing. 1889	1 00
72	List of Geographical Positions 1883	.75
9	The New American Practical Navigator. Edition of 1890	2 25
13	Bowditch's Useful Tables 1890	1.25
17	Projection Tables 1869	1.50
8	Magnetism of Ships and the Deviations of the Compass. By Poisson, Airy, Smith, Evans, and Randall, with other papers and documents. Edited by B. Franklin Greene. 1867	3 00
8a	Magnetism of Ships and the Deviations of the Compass Comprising the three reports of the Liverpool Compass Commission, with additional papers by Mr Archibald Smith, F. R. S., etc, and Staff-Captain F J Evans, R N 1869	3 00
71	Azimuth Tables for parallels of latitude between 61° N and 61° S. 1883	4 25
66	Arctic Azimuth Tables for parallels of latitude between 70° and 88° 1881	.80
62	Finding the Compass Error on board Ship Greene 1875	2.75
4	The Way to Avoid the Center of our Violent Gales 1868	15
57	Tables for finding the Distance of an Object by two Bearings (Pamphlet) 1874	.20
49	The Route of Mail Steamers between the English Channel and New York. 1873 (Pamphlet)	.20
87	International Signal Code. Edition of 1890	3 00
95	The Average Form of Isolated Submarine Peaks 1890	.70

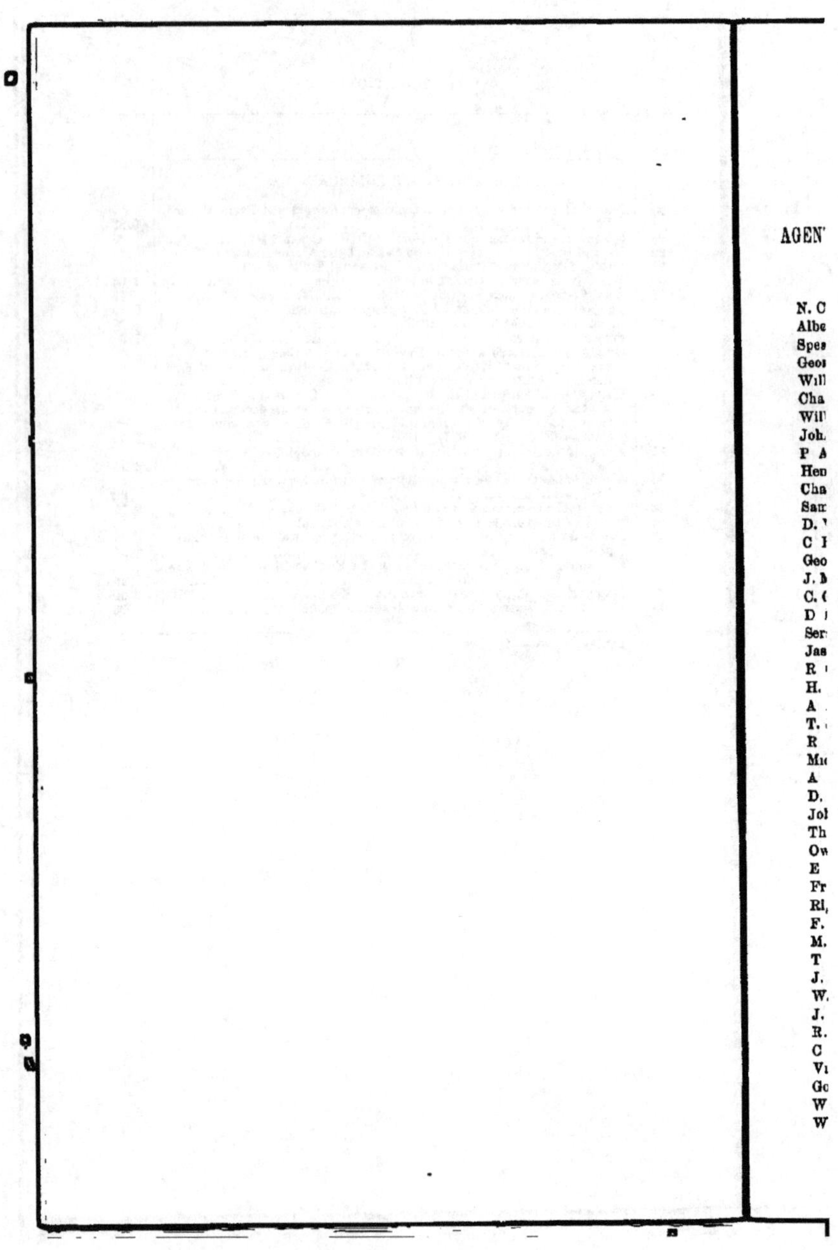

CPSIA information can be obtained
at www.ICGtesting.com
Printed in the USA
LVHW082155141220
674202LV00005B/32

9 781345 552782